THE CHALLENGE
OF CHINA AND JAPAN

This book, part of a college-level audio/print course in international studies, was developed by the Global Understanding Project at National Public Radio in cooperation with National Media Programs, University Extension, University of California, San Diego. Funds for the preparation of print and audio materials were provided by The Annenberg/CPB Project, which was established in 1981 by a grant to the Corporation for Public Broadcasting from the Annenberg School of Communication.

 An Annenberg CPB/Project

THE CHALLENGE OF CHINA AND JAPAN

Politics and Development in East Asia

edited by
Susan L. Shirk

With the Assistance of Kevin Kennedy

PRAEGER SPECIAL STUDIES • PRAEGER SCIENTIFIC

New York • Philadelphia • Eastbourne, UK
Toronto • Hong Kong • Tokyo • Sydney

Library of Congress Cataloging in Publication Data

Main entry under title:

The Challenge of China and Japan.

Designed to serve as the textbook for an audio/print course developed by the Global Understanding Project at National Public Radio, in cooperation with National Media Programs, University of California, San Diego.

Bibliography: p.

1. China—Addresses, essays, lectures. 2. Japan—Addresses, essays, lectures. I. Shirk, Susan L. II. Wood, Linda C., 1945– . III. Kennedy, Kevin.

DS706.C456   1985   951   84-24862
ISBN 0-03-071798-1

ISBN 0-03-071799-X (pbk.)
ISBN 0-03-071801-5 (instructor's manual)
ISBN 0-03-071802-3 (study guide)

Published in 1985 by Praeger Publishers
CBS Educational and Professional Publishing
a Division of CBS Inc. 521 Fifth Avenue, New York, NY 10175 USA
© 1985 by the Corporation for Public Broadcasting
and The Regents of the University of California.

56789 052 987654321

Printed in the United States of America
on acid-free paper

Acknowledgments

UNIT I

Steven M. Goldstein, Kathrin Sears, and Richard C. Bush, "China: The Land and the People." Excerpted by permission of the China Council of The Asia Society from Steven M. Goldstein, Kathrin Sears, and Richard C. Bush, *The People's Republic of China: A Basic Handbook*, 4th edition (New York: Learning Resources in International Studies, 1984), pp. 8–10, 111–117, 153–158.

Maurice Meisner, "Maoism and Socialism." Reprinted (in excerpted form) with permission of The Free Press, a Division of Macmillan, Inc. from *Mao's China: A History of the People's Republic* by Maurice Meisner. Copyright © 1983 by The Free Press.

"Deng's Quiet Revolution." Excerpted from two articles, "Deng's Quiet Revolution" by Larry Rohter with Melinda Liu, and "Great Expectations" by Tom Morganthau with Melinda Liu, Larry Rohter, and Barbara Slavin, *Newsweek*, April 30, 1984. Copyright 1984, by Newsweek, Inc. All Rights Reserved, Reprinted by Permission.

Robert E. Ward, "The Foundations of Japanese Politics." From Robert E. Ward, *Japan's Political System*, 2nd Edition, © 1978, pp. 28–56. Excerpted by permission of Prentice-Hall, Inc., Englewood Cliffs, New Jersey.

J. A. A. Stockwin, "The Japanese Economy Today." From *Japan: Divided Politics in a Growth Economy* by J. A. A. Stockwin, by permission of W. W. Norton & Company, Inc. and Weidenfeld (Publishers) Limited, London. Copyright © 1975, 1982 by J. A. A. Stockwin.

UNIT II

Edwin O. Reischauer, "The Coming of Chinese Civilization." From *Japan Past and Present, Third Edition, Revised*, by Edwin O. Reischauer. Copyright 1946, 1952, © 1964 by Alfred A. Knopf, Inc. Reprinted by permission of Alfred A. Knopf, Inc. and Gerald Duckworth & Co. Ltd.

John King Fairbank, "The Nature of Chinese Society." Reprinted by permission of the author and publishers from *The United States and China*, 4th ed., by John King Fairbank, Cambridge, Mass.: Harvard University Press, Copyright 1948, © 1958, 1971, 1972, 1979 by the President and Fellows of Harvard College, © 1976 by John King Fairbank.

John King Fairbank, "Confucianism and the Chinese Political System." Reprinted by permission of the author and publishers from *The United States and China*, 4th ed., by John King Fairbank, Cambridge, Mass.: Harvard University Press,

Kozo Yamamura, "Behind the 'Made in Japan' Label." From *Politics and Economics in Contemporary Japan*, published by Kodansha International, 1983. Reprinted by permission of the publisher.

UNIT III

John King Fairbank, "China's Response to the West." Reprinted by permission of the author and publishers from *The United States and China*, 4th ed., by John King Fairbank, Cambridge, Mass.: Harvard University Press, Copyright 1948, © 1958, 1971, 1972, 1979 by the President and Fellows of Harvard College, © 1976 by John King Fairbank.

John King Fairbank, Edwin O. Reischauer, and Albert M. Craig, "Japan's Response to the West." From Fairbank-Reischauer-Craig: *East Asia: The Modern Transformation*. Copyright © 1965 by Houghton Mifflin Company. Used by permission.

Marion J. Levy, Jr., "Contrasting Factors in the Modernization of China and Japan." Excerpted from *Economic Development and Cultural Change*, Volume 2, 1953–54, pp. 178, 184, 186–192, by permission of The University of Chicago Press. © 1953 by The University of Chicago. All rights reserved.

UNIT IV

Hans H. Baerwald, "Parties, Factions, and the Diet." From *Politics and Economics in Contemporary Japan*, published by Kodansha International, 1983. Reprinted by permission of the publisher.

Robert E. Ward, "Japanese Political Parties." From Robert E. Ward, *Japan's Political System*, 2nd Edition, © 1978, pp. 109–111. Reprinted by permission of Prentice-Hall, Inc., Englewood Cliffs, New Jersey.

Franz Schurmann, "The Chinese Communist Party: Structure and Organization." Excerpted from *Ideology and Organization in Communist China*, 2nd Edition, by Franz Schurmann. Copyright © 1966, 1968 by the Regents of the University of California. Reprinted by permission of the University of California Press.

A. Doak Barnett, "Party Leadership and Control." Excerpted from *Cadres, Bureaucracy and Political Power in Communist China*, © 1967, Columbia University Press. Reprinted by permission.

John Bryan Starr, "The Party and the State in China." Specified excerpt (pp. 203–205) from *Ideology and Culture: An Introduction to the Dialectic of Contemporary Chinese Politics* by John Bryan Starr. Copyright © 1973 by John Bryan Starr. Reprinted by permission of Harper & Row, Publishers, Inc.

"The Building of the Chinese Communist Party." Excerpts from *Beijing Review,* No. 28, July 12, 1982. Reprinted by permission.

"Socialist Modernization and the Changing Communist Party." Excerpts from *Beijing Review,* No. 37, September 13, 1982. Reprinted by permission.

UNIT V

Michel Oksenberg, "The Political Leader." Excerpted from *Mao Tse-Tung in the Scales of History,* edited by Dick Wilson. Copyright 1977 by Cambridge University Press. Reprinted by permission.

Michel Oksenberg and Richard C. Bush, "From Revolution Toward Reform." Reprinted by permission of Westview Press from *China Briefing,* 1982, edited by Richard C. Bush. Copyright © 1983 by The Asia Society, Inc.

Kent E. Calder, "Dynamics of Conservative Leadership in Postwar Japan." Excerpted from Kent E. Calder, "*Kanryō* vs. *Shomin:* Contrasting Dynamics of Conservative Leadership in Postwar Japan," *Political Leadership in Contemporary Japan,* edited by Terry Edward MacDougall (Ann Arbor: Center for Japanese Studies, The University of Michigan, 1982), pp. 1–22. Reprinted by permission of the publisher.

Robert E. Ward, "Political Leadership in Contemporary China." Excerpted from Robert E. Ward, *Japan's Political System,* 2nd Edition, © 1978, pp. 135–140. Reprinted by permission of Prentice-Hall, Inc., Englewood Cliffs, New Jersey.

Gerald L. Curtis, "The 'New Japanese' Leaders." Excerpted by permission of Foreign Affairs, Spring 1981. Copyright 1981 by the Council on Foreign Relations, Inc.

UNIT VI

Chalmers Johnson, "The Japanese 'Miracle'." Excerpted from *MITI and the Japanese Miracle: The Growth of Industrial Policy, 1925–1975,* by Chalmers Johnson with the permission of the publishers, Stanford University Press. © 1982 by the Board of Trustees of the Leland Stanford Junior University.

Sam Jameson and Tom Redburn, "Inside MITI: How Japan Forges Industrial Consensus." From the *Los Angeles Times,* May 23, 1983. Copyright, 1983, Los Angeles Times. Reprinted by permission.

Steve Lohr, "How Japan Helps Its Industry." Excerpted from "How Trade Ministry in Japan Promotes the Nation's Industry," by Steve Lohr, *The New York Times,* May 18, 1983. Copyright © 1983 by the New York Times Company. Reprinted by permission.

Chu-yuan Cheng, "Formulation and Implementation of Central Plans." Reprinted by permission of Westview Press from *China's Economic Development: Growth*

UNIT VII

UNIT VIII

UNIT IX

Masataka Kosaka, "The International Economic Policy of Japan." Excerpted from *The Foreign Policy of Modern Japan,* edited by Robert A. Scalapino. Copyright © 1977 by the Regents of the University of California. Reprinted by permission of the University of California Press.

"Liberalization of Agricultural Produce." From *The Oriental Economist,* June 1982. Reprinted by permission.

Susan L. Shirk, "The Domestic Political Dimensions of China's Foreign Economic Relations." Reprinted by permission of Westview Press from *China and the World: Chinese Foreign Policy in the Post-Mao Era,* edited by Samuel Kim. Forthcoming from Westview Press, Boulder, Colorado.

UNIT X

Michael Parks, "China—The Rural Road to Prosperity." From the *Los Angeles Times,* May 19, 1983. Copyright, 1983, Los Angeles Times. Reprinted by permission.

Stewart Fraser, "One's Good, Two's Enough." From *Far Eastern Economic Review,* July 9, 1982. Reprinted by permission.

P.-C. Chen and Adrian Kols, "Population and Birth Planning in the People's Republic of China." Excerpted from Chen, P.-C. and Kols, A., "Population and Birth Planning in the People's Republic of China," *Population Reports,* Series J, Number 25, January–February 1982, pp. J-605-607. Population Information Program, The Johns Hopkins University, Baltimore, Maryland 21205, USA. Reprinted by permission.

Bernard Bernier, "The Japanese Peasantry and Postwar Economic Growth." Excerpted from "The Japanese Peasantry and Economic Growth Since the Land Reform of 1946–47," by Bernard Bernier, *Bulletin of Concerned Asian Scholars,* Vol. 12, No. 1 (January–March 1980), pp. 40–52. Reprinted by permission.

UNIT XI

Margaret A. McKean, "Japan's Energy Policies." Excerpted from *Current History,* November 1983. Copyright © 1983 by Current History, Inc. Reprinted by permission.

Christopher M. Clarke, "China's Energy Plan for the 80s." Excerpted from *The China Business Review,* and reprinted with permission from the National Council for US-China Trade.

Thomas Fingar, "Energy in China." Excerpted by permission of the China Council of

lapino. Copyright © 1977 by the Regents of the University of California. Reprinted by permission of the University of California Press.

Gerald L. Curtis, "Japanese Security Policies and the United States." Excerpted by permission of *Foreign Affairs*, Spring 1981. Copyright 1981 by the Council on Foreign Relations, Inc.

June Teufel Dreyer, "China's Military Power in the 1980s." Excerpted by permission of the China Council of The Asia Society from "China's Military Power in the 1980s" by June Teufel Dreyer. Washington, D.C.: The China Council of The Asia Society, 1982, pp. 1–23.

UNIT XV

A. Doak Barnett, "China's International Posture: Signs of Change." Excerpted by permission of the China Council of The Asia Society from *China's International Posture: Signs of Change* by A. Doak Barnett (The China Council of The Asia Society, July 1982).

Gerald Segal, "China and the Great Power Triangle." Taken from "China and the Great Power Triangle," by Gerald Segal, originally published in *The China Quarterly*, No. 83 (September 1980), pp. 490–502. Reprinted by permission.

J. A. A. Stockwin, "Issues of Foreign Policy and Defense." From *Japan: Divided Politics in a Growth Economy* by J. A. A. Stockwin, by permission of W. W. Norton & Company, Inc. and Weidenfeld (Publishers) Limited, London. Copyright © 1975, 1982 by J. A. A. Stockwin.

Gerald L. Curtis, "Japan's Foreign Policies." Excerpted by permission of *Foreign Affairs*, Spring 1981. Copyright 1981 by the Council on Foreign Relations, Inc.

Development Team

Academic Project Coordinators

Susan L. Shirk, Ph.D.
Associate Professor of Political Science
University of California, San Diego

Mary L. Walshok, Ph.D.
Dean, University Extension
University of California, San Diego

Chief Academic Consultant

Susan L. Shirk
Associate Professor of Political Science
University of California, San Diego

Special Consultant

Chalmers Johnson, Ph.D.
Walter Haas Professor of Asian Studies
University of California, Berkeley

Editorial Director

Linda C. Wood
National Media Programs
University of California, San Diego

Chief Research Associate and Associate Editor

Kevin Kennedy
University of California, San Diego

Project Director

Lynn Fontana, Ph.D.
International Studies
National Public Radio

Project Coordinator

Yvonne Hancher
National Media Programs
University of California, San Diego

Research Assistant

Judith C. Hyde
National Media Programs
University of California, San Diego

Advisory Committee
Global Understanding Project

Dr. Rose L. Hayden
Executive Director
National Council on Foreign Languages
and International Studies

Mr. James R. Mahoney
Director, International Services
American Association
of Community and Junior Colleges

Ms. Carol Katzki
Associate Director
National University
Continuing Education Association

Dr. Sheilah Mann
Director, Educational Affairs
American Political Science Association

Dr. F. Stephen Larrabee
Professor, Department of Government
Cornell University

Mr. Timothy Plummer
Director, Education and Communications
Asia Society

Dr. Frank Wolf
Associate Dean, School of General Studies
Columbia University

Contents

Preface

The Challenge of China and Japan: Politics and Development in East Asia is designed to serve as the primary textbook for the audio/print course, "The Challenge of China and Japan," developed by the Global Understanding Project at National Public Radio. The book was edited by Dr. Susan L. Shirk of the University of California, San Diego, with assistance from Linda C. Wood and Kevin Kennedy, in association with National Media Programs, University Extension, University of California, San Diego.

The primary goal of the Global Understanding Project is to provide adult learners with opportunities to explore and better understand some of the more pressing global political issues of our time. The course materials developed for "The Challenge of China and Japan" include a combination of both audio and print materials. The audio component consists of fifteen half-hour audio programs, produced on location in China and Japan. Each program features commentaries by authorities on East Asian affairs as well as interviews with Chinese and Japanese policymakers, government officials, and people on the street who share their views on a wide range of contemporary problems and policy issues.

The print component consists of this anthology, a study guide, and a faculty manual. The readings included in this anthology have been drawn from a variety of scholarly, popular, and government sources. Although the book is primarily intended to be used in conjunction with the other materials developed for this course, it is also hoped that it will represent an important addition to the general body of literature on East Asian studies. The study guide and faculty manual are designed to assist students and educators in making the most constructive use of the course materials.

The Global Understanding Project was funded by the Annenberg/CPB Project, which was established in 1981 by a grant to the Corporation for Public Broadcasting from the Annenberg School of Communication. The two major goals of the Project are 1) to demonstrate the use of telecommunications systems for addressing unique problems of higher education and 2) to create one or more significant collections of innovative, high-quality, college-level materials.

Introduction

The Challenge of China and Japan: Politics and Development in East Asia is designed to introduce the reader to the political and economic institutions of China and Japan and to explore the different ways these two countries have approached similar problems of public policy. While China and Japan have common cultural origins and are neighbors in East Asia, they have different geographies, have experienced different histories, have achieved different levels of development, and, of course, have very different political and economic systems. How have two such different societies grappled with issues like industrial productivity, foreign trade, energy supplies, and national defense?

Comparisons of the ways China and Japan have addressed these and other policy issues highlight the institutional differences between the two countries. Japan is a developmental state in which the government plays an active role in guiding a market economy. China is a command economy in which the government plans and administers all economic activity. Japan is an electoral democracy in which the Liberal Democratic Party is preeminent. China is an authoritarian state dominated by the Communist Party. These fundamental institutional differences shape the policymaking process and the actual policy choices we find in China and Japan today.

Another important theme of this book is the continuing influence of traditional patterns of thought and behavior in both China and Japan. In neither country have traditional values been abandoned in the rush to achieve modernity. Traditional cultural orientations continue to influence the style of politics and policy debates. And the lessons of history are still being applied to contemporary situations. In particular, the stances of China and Japan toward foreign nations are rooted in their different historical responses to the West.

The first half of the book introduces the reader to the political institutions of China and Japan. Unit I provides an overview of the differences between China and Japan, emphasizing the contrast in their natural geographies, level of economic and technological development, and living standards. Units II and III describe the cultural and historical patterns which shape the context of contemporary politics. The institutions of the Chinese and Japanese political systems—political parties, national executives, bodies which determine economic policy, and bureaucracies—are examined in Units IV through VII.

The second half of the book moves from the institutions of Chinese and Japanese government to an analysis of the way these institutions have responded to common problems. Units VIII through XIV focus on specific issues—industrial policy, foreign trade, agriculture, energy, education, social welfare, and military defense—and the different ways they have been addressed by Chinese and Japanese policymakers. Finally, Unit XV examines

the foreign policies of China and Japan toward the United States and the
Soviet Union, and addresses the question of how the relations between
these two very different nations will shape the future of East Asia.

Unit I

China and Japan Today

Drawing comparisons between China and Japan is no simple task. These two Asian nations—one of the world's most populous country, the other the world's third most powerful economic entity—could not be more different. Yet, in many ways, they could not be more alike.

The People's Republic of China (PRC) now ruled by the heirs of the late Chairman Mao Zedong (Mao Tse-tung), has been under Communist rule since 1949. Since that time, the Communist Party has pervaded literally every aspect of Chinese life— political, social, and economic. And because China is an authoritarian state, there are no institutional means whereby the people can influence government decisions. Although welcomed by the masses of urban and rural poor in 1949, the Chinese Communist Party (CCP) is now facing a crisis of leadership. The failure of many of the Party's economic policies, such as the Great Leap Forward of the 1950s, and the ten years of political conflict and chaos engendered by the Great Proletarian Cultural Revolution (1966) have left the Chinese economy in a shambles. In recent years, the Chinese people have become increasingly dissatisfied with the country's stagnating standards of living.

The present Chinese leadership, which consists of Deng Xiaoping, Premier Zhao Ziyang, and Party Secretary Hu Yaobang, has established economic progress and modernization as the foundation for the legitimacy of Party rule. Since 1978, these leaders have implemented a series of economic and political reforms that promise to transform Chinese agriculture, industry, technology, and military policies. However, many of these reforms have already met with political opposition from former Mao supporters as well as from other groups who have personally suffered under the new policies. While the present leadership appears to be secure and continues to enjoy popular support, political conflicts are certain to continue and will undoubtedly affect many areas of public policy in the years to come.

Japan's domestic political picture appears to be more stable than China's, but this appearance of stability masks a wide variety of problems ranging from inadequate social welfare provisions to increasingly divisive debates over military spending. Despite these problems, Japan has enjoyed an unusual degree of domestic political stability, in part because of the long and continuing role of the Liberal Democratic Party (LDP). Formed in 1955, the LDP has dominated the democratic political process in Japan for almost forty years and has played a leading role in directing the growth of the Japanese economy. Yet, the LDP is itself a divided party. Strong factional allegiances require the party to operate through a time-consuming process of consensus building, but as Japan faces increasingly complex and difficult policy choices, that consensus becomes more and more difficult to achieve. Today, Japanese leaders are confronted by a dizzying array of potentially explosive problems. The nation is not only attempting to develop an international posture that is congruent with its spectacular economic success, it is also trying to decide how to best develop such a posture without returning to the kind of militarization that many hold responsible for the devastation of World War II. American demands for increased defense spending, while somewhat justified by Japan's growing economy, must be explained and defended to the Japanese public, which has favored a pacifist approach since the end of the war. Any increases in defense spending will undoubtedly be subject to the scrutiny of vocal interests demanding better and more comprehensive social services.

China and Japan share much more than difficult political choices and potentially divisive political conflicts. As Asian nations, the two countries share many aspects of history and culture. Their written languages are similar, suggesting a common origin. Philosophically, both have been influenced by successive waves of Confucianism, Buddhism, and Taoism and so both societies place great importance on the virtues of family, loyalty, and consensus. Moreover, both have a long history of bureaucratic administration, predating any similar development in the West.

Physically, both peoples are classified as variants of the Mongoloid race and, as such, have jointly experienced the humiliation and debasement of Western discrimination and imperialism. Yet their positions as the two dominant political powers in East Asia have at times made them enemies. Moreover, their differing responses to the intrusion of Western powers have led them, in recent times, down diverse paths of political and economic development. Today, China and Japan coexist in the most rapidly developing region of the world. In their search for answers to different though perhaps complementary issues of economic development, the two countries have begun to reach out to one another. In their uniqueness, they have found cause for cooperation.

This unit provides a general introduction to political, social, and economic life in present-day China and Japan. The readings focus on a number of issues related to political and economic trends in each country. Population, natural resources, social conditions, and recent developmental experiences are among the specific topics to be explored.

China and Japan are geographically separated by the Sea of Japan. Japan is made up of four main islands and thousands of smaller ones. The four islands of Hokkaido, Honshu, Shikoku, and Kyushu, together with the smaller islands, are home to 118 million people. Over 85 percent of the landmass is mountainous, so that the population is concentrated along the highly urbanized and densely populated eastern coast. Fully 75 percent of the Japanese people live in the Pacific Coast region, with a population density of 737 people to the square mile.

China is the largest nation in Asia, sharing its borders with eleven other countries. Claiming one quarter of the world's population, or approximately 1.2 billion people, China is often perceived as overcrowded. And although China *is* densely populated (many areas are more dense than cities in the United States), it is not as densely populated as Japan. Under a conscious policy of restricted urban growth, 80 percent of the Chinese population still resides in rural areas. However, in recent years, serious measures have been taken to curtail rural population growth. In fact, birth control and family planning policies have been identified by the Chinese leadership as key requirements for modernization. In

Japan, where legalized abortions outnumber births, no such administered birth control policy is necessary.

China, with its larger landmass, has vast amounts of undeveloped natural resources. Self-sufficient in coal, oil, iron, most types of food, and natural fibers, China has often been able to close its doors to the rest of the world. And, until the 1970s, the Chinese have done just that, ignoring Western demands for trade and commerce. However, the failure of recent economic policies has led to an increased willingness on the part of the Chinese leadership to open its doors to trade with other countries. Even before the 1970s, China began importing sizeable quantities of grain from abroad. Current targets for economic growth clearly presuppose an expanded trade with foreign nations and increased imports of foreign technology, capital, and expertise. However, this "open door" policy has already proved to be a source of domestic political conflict.

Trade policy is a source of domestic political conflict in Japan as well. Japan's dependence on massive quantities of imported oil has been recognized as a serious vulnerability since the Arab boycott of 1973, and today Japan is actively seeking alternative energy supplies. But Japan's efforts to achieve energy independence have been impeded by its trade partners, many of whom feel that the country's policy of export promotion and domestic protectionism is blatantly unfair. Japan is being increasingly pressured to liberalize its trade policy and to increase the openness of its domestic market to foreign goods.

Until recently, China has made no significant effort to seek foreign exchange. But the present Chinese leadership is actively seeking foreign investment, export markets, and aid. Still, despite recent increases Chinese exports do not even begin to approach the export level reached by Japan in the 1960s. In fact, economic statistics show that China falls far short of 1960s Japanese levels in all areas of foreign trade. Much of this differential can be traced to the alternative methods of economic development employed by the LDP and the CCP.

Japanese leaders since the Meiji Restoration and especially since the end of World War II have followed a policy of "administrative guidance." In effect, this is a policy of cooperation between government and most businesses in which governmental bureaucrats encourage businesses—through tax, investment, and other incentives—to invest in high-growth areas and to reduce production and investment in less efficient sectors of the economy. Much of this guidance has been provided by the staff of the Ministry of International Trade and Industry (MITI), though all levels of government have been involved. Clearly, these policies have produced great successes.

China, on the other hand, is a command economy in which all productive capacity has been under the direct administration of the Communist Party since the early 1950s. Through a "parallel structure" of state and Party, every enterprise, farm, and market has been subject to national price, labor, wage, and allocation and distribution policies. Such overcentralization in economic administration has stifled initiative and innovation, prevented effective quality control, produced bottlenecks in supplies and transport, and resulted in low labor productivity. Today, the political leaders of the PRC are struggling to find alternatives to the centrally planned economy. Many of the reforms in economic policy since 1978 have aimed at incorporating market mechanisms into the planning system without jeopardizing Communist Party control of the state. The most dramatic change has been the return to family farming after so many years of collectivized farming.

The different results of these starkly contrasting developmental approaches are clearly revealed in the statistics on economic performance. Japan has a GNP of almost $980 billion and is expected to become, at least in terms of per capita income, the world's wealthiest nation sometime in the 1990s. China, with a population ten times as large as Japan's, has a GNP of only $444 billion and is expected to remain one of the world's poorest nations until the end of the century. Today, Japan produces more motorcycles, cameras, ships, and synthetic fibers than any other country in the world, and is presently competing with the United States to secure a place in such high-technology fields as fiber optics, communications, and the development of artificial intelligence in computers. China has the world's largest hog population.

These statistics, while humorous, point to important differences in the two nations' economies. Whereas approximately 70 percent of the Chinese workforce is engaged in agriculture, only about 13 percent of the Japanese workforce is so employed. Ninety-five percent of the Japanese GNP is generated by industry and services whereas the Chinese GNP is composed of 69 percent manufacturing and service related products and 30 percent agricultural goods.

An important factor in this differentiation is the sad lack of efficiency in the Chinese economic system. While the rate of industrial growth in China since 1949 has matched the Japanese postwar rate of 12 percent, China's growth has been lopsided. Consumer goods industries and agricultural production have stagnated and waste and poor quality have continued to plague planners. While both nations have had high rates of capital investment, at times exceeding 35 percent of the national income, the Japanese, free of the frequently catastrophic ebb and flow of Chinese economic policy, have targeted their investment wisely and received much more "bang" for their "yen." And although Japan has far fewer natural resources than its neighbor, the Japanese have outperformed the Chinese in almost every industry. Consider, for example, that Japan produces 102 million metric tons (mmt) of steel to China's 32 mmt and generates 494 billion kilowatt hours of electricity to China's 257 billion.

There are also dramatic differences in living standards in the two countries. While a majority of Japanese families own refrigerators, China can produce only 56,000 per year. Ninety-five percent of Japanese families own at least one television, usually color, whereas in China, there is only one television for every 100 people. There are 2.3 users for every Japanese telephone; in China, there are some 320 users for every unit. Despite these differences, it should be noted that China's output of consumer goods is steadily increasing, though it is still far from meeting domestic demand.

Considering its lower level of development, China has achieved an impressive record in the area of social welfare provisions. Life expectancy in China is 68 for men and 70 for women, remarkable statistics for an underdeveloped nation. In Japan, the respective rates are 70 and 76. Health care in China is available to a large number of people through such experimental programs as rural "barefoot doctors" and urban paramedic teams. Japan's system, while adequate, is in some areas well below the levels of other advanced industrialized states. Eighty percent of Japanese hospitals are considered ill-equipped for advanced medical care, not so much in terms of technology or machinery as in terms of physical plant and trained personnel.

Japanese pensions and old-age care are similarly inadequate. The government has traditionally depended on businesses to provide their employees with health, retirement, and other benefits. However, only a third of the Japanese workforce is covered by such policies as "permanent employment." The remainder, usually employed in smaller firms, are entitled to only limited unemployment compensation, pension benefits, or welfare. Recently, the public has begun to demand more comprehensive social welfare provisions. But it is unclear whether and how the government will respond to these demands, though some policy makers have voiced support for an increased governmental role in the provision of public services.

In China, social welfare policy is evolving in quite the opposite direction. Recent economic reforms have destroyed many of the cooperative rural organizations that traditionally provided "cradle-to-grave" medical and educational benefits for their members. In urban areas, new policies are seriously threatening the "iron rice bowl" security of guaranteed employment. Increasingly, the government is seeking ways to "privatize" the supply of social services. This is especially true in rural education.

In the area of overall education policy, China compares well with Japan, especially considering its lower level of development. China has to educate almost 200 million students whereas Japan must only educate 21 million. China has a literacy rate of 66 percent as compared to Japan's universal literacy. But it should be noted that whereas Japan has almost mass higher education, the smaller number of universities in China prevents many qualified students from gaining admission (less than 3 percent of the age group can attend university). Again, reform policies in China have shifted the emphasis from quantity to quality, and meritocratic criteria are being increasingly substituted for the political evaluations that were so common during Mao's reign. The Japanese, meanwhile, are primarily concerned with the competitive pressures students are forced to endure, and more attention is being paid to the stress the educational structure places on students than on the quality and availability of educational opportunity.

Interestingly, in many ways, China and Japan appear to be changing places. In the future, China and Japan will face vastly different problems. The Japanese population is aging. Over half of the population is 30 or older. The elderly are putting an increasing amount of pressure on the government to respond to their needs. In today's changing Japan, the elderly find little refuge in the nuclear family and thus are demanding better protection and security in their old age. China, conversely, must respond to the needs of its predominantly young population, 60 percent of whom are under 25, and is seeking ways to provide gainful employment, increased educational opportunities, and a legitimate rationale for Communist Party rule for this dissatisfied and highly volatile sector of society.

Additionally, both China and Japan are seeking ways to respond to a changing global environment that more and more frequently intrudes into the domestic political context. China must discover ways to renew its friendship with the Soviet Union while at the same time satisfying the requirements of improved technological and economic relations with the United States. Japan, which has not signed a peace treaty with the USSR, must balance its close alliance with the United States with the recognition that the United States is not the hegemonic power it was immediately after World War II. Its economic success has altered the expectations of its allies, many of whom, like the United States, now expect Japan to play a greater role in global politics and Western defense.

In China, military policy is as much subject to domestic forces as it is to international pressures. The People's Liberation Army (PLA) is becoming increasingly queasy about current economic and political reforms. Some observers even consider the PLA to be a hotbed of resistance. But whether or not this is true, the present Chinese leadership must find ways to respond to the demands of the military without jeopardizing economic programs or political reform. Japan's military policy is likewise subject to both domestic and international forces. Its major ally, the United

States, is pressuring Japan to increase its military spending. However, such demands must conform to the desires of a Japanese population that has not forgotten the atomic nightmares of Hiroshima and Nagasaki.

In the realm of economics, Japan must move away from those industries which were responsible for its past success toward the new, largely unexplored realm of high technology. A key concern of Japanese leaders is how to shift from a policy of imitative technology to one that emphasizes a more independent approach to research and development. China, on the other hand, must find ways to secure its economic future. This requires that the politically sensitive issues of foreign aid, investment, and technology transfer be addressed. Japan is one possible source of such economic aid, just as China is an attractive market for Japanese industries. However, closer economic relations are dependent on both international and domestic political factors. For now, the two nations share warm relations and the possibility of increasingly friendly cooperation in the future. In many ways, their economies complement each other. The Chinese are rich in resources, poor in technology. And while Japan's technological sophistication equals that of any industrialized economy in the world, the Japanese nation is extremely poor in natural resources. In some policy areas, the two nations may have much to learn from one another. Clearly, the potential for growth and stability is great, both in terms of domestic situations and bilateral relations. However, that future is largely dependent on how the leaders of the two nations choose to solve the problems presently confronting their respective societies.

Steven M. Goldstein, Kathrin Sears, and Richard C. Bush in "China: The Land and the People," examine several different aspects of contemporary Chinese life, including the physical environment, recent economic reforms, and daily life. Maurice Meisner, in "Maoism and Socialism," discusses some of the distinguishing features of Chinese socialism, emphasizing the role of Mao and the CCP in unifying and transforming China into a rapidly modernizing state. The authors of "Deng's Quiet Revolution" describe the dramatic social, political, and economic reforms that have been initiated in China since the death of Mao, and their impact on Chinese society.

In "The Foundations of Japanese Politics," Robert E. Ward provides a general overview of Japan and the Japanese people, focusing particularly on the forces that have shaped present-day political realities. J. A. A. Stockwin examines some of the important factors that contribute to Japan's spectacular postwar economic growth in "The Japanese Economy Today."

1

China: The Land and the People

Steven M. Goldstein, Kathrin Sears, and Richard C. Bush

In these excerpts from *The People's Republic of China*, authors Goldstein, Sears, and Bush examine several different aspects of physical, economic, and social life in contemporary China. They describe how China's physical environment and human population have posed serious problems for the Chinese leadership in recent years and have limited economic growth. They also consider China's economic performance since 1949, economic policy since Mao, and the role of foreign trade in China's domestic modernization program. Finally, they describe the role of the family in China today, opportunities for women, the role of work in Chinese daily life (particularly emphasizing differences between urban and rural dwellers), housing, recreational activities, and other aspects of contemporary Chinese social and cultural life.

Chinese leaders throughout the 20th century have shared the goal of building a strong and prosperous country. And sooner or later they have had to come to grips with the limits to economic growth posed by China's physical environment and human population. Past episodes of visionary optimism have given way to the recognition that geography and demography dictate a "Chinese-style" modernization strategy, characterized by a moderate pace and moderate expectations.

The Physical Environment

The Chinese land mass (3,692,244 square miles) descends from the Himalayan highlands to the sea in a series of steps: the first is the Tibetan plateau, the second the western uplands, and the third a vast and fertile agricultural plain. The lower the elevation, the more suitable for human habitation. This land mass is subject to a variety of climates, ranging from continental in the west to maritime in the east, and from subpolar in the north to subtropical in the south....

A number of major river systems cut their way through the land mass, carrying water and silt necessary for agriculture. But the rivers can be a mixed blessing: inadequate flow reduces the area under cultivation; silting raises the level of the river and produces deltas as the rivers near the sea. Water resource management—facilitating irrigation and preventing floods—has thus been an age-old Chinese problem. Because of the uneven rainfall distribution, irrigation is the primary water management task in the north, flood control in the south.

A comparison with the American physical environment is instructive. China is slightly larger than the United States, and the two countries are roughly comparable in north-south range and in extent and diversity of topography and climate. But China has greater extremes of climate and larger areas that are unproductive and uninhabitable; cultivated land area in China is only 70 percent that of the United States.

Economic Potential

China's physical environment influences profoundly its economic potential. In agriculture there are three very general land-use patterns. A diagonal line drawn from northeast to southwest would halve the country. In the high and dry land to the west of the line, stock raising and oasis cultivation predominate. The eastern half contains the other two regions, north and south of the Jinling mountains/Huai valley dividing line. In the relatively dry northern zone, single cropping of grains like wheat and millet is the rule, although summer rice is common in some areas. With its wetter and warmer climate the southern zone supports multiple cropping of rice and commercial crops.

Well endowed with mineral and energy resources, China has great industrial potential. Before 1949, industrial development took place in major coastal and riverine centers that had higher population densities, better transportation and financial facilities, and some foreign presence. Particularly important were southern Manchuria, led by Shenyang and Dalian (Dairen), and the lower Yangzi (Yangtze) valley, dominated by Shanghai. Once order and central control were restored in 1949, industrialization began in a number of other centers. Nevertheless, development of both extractive and manufacturing industries still requires hard choices among competing priorities: accommodating regional diversification, minimizing investment in transportation facilities (already available in older centers), and promoting national security.

Human and Political Geography

China's population is the largest in the world, but how large is still a question. After years of providing only rounded figures, the Chinese government is again announcing specific estimates. The one billion mark was broken in mid–1980, and a detailed census was taken in 1982, the first in 29 years....

China's population is not only large, it is also distributed unevenly over the landscape. It is concentrated in the area east of the diagonal line referred to above, concentrated in fertile, low-land agricultural areas, and along rivers and transportation arteries. Thus, one-fifth of the globe's population must support itself on land that is about 12 percent arable. (Again, there is an interesting contrast with the United States: China has many rural areas just as densely populated as urban America.)

At present, the age distribution of the population also poses problems. ... [A]pproximately 46 percent of the population is under twenty years of age, consuming much more than they are producing. Moreover, the percentage of women in the 20–50 childbearing years—now about 38 percent—will grow over the rest of the century. Chinese population specialists have estimated that the population could quadruple in the next century if each fertile woman bore three children.

In view of these factors—high absolute numbers and uneven age and spatial distribution—the PRC government has intensified its already vigorous birth control program. The previous policy—encouraging late marriage and distributing free contraceptives—did reduce birth rates when it was strictly implemented, but it did not reduce population growth enough in the eyes of the present leadership. In 1980 the "one-child family" policy was introduced along with a system of benefits and penalties to encourage compliance. One-child families are given priority in housing, medical care, and education. Working mothers who pledge to have only one child are given longer maternity leaves. And intense social pressure is often brought to bear on couples to comply with the one-child family program. The birth of a second child can result in lack of access to nursery schools, salary reductions, or fines. Despite these measures, resistance to the one-child family program is common, especially in rural China. Traditional preference for male children has resulted in instances of female infanticide in some areas. Perhaps more significant for the ultimate success of the one-child family policy, is the disincentive provided by the introduction, in 1979, of the responsibility system in the countryside. The greater freedom given to the household to produce for its own use encourages peasant families to have more, rather than fewer, children as a way to increase the number of individuals contributing to total family income. Compliance with the one-child family program is thus stymied not only by traditional values but also, ironically, by the current economic reforms.

Although over 80 percent of the population lives in the countryside, China has many large cities, more in fact than the United States. To guarantee food supplies, Chinese municipalities include rural areas within their jurisdiction. Cities have both an economic role, as centers of manufacturing and distribution, and a political function, as links in the administrative chain of command.

The province is the most important subnational administrative unit. The PRC has 29 provincial-level units, most of them of substantial area and population. There are two special categories. One is the autonomous region, of which there are five. These have large minority populations who have received at least nominal guarantees that certain aspects of their culture will be preserved. The other special category is the centrally administered city, of which there are three: Beijing (Peking), the national capital; Tianjin (Tientsin), its port; and the great industrial and commercial metropolis of Shanghai. Like other municipalities, these units consist of the dominant city and the surrounding suburban and rural hinterland. At times during the PRC's history six regional units composed of several provinces have played an important role; over the long term, the central government, fearing the emergence of "independent kingdoms," has let power flow to the regional level only in special circumstances.

The people of China are ethnically and linguistically diverse. Although ethnic Chinese (Han) constitute 94 percent of the population, the 55 "national minorities" recognized by the government constitute 60 million people. Thirteen have populations exceeding one million. Minority peoples live mainly in a belt that surrounds the core Han population on the south, west, and north. They vary greatly in degree of integration with Chinese society and culture, though the pace of integration is faster now than in the past. As noted above, some minorities have "autonomous" provincial-level units; lower level units have been created for smaller concentrations.

Linguistic divisions occur not only between the Han and minorities, but also among the Chinese speakers themselves. The basic division in spoken Chinese is between the Mandarin dialect of north and central China and the numerous non-Mandarin dialects of the southeast. These "dialects" are really different languages, as different, say, as Italian and Spanish. Mandarin itself divides into different dialects, which are sufficiently dissimilar in pronunciation to cause some communication problems. The written language is the same for all these Chinese language groups, and a single national spoken language (called *pu'tonghua* [common speech]) is taught in all schools. Eventually, all PRC citizens will be able to converse in this official dialect, which is based on northern Mandarin. For the foreseeable future, however, *pu'tonghua* will remain a second language for close to 40 percent of the population.

ECONOMIC DEVELOPMENT AND FOREIGN TRADE

The Economy Since 1949

The Communist Party in 1949 faced an economy on the brink of collapse. Two decades of war had ravaged the small industrial sector and reduced the food supply. Hyperinflation had devalued the currency; commercial links between urban and rural areas were disrupted; and communications were in disrepair. Thus, the first task for the regime was economic rehabilitation. During the first few years of the Communist regime, private enterprise was permitted in the rural and urban areas in order to put the economy back on its feet.

In 1953 the leadership felt that the economic situation had stabilized enough to permit the launching of the First Five-Year Plan. The plan was based on the Soviet model in both its organizational nature and economic priorities. Heavy industry received the lion's share of investment and consumption was curtailed to permit the accumulation of capital. Light industry and agriculture received little financial support from the state. Organizationally, private enterprise in the urban areas was replaced by state ownership and agricultural collectivization in the countryside was accelerated. The economic system was managed from Beijing by a highly centralized plan implemented by national ministries.

By 1956 the Chinese leadership was rethinking the applicability of the Soviet model, some seeking greater investment in agriculture and a certain degree of decentralization. Mao, along with the majority of the Party's top leadership, had other ideas. The result was the Great Leap Forward of 1958 to 1961. Under this plan heavy industry would grow at an even more accelerated pace—but still at the expense of agriculture. The rural sector would provide the capital for heavy industry as well as its own developmental needs by yet greater production. The key to the program's success was the communes. These organizations, with their emphasis on egalitarianism and their ability to mobilize large numbers of peasants, were intended to provide greater rural productivity and savings. Moreover, their claim to be a yet higher stage of socialist development made them ideologically appealing to many within the leadership, most prominently Mao.

The Great Leap Forward was a disaster. Millions may have died due to food shortages. Communist support among the peasantry clearly suffered. From 1961 to 1966, the Party leadership engaged in a dramatic salvage operation. The authority of the communes was weakened, private plots were restored, and the peasantry was paid according to work performed. In the economy as a whole there was talk of decentralization, and a larger share of the state's investment funds was directed into agriculture.

However, beneath these changes in the economy, cleavages among the leaders of China were developing. Mao was becoming concerned about the social and ideological effects of the new economic strategy. Others, while not indifferent to this issue, felt that economic construction had to continue to take first priority. By 1966 Mao's concerns had become so profound that he promoted the Cultural Revolution.

Unlike the Great Leap Forward, the Cultural Revolution was not concerned primarily with economic issues. However, many of its ideological and social currents clearly touched the economy. Naturally, the turmoil was disruptive, particularly in respect to the nation's transportation network. More specifically, worker morale in urban and rural areas was damaged by what was perceived as an arbitrary and unfair wage system which did not reflect seniority or provide raises for ten years. Finally, the nativist mood severely limited regularized economic relations with foreign countries. Despite efforts by Zhou Enlai and Deng Xiaoping to reverse some of the currents of the Cultural Revolution in the early 1970s, any basic change had to await Mao's death in September 1976.

Amid these kaleidoscopic changes, how did the Chinese economy perform in the aggregate over the nearly three decades from 1949 to 1976?

First, China has generally experienced strong, sustained economic growth. Over the 1952–1978 period, average annual growth rates were 6 percent for gross national product, 11 percent for industry, and 2 percent for agriculture. If 1970 is taken as the base year, the annual growth rates were 7 percent for GNP, 9 percent for industry, and 3 percent for agriculture. These rates compare favorably with other large developing countries.

Second, poor performance in agriculture has inhibited growth. Given only a 2 percent growth rate, the food supply has held even with population growth. Though China is currently a net food exporter, it has imported grain since the early 1960s to insure sufficient reserves.

Third, economic growth has been interrupted by three periods of recession. By far the most severe was in 1959–62, when bad weather, withdrawal of Soviet aid, and dislocations caused by the Great Leap Forward led to absolute declines in GNP, industrial production, and agricultural production. There was another dip in 1967, due mainly to disruptions of the Cultural Revolution, and a period of stagnation in 1975–76 caused by the political conflict preceding Mao's death.

Fourth, despite the strong economic growth overall, living standards have not improved. The lack of attention to demand in production planning and problems in the planning system in general have contributed to waste and the stockpiling of unmarketable goods.

Post-Mao Economic Policy

Under the banner of the "four modernizations," Mao's successors pledged to reduce China's backwardness in industry, agriculture, national defense, and science and technology by the end of this century. The annual growth targets initially proposed were very ambitious: over 10 percent in industry and over 4 percent in agriculture. Rapid mechanization of agriculture and a broad expansion of heavy industrial plant—in part through foreign imports—were the central features of the strategy.

By late 1978 the leadership realized that the new goals were inappropriate to China's resources and conditions. It embarked on a policy of "readjustment" to rectify a number of problems. One of these was a serious decline in labor productivity, due to a variety of factors including stagnation in personal income, insufficient managerial capability, and planning difficulties. As a solution, economic planners have tried to raise consumption capabilities and opportunities by shifting investment priorities. As investment in capital construction has gradually stabilized, personal incomes have grown, especially in the countryside. Furthermore, the government has sought to shift investment funds away from heavy industry towards agriculture (to increase the food supply), light industry (for exports and to satisfy pent-up consumer demand), and transportation and energy resources. Importing foreign technology continues, but within the context of China's ability to pay. Growth targets recently have been more modest: in 1983, for example, both agricultural and industrial output were to rise at about 4 percent, with production in light industry to exceed slightly that in heavy industry. According to Chinese sources, the actual rate of growth of heavy industrial output was 13 percent, and 8.4 percent for light industry. Growth in industrial output in 1984 is expected to exceed 5 percent.

The leadership realizes that investment in energy resources is an essential guarantee of continued economic growth. From 1976 to 1983, every 1 percent of increase in industrial output required a 1.35 percent rise in the energy supply. Potentially, China has abundant resources of coal (the primary fuel source), oil (increasingly important in the 1970s), and hydroelectric power. But the capacity to exploit these resources has been lacking, and supply has stagnated in recent years. Aggravating the situation is a low ratio of efficiency in fuel utilization (in the 25–30 percent range). In the short term the government has spurred a conservation effort; for the long term it plans to use foreign technology to exploit offshore oil and onshore coal, and develop a nuclear power capability. Implementing these plans, which will mean China's closer involvement in the international economy and substantial joint venture arrangements, or possibly, foreign private investment in China, will not be an easy matter.

The post-Mao leadership has also experimented with changing the relationship between state-owned and collective enterprises and, increasingly after 1978, allowing very small private businesses to be organized. China's industrial economy has a dualistic structure, with a large number of state-owned enterprises under the control of central and lower level governments, and a much larger number of collective enterprises. The state-owned enterprises receive the bulk of available capital, are responsible for most of the output, and have a close relationship with the government. Until recently, state-owned enterprises remitted all their profits to the government, which in turn provided grants to underwrite any new investment. These remittances constitute the largest share of the state's revenue base, and economic construction (capital investment) has been the largest item of government expenditure. The regime's relationship with collective enterprises has been less direct and more ideological. In politically radical periods, rural small-scale industries have been praised for their contributions to self-sufficient rural development, while some urban ones have been restricted on the grounds that they represent vestiges of "capitalism." In more pragmatic periods, questions are raised about the efficiency of rural enterprises while urban ones are encouraged in order to fill gaps left by state-owned units and reduce urban unemployment.

The current leadership has returned to the approach of past periods of pragmatism, even to the point of legitimizing individual entrepreneurship. It has also questioned whether the close relationship between the government and state-owned enterprises, copied from the Soviet Union in the 1950s, is suited to China's conditions. To better link investment and performance, a number of experiments were tried during 1979 and 1980. Material incentives to increase efficiency and profitability were created by allowing many enterprises to retain a portion of their after-tax profits for reinvestment, bonuses, and worker services. Bank loans became a growing source of funds for new investment and means to encourage improvements in managerial and technical skills. For, if an enterprise did not use borrowed money efficiently, it would be less likely to get more. Instead of relying primarily on administrative mechanisms to distribute goods, planners allowed a greater role for market forces.

These limited experiments with market socialism were controversial. As in the political sphere, implementation of the reforms was shaped, and in some cases driven off course, by existing arrangements. Lower levels used their new freedom to increase rather than restrain new investment, and an irrational price system made it difficult to measure which enterprises were truly efficient. As profit deliveries to the government declined, due to the new policy of allowing some enterprises to retain part of their earnings, the central deficit rose dramatically to RMB 17 billion in 1979—15.4 percent of total revenues—and RMB 12.1 billion in 1980—10.5 percent of budgeted revenues. . . . The deficit was exacerbated by the steep increase in 1979 in the prices paid by the government for agricultural output. A greater number of investments at the local level and the provision of a 5 yuan subsidy to each urban worker to counteract rising consumer prices fed an inflationary spiral. In late 1980, in an effort to curb inflation, the government reduced central investments, halted further extension of the enterprise profit-sharing reforms, ended the bank loan reforms, and increased price controls on consumer goods. The result was a further expansion of the central deficit as industrial output and profitability declined. From the second half of 1981, controls on profits were relaxed once more and enterprises allowed to retain a portion of their after-tax profits. In 1983 this system of contracted profit payments to the government was supplemented by taxes on capital, sales, and income.

Despite these various adjustments, problems remain. Tension between central and local governments over relative shares of enterprise profits and influence over management remains an undercurrent in all policy revisions. The government continues to be frustrated by its inability to control local-level investment once enterprises are allowed to retain a portion of their earnings. Yet, profit sharing in some form seems necessary if production is to increase. Real future progress in industrial reform hinges upon a major reworking of the price system, a delicate task in any economy.

Finally, while anxious to maintain central control over the largest, most profitable enterprises, state policymakers seem willing to relax control over medium- and small-sized enterprises. Whether the government will be able to achieve economic growth by introducing a more market-oriented approach into some industrial firms, while retaining a centrally planned system in other enterprises, is yet to be demonstrated.

In the agricultural sector, the post-Mao leadership has been very successful in linking incentives to performance. In order to raise output and incomes, the government has improved rural-urban terms of trade, expanded private plots, liberalized crop management and generally allowed the lowest levels more freedom in production decisions. No longer is there a stigma attached to making money, and rural producers have taken full advantage of the change in climate.

Under the new "responsibility system," individuals, households, or work groups are assigned parcels of land in return for their delivery of a certain amount of output to the government. After fulfilling the terms of the contract, the individual, household, or group is free to consume or sell any remaining output. The significant change which the "responsibility system" has introduced is to make the peasant household the level at which income is determined, a role previously played (since 1962) by the production team. The land worked by the peasant household remains collective property, however, and cannot be sold by the individual although a tenure of 15 years is now guaranteed. Introduction of the "responsibility system" has been matched by easier credit terms and an increase in purchase prices for some items. The result has been a rise in productivity, the re-introduction of non-agricultural activities such as animal husbandry, fishery, or forestry (called "side-line" activities by the Chinese), crop diversification, and larger incomes.

Despite the apparent success of the agricultural reforms in raising productivity and incomes, there is resistance to the program by those worried about the creation of a gap between rich and poor households and restoration of class divisions in the countryside. There is also concern among some central leaders that the state plan will be weakened by giving peasant producers too much independence. Peasant reaction to the reforms also varies depending upon the extent to which they perceive that instituting individual responsibility will rob them of the benefits of collectivized activities, such as large-scale construction or water conservation projects.

The Role of Foreign Trade

China's international trade has increased gradually over the years, dropping only during the periods of recession noted above. Although China is not pursuing a development strategy of export-led growth like Singapore and South Korea, it shares their status as a "newly industrializing country" in that its exports are primarily industry-related commodities. On the import side, China depends on international markets for advanced technology, supplemental food supplies, and agricultural raw materials. This dependence, and Sino-Soviet enmity since 1960, have caused a dramatic change in China's list of trading partners, with Japan and the West replacing the Soviet-bloc countries, the principal partners of the 1950s.

The United States embargoed trade with China from 1950 to mid-1971. Commerce jumped in 1973 and 1974, primarily because of American wheat and cotton exports, then fell for three years for political and economic reasons. From 1977 to 1980, two-way trade between the United States and China rapidly developed, doubling every year. In 1981 two-way trade increased more modestly, from 4.8 to 5.4 billion, and then fell in 1982 to 5.1 billion and in 1983 to 4.4 billion. Despite the generally upward trend in trade relations between the United States and China, and in China's international trade relations in general, the process of developing foreign trade has not been a smooth one for post-Mao China.

In 1978, as part of the ten-year plan launched by Hua Guofeng, China went on a buying spree, contracting to purchase plant and technology from abroad in quantities far exceeding financial capabilities. During the first six months of 1979, reevaluation of China's domestic economic plans and foreign trade practices resulted in the cancellation of $2.6 billion in contracts with Japanese companies and institution of a moratorium on the signing of new purchasing contracts with foreign firms. Six months later, the Japanese contracts were restored and the importance to China of foreign trade and investment relations was underlined by the announcement of a new law governing joint ventures.

In 1980 foreign trade increased dramatically, at least in part due to the decentralization of foreign trade decision-making authority from central trade bureaus to individual production enterprises. This decentralization was a part of the larger reform program, noted above. The result was an enthusiastic scramble by Chinese enterprises to purchase items from abroad. For the government, however, decentralization decreased its ability to control the flow of foreign exchange or to set trade plans. In response, in early 1981, the Chinese government again cancelled contracts with foreign suppliers and moved to reinstate central control over the trading of various commodities. While total two-way trade declined in 1982, the effect on some countries (such as the United States where the volume of two-way trade fell from 5.4 to 5.1 billion) was not dramatic.

The United States remains China's third largest trading partner, after Japan and Hong Kong. While grain is the predominant U.S. export to China, fertilizers, logs, and lumber are sold in large quantities. The Reagan administration's decision in June 1983 to loosen export restrictions on high technology items, and continued Chinese interest in boosting their modernization effort by importing technology, may lead to future expansion in trade in that area. United States imports from China are led by petroleum products and textiles. The latter have been a continuing sore spot in Sino-American relations. Pressure from U.S. textile producers for protectionist restrictions on Chinese imports, and the Reagan administration's announcement in December 1983 of general support for implementing tighter controls, may limit future expansion of U.S. textile purchases. In contrast, business relations between the United States and China show some potential in the field of energy exploration. Foreign oil companies are being allowed to participate in joint oil exploration ventures, and at least one American company is involved in a coal mining operation in China.

Several factors still restrict the development of China's international trade. The composition of Chinese exports (primarily agricultural products and light manufactured goods) limits the scope of international demand. Demand for Chinese products is also subject to the effect of future world recessions (oil is the only possible exception, but the extent and quality of China's reserves is still uncertain). Limited demand and the need to import grain restrict the foreign exchange China has available for purchasing foreign technology. To deal with this problem, China is increasingly encouraging joint ventures, compensation trade, and concessionary aid. Indeed, in 1984 China plans to purchase 1 billion worth of foreign technology, financed in large part by loans from international lending organizations.

Since 1980, when China became a member of the World Bank and the International Monetary Fund (replacing Taiwan), the country's integration into the international financial system has increased. In 1981 a special domestic investment bank was created to channel loans from the World Bank to China's enterprises, and the Bank provides funding for other projects as well. China has applied to become a member of the Asian Development Bank, but approval hinges on resolution of the question of Taiwan's status (already a member) should China be admitted. In December 1983 China agreed to participate in the Multi-Fibre Arrangement (MFA) which, as part of the General Agreement on Tariffs and Trade (GATT), governs international textiles trade. The quota terms which China receives under the MFA is an important source of conflict in China's trade relations with the European Economic Community. Finally, China is encouraging foreign investment by opening special economic zones (SEZ) in Guangdong and Fujian provinces and Shanghai municipality. In 1984 similar status is extended to fourteen other areas in China. Foreign entrepreneurs are eligible for tax breaks and loans form the Bank of China if they invest in the special zones. A variety of arrangements are available to foreign investors in these areas including wholly owned or joint ventures, compensation trade, licensing, leasing, or co-production. The zones are viewed by the Chinese as a way to attract foreign capital and technology and to train personnel.

These innovations are a radical departure from the cash-and-carry approach of the Maoist era. While designed to support the domestic modernization drive, they also increase China's contact and enmeshment with the capitalist world. Like the technology-based developmental strategy as a whole, China's increasing integration into the international economic system could become a politically explosive issue domestically if it does not produce favorable results soon.

DAILY LIFE

Trying to describe the daily life of a society of one billion people is presumptuous at best[, particularly in view of] ... China's great variety and the Chinese people's range of life styles. Most foreigners can make only general observations.

Families and Organizations

The family is an important institution in China today, though very different from what it was thirty years ago. Reforming the family system was high on the CCP's immediate post-1949 agenda: land reform and confiscation of firearms deprived the clan of its power, and a marriage law ended flagrant abuses against women. Subsequently, demographic changes have caused the extended family to decline. But Chinese today still spend much of their time as members of family units. The family is still a principal institution for production, savings, consumption, and socialization. And in many ways, it is perhaps more cohesive, more closely knit, and more a part of the social fabric today than it was in 1949. The post-1949 restoration of political and economic stability made the forced breakup of families less likely. Public health measures and better diet have increased the number of generations living at the same time. Severe restrictions on migration within the country have discouraged family members from seeking employment away from their kin. Because they provide a foundation of social order, facilitate savings, and instill discipline, China's approximately 200 million family units are a significant resource in fostering development.

But unlike three decades ago, Chinese now live in a world of organizations that are linked directly or indirectly to the state. Everyone is a member of a work unit or a residential unit—in many cases the two are the same. An individual's work unit—*danwei*—defines one's social status; sets the level of income, health care, and old-age pension; provides (in cities) ration coupons for scarce basic commodities; may regulate the purchase of durable consumer goods; authorizes marriage; and even attempts to regulate the conception of children. One's unit often also provides a family-like social support. Organizations are responsible for a wide range of other social activities—schools for education, medical facilities for health care, urban housing offices for living space, retail outlets for consumer goods, the police and the courts for social control, and the Communist Party and mass organizations for political indoctrination.

Women

Before 1949 women in China had only limited educational and employment opportunities, could not marry freely, and were subject to the authority of their own families and their spouse's family after marriage. While advanced age led to greater social status for women as well as men and educational opportunities were made available to some women, particularly in wealthy or well-educated families, in general, life was delimited by the traditional priority given to males.

After 1949 the promulgation of the new marriage law in 1950 which legalized freedom of choice for both men and women, and continuing efforts to convince the population that women "hold up half the sky," did much to improve the social status of and the opportunities available to women in China. The number of women in government positions has increased dramatically in the last 30 years, although the total remains small. Only one woman, Zhou Enlai's widow Deng Yingchao, is a full member of the Politburo.

Women do, however, play a particularly active role in local level organizations, such as street committees, and in supervising the implementation of birth control policies. The All-China Women's Federation, headed by Kang Keqing, has responsibility for transmitting policies which affect women and representing women's interests to some extent. In recent years, the Federation has conducted surveys on women's domestic, professional, and social roles, but the impact of such studies on policymaking remains unclear.

Women workers predominate in certain sectors, such as textiles, light industry, and precision machine tools, and comprise an increasing percentage of the work force in the electronics industry. However, in many industries technical and higher level staff positions are still more often filled by men, while women are assigned to lower paying assembly-line or support jobs, such as operating cranes.

In the countryside, under the previous system of calculating individual income on the basis of work points, in general a woman could earn a maximum of eight work points for a day's labor, as compared to ten for a man. Some women "shock workers" could, however, earn more. The recent "responsibility system," which sets quotas for households or work groups, provides an alternative to the disparity in total points which most women and men were eligible to earn. Under both the work point and responsibility systems, the head of household is made responsible for allocating family income, rather than directly assigning income to the individual.

In short the opportunities—educational, social, and professional—available to women have increased since 1949. However, problems remain: There are indications that the "responsibility system" reinforces the traditional preference in rural areas for male children, forced marriages are not unknown, a substantial proportion of the urban unemployed are women, and most importantly of all, it is not clear that intrinsic attitudes about the social role of women have been changed by the revolution.

Work

The type of work dictates much about the individual's daily life and the extent to which organizations impinge on it. In the composition of its labor force, China is still very much an agricultural country. Three-fourths of the labor force works in farming, one-tenth in the manufacturing sector, and the remainder in the service sector. As in many developing countries, creating new jobs in China's cities has not kept pace with even the natural increase of the urban population. . . . [L]ess than half-a-percent of the labor force has moved out of agriculture each year.

The government has taken a variety of measures over the years to minimize urban unemployment and the social problems it engenders. There have been strict controls on internal migration since the late 1950s. Beginning in the early 1960s, millions of urban middle school graduates have had to settle on communes and state farms at varying distances from their home cities for varying lengths of time. The resettlement rate rose in 1968 (to restore order after the turmoil of the Cultural Revolution) and then again in the mid-1970s. The post-Mao leadership deemphasized this very unpopular program, but soon faced a rise in urban unemployment—about 20 million persons by March 1979 (20 percent of the urban population). The government is now permitting private citizens to establish individual and partnership enterprises, especially in handicraft and service trades, to reduce the number of young people out of work.

There is a sharp contrast between city and countryside in the organization of work. In the rural areas, the changes have been most dramatic. For example, a peasant in his or her mid-50s today has lived through several very different kinds of work environments. In the immediate post-revolutionary period, the Communists carried out a policy of land reform and the norm was privately owned family farms. By the early 1950s, the CCP was encouraging cooperation among families while still recognizing peasant ownership of land and livestock. In the mid-1950s, Soviet-style collectivization was carried out with ownership of land and livestock passing to the collective (a village of number of villages), with the peasant being paid from the proceeds of common labor. In the late 1950s came the communes. Peasants were organized into multi-village work units and were often paid the same wage regardless of work done or individual productivity. By the early 1960s, the basic work unit was the multi-family team (20–40 families). Although some private family plots were allowed, most income came from the fruits of this collective labor, and was distributed to individuals according to work done after provisions had been made for expenses, reserves, and welfare services.

In 1979 yet another dramatic change took place; the so-called "responsibility" system which allows peasant production groups, households, or individuals to sign contracts for what they will produce for the state and retain the surplus for their own use. As a result, the proportion of family income earned from above-contract production and non-agricultural activities has greatly increased in some areas. The role of the team in managing labor in the countryside has been reduced by the reform, and it remains uncertain whether teams receive any income from the production activities of peasant households. Once again, the family has become the basic economic and work unit in the Chinese countryside. Despite a general rise in income in rural areas, the decline in collective funds may have a critical effect on old or disabled people who previously have relied on team welfare for support.

Recently, individuals or families have been permitted to establish small private enterprises. However, in urban areas the vast majority of organizations—factories, stores, schools, government offices, and so forth—are still "owned by the whole people" and run by the state. These tend to be large, formal organizations in which the family as an institution plays a much more limited role than in the countryside. The work week is usually six eight-hour days. Monthly wages are paid according to the relevant salary scale. In some cities, employees also receive supplemental payments to compensate for a higher cost of living. The wage program originally set out in the mid-1950s called for wage increases every two to three years for most workers. In fact, no raises based on work evaluations were given from 1963 to 1977. Workers did receive bonuses, but they were not tied to skills or achievement. The result was a decline in real wages and deadening of motivation. Wage adjustments since 1977 have increased the incomes of a majority of China's industrial workers and efforts are being made to link raises and bonuses to performance.

In sum, work creates two very different styles of life in China. In agriculture, the hours are long and irregular, and hard physical labor is the norm. In the urban areas, one's job is still quite time-consuming, but the hours are more regular and there are many exceptions to physical labor. In the countryside, production is now based on the household unit. In urban areas, most workers remain employees of collective or state-run enterprises, though an increasing number of individuals (particularly the young unemployed) are starting up very small businesses of their own. While rural inhabitants still envy the wide variety of consumer goods available in the cities, urban residents may become increasingly jealous of the high incomes earned by many peasants participating in the "responsibility" system.

Residence

City and countryside also differ considerably in the housing available to families, and in the degree of neighborhood organization. Rural dwellers usually own their own homes (but not the land on which they sit), may build new ones, and may transfer ownership to their children when they die. Depending on the family's wealth, houses range from mud huts to spacious two-story brick homes.

Urban residents must put up with more crowded conditions. They either live in traditional one-story houses or in multi-story apartment buildings. There are some enterprises that provide quarters for their employees, but many urban residents rent housing from the municipal government. The supply of urban housing has not kept pace with population growth, and families must live in very tight quarters. According to government statistics, residents of 192 municipalities have 3.6 square meters of living space per capita, a decline from the early 1950s. The government is investing more in new housing, but not enough to quickly alleviate the shortage.

Concerning community organization, rural areas are much less complex than cities. Production teams, equivalent to a small natural village or part of a large one, are the basic units. In some parts of China, the production team is composed of members with the same surname. In cities, separation of work and residence is the norm, and municipal governments have extended organizational tentacles into urban neighborhoods, both to maintain social control and to mobilize the populace. Fifteen to 40 households form a resident's small group, which is under the jurisdiction of a residents' committee supervising up to several hundred households. The next level is the neighborhood committee, which controls several residents' committees and probably several thousand people. Units at each level work under the supervision of police and various administrative agencies. Direct official intervention occurs only for the most serious cases, however.

Generally speaking, the organizational networks that most affect daily life—both work and residential, in both city and countryside—encourage individuals to solve problems within their immediate social context.

Leisure

The demands of work and household leave Chinese relatively little time for leisure, and the quantity and quality of recreational activities have varied over time. The low point was certainly the Cultural Revolution decade (1966–76): Offerings in the arts were few and didactic, and many parks and monuments were closed on the grounds that they might foster "feudal" thinking. But since the fall of the "gang of four," there has been substantial liberalization in the cultural realm. Entertainment is no longer taboo in the performing arts (though a political message often remains), and the number of movies, plays, and operas—some of which are foreign—has greatly increased. In the fine arts, both traditionalism and a searching modern eclecticism are permitted. Literature has become an important vehicle for personal expression. Museums and reopened traditional cultural sites appeal to the Chinese pride in their long past. Spectator sports continue to be popular and are an outlet for patriotic enthusiasm as China enters more international competitions. Radio and, increasingly, television bring varied cultural fare into units and households. Limits to cultural liberalization remain, however. Literature and the arts has continued to be a sensitive area politically. In 1981 sharp criticism was directed at the screenplay "Bitter Love," and in the fall of 1983 a more general campaign was launched against "spiritual pollution." While the campaign had decelerated by early 1984, it provided a potent reminder that freedoms in cultural expression, in social behavior, and even in personal fashion, must be expanded gradually if they are not to alarm those concerned that China's contact with the West may introduce inappropriate ideas, values, and practices.

Restoring Political Bonds

The liberalization of culture is part of a broader effort to recreate public confidence in the regime. Over the last three decades, the Communist Party lost much of its originally broad mandate to transform the country's social and political life. Especially among those born after 1949, there is skepticism—how much is impossible to measure—about whether the government can bring a change for the better.

The relatively low standard of living and limited career opportunities—problems common in most developing societies—are partly responsible for these attitudes. But China's unique political history also plays a role. A final verdict has yet to be rendered on the Cultural Revolution era, but there is substantial evidence that it wreaked havoc with the lives of many and created a social climate of cynicism and anxiety.

The post-Mao leadership has taken some specific steps to reduce its political liabilities and reknit old loyalties. It has cancelled class labels assigned during the social and political transformations of the 1950s and 1960s, and forbid discrimination in employment, social services, and political participation on the basis of class. Revival of legal institutions and training is seen as a way to reinstate confidence in authority based on rules of due process rather than arbitrary force. And regularized popular participation is being encouraged in many areas through introduction at the county level of direct election of deputies to people's congresses.

On the surface, the shape of daily life in China will probably not change radically in the foreseeable future. The great majority of Chinese will, as they do now, have to work hard to guarantee a standard of living that ranges from basic subsistence to moderate comfort. They will continue to live in close quarters with families and neighbors, relying on time-tested ways of maintaining social harmony. Like others in the modern world, they must find personal orbits in a universe of organizations that create opportunities while imposing controls. But whether they have confidence in their government will depend on its success in raising the general standard of living and guaranteeing some measure of personal autonomy.

2

Maoism and Socialism

Maurice Meisner

In this selection from *Mao's China*, Meisner discusses some of the unique features of Chinese socialism. He credits Mao and the Communist Party of China with the unification and economic transformation of China into a powerful and rapidly modernizing nation state. Like other socialist countries, China after 1949 quickly nationalized all means of production. The state administration was seen as the only agency capable of promoting rapid industrialization of China's agricultural-based economy. However, unlike the leaders of the Soviet Union and the socialist states of Eastern Europe, Mao was as concerned with transforming China into a socialist society as with building a modern economy. He was particularly concerned with the struggles against bureaucratism, which lay at the very heart of the development of socialism and the transformation of the Chinese people into "new socialist" men and women. Meisner argues here that concern with these issues has prevented the differentiation of vocational and political ethics (meritocracy versus virtuocracy), has narrowed socioeconomic inequalities, and has avoided the separation of bureaucrats from the people they serve.

Still, there are political preconditions for the full realization of socialism that China has not yet met. Democratic processes and institutions are not present in contemporary China. Despite political movements such as the Hundred Flowers campaign (1957–58) and the Cultural Revolution (1966–69), authoritarianism and totalitarianism are still the essential characteristics of societal-state relations. Therefore, Meisner concludes, Mao's legacy is an ambiguous one. The tension between economic progress and political backwardness is the primary contradiction facing the post-Mao leadership—and, if Meisner is correct, it is one that will not be easily resolved.

When the Chinese Communists came to power in 1949 they promised not one revolution but two—a bourgeois revolution and a socialist one. The former, left unfinished by the old regime, was accomplished swiftly by the new one. In the early 1950s the Communists rapidly fashioned China into a modern nation-state and instilled her people with a strong sense of national identity and purpose. The long-delayed agrarian revolution was completed with the conclusion of the land-reform campaign in 1952, liberating the great majority of the Chinese people from the most inhumane forms of economic exploitation and social oppression imposed by the modern persistence of traditional rural social class relationships. Territorial unification, the establishment of a strong centralized state and a national market, and the abolition of precapitalist relations in the countryside created, in turn, the essential preconditions for the development of modern productive forces; the enormous human and material resources latent in the vast land soon were harnessed to bring about the modern industrial and technological transformation of a backward and hitherto stagnant economy.

What was accomplished during the early years of the People's Republic was essentially the program that Sun Yat-sen had set forth at the beginning of the century: national unification, "land to the tiller," and a plan for modern industrial development. And the Communists, to whom the task of implementing that program fell, justly can claim to be the true heirs of that most eminent of modern China's bourgeois revolutionaries. The fruits of that now-completed bourgeois revolution are apparent. China, long (and not long ago) among the most wretched and impoverished of lands, today stands in the world as a powerful, independent, and rapidly modernizing nation. . . .

More than two decades have passed since the Chinese Communists announced the inauguration of the socialist phase of the revolution. Have they succeeded in creating a socialist society, as they claim? Is the People's Republic, as its leaders declare, a state under "the dictatorship of the proletariat," a country in the "transitional" stage between socialism and communism? The close of the Maoist era is an appropriate time to ask these questions, although it is perhaps still too early to provide any definitive answers. Nonetheless, some tentative observations might be offered.

The socio-economic changes that have transformed China in the years since 1949 cannot easily be subsumed under the rubric of "the modernization process," however broadly one may choose to define that rather vague term. "Modernization," after all, does not typically entail the abolition of private property. Yet it is precisely the absence of private ownership over the means of production that crucially characterizes contemporary Chinese society. The nationalization of the urban economy and the collectivization of agriculture in the 1950s have proved to be irreversible measures, and they are necessary (if not necessarily sufficient) conditions for socialism.

The abolition of private property was accompanied by an intensive drive for industrialization, and the latter of course lies at the heart of anyone's concept of modernization. But industrial development has proceeded under state direction and ownership, and the process was conceived not simply as an end in itself but as a means to achieve socialist ends, as the essential means to build the material base upon which any future socialist society inevitably must rest. Indeed, perhaps the most unique and noteworthy feature of that process has been the Maoist attempt to reconcile the means of modern industrialism with the ends of socialism. In China, as in the Soviet Union, rapid industrialization rapidly produced new forms of social inequality: the growth and stratification of new bureaucratic and technological elites; the exploitation of the rural areas for the benefit of the industrializing cities; and a tendency for the industrial values of economic rationality and bureaucratic professionalism to become the dominant social values, subordinating the socialist values and goals which industrialization originally was intended to serve.

What has been distinctively "Maoist" about the Maoist era has been an effort to avoid (or at least mitigate) the social and ideological consequences of industrialization by attempting to pursue modern economic development in a fashion consistent with the achievement of Marxist goals. Rejecting the comfortable but illusory Soviet orthodoxy that the combination of nationalization and industrialization automatically guarantees the arrival of a socialist society, Maoists have demanded that modern economic development must be accompanied by (and perhaps preceded by) a "continuous" process of the revolutionary transformation of social relationships and popular consciousness, a demand that socialist organizational forms and communist values must be created in the very process of constructing the material prerequisites for the new society. That demand, expressed in its most pristine form in the ill-fated Great Leap Forward campaign, since has found more lasting expression in such policies as those which aim to combine industrial with agricultural production, combine education with productive labor, and oblige officials and intellectuals to periodically engage in work on farms or in factories—and perhaps most importantly, in the program for the industrialization of the countryside. These policies were conceived not only (or even primarily) for their economic efficacy but with classic Marxist aims in mind: the reduction of the age-old distinctions between mental and manual labor, between workers and peasants, and between town and countryside. At the close of the Maoist era, China is far from realizing these ultimate goals, but the striving to achieve them has served to narrow the range of socioeconomic inequalities, to prevent the differentiation of a professional vocational ethic from the Maoist political ethic, and to forestall the stratification of bureaucratic elites separated from the masses. In general, the thrust of Maoist policies pursued over the past quarter-century has been specifically socialist and not generally "modernistic."

Yet if the Maoist era established many of the socioeconomic preconditions for socialism, it did not create its no less essential political preconditions. For socialism involves more than the abolition of private property and more than a general social leveling. Socialism means, if it is to have any genuine meaning, a system where political power is exercised by the masses of the producers themselves, permitting them to control the conditions and the products of their labor. The dictatorship of the proletariat, as socialism, or the "lower phase of communism," is defined in Marxist theory, is a time marked by a process whereby the social powers usurped by the state are returned to society as a whole; more specifically, it is a period when the state, both as a repressive instrument and in its constructive functions, takes the form of what Marx termed "the self-government of the producers." In what has passed for "the dictatorship of the proletariat" in Maoist China, these socialist political conceptions and forms have been absent in both theory and practice. If Maoism is a doctrine that has confronted the dilemma of reconciling the means of modern economic development with socialist ends, it is not a doctrine that recognizes that popular democracy is both the means and the end of socialism.

There were two crucial periods in the history of the People's Republic when the critical problem of the relationship between state and society was raised and presented for solution. During the Hundred Flowers campaign Mao himself posed the question of the contradiction between "the leadership and the led," and from the movement itself there came widespread demands for political democracy and intellectual freedom. But the demands were suppressed and the contradiction between rulers and ruled remained unresolved. The Cultural Revolution launched a wholesale attack against party and state bureaucracies and at first seemed to promise the reorganization of political power in accordance with the Marxist principles of the Paris Commune. But the promise was aborted and the Cultural Revolution concluded with the total reestablishment of the rule of the Leninist party. If Mao can be credited with initiating the Hundred Flowers campaign and the Cultural Revolution, he also must bear the historical responsibility for their failure to initiate processes to transform the state from the master of society into its servant. . . .

The legacy of Mao is thus an ambiguous one, for it is marked and marred by a deep incongruity between its progressive socio-economic accomplishments and its retrogressive political features. On the one hand, Maoism has thrown off Stalinist orthodoxies and methods in forging a new pattern of economic development which has, on balance, moved Chinese society in a socialist direction. On the other hand, it has retained essentially Stalinist methods of bureaucratic political rule, generated its own cults, orthodoxies and dogmas, and consistently suppressed all forms of intellectual and political dissent. Mao, to be sure, regarded bureaucracy as the greatest of evils, but his weapon to combat the phenomenon was to rely on his personal prestige and the forces he could rally under his own banner. Neither in theory nor practice does the Maoist legacy include institutional safeguards against bureaucratic dominance.

The new rulers of the People's Republic, whoever they ultimately may turn out to be, will surely wrap themselves in the mantle of Maoism; they will certainly continue the modern economic development of China, and they even may do so through Maoist methods, although the latter can by no means be taken for granted. But the question that will determine the future course of China's social development is not simply whether Mao's successors will inherit his legacy, for as a socialist legacy it is politically deficient. The real question, at least insofar as the possibility of socialism is concerned, is whether new and future generations of Chinese will enrich and develop that legacy in a manner that will make China politically democratic and intellectually free. For the absence of political and intellectual freedom precludes the possibility that political power will take the form of "the self-government of the producers," the only form that will permit the Chinese people to bring about their own emancipation, the form that is both the essential condition of socialism and the essential precondition for its genuine emergence and development.

The prospects for such a democratic evolution are hardly promising, for not only are the necessary political prerequisites absent in Chinese Communist reality but the need for them is unrecognized in Chinese Communist theory. Indeed, at the close of the Maoist era, Chinese socio-historical conditions powerfully favor the further growth of an autonomous bureaucratic state standing over higher above society. First and foremost among those conditions is the absence of a dominant social class capable of restraining the independent power of the state. In original Marxist theory it was assumed that political power in a postrevolutionary society would be exercised by the proletariat and would be employed for universalistic ends, the creation of a classless and stateless society. In lieu of a politically active proletariat (or its functional equivalent), the socially egalitarian results of the Chinese Revolution, far from initiating a process leading to the "withering away" of the state, ironically have created conditions for the state to become all the more powerful. The postrevolutionary history of China offers abundant contemporary evidence to support Max Weber's proposition that "every process of social leveling creates a favorable situation for the development of bureaucracy."

To this general condition there must be added several specific factors conducive to bureaucratic autonomy and supremacy: the persistence of old Chinese bureaucratic traditions and habits; the bureaucratic elites and mentalities fostered by modern industrialism; the elitist implications of Leninist principles of party organization, now fully restored; and, what has gone hand in hand with the latter, the political apathy of the masses since the Cultural Revolution. And perhaps the passing of Mao has removed the last and greatest barrier to the bureaucratic institutionalization of the Chinese Revolution.

Thus China finds itself in that misty historical realm of socioeconomic orders that are neither capitalist nor socialist and are sometimes simply labeled, for want of any better term, "postcapitalist." The People's Republic is not simply capitalist because it is a society which has abolished the essential condition of capitalism—private property and private ownership of the means of production. And it is not genuinely socialist because the masses of producers do not have the means to control the products of their labor, nor do they control the state that has become the economic manager of society and that stands above them. . . .

If China is unlikely to go back to the old world, it is not necessarily the case that she will move forward to a new socialist world. "Wandering" can become a more or less permanent state of affairs and "postcapitalist" societies can crystallize into new forms of bureaucratically dominated social orders, as the history of the Soviet Union demonstrates. During the Maoist era, the impetus for socialism and the struggle against bureaucracy came from the top, principally from Mao himself. That impetus struck responsive chords in Chinese society and Maoist goals were pursued through the mobilization of the masses for radical social change. It is highly improbable that any similar impetus will come from the leaders of the post-Maoist order, for they are men who are essentially the managers of a powerful party-state bureaucracy that has a strong interest in its own self-preservation, and thus a vested interest in the political apathy of the masses. If much of the Maoist era was guided by the principle of "permanent revolution," it is likely, at least for the foreseeable future, that the post-Maoist era will be marked by the permanence of bureaucracy and its dominance over society.

3

Deng's Quiet Revolution

Newsweek

These excerpts focus on some of the social, political, and economic reforms that have been initiated in China since the death of Mao. The economic stagnation of the Cultural Revolution decade (1966–76) has given way to an era of pragmatism and an explosion of entrepreneurial activity unknown in China since 1949. Under Deng Xiaoping's economic reforms, profit and efficiency, rather than political loyalties, are the measuring rods of success. The "iron rice bowl" of guaranteed wages has been "cracked" if not broken. Managers have greater autonomy, consumers have more choices among higher quality goods, and foreign companies are investing in Special Economic Zones—transferring to China some of the world's most advanced technologies.

Of course, such reforms are not without unintended consequences. The importation of "decadent" Western values is at the heart of political conflicts between pragmatists and leftists. Corruption is on the rise. And rural cadres find themselves without any meaningful political role as more and more peasant households join in the "household responsibility" system of production. In short, economic reform has in many ways highlighted the need for political reforms. Central government subsidies, bureaucratic conflicts over price and distribution policies, and growing income disparities make further economic reforms very difficult. The army, former Maoists in the Communist Party, and certain government ministries are all sources of political resistance to Deng's policies. And as economic liberalization moves slowly forward, the demands of discontented intellectuals and unemployed youth are being increasingly voiced.

Still, these conflicts and demands are being openly discussed and debated. Juvenile delinquency, sexual inequality, and artistic freedom are hotly contested social problems. As these issues come to center stage, Chinese leaders may find it more and more difficult to import Western technology while restricting the influence of Western values.

[T]oday the pragmatism of Deng Xiaoping, not the revolutionary fervor of Mao Tse-tung [Mao Zedong], governs China. To put the energies of 1 billion Chinese to better use, Deng and his loyalists are trying some starling economic experiments. The effects are creeping into almost every aspect of Chinese life. To stimulate growth, competition and efficiency, market forces once derided as "capitalist tails that must be chopped off" are being grafted cautiously onto China's planned economy. The byword of Deng's great leap upward is not Marx's dictum "from each according to his abilities, to each according to his needs." The motto adopted by the Chongqing Iron and Steel Works comes closer to its spirit: "The more you work, the more you get."

In his old age, Deng has not become a follower of Adam Smith: Marxism-Leninism remains the ideological foundation of Deng's "New China." But he *is* tolerating some striking lapses from Leninist orthodoxy. The Chinese economy is dramatically "enlivened," as the Chinese press likes to boast. The dour Peking streets of the Maoist era are full of privately owned food stalls and bicycle-repair shops, itinerant vendors and even hairdressers. At the gates of the Forbidden City, enterprising private photographers hustle tourists from the countryside. Peking Opera performers have agreed to lower salaries in return for a percentage of box office receipts. In Henan, retired doctors are forming private clinics. In Shenyang, a drab city in Manchuria, 18-year-old Guan Changzhi has opened a private four-room hotel equipped with radios, televisions and a washing machine.

The state commercial system—described by Peking's Guangming Daily as "a pool of stagnant water"—is suddenly gushing like a spring flood. State banks make low-interest loans to small businesses. Management and technical advice comes free from once scorned retired executives. The so-called "Patriotic Capitalists"—members of the pre-1949 business elite who elected to stay on in revolutionary China—are back in style. . . .

Over it all rules Deng, who prides himself as merely a practical thinker—a leader out to "seek truth from facts." His pragmatic revolution has its limits. The levers of totalitarian power remain firmly in the hands of the Communist Party. Deng is experimenting mostly on the system's margins, where he can buy quick results at relatively little political cost. The question is always whether his ambitions exceed his reach. There have been delays in much-needed price reforms apparently because the leadership fears that a lurch toward reform will produce Polish-style unrest. Heavy industry continues to gobble up scarce investment funds. Few old-line managers have lost their jobs, despite a government study that found 70 percent of them to be unqualified. But if Deng is cautious, he is no less persistent.

Under Deng, China is forging erratically toward the "four modernizations" in agriculture, industry, science-technology and the military. The leader is sticking to his "open door" policy to attract foreign know-how and capital. He is fighting off stubborn opposition in the party—and even some of his closest colleagues are tempted to retreat to the familiar safety of the Stalinist economic models. Deng's remedy remains the flash point of China's domestic debate: ideology has its place, the message seems to be, but what matters most are results.

History may provide Deng's most compelling case for change. In the 1950s, communist China and capitalist Taiwan had almost the same per capita income; today the average Taiwanese earns about $2,000 a year— more than 10 times the income of his counterpart on the mainland. To stimulate his catch-up program, Deng's government has introduced a package of incentives called the "Responsibility System." In the old days, Mao relied on guaranteed jobs and fixed wages; but Deng's new strategy penalizes workers for their company's losses and rewards them for profits. . . .

QUALITY

Under Deng, managers also have won greater authority over production. Peking's quotas are no longer quite so demanding. "Before 1979 the Central Government never considered the profits a factory made, and because of that the quality of products was very low," says Li Qian, an economic director of the huge Chongqing Iron and Steel Works. "Now, though, the state emphasizes the profit factor greatly, and if the quality of your product is low, people will refuse to buy."

People can make the choice because these days they have money to spend—and the Chinese are becoming avid consumers. According to official figures, retail sales in China reached $142 billion last year, a 10.5 percent increase over 1982's record total. Production of television sets rose 10 percent to 6.8 million, cassette players increased 39 percent to 4.8 million units, washing machines climbed 44 percent to 3.6 million. Refrigerators, electric rice cookers, floor fans, sewing machines and radios have also become prized items.

Keeping up with this exploding consumer demand has required readjustments in Chinese industry. Defense plants that once produced tanks have been retooled to make washing machines and refrigerators. . . .

INCENTIVES

To spur efficiency—and to bring in badly needed foreign capital and technology—China is developing special economic zones. The four coastal areas in the south receive special incentives, including a corporate tax rate half that of the rest of China, exemption from import duties on raw materials and more leeway for managers. Unlike their counterparts elsewhere in China, executives in the zones have powers to pay piecework wages, to hire and fire employees and to negotiate their own contracts. The zones cannot compete with more attractive business climates in Hong Kong, Taiwan, Singapore and South Korea. But by the end of 1983, the four zones had lured $2.8 billion in foreign investment—nearly half the national total.

The zones are obviously another kind of China. In Shenzhen, just across the border from Hong Kong, factories, a floating hotel and a fishing village are prospering. Nearby, construction of China's first Club Med is under way, and Shenzhen also boasts a lavish Chinese-style resort called the "Honey Lake Country Club" complete with a 2,000-seat Cantonese opera theater and an amusement center where long-haired Chinese youths cruise in bumper cars and play electronic five-card stud. To seal the rest of China off from such "decadent" influences, the authorities are erecting an internal border: a 50-mile-long barrier with spotlights, barbed wire and land and sea checkpoints.

RATS AND KINGS

Deng's program has other consequences. The combination of surging demand and short supply has prompted a rapid expansion in the underground economy. Newspapers are rife with reports of "grain rats," "cigarette tigers" and "coal kings" who use their access to commodities and raw materials to extort such items as television sets or bicycles from purchasing agents at stores and factories. This year it was revealed that one coal distributor had refused to ship fuel to a plant in Zhejiang Province until the buyers sent a set clothes, five bookcases and nine pieces of furniture to his home in Shanghai. In the northern city of Tianjin, doctors halted a cancer patient's chemotherapy at midpoint and forced him to leave the hospital until his relatives sent the staff food and other gifts.

But corruption is only a minor byproduct of the surge of private initiative. Of all Deng's changes, none has affected more people than the revolution in the countryside. Until 1979, 800 million peasants had to endure the collectivization of land. A policy of "eating from one big pot" has always dulled initiative. But over the last five years, strict government controls have been eased. "The Chinese peasant is a pretty smart agricultural person; the Chinese political cadre is a pretty dumb agricultural person," says University of Michigan Sinologist Robert Dernberger, "so the transformation has proved to be a pretty smart move." Peasants have responded with a burst of energy that has doubled rural living standards and produced bumper harvests: in 1983, China's grain output reached a record 388 million tons—larger than America's production.

As in the cities, the key to this rural revival is to foster responsibility. The state signs work contracts with peasant households or teams to take over tasks such as breeding poultry or cultivating orchards. A basic quota is set, which must be turned over to the state. But beyond that, peasants are free to pocket most of their proceeds. This "specialized household" system permits peasants to decide not only how much time and money they will spend on each crop, but also when, where and how much they will get for the produce they need not turn over to the state. . . .

PRICE QUOTATIONS

Now that China's peasants have permission to use their ingenuity, they are busy innovating. Last year, Sichuan potato farmers unhappy with slack local demand chartered a pair of cargo planes and flew off to Tibet, where their spuds earned a substantial profit. Perhaps most remarkable of all is the appearance of rural telephones—installed at much cost by farmers who want up-to-the-minute weather reports and price quotations from nearby market towns.

The principal obstacles to change are as much political as economic. Many cadres that have seen their authority reduced are resisting the reforms. And because of the twists and turns of policy over the last 35 years, many peasants have doubts about how long the good times can last. Newspapers report that peasants refuse to turn up to receive awards, apparently out of fear that they could become targets if political winds shift again. An even more fundamental concern among peasants is the status of their contracts, some of which are now coming up for renewal. Peking has sought to soothe such worries by issuing "central document No. 1" in January, which states that the contracts can be extended to 15 years, or even longer.

High party officials have indicated that they intend to press ahead with—and expand—incentives, even if there is sometimes grumbling about income disparities. "For a long time we have worried about the division between rich and poor in the countryside, [but] egalitarianism does not accord with objective laws of development," Heilongjiang's party secretary, Li Lian, said recently. Li also supported "abolishing the state monopoly over purchasing and marketing." And he advocated "allowing prices to float according to supply and demand."

SUBSIDIES

Such brave words are one thing; the real test of Deng's revival scheme is something much more. Will he actually stake China's economic future—and his regime—on the drift of free-market wages and prices? So far he has done the opposite: in his first great modernization, agriculture, he has used wage-and-price *subsidies* to fuel production. In an early reform, the government hiked the prices it paid for farm goods by 20 percent, a quick-fix effort to raise rural living standards. Next, to cushion the impact of higher prices on consumers, Peking granted each urban worker a $3-a-month subsidy. As a result, agricultural grants now comprise more than 70 percent of total government subsidies, which themselves devour nearly 45 percent of Peking's revenues.

China cannot afford to continue such largesse indefinitely; in recent months, state investment in rural improvements has dropped by 40 percent. The leadership is counting on the peasants themselves to promote further agricultural growth, reinvesting their profits in crops and machinery. But so far many peasants have used their money to improve the only asset the state has never subsumed: their homes. So what have Deng's massive agricultural subsidies bought? Perhaps little more than a one-time spurt in production.

Meantime, Deng's subsidies have only sharpened the price disparities that have distorted the entire Chinese economy. Prices for a wide spectrum of goods—from construction material to flour to ice cream—have soared willy-nilly. The cost of some crucial commodities, however, has remained fixed. Domestic coal prices, for example, have not risen for 30 years, forcing the mines to operate on red-ink budgets. The problem is that in China, as everywhere else, price reform makes for volatile politics. Raising prices to meet production costs might set off coal riots, for instance, that would rival the Polish meat riots in intensity.

All the same, Deng cannot afford to introduce wage-price reforms too cautiously. To have any major impact, he must drastically reduce subsidies, alter wage scales and introduce tax-and-investment reforms almost simultaneously. An opportunity may come in the autumn, when a Central Committee plenum is expected to meet, and might endorse another round of economic reforms.

Even if he performs magic on China's wage-and-price disparities, Deng's economic problems are just beginning. To meet his ambitious overall goal—quadrupling China's 1981 output by the end of the century—he must maintain the nation's economic growth rate of about 7 percent a year. The burden will again fall on agriculture, which will need more irrigation facilities, more chemical fertilizers, more roads and stronger seed strains among other things. These efficiencies might generate a trend away from fragmented family plots back to larger fields. Encouraging peasants to loosen some of their newly won control over the land is one major problem. Persuading them to help finance the new projects is just as unlikely.

Even in the best of circumstances, Deng's schemes are bound to widen the gaps between China's rich people and its poor—and between its prospering regions and its impoverished areas. Beyond the well-publicized success stories exploding across the countryside, such backwaters as Gansu and Guizhou provinces remain poorer than Bangladesh. In the industrial areas, ideas perfected in Deng's four special economic zones already are being expanded to 14 cities along the coast, a trend that reminds some disgruntled Chinese of the "treaty port" concessions of Peking's dynastic days. Now other areas are clamoring for more autonomy and similar special treatment, and Peking is preparing to grant limited special economic rights in such far-flung regions as Qinghai and Ningxia in an attempt to attract foreign investment.

OVERFLOW

China has another big headache—surplus labor. Deng's reforms have released 1 peasant in 3 from full-time work in the fields, according to one Chinese economist, and the ratio is increasing. So far many of these peasants have found work in the new rural factories, stores, transport companies and other services. But there is not room for the rural overflow in China's cities—at least until the government can realize its distant goal of building industrial satellite enclaves around the major metropolises. If productivity continues to rise, Deng's reforms might conceivably produce a rarity for China: the unemployed peasant.

Throughout China's long history, of course, peasants have been forced to adapt to innumerable shifts of bureaucratic policy. That experience has helped them steel themselves against the upheavals of Deng's pragmatic reforms. Deng faces problems enough in the economic reverses that surely lie ahead—and from the hard-liners still lurking in the party, state bureaucracy and Army. But in many parts of China, both rural and urban, the mood is optimistic. At the Heavenly Garden commune, peasant woman Liu Wen-fan, for one, has even decided to invest more heavily in pigs and vegetables. "Before, we could plant only grain," she says. "Now we can plant whatever we like, and in that way we can earn money." For peasants and workers who remember all too well the hard times of the recent past, that modest advance is the cutting edge of Deng's revolution. . . .

Measured by the memories of artists . . . or by the disillusionment of its urban youth, or by the muffled discontent of its 500 million women, China is something less than a people's paradise. The excesses of the Cultural Revolution are past, buried with Chairman Mao. The government of Deng Xiaoping has expanded economic incentives, ended the pogrom against "capitalist roaders" and praised the efforts of the nation's scientific and technical elite. But officials in Peking still regard the intelligentsia with suspicion. Although there is lip service aplenty about the changing role of women, centuries of tradition, together with some of Deng's economic reforms, conspire to keep Chinese women in their place. And if China's future depends on the next generation, the government has many problems. . . .

[E]ven if, officially, a communist society cannot have unemployment, government officials concede that China has significant numbers of *dai ye gingnian*—job-awaiting youths. Almost entirely, they are to be found in the cities. There is an increase in urban crime, though mild by the standards of the West. There is suicide, and there is China's own pallid version of juvenile delinquency—gangs on motorbikes, young men in black leather jackets and a tendency toward what strikes strait-laced Chinese commentators as "debauchery." One distressing trend, the official journals say, is the new taste for "yellow" (pornographic) music from the West—which includes both Led Zeppelin and John Denver.

One encouraging aspect of the Deng regime's liberalization is that, for the first time in years, such social problems are being discussed with relative candor. Chinese officials see three main reasons for their problems with urban youth: the lack of jobs, the influence of the West and the Cultural Revolution. One article last summer blamed the "disastrous" Cultural Revolution for "the rapid increase of juvenile delinquency," explaining that under the "Gang of Four" "many young people lost parental care as their families were broken, and many others, with their pious belief in what they were doing, devoted themselves to the 'Great Revolution'." Since then, says one official researcher, China's mass media have "spent too much time on the positive aspects of the West. Young people saw only the cars, the beautiful houses and the color television sets, but not the other evils of capitalism . . . this has made them doubt the superiority of socialism."

China's youth problem, however, doesn't end there—for the nation's educational system is almost savagely meritocratic. China's young people face a draconian selection process on their way to a university education: two-thirds are winnowed out between primary school and secondary school, and only nine-tenths of 1 percent make it to college. Then there is *fen pei*—divide and send—the moment when university graduates are assigned to their first jobs. "It is a very divisive time," says a foreigner who teaches at a university in Peking. "Students who have been friends for years become enemies over jobs."

The government has announced its intention to improve the quality of teaching at all levels, to double university enrollment by 1990 and to allow better-qualified graduates some choice in their first job assignments. But some Western observers are skeptical that the government can do enough: Deng's educational policy, says Ann Arbor sociologist Martin Whyte, "is a wager on the most capable. The problem is what it does to everyone else." . . .

Chinese women have made great strides toward equality in the labor force: 40 million women hold jobs in urban areas, and 150 million are at work in the countryside. But the percentage of women who hold upper-level or professional posts is still very low, and women are a minority among university students. According to both Chinese and Western analysts, it is commonplace for women applicants to face much stiffer requirements than men for admission to universities—and for working women to subordinate their careers to their husbands'.

Change is coming slowly, amid reminders of the oppressive past. "Although a number of female scientific workers are dissatisfied with this state of affairs, they cannot do anything about it," a recent study in the official journal Sociology concluded. "In their opinion, it is very difficult to change the view . . . that the wife should mainly shoulder the housework."

At 35, sculptor Wang Keping is a veteran traveler on China's road to modernization. In the 1960s, during the Cultural Revolution, Wang helped denounce foreign influence as a member of the Red Guards—and in the late '70s, during the days of post-Maoist liberalization, he became a leader of a group of avant-garde artists known collectively as "the Stars." When the Stars defied a government crackdown to exhibit their works in Peking. Wang's political sculptures were among the most controversial. A piece called "Idol," for example, depicted a Buddha-like head with a drooping eye, a wart on the chin and a five-pointed star on its cap; it was unmistakably a satire on the cult of Chairman Mao.

Probably no group has been buffeted as much by the shifting winds of Chinese politics—and today, China's artists and intellectuals are thankful simply to have survived. During the Cultural Revolution, the intelligentsia was reviled as the "stinking ninth category" of the enemies of Maoism; latter, leading dissidents were jailed for crimes against the state. And when, last fall, the government announced a new campaign against "spiritual pollution," many expected a revival of terror; the campaign was suspended, and its prime enforcer, party propaganda chief Deng Liqun, has fallen out of favor.

The bottom line seems to be that intellectual freedom will be tolerated—within limits. Mass media and the state television network are closely scrutinized by censors; even novelists must walk a careful line. "By Chinese standards, the intellectuals' situation is much better than at any time since the 1950s," says author Liang Heng. "That still doesn't mean you can speak freely." Liang's American wife and coauthor, Judith Shapiro, says, "Deng wants to open the doors to the West for its science and technology, but he doesn't want to let thought in. You can't have one without the other." That may be so in the long run—but for now, China's intellectuals are taking nothing for granted.

4

The Foundations of Japanese Politics

Robert E. Ward

In these excerpts from *Japan's Political System,* Ward describes some of the basic features of Japan and Japanese society. He discusses the geography of Japan, its low percentage of arable land, the losses of territory during World War II, and some of the social ramifications of being an island nation with clearly defined borders. One of these is an unusually strong sense of national identity and group consciousness, though this is as much a result of the homogeneity of the people as it is of insularity.

In terms of population, Japan is culturally and ethnically homogeneous. Koreans, Chinese, Americans, and other immigrants account for less than 1 percent of the total population. The central cleavage is therefore not ethnic, but generational. Improved medical care has greatly increased the average life expectancy in Japan, creating tensions between nonproductive seniors and younger workers. These tensions have been exacerbated by the tendency toward nuclear families and by the lack of significant social welfare provisions for the elderly.

Despite ethnic homogeneity, urban-rural cleavages are an important fact of Japanese political life. Rural farmers, despite their relatively small numbers, are a potent political force in Japan's dominant Liberal Democratic Party (LDP). Because of representation rules for the Diet (Parliament), urban voters are underrepresented. (Occupational differentiation is a contributing factor in this political cleavage.) The differences in rural-urban occupation lead to significant differences in income distribution, with urban workers being far better paid than their rural counterparts. (Wage differentiation is also very pronounced by economic sector and gender.) Still, class stratification does not appear to be of primary importance in contemporary Japanese politics.

GEOGRAPHY

The most obvious geographic facts about present day Japan are that it is small and insular. Its total area is 372,393 square kilometers or 143,781 square miles. This is small compared to the United States (9,519,622 square kilometers or 3,675,547 square miles), the Soviet Union (22,272,200 square kilometers or 8,599,300 square miles), or China (9,561,000 square kilometers or 3,691,500 square miles). It is not small, however, when compared to the United Kingdom (244,004 square kilometers or 94,211 square miles), West Germany (248,534 square kilometers or 95,959 square miles), or France (543,998 square kilometers or 210,039 square miles). In Japan, however, there is an important distinction between the total area of the country and the generally useful or arable land. Only about 16 percent of Japanese territory is arable. In terms of this more meaningful index, Japan suffers a great handicap. The United States has 20 percent arable land; India, 50 percent; the United Kingdom, 30 percent; West Germany, 34 percent; and France, 39 percent. Among the major states, only the People's Republic of China (11 percent arable land) and the Soviet Union (10 percent) may be in less advantageous positions, although the current accuracy of these percentages is somewhat dubious.

To make matters worse, Japan's national territory has greatly decreased as a result of its defeat in World War II. Japan lost Formosa, the Pescadores Islands, Korea, the Kwantung Leased Territory, and the South Seas Mandated Islands—all of which were formerly a part of the empire (Manchukuo was technically independent). There is little present prospect that southern Sakhalin or the Kuriles will be voluntarily returned by the Soviet Union, although Japan has not yet formally accepted this loss. Until recently Japan had also suffered the loss of administrative control over the Ryukyu (Okinawa) and Ogasawara (Bonin) islands. While acknowledging Japanese "residual sovereignty" over these two island groups, the United States had occupied and administered both—largely for strategic reasons— since the end of World War II. . . . The only territorial claim resulting from wartime losses that Japan is currently pressing, therefore, is that against the Soviet Union with respect to the southern Kurile Islands. . . .

The bulk of Japan's present territory is accounted for by the four main islands of Hokkaido, Honshu, Shikoku, and Kyushu. There are also more than 3,300 smaller islands within the national boundaries. Japan is a country of islands and mountains, a fact that has profoundly affected the political character of the country. In the first place, it shapes the political unity of the country. Although Japan is a relatively small state, it is not unified and homogeneous. The islands and the mountains have historically made land communications rather difficult and have produced well-developed patterns of regionality. These regions have traditions and histories of their own and have usually had some sort of political identity as well. In modern political terms, Japan was not really effectively unified until the Restoration (1868), and even today this long history of political decentralization and localism has identifiable political importance and consequences.

Second, the insularity of the country seems to have affected its political history in several significant ways. It has, for example, given Japan a sharply defined national frontier, so unlike the broad and shifting bands of territory that have historically constituted China's frontiers. This has tended to give to the Japanese a sense of group identity, against outsiders at least, and—when joined with the development of a serious foreign and imperialist threat to their collective security, as was the case after Perry had reopened Japan in 1854—has provided fertile ground for the rapid emergence of strong nationalist feelings. Some would go further and claim that this historic isolation from extensive foreign contacts, made possible by Japan's insular condition, also partly accounts for certain narcissistic qualities in Japanese culture, as well as for the alleged inability of the Japanese to view either themselves or their relations with foreign countries objectively. National isolation may also explain the Japanese tendency to alternate between poles of aggressive self-assertion and a sort of collective inferiority complex in its relation to Westerners and Western culture.

Whatever the merits of such speculations about the Japanese national character, it is certainly true that geography has endowed Japan with a degree of national security that is almost unique in the history of the greater states. It is approximately one hundred thirty miles across the Straits of Tsushima to Korea, Japan's closest continental neighbor. It is about four hundred seventy-five miles across the Yellow Sea to the Chinese coast. Japan's safety from invasions from the continent is thus far greater than that of Great Britain, lying twenty-odd miles from the shores of France. Prior to 1945, no one had successfully invaded Japan since the ancestors of the present Japanese race did so in prehistoric times. This fact has had two prime consequences for the Japanese. First, until 1854, it enabled them to turn on and off almost at will the stream of intercourse with the Asian continent or with the rest of the world. It made possible, for example, the effective adoption of a deliberate policy of national seclusion for almost two hundred fifty years prior to 1854. Second, it enabled the Japanese throughout most of their history to concentrate exclusively and almost fiercely on domestic political issues, domestic power struggles, and internecine strife, with little or no concern for the effect this might have on the external safety of the nation. National security carried to this extent is unparalleled among the other great states of modern history. It is hard to specify precisely the consequences of this unique national experience, but the question certainly ought to be posed.

In basic resources, Japan is in many respects a poor country. In recent years, it has had to import all its bauxite, natural rubber, phosphate rock, nickel, uranium, cotton, and wool. Also, Japan has to import 99 percent of its crude petroleum and iron ore, 80 percent of its copper, 79 percent of its coking coal, 80 percent of its lead and zinc, and 60 percent of its lumber. Japan suffers similar deficiencies in food, although in the past decade rice imports and all but 1 percent of vegetable imports have been eliminated.

TABLE 4–1   Average Annual Increases in Gross National Product

Country	1950–60	1960–70
Japan	9.1%	11.3%
West Germany	7.9	4.7
France	4.5	5.6
United Kingdom	2.8	2.7
Italy	5.6	5.7
United States	3.2	4.2

Source: Adapted from OECD sources.
Note: Calculated at constant prices.

Japan continues, however, to import 100 percent of its coffee, 80 percent of its sugar, 96 percent of its soybeans, 92 percent of its wheat, and 82 percent of its barley. On a value basis, Japan's index of self-sufficiency in foods has hovered around 73 percent in recent years. In 1960 it was 90 percent. On a caloric basis, Japan imports about 50 percent of its food supply. . . .

POPULATION

The Japanese Government conducts a formal census every five years. The most recent of these indicates that as of 1 October 1975 the population of Japan was 111,933,818. This figure takes into account the retrocession to Japan by the United States in 1972 of control over the prefecture of Okinawa, which added about 969,000 people to Japan's total population. The current Japanese population is, therefore, more than three times that during the Restoration (1867–68) and a little more than double that of 1920.

Japan has the sixth largest population of any contemporary state— ranking behind China, India, the Soviet Union, the United States, and Indonesia, in that order. This population is distributed, however, over only 372,393 square kilometers of national territory, yielding a 1975 pattern of 297 people per square kilometer. In national terms this is one of the highest population densities in the world, exceeded only by Singapore, the Republic of Korea, the Netherlands, and Belgium. A somewhat more meaningful figure, however, is the distribution per square kilometer of arable land. In 1975 this amounted to 1,982 persons, one of the highest such ratios in the world. In 1975 male members of the Japanese population had a life expectancy at birth of 71.7 years and females of 76.9 years, figures somewhat more favorable than our own and among the highest in the world.

TABLE 4-2 Gross National Product and Per Capita National Income for Selected Countries

Rank	Country	Base year	Gross national product (in billions of U.S. dollars)	Rank	Country	Base year	Per capita national income (U.S. dollars)
1	United States	1974	$1,397.4	1	Sweden	1974	$6,693
2	Japan	1974	465.4a	2	United States	1974	6,030
3	West Germany	1974	412.4	3	West Germany	1974	5,874
4	France	1974	298.0	4	Denmark	1974	5,828
5	United Kingdom	1974	191.2	5	Canada	1974	5,634
6	Italy	1974	149.6	6	Belgium	1974	5,424
7	Canada	1974	142.1	7	Norway	1974	5,222
8	Brazil	1973	76.1	8	France	1974	5,037
9	Argentina	1973	75.5	9	Netherlands	1974	5,034
10	Netherlands	1974	74.3	10	Switzerland	1973	4,697
11	Australia	1974	66.7	11	Australia	1974	4,635
12	Mexico	1974	65.0b	12	Finland	1974	4,431
13	India	1973	64.6b	13	Iceland	1973	4,313
14	Spain	1973	62.3	14	Austria	1974	4,274
15	Sweden	1974	60.5	15	Luxembourg	1973	4,271
16	Belgium	1974	57.3	16	New Zealand	1973	3,896
17	Switzerland	1974	54.9	17	Japan	1974	3,497b

Source: Adapted from International Monetary Fund, *International Financial Statistics*, February 1976.
aFigure for Japan based on Prime Minister's Office, Economic Planning Agency data in *Nihon Kokusei Zue*, 1976, p. 87.
bGross Domestic Product

47

The postwar population history of Japan is unique (see table 4–3). Immediately after the war, as a result of the demobilization of the armed forces and the repatriation to Japan of about six million Japanese soldiers and civilians resident in other parts of Asia, the national birth rate per thousand of population soared to 34.3, a figure very close to the record high of 36.3 in the 1920s. Thereafter, it declined steadily to 16.9 per thousand in 1961, one of the world's lowest rates. By 1974 it had risen to 18.6 per thousand. Along with this rapid decline in the birth rate has been an equally impressive decrease in the death rate per thousand; it dropped from 14.6 to 6.5 per thousand between 1947 and 1974, largely because of improved medical services and a national health insurance program. These rates compare favorably with those of the United States and the major countries of Western Europe. The result of such developments has been a sharp decline in the rate of natural annual increase of the Japanese population, from a postwar high of 21.6 per thousand in 1948 to a low of 7.0 in 1966. More recently, however, the rate has risen again to 12.1 in 1974. Thus, a population that was increasing by such fantastic annual increments at 4.99 and 3.10 percent in the 1946–47 period of repatriation has in recent years been increasing at a rate of slightly over 1 percent per year. The official projections, which have not been notably reliable in the past, anticipate total populations of 115,972,000 in 1980; 124,744,000 in 1990; and 131,838,000 in 2000.

The abrupt decline in national rates of natural increase is unprecedented in modern demographic experience. It was due in the first instance

TABLE 4–3 Increase in Japan's Population, 1920–75

Year	Population	Increase over preceding census Number	Percentage	Average annual increase (%)
1920	55,963,053	—	—	—
1925	59,736,822	3,773,769	6.7	1.3
1930	64,450,005	4,713,183	7.9	1.5
1935	69,254,148	4,804,143	7.5	1.4
1940	73,114,308	3,860,160	5.6	1.1
1947[a]	78,101,473	5,561,744	7.7	1.1
1950	84,114,574	5,098,164	6.5	2.1
1955	90,076,594	5,962,020	7.1	1.4
1960	94,301,623	4,225,029	4.7	0.9
1965	99,209,137	4,907,514	5.2	1.0
1970	104,665,171	5,456,034	5.5	1.1
1975	111,933,818	7,268,647	6.9	1.4

Source: Adapted from Office of the Prime Minister, Bureau of Statistics, *1975 Population Census of Japan, Preliminary Count of Population*, Tokyo, December 1975, p. 6.
[a]Due to postwar conditions there was no regular census in 1945. The 1947 count is used in its stead. The population of Okinawa is excluded from the 1947–70 censuses.

to the economic hardships of early postwar days plus the enactment in 1948 of a Eugenics Protection Law that legalized abortion and made it readily and cheaply available to persons desirous of limiting the sizes of their families. In a number of recent years there have been more than one million registered abortions in Japan. Adding to these the sizable number of unregistered abortions, the resulting figure may well come close to or surpass the total number of live births occurring annually in Japan. Since 1952, the increasing popularity of contraception as a means of limiting family size has reinforced the effect of abortion on the declining birth rate. The rise in the rate of increase in the population between the 1970 and 1975 censuses is attributable largely to what the Japanese call the "second baby boom." Most of the women born during the first postwar "baby boom" around 1947 became mothers during this five-year period.

As a consequence of these developments, the basic nature of Japan's population problem has changed several times in the postwar period, and the resulting political and economic problems have changed accordingly. The initial postwar difficulties associated with an unchecked growth of population were resolved by the late 1950s. They were promptly succeeded, however, by the new problem of a population structure weighted increasingly toward the working population (ages fifteen to sixty), a segment that accounted for 61 percent of Japan's total population by 1960. It was calculated at the time that it would be necessary to find approximately one million new jobs per year to meet the employment needs of this group. For an economy that had only recently recovered from the shock and losses of war, this was a daunting prospect. This problem, however, was solved by the explosive growth of the Japanese economy in the mid- and late-1960s. By the early 1970s, Prime Minister Sato was actually complaining about a labor shortage in Japan, suggesting that the birth rate was too low for the country's economic needs and considering the advisability of positive measures by the government to encourage larger families. At the same time, Japanese firms were beginning to establish assembly plants abroad to carry on the more labor-oriented aspects of production.

The newest version of the Japanese population problem is the increase in the proportion of the population aged sixty-five or more. In prewar times this segment held fairly steady at about 3–4 percent of the population. Between 1950 and 1975, it increased steadily in size from 5.3 million (5.7 percent of the total population) to 8.8 million (7.9 percent). It continues to rise sharply. Furthermore, the entire over-sixty portion of the population increased at a quinquennial rate far in excess of rates for the newborn to aged fourteen (1.6 percent) or aged fifteen to fifty-nine (about 6.5 percent) groups: the actual rate for the five-year period between the 1965 and 1970 censuses was about 19 percent. This shift in the age structure will greatly inflate the national need for programs such as social welfare and old-age and health insurance. A massive change in population balance and characteristics of this sort poses basic problems for both the economy and the polity. They define some of the most basic issues of politics and significantly affect the style as well as the content of the political power struggle. The problem is particularly acute for Japan because the traditional system of care for the aged by their family is only now being supplanted by new and quite inadequate measures of public assistance.

One further aspect of Japan's population structure that deserves notice at this point is the number of households. The significance of such a statistic derives from the traditional centrality of the family in Japanese society and from the greater prevalence in earlier times of "extended" as opposed to "nuclear" families. The nuclear family consists of father, mother, and children; the extended family of this nuclear group plus members of other generations or collateral kin. While it has never been true that families and what Japanese call "ordinary households" are strictly equivalent groups, it is still possible to gain some insight into the fractionalization of traditional family life, the increasing ascendancy of the nuclear as opposed to the extended family, and by extension, the process of individuation through an examination of the household section of census statistics.

The number of "ordinary households" in Japan and the average number of individuals comprising such households has changed. There has been a steady increase in the number of individual households and a corresponding decrease in their average size. Implicit in this is an increase in both the popularity and the normalcy of nuclear family life, which would undoubtedly be considerably more pronounced if housing were cheaper and easier to find in the crowded conditions of postwar Japan. The increase in nuclear families also tells a good deal about the sorts of basic change in the circumstances of daily life that accompany the process of modernization. It has, of course, important consequences for Japan's political system. The older solidarities of political attitudes and behavior that characterized the more stable family and community scenes of earlier times are breaking down, and at the very least, the forces favoring deviance from the more traditional modes of political attitudes, values, and behavior are being substantially enhanced.

ETHNIC CHARACTERISTICS

Japan has a remarkably homogeneous population. Although hybrid in their historic origins, the latest available statistics indicate that of a total population of about 112 million in 1975, only 745,565 (0.7 percent) belonged to registered minority groups. Of this number, 643,096 (86 percent) were Koreans, 47,677 (6 percent) Chinese, and 21,045 (3 percent) Americans. The figures for all other nationalities were insignificant. Although these figures exclude foreigners who have assumed Japanese citizenship (and thus substantially understate the Korean element in the population), there is no other major nation with so small an admixture of identifiable minority elements. Japan is in an ethnic sense 99.9 percent "pure." This helps to explain the strong nationalism frequently displayed by the Japanese in modern times. Their geographical isolation, common language, and long history combine with racial homogeneity to facilitate the development of a very strong "in-group" feeling against foreigners. The result is a nation that, although subject to a number of domestic cleavages, has in the past usually presented a strong and united front to the rest of the world. This same degree of "purity" also affords Japan the most unusual luxury of almost complete freedom from the stresses and problems of ethnic politics that currently afflict so many other societies.

SECTIONALISM

A distinction must be made between Japan's outward-facing and inward-facing character. Racial homogeneity and nationalism have not precluded the development of political, cultural, and economic sectionalism. Japan's premodern past lies very close to its present; the Restoration occurred just over one hundred years ago. Most of Japan's national history before that was more local than nation-centered. Geography conspired with feudalism and the limitations of premodern communications to insure such a result. The Restoration originally centered around four principal southwestern clans, that is, around specific regions or sections of the country. Until well into the present century, the new system of government established by the Meiji oligarchy was denounced by its opponents as clan-dominated. Sectionalism has thus played a continuous and important role in Japanese political history. Today, sectionalism is still important in an understanding of Japanese politics but in a somewhat different guise. Clan affiliations are largely forgotten, but domestic differences in language, culture, tradition, and economic characteristics and interests reinforce the distinctly regional quality of most politicians' sources of political support in a way that provides a role for sectionalism in the political process. As politicians grow more responsive to local interests and pressures, the importance of sectional considerations may increase rather than diminish. Today, however, they are cast in terms of competitive economic or political advantage rather than traditional loyalties.

URBAN-RURAL DISTRIBUTION AND EMPLOYMENT CHARACTERISTICS

Throughout much of Asia, the distinction between city-dwelling and country-dwelling is of fundamental importance. Asian societies are predominantly agrarian, and most of the people are farmers living and working in the countryside. Cities, although by no means new, usually account for minor proportions of the total population. Yet as the modernizing process takes hold in these countries, the urban sector of the population steadily grows in size and changes its social characteristics. Industrialization occurs first in the cities; migrants flow in from the surrounding countryside; foreigners and foreign ideas gain a foothold; and old ways and old social relationships begin to break down. In short, the city becomes the vanguard of change from a traditionally organized to a modern society, whereas the countryside—less directly subject to many of the forces of change—tends to cling more closely to the established an traditional ways. This process has political as well as economic and social consequences. In Japan, for example, the urban population has definitely been more receptive to political innovation than the rural population. Liberalism, socialism, communism, the Clean Government Party, the local autonomy movement, and many other new political movements have been primarily identified with the urban population, at least in their early stages.

The urban portion of the Japanese population has steadily increased.... As recently as 1950 there were only four cities (Tokyo, Osaka, Nagoya, and Kyoto) with populations in excess of one million; today there are ten (the preceding four plus Yokohama, Kobe, Kitakyushu, Sapporo, Kawasaki, and Fukuoka). In 1975 they accounted for 20.7 percent of Japan's population. Tokyo is perhaps the world's largest city with an overall population in 1975 of 11,669,167—8,642,800 of whom live within the twenty-three wards (ku) of the city proper. It is interesting to note in the recent census that cities with populations over one million—the true metropolises of Japan—dropped slightly in their share of the total population from 21.6 percent in 1970 to 20.7 percent in 1975, indicating that the very largest cities may be reaching their limits of growth.

The environs of these major cities continue to grow dramatically, however, giving rise to doughnut-shaped rings of areas of very high growth rates. A phenomenon called the Tokaido Corridor or Belt consists of the Tokyo Metropolitan Region (the prefectures of Tokyo, Kanagawa, Saitama, and Chiba with a population of 27,037,267, or 24.1 percent of Japan's total population), the Osaka Metropolitan Region (Osaka, Kyoto, Hyogo, and Nara; 16,772,885, or 14.9 percent), the Chukyo Metropolitan Region (Aichi, Mie, and Gifu; 9,417,461, or 8.4 percent), and Shizuoka (3,308,796, or 2.9 percent). The result is an almost continuous megalopolitan belt from Tokyo to Kobe with a population of 56,536,409, or 50.5 percent of Japan's total population. These twelve very heavily settled prefectures, therefore, account for over half of the overall population of Japan's forty-seven prefectures. This sort of phenomenon is not unique to Japan. One encounters a similar pattern on a smaller scale in the Boston–New York–Philadelphia–Washington Corridor in the United States.

Since there has been no appreciable change in the Japanese population due to permanent immigration or emigration, the reciprocal of this pattern of rapid growth in the major metropolitan areas has been a heavy drain on the population of the more rural portions of Japan. Most of the increase in urban population has been attributable to domestic migration from the countryside. This process began to slow down in the early 1970s....

TABLE 4–4 Urban-Rural Population Distribution

Census year	Population			Percentage		Densely inhabited districts		All other districts	
	Total	All cities	All rural	All cities	All rural	Population	Percentage	Population	Percentage
1920	55,391,481	10,020,038	45,371,443	18.1	81.9				
1925	59,179,200	12,821,625	46,357,575	21.7	78.3				
1930	63,872,496	15,363,646	48,508,850	24.1	75.9				
1935	68,661,654	22,581,794	46,079,860	32.9	67.1				
1940	72,539,729	27,494,237	45,045,492	37.9	62.1				
1945	71,998,104	20,022,333	51,975,771	27.8	72.2				
1947	78,101,473	25,857,739	52,243,734	33.1	66.9				
1950	83,199,637	31,203,191	51,996,466	37.5	62.5				
1955	89,275,529	50,288,026	38,987,503	56.3	43.7				
1960	93,418,000	59,333,000	34,084,000	63.5	36.5	40,830,000	43.7	52,589,000	56.3
1965	98,281,000	66,919,000	31,356,000	68.1	31.9	47,261,000	48.1	51,014,000	51.9
1970	103,720,000	74,853,000	28,867,000	72.2	27.8	55,535,000	53.5	48,185,000	46.5
1975	111,933,818	84,961,894	26,971,924	75.9	24.1	63,822,648	57.0	48,111,170	43.0

Source: Derived from *1965 Population Census of Japan; 1970 Population Census of Japan;* Sorifu Tokeikyoku, *Waga Juni no Jinko,* 1970, p. 23; and *1975 Population Census of Japan, Preliminary Count.*

[a]Starting with the 1960 census, the Japanese government introduced the concept of "densely inhabited districts," defined as a group of contiguous enumeration districts with a population density of 4,000 inhabitants or more per square kilometer lying within the boundaries of a city, town, or village that itself has a population of 5,000 or more inhabitants. This is a more meaningful measure of urban dwelling circumstances than the earlier system that was based on the distinction between political units denominated as cities (*shibu*) — and therefore "urban" — and those denominated as towns or villages (*gumbu*) — and therefore "rural." In fact many parts of areas designated technically as cities (*shibu*) are notably rural.

A further and more precise insight into the urban-rural characteristics of the Japanese people may be gained from an analysis of their occupational characteristics. The changes are remarkable. For example, in 1920 the total labor force was 26,966,000, and 53.6 percent were employed in the primary or typically rural industries (agriculture, forestry, and fishing), 20.7 percent in the secondary industries (mining, construction, and manufacturing), and 23.8 percent in tertiary or service industries (trade, finance, communications, government, services, and so on). In other words and in occupational terms, more than one-half of the Japanese population was still rural. By 1975 the size of the labor force had increased to 54,380,000. Of this number only 13.9 percent were still engaged in the primary industries, 34.4 percent were in secondary employments, and 51.7 percent in tertiary. Obviously an enormous shift had occurred. Less than one-seventh of the labor force was still engaged in the traditional rural occupations, but more than one-half were in the service industries. A solid one-third were engaged in the secondary industries. Basic changes of this sort in a society's employment characteristics and urban-rural distribution patterns prepare the way for profound shifts in the sociopolitical attitudes, values, behavior, and potentialities of the Japanese people.

INCOME DISTRIBUTION

The economic characteristics of a nation's population vitally affect the country's political attitudes and behavior. Economic dissatisfaction is conducive to political dissatisfaction that may, under appropriate circumstances, lead to political instability and change. In the case of Japan, there can be no doubt that the country's remarkable prosperity in recent years has had a great deal to do with the stability of its political system. Should these economic circumstances change markedly for the worse, corresponding political changes would undoubtedly follow, although it is difficult to foresee their specific nature.

The gross facts of income distribution in Japan are as follows. National income has risen steadily and sharply during the postwar years. During the period from 1948 to 1964, for example, Japan's national income rose from ¥1,961.6 billion ($5.4 billion) to ¥20,522.5 billion ($57 billion), a more than tenfold increase in sixteen years. Not all of this represents a real improvement, however, since it was accompanied by a considerable measure of inflation. If this is compensated for by including changes in the general price index (which until 1964 was based on average prices in the years 1934–36), the real national income increased from approximately ¥9.5 billion ($2.7 billion) to ¥46.6 billion ($13.3 billion), almost a fivefold increase, while real national income on a per capita basis increased in terms of 1934–36 prices and exchange rates from about ¥118 ($34) to about ¥480 ($137), a fourfold increase.

After 1964 the period of explosive growth in the Japan economy got under way with the results set forth in table 4–5. For our purposes, the most meaningful of these figures are those giving gross national product on a per capita basis. Even discounting these for inflation and changes in the value of the yen, it is obvious that the circumstances of the Japanese people have on the average improved markedly in recent years. The 1970 figure, for example, is in real terms about the same as that for Great Britain and substantially better than that for Italy. Similar cross-national comparisons are difficult for more recent years because of the distorting effects of floating exchange rates, high but differential rates of inflation, and Japan's abandonment of the 1965 base for the calculation of constant prices, but even so, there continued to be notable improvements in real per capita income. The 1973 figures, for example, show an increase of 7.1 percent over those for 1972 after discounting for price increases.

While there is no doubt that practically all Japanese have benefited appreciably from their country's increasing affluence, these benefits have differed from sector to sector of the population. For example, there are substantial differences from one part of the country to another. To take an extreme case, a 1973 report on the distribution of per capita incomes by prefecture showed a gap of more than ¥832,000 ($2,770) between Tokyo's average of ¥1,417,000 ($4,723) per year and Kagoshima's figure of ¥586,000 ($1,953). Only four prefectures—and these the most metropolitan—had average per capita annual incomes in excess of ¥1,000,000 ($3,333), whereas eight—and these the most rural and remote—had averages below ¥700,000 ($2,333). Thus in terms of average income, it makes a good deal of difference where one lives in Japan. There continue to be marked urban-rural differences with respect to income.

There is also a difference in the monthly earnings of employees of different-sized firms. In 1973, for example, the average monthly wage of workers for firms with 10 to 99 employees was ¥80,000 ($267); for firms with 100 to 999 employees, ¥90,400 ($301); and for firms with more than 1,000 employees, ¥106,500 ($355). There are still significant differences in

TABLE 4–5   Gross National Product and Per Capita Income, 1965–74 (in billions of dollars)

Item	1965	1970	1972	1973	1974	1975
Gross National Product	$ 88.8	$ 197.1	$ 322.3	$ 407	$ 454	$ 488
Gross National Product per capita	928	1,957	2,949	3,547	4,133	4,432

Source: Adapted from Office of the Prime Minister, Bureau of Statistics, *Japan Statistical Yearbook 1976*; and Morgan Guaranty Trust Company, *Basic Economic Indicators, Japan.*

income attaching to employment by firms of different sizes. However, these are now far smaller than has typically been the case in the modern Japanese economy; they were truly major until the growing labor shortage after the mid-sixties began to increase rapidly the wages of all employees, notably those of the formerly depressed "small and medium industries." In this connection the extraordinary recent increases in the average wages of unionized labor in Japan should also be noted. These were, of course, intended to compensate for the very high rate of inflation. The average wage increase amounted to 20 percent in 1973 and 32 percent in 1974, dropping to about 14 percent in 1975.

The Japanese system of wages is also characterized by quite pronounced generational differences in pay levels. To an unusual degree, wage scales in Japan are directly proportional to age and seniority. In 1973, for example, wages for employees aged eighteen to nineteen started at about ¥62,000 ($207) per month and peaked for males aged forty to forty-nine at about ¥135,000 ($450). Wages fell off very slightly for the group aged fifty to fifty-nine and quite markedly for those over sixty, for whom continued employment is apt to be regarded as a form of social security. There tend to be relatively few exceptions to this gradual escalation of salaries over time, and as might be expected, there is resentment among some younger workers who feel that more recognition should be accorded to performance and less to seniority.

Generational inequities in pay levels are not nearly as pronounced as those in terms of the sex of employees. On the average, the pay scale of women in Japan starts low and remains low. For example, the 1973 average wage level for female employees was ¥56,400 ($188) per month, some ¥51,600 ($172) less than the average of ¥108,000 ($360) received by male workers. Thus, the average male worker was paid almost 48 percent more than the average female worker. In general women are neither highly regarded nor well paid in Japanese industry, although the slow beginnings of change are evident.

Income distribution in Japan, as elsewhere, is obviously stratified in a number of different ways: by geography, by size of firm, by age and seniority, and by sex. In each case, the political consequence is the creation of actual or potential grievances capable of lending themselves to exploitation for partisan purposes. The degree to which these have become real issues in Japanese politics varies greatly. Differences between urban and rural income levels, for example, have long been a major political problem in Japan. They underlie the "military revolts" of the 1930s, while in more recent times they lie at the heart of the highly controversial, and very costly, program of governmental subsidies to the rice farmers of Japan. The women's movement is also something of an issue in contemporary Japanese politics, but it has not been particularly successful in pressing for equal pay for equal work. The same is true for the seniority system. These problems have the capacity to become vibrant political issues in Japan.

CLASS STRUCTURE AND MOBILITY

... In Japan as elsewhere, satisfactory definitions of precisely what is meant by such terms as upper, middle, and lower classes—or their many variants—are lacking, and there is not enough information to determine what proportions of the population should be assigned to which classes. Insofar as one's class status is a product of socioeconomic status, however, it may prove useful to review the 1975 census findings (see table 4–6).

Whatever may be its precise characteristics, present Japanese class structure is the product of a series of quite unusual historical forces. To begin with, a century ago Japanese society was very rigidly stratified into a four-class hierarchy, ranging from the samurai, or warrior class, at the top through the peasantry and artisans to the merchants at the bottom. Although this ranking frequently did not accord with the actual distribution of wealth or influence in late Tokugawa times, it did represent a very important aspect of the status and value system of the time. It was legally abolished only after the Restoration of 1868. The social and economic tumult of early and mid-Meiji years (roughly 1868–1900) brought with it very considerable changes in class structure. ...

World War II and Japan's defeat and occupation brought with it another great period of social change that is still in process. At the upper levels of society, the hereditary aristocracy and the military elite were eliminated from positions of leadership. The big business element was shaken up. Many political leaders were purged from politics, at least temporarily. Only the

TABLE 4–6 Socioeconomic Groups in the Japanese Population Aged Fifteen Years and Over (1975)

Socioeconomic group	Number	Percent
1. Farmers, fishermen, and associated family workers	7,253,300	8.6
2. Company and corporation executives	1,128,500	1.3
3. Business proprietors	2,998,200	3.5
4. Professionals, engineers, and technicians	2,108,300	2.5
5. Teachers, religious workers, and liberal professions	1,965,600	2.3
6. Managers, administrators, and clerical workers	9,860,800	11.6
7. Sales and service employees	8,742,500	10.3
8. Skilled, semiskilled, and unskilled workers	17,733,700	21.0
9. Protective service workers	737,800	0.8
10. Home job workers	612,200	0.7
11. Pupils and students	7,399,300	8.7
12. Housekeepers	16,707,200	19.7
13. Not employed	7,452,800	8.8
Total	84,700,200	100.0

Source: Adapted from Sorifu Tokeikyoku, *Nihon Tokei Nenkan, 1976*, pp. 32–33.

bureaucracy remained largely immune from the most drastic aspects of the great reconstitution of Japan's political elite. At lower social levels, even more massive and important changes have taken place. Before the war, the Japanese middle class was, by Western standards, small in both numbers and sociopolitical importance. Since the war, it has expanded enormously in both size and importance. In the cities, this development has resulted from the postwar development and diversification of Japanese industry, commerce, and government, the improved status and welfare of employees in general, and the economy's growing prosperity since 1952. In the countryside, it has been the product of land reform, technical improvements, and prosperity. As the middle class has expanded, the lower class has diminished. It now constitutes a much smaller proportion of the total population than before the war.

Precise information is lacking, but income statistics, consumers' purchases, the results of polls, biographical data, and a variety of other indicators testify that recent years have witnessed an almost unprecedented amount of upward social mobility in Japan. The specific political consequences of this social surge forward are rather hard to identify, however. Class by itself does not, in Japan, provide a very satisfactory explanation of popular political attitudes or behavior. Major segments of the population are not particularly class conscious politically. Conservative political allegiances are by no means based primarily or exclusively on "the middle class," nor are radical allegiances very closely correlated with "lower-class" or "proletarian" status. In fact, one fascinating aspect of Japanese politics is the extent to which the Japan Socialist and Communist parties derive support from the middle class. Given the general trend of recent developments, moreover, it is improbable that class consciousness will become a major political factor. A prolonged and serious depression or other comparable national disaster could, however, enhance its importance. . . .

EDUCATION

This high level of national educational attainment is one of Japan's great strengths. By 1970, for example, 51.6 percent of the entire population aged fifteen and over had completed the compulsory years of education, 30.1 percent had completed higher secondary schools or their equivalent, and 8.4 percent had completed a junior college or college education. These are proportions exceeded only in the United States. These high levels of education have important consequences for both politics and Japanese society in general. To an unusual degree the Japanese educational system operates on a basis of demonstrated accomplishment and merit. While no system eliminates completely the educational advantages conferred by family wealth or high socioeconomic status, the Japanese system has succeeded in doing so to an unusual degree. Higher and specialized education of excellent quality is still relatively cheap and generally accessible in Japan, and the admission standards involved are ruthlessly and fiercely meritocratic. Indeed, the popular complaints about higher education in Japan today center less upon its quality than upon the cruelty to children entailed in the long series of grueling entrance examinations, known as "examination hells." These start with kindergarten and continue through college and must be successfully passed before a student can be admitted to one of Japan's more prestigious universities—which, incidentally, tend to be public rather than private. Careers in the national higher bureaucracy are highly valued in Japan. They are open—again on the basis of rigorous entrance examinations—only to the most outstanding graduates of Japan's finest universities. These strictly merit-oriented standards make it possible for brilliant students from poor families to have more frequent access to high-level positions than is common in many other societies. The same standards insure a very high level of intellectual capacity and talent in Japan's higher bureaucracy.

Japan's consumption of the mass media is correspondingly high. In 1973, for example, the Japanese were purchasing 537 daily newspapers per one thousand people, a figure in excess of the United States' figure of 300. In 1971, the Japanese published 26,595 separate titles of new books and reprints, a figure substantially in excess of that for the United States. Japan also produced more feature length films than any other country in the world. Practically every household had a radio, and 82 percent had a television (42 percent were color). Japan is literally saturated by the out-pourings of the mass media, most of which devote a considerable amount of space or time to subjects directly or indirectly related to politics. Whatever their political views and behavior, the Japanese are exposed to a substantial amount of political information and stimulation, even by the most advanced Western standards.

It is important to note that much of what the average Japanese reads in the press is critical of the government and its policies. The relationships between government and the printed media in Japan are complex and interesting. The press is largely national to an extent unknown in the United States. Three major daily papers dominate the national market: the *Asahi* and the *Yomiuri* with circulations in excess of six million each, and the *Mainichi* with a circulation of about 4.5 million. These three papers blanket the entire country. The closest American analogy would probably be the *New York Times,* which is nationally read but has a circulation of only 843,000.

In general the Japanese press conceives its mission as involving systematic and continuous criticism of the government in power. Seldom does one encounter words of praise or confidence concerning governmental performance, capacity, or plans. To a degree this vested hostility is moderated in practice by the close personal relationships that often develop between Japanese reporters and the politicians and bureaucrats of the party or ministry in which they specialize. Japanese reporters specialize to a far greater extent than is customary elsewhere; the Diet and every ministry has regularly assigned to it a group of particular reporters from the major papers who constitute that agency's "press club." Only these reporters have routine and favored access to the personnel and news of that particular agency—a cause of constant complaint by the foreign press representatives stationed in Japan. The effect of this close relationship seems to be, in some cases at least, a moderation of the types and intensity of the criticism carried by the press. Still, the overall tone is with few exceptions distinctly antigovernmental.

The political content of television differs from the press in the sense that the emphasis on politics in news telecasts is considerably less intense and the treatment more factual and neutral. To some extent, however, this relative neutrality is compensated for by the number and popularity of what the Japanese call *zadankai,* panel shows with a political focus. These often tend to be antigovernmental in content and emphasis. The use of television in connection with election campaigns is, by American standards, almost completely colorless. A very limited amount of television time is allocated by law to each candidate, and no one can buy or otherwise acquire more for campaign purposes. . . .

RELIGIOUS AFFILIATIONS

For most Japanese, religious attitudes and persuasions do not seem to have an appreciable effect on their political attitudes or behavior. This is a rather surprising development because of the political uses to which prewar Shinto was put, because of the seeming importance of organized religion in postwar Japan, and because many Westerners expect a people's religious affiliations to affect their politics. The symbols of religion are everywhere in Japan—temples, shrines, priests, and pilgrims. The average Japanese is a registered member of some faith and is usually a member of two faiths, the Buddhist and the Shinto, at the same time (only about 0.5 percent of the population is Christian). This dual allegiance, however, normally carries with it rather modest doctrinal and spiritual commitments. Religious considerations do not seem to be influential in the average person's decision making, particularly political decisions.

There are, of course, exceptions to this generalization. The political militancy of national Shintoism before the war, with its emphasis on the divine descent of the emperor, on Japan's world mission, and on the citizen's duty to be unquestioningly loyal and obedient, is found today in a scattering of small right-wing bands. A few of the "new religions" have strong political views or programs that they strive to impart to their followers. The *Sokagakkai* is the most notable of these. It claims a membership of more than sixteen million, but sophisticated observers are inclined to place its active or meaningful membership at somewhere between three and five million. The *Sokagakkai* has also established its own political party, the *Komeito* or Clean Government Party, that is currently the third largest group in the

House of Councilors and the House of Representatives. The official relationship between the religious movement and the *Komeito* was formally severed in 1972, however, and the party's candidates now present themselves in an ostensibly secular guise. This is the only significant political party in Japan that has explicitly religious antecedents or connections.

5

The Japanese Economy Today

J. A. A. Stockwin

The factors underlying the so-called "economic miracle" that occurred in Japan between the 1950s and 1970s have been the subject of worldwide interest and study. But, as Stockwin points out here, most economists agree that there is no easy explanation for Japan's spectacular economic success. From the atomic ashes of Hiroshima and Nagasaki, Japan emerged in the postwar years as an economic dynamo, and is now the world's third largest economy, after the United States and the USSR. Stockwin argues that high rates of capital investment, willingness to import technology, high levels of personal savings, weak labor organizations, low wages, global expansion, and an educated and highly skilled work force are all responsible for Japan's rapid postwar recovery and expansion. However, most important is the "administrative guidance" provided by such government agencies as MITI (Ministry of International Trade and Industry). Rates of investment, technology transfer, and production capacity are all areas in which government and industry cooperatively plan and direct the economy. Still, this spirit of cooperation, argues Stockwin, masks serious political cleavages resulting from the fast pace of economic development. Nevertheless, he adds that historical, economic social, and cultural factors would indicate continued stability and growth for Japan in the immediate future.

Despite the serious economic problems affecting Japan between 1974 and 1981, it was still the case that no other country had achieved such spectacular economic progress since the 1950s. Few would have dared to predict, after her defeat in 1945, that within a quarter of a century Japan would have created one of the three largest economies in the world. Already by the early 1970s only the United States and the Soviet Union had economies that in terms of gross national product were bigger than that of Japan. The resilience of the economy and its capacity to adjust rapidly to adverse circumstances were graphically illustrated by the fact that although economic growth turned negative for a year or so following the OPEC oil crisis of 1973–5, by 1975 steady economic growth had been resumed at a lower but still impressive level. Whereas between the mid-1950s and early 1970s the growth of GNP averaged an annual 10 percent, between 1975 and 1980 it was averaging around 5 to 6 percent per annum.

In some respects, it is true, Japan lagged further behind than her GNP would indicate. Social services, and that part of the economy known as the 'social infrastructure' (roads, sewerage, housing and the like), had been seriously neglected when compared with the attention given to them in other advanced economies. Gross neglect of the environment, particularly during the 1950s and 1960s, had caused some appalling tragedies. Living standards, though they had risen rapidly and continued to rise, were still probably rather lower than those of a few countries whose GNP was smaller, and were being affected by inflation. Moreover, the economy was exceedingly dependent on foreign supplies of oil (99 percent of total requirements were imported), and heavily dependent of foreign countries for most other raw materials. As the cost of imported oil rose rapidly in the late 1970s and early 1980s, so the need to expand overseas markets further increased, and Japanese export drives were apt to cause difficulties with the United States, Europe and elsewhere. National security, in an economic as much as in a military sense, was a prime concern of Japan's policy-makers as the nation entered the 1980s. Nevertheless, in many of these problem areas considerable progress had been made. . . .

The reasons for the Japanese economic 'miracle' of the 1950s to 1970s have been quite widely studied by economists, who for the most part agree that there is no simple or single-factor explanation of it. Yet although there may be dispute about the relative weights which ought to be given to each of them, it is clear that certain factors were particularly important.

Perhaps the most crucial is the high rate of productive investment carried out by industry. As a percentage of GNP, fixed capital formation during the 1950s and 1960s was on average over 30 percent (substantially more than any other comparable economy), and very little of it went into types of investment, such as housing, that were not directly productive. This in itself, however, needs explaining, and the explanation is far from simple. A number of factors were involved. One was the extent to which Japanese industry over the period was willing and able to import foreign technology, purchased through licensing agreements, and develop it, incorporating improvements and adaptations. This had the twin advantages of minimizing research costs and enabling industry to incorporate the latest techniques developed overseas, without delay. Given also the willingness of businessmen to replace existing plant early (and this was no doubt initially connected with the fact that industry had had to start virtually from scratch with new equipment after the end of the Second World War), this resulted in an astonishingly rapid and sustained rise in productivity.

In its pursuit of growth, Japanese industry enjoyed what in retrospect seems like a uniquely favourable set of circumstances. The level of personal savings was extremely high, not so much because of any innate Japanese quality of thriftiness, as because the average individual needed to provide substantially for his own and his family's social welfare, as well as for his children's education. Channelled largely through the banking system, such savings provided industry with the funds for investment. Industry's bill for wages also remained moderate throughout the period, as productivity ran well ahead of wage increases. This was principally a result of the relatively low bargaining power of labour, which was organized for the most part in enterprise unions which in day-to-day bargaining with their employers would usually accept moderate wage settlements. Yet another factor was the buoyancy of Japanese exports, whose rate of increase was well in excess of the overall rate of growth of world trade. The free trading atmosphere of international economics in the 1960s was peculiarly favourable for the expansion of Japanese exports, and a number of key growth industries experienced fast growth in their export markets: These industries were largely those with high technology content, where productivity was rapidly rising and prices were highly competitive.

Other factors may be mentioned more briefly. The work force was well educated and technologically skilled. There was a substantial pool of labour ready to be absorbed into industry from less productive occupations including agriculture. Taxation was moderate and defence spending low, while there had been 'windfall gains' from the Korean and Vietnam wars.

Finally, however, it is necessary to mention a factor of major and somewhat controversial significance, namely, the role of government in the expansion process. There has been some misunderstanding of the nature of Government's role in economic management. It was not true, for instance, that the Government usurped the function of the industrialist to the point of making his day-to-day business decisions for him. The independent strength and purposiveness of the major Japanese companies is well known. Nevertheless, on many matters vitally affecting business conditions and the overall guidance of the economy, the Government occupied a key position. The Ministry of International Trade and Industry (MITI) took the initiative over a long period in relation to the pace of import and capital liberalization, and the purchase of foreign technology. Through 'administrative guidance' the nature and direction of an industry's investment programme, or the number of independent operators in a given industry, was capable of being influenced by government sources (particularly MITI).... [T]he important factor making such influence possible was the ability of government and industry to co-operate with each other, despite constant jockeying for position between different sections of both. In broad terms, the ability of government and industry to co-operate was premised upon the existence of stable conservative government, which predominated from the end of the Second World War. The long-term supremacy of the conservative business-oriented forces in Japanese politics was conducive in the circumstances of the time to sustained economic growth.

The economic environment of the 1970s was considerably more complex for Japan than that of the 1960s. Apart from the overriding problem of oil, which has already been mentioned, international trade as a whole was growing more slowly, wide fluctuations in the relative values of major currencies reflected a general mood of instability, and protectionist pressures had strengthened in several of Japan's major trading partners. Considerable progress had been made towards the internationalization of the Japanese economy, though the Government was reluctant to relax practices and alter institutional arrangements in such a manner as to render its economic policies less effective. Domestically, the intense wage-cost pressures which followed the 1974–4 oil crisis gave way to more moderate union demands, influenced by increased (though still relatively low) levels of unemployment and underemployment. Faced with reduced economic growth and an ageing population structure, firms were finding it harder to maintain intact the permanent employment system with its regular seniority increments for regular employees, so that various medifications of the system were making their appearance. One result of this was less harmonious labour relations in some sectors of the economy. Stuctural adjustment, however, continued apace, and productivity increases, though much lower than a decade earlier, were high relative to other advanced economies. Japan was now a world leader in many areas of technology, and rather than buying foreign patents, as she had largely done in the 1950s and 1960s, she was putting much greater resources than previously into her own research and development. The Japanese economy, in other words, was under much greater strain than it had been a decade earlier, but was also better equipped to withstand such strain.

When we turn, however, from economics to the broader field of politics, a substantially different logic is seen to apply in which conflicts and divisions abound, but consensus is laboriously reached or solutions are imposed. Japan is a seriously divided polity, although the divisions were partially concealed by a long period of conservative government. Vexed problems, left over from the Occupation period, or resulting from the forced pace of Japan's development, remainedd largely unresolved, and a way to their solution was by no means clear. There was thus a latent and sometimes overt tension in Japanese politics, even though in comparison with many other countries it was remarkably stable.

The juxtaposition of conflict and consensus, tension and stability, was probably the aspect of Japanese politics and government which was least easy to understand from the outside. . . .

Japan in modern times experienced two periods of massive change, the first at the time of the Meiji Restoration of 1868, and the second following her defeat at the hands of the Allied powers in 1945. It was largely the radical change of direction brought about by these two 'revolutions' which led some Western writers to suspect that the Japanese character was particularly prone to adopt sudden massive shifts in political outlook without worrying unduly about the inconsistency of old and new approaches. Thus, it was suggested, Japan could once more, in certain circumstances, radically change the direction of national policies from those of the period since the Occupation.

This, however, is not a particularly convincing argument, at least on the evidence of political events hitherto. Underlying the discontinuities of recent political history may be found a strong element of continuity. Breaks with the past are seldom complete, as a comparison of the habits, personnel and themes of Japanese politics before and after the Second World War will readily reveal. There is no counterpart in Japanese experience to the Bolshevik Revolution of 1917. Rather than the wholesale replacement of political leadership and radical reshaping of institutions and philosophies to which that event gave rise, political change in Japan even at its most radical point stopped short of a severing of links with what went before.

In part, this may well be largely a question of the character of political control in recent Japanese history. Despite the pace and scope of economic, social and political change since the middle of the nineteenth century, Japan never experienced anything resembling a revolution from below. Political activists from lower social strata at times acted as a catalyst for quasi-revolutionary changes (as in the case of the ultra-nationalist groups of young officers—many of peasant origin—who were active in the 1930s), but the political controllers, whether they were conservative or radical in outlook, always constituted a fairly self-conscious élite of people possessing high status in the society. This is as true of Japanese politics in the 1980s as it was in earlier periods, although the method of recruiting the élite is now substantially meritocratic. The politics of competing class-based parties, alternating in government, is a model that did not emerge as viable in Japan, even though in the postwar period the forms of party competition appeared to be based on the major premise that this was how the system ought to work. The reasons for this and the prospects for change will be explored in a later chapter.

Japan, it is sometimes remarked, is an oriental, not a Western, country. Some writers have argued that since the Japanese polity has a cultural context radically different from that of any of the major Western powers, one should not expect that polity to behave according to the normal expectations of Western political observers. There is some truth in this, even though writers who press this point tend to forget that each Western polity also has unique elements in its political structure. On the other side it is arguable that Japan, as a modern industrial state, with a technologically skilled population, vast industrial output and a sophisticated network of communications, should have much in common politically with other similarly advanced states. A priori, it should have more in common with them than will less developed societies elsewhere in Asia, despite some cultural and social similarities with the latter.

It is important not to become bemused by this problem. As we have already hinted, Japan has a richness of political experience and tradition comparable to that of Britain, France or the United States. Japanese political culture is neither untouched by Western influences, nor a mere carbon-copy of any other political culture. The mere fact that Japan is an industrial-ized society does not mean that it is just the same as any other industrialized society, but neither is it unaffected by pressures common to all industrial-ized states. It should be possible to attempt an analysis of Japanese govern-ment and politics using a frame of reference which owes much to Western models. Since, however, there are significant features of Japanese social or-ganization and cultural attitudes which *are* peculiar to Japan (or at least are not exactly replicated elsewhere) due attention must also be paid to these. Certain aspects of political behaviour and organization were undoubtedly formed in the mould of a social culture which emphasized group cohesive-ness and local loyalties. Other aspects can illuminated if one realizes that parts of the traditional culture held achievement in high esteem. The group, however, rather than the individual, was and is widely regarded as the en-gine of achievement, although by the early 1980s the accuracy of the gen-eralization was under attack in some quarters.

Neither the dynamism of the Japanese economy, nor the persistent fragmentation of political life into cliques and factions can be properly understood without an awareness of the social context (including an appre-ciation of the extent to which it is changing). The whole nature of decision-making is profoundly affected by social and cultural norms which are re-cognizably Japanese, even it to an extent they have their counterparts else-where. Once again, however, this is true of politics in any state one cares to name. There is a mixture of influences, social, cultural, political and eco-nomic, which has to be analysed in depth in order to gain some understand-ing of how the system works, has worked, and is likely to work in the future.

In any case it would be wrong to suggest that cultural peculiarities are the only thing which have given an element of uniqueness to Japanese po-litical patterns. Since the nineteenth century the nation's economic circum-stances have also had a profound effect upon its politics. . . .

The challenge of economic backwardness has by now been substan-tially overcome (although vulnerability in respect of oil supplies and sup-plies of other raw materials remains), and by this token the Japanese polit-ical experience tells a story of spectacular success. Whatever the successes and failures of Japanese economic management over the past century, one thing that is certain is that national economic imperatives have crucially shaped the character of the polity and the perceptions of political leaders. Many of Japan's leaders perforce developed certain habits of mind and cer-tain kinds of political arrangement adapted to the governing of a resource-poor nation, dependent upon making the best of meagre natural advantages, so as to survive in a competitive economic and political environment. These economic imperatives, reinforced, it must be added, by straightforward power considerations, have probably been as important as the social and cultural background in promoting basic continuities in Japanese politics.

In one sense economic pressures have tended to work in a similar direction to traditional social characteristics of the Japanese people. The natural poverty of the nation, coupled with its geographical and historical isolation, have served to foster a strong sense of national vulnerability and even inferiority. This in turn tended to facilitate a sense of cultural uniqueness and group-togetherness, which as seized upon by the political leaders of the Meiji period (1868–1919) as a means of cementing nationalism, including national purpose and national discipline. Only since the emergence of an increasingly affluent society and a more internationally oriented economy in the 1960s and 1970s have forces been set in motion which could radically alter in a more relaxed direction the style of exercising power and the extent of political participation. Even here we are witnessing determined resistance by the 'old guard.'

There are two particular aspects of continuity in Japanese politics which are significant in this context. One is the habit of close co-operation between government and business, which has led to a unique blend of private enterprise and political direction. Although the extent of this in the most recent period and indeed also in the Meiji period has sometimes been exaggerated, it is none the less true that Japanese industrialization was begun largely on government initiative, and political leaders continued to involve themselves closely in its progress.

The second area of continuity is the great influence of government bureaucracy in political decision-making. Essentially this was part and parcel of the doctrine of a strong Executive enshrined in the Meiji Constitution of 1890. The power of the bureaucracy, however, remains strong in practice under the 1947 Constitution, even though its relative position has been somewhat attenuated. The idea that the Executive should be strong, which not even the American Occupation was able to transform, may also be traced to a deep-seated instinct among government officials that the economy, despite its superficial advances, was too vulnerable to risk political relaxation.

The economy, however, has grown so rapidly in recent years that talk of economic vulnerability in the old sense in anachronistic, although the problem of energy and raw material supplies has yet to be overcome, if indeed a 'solution' is possible. Issues have become more complex, and between 1976 and 1980 the political system went through a period of marked instability, with the ministerial party only barely maintaining a parliamentary majority. Even though the 1980 general elections spectacularly restored conservative dominance over the national Diet, relationships between the electorate, pressure groups, political parties, the Diet and the government bureaucracy were undergoing considerable change. Japanese politics was becoming if anything more dynamic, and the constellation of forces within government, though heartened by its electoral victory and by a conservative mood in the electorate, needed to exhibit fine political judgement if is was to retain fully effective power on a long-term basis. Whatever form the distribution of political power might assume in the future, the adaptability of the present system was being continuously tested.

Unit II

China and Japan Yesterday: The Cultural Background

China and Japan share many cultural attributes. Since early in the sixth century Japan has been greatly influenced by its larger and more powerful neighbor. The inhabitants of the Japanese islands saw in the glory and splendor of Tang dynasty China a model to be emulated. Chinese characters, literary forms, painting styles, and philosophy were transmitted across the Sea of Japan with little or no modification. However, the Japanese were able to maintain a degree of independence in the development of religious and political institutions.

The indigenous religion of Japan is Shinto. In its most primitive aspects Shinto resembles a type of nature-worship. Its most important myths concern the founding of the Japanese nation and constitute the basis for the belief in the "divine" nature of the Emperor. But Shinto has been adulterated by waves of missionaries from China espousing Confucianism, Taoism, and Buddhism. Ongoing disputes have occurred over the extent to which these foreign faiths should be incorporated within the overarching structure of the Shinto religion.

Likewise, similar conflicts have arisen in the realm of Japan's political institutions. The Tang dynasty's practices of centralized administration and the appointment of local officials by the central bureaucracy were also adopted by Japanese leaders, although in a somewhat modified form. Yet the strength of existing local leaders, a strength arising from powerful clan ties, prevented the full implementation of Chinese-style centralized control. By the ninth century, the Tang dynasty had fallen into a state of decay, and a primitive kind of nationalism began to develop within the Japanese political elite. The emphasis on native institutions further weakened the imported political forms. Local leaders gained increased power and the centralized administration degenerated into feudalism.

This unit traces the history of Chinese influence on Japanese cultural, religious, and political institutions from the time of the Tang dynasty in the sixth century to the advent of Japanese feudalism in the tenth century, and introduces some of the more important elements of traditional Chinese and Japanese social structure. As Edwin O. Reischauer points out in "The Coming of Chinese Civilization," Chinese influence on Japan during this period was greatest in the area of culture. The Japanese imitated Chinese styles of painting, writing, and poetry and borrowed heavily from the Chinese language. They also adopted many of China's religious and political practices but by the tenth century had begun to place greater emphasis on indigenous cultural forms, religions, and political institutions.

In "The Nature of Chinese Society," John King Fairbank outlines the salient features of Chinese social structure and ideology and examines China's traditional family structure and its relation to thé state. In "Confucianism and the Chinese Political System," Fairbank discusses the bureaucracy, Confucianism, and the Chinese legal system, showing how Confucian principles provided an ethical basis for governance in China.

Finally, in "Behind the 'Made in Japan' Label," Kozo Yamamura identifies some of the socio-cultural factors that have contributed to Japan's rapid economic growth. An important question to be kept in mind is why China and Japan have developed along such different paths. This is an issue that relates not only to the traditional societies but also to the changes brought about by modernization. The continuing impact of cultural values on contemporary behavior can be seen in many areas—for example, in the Japanese work ethic and in the Chinese conception of rule by virtue and not by law. In Unit III, we will examine the very different responses made by China and Japan to the expansion of the West into East Asia beginning in the eighteenth and nineteenth centuries. The readings in this unit will provide the basis for comparing those responses.

6

The Coming of Chinese Civilization

Edwin O. Reischauer

In this selection from *Japan, Past and Present,* Reischauer traces the history of Chinese influence on Japanese cultural and political institutions—from the time of the Tang dynasty in the sixth century to the advent of Japanese feudalism in the tenth century. As he points out, this influence was particularly strong in the area of culture. The Japanese imitated Chinese styles of painting, writing, and poetry, and borrowed heavily from the Chinese language. However, by the tenth century, the Tang dynasty in China had entered a period of rapid decline, which prompted the Japanese to place greater emphasis on indigenous cultural forms, religions, and political institutions. Eventually, the centralized administration borrowed from the Chinese mainland deteriorated and was replaced by the rule of local nobles.

The peoples of northern Europe have always been conscious of their double heritage—their primitive Teutonic ancestry and the cultural legacy of ancient Greece and Rome. Similarly, the Japanese have a double historical heritage—the primitive stock of early Japan and the civilization of China. As in northern Europe, true history only started for Japan when the broad stream of a highly developed civilization reached its shores and, in a new geographic setting, combined with the simple native traditions of a primitive people to form a new culture, derived directly from the old civilization but differentiated from it by new geographic and racial ingredients. . . .

China's history as a highly civilized part of the world reaches back to the second millennium before Christ. Its first great period as a colossal military empire came during the period of Rome's greatness, roughly from about 250 B.C. to 200 A.D. An era of political disunion and disruption followed, and came to an end only in the second half of the sixth century, when a new and greater Chinese empire emerged from the chaos of three centuries of civil wars and barbarian invasions. The new Chinese empire was far richer and stronger than the first. In fact, during the seventh and eighth centuries China was, with little doubt, the richest and most powerful land in the whole world. This period was known by the dynastic name of T'ang, a period of unprecedented grandeur and might, and of brilliant cultural attainments. It is small wonder that the primitive Japanese in their isolated island country felt the reflected glory of the new Chinese empire and awoke to a new awareness of the great land across the sea.

The start of the heavy flow of Chinese influence to Japan is usually dated about 552, the year when the Buddhist religion is said to have been officially introduced to the Yamato clan by a missionary from a kingdom in southern Korea. Actually, Buddhism had probably entered Japan even earlier, but this incident affords a convenient date to mark the time when the Japanese first started consciously to learn from the Chinese.

During the next few centuries Buddhism served as an important vehicle for the transmission of Chinese culture to Japan. Buddhism is by origin an Indian religion. It had slowly spread to China and had won a place of importance in Chinese culture during the troubled era between the two great empires. It was a vigorous missionary religion at that time, and missionary zeal carried it beyond China to Korea and from there to Japan. Korean, Chinese, and even occasional Indian priests came to Japan from the sixth to eighth centuries. In turn, scores of Japanese converts went to China to learn more of the new faith. Returning from the continent, these Japanese student priests, even more than foreign missionary teachers, took the lead in transmitting to Japan the new religion and many other aspects of Chinese civilization. They were the true pioneers in planting and nurturing in Japan the borrowed culture of China.

In the second half of the sixth century Buddhism and other new influences from abroad so affected the Yamato clan that clashes broke out between factions favoring the acceptance of Buddhism and other continental ideas and opposition groups which resisted the new religion and all change. The victory of the pro-Buddhist faction in about 587 cleared the way for a more rapid importation and acceptance of Chinese ideas and knowledge, and under the able leadership of the crown prince, Shotoku, many startling reforms were undertaken.

One of the most important innovations of Prince Shotoku was the sending of a large official embassy to China in the year 607. This embassy, and many others following its precedent during the next two centuries, played a vital role in the great period of learning from China. Although their immediate political significance was slight, and the economic importance of the exchange of goods carried on under their auspices was limited, the cultural influence of the embassies was tremendous. The Japanese leaders, showing extraordinary wisdom for a people only just emerging into the light of civilization, carefully chose promising young scholars and artists to accompany the embassies in order to study at the sources of knowledge in China. These young men, selected for their knowledge of Chinese literature, philosophy, history, or Buddhist theology and ritual, or for their skill in the arts of painting, poetry, or music, studied in China during the year of the embassy's stay, and some remained in China for a decade or two between embassies. Upon their return to Japan, they became leaders in their respective fields, the men most responsible for the successful transmission to this isolated land of the science, arts, and ideals of the great continental civilization. ...

Under the influence of Chinese ideas, the Japanese for the first time conceived the idea of the Yamato state as an empire, and at that, an empire on an equal footing with China. Prince Shotoku even dared to phrase a letter to the Chinese emperor as coming from the Emperor of the Rising Sun to the Emperor of the Setting Sun. With the new imperial concept, the ruler of the Yamato state for the first time assumed the dignity and majesty of an emperor. The priest-chief of the clan became in theory all-powerful, an absolute monarch in the Chinese tradition. But he did not lose his original role as high priest. He retained a dual position. Even today the Japanese emperor is in theory the Shinto high priest of ancient Yamato tradition, and at the same time the all-powerful secular ruler of Chinese tradition.

Possibly also under the influence of Chinese social concepts and of the Chinese prejudice against ruling empresses, the ancient custom of rule by women came to a definite end in Japan in the first half of the eighth century, after an unfortunate incident between a ruling empress and a Buddhist priest. Only many centuries later, long after the imperial line had become politically insignificant, did women again appear on the throne. Japanese women, who in the earliest times had enjoyed a position of social and political dominance over men, gradually sank to a status of complete subservience to them. Their rights and influence in early feudal society seem still to have been considerable, but in time even these rights were lost, as the women of Japan became socially and intellectually mere handmaids of the dominant male population.

Below the emperor the Japanese created a complex central government patterned after the tremendous centralized administration of T'ang China, one of the most highly developed and complex governments the world has ever seen. Under a Supreme Council of State, with its Prime Minister and Ministers of the Left and Right, were eight ministries, in concept not unlike the departments of our own government. Under the ministries in turn came scores of bureaus and other offices. ...

The creation of a central government in Japan based on Chinese models was an easier task than the creation of the Chinese type of provincial administration. Clan spirit and clan autonomy were still too strong to tolerate the direct rule of all parts of the land by a bureaucracy dispatched to the provincial centers from the court. But the Japanese at least created the outward forms of the Chinese provincial system. The land was divided into prefectures and sub-prefectures, and over these were placed officials with high-sounding titles. Since most of these provincial posts, however, were given to local aristocrats, control from the central government remained vague and probably subject to the tolerance of local leaders. ...

The process of learning and borrowing from China was of course not limited to the political field. In fact, what the Japanese were learning at this time in cultural and intellectual fields had much more prolonged influence in Japan than did the borrowed political institutions. The latter for the most part decayed rapidly, and eventually disappeared in all but name, but many of the religious concepts, artistic skills, and literary forms learned during these centuries, far from losing their original vigor, developed and helped form the basic cultural patterns of later ages.

After the triumph of the pro-Buddhist faction at the Yamato court in the second half of the sixth century, this continental religion enjoyed the uninterrupted favor of the central government. Splendid temples were erected at government expense; impressive Buddhist ceremonies were sponsored by the court and the noble families. Many a Japanese emperor retired from the heavy burdens of his dual secular and religious role to the more peaceful life of the Buddhist monk. As was the case with so much else in the newly imported continental culture, the influence of Buddhism was still weak in the provinces, but in the capital district the new religion was supreme, and enjoyed official favor far greater than that afforded even the native cults of Shinto. . . .

In art, the Japanese could have had no better teachers than the Chinese, but in the field of writing Chinese influence was less happy. Japanese is a language of simple phonetic structure and highly inflected words. Hence it can be easily written by phonetic symbols, and these are necessary to represent the language properly. The Chinese writing system, on the other hand, leaves little possibility for phonetic transcription or for the representation of inflections. Since Chinese lacks inflection and since in ancient Chinese the words tended to be monosyllabic, the Chinese found it possible to use a writing system in which each monosyllabic word or word-root is represented by a special symbol, called a character or ideograph. These characters range from a simple line, — to represent "one," to more complex characters, [having as many as] twenty-five strokes. . . .

Because of the difficulties involved and also because of the tremendous prestige of all things Chinese, the ancient Japanese made little effort to write their own language. Proper names and brief poems in Japanese were spelled out laboriously with one Chinese character used phonetically for each syllable, but little else was attempted. Instead the Japanese wrote in pure and often reasonably good classical Chinese. Using Chinese much as medieval Europeans used Latin, they wrote their histories, geographies, law books, and official documents of all sorts. They even attempted to imitate Chinese literary forms, and men of education prided themselves on their ability to compose poems in Chinese. . . .

THE GROWTH
OF A NATIVE CULTURE

The period of greatest learning from China lasted from the late sixth century until the early ninth century, when a subtle change began to take place in the attitude of the Japanese toward China. The prestige of all things

Chinese remained great, but the ninth century Japanese were no longer so anxious to learn from China or so ready to admit the superiority of all phases of Chinese civilization over their own.

One reason for this slowly changing attitude toward Chinese culture was the political decay of T'ang, which became marked as the ninth century progressed. Perhaps even more fundamental was the intellectual growth of the Japanese themselves, resulting in a gradual reassertion of a spirit of cultural independence. Three centuries of assiduous learning from the Chinese had created, at least in the capital district, a cultured society with its own political and social institutions, patterned of course after Chinese models but changed and adapted to fit Japanese needs by over two centuries of conscious experimentation and slow unconscious modification. The Japanese were no longer a primitive people, overawed by the vastly superior continental civilization and eager to imitate blindly anything Chinese. Japan was reaching a state of intellectual maturity and was ready to develop a culture of its own. . . .

The slow rise of native Japanese culture is perhaps best observed in the development of an adequate means of writing the native tongue. This writing system was developed slowly during the ninth and tenth centuries by the process of using certain Chinese characters in greatly abbreviated form as simple phonetic symbols devoid of any specific meaning in themselves. Since the Chinese characters each represented one monosyllabic word or word-root, the phonetic symbols derived from them normally stood for a whole syllable, such as *ka, se,* or *mo.* The result was a syllabary [called *kana*] and not an alphabet, such as our own system of writing. . . .

Political Institutions

Although the appearance by the tenth and eleventh centuries of a new and distinctive Japanese culture was perhaps best seen in the literature of the time, it was evident in other fields also. The arts of painting, sculpture, and architecture all showed definite and sometimes marked signs of Japanese characteristics quite distinct from the original Chinese patterns, and political and social institutions changed so radically as to bear little resemblance to the Chinese prototypes.

The key figure of the Chinese political system was the bureaucrat, the scholar-civil servant who operated the complicated central government and went out to the provinces to collect taxes and maintain order. Thousands of these bureaucrats were required, and the recruiting of wise and capable men for the higher posts was a matter of crucial importance to the whole state. For this purpose, the Chinese had developed a system of civil service examinations. It centered around the great central university at Ch'ang-an where periodic examinations were given on classical subjects. Candidates who succeeded best in the examinations went directly to high government posts. In this way, men of scholarly talents from all walks of life could reach positions of responsibility, and among the educated classes a vital tradition of public service was built up.

The Japanese borrowed only the outward forms of this system. With their strong traditions of clan loyalty and hereditary rights, they could not bring themselves to accept its spirit. They created a central university where the Chinese classics were studied and examinations were held, but only in rare cases did scholars with little family backing attain positions of much responsibility. In the provinces, political authority remained in the hands of local aristocrats masquerading as civil servants appointed by the central administration, while at the capital courtiers of noble lineage held most posts of importance, leaving to the scholar bureaucrats the humbler clerical jobs.

In China, the central government was constantly kept busy fighting the natural tendency for the tax-paying peasants and their lands to gravitate into the hands of powerful families with sufficient influence at court to protect their holdings from the encroachments of tax collectors. In Japan, this tendency was even stronger, for there was no powerful civil servant class to protect the interests of the state, and local aristocrats, in key positions as provincial officers, joined with court nobles in despoiling the public domain. . . .

Tax-free manors grew and expanded during the eighth and ninth centuries until, by the tenth, the national domain had virtually disappeared. With its disappearance, the income of the state from taxes, the economic basis for the Chinese form of centralized government, dwindled to almost nothing. As a result, provincial governmental agencies, which had never been strong, withered away almost completely, leaving behind imposing but meaningless administrative titles, such as Governor or Vice-Governor. Even the central administration became largely an empty shell, a great paper organization with court nobles sporting high titles but with little working personnel, scanty funds, and greatly reduced functions of government. The complex system of rule through eight ministries was for all practical purposes abandoned, and new and simplified organs of government were developed to handle what few political duties the central government still had.

The net result of all this was that centralized government ceased to exist for most parts of Japan. Each estate, freed from encroachment by tax collectors and other state agents, became a small autonomous domain, a semi-independent economic and political unit. The contacts it had with the outside world were not with any government agency but with the great court family or monastery which exercised a loose and distant control over it.

The noble court families and monasteries became, in a sense, multiple successors of the old centralized state. Any centralizing forces in the economic and political life of Japan were represented largely by them and not by the bureaus of the central government. These families and monasteries became to a certain degree states within the hollow framework of the old imperial government, each supported by the income from its own estates and, through family government or monastery administration, exercising many of the functions of government in its widely scattered manors throughout the land.

The imperial family, though retaining great prestige because of its past political role and its continuing position as leader in the Shinto cults, became in fact simply one among these central economic and political units. It exercised a theoretical rule over a shadow government, but in reality it controlled only its own estates and lived on the income from them, and not from government taxes. In time, even control over its own private affairs was lost, as one of the court families, the Fujiwara, gradually won complete mastery over the imperial family by intrigue and skillful political manipulations.

7

The Nature of Chinese Society

John King Fairbank

Here, Fairbank outlines the various features of the Chinese social structure, focusing particularly on the bifurcation of the rural and urban classes. After examining the traditional family structure and its relation to the state, he turns to the gentry and considers both the economic and political role of this important stratum. Finally, he discusses the issue of mobility between the peasantry and the gentry, as well as within the gentry itself.

SOCIAL STRUCTURE

Since ancient times there have been two Chinas—the myriad agricultural communities of the peasantry in the countryside, where each tree-clad village and farm household persists statically upon the soil; and the superstructure of walled towns and cities peopled by the landlords, scholars, merchants, and officials—the families of property and position. There has been no caste system, and the chance to rise from peasant status has not been lacking. Yet China has always remained a country of farmers, four-fifths of the people living on the soil they till. The chief social division has therefore been that between town and countryside, between the 80 percent or more of the population who have stayed put upon the land and the 10 or 20 percent of the population who have formed a mobile upper class. This bifurcation still underlies the Chinese political scene and makes it difficult to spread the control of the state from the few to the many.

If we look more closely at this inherited class structure, we note that the upper levels have included really several classes—the land-owning gentry, the scholar-literati, and the officials, as well as the merchants, the militarists and their hangers-on. This composite upper stratum has been the active carrier of Chinese culture in its many aspects. Within this minority segment of the Chinese people have been developed and maintained all the literature and most of the fine arts, all the higher philosophy, ethics, and political ideology of the state, the sanctions of power, and much of the wealth that accompanied them. Culture has filtered down to the masses. . . .

The Chinese family has been a microcosm, the state in miniature. The family, not the individual, has been the social unit and the responsible element in the political life of its locality. The filial piety and obedience inculcated in family life have been the training ground for loyalty to the ruler and obedience to constituted authority in the state.

This function of the family to raise filial sons who would become loyal subjects can be seen by a glance at the pattern of authority within the traditional family group. The father was a supreme autocrat, with control over the use of all family property and income and a decisive voice in arranging the marriages of the children. The mixed love, fear, and awe of children for their father was strengthened by the great respect paid to age. An old man's loss of vigor was more than offset by his growth in wisdom. As long as he lived in possession of his faculties the patriarch possessed every sanction to enable him to dominate the family scene. He could even sell his children into slavery. In fact, of course, parents were also bound by a reciprocal code of responsibility for their children as family members. But law and custom provided little check on parental tyranny if they chose to exercise it.

The domination of age over youth within the old-style family was matched by the domination of male over female. Chinese baby girls in the old days were more likely than baby boys to suffer infanticide. A girl's marriage was, of course, arranged and not for love. The trembling bride became at once a daughter-in-law under the tyranny of her husband's mother. In a well-to-do family she might see secondary wives or concubines brought into the household, particularly if she did not bear a male heir. She could be repudiated by her husband for various reasons. If he died she could not easily remarry. All this reflected the fact that a woman had no economic independence. Her labor was absorbed in household tasks and brought her no income. Peasant women were universally illiterate. They had few or no property rights. Until the present century their subjection was demonstrated and reinforced by the custom of foot-binding. This crippling practice by which a young girl's feet were tightly wrapped to prevent normal development seems to have begun about the tenth century A.D. The "lily feet" which it produced through the suffering of hundreds of millions of young girls acquired great aesthetic and erotic value. In practice bound feet kept womankind from venturing far abroad. . . .

Status within the family was codified in the famous "five relationships," a doctrine emphasized by the Confucian philosophers. These five relationships were those between ruler and subject (prince and minister), father and son, elder brother and younger brother, husband and wife, and friend and friend. To an egalitarian Westerner the most striking thing about this doctrine is that three of the five relations were within the family, and four of the five were between superior and subordinate. . . .

Chinese well habituated to the family system have been prepared to accept similar patterns of status in other institutions, including the official hierarchy of the government. One advantage of a system of status (as opposed to our individualist system of contractual relations) is that a man knows automatically where he stands in his family or society. He can have security in the knowledge that if he does his prescribed part he may expect reciprocal action from others in the system. It has often been observed that a Chinese community overseas tends to organize its activities and meet new situations in a hierarchic fashion. . . .

Contrary to a common myth, a large family with several children has not been the peasant norm. The scarcity of land, as well as disease and famine, has set a limit to the number of people likely to survive in each family unit. The large joint family of several married sons with many children all within one compound, which has usually been regarded as typical of China, appears to have been the ideal exception, a luxury which only the well-to-do could afford. . . .

The Chinese gentry can be understood only in a dual, economic-and-political sense, as connected both with landholding and with office holding. The narrow definition, following the traditional Chinese term *shen-shih,* confines gentry status to those *individuals* who held official degrees gained normally by passing examinations, or sometimes by recommendation or purchase. This has the merit of being concrete and even quantifiable—the gentry in this narrow sense were degree-holders, as officially listed, and not dependent for their status on economic resources, particularly landowning, which is so hard to quantify from the historical record.

Yet in an agrarian society one can hardly ignore the importance of landholding as one source of upper-class strength, much as one may wish to avoid the Marxist exaggeration of the role of economic relations. The main point about the gentry as individuals was that they were public functionaries, playing political and administrative roles, in addition to any connection with the landlord class. Yet, being Chinese, they were also enmeshed in family relations, on which they could rely for material sustenance. This political-economic dualism has led many writers to define the term gentry more broadly, as a group of *families* rather than of individual degree-holders only. Both the narrow and the broad definitions must be kept in mind.

Looked at descriptively, the gentry families lived chiefly in the walled towns rather than in the villages. They constituted a stratum of families based on landed property which intervened between the earth-bound masses of the peasantry, on the one hand, and the officials and merchants who formed a fluid matrix of overall administrative and commercial activity, on the other. They were the local elite, who carried on certain functions connected with the peasantry below and certain others connected with the officials above. . . .

The view taken here is that the degree-holding individuals were in most cases connected with landowning families, and the latter in most cases had degree-holding members. Until the subject is clarified by further research we can only proceed on the assumption that, in general and for the most part, the gentry families were the out-of-office reservoir of the degree-holders and the bureaucracy. The big families were the seedbed in which officeholders were nurtured and the haven to which dismissed or worn-out bureaucrats could return.

If we turn to the narrower and more concrete, political-administrative definitions of the gentry, we find that in each local community the gentry as individuals, in the basic sense of literati or degree-holders, had many important public functions. They raised funds for and supervised public works—the building and upkeep of irrigation and communication facilities such as canals, dikes, dams, roads, bridges, ferries. They supported Confucian institutions and morals—establishing and maintaining schools, shrines and local temples of Confucius, publishing books, especially local histories or gazetteers, and issuing moral homilies and exhortations to the populace. In time of peace they set the tone of public life. In time of disorder they organized and commanded militia defense forces. From day to day they arbitrated disputes informally, in place of the continual litigation which goes on in any American town. The gentry also set up charities and handled trust funds to help the community, and made contributions at official request to help the state, especially in time of war, flood, or famine. So useful were these contributions that most dynasties got revenue by selling the lowest literary degrees, thus admitting many persons to degree-holding status without examination. While this abused the system, it also let men of wealth rise for a price into the upper class and share the gentry privileges, such as contact with the officials and immunity from corporal punishment.

The position of the gentry families as the reservoir from which most of the individual scholar-officials emerged may explain why officialdom did not penetrate lower down into Chinese society. The imperial government remained a superstructure which did not directly enter the villages because it rested upon the gentry as its foundation. The many public functions of the local degree-holders made a platform under the imperial bureaucracy and let the officials move about with remarkable fluidity and seeming independence of local roots. Actually, the Emperor's appointee to any magistracy could administer it only with the cooperation of the gentry in that area. All in all, in a country of over 400 million people, a century ago, there were less than 20,000 regular imperial officials but roughly one and a quarter million scholarly degree-holders. . . .

The scholar class produced by mastery of the characters was closely integrated with both the gentry families beneath it and the official system above. When successful as a degree-holder and perhaps an official, the scholar found his channel of expression and achievement through the established structure of government. He could become an official, however, only by mastering the official ideology of the state as set down in the canonical works of the Chinese classics. These texts were part of a system of ideas and ritual practices in which the scholar-official learned and applied the Confucian rules and attitudes on the plane of verbal conduct while participating in the personal relationships, political cliques, organized perquisites, and systematic squeeze which distinguished the official class on the plane of practical action. . . .

In a society which seems to us remarkable for its emphasis upon personal relations, the Chinese examinations appear to have been amazingly impersonal and universalistic. When the system was functioning effectively at the height of a dynasty, every effort was made to eliminate personal favoritism. Candidates were locked in their cubicles, several thousand of which in long rows covered a broad area at each provincial capital. Papers were marked with the writer's number only. Such precautions were, of course, necessary for the maintenance of any rational and objective standards in the selection of candidates for office. They expressed the Chinese ruler's genuine need of talented personnel to maintain an efficient administration. Once the best talent of the land had been chosen by this impersonal institution, however, it was then perfectly consistent that the officials should conduct a highly personal administration of the government, following a "virtue ethic" which attached importance to the qualities of individual personality rather than a "command ethic" which laid emphasis upon an impersonal and higher law.

The fact and the myth of social mobility in the Chinese state are still matters of debate. Most dynasties which supported the examination system as a mechanism for the selection of talent gave extensive lip service to the myth that all might enter high position, depending only upon ability. Western writers for long assumed that the Chinese examinations were a really democratic institution, providing opportunity for the intelligent peasant to rise in the world. In fact, however, this seems to have happened rather seldom. The many years of assiduous study required for the examinations were a barrier which no ordinary peasant could surmount. The legend of the villagers who clubbed together to support the studies of the local peasant genius has been an inspiring tradition. But it was not an every day occurrence. . . .

[L]andlords, scholars, and officials were all parts of a composite ruling class. Landowning families, having some agricultural surplus, could give their sons leisure for study to become scholars. Scholars, with a mastery of classical learning, could pass examinations and become officials. Officials, with the perquisites and profits of bureaucratic government, could protect and increase their family landholdings. The structure was flexible, automatically self-perpetuating and very stable.

8

Confucianism
and the Chinese Political System

John King Fairbank

In these excerpts, Fairbank examines the historical influence of Confucianism on the development of the Chinese bureaucracy and legal system. Bureaucrats were all trained in Confucian principles, which provided the ethical basis for governance in China. The Confucian conception of "righteousness" was transferred to the realm of law. Leaders were expected to rule by moral example and not by regulation or statute. Despite this official ideology, regulation of the bureaucracy was quite intense. Moreover, the so-called "law of avoidance" coupled with overcentralization hindered innovation and encouraged conformity at lower levels of the state bureaucratic structure.

If we take [the] Confucian view of life in its social and political context, we will see that its esteem for age over youth, for the past over the present, for established authority over innovation, has in fact provided one of the great historic answers to the problem of social stability. It has been the most successful of all systems of conservatism. For most of two thousand years the Confucian ideology was made the chief subject of study in the world's largest state. Nowhere else have the sanctions of government power been based for so many centuries upon a single consistent pattern of ideas attributed to one ancient sage.

CONFUCIAN PRINCIPLES

The principles of Confucian government, which still lie somewhere below the surface of Chinese politics, were worked out before the time of Christ. Modifications made in later centuries, though extensive, have not been fundamental.

First of all, from the beginning of Chinese history in the Shang and Chou periods (from prehistoric times before 1400 B.C. to the third century B.C.) there was a marked stratification into the classes of the officials and nobility on the one hand, and the common people on the other. . . .

In the second place, Confucianism has been the idealogy of the bureaucrat. The bureaucratic ruling class came into its own after the decentralized feudalism of ancient China gave way to an imperial government. . . .

Government by Moral Prestige

Confucius and his fellow philosophers achieved their position by being teachers who advised rulers as to their right conduct, in an age when feudal princes were competing for hegemony. Confucius was an aristocrat and maintained at his home a school for the elucidation and transmission of the moral principles of conduct and princely rule. Here he taught the upper class how to behave. . . .

[The] complex system of abtruse rules which the Confucians became experts at applying stemmed from the relationship of Chinese man to nature. . . . This relation had early been expressed in a primitive animism in which the spirits of land, wind, and water were thought to play an active part in human affairs. . . . In its more rationalized form this idea of the close relation between human and natural phenomena led to the conception that human conduct is reflected in acts of nature. To put it another way, man is so much a part of the natural order that improper conduct on his part will throw the whole of nature out of joint. Therefore man's conduct must be made to harmonize with the unseen forces of nature, lest calamity ensue.

This was the rationale of Confucian emphasis on right conduct on the part of the ruler, for the ruler was thought to intervene between mankind and the forces of nature. As the Son of Heaven he stood between Heaven above and the people below. He maintained the universal harmony of man and nature by doing the right thing at the right time. It was, therefore, logical to assume that when natural calamity came, it was the ruler's fault. It was for this reason that the Confucian scholar became so important. Only he, by his knowledge of the rules of right conduct, could properly advise the ruler in his cosmic role.

The main point of this theory of "government by goodness," by which Confucianism achieved an emphasis so different from anything in the West, was the idea of the virtue which was attached to right conduct. To conduct oneself according to the rules of propriety or *li* in itself gave one a moral status or prestige. This moral prestige in turn gave one influence over the people. "The people (are) like grass, the ruler like the wind"; as the wind blew, so the grass was inclined. Right conduct gave the ruler power.

On this basis the Confucian scholars established themselves as an essential part of the government, specially competent to maintain its moral nature and so retain the Mandate of Heaven. Where the Legalist philosophers of the Ch'in unification had had ruthlessly efficient methods of government but no moral justification for them, the Confucianists offered an ideological basis. They finally eclipsed the many other ancient schools of philosophy. As interpreters of the *li,* they became technical experts, whose explanations of natural portents and calamities and of the implications of the rulers' actions could be denied or rejected only on the basis of the classical doctrines of which they were themselves the masters. This gave them a strategic position from which to influence government policy. In return they provided the regime with a rational and ethical sanction for the exercise of its authority, at a time when most rulers of empires relied mainly upon religious sanctions. This was a great political invention. . . .

BUREAUCRACY

One key to the understanding of the Communist administration in China is the fact that the old imperial government was a bureaucracy of the most thoroughly developed and sophisticated sort. To the American who has confronted the problems of bureaucracy only recently, the effort of modern Chinese to escape from the evils and capitalize upon the good points of their own bureaucratic tradition is a matter of absorbing interest. . . .

Central Controls

Given this network of officials, connected by a flow of documents and persons along the postal routes, it was the problem of the capital to stimulate the local bureaucrats to perform their functions and yet prevent them from getting out of hand. This control was achieved by the application of techniques common to bureaucracies everywhere, in addition to the special measures . . . whereby the Manchus sought to preserve their dynasty.

Among these techniques the first was the appointment of all officers down to the rank of district magistrate by the Emperor himself. This made them all aware of their dependence upon the Son of Heaven and their duty of personal loyalty to him. Circulation in office was another device. No official was left in one post for more than three years or at most six years. Ordinarily when moving from one post to another the official passed through the capital and participated in an imperial audience to renew his contact with the ruler.

Thus Chinese officialdom was a mobile body which circulated through all parts of the empire without taking root in any one place. In this it was aided by its reliance upon the Mandarin (Peking) dialect as a lingua franca of universal currency in official circles. Frequently an official would arrive at his new post to find himself quite incapable of understanding the local dialect and therefore the more closely confined to his official level.

One means to prevent officials taking local root was the "law of avoidance" according to which no mandarin could be appointed to office in his native province, where the claims of family loyalty might impair devotion to the imperial regime. . . .

The evils inherent in bureaucracy were all too evident. All business was in form originated at the bottom and passed upward to the Emperor for decision at the top, memorials from the provinces being addressed to the Emperor at the capital. The higher authority was thus left to choose alternatives of action proposed, and yet the proposal of novel or unprecedented action was both difficult and dangerous for the lower official. The greater safety of conformity tended to kill initiative at the bottom. On the other hand the efficiency of the one man at the top was constantly impaired by his becoming a bottleneck. All business of importance was expected to receive his approval. All legislation and precedent were established by his edict. Modern China still suffers from this tradition.

In view of the complete and arbitrary power which the imperial bureaucracy asserted over the whole of Chinese life, it is amazing how few and how scattered the officials were in number. The total of civil officials for whom posts were statutorily available, both at the capital and in the provinces, was hardly more than 9000. The military officials were supposed to number only about 7500. It is true, of course, that there were a great many supernumerary or "expectant" officials who might be assigned to various functions without receiving substantive appointments. There was also the vast body of clerks and factota necessary for the copying, recording, negotiating, and going and coming in each Chinese official's establishment or "yamen." Down to the gatemen, runners, and chairbearers, these human elements in the official machine no doubt totaled millions. But if we look for the men of genuine official status who could take official action and report it in the hierarchy as representatives of his imperial majesty, we find them few and thinly spread, totaling at a rough estimate hardly more than 30 or 40 thousand "officials" at most, ruling over a country of about 200 million which grew to perhaps 400 million by the middle of the nineteenth century. Of the nine ranks, for example, the seventh rank near the bottom of the scale began with the district magistrate who was responsible for a population on the order of 250,000 persons. This relative smallness of the imperial administration no doubt reflects the fact that it depended upon the gentry class to lead and dominate the peasantry in the villages. . . .

[The] Chinese concept of law was fundamentally different from legal conceptions in the West. It began with the ancient Chinese idea of the order of nature, the necessity of human actions harmonizing with it, and the ruler's function of maintaining this harmony. Since the ruler swayed the people by his virtuous conduct and moral example, not by law, it was felt that enlightened and civilized persons would be guided by such an example without the need of regulations. Punishment was necessary in this theory only for barbarous and uncivilized persons who could not appreciate the ruler's example and must be intimidated. Rewards and punishments were useful in order to make clear the activities proper to each person according to his status. But they were always considered in theory a secondary means of securing people's right conduct. The object was to "punish only to be able to stop punishing." . . .

This nondevelopment of Chinese law along lines familiar to the West was plainly related to the nondevelopment of capitalism and an independent business class in the old China. There was no idea of the corporation as a legal individual. Big firms were family affairs. Business relations were not cold impersonal matters governed by the general principles of the law and of contract in a world apart from home and family. Business was a segment of the whole web of human friendship, kinship obligations, and personal relations which supported Chinese life. In old China the law, sanctity of contract, and free private enterprise never became a sacred trinity.

9

Behind the "Made in Japan" Label

Kozo Yamamura

In these excerpts from *Politics and Economics in Contemporary Japan,* Kozo Yamamura discusses the socio-psychological characteristics of the Japanese people, and shows how Japan's homogeneity, vertical organization, and strong emphasis on the group create an environment that is particularly conducive to coordination of information, planning, and execution. These characteristics, Kozo argues, form the basis of the Japanese "cultural contract," which includes such features as life-long employment and consensual decision making (*ringi*). He concludes by raising some questions concerning the ability of the Japanese to adapt to a changing international environment.

It is ignorant and chauvinistic to claim that one's own culture is superior to another's. What one can say is that some cultures are better suited to certain activities than others. We often say, for example, that the American cultural milieu encourages an individualistic and competitive spirit which is highly adapted to achieving individual excellence in many endeavors, including economic growth through competition. That is, one may acquire a fairly well-defined cultural image of each nation which will convey with some accuracy the specific strengths (or weaknesses) of each culture with regard to industrial economic activities.

In this sense, I believe that we can say that Japanese culture, or its social capability, is well suited to activities which demand (1) close coordination of all available information, (2) finely coordinated planning and execution involving many parts of a firm or a number of firms, (3) meticulous attention to details, and (4) organizational ability to distribute collective gains to reward the participants in coordinated activities in such a way as not to stifle the inherent competitive spirit of each individual participant.

On the other hand, this would indicate that Japanese society is not an ideal setting for innovative or inventive activities that depend upon a flash of insight by a strong-willed individual who pursues his goal even against the doubts expressed by his colleagues, or for a rugged individualist who, perhaps by trial and error, accomplishes his chosen course for his own satisfaction. In other words, individuals who are not inclined to observe the numerous strict rules and procedures required for the close coordination and smooth functioning of the intricately balanced organization characteristic of Japanese society will find the rigidly circumscribed rules for close interpersonal relationships oppressive.

On the other hand, Japanese society is ideally suited for the production of goods for which the fundamental technology has already been invented elsewhere, and for which the efforts needed to maximize gains (GNP and individual income) are best pursued collectively. . . . Socio-psychological factors and institutions . . . are significant in influencing and even determining the basic organizational structure and behavioral characteristics of Japanese society and firms[:]

1. Japan is a "vertical" society in which the upper-lower hierarchical (i.e. vertical) order among men of unequal social standing dominates horizontal relationships among equals. A Japanese spends most of his daily life in situations where he must be clearly aware of his relative ranking. Or, in the words of Professor Nakane Chie, a well-known Japanese social anthropologist:

> In everyday affairs a man who has no awareness of relative rank is not able to speak or even sit and eat. When speaking, he is expected always to be ready with differentiated, delicate degrees of honorific expressions appropriate to the rank order between himself and the person he addresses. The expressions and the manner appropriate to a superior are never to be used to an inferior. Even among colleagues, it is only possible to dispense with honorifics when both parties are very intimate friends.

Because of the overwhelmingly vertical nature of the society which dominates their lives from childhood, the Japanese function best in situations in which relative rank order is clearly established. This means that if a Japanese finds himself in a circumstance in which rank order is not clearly established, he will take infinite pains to establish it for his psychological comfort. The need for an established rank order is such that "even a set of individuals sharing identical qualifications tends to create a *difference* among these individuals." Anyone who has ever visited Japan is familiar with numerous examples of the processes by which Japanese quickly establish at the first meeting their relative rank order, methods ranging from exchanging name cards (which invariably carry the person's title) to discreet questioning as to the other's age, occupation, and the school from which he was graduated.

This rigid, vertical social structure is a product of the past that has come to be well-entrenched in modern Japanese society, and must always be kept in mind in discussing the managerial structure and behavioral patterns observed in Japanese firms.

2.   Another, better known "fact of life" in Japan is that social characteristic which has been variously termed paternalism, groupism, and familyism. This aspect of Japanese society originated in the strong tradition of *ie* or the "house." Simply put, this is the Japanese socio-psychological tendency which emphasizes (in the sense of protecting, cherishing, finding needs for, or functioning best in) "us" against "them." In the context of this essay, a firm may show this characteristic by being "paternalistic" toward its employees. Paternalism can take the form of providing various welfare programs, fostering group cohesion by providing housing for employees to live in as neighbors, holding daily pre-work sessions to recite company mottos, conducting seminars at a Zen temple, etc. Employees, for their part, place the success of the *ie* (their company, department, or section) above everything. Even an employee's family takes second place (in terms of time, mental energy, and emotional output) to his group at work. What is important is that, in Japan, this can be said even of factory workers. The ultimate form of this is the well-known lifetime employment system which is still accepted as the norm in Japan. The *ie* guarantees lifetime security, and demands total dedication in return.

This, along with its vertical organizational quality, results in a facet of Japanese society which is important in the context of this essay. That is, the person's hierarchical rank order is fixed for life, and not only is any sign of disregarding it repugnant to the harmony within an *ie,* but it is also extremely costly to ignore. In understanding the Japanese process of decision-making, this is of crucial importance. Though this brief observation of this important facet of Japanese life must suffice here, it should be made explicit that no purely economic explanation of this Japanese characteristic—such as the long-run maximization of profit or income, or labor conditions—can ever hope to suffice. The importance of *ie* is psychological as well as economic.

3.   After a discussion of the vertical nature of society and the importance of the *ie,* it is easy to understand the institutions of lifetime employment and the seniority system—in the Japanese senses of these terms. Lifetime employment is only a socially expected form of membership in an *ie,* and seniority is the handiest and socially least costly (least disruptive of harmony) indicator which can be used in establishing rank order. Economic explanations of these institutions can be only partial. Though we need not describe these two well-known institutions further, we should add that they form the basis of the view which might best be summarized as "men over organization," that is, employees matter above all else in firms. As long as the functioning of a firm is circumscribed by the lifetime employment and seniority systems, the most important thing is to hire "good" men because they will in time rise to become the decision-making officers of the firm.

4.   The *ringi* system of decision-making, widely used in bureaucracy, firms, and many other organizations, is a natural one for the society we have just described. For firms, this is a system by which any change in the routines, tactics, and even overall strategy is originated by those persons who

are directly concerned with the change. The final decision is made at the top level only *after* an elaborate examination of the proposal and its acceptance or rejection by consensus at every echelon of the managerial structure. This process of consensus-building involves at first one's immediate colleagues. If a consensus is obtained, then the proposal goes to the head of that group, who will then circulate it among the heads of departments (or sections) that will be directly and indirectly affected by the proposed change. If a go-ahead is obtained at this level (or after a few more layers of consensus-building, if necessary to reach the top level) it will finally go to the top for sanction.

The system is ideally suited to Japanese firms because it assures harmony within an *ie* and enables senior (but not necessarily more capable) men to occupy higher-ranking positions. At the same time, the cohesion of the group is strengthened because no one person is to blame should the change end in failure. In any event, informal consensus-building is much more efficient in getting the best perspective than a committee which would be dominated by a senior presiding chairman whom others would be reluctant to oppose. In public as well as in private, a subordinate will exercise the greatest caution in efforts to change his senior's mind. The process is extremely delicate and often time-consuming, but to most Japanese, the advantages of the *ringi* system are more important than the slowness of the process, its unsuitability for long-range planning (strategy), and (from the Western point of view) its other shortcomings. The system is changing and is being complemented by other methods of decision-making, but it is still used widely by the largest firms even today.

5. As is evidenced in various forms of Japanese art—such as bonsai and architectural designs—the Japanese exhibit an intense interest, even fascination, with detail and subtle distinctions of color and shape. I believe it is also accurate to say that this concern for detail and nuance is seen also in their interpersonal relationships and communication. . . .

6. Finally, I should again remind readers that Japan is an extremely homogeneous and cohesive society in terms of basic values, ethnic origin, language, and many other dimensions. This fact is well known and often discussed, and plays, as will be argued below, an important role in the workings of Japanese firms and the interrelationships among firms.

If the preceding characterization of the socio-psychological characteristics of the Japanese is accurate, one can readily see why such a society might excel in industrial production through the close coordination of information, coordinated execution of plans, attention to details, and the evocation of maximum efforts by individuals in collective teamwork.

Of all the socio-cultural attributes which contribute to the effectiveness of Japanese industrial firms, the sense of the group—the *ie*—which is shared by both employers and employees is perhaps the most important. Though labor mobility has risen during the past decade, an overwhelming majority of Japanese hope and expect that their employment with a firm will be permanent. To say the least, even today there is a strong presumption on the part of employees at larger industrial firms that they will work for the same firm and with the same colleagues until retirement. An employee is fully justified in believing that his employer will terminate his employment only as a last resort, even in a recession. When asked "To whom is your obligation greatest in order to assure the success and the growth of your firm?" virtually all Japanese employers will say it is to their employees rather than to their stockholders. The better one knows Japanese society, the less likely one is to dismiss this as merely a stock answer for public relations purposes.

To be sure, this implicit "cultural contract" is by no means always harmoniously adhered to. Japan has labor unions, strikes (though many less than in other industrial economies), dismissals, and bankruptcies. But the "cultural contract" serves as a strong force in determining the conduct and behavior of both employees and employers, and the presumption of both is of a life-long association.

From the assumption that all members of a firm belong to an *ie* (the firm) and that the membership is permanent may be derived several crucial attributes which are extremely important to efficient production. As long as one's employment is guaranteed, there is little reason to object to the adoption of new technology. If a job becomes obsolete as a result, the company will shift the employee to another task within the firm. Of course, given the permanent employment system, the firm is also willing to undertake the retraining of the employee at its own expense so that employees whose skills become obsolete may still be used productively within the firm.

With the prospect of a life-long association, there is a premium on harmonious relationships with one's colleagues, superiors, and subordinates. There is little temptation to seek exclusive recognition or to monopolize credit for a success when this would mean incurring the jealousy or ill-will of others. Harmony is thus cherished, and consensus is sought wherever possible.

In Japan, the task of obtaining consensus and maintaining harmony is easier than in other nations because of the homogeneity of values, ethnic origins, language, and many other factors. To repeat, perhaps the most prominent characteristic of the corporate culture of the Japanese firm is that the Japanese are prepared to go a long way to preserve harmony, consensus, and identity of goals.

A necessary part of success at preserving these social goals is the maintenance of constant communication, i.e., intense "dialogue." Inadequate explanations or incomplete information can be a cause of disharmony, misunderstanding, and the inability to obtain consensus. Thus Japanese take great pains, during and even after work hours, to communicate with each other. Firms supplement the *ringi* system with discussion groups, study sessions, seminars, company-sponsored outings, frequent nights out for "the boys from the same section," etc. The members of an *ie* are expected to remain in very close contact with each other. However, despite the harmony and closeness of the members of a firm, observance of the vertical authority structure is deeply ingrained, so that formal lines of communication, channels of authority, and protocol for the exchange of views are not compromised. A vertical society also yields the added benefit of minimizing disciplinary problems, as the rationale of the structure and the source of authority is readily understood by all and most can expect, in time, to climb the ladder of authority themselves.

Above all, a Japanese firm with these characteristics can expect the maximum effort from its employees. The success of their *ie,* through increased efficiency and performance, is important not only in perpetuating their employment but also in increasing their income and prestige. The more successful one's firm, the larger one's wages, bonuses, and pride in working for a large and prosperous firm. To cite only two examples: employees at Toyota have decided to work on weekends to meet the demand for their cars; and the Ministry of Labor as late as the summer of 1978 issued a pamphlet urging employees to take all paid vacations to which they are entitled, whereas at present only 50 percent do so. . . .

Visibly slowed economic growth is already severely testing the institution of permanent employment and the seniority system of promotion. In the increasingly competitive post-OPEC era, the luxury of the time-consuming *ringi* system can less and less be indulged as more and quicker decisions are called for; more firms are becoming aware that the virtues of cooperative and harmonious teamwork can be preserved only at the cost of detracting from the innovative efforts which now need to be encouraged more than ever; the new generation of employees seems to take less pride in their firm or in *keiretsu* than their fathers did; the ability of Japanese firms going abroad to "transplant" their corporate culture is in serious doubt at best; etc. The implications of these recent developments for the near future of the Japanese economy may prove to be profound.

Culture can be likened to athletic skill. Often a superb baseball player can hope to be only a mediocre football player. Skills suitable for one game are transferable to another only with great difficulty. Japanese culture could very well be in the position of the baseball player as the rules of the game of international competition—if not the game itself—are changing rapidly. Will Japanese culture successfully adapt to the new game? Or will it fail to adapt and thus limit its success in the international markets? These are questions which I believe are worth pondering instead of merely bewailing the current trade deficit with Japan and condemning "Japan, Inc." for its large trade surplus.

Unit III

China and Japan Yesterday: _____ Response to the West _____

The apparently similar societies of China and Japan met the challenge of the West in the nineteenth century in sharply contrasting ways. In their responses to superior Western military power, based on new technologies and industrialization, the two peoples established patterns of action that not only had a profound impact on their subsequent development but that continue to be significant today.

The Chinese were slow to grasp the need for modernization and clung to traditional values in a futile attempt to resist Western encroachments. Failure to implement meaningful reforms, however, resulted in peasant rebellions and finally in revolution and overthrow of the monarchy in 1911. This pattern, repeated again when the Communists came to power in 1949, is one that continues to haunt China's leaders.

In contrast to China, Japan quickly recognized the need for change and, choosing to emulate the West, built a modern industrial society that soon rivaled that of its Western intruders. Its reliance on continuous reform as a means of effecting change without revolution remains a characteristic pattern of response in contemporary Japan. In further contrast to the Chinese, for whom the question of cultural borrowing from abroad is politically very controversial, the Japanese borrow liberally from other cultures simply as a matter of course.

This unit provides an historical context in which to examine the evolution of political and economic life in China and Japan since the nineteenth century. Through a comparison of political and economic structures in the two countries prior to their opening to more extensive contact with the West, the unit sheds light on fundamental differences between China and Japan that led to such contrasting patterns of response to the Western challenge.

In "China's Response to the West," John King Fairbank traces the gradual expansion of the Western presence in China from tolerated "tributary" traders to virtual overlords. Late efforts to modernize fell short as reformers, failing to understand the fundamental strength of the Western challenge, relied on a restoration of traditional ideals and, as Fairbank points out, change came only with revolution. Authors John King Fairbank, Edwin O. Reischauer, and Albert M. Craig tell a very different story in "Japan's Response to the West." They describe how Japan's more dynamic social and political system made possible a prompt decision to imitate the West and facilitated rapid modernization. Marion J. Levy, Jr., provides a detailed analysis of these underlying cultural differences in "Contrasting Factors in Modernization in China and Japan." He points particularly to differences in family loyalties and opportunities for social mobility in accounting for the individual initiative, flexibility, and receptivity to change which made Japan more successful in confronting the West.

10

China's Response to the West

John King Fairbank

In these excerpts from his now classic 1962 study, *The United States and China*, Fairbank describes the cultural and political factors underlying China's ineffectual policy of resistance to the West, and traces the transition from the early "Canton system," through which European mercantilists established a foothold in imperial China's "tributary trade," to the punitive treaty system of trade imposed on China by Western military force. He then analyzes the ultimate failure of the Manchu restoration of traditional politics after the Taiping Rebellion, a conservative restoration that inhibited China's response to the West, and the hopelessness of China's "half-way" effort to modernize through reform from above. Without meaningful reform, revolution became the only route to necessary change.

The West approached China in modern times through the medium of China's foreign trade. The Western impact can be understood only against this commercial background. The sixteenth-century Portuguese and the seventeenth-century British adventurers and merchants who opened the China trade discovered unknown regions, just as their colleagues of the same generations were opening up the New World. The all-important difference was that Eastern Asia, far from being a virgin continent, was already the center of an enormous and ramified commercial life of its own. The early Western ventures of exploration and trade were but small increments in channels of commerce already centuries old. . . .

Early Maritime Contact

After the Portuguese entered the channels of China's maritime commerce, from 1514, they began a process of trade and evangelism which was to culminate three centuries later in the unequal treaty system of our own day. The chief focus of the new Sino-European relationship was trade. The Portuguese carried the silks of China to Japan as well as the spices of the Indies to Europe. Their commercial empire was built on a far-flung network of fortified trading posts, in India, at Malacca, at Nagasaki and after 1557 at Macao near Canton. Development of bigger ships and guns and of skill in navigating by compass, astrolabe and written sailing directions gave the Portuguese their century of supremacy in the eastern seas. They were eclipsed in the seventeenth century by the Dutch and British, whose East India Companies were better organized and financed, but the same network of trading posts continued to facilitate European penetration of the Far East. Each one was an outpost containing the seeds of empire—claims to national sovereignty, zeal for Christian evangelism, demands for Western legal practices, fluid capital funds and superior military technology—all planted on Oriental shores and ready to sprout when conditions permitted.

The Spanish from Manila and the Dutch from Batavia soon expanded over the adjacent territories to create colonial domains. But Japan and China, being centralized empires already, were able to keep the Europeans quarantined for the time being at designated ports like Nagasaki, Macao, and Canton, which became the predecessors of the nineteenth-century treaty ports. . . .

THE TRIBUTE SYSTEM

To understand the one-sidedness and inequality of the unequal treaties which the Western powers imposed upon the Chinese empire, one must look at the ancient tribute system which China first imposed upon Western visitors. This old Chinese system was in some ways just as unequal as the treaty system which supplanted it.

The tribute system was an application to foreign affairs of the Confucian doctrines by which Chinese rulers gained an ethical sanction for their exercise of political authority. Just as the virtuous ruler by his moral example had prestige and influence among the people of the Middle Kingdom, so he irresistibly attracted the barbarians who were outside the pale of Chinese culture. To a Confucian scholar it was inconceivable that the rude tribes of the frontier should not appreciate China's cultural superiority and therefore seek the benefits of Chinese civilization. Since the Emperor exercised the Mandate of Heaven to rule all mankind, it was his function to be compassionate and generous to all "men from afar." The imperial benevolence should be reciprocated, it was felt, by the humble submission of the foreigner.

Once the latter, however, had recognized the unique position of the Son of Heaven it was unavoidable that these reciprocal relations of compassionate benevolence and humble submission should be demonstrated in ritual form, by the ceremonial bestowal of gifts and of tribute respectively. Tribute thus became one of the rites of the Chinese court. It betokened the admission of a barbarian to the civilization of the Middle Kingdom. It was a boon and privilege, and not ignominious. As the original Chinese culture-island spread through the centuries to absorb barbarian tribes, the formalities of tribute relations were developed into a mechanism by which barbarous regions outside the empire might be given their place in the all-embracing Sinocentric cosmos.

When Europeans first came to China by sea these formalities were naturally expected of them. According to the collected statutes of the Manchu dynasty, a tributary ruler of a foreign state should receive an imperial patent of appointment which acknowledged his tributary status. There should also be conferred upon him a noble rank and an imperial seal-for use in signing his memorials, which should be dated by the Chinese calendar. When his tribute missions came, they should be limited in size to one hundred men, of whom only twenty might proceed to the capital, by the imperial post. At the capital the mission was lodged, carefully protected and entertained. Eventually it was received in audience by the Emperor. This was the time of all others when the tribute envoys performed the kowtow.

Early European envoys, like the unhappy Hollanders who presented tribute at the Manchu court in 1795, were inclined to feel that this calisthenic ceremony more than offset the imperial benevolence which filtered down to them through the sticky hands of the officials who had them in charge. The full kowtow was no mere prostration of the body but a prolonged series of three separate kneelings, each one leading to three successive prostrations, nose upon the floor. The "three kneelings and nine prostrations" left no doubt in anyone's mind, least of all in the performer's, as to who was inferior and who superior. Egalitarian Westerners usually failed to appreciate that this abasement of the individual who kowtowed was a normal aspect of the ceremonial life in a society of status. The Emperor kowtowed to Heaven and his parents, the highest grandees kowtowed to the Emperor. In a less formal way friends might kowtow to each other, as polite Japanese almost do today. From a tribute bearer it was therefore no more than good manners.

The secret of the tribute system was the fact that it had become a vehicle for trade. The Ming chroniclers, by including the long defunct Roman East, fictitious principalities, and border tribes, had listed more than 120 tributaries. The Manchus put the border tribes under a special office and reduced their list of genuine tributaries to less than a dozen including the still shadowy countries of the "Western Ocean" whose merchants had already appeared at Canton. Because the Manchu empire chiefly sought stability in its foreign relations, it dealt only with neighboring countries or with those who came to China. If foreign merchants came and their ruler wanted to promote their trade, he could present tribute. It was as simple as that. . . .

The old Canton trade in its heyday (c. 1760–1840) was carried on under a working compromise between the Chinese system of tributary trade and European mercantilism. During the Napoleonic wars one of the great survivors of the mercantilist era, the British East India Company, based on India, beat out its Continental competitors and brought the growing tea-exports of Canton into a profitable triangular trade between England, India, and China. Fleets of East Indiamen voyaged annually from London to Canton, where the Company by its charter monopolized all British trade and dealt with a comparable monopoly on the Chinese side—a licensed guild of about a dozen firms, or "hongs." These hong merchants were responsible to the imperial officials for the foreign trade and traders. The latter in turn were restricted by various regulations which, for example, confined them largely to their factories and kept them outside the walls of Canton. Thus by mutual agreement during the greater part of the century, in spite of continual disputes, the old Canton trade proved mutually profitable within the limits imposed by two, Chinese and foreign, systems of trade regulation.

Western expansion, and free trade in particular, disrupted the Canton system after the East India Company (E.I.C.) lost its monopoly of Britain's China trade in 1833. Unfortunately for the repute of private enterprise in the Orient, it reached the China coast at this time chiefly in the form of the opium trade conducted by private traders. This historical circumstance has poisoned Sino-Western relations ever since.

The opium was grown and taxed chiefly in areas under E.I.C. jurisdiction in India. Opium was carried to China by private British and Indian traders, as well as by Americans who competed as best they could by buying opium in Turkey. They usually found Chinese merchants and mandarins eager to flout the Emperor's prohibitions of smoking and importation. The result was an illegal trade openly connived at by British, American, Chinese, and other merchants and officials—too valuable to the British Indian exchequer to be refrained from, too necessary to the balancing of the tea export trade to be given up by the merchants, and too profitable to them and to venal Chinese officials to be easily suppressed. . . .

THE TREATY SYSTEM

The legal structure established by the unequal treaties in the period 1842–1860 resulted directly from the two wars fought by the British against the Ch'ing government. The first in 1840–1842, which has been called, particularly in China, the Opium War, resulted directly from the doughty Commissioner Lin Tse-hsu's vain effort to suppress the drug trade at Canton. But the British expeditionary force was sent to Canton and thence up the coast to secure privileges of general commercial and diplomatic intercourse on a Western basis of equality, and not especially to aid the expansion of the opium trade. The latter was expanding rapidly of its own accord, and was only one point of friction in the general antagonism between the Chinese and British schemes of international relations.

The principles embodied in the Treaty of Nanking in 1842 were not fully accepted on the Chinese side and the treaty privileges seemed inadequately extensive from the British side. Consequently the treaty system was not really established until the British and French had fought a second war and secured treaties at Tientsin in 1858. Even then the new order was not acknowledged by the reluctant dynasty until an Anglo-French expedition had occupied Peking itself in 1860. The transition from tribute relations to treaty relations occupied a generation of friction at Canton before 1840, and twenty years of trade, negotiation, and coercion thereafter.

Although the new treaties were signed as between equal sovereign powers, they were actually quite unequal in that China was placed against her will in a helpless position, wide open to the inroads of Western commerce and its attendant culture. By the twentieth century, after three generations of energetic Western consuls had developed its fine points, the treaty structure was a finely articulated and comprehensive mechanism. It was based first of all on treaty ports, at first five in number, and eventually more than eighty.

The major treaty ports had a striking physical and institutional resemblance to one another. Each had a crowded, noisy bund and godowns (warehouses) swarming with coolies, who substituted for machinery, under the supervision of Chinese compradors (business managers), who managed affairs beneath the overlordship of the foreign taipan (firm managers), teatasters, and other personnel. . . .

Extraterritoriality

This legal system, under which foreigners and their activities in China remained amenable to foreign and not Chinese law, was not a foreign nor a modern invention. In a manner rather like that of the Turks at Constantinople, the Chinese government in medieval times had expected foreign communities in the seaports to govern themselves under their own headmen and by their own laws. This had been true of the early Arab traders in China. The British and Americans at Canton before the Opium War demanded extraterritoriality because they had suffered from Chinese attempts to apply Chinese criminal law to Westerners, without regard for Western rules of evidence or the Western abhorrence of torture. But most of all the foreign traders needed the help of their own law of contract.

As applied in the treaty ports, extraterritoriality became a powerful tool for the opening of China because it made foreign merchants and missionaries, their goods and property, and to some extent their Chinese employees, converts, and hangers-on all immune to Chinese authority. France in particular undertook the protection of Roman Catholic missions and communicants. All this was, to say the least, an impairment of Chinese sovereignty and a great handicap to China's self-defense against Western exploitation. The Japanese, who were saddled with the same system also, after 1858, made tremendous efforts to get out from under it and did so by the end of the century.

A further essential of the treaties was the treaty tariff which by its low rates prevented the Chinese from protecting their native industries. Since, for various reasons, the administration of the low treaty tariff was not effective in Chinese hands, a foreign staff was taken into the Chinese custom house. . . .

THE TAIPING REBELLION AND THE RESTORATION OF CONFUCIAN GOVERNMENT

The Chinese revolution of today really goes back to the Taiping Rebellion of 1851–1864, a full lifetime before Marxism entered China. The Taiping rebels were mainly peasants. They never heard of the Communist Manifesto. Yet modern China's revolution is unintelligible without reference to the Taiping effort to destroy Confucianism, and why it failed.

This great upheaval arose from a background of population pressure, which had increased the insecurity of life and the vulnerability of the populace to drought, flood, famine, and disease. These in turn presented the creaking machinery of government with problems which it could not meet—flood control, famine relief, increased need for taxes, increased difficulty in getting them. Then, as now, official self-seeking produced inefficiency. Governmental incompetence bred loss of confidence on the part of the people.

The Emperor's inability to expel the British barbarians in 1842 or to check the connivance of Chinese merchants and pirates with the foreigner in the import of Indian opium, shook the imperial prestige. In 1846–1848 flood and famine were widespread among China's expanded population. It is not surprising that a great uprising finally began in 1851. . . .

. . . In 1860 the Ch'ing dynasty seemed on the point of collapse, beset by a recrudescence of Taiping military vigor in the lower Yangtze region and by the Anglo-French invasion and capture of Peking. Yet just at this point there emerged new Manchu leaders under the regency of the young Empress Dowager (Tz'u-hsi). By accepting the Western treaty system and supporting the conservative Chinese scholar-generals in the provinces, they achieved the suppression of the Taipings by 1864 and gave their dynasty a new lease on life. A small Sino-foreign mercenary army, led by an American and then a British commander (F. T. Ward of Salem, and the famous C. G. "Chinese" Gordon) helped defeat the rebels around Shanghai; but the victory was essentially a Chinese one. . . .

. . . During the 1860's the components of the traditional Confucian state were energized to function again: a group of high-principled civil officials, chosen by examination in the classics and loyal to the reigning dynasty, sternly suppressed rebellion and ministered benevolently to the agrarian economy and the popular welfare. Order was restored in the central provinces, armies were reduced, taxes remitted, land reopened to cultivation, schools founded, and men of talent recruited for the civil service. While reviving the traditional order in this fashion, the Restoration leaders also began to Westernize. They set up arsenals to supply modern arms, built steamships, translated Western textbooks in technology and international law and created a proto-foreign office in the form of a special committee (the Tsungli Yamen) under the Grand Council. In these efforts they were aided by the cooperative policy of the Western powers, whose imperialist rivalries did not become intense until the 1870's. Yet in the end this renewed vitality within the Ch'ing administration showed both the strength and also the inertia of the traditional Chinese polity—it could not really be modernized but could function effectively only on its own terms, which were now out of date. . . .

Yet in spite of the influx of Western trade and the evident commercial power of the foreigners, the Restoration leaders clung conservatively to the economic principle of the preeminence of agriculture as the basis of state revenue and popular livelihood. They had no conception of economic growth or development in the modern sense but were austerely anti-acquisitive and disparaged commerce, including foreign trade, as non-productive. Rather, they tried to set before the peasantry and bureaucracy the classical ideals of frugality and incorruptibility, so that the product of the land could more readily suffice to maintain the people and the government. To assist agriculture, they reduced land taxes in the lower Yangtze region, but did not try to lower rents or prevent landlordism. They tried to revive the necessary public works for water control, but could not control the Yellow River any better than their predecessors.

The Restoration lost vitality after the 1860's for many reasons. Its leaders were conscientiously reviving the past instead of facing China's new future creatively. They could not adequately inspire the lower levels of their bureaucracy nor handle the specialized technical and intellectual problems of modernization. The very strength of their conservative and restorative effort inhibited China's response to the West.

THE SELF-STRENGTHENING MOVEMENT

The Confucian way of life was undermined first of all by the fire power of foreign cannon. During the first Anglo-Chinese war in 1840–1842 the British had used on the coast of China a shallow-bottomed paddle-wheel iron steamer called the *Nemesis*. It carried swivel cannon fore and aft and was capable of moving into the wind and against the tide in a manner disastrous to China's fortunes. Chinese officials like Commissioner Lin Tse-hsu, who were given the job of pacifying the new barbarians from the West, could not but be impressed with this mechanism. At Canton in 1840 Lin led the way in study of the West, securing translations of Western periodicals, patronizing an American missionary hospital, and experimenting in the construction of cannon and gunboats. Under the British impact Chinese officials in the coastal provinces made extensive preparations for coast defense, at least on paper, and several others followed Lin's example in studying Western geography and arms.

In contrast to the Japanese, however, these Chinese officials of the 1840's were unable to initiate changes to meet the foreign menace once the British had been pacified. During the two decades following the first war with Britain no fundamental progress was made in learning Western technology for military purposes, much less in accepting Western ideas generally. Lin himself, although plainly convinced of the need of Western arms by his experience at Canton, later hid his views because they were unpopular, and thus failed to warn his countrymen of dangers they refused to acknowledge.

Meanwhile, however, the great rebellion created profound changes in the Chinese government, primarily by shifting the center of gravity from the capital to the province both in financial and in military affairs. With Peking cut off from its richest provinces, it was left for local Chinese gentry leaders to raise the funds and the armies with which to suppress the rebels. The result was that trade taxes began to compete with the land tax as the government's staff of life, while personally-led regional armies began to supplant the effete imperial forces. . . .

Both in the provinces and at Peking the new trade revenues financed new efforts to deal with the Western invaders. Manchu and Chinese officials worked as one to strengthen the Chinese position by imitating Western mechanisms. This movement for "self-strengthening," as it was called, was posited on the attractive though fallacious doctrine of "Chinese learning as the fundamental structure, Western learning for practical use"—as though Western arms, steamships, science and technology could somehow be utilized to preserve Confucian values, instead of destroying them. In retrospect we can see that the latter was inevitable—gunboats and cotton looms bring their own philosophy with them. But the generation of 1860–1900 clung to the frustrating shibboleth that China could leap half-way into modernization. Under the slogan of "self-strengthening" they therefore began the adoption of Western arms and machines, only to find themselves sucked into an inexorable process in which one Western borrowing led to another, from machinery to technology, from science to all learning, from acceptance of new ideas to change of institutions, eventually from constitutional reform to republican revolution. The fallacy of half-way modernization, in tools but not in values, was in fact apparent to many conservative scholars, who therefore chose the alternative of opposing all things Western. With policy discussions dominated by these die-hards (who opposed Westernization as fervently as we oppose totalitarianism, but with much less chance of success) and the half-way modernizers (who usually had the responsibility for taking action), there was little chance for a third course of drastic revolutionary change. . . .

REFORM AND REVOLUTION

. . . Not until Japan had unexpectedly defeated the Chinese empire in 1895 and the European powers had extorted leaseholds and concessions in the three years following were genuine institutional changes attempted.

Even then, the objective was still not fundamental change but merely intensified "self-strengthening" by the use of foreign methods. The reformers still
took the position that the fundamental values in Chinese society should
remain unchangeable but that the laws and institutions were changeable
and must be made to take account of the West. . . .

The Hundred Days of [Reform in] 1898 produced consternation
among the officials high and low. It mattered little that the constitution
envisaged by the reformers would hardly limit the ruler's power, even
though it espoused the rule of law—the fact was that too many officials felt
themselves too closely endangered by these sudden changes. The Manchu
Empress Dowager, Ts'u-hsi, who had been in retirement for the past decade,
was able with military support to effect a *coup d'etat,* depose the unfortunate Emperor, declare herself regent, and rescind all his edicts. Six of the
reformers were executed. [Others] fled to Japan.

No incident could have dramatized more effectively the hopelessness
of modernizing China through gradual reform from above. The defeat of
1895 and the fiasco of 1898 together gave the first great impetus toward
revolutionary change. From then on, efforts at political revolution ran parallel to those for constitutional reform. . . .

The Revolution

A revolutionary attempt at Canton in April 1911 was put down with
the execution of the famous seventy-two martyrs. This constituted Sun Yat-
sen's tenth failure. The next plot was planned in Hankow in October 1911.
The plot was accidentally discovered when a bomb exploded in the revo-
lutionists' warehouse. This precipitated the uprising of October 10, since
celebrated as the birthday of the Republic, the "double ten" (tenth day of
the tenth month). . . .

11

Japan's Response to the West

John King Fairbank,
Edwin O. Reischauer,
and Albert M. Craig

Japan's success in maintaining its independence by emulating the West was possible because of cultural characteristics that were markedly different from China's, despite surface similarities. In this selection, three distinguished Asia scholars describe how Japan's particular feudal social organization and centralized political system made rapid modernization possible. With the Meiji restoration of direct imperial rule, flexible and pragmatic leadership allowed Japan to meet the West on equal terms while at the same time retaining its unique cultural identity.

JAPANESE RESPONSIVENESS

The uninterrupted interest of Europeans, ever since the late Ming dynasty, in trade and missionary activity in China was not paralleled by a similar interest in Japan. In 1639 Japan adopted a policy of strictly limited contact with the outside world, and thereafter all but dropped out of the consciousness of Occidentals. Even the Catholic missionaries eventually gave up their fruitless attempts to re-enter the country, and few Western ships reached Japanese waters. The only important exception was the annual Dutch vessel from Indonesia to the Dutch trading post on the island of Deshima in Nagasaki harbor. This Dutch trade, some carefully controlled commerce with Chinese merchants at Nagasaki, and a restricted flow of trade by way of the island of Tsushima to Korea and through the Ryūkyūs to China, formed the only contact between Japan and the outside world. Europeans simply accepted the inaccessibility of the islands as a fact of political geography. Absorbed in their expansion into other, much larger areas in Asia, they came to regard Japan as a small, poor country of little interest.

But in the closing years of the eighteenth century and the first half of the nineteenth, the increased activity in China was reflected in a sharp increase in Western pressures on Japan. Now, after a century and a half of Japanese isolation, Western ships began to appear in Japanese waters. Soon the nations of the West were demanding that the Japanese follow China and open their country to commercial and diplomatic relations. This was eventually achieved through the establishment of much the same unequal-treaty system as had been imposed on China. Commodore Perry of the United States led the way by facing the Japanese with unchallengeable naval power in 1853 and extracting from them the next year a treaty of friendship and limited trade relations. Then in 1858 the American consul, Townsend Harris, concluded a treaty opening Japan fully to trade. Both of these American treaties were followed by similar ones with the other interested Western nations.

As compared with the Chinese experience, however, the initial impact of the West on Japan in the middle of the nineteenth century was gentle. No wars were fought, no smuggling trade developed, no territory was forfeited. Not a single man was killed on either side during Perry's expedition to Japan, and the commercial treaties were negotiated amicably around a table. And yet Japan's response was far quicker and greater than that of China. Within a decade of the signing of the Harris treaty, the Japanese government had fallen, to be replaced by a regime of a radically different sort. Within another decade the whole feudal system of seven centuries' standing had been swept into the discard, and Japan was well launched on a series of astonishing reforms that were soon to make it a modern power.

This startling paradox—that Japan's greater response followed a less violent impact than in China—has posed difficult questions of historical interpretation. What forces at work in Japan produced so great a ferment? Obviously Japan in the mid-nineteenth century, even though it had derived a large part of its higher culture from China, was a very different country, capable of very different responses to the Western challenge.

Predisposing Factors

Insularity had from early times made the Japanese very much aware of their cultural and technological borrowings from the continent, even though the sum of such borrowings was probably no greater and possibly considerably less than in other countries of comparable size. Having early sent missions overseas to borrow from T'ang China, the Japanese were aware that useful things could be learned from abroad, and so found it easy to accept the idea of learning from the West. The Chinese normally assumed the opposite, and therefore were slow to appreciate what might be learned from the "barbarian" Occident.

The geographical isolation of Japan, as well as its distinctive language and feudal society, had also made the Japanese acutely aware that despite their heavy cultural debt to China they were a separate ethnic and political entity. In short, they already had a strong sense of separate identity which amounted to a feeling of nationalism. They assumed a plurality of countries in the world and made no claim to universal rule. In the nineteenth century, while the Chinese found the multi-state, international system of Europe wholly unacceptable, the Japanese could quickly understand and accept it, and begin to act accordingly.

The organization of their society also gave the Japanese a greater propensity to respond to Western influences. The hierarchical, feudal society of Japan was bound by vertical ties of loyalty. These reached from shogun to daimyo to samurai, and even in a sense to peasants who felt obligated to their superiors for benefits received. The actual social ties were reinforced by the Confucian ethic prescribing duties according to status and by the Japanese emphasis on reciprocal obligations. This pyramidal structure of loyalties had created a unifying, centripetal political tendency, visible since the sixteenth century, that was held in check only by the Tokugawa decentralization of power within the system of feudal fiefs, or *han.*

In China, by contrast, though the top level of administrative organization under the emperor was more centralized, loyalties even within the bureaucracy were more diffuse: obligations to family or to local community competed with duty to emperor and to society. The Chinese commitment to their traditional way of life, their "culturalism," served less well than Japanese feudal loyalty (even in the less centralized Tokugawa state) to produce the unity necessary for a modern nation.

The feudal character of Japanese society also led to a different appreciation of Confucianism than in China. The Japanese accepted the metaphysical and ethical system of Sung China, Chu Hsi's Neo-Confucianism. But China since the Sung dynasty had interpreted the Confucian Classics in such a way as to reconcile them with bureaucratic government. Japan rejected this interpretation and emphasized the "feudal" character of the ideal society depicted by the sages. This they saw as very similar to their own Tokugawa society. Thus the Classics were put to different uses in the two countries.

In Japanese feudal society, status depended overwhelmingly on birth, and yet the Confucian political and social doctrines which permeated Japanese thinking asserted the moral potential inherent in all men. The contrast between hierarchic feudalism and some of the egalitarian doctrines of Buddhism was even greater. Thus there was not the same unity of theory and practice as in China and hence perhaps less stability. Ambitious men, if denied high status, would seek distinction through achievement. The energies that such stirrings produced were all the more dynamic because they were channeled within and subordinated to the ends of the group. In sociological terms, the Japanese can be called goal-oriented, the Chinese status-oriented. This is one reason why, in the face of the Western menace in the nineteenth century, many Chinese tried to control the situation by playing traditional roles, while the Japanese generally reacted by seeking specific objectives. . . .

Not only were the Japanese leaders much better informed than the Chinese about Western science; as feudal military men they had a more realistic understanding of military technology than did the scholar-gentry leadership of China. The Japanese did not have to be humiliated in bitter defeat before they could recognize their own military inferiority. At least some of them could see clearly, from the displacement of Western ships, the size and range of Western guns, and the strength of Western forces in the wars in China, that Japan was no match for the intruders.

Another underlying reason for the speed of the Japanese reaction was the relative smallness and accessibility of the islands and the close contacts maintained among all parts of the country. Perry's ships sailed within sight of Edo, the capital of the feudal government, and most of the other large cities were equally vulnerable from the sea. Although the country was divided into many autonomous feudal domains, the control system required the various lords and a large number of their retainers to spend alternate years in Edo (the *sankin kōtai* system). This brought the leadership into much closer contact than was afforded in China by the dispatch of officials from the capital to the provinces, even though the political structure of China was more highly centralized. Within a few weeks of Perry's arrival the whole country knew of this momentous event. Within four or five years, vigorous responses were coming from many areas, not merely from a few harried officials in a large bureaucracy or from residents of some port city remote from the capital.

The Diversity of Responses

Japan's responsiveness to Western contact seems actually to have been a variety of responses, only some of which proved successful and emerged as the new trend. Just because of this greater diversity, Japan was better able than China to find and pursue lines of action that proved meaningful and effective.

The feudal system itself made for this greater variety of response. The Tokugawa political structure, unlike that of China, was composed of units of various degrees of autonomy. After 1600 the Tokugawa shoguns had established their supremacy as feudal lords over the whole country, ruling a great central domain and indirectly controlling the rest of the land from Edo. But by the middle of the nineteenth century the emperor's court at Kyōto, as the theoretical source of the shogun's authority, was beginning to show signs of intellectual independence, though the shogunate still supported and controlled it. The bulk of the country was divided into about 265 *han,* or feudal domains, some of which showed even greater intellectual independence than the court. . . .

The division of political authority meant that, under Western pressure, reactions varied. The responses at the imperial court, the shogunal capital, and the many castle towns of the major daimyo ran the gamut from intransigent opposition to open-minded acceptance of foreign intercourse.

Even the class divisions contributed to this diversity of response. In theory, there were four classes: the samurai or warrior class of soldiers, administrators, and intellectuals at the top; then the peasants, artisans, and merchants, in that order. But actually there were only two main classes, samurai and commoners, though each was divided into many strata. Samurai and commoners were kept strictly apart both socially and in their functions in society. Men raised as peasants or townsmen had no chance of political and social eminence, and so developed somewhat different concepts of economic enterprise and service than did most samurai. Their responses to Western stimuli often differed from those of the ruling class.

The wide diffusion of education also made for a diversity of responses. The samurai class, constituting some five or six percent of the population, was roughly five times the proportional size of the degree-holding gentry class in China. It was no narrow feudal aristocracy of the European type but a rather broad upper class of education and traditions of leadership. While the political hierarchy was rigidly fixed and in theory all powers were determined by heredity, in actuality the various *han* governments had developed into widely based bureaucracies. Just as the shogun's chief administrators were drawn from the "hereditary" daimyo, so the chief administrators under each daimyo were drawn from his major hereditary vassals, usually called "family elders" (*karō*). But most of the daimyo, like the shoguns, were little more than figureheads, and only rarely did their chief officers take political initiative. Lower officers, often of rather humble origin inside the samurai class, were not infrequently the chief formulators of policy, which they carried into effect by winning formal approval from the daimyo and "family elders." *Han* bureaucracies at times became divided into rival factions clustering around statesmen of this type, and "reform" and "conservative" parties might alternate in power.

Given this sort of bureaucratic politics within the *han*, it is not surprising that large numbers of samurai reacted strongly to the Western challenge, struggling with one another to determine the response of their respective *han* governments. . . .

Behind the various responses to Western contact we can discern a pervasive concern for the fate of the nation. The Japanese were determined to preserve their independence, and the concept of national interest, though variously understood, was a basis on which some responses were sorted out as more meaningful or effective than others, and accordingly found greater support and shaped national policy. Certain reactions to Western technological superiority and military might did not work, whereas other efforts were highly successful and catapulted their advocates to positions of power. . . .

JAPAN'S CAPACITY TO MODERNIZE

Once Japan was launched on the course of modernization, certain underlying conditions made possible rapid progress, though most of these conditions had existed for at least a century without seriously affecting the Tokugawa regime. Without pressure from the West, which revealed its military and political weakness, the Tokugawa system might have continued another century or more.

It is useful to distinguish here, as with China, between long-range domestic trends and immediate foreign stimuli. The startling difference between Japan's response and that of China lies precisely in the domestic conditions in the two countries before their "opening" to more extensive Western contact. Some of these conditions in Japan had been developing over a long period. The tradition of "Dutch learning," for example, not only contributed to Japan's responsiveness to the West but also gave Japan a head start with the Western science and technological modernization that most Asian countries lacked. Another example was the long-term trend toward more centralized government. Although *han* administration was in theory autonomous, actually a high degree of central control had evolved. Similarly, within the shogunate and the various *han,* the ruling class, though of feudal warrior origin, had developed the kind of bureaucratic experience and tradition required in modern government.

Why Japan alone among Asian countries in the nineteenth century responded to the West with a clear sense of nationalism is an interesting question. One major reason was the peculiar relationship of Japan to China. As a sub-unit within East Asian civilization, Japan early realized its smallness compared to the whole cultural unit and perhaps in compensation began to emphasize its "uniqueness" and "superiority." . . .

. . . The great economic development of the Tokugawa period made economic modernization easier. Feudalism, far from having retarded this growth, seems to have been a major cause of it. Townsmen and peasants, barred from political power by the feudal class system, did not dissipate their energies in political and social efforts, but devoted themselves to economic advancement. Furthermore, they were better protected by feudal custom and the disdain of the ruling class for economic activities than was true in the rest of Asia, where autocratic rulers had few compunctions about taking over lucrative commercial undertakings. As a result, Japanese merchants were able to make long-range investments with greater security than were their counterparts in most of Asia. Rich Japanese peasants, instead of investing in more land, the only relatively safe investment in most of Asia, put their wealth into trade and industry, which brought larger profits. . . .

Thus by the nineteenth century the Japanese probably had the most advanced and thoroughly monetized economy in Asia and were well prepared for further economic development. They had little trouble understanding and adopting the commercial and industrial patterns of the West—and here again they had a running start at modernization.

Social Conditions

By the nineteenth century the feudal class structure had become outmoded and could be discarded with relative ease. Two centuries of peace had eroded the martial spirit and the bonds of loyalty on which it depended. The samurai had been transformed from feudal warriors into a salaried class of professional soldiers and administrators, arrogant by tradition but frustrated by poverty. Power and status were still determined largely by birth, but the more able and ambitious of the lesser samurai chafed under the system and often sought to escape its limitations by abandoning their hereditary duties for less restricted careers as scholars—sometimes of "Dutch learning"—or as military experts. The ambition of certain samurai of humble birth was the force most subversive to feudalism in the turmoil that followed Perry. . . .

The Imperial System

A final factor that speeded modernization was the peculiar status of the imperial institution. Whereas the Chinese eventually had to rationalize modernization by accepting strange foreign ideologies, the Japanese could justify it as strengthening a venerable native institution understood by all. The myth that change was merely part of the restoration of the direct rule of the emperors, after more than seven centuries of aberration, made it easier to sweep aside a regime that had ruled successfully for two and a half centuries and a political and social system of even longer duration. Only this myth made many otherwise distasteful features of modernization tolerable. . . .

EARLY CONTACTS WITH THE WEST

In both China and Japan antecedent domestic conditions helped shape the response to foreign stimuli. But the actual opening of each country was brought about mainly by the application of Western power or the threat of it. In Japan as in China, it took the impact of Western military strength to crack the framework of the old system and reveal its inability to cope with the new situation. . . .

THE TRANSFORMATION OF SOCIETY

Industrialization as well as political and military modernization depended on new skills, new attitudes, and broader knowledge among the Japanese people. The new leaders had realized from the start that social and intellectual modernization was prerequisite to successful innovation in other fields. But in the social and intellectual areas, as in economics, the responsiveness of thousands of individuals from all classes was more important in the long run than the planning of the authorities. . . .

THOUGHT AND RELIGION

... [T]he Meiji leaders might best be described as pragmatists and utilitarians, ready to adopt whatever techniques, institutions, or ideas seemed useful. They had the advantage of being in complete agreement on their ultimate objective and of having the support of most thinking Japanese. The country was to be made strong enough to withstand foreign domination and to win equality. The trial-and-error experience of the late Tokugawa period had shown that the best way to create "a rich country and a strong military" was to centralize Japan politically by means of the convenient imperial symbol and to modernize it by borrowing from the West. But no one as yet had a formula for modernizing an underdeveloped nation, and the leaders, faced with a confused and rapidly changing situation, were flexible rather than doctrinaire about the best way to achieve their ends. ...

THE INTRODUCTION
OF REPRESENTATIVE INSTITUTIONS

The introduction of democratic institutions was perhaps the most surprising innovation of the Meiji period, because the Japanese had in their background no trace of representative government either in theory or in practice. ...

Demands for the sharing of political power, though a major historical source of democracy in the West, did not force democratic institutions on a reluctant government in Meiji Japan. The governing group had gained such complete and rapid mastery over the nation, and the whole concept of democracy was so unfamiliar to most Japanese, that the new regime at first did not have to worry about such outlandish ideas.

Rather, democratic institutions were introduced chiefly because many government leaders felt that Japan had something to gain from them. They were influenced by prevalent Western beliefs in the triumph of democracy as part of the inevitable course of progress. They saw the specter of the French Revolution as the fate of any too-autocratic regime. They also noted that strong and advanced countries like Great Britain, France, and the United States based their national strength on democracy, while democratic ideas had some currency in all of the more modernized nations. Assuming that representative institutions, like machine production, were among the reasons for the power and dominance of the Occident, most of the government leaders felt impelled to introduce at least some aspects of parliamentary government as a means of modernizing and strengthening the nation. The introduction of democratic institutions, they also felt, would help win the esteem of the West and bring nearer the day of Japan's acceptance as an equal. ...

12

Contrasting Factors in the
Modernization of China and Japan

Marion J. Levy, Jr.

In these excerpts, sociologist Marion J. Levy, Jr., focuses on the social and political advantages Japan enjoyed, in contrast to China, in achieving effective modernization. In Japan, loyalty to the Emperor took precedence over strong family ties, making it easier to effect change from above than in China, where the family claimed first allegiance. While China's open social system drained capital and talent away from trade, Japan's closed social system fostered development of a strong merchant class, which facilitated capital investment in industrialization. Levy details the heroic reforms undertaken by Japan's new Meiji government, which rapidly carried forward the development of the modern industrial society necessary for military strength and continued independence.

The initial stage taken for Japan can be set up for the purposes relevant here by contrast with that of China. There were, or course, many similarities. Both of these societies were predominantly agrarian in their systems of economic production. In both cases the non-agrarian members of the society found their basic means of support in the goods and services produced by the peasants. The peasants in "traditional" Japan were also to a very high degree self-sufficient in the matter of production and consumption and received little in return for the portion of their production that was received by others. Certainly they did not receive goods and services from the non-farmers in the society that permitted or accounted for a rise in the net productivity of agriculture. In the system of production of "traditional" Japan there were no elements of modern industrial production. As in China relationships in most spheres, and certainly in the economic aspects of action were to a very high degree traditionally determined. People were selected for relationships primarily on the basis of who they were rather than what they could do with certain peculiar and important exceptions as will be seen below. The relationships among individuals contained many specific obligations and rights, but they were in strategic respects only vaguely defined and delimited. The great emphasis in relationships was not upon what was specifically covered but rather upon whom a given individual stuck with, to whom he owed loyalty, under any and all possible conditions, whatever they might be. As in China the vast majority of people lived very close to the margin of subsistence for the society, and a relatively small group lived on a comparatively luxurious basis. The family was a fundamental unit of solidarity in Japan as in China, and many of the decisions and activities of daily life were family oriented. As will be seen below, however, action in Tokugawa Japan was not in the last analysis nearly so overwhelmingly family oriented as in the case of China. In fact family orientation took a clearly secondary position relative to another solidarity orientation. . . .

In Japan loyalty to the feudal hierarchy took clear precedence over loyalty to one's family. This did not mean that loyalty to one's family was unimportant. It was tremendously important. It did mean, however, that one had two means of control over the deviance of individuals, control as in the Chinese case through the family organization and direct control through the feudal hierarchy. One of the implications of this dual hold on the individual was that the possibility of "individualism by default" was minimized. Even if an individual were to lose or be separated from his family, he could not lose or be separated from the entire hierarchy of persons in positions of power over him. One of the most important arguments used in the amazingly peaceable deposition of the Shogun was, of course, to the effect that the Shogun had himself violated his loyalty to his overlord, the Emperor. The emphasis on the loyalty was never denigrated. The people were simply told that this loyalty was due directly to the Emperor and his officials and hence to the Japanese nation and not to the Shogun. . . .

The general hypotheses of this paper include two of special importance. The first is that the differing systems of control over individuals in China and Japan made for much of the difference in their respective experiences with industrialization. The second is that what on the surface in the early nineteenth century might have seemed like comparatively small differences in the roles of the merchants in the two societies was also of special importance in the different experiences of the two countries. This difference between the merchants was directly related to the general and the specific characteristics of feudalism in Japan. As regards the general characteristics the most important factor for present purposes is the closed class character of "traditional" Japanese society by contrast with that of Chinese society. In both societies the merchant role was, ideally speaking, one of extremely low prestige. Actually in both societies, as has been noted above, the merchants were often powerful and even respected. But in Chinese society the open class character of the social system held out to all merchants the possibility of achieving for their families, if not for themselves, the genuinely ideal social position for the entire society. By following the proper preparations and procedures the individual could acquire gentry status, and with him his family could do so as well. Thus, there was motivation aplenty for merchants to spend capital as well as income to acquire either by graft or education or both a different status for their sons or even in some cases for themselves. There was, therefore, a flight of talent from the merchant field in China and with it a flight of funds. Such flights were not features of the Japanese case. No matter how much he might wish to do so, a merchant could not become a member of the nobility. He might become the power behind the throne of a daimyo, but he could not become one, nor could his family after him acquire that status. . . .

. . . The feudal relationships of individuals to the land were an important part of social position in Japanese society, but land could correspondingly not be bought and sold with any general freedom, at least ideally speaking. This meant that many actual transfers of land were exceedingly vulnerable to confiscation. These limitations on the acquisition of land either as a symbol of social status or as a category of investment meant that one of the most prominent forms of capital flight from merchant uses in China was virtually out of the question in Japan. Talent could not be readily drained from the field because of the class system. Capital could not be readily drained from the field either, because of the closely associated restrictions on the holding of land. The merchants of Japan could not seek to minimize their vulnerability to the political hierarchy by either a personal or capital flight from merchant pursuits. Through no virtue of their own, perhaps, they were forced to think in terms of buying and selling and production and reinvestment. Their hope for security lay in being more and more successful merchants and in having their successors continue in that vein. . . .

As in the case of China the transitional period in Japan was compounded of the disintegration of the old order and the introduction of the new forces. The new forces were virtually identical. The old order was different, however, and in the transitional stage in Japan industrialization made dramatic headway which was not the case in China. Furthermore the transition was made without the chaotic state of affairs that has characterized China. Here we shall first examine the disintegration of the old order prior to the introduction of the new.

It is perhaps not an exaggeration to state that the disintegration of the old order is best mirrored for present purposes in the rise in actual power and importance of the merchants. They made their position, ideally a minor interstitial one, the kingpin of the whole system. The daimyo relied upon them for their needs of exchange, and their reliance made the merchants powerful and the nobles dependent upon them. Outside of the peasant households and outside of the strictly agrarian pursuits all other aspects of production and consumption came to revolve around the merchants. The artisans produced for the wealthy and for other artisans. They depended for food on the production of rice and other staples by either the farmers or the fishermen of a given daimyo. The upper classes depended upon the artisans for much of what they consumed. The scale of operations precluded barter as a daily means, and the merchants provided the facilities to make barter unnecessary. They not only traded; they financed production and consumption; they developed banks; they created commodity markets and dealt in futures as well as concrete goods; and they became in short general entrepreneurs for endeavors of all sorts. It is not a matter of chance that the zaibatsu of modern Japan, who grew out of these merchants roles, characteristically built industrial and economic empires of the most diverse sorts. In the modern West such great family enterprises as have grown up have tended to specialize to a much greater degree in, say, banking or insurance or even the industrial production of a particular sort of product with others added primarily if germane to that original one. . . .

. . . The actual opening of Japan that was forced by Perry was not of course a part of Japanese operations, but it was not totally unexpected, and its possible significance for the future of Japan was grasped at once. The closure of Japan was one of the techniques by which the Tokugawa hoped to hold back change and incidentally to forestall changes brought about by foreign contacts raising the possibility of foreign allies for rebellious nobles—a possibility that might have broken the rather thorough system of control devised by the Shogunate. But all through the period of closure the Tokugawa kept a window to the West in the carefully restricted Dutch trading concession. This was so restricted as to offer the Dutch no uncontrolled basis for influencing the people at large as existed in China even before the Opium Wars forced even more contacts to be made available. One of the exactions placed on the Dutch was a periodic report on what transpired in the Western world. Scholars today may laugh at the naivete of some of the ideas of the West held by the Japanese in power in those days, but the fact remains that they knew a great deal more about the West than the West knew about Japan. They were particularly impressed by the apparent ease and avidity with which the Western powers took over control of those parts of the world that lacked even the beginnings of industrialization and yet were strategic for it in terms of raw materials, markets, transportation, etc. The manner of Perry's appearance in Japan was to many of the Japanese a sign that their time had come unless they moved to prevent it. . . .

. . . But the devotion of the leaders, at least, to rule of Japan by Japanese was certainly intense in the middle of the nineteenth century, and apparently had been so for centuries past. The Japanese who seized control from the Tokugawa were determined to prevent the domination of Japan by outside forces. In the period interstitial to Perry's appearance and the restoration of the Emperor, the power of the West was studied in Japan, and Japanese went abroad to see for themselves. They were given conclusive evidence by the West of the importance of armies and fleets in these matters in a series of incidents in which victory went inevitably to the West. . . .

Reforms followed the Restoration of the Emperor (formally dated as 1868) quickly. The men in power understood that an army and fleet of the modern sort were necessary if Japan were to escape absorption. A conscript army of peasants was organized and trained—a radical departure for Japan in which the right to bear arms was the prerogative par excellence of the upper classes. . . .

The new rulers understood that a modern army and fleet were minimal requirements if Japan was to escape foreign domination. They also realized that a modern heavy industry was necessary if Japan was to be able to support a modern military establishment without dependence upon foreign powers. They understood even more. They understood that one of the major avenues of encroachment by the modern Western nations in other "underdeveloped" countries had been via the protection of their investments in these areas. The new rulers of Japan early faced up to the-problem of building up these necessary industrial facilities without resort to financing from abroad with all the footholds that sort of a relationship offered to foreign governments. The problem posed for them by this point of view was a serious one. In the first place the scale on which these industries had to be set up precluded the easy transformation of capital from prevailing forms to the modern ones. In the second place the Japanese had initially at least to seek their capital equipment abroad, since they lacked the means of making it at home. Finally, and perhaps most difficult of all, the sort of heavy industry necessary to serve as a basis for the independent maintenance of a modern army and fleet was uneconomic in Japan. Because of the relative lack of good coal and iron deposits in Japan proper, it was cheaper for Japan to buy heavy industrial goods abroad than to produce them at home. But buying them abroad would make and would keep Japan more and more vulnerable to the interests of her foreign sources of supply of these commodities. National interest from the point of view of the Japanese required the subsidization of these industries at any cost. The maintenance of a modern army and fleet was another economic strain on Japan. Armies and fleets may be justified on many grounds, but they are always net drains on the effective material productivity for other uses of any country. Economically they are never justified save by a consideration of the spoils of conquest that they may make possible or by a consideration of the costs of the conquests they prevent. It was the prevention of conquest by outsiders that initially at least motivated the money and effort spent on army and fleet in Japan.

The Japanese feat came as close to being one of lifting oneself by one's bootstraps as the modern world has ever seen. They started close to bankruptcy, used almost no foreign capital, established uneconomic heavy industries, organized and maintained a modern military and naval establishment, changed their governmental system radically, altered their system of production and consumption of goods and services to one in which modern industry was strategic, erected and conducted many highly profitable modern enterprises, made literacy of a sort virtually universal, and taught their people to operate effectively in terms of types of relationships that had been relatively unimportant and unknown in the Tokugawa period. They did it all with virtually no internal bloodshed or disintegration of major proportions, and they were very far along with the job in no more than five decades. The problems they posed themselves required even tighter controls on the process than industrialization would have in another context in which the utilization of loans and other help from abroad would not have been excluded or in which natural resources furnished a better material basis for industrialization than they did in Japan. . . .

The transition had to be kept smooth. The Japanese were well aware that civil strife was a well understood fishing ground for foreign nations. Their own expulsion of Europeans some centuries before had been intimately tied up with the participation of these Europeans in Japanese domestic struggles for power. The Japanese also had China as a constant warning to them. China had all the obvious possibilities for industrialization that Japan had plus infinitely better raw material resources and even cheaper labor. But China lacked the ability to organize and maintain tightly a planned program for industrialization, and most of the things Japan's leaders feared for Japan happened to China. In fact Japan herself in her initial tests of her progress was an outstanding participant in the exploitation of China's weakness. . . .

Unit IV

Political Parties

Political parties in China and Japan differ from American political parties in a number of striking ways. In China, the Communist Party (CCP) has an absolute monopoly on political power; it does not engage in electoral competition with other parties at all. Japan has democratic elections among different political parties, but the country has been ruled almost without interruption since World War II by the Liberal Democratic Party (LDP).* The longevity and strength of the CCP and the LDP have not only shaped the political processes of their respective nations, they have also affected the structure and nature of the parties themselves.

This unit examines political parties in China and Japan—their structure, functions, and ideologies, the electoral processes that underlie them, their role in the policymaking process, and changing trends in present-day party politics. In "Parties, Factions, and the Diet," Hans H. Baerwald traces key developments in the Japanese political system since the end of World War II, and shows how factionalism and internal disunity within the country's major parties have influenced the recent evolution of political life in Japan.

Japan is a democratic nation that has been governed by one party since 1945. Except for a brief interlude of Socialist rule in 1947–48, neither the Communists, the Komeito, nor any other party has managed to break the monopoly of LDP power. However, as Robert E. Ward points out in "Japanese Political Parties," the popular strength of the LDP has been steadily declining since 1958. Yet consistently high levels of support among rural inhab-

---

*The LDP in its present form was created in 1955 when the Liberal Party and the Japan Democratic Party merged.

itants, farmers, and big business, along with the relative weakness of the opposition parties, suggest that the LDP is in no immediate danger of losing its current majority status.

In China, the CCP has an even more secure grip on the leadership of the country. As Franz Schurmann explains in "The Chinese Communist Party: Structure and Organization," the parallel structure of the Party and state allows the CCP to oversee even the most minor details of political and social life in China. One of the most important instruments for maintaining this control is the so-called "study" system. In "Party Leadership and Control," A. Doak Barnett describes how regular study sessions, in which "criticism" and "self-criticism" are practiced, indoctrinate Party members and nonmembers alike. Combined with Party control of the media, frequent political campaigns, and especially Party control over all personnel appointments, these study groups inculcate Communist political values in the masses and encourage obedience and conformity.

Neither the CCP nor the LDP is without its share of problems. In Japan, where political parties tend to be parliamentary parties* rather than mass membership organizations, contact between party leaders and the electorate occurs only at election time (although individual politicians do have their own citizen support groups). Moreover, the hierarchical organization common to many aspects of Japanese society further contributes to the "communications gap" between voters and party representatives. As conditions change in Japan in response to growing urbanization, international economic competition, and global politics, this lack of contact between politicians and voters could develop into a serious problem for the LDP. Already, there is evidence of much greater activity on the part of interest groups concerned with social welfare, women's rights, job security, and nuclear weapons. These groups, if unable to influence distant representatives through existing channels, may eventually turn to other, more effective means of influencing government policy,

---

*Parties whose members are primarily elected officials rather than ordinary citizens.

which in turn could produce significant changes in the existing political process.

In contrast to Japan, the problem in China is not too little contact between the governed and the governors, but rather too much contact. In "The Party and the State in China," John B. Starr focuses on some of the problems that arise from the CCP's involvement in so many aspects of Chinese life, particularly the problem of divided authority between the Party and the state. Finally, two selections from the *Peking Review,* "The Building of the Chinese Communist Party" and "Socialist Modernization and the Changing Communist Party," describe how the present leadership of the CCP is moving towards reforming the Party structure and changing its role in order to recover the prestige and legitimacy among the people which it lost during the era of the Cultural Revolution. How effective and permanent these reforms will be, however, still remains to be seen.

13

Parties, Factions, and the Diet

Hans H. Baerwald

The Japanese political party system has undergone a series of transformations since the end of the Second World War. In this selection Baerwald traces the evolution of Japan's political parties from the postwar period to the present, stressing the importance of factions, the "real actors in intra-party politics in Japan," in shaping present-day political realities. Baerwald pays special attention to the Liberal Democratic Party (LDP), which has been the ruling party in Japan for almost forty years, and analyzes the role of factionalism in sustaining the LDP's power. After examining the factors that give rise to factionalism, he argues that factions are actually advantageous to the Japanese political system in that they make the political arena more open and competitive and prevent the LDP from becoming authoritarian. Moreover, he contends, because the various factions within the country's major governing party represent a broad spectrum of views, they make it possible for different segments of the Japanese public to influence policies and legislation through their representatives inside the party.

In the byways of Tokyo's Akasaka district just down the hill from the Diet Building are to be found numerous *ryōtei,* a term which is inadequately translated as "restaurants." Delicious food is served, and possibly far more importantly private rooms are provided for discreet conversations among Japan's political elite. In the last quarter century a sprinkling of political party leaders has always been included; it was not always so. In prewar Japan, effective power was in the hands of higher-class civilian bureaucrats (*buchō*—department manager upwards), corporation executives and senior echelons of the military. Today, the civilian bureaucracy may still constitute Japan's governing class, but it is the political party leaders who rule. Lest it be forgotten, the Diet is the instrument through which these politicians exercise their power.

Japan's political party system has undergone a number of transformations since the end of the Pacific War. In the immediate aftermath of defeat, a multi-party system emerged. There were two major conservative parties which adopted the names "Liberal" and "Progressive" (also "Democratic") and were the descendants of the prewar Seiyūkai and Minseitō respectively. Around the center of the ideological spectrum a number of minor parties emerged, of which the most significant was the "Cooperative Party" (later called the "People's Cooperative Party") under the leadership of Miki Takeo. He and his followers ultimately joined the conservatives. The Socialist Party of Japan (SPJ) quickly established itself as the major left-wing force by bringing together various strands of the prewar non-Communist left. In addition to the Japanese Communist Party (JCP), which for the first time was accorded legal status, a large number of splinter parties ran a substantial number of candidates (most of whom were unsuccessful) in the three elections held under the Occupation (1946, 1947, and 1949). Of these, only the Communists established a foothold, but one which they soon lost. It took more than twenty years for them to recover and to become a national party again.

This multi-party structure lasted until 1955 when, during a banner year, the conservatives merged into a unified Liberal Democratic Party (LDP) six months after the Socialists (who had split into "Right" and "Left" parties) in 1951 had reunited. Japan's political party system seemed to be evolving into a relatively stable two-party structure during the last half of the 1950s. Power, as measured in number of seats in the Diet, was notably unequal between the two parties, with the LDP coming close to winning two-thirds and the Socialist not quite one-third of the seats, the remainder going to a small offshoot of the SPJ and to the Communists. It was . . . more properly labeled a one-and-a-half party system.

A new and far more permanent split in the Socialist Party—from which the Japan Democratic Socialist Party (DSP) under Nishio Suehiro emerged as a separate entity—ushered in the 1960s. And by the middle of the decade, Sōka-Gakkai (Value-Creation Society), a neo-Buddhist religious group, spawned Kōmeitō (Clean Government Party), which carved out a distinctive but ideologically imprecise niche for itself. In the interim, the Communist Party had been slowly and painfully rehabilitating itself from the debacles of Cominform criticism and the "Red" Purge as a force in Japanese politics. These efforts paid off handsomely in the December 1972 House of Representatives election, when it won the largest number of seats ever (39 plus one "Independent"), thereby surpassing both the Kōmeitō and the Democratic Socialists. These developments did not alter the basic shape of Japan's party system, however. As has been the case for nearly the entire postwar period, and most definitely so since 1955, the conservatives in the LDP held a preponderant share of power and the Opposition was, by comparison, weak and fragmented. . . .

An unevenly-shaped tripod supports the LDP. Financiers and industrialists provide financial support, either directly or through such organizations as the Keidanren (Federation of Economic Organizations), Nikkeiren (Japan Federation of Employers' Associations), and Keizai Dōyūkai (Japan

Committee for Economic Development). Farmers, fishermen, white-collar workers and junior executives make up the core of the *kōenkai* ("supporters' societies") which provide the votes. The bureaucracy provides policy and legislative guidance, and also serves as an incubator for LDP candidates. Each leg of this tripod is important and serves a dual function; each is a prop, and the hollow interior of each serves as a pipe through which demands are sent up to the leadership. It must be understood that these demands, or signals, are often contradictory. Finance Ministry bureaucrats may promote trade liberalization as a means of coping with balance of trade surpluses, and thereby possibly offsetting the need for yen revaluation, while Ministry of International Trade and Industry bureaucrats may contend that such a cure is worse than the disease. What is important is that these groups with demands who serve as props and thus have access to the pipelines have more influence upon the councils of the LDP than those who do not.

The Socialist and Democratic Socialist parties have trade union federations as the bases of their organizational and voting strength. Sōhyō (General Council of Japanese Trade Unions) does for the SPJ what Dōmei Kaigi (Japan Confederation of Labor) does less successfully for the DSP. Endless debates take place in both parties and the union federations with which they are affiliated concerning the advantages and disadvantages of their dependence. While neither seems willing or able to cut the mutually beneficial umbilical cords, it goes without saying that these ties also impose constraints. For the political parties, it means that ideological orientations of the union leadership must be respected even if doing so might limit the pool of potential supporters. For the unions, it means that their influence over public policy remains relatively negligible so long as the parties with which they are affiliated are parts of a permanent Opposition. Most important, it means that the trade union movement has considerably less influence in the policy-making process than the size of the trade union electorate would appear to warrant. . . .

One overriding feature of Japanese political parties renders the foregoing description incomplete, accurate though it may be if attention is accorded only to the formal votes that are cast. Appearances of unity within each of the parties during formal decisions in the Diet are deceptive, for they hide the intense bargaining that has taken place inside the parliamentary parties at earlier stages of the policy-making and legislative processes. Especially in the cases of the LDP and SPJ, the facade of unity during Diet votes that each party seeks to project to the public obscures the considerable amount of strife that exists fairly constantly in each. It is the factions (*habatsu*) which are the real actors in intra-party politics in Japan. Their importance, especially in the LDP, cannot be overemphasized. It is the factions which have provided the most crucial leavening element in what might otherwise have become an LDP bulldozer and a relatively dull scene. . . .

That the LDP is a coalition of factions has become a cliche. Nonetheless it bears repetition if for no other reason than that America's most distinguished Ambassador to Japan, Dr. Edwin O. Reischauer, at his farewell press conference in Tokyo's Ōkura Hotel in effect scolded some of the American journalists (and others like myself who were present at the occasion) for being excessively concerned with factionalism in their analyses of Japanese politics. It seems to me that too little attention is accorded to factionalism by either foreign journalists and scholars in writings about or discussing that country's politics. Therefore I would like to invite the reader's attention to the question not of whether, but of why there are factions in the LDP and why they are influential.

First of all, the LDP is like a major river into which various tributaries have flowed. Even in terms of the simplest schematic representation, it is necessary to mention that each of the two major conservative parties that combined to form the LDP, that is, the "Liberal" and "Democratic" parties, brought with them their own internal divisions. Hence, the concept of the LDP as two parties brought together under one name is an oversimplification; the Liberal Party had been divided into the Hatoyama and Yoshida wings, and the Democratic Party had gone through a number of different incarnations in the immediate postwar years, each leaving its mark. Given the importance that is accorded to group loyalty in Japan, it is therefore not surprising that there are rivalries among those who trace their initial allegiance to various wings and incarnations. All of the LDPers may quite properly be labeled as conservatives, but the meaning of that label is imprecise and covers a broad spectrum of attitudes. Opposition to the "progressives" is the principal ingredient that holds them together, as is evidenced by the fact that the LDP came into existence in response to the—temporary—reunification of the Socialist Party.

A second factor, which is becoming considerably less important as the years go by and mortality takes it toll, is the conflict between those conservatives who were temporarily removed from active political life under the Occupation-induced purge of militarists and ultranationalists and those who had emerged as leaders during the years that their brethren were *persona non grata.* Hatoyama Ichirō, the unifier of the conservatives and first president of the LDP, had been declared "undesirable" by the Occupation on the eve of his election as Prime Minister in the spring of 1946. At the time, an agreement was ostensibly made between himself and his successor, Yoshida Shigeru, that when Hatoyama would be permitted to return to active political life, Yoshida would restore to him the reins of power. This well-publicized "secret" agreement was not honored by Prime Minister Yoshida. Earlier supporters of these gentlemen encountered some difficulty, understandably enough, in becoming happy swimmers in the same LDP stream.

A third factor, also exemplified by the Hatoyama-Yoshida split, was and remains the substantial difference in orientation between those who entered political life through participation in local, prefectural or national legislatures as opposed to those who entered from the bureaucracy. In Japanese parlance, this is referred to as the division between *tōjin* (partymen) and the *kanryō* (bureaucrats). If Hatoyama epitomized the *tōjin* by having been re-elected thirteen times to the House of Representative, Yoshida was the archetype of the ex-bureaucrat who came to dominate the LDP in the post-war period. Indeed, nearly all of the Prime Ministers have been drawn from the latter ranks.... In this context, the accession of Tanaka Kakuei to the presidency of the LDP and Prime Ministership in the summer of 1972 was a minor revolution. He was not an ex-bureaucrat—and his formal education had ended with elementary school....

Seiji shikin (political funds), or to put it less elegantly *o-kane* (money) provides the fourth factor contributing to factionalism in the LDP. While the party is generally conceded to be the wealthiest in Japan, ... its wealth is insufficient to support all of its endorsed candidates adequately. By the same token, few candidates can make up out of their own pockets the difference between what the party provides and what is required. Substantial sums are involved....

Hence, an aspiring candidate for a Diet seat, after receiving official party funds and contributions from his local supporters, usually finds it necessary to approach one of the faction leaders for about 25% of his campaign budget. Conversely, one of the principal prerequisites for becoming a faction leader (*oyabun,* literally translated "boss") is the ability to raise political funds....

The amount of money a faction leader has access to obviously influences the number of LDPers, either as candidates or elected Dietmen, he can help to support, and who are therefore likely to become his followers. This factor becomes particularly salient at LDP conventions. Contests for the coveted post of party president, which automatically brings with it the Prime Ministership so long as the LDP retains its majority in the House of Representatives, are rarely charades. Alliances which are made, coalitions which are built, promises which are kept—and occasionally broken—during the course of these elections for LDP president provide the fifth reason for the persistence of factionalism.... If the leader has many followers, his ability to bargain with other faction bosses is enhanced, as is his ability to declare his own candidacy for the office of party president. However, the larger the number of his followers, the greater is the drain on his financial resources. Former LDP Vice-President Kawashima Shōjirō maintained that the optimum factional size was 25 Representatives. It was his contention that a faction boss could not provide adequate services to his followers if the faction's size exceeded that number. By "services," he was understood to mean financial support and assistance in securing for his followers Cabinet portfolios, Diet Committee chairmanships, parliamentary vice-ministerships, or important party posts. Less than 25 members would result in a loss of influence and bargaining power with the party president or the other faction bosses. Yet, the record indicates that for a leader to have a reasonable chance for success in running to win for the party's presidency ... the minimum number in his faction must be around 45 members in the House of Representatives.... Regardless of how questions of money and factional size are dealt with, it is clear that contests for the party presidency serve to perpetuate whatever tendencies toward factionalism may already exist.

The unique medium-sized multiple-member district system under which candidates for Japan's House of Representatives are elected provides the sixth factor promoting factionalism. There are 124 districts, each returning three, four, or five members, depending upon the district's population. Voters write the name of one candidate on blank ballots, thus precluding multiple or weighted voting. It is a system which seems to have been peculiarly well-designed to drive campaign managers and their candidates to distraction and despair, and which is exceptionally well-suited to exacerbating intra-party factional strife. Not all parties run more than one candidate per district, of course. For example, until the December 1972 election the JCP had always run only one, but broke with tradition by running two in Kyoto's 1st constituency. Both won.

The LDP, however, must run more than one candidate per district since the mathematics of winning a majority of seats in the House of Representatives requires it to do so. The House currently has 491 districts; a bare majority would be 246; but there are only 124 districts. Hence, it is necessary to have two successful LDP candidates per constituency at the very least. Complicating these calculations is the declining strength of LDP support in urban districts. For example, there was one urban district, Aichi's 6th (the city of Nagoya) in which no LDP member won in 1972. In effect, this means that the LDP must run more than two candidates in certain rural districts where "conservative" sentiment remains strong. . . .

As has become amply clear by now, each district has its own characteristics. In nearly all of them, intra-party factional strife tends to be more important than the ostensible battle among the different parties. While these battles between presumed comrades-in-arms can be destructive of party unity (more on that later), they can also . . . serve to turn out the vote in contests which might otherwise induce voter apathy. Whatever the final balance of pluses and minuses one might wish to draw up, one point is clear: multiple-member constituencies do tend to promote factionalism within the LDP.

The seventh and final factor contributing to factionalism in the LDP is the most difficult to pin down because of its quicksilver properties. What is involved is the whole matter of public policy and the issue of tactics to be employed by the LDP towards the parties of the Opposition. LDPers tend to be highly pragmatic in their approach to politics, or to put it another way, are perfectly willing to permit others the privilege of being ideological or principled. (No implication is intended that ideology and principle are synonymous.) Yet, questions of policy do occasionally contribute to factional strife. Approval of the revised Security Treaty with the United States in the spring of 1960 was one such issue, as was the whole question of China policy. On the latter, for example, it was generally conceded that most of the so-called "Taiwan Lobby" supported Mr. Fukuda, whereas most of those favoring the re-establishment of relations with the People's Republic of

China (PRC) were backers of Mr. Tanaka in the July 1972 Convention of the LDP. It would be totally misleading to conclude that this division over an issue of policy was the determining factor in trying to explain why Tanaka emerged victorious. At most it was marginal and quite possibly largely fictitious in that even if Fukuda had won he too would have undertaken a rapprochement with the PRC. There might have been a slightly different timetable involved, and there might also have been certain differences in nuance in the Japanese government's dealings with Taiwan. On elements of basic substance there would have been virtually no difference.

What creates perplexity in attempting to assess the influence of policy as an element in factional strife is its ambiguity. That is to say, one is never certain whether advocacy of an alternative policy contributes to factional strife or, conversely, that the requirements of factionalism demand the espousal of substitute ideas. It has not been uncommon for individuals to change their stands in accordance with whether they were moving into or out of the mainstream coalition in the party. If nothing else—and, on occasion this can be of more than passing consequence—factionalism does assist in the ventilation of alternative approaches to questions of public policy. Whether this process actually promotes factionalism cannot be conclusively answered. . . .

There can be little doubt that factionalism exists as a fact of life—probably the basic fact of life—in Japanese politics. Disagreements arise, however, over the worth of its continued existence in the conduct of that country's politics. Many members of the academic and intellectual communities criticize factionalism because, for them, the *batsu* are an atavistic remnant of Japan's feudal past. Furthermore, they contend that Japan's political party system cannot become modern or truly rational so long as these factions—which by their very nature tend to emphasize the role of personality in politics and the bonds of loyalty between a leader and his followers (the *oyabun-kobun* relationship)—interfere with the goal of doing what is best for Japan. Policies cannot be developed and decisions cannot be made on the basis of some abstract notion of rationality, it is averred, so long as factionalism interferes by introducing the presumably non-rational personal element into the political process.

I disagree, and for several reasons. The structure of the Japanese political party system is the basic element. There is every likelihood that the Liberal Democratic Party will continue to be the majority—and hence governing—party for the foreseeable future, given the relative weakness and disunity of the Opposition parties, i.e., the SPJ, DSP, Kōmeitō and JCP. For the time being, they have extremely limited prospects of becoming a majority if for no other reason than that they are divided.

Second, if the foregoing is a reasonably accurate forecast of trends of Japanese politics, then the LDP—if it were an absolutely united party—might become authoritarian or its president (in his capacity as Prime Minister) might become dictatorial. While this latter contingency is unlikely, given the submergence of the individual in the group which in itself has provided a barrier against dictatorship in Japan, oligarchical authoritarianism is a danger against which factionalism has been, and has every prospect of continuing to be, an important protective shield.

Third, factions allow different segments of the Japanese public to have influence, and thereby allow alternative ideas, policies and legislative proposals to have supporters and opponents inside the party which governs Japan. It is inside the majority party, in the pre-parliamentary negotiations, that the fundamental decisions are made, and it is therefore vital that alternative proposals be ventilated at that stage of the policy-making process. One can of course argue that even with the existence of factions in the LDP the spectrum of views which have their spokesmen in the highest policy-making councils of the Japanese government is insufficiently broad. That may be true in ideal terms. Relatively speaking, however, so long as factions exist there will certainly be a broader spectrum of views which must be taken into account than if they were abolished.

In conclusion therefore, factions and factionalism contribute their share to making Japanese politics more open and competitive. In the context of Japan's political party system, factionalism is not only advantageous, but also eminently rational. Furthermore, only by coming to terms with the intra-mural disputes that take place within the political parties themselves can one come to grips with the realities of Japanese politics.

14

Japanese Political Parties

Robert E. Ward

In this brief selection, Ward describes the general characteristics of Japanese political parties. In contrast to the United States,
where political parties are mass organizations, political parties in
Japan are essentially parliamentary parties. Outside of elections,
the typical Japanese citizen has little or no contact with political
leaders and government officials. The two largest parties in the
country, the Socialists and the Liberal Democratic Party, both suffer from severe factionalism and internal disunity. And the LDP,
which has ruled Japan almost without interruption since World
War II, is losing its strength at the polls. As Ward suggests here,
these factors could eventually combine to alter the political process in Japan.

GENERAL CHARACTERISTICS OF JAPANESE PARTIES

There are several characteristics of the general political party situation
in Japan. First, none of the parties—except perhaps the Clean Government
and Communist parties—are truly mass membership organizations. They
notably lack solid bases in popular involvement and support. They normally
operate in Tokyo and among circles limited almost exclusively to professional politicians and administrators. They are essentially parliamentary parties. Their prime focus of interest is the lower house of the National Diet
and what goes on there. Only during election campaigns do they engage in
massive and sustained contact with the people. They are increasingly aware
of the unsatisfactory nature and the dangers of this sort of relationship with
the electorate and are seeking more meaningful forms of association. So far
they do not seem to have found them. This is true of both conservative and
progressive parties, with the previously mentioned exceptions.

Second, the two largest parties are internally disunited. Both the Liberal Democrats and the Socialists are really congeries of factions held together primarily by the tactical requirements of effective campaigning and
parliamentary competition. Within both parties there is a great deal of disagreement on major issues of policy and program. Neither the Liberal Democratic Party nor its several factions may be said really to have a basic pro-

gram. The party's politics are pragmatic and professional rather than ideological. The Socialists, primarily ideological in their orientation, share some common theoretical ground among themselves, but differ so fiercely over the all-important means of translating theory into practice that they are at least as disunified as their opposition. Indeed, it seems to be easier for the practical conservatives to reach agreements on particular political issues than for the more theory-oriented progressives to do so. The results of such a situation are constant instability and strife within each party. The first concern of a party leader must be the careful nursing of the factional coalition that supports him in power; the loss of even one element may well be fatal to his leadership. These are not circumstances conducive to strong, continuous, or courageous party leadership. As a consequence, although the parties—or, more specifically, their leaders—increasingly discuss and suggest national policies and formulate these as bills for parliamentary adoption, the policies are almost certain to represent the end product of an elaborate series of compromises. Between the two largest parties, the fundamental differences in their political orientation produce a marked and dangerous lack of common ground. A rigorous, theoretical approach to politics confronts a hostile and pragmatic approach. The terms and levels of discourse are different, and on issues judged to be basic, both sides are inflexible. Pitched battles rather than parliamentary processes are frequently the result.

It should also be clear that Japan does not have a two-party system in the American sense. Only once since 1945, and then briefly, have the Socialists been able to form a Cabinet—and that was a weak coalition. Instead, Japan has a multiparty system in which one party, the Liberal Democratic Party, has been constantly in power. There is no present indication that the Japan Socialist Party's circumstances will undergo a marked improvement in this respect. In fact, if anything, their prospects of gaining power have on the whole been steadily deteriorating since 1958.

Considering the weakness of the Socialist Party and the fierce hostilities, suspicions, and rivalry that beset the five opposition parties collectively, some understanding of the basic immobilism of Japanese party politics begins to emerge. The Liberal Democrats and their predecessors have been able to rule without interruption since 1948 partly because of a lack of any credible alternative. Despite this advantage, the Liberal Democratic share of the popular vote has declined steadily from 57.8 percent in the 1958 general election to 41.8 percent in 1976. Adding to these figures the proportion of the vote for independent candidates that really should be counted for the Liberal Democrats, the party's total was somewhat improved to 46 or 47 percent. That was still dangerously less than a majority. It is really the superior campaigning skills of the party that have maintained for it a working majority in the lower house. In the 1972 election, for example, the Liberal Democratic Party was able to translate 46.8 percent of the popular vote into control of 55.1 percent of the seats—this does not include the eleven successful independent candidates who joined the Liberal Democrats immediately after the election. After the 1976 election, however, this ruling margin—even after some thirteen victorious independents were added—had shrunk to 51.2 percent of the seats (262 of a total of 511). Adding to this dwindling measure of success at the polls the adverse consequences of a succession of highly publicized scandals involving Liberal Democratic leaders, the apparent ending of the boom economy so long sustained in Japan, the impact of an unusually prolonged recession, a hostile press, the advent of the New Liberal Club, and sheer public boredom with the party after some thirty years in power in one guise or another, it is now conceivable—some would say probable—that the Liberal Democrats will fail to obtain a working majority of the seats in the lower house in some election in the near future. Somewhat less serious, but probably more imminent, would be a similar loss in the House of Councilors.

Should either of these events occur, Japan would be faced with the prospect either of a certainly unstable minority government or of the need to patch together some sort of coalition government with a working majority. The preceding sections have dealt with the problems of forming such a coalition from the present opposition parties as long as the Liberal Democratic Party retains anything approximating one-half of the seats. The remaining alternatives are clear. Either several of the existing parties could split up and recombine into a new majority party—probably the left wing of the Liberal Democratic Party, the New Liberal Club, and all or some elements of the Democratic Socialist, Clean Government, and Japan Socialist parties—or the present Liberal Democratic Party could enter into a coalition that would insure it the dominant position in the group with one or more of the previously mentioned parties. Of the two, the latter alternative currently seems a bit more probable in the near future. It is difficult to see, however, how such a development would improve the quality of governance in Japan. It would probably serve to make decisions and actions even more difficult and time-consuming than they are at present.

15

The Chinese Communist Party: Structure and Organization

Franz Schurmann

The Chinese Communist Party resembles the Soviet Party model in a number of ways, particularly in the "parallel structure" of its Party and state institutions. As Schurmann explains in these excerpts, each administrative or productive unit in the Chinese state has an equivalent unit in the Party structure, which is responsible for communicating central decisions as well as for overseeing the unit's activity. This enables the Party to exercise direct control over all aspects of Chinese life. Schurmann goes on to describe how policies are made in China, pointing out that because lower-level Party units enjoy a certain amount of autonomy in implementing policy, local authorities can directly influence policymaking decisions.

THE STRUCTURE OF THE PARTY

The formal structure of the Chinese Communist party is essentially like that of the Soviet Communist party. It is hierarchically organized, which means that the whole structure resembles a pyramid. It has a far-flung base ramifying throughout the society and culminating in an apex where supreme power resides. The Party stands in alter-ego fashion alongside every organized unit of state and society. Wherever there is a factory, bureau, school, production brigade, military company, there also is a unit of the Communist party. This parallelism makes it possible for the Party to exercise direct leadership over every unit of organization to which it is linked. Linkage is created by the fact that leaders of the organizational unit are members of the Party and thus subject to Party discipline. . . .

The Central Organizations of the Party

The National Party Congress theoretically represents the source of authority and the agent of legitimation of the operative central organizations of the Party. . . .

The Party congresses have the important function of adopting long-term policy lines for coming periods. The long intervals between Party congresses usually reflect the inability of the Party to emerge with an over-all Party line. Indeed, the setting of "line and policy" is explicitly stated in the Party Rules as one of the major functions of the Party congresses. The Party congresses also ratify changes in the membership of the Central Committee, thus revealing something about the constellation of power at the supreme level. The adoption of new policy decisions is always preceded by long reports from the leadership which sum up the existing situation in various sectors of national life and point the way toward the future. Thus, far from being a ritual, the Party congresses mark decisive periods in the political development of Communist leadership.

The National Party Congress legitimates the appointments to the Central Committee of the Party. The Central Committee includes all top leaders of the Party. It meets in plenary session only on special occasions, which are marked by the announcement of new policy decisions worked out in the Politburo or the Standing Committee. Plenary sessions are attended not only by full and alternate members, but as the occasion demands by others, such as provincial Party cadres. . . .

The form that these various meetings takes clearly is an indication of top-level power politics. The fact that some of these meetings are not announced or that no communiques are issued indicates that no hard and fast policy line was adopted. But one thing is certain: If a plenum of the Central Committee is announced, this means that a policy decision has been made. Such plenums thus take on the form of meetings that discuss policy in operational terms. Invited to those meetings are all those directly responsible for implementation, such as local Party secretaries. One would presume that the ideal pattern of decision-making is that the Politburo makes the policy decision and the Central Committee discusses modifications and operational measures. But it may not always be so. Judging from the length of many of these meetings, vigorous discussion goes on. Long reports are read, and participants break up into small group sessions to discuss them. The intriguing question is whether these enlarged sessions ever lead to a reversal or decisive modification of a decision made by the Politburo. . . .

Little is known about the functions of the different departments and committees of the Central Committee. The Party Rules (Article 34) state only that "the Central Committee, through Party fractions in central state organs and in national people's bodies, directs the work of these organizations." All members of the Central Committee who hold high governmental position are members of the so-called Party fractions. Departments and committees of the Central Committee presumably are in constant contact with these fractions and serve as coordinating bodies. Basic administrative decisions are made by the Party fraction. Almost nothing is known about decision-making and discussion within the Central Committee itself. Political analysis of the workings of the Central Committee or of the Politburo is usually based on knowledge of the organizational functions, opinions, and personal history of the members (so far as they are known), and known changes in the composition of the Central Committee or the Politburo.

Party activity at regional levels has always been of great importance in carrying out policy. Lower-echelon Party organizations are not just manipulated from the center. In particular since the Yenan period [Yenan, in Northern Shensi province, was the Communists' wartime revolutionary headquarters in the late 1930s and 1940s. During this period, Mao set the tone for CCP leadership.], the Communists stressed the "creativity and autonomy" of lower-echelon Party units. The importance of the provincial and local party organizations can often be seen in the accounts of meetings of Party organizations at these levels. Such meetings are rarely stereotyped affairs in which Party secretaries simply inform Party cadres of the decisions made at the center. They are instead marked by vigorous discussion, in which Party cadres report on conditions in their own areas and suggest ways by which general policy can be translated into concrete action. Party meetings, like other meetings in Communist China, tend to follow a certain pattern. The meetings start with a general report by the highest-ranking Party cadre present and are then followed by particular reports from local Party cadres. These are interspersed with small-group discussions in which concrete problems are hammered out, and solutions decided on which can be incorporated into the final resolutions. . . .

Basic-Level Party Organization

Basic-Level Party units constitute the lowest echelon of Party organization, although not its smallest units. The concept of basic-level unit is important in both the Soviet Union and Communist China. It is at the basic level that state meets society. The Chinese divide society into units of production and units of territory; the former are based on a production system, the latter are geographical units. There also are basic-level units of the state administration. The nature and size of the basic-level organization of the Party is thus determined by the unit of production, territory, or administration to which it is attached. Article 47 of the 1956 Party Rules indicates what the basic-level units of production, territory, and administration are, and hence the nature of the corresponding basic-level units of Party organizations: "In each factory, mine, or other enterprise, in each *hsiang* or nationality *hsiang,* in each town, in each agricultural producers' cooperative, in each organ of the state administration, school, or street, in each company within the People's Liberation Army, and in other basic level units, whenever there are more than three regular Party members, one must establish a basic-level organization of the Party." The basic-level units thus are: factory, mine, other enterprise, *hsiang,* town, cooperative, state organ, school, street, military company. When the communes were formed, they became basic-level units.

16

Party Leadership and Control

A. Doak Barnett

All Chinese citizens are required to attend regular meetings where they study Marxist theory, government policy, and/or Communist Party history. These study sessions typically take place in groups of ten to twenty people who live or work together. In this selection from his classic study, *Cadres, Bureaucracy, and Political Power in Communist China,* A. Doak Barnett describes the importance of these "study" sessions to Communist Party control and leadership, and shows how they encourage obedience and conformity through the use of "criticism and self-criticism." Although criticism sessions are fairly routinized during periods of political calm, they increase in intensity during political campaigns. More often than not, people conform to authorized norms in order to avoid being targeted during one of these frequent campaigns.

INDOCTRINATION:
THE "STUDY" SYSTEM

One of the most important instruments for Party leadership and control over all personnel in Ministry M—as in virtually all institutions in Communist China today—was a system of regular indoctrination labeled "theoretical study" (*li lun hsüeh hsi*). One half-day every week, Saturday afternoon, was set aside for this directed study, in which all Party and non-Party cadres had to participate. The aim was both to educate all cadres in a positive sense and to exercise tight ideological control over them.

The ministry's Party Committee, and most particularly its propaganda committeeman, was responsible for directing the program of study; but it obtained the collaboration of the Personnel Bureau in organizing the entire staff of the ministry into small groups, and instructions and materials for study were issued through the bureau. The study groups, each with a designated head, generally consisted of ten to twenty persons, and they contained both Party and non-Party cadres. Sometimes they were established on the basis of the sections and divisions in which the cadres worked. At other times, however, persons were specially assigned to study groups by the Personnel Bureau on the basis of their educational level and ideological sophistication. In Ministry M, there were three levels of groups—referred to simply as higher, middle, and lower—with different study programs for each. The higher-level groups, composed almost entirely of college graduates, dealt with fairly advanced questions of Marxist-Leninist theory; the middle-level ones placed more stress on specific political and economic policies and problems; and the lower-level groups concentrated on subjects such as the history of the Communist movement in China. In Ministry M, some special groups were also established for cadres of the rank of division chief and above, regardless of their educational or ideological level; one explanation given for this by ex-cadres was the belief that some of the poorly educated "old cadres," who held many leading posts in the ministry, might have been embarrassed if they had been mixed with ordinary cadres whose grasp of ideological problems exceeded theirs. However, section chiefs apparently were always assigned to regular study groups along with ordinary cadres.

As was true in the case of political study in the Party branches, materials for these general study groups included both designated Party publications and other specially prepared and mimeographed materials provided by the Party Committee and the Personnel Bureau. Periodic lectures were organized, but small group discussion, including criticism and self-criticism, was considered to be the most important element in the study process, and Party and YCL [Young Communist League] members, as well as activists hoping to join the Party, invariably played leading roles in it. Active participation was expected of everyone, though, and persons showing lack of interest risked exposure to organized group criticism. Over time, however, this group indoctrination process tended, perhaps not surprisingly, to become routinized. During certain periods group discussion was irregular, and a substantial amount of time was allotted to self-study, during which individuals could simply read designated materials at their own desks. The process became routinized, also, in the sense that many ordinary cadres who had participated for years in such study found it increasingly dull and boring, and in periods of comparative political relaxation, when the general level of tension in China dropped, they sometimes simply went through the proper motions, without devoting serious attention to it. However, although political study could become somewhat routinized during periods of relaxation, such periods never lasted for long, and when the regime promoted one of its major political campaigns, as it did at fairly regular intervals, the indoctrination of cadres in the entire bureaucracy was greatly intensified and had to be taken seriously by all cadres.

The Party Committee, as part of its general propaganda program within the ministry, also ran a regular "wall newspaper," focusing on internal news and information. It was a handwritten paper, posted periodically on a large board near the ministry's main entrance. And during campaigns the walls of the ministry were plastered with posters and "large-character newspapers" (*ta tzu pao*) written by ministry personnel.

POLITICAL CAMPAIGNS

The importance of major political campaigns in China can hardly be overstated, in terms of their effects on the bureaucracy as well as on relations between the regime and the population as a whole. Both the cumulative effects of past campaigns and the conscious or unconscious anticipation of future campaigns have helped to create the special psychological milieu in which members of the bureaucracy operate.

Over the years, national political campaigns have occurred at frequent intervals. Some "rectification" (*cheng feng*) campaigns have been aimed primarily at cadres in the Party and government bureaucracies, and have been designed to tighten discipline as well as to combat bureaucratization and various sorts of "bourgeois" or other undesirable influences which the regime's top leaders regard as corrosive and subversive. Other campaigns have been massive, nation-wide, Party-directed struggles against designated class enemies (e.g., landlords, capitalists, counterrevolutionaries). Even though the major targets of these campaigns have been groups outside the bureaucracy, the cadres have been affected in many ways. Not only have the cadres been fully mobilized to participate in these campaigns, but, because many, if not most, have themselves had connections with the target groups, they have been affected by actual or potential "guilt by association." Consequently each campaign has been a period in which the cadres' loyalty to the regime has been tested, and all cadres have been pressured to cleanse and purify themselves of subversive "feudal" or "bourgeois" influences of the past.

Every major campaign has involved enormous organizational activity, and has introduced a period of apprehension, anxiety, and tension with the bureaucracy as well as throughout society as a whole. Generally, with the bureaucracy, political study has been dramatically increased until, at the peak of such a campaign, normal work has come virtually to a halt while everyone has devoted almost full time for weeks—and sometimes months—to endless group discussion, usually culminating in tense, emotional "struggle meetings" (*tou cheng hui*).

In Ministry M, special *ad hoc* leadership organizations were established by both the Party Committee and the Personnel Bureau to manage each major campaign. In one major campaign, for example, the Party unit responsible for organizing all campaign activities consisted of five men and was popularly referred to as the "Five-Man Small Group" (*wu jen hsiao tsu*). Under its direction, the Personnel Bureau set up a special campaign staff office (*X yün tung pan kung shih*) which was also composed wholly of Party members. Both of these organizations devoted full time to organizing and directing propaganda meetings, large lectures, small group sessions, and "struggle meetings."

In many campaigns, special campaign indoctrination meetings slowly increased until they occupied about half time, and finally full time for perhaps a month or two. As a campaign progressed, emphasis shifted from fairly generalized propaganda and indoctrination to increasingly emotional discussions in which everyone had to engage in criticism and self-criticism. Finally, a climax was reached when a number of specific cadres were singled out and made the targets of mass public denunciation within the ministry in huge "struggle meetings." In major political campaigns there had to be specific human targets to "struggle" against; errors and evils, as well as virtues, had to be personified.

These "struggle meetings," as described by ex-cadres from central ministries who have participated in them, are psychologically unnerving, even terrifying, experiences for all who take part, whether as targets of abuse or simply as observers. They are carefully planned and directed by Party personnel, and the hapless victims are pilloried with torrents of abuse in a succession of public meetings that may last several days. The victims must stand with bowed heads while accusations are shouted at them; and in contrast to some other types of criticism meetings, such as "debate meetings" (*pien lun hui*), they cannot speak in self-defense except when specifically instructed to do so by the Party leaders directing the meetings. The charges made in these accusation meetings generally include ones to which large numbers of cadres in the audience may feel vulnerable—e.g., charges of having a politically tainted past or of holding wrong general attitudes— and consequently it is fairly easy for many cadres to identify themselves secretly with the victims. Those who do so often feel under the greatest compulsion to join publicly in the denunciations, fearing that failure to do so might suggest that they secretly sympathize with the persons under attack.

The effects of these campaigns within the bureaucracy are subtle and far-reaching. By dramatically demonstrating the Party's power to determine the fate of every cadre, and by clearly defining attitudes and behavior that are unacceptable to the Party, they create strong incentives for all cadres to submit to the Party's authority in order to minimize the risks of being singled out for punishment. Ex-cadres assert that even in periods of relaxation, all cadres consciously or unconsciously anticipate the recurrence of political campaigns in the future. Non-Party cadres, in particular, feel that they are under continuous scrutiny by the Party members in their organization and that any tendency to challenge the Party's authority, or even any clash of personality with ordinary Party members, may make them vulnerable to political attack in some future campaign. This strongly reinforces the tendencies of most non-Party cadres to be deferential and responsive to the opinions of Party members and clearly strengthens the authority of the Party.

17

The Party and the State in China

John Bryan Starr

The problem of divided authority between the Party and the state is of central concern to present-day Chinese leaders. In these excerpts, Starr argues that the state structure in China is much more than a mere facade; in his view, it is an institutional framework that while not wholly distinct from the Party nonetheless enjoys a certain degree of autonomy. At the lower levels of government, this inherent division of authority often leads to a struggle between state officials and their overseers in the unit's Party "fractions." At the higher levels, the problem is not one of divided authority, but rather one of conflicting authority since high-level state officials, most of whom are also Party members, experience a conflict of interests in the making of policy.

The problem of divided authority as between Party and state is one for which several different resolutions have been put forward during the period since the adoption of the Constitution in 1954. The state structure as set up under this Constitution owed a great deal to the influence of the Soviet model. As a result the basic framework gives the impression of a strong commitment to the principle of parallel hierarchies. This strong commitment has never been manifested in the actual operation of the system, however. To understand the relationship between Party and state, it is crucial to understand at the outset the fallacy of two conflicting interpretations of that relationship. First, the state structure is not merely a facade created to cloak Party control of the affairs of state. Second, the two structures do not represent two wholly distinct and competing *loci* of political power in the system.

The state structure has always been conceived of in China as the implement by means of which Party-determined policy is put into practice. On the other hand, as our own experience with bureaucracy continues to demonstrate, organizations and their members are highly resistant to being reduced to mere implements and thereby subordinating their own goals and interests. Consequently, policies are altered as a result of the way in which they are implemented. The purpose of Party supervision of the state structure is thus to minimize this distortion that it is not sufficiently powerful to eliminate.

At the level of the central government, the problem of divided authority between Party and state takes a slightly different form than in the lower levels. Within the ministries and committees of the State Council, the majority of the leaders are themselves Party members. At lower levels of the state structure the proportion of Party members is correspondingly lower. Where the parties to a decision are all Party members it is a question of determining whether those parties acted in their capacities as Party members or in their capacities as members of the government. In the case of decisions taken by a group consisting of some Party members and some nonmembers, the situation is more often one of conflicting authority.

Party authority within government organs is not vested in the Party branch of that organ but with the Party "fraction" (*dangzu*). Whereas the Party branch includes all of the Party members within the organ—a relatively large group in many government organs—the Party fraction is a small group of a half-dozen or so of the leading Party members of a state organ. The fractions were originally set up as control agencies to oversee the ideological purity of Party members within the state organs. The party branches within these organs, in turn, were charged with overseeing the operation of the organs themselves. Over the course of time, however, the fractions and branches have exchanged functions: it is now the fraction that exerts direction over the work of the organ, while the Party branch is reduced to the function of attending to the ideological purity of its own members. Because the fraction normally includes the leading figures of the state organ, the Party fraction constitutes a kind of board of directors among whom important decisions are taken. Clearly a non-Party leader within the state organ would be at a disadvantage, given the role of the Party fraction, unless of course the Party fraction was dependent upon his greater command of the technical details of the operation of the organ.

Party control is also exerted through the close supervision of personnel management. Virtually every cadre involved in personnel management is a Party member. The handling of personnel records as well as all the other aspects of managing personnel within the state organs is considered to be sufficiently sensitive work to require direct and complete Party supervision.

The checking of bureaucratization within the state organs was, as we have seen, originally the function of a separate committee and later that of a ministry devoted to supervision. Once this task was assumed by the Procuracy, however, it was gradually phased out as a function of the state structure, for the Procuracy itself was in process of losing its independence and falling more and more completely under Party control. As a result, bureaucratization in the Chinese political system is most often counteracted by campaigns rather than by some form of routine control. The campaign is seen as better suited to the task of controlling bureaucratization than would be the use of a permanent organ devoted to the task since that organ would itself be subject to routinization and bureaucratization.

18

The Building of the Chinese Communist Party

Peking Review

In these excerpts from an interview that appeared in the *Peking Review* in 1982, a leading comrade of the Organization Department of the Party Central Committee describes the changes that have taken place in the Chinese Communist Party since its founding in 1921. He also discusses current qualifications for membership in the Party, the role of the Party in Chinese life, and the series of reforms that are being initiated as part of the new leadership's program for modernizing China's economic and political institutions.

Question: How many members does the Chinese Communist Party have? Will it continue to expand its organization?

Answer: The Chinese Communist Party was established in light of the needs of the Chinese people's revolution. During the 61 years of revolutionary wars and construction in China, the Chinese Communist Party has grown in size and strength. It began with some 50 members and now it has more than 39 million. Along with the development of revolution and socialist construction, it is bound to continue growing and developing.

Q: Who are qualified to be Party members? How about the procedures? . . .

A: Any Chinese worker, peasant, soldier, intellectual or any other revolutionary who has reached the age of 18 and who supports the Party programme and accepts the Party Constitution, is willing to join a Party organization, work actively in it, carry out the Party's decisions and pay membership dues on time, can apply for membership in the Communist Party of China. A Party member should study hard, serve the people wholeheartedly, play an exemplary vanguard role in work, be truthful and honest to the Party, observe Party discipline, put the Party's interests above everything else, be ready to sacrifice everything he or she has and strive all his or her life for the realization of the communist cause.

Applicants for Party membership must go through the procedure for admission, which includes: An applicant must be recommended by two full Party members who should earnestly brief a Party branch on the applicant, and the applicant must be examined by the Party branch which should seek extensive opinions inside and outside the Party. The applicants may become a probationary member after being accepted by the general membership meeting of the Party branch and being approved by the next higher Party committee. Before approving admission for an applicant, the higher Party committee must appoint someone to talk with the applicant and carefully examine his or her case. If he or she is qualified for Party membership, the committee should give its approval.

The Party Constitution stipulates that the probationary period of a probationary member is one year. The purpose is mainly to make further efforts to educate and observe him or her. During this period the Party organization concerned should further observe the member and set right his or her motives to join the Party, so as to exclude those who are not qualified to join the Party and ensure the quality of Party members. . . .

Q: How does the Party play its leading role in the period of socialist construction?

A: The Chinese Communist Party is the ruling party. To uphold and improve the leadership of the Party and to steadily raise the Party's militancy is the basic guarantee for our socialist modernization drive and for realizing the reunification of the motherland and defending our country's independence and security. The Party does not exercise leadership by issuing orders or using mandatory administrative means, but by using Marxism-Leninism and Mao Zedong Thought and its correct propositions and actions to educate and influence other organizations and people to conscientiously support the Party, have faith in the Party, accept the leadership of the Party and to work hard for the realization of the Party's propositions.

Specifically speaking, the Party's leading role is exercised through different ways. First, leading organs of the Party must formulate and implement a correct line, principles and policies. Second, through the work of its organizations at different levels, the Party co-ordinates relations in various fields and unites all forces under its line and goals. Third, the Party relies on all its members to play backbone and exemplary roles in political and social life. . . .

Q: Why is emphasis being placed on consolidating the Party's work style at the present time?

A: The Communist Party of China is a ruling party. As Vice-Chairman of the CPC Central Committee Chen Yun pointed out, the style of work of a ruling party is a matter of life-and-death importance.

During the revolutionary war years, everyone who joined the Communist Party was willing to bear hardships, take risks and, if necessary, sacrifice his or her life. Things have changed since the revolution succeeded. The people showed gratitude to us and the bourgeoisie came forward to flatter us. It is very easy for people within our Party to become arrogant and begin to seek pleasure. Some opportunists and careerists may have wormed their way into the Party, taking advantage of the Party's position to line their pockets. The 10 chaotic years of the "cultural revolution" clearly proved that a ruling party would become divorced from the masses if it does not maintain its good style of work and does not follow the principle of democratic centralism. Conspirators and careerists will be active and the Party may face the danger of changing its character and political colour.

After years of efforts, the Party's style of work has begun to take a turn for the better. But this does not mean that a fundamental change has taken place. For instance, an extremely small number of Party cadres doubt the line of the Party Central Committee, with some publicly singing different tunes. A number of Party members have grown individualistic. An extremely small number of them, corrupted by capitalist ideas, have become criminals. Some Party organizations have forfeited their role as fighting bastions. . . .

Q: How will Party members be educated in the future?

A: According to our experience in building up our Party over the past decades, the Party's power does not depend upon the number of members, but the quality of the Party members. We have always emphasized the importance of ideological building to the Party's development. Half of our present members joined the Party after 1966 when the "cultural revolution" began. When Lin Biao and the gang of four were holding sway, inner-Party life was extremely abnormal. These comrades had no chance to receive Party education. They lack the experience of strict Party life. Many of them do not fully understand the basic knowledge of the Party, its rules, discipline, fine traditions and style of work. In the meantime, some of those who joined the Party much earlier have become lax and are not strict with themselves.

At present, our Party is leading the people of all nationalities in building socialist ethics and material civilization.

19

Socialist Modernization
and the Changing Communist Party

Peking Review

These excerpts from another article published in the *Peking Review* shed further light on contemporary problems in Chinese party leadership and control. Under the new leadership's program for reforming the country's political and economic institutions, party control over production is being reduced; younger, better educated, and more proficient members are being sought and recruited, while older, politically appointed cadres are being eased out of office.

To solve correctly the question of the Party leadership over government organs and over enterprises and institutions is a highly important task in the organizational reform. It is necessary to achieve a proper division of labour between the Party and the government and between Party work and administrative and production work in enterprises and institutions. The Party is not an organ of power which issues orders to the people, nor is it an administrative or production organization. The Party should, of course, exercise leadership over production, construction and work in all other fields, and for this leadership to be fully effective it must be exercised in close connection with professional work by cadres who are professionally competent in such work. But Party leadership is mainly political and ideological leadership in matters of principle and policy and in the selection, allocation, assessment and supervision of cadres. It should not be equated with administrative work and the direction of production by government organizations and enterprises. The Party organizations should not take everything into their own hands. Only in this way can the Party ensure that the government organs and enterprises do their work independently and effectively, and can the Party itself concentrate its efforts on the study and formulation of major policies, the inspection of their implementation and the strengthening of ideological and political work among cadres and the rank and file both inside and outside the Party. For long-standing historical reasons, some members of our Party committees think that there will be nothing for them to do if they don't handle concrete administrative work—

this is an erroneous idea that impairs Party building and weakens the Party's leading role. From now on, Party committees at all levels should frequently study and discuss the Party's major policies and principles regarding socialist construction, matters involving the ideology and education of cadres, Party members and the masses, the ideological tendencies of cadres and their observance of discipline, the improvement of the Party organization and the recruitment of new members, and so on. Of course, while the division of labour between Party and government is emphasized, major policy decisions concerning government and economic work must still be made by the Party, and all Party members working in government organizations, enterprises and institutions must resolutely submit themselves to Party leadership and carry out the Party's policies.

To ensure that the ranks of the cadres become more revolutionary, younger in average age, better educated and more professionally competent is a long-established principle of the Central Committee of the Party. During the organizational reform, we will relieve our many veteran cadres who are advanced in age of their heavy responsibilities in "front line" posts and at the same time enable them to continue their service to the Party, the state and society by utilizing their rich experience in leadership work. We will promote large numbers of energetic young and middle-aged cadres who possess both political integrity and ability to various leading posts in good time, so that they can be tempered over a longer period practically and effectively by working with older cadres and taking over responsibilities from them and so that the leading bodies at all levels can continuously absorb new life-blood and talent to maintain their vigour. As for persons who rose to prominence by "rebellion," who are seriously factionalist in their ideas, who have indulged in beating, smashing and looting, who oppose the line followed by the Party's Central Committee since its Third Plenary Session, or who have seriously violated the law and discipline, we must remove with a firm hand those among them who are still in leading posts. . . .

We must work strenuously to strengthen the education and training of cadres in order to prepare large numbers of specialized personnel needed for socialist modernization. In the future, in our use and promotion of cadres, we must attach importance to educational background and academic records as well as to experience and achievements in work. Party schools at all levels, cadre schools run by government organizations and enterprises, and especially designated institutions of higher learning and specialized secondary schools should all, as required by socialist modernization and in their different capacities, revise their teaching plans and shoulder the regular training of cadres. All functionaries on the job should be trained in rotation. After such training, appropriate adjustments can be made in their jobs through assessment of their actual performance. The training of all cadres in rotation is an important strategic measure for enhancing their quality. . . .

Our Party is a party of the working class, and it must make a point of relying on the masses of workers. The composition of the working class in China has undergone a big change in recent years, with large numbers of new workers replacing old ones. Many old workers who are Party members have retired, many young people have joined the ranks of the working class, and group after group of workers who are Party members have been transferred to managerial jobs. As a result, there are fewer Party members on the production front, and the harder the labour, the smaller the number of Party members. This grave situation has weakened the direct link between the Party and the industrial workers. From now on, we must greatly strengthen Party work on the production front, encourage Party members fitted for working there to do so, and at the same time admit into the Party outstanding workers who are qualified for membership. The Party's work in the trade unions must be greatly strengthened so that they become a strong transmission belt between the Party and the masses of workers. . . .

Our party is the vanguard of the Chinese working class; it has been nurtured over the years by Marxism-Lenimism and Mao Zedong Thought and has matured through repeated tempering by successes and failures. . . .

However, the pernicious influences of the 10 years of domestic turmoil have not yet been eradicated, and there has been some increase in the corrosive inroads of exploiting-class ideologies under new conditions. It is true that impurities in ideology, style and organization still exist within the Party and that no fundamental turn for the better has as yet been made in our Party style. In the leadership work of some Party organizations signs of flabbiness and lack of unity abound. Some primary Party organizations lack the necessary fighting capacity, and some are even in a state of paralysis. A small number of Party members and cadres have become extremely irresponsible or seriously bureaucratic; or live a privileged life and abuse the powers entrusted to them to seek personal gain; or commit acts of anarchism and ultra-individualism in violation of Party discipline; or obdurately indulge in factional activities to the detriment of the Party's interests. A few Party members and cadres have even sunk to corruption, embezzlement and other malpractices, committing serious economic crimes. In addition, a small remnant of the followers of the Lin Biao and Jiang Qing counterrevolutionary cliques still usurp some leading positions and are waiting for a chance to stir up trouble. All these phenomena have greatly impaired our Party's prestige. While we must not allow any exaggeration of this dark aspect of our Party, on no account should be afraid to expose it. For ours is a staunch Party; we have ample healthy forces on our side to wage an uncompromising struggle against the dark aspect and are confident of our victory in the struggle.

The style of a political party in power determines its very survival. To achieve a fundamental turn for the better in the style of our Party, the Central Committee has decided on an overall rectification of Party style and consolidation of Party organizations, which will proceed by stages and by groups over a period of three years beginning from the latter half of 1983. This task will undoubtedly be of primary importance to the Party, and it requires very careful attention and preparation and should be carried out step by step in a planned way. The key link in accomplishing this work must be throughgoing ideological education throughout the Party. In conjunction with the study and implementation of the report and the new Party Constitution to be adopted by this Party congress, the whole Party should study the Resolution on Certain Questions in the History of Our Party Since the Founding of the People's Republic of China and the Guiding Principles for Inner-Party Political Life, and carry on an education in the basic theories of Marxism-Leninism and Mao Zedong Thought, in the ideal of communism and the Party's line, principles and policies and in essential knowledge concerning the Party and the requirements for Party membership. We must lay stress on getting every member to understand clearly the character, position and role of the Party and to realize that all Party members have only the duty to serve the people diligently and conscientiously, and no right whatsoever to take advantage of their power and positions to "fatten" on the state and on the masses. In matters of organization and leadership, the consolidation will start with the leading organs and cadres and then proceed, from top to bottom, with the leading bodies at different levels which have already been consolidated leading the consolidation of the subordinate and primary organizations. Bad elements must on no account be permitted to take this as an opportunity to frame and attack good people. We must act in, and develop further, the spirit of the Yanan Rectification Movement of 1942, follow its principle of "learning from past mistakes to avoid future ones and curing the sickness to save the patient" and its twofold objective of "clarity in ideology and unity among comrades" in unfolding earnest criticism and self-criticism, and take appropriate measures to solicit opinions from the masses outside the Party. In the final stage, there will be a re-registration of all Party members and, in strict accordance with the provisions of the new Party Constitution, those who still fail to meet the requirements for membership after education shall be expelled from the Party or asked to withdraw from it. At the same time, concrete measures should be worked out to strengthen and improve Party leadership so as to effect an improvement in the work of Party organizations at all levels.

Through the proposed consolidation of the Party, we must further normalize inner-Party political life, place an effective check on unhealthy tendencies and greatly strengthen the ties between the Party and the masses. In this way, we will certainly achieve a fundamental turn for the better in our Party style.

Unit V

_____ Political Leadership _____

Pragmatism is a hallmark of contemporary political leaders in both China and Japan. Prime Minister Yasuhiro Nakasone and the Liberal Democratic Party (LDP) rule Japan through a process of negotiation and consensual decision making. Demands from constituents, local political leaders, businessmen, and bureaucratic interests are all filtered through the brokerage process. Many analysts believe the Chinese system to be similar in this respect, even though its political system is not democratic. The triumvirate of Deng Xiaoping, Premier Zhao Ziyang, and Party Secretary Hu Yaobang must satisfy the demands of Party cadres, industrial ministries, urban workers, and technical elites. While it is not clear how these demands come to be articulated, it is apparent that policy and decision making are frequently a matter of compromise and consensus among competing interests.

Since the end of the American Occupation, the Liberal Democratic Party has dominated the political process in Japan. Its leaders have usually been the leaders of the nation as well. The stability of this rule has been one factor in the emergence of clearly identifiable career patterns for government officials. A bureaucratic background is a valuable asset in a system in which the professional bureaucrat plays a central role in the policymaking process. Japanese leaders, by and large, tend to be recruited from the bureaucracy, although they are increasingly professional politicians or businessmen. Indeed, experience in bureaucratic procedures has always been an important leadership skill in a society whose values emphasize bargaining, compromise, and consensus. Such skills become increasingly important in a modern industrialized state where so much depends on being able to effectively bargain over budgets, public works, and state subsidies.

The recruitment of bureaucrats to political leadership positions is one factor in Japan's success in identifying national objectives and then in pursuing these objectives with maximum efficiency. The practice of "administrative guidance," discussed by J. A. A. Stockwin in Unit I, depends on the cooperation between bureaucrats and political leaders. However, the consensual decision making that has been a distinctive feature of Japanese postwar politics may be changing. More and more, Japan's leaders are professional politicians who have little or no bureaucratic experience. In addition, groups such as women and the Korean minority in Japan are making increasing demands on a political process that has traditionally ignored them. Electoral support for LDP representatives has consistently declined in recent elections and may foreshadow not only the end of LDP predominance but the end of national consensus as well.

Unlike Japan, China since 1949 has not always been governed by consensus. Chairman Mao Zedong was the preeminent voice in Chinese politics from 1949 to 1976. His rule was interrupted in 1959 when his economic policies led to catastrophic imbalances in the Chinese economy. When the failure of the "Great Leap Forward" of 1958 forced Mao to retire from active involvement in governmental affairs, his leadership position was assumed by Liu Shaoqi, who, together with Chou En-lai (Zhou Enlai) and Deng Xiaoping, led China during the early 1960s. During this period, economic recovery and expansion were considered fundamental objectives of the Communist state and Party. Mao objected to this emphasis on economic goals over political ones and feared the return of capitalism to China. He argued that "a handful of capitalist roaders" had infiltrated the Party and state structures. In 1965, he launched a Socialist Education Movement for the purpose of intensifying political education. When he felt that his efforts were being undermined by other members of the leadership, he called upon his supporters and the youthful Red Guards to "bombard the headquarters" of revisionist leaders.

For three years, from 1966 to 1969, the Great Proletarian Cultural Revolution raged through most of urban China. The Red Guards were divided along class lines between students of a "red," or good, class background, such as workers, peasants, party members, and military families, and students with a "black," or bad, class background, such as intellectuals, former landlords, or suspected members of rightist families. These factional conflicts, in addition to being employed as a weapon in the leadership struggle, also had dire consequences for the Chinese economy. Production in urban factories declined precipitously as many workers stayed home to avoid the political struggles of the workplace. Schools closed and some did not reopen for ten years.

In 1969, the People's Liberation Army was called in to quell a situation that threatened to erupt in civil war. But even after order was restored, there was considerable conflict at the elite level. For seven years, Maoist supporters in the Party and state, along with high-ranking officials of the PLA, dominated the political arena while supporters of Liu Shaoqi and other politically moderate factions struggled for control of the state. With the deaths of Zhou Enlai and Mao Zedong in 1976, the leadership struggle gained new intensity. The Maoist "Gang of Four," consisting of Mao's wife Jiang Ching, Yao Wenyuan, Wang Hongwen, and Zhang Chungiao, attempted to succeed Mao and take control of the nation. But with Mao gone, their power base was weakened. The army turned against them and they were arrested shortly after Mao's death. Then Hua Kuo-feng assumed control of the government.

Hua's economic policies proved too ambitious, and since 1978 the more cautious stance of Deng has predominated in Chinese policy making. Deng's style of leadership offers a stark contrast to that of Mao. Where Mao fostered tensions in order to identify contradictions in society which could then be resolved, Deng emphasizes economic rationality and has made economic performance the main criterion for judging policy. Deng has used Mao's slogan "Seek truth from facts" as a foundation for promoting pragmatism over ideology. In so doing, he has intensified competition among economic interests, regions, and ministries. Increasingly in China, as has been the case in Japan, the satisfaction of these competing interests is a basic responsibility of the political leadership. Deng and his supporters must find ways to bridge the cleavages in Chinese society even as they intensify. Such a responsibility demands exceptional brokering skills. Indeed, as in Japan, seniority, political connections, and background are all important factors in the selection of leaders.

In both China and Japan, postwar leadership has been dominated by one party. In China, despite the totalitarian power of the Communist Party, conflict and leadership struggles have plagued the policy process since the early 1960s. The LDP, while also subject to factional struggles and constrained by the additional demands of electoral constituencies, has had much greater success in achieving essential unity in identifying goals and formulating policies to achieve them. In both cases, bargaining skills are important.

The readings in this unit focus on various aspects of leadership in present-day China and Japan. Michel Oksenberg, in "The Political Leader," argues that Mao's leadership skills concentrated on fostering tensions among subordinates and within policy arenas and then resolving the contradictions that arose as a result of those tensions. In "From Revolution to Reform," Michel Oksenberg and Richard C. Bush analyze recent changes in China's political climate and shed light on some of the major problems and challenges facing present-day Chinese leadership.

Kent E. Calder provides a detailed analysis of the role of brokerage in the Japanese political process in "Dynamics of Conservative Leadership in Postwar Japan." Then, in "Political Leadership in Contemporary Japan," Robert E. Ward examines the three major groups from which Japan draws the majority of its leaders—businessmen, politicians, and bureaucrats—noting that the criteria for political leadership in Japan are such that women and minority groups are effectively barred from top-level positions within the Japanese government.

Both China and Japan seem to be "professionalizing" their leaders. As Gerald L. Curtis points out in "The 'New Japanese' Leaders," there is a growing trend in Japan toward selecting leaders from the ranks of politicians, rather than from the bureaucracy, as has been the norm in the past. In China, leaders and cadres are being chosen for their technocratic skills, and expertise more than political acuity is the new criterion for recruitment and promotion with the Chinese Communist Party.

20

The Political Leader

Michel Oksenberg

In this selection, Oksenberg discusses Mao's role in the policymaking process and identifies five qualities of Mao's style and leadership. Mao believed in the dialectical development of policy, emphasizing first one issue then another. He fostered tensions among his subordinates in order to prevent bureaucratization. He maintained control over such key policy areas as agriculture, culture, and foreign policy. He concentrated most of his energies on controlling the policy process rather than on achieving specific policy goals. And he cultivated popular support for his policy orientation as well as for himself. The exact nature of Mao's role in the policymaking process is still being debated. As Oksenberg notes, there is an ongoing dispute between scholars who think Mao played a dominant role and those who believe him to have been a balancing factor among competing groups. Oksenberg suggests that Mao's role probably included both of these descriptions and differed according to the policy in question.

How did Mao Tse-tung organize and employ power? How did he seek to dominate and draw upon his colleagues? How did he rule his nation? What was the pattern of interaction between Mao and those he sought to influence? These are the fascinating questions to be addressed in this essay. . . .

MAO'S PATTERN OF RULE

Mao's concepts of power and leadership gave basic shape to his pattern of rule. Five qualities particularly marked his reign: (1) the pursuit of a "zig-zag" strategy of development; (2) the fostering of tensions among his subordinates; (3) the retention of certain key decisions in his hands; (4) the careful cultivation of a popular image; and (5) the effort to control not so much political outcomes as the process of policy-making by determining communication channels, personnel appointments and military deployment. . . .

A Dialectical Process of Development

One of the most striking aspects of Chinese politics during Mao's era was the alternation between a period of social ferment, mass mobilization, unleashed advance and conflict on the one hand, and a period of consolidation, institutionalization, planned advance and reconciliation on the other. . . .

It seems fair to conclude that, although other factors helped generate the oscillations, to the extent his power allowed, Mao deliberately piloted China along this fluctuating course. He saw it as the only way to maintain his quest for the irreconcilables, letting the emphasis shift from economic growth to cultural change to economic growth, from freedom to discipline to freedom, from democracy to centralization to democracy, and from struggle to unity to struggle. The development was supposedly dialectical, with each stage representing a closer approximation to the ultimate synthesis.

Mao explicitly acknowledged his approach on many occasions. One European diplomat, who saw Mao towards the end of the Cultural Revolution, for example, claims that in their conversation, the chairman had likened his approach to rule to making broth. Every so often, Mao apparently said, one had to throw more logs on the fire to heat up the cauldron to make the impurities bubble to the surface. . . .

In sum, Mao viewed the process of social change as the object of grand strategy, with the fomenting of high tides of development central to his design. Those eras of ferment, with their induced and controlled spontaneity, revealed to the leaders the underlying grievances of the people. The energies unleashed through the outpouring of hostility could then be channelled in directions which the leaders deemed advisable. Mao also made use of those eras to test the mettle of his associates and to recruit new cadres into the ranks, for he felt that such times revealed the capacity of the leaders to handle raw social forces no longer mediated by institutions. The clearest instance of Mao's principle in action came during the Cultural Revolution. On the eve of that upheaval, Mao had stated:

> Successors to the revolutionary cause of the proletariat come forward in mass struggles and are tempered in the great storms of revolution. It is essential to test and judge cadres and choose and train successors in the long course of mass struggles.

It should be stressed, however, that when Mao called for an era of struggle, he was not sure of the result. Further, he recognized that risks were entailed:

excessive violence, disruption of production and so on. But he judged the risks to be necessary.

Fostering Political Tensions among Subordinates

To recapitulate with an obvious but sometimes neglected point, Mao could not and did not rule China alone. He, perforce, relied on his Politburo associates and the vast bureaucracies under their command to transfer his guidelines into action. Mao, therefore, faced the challenge of structuring the political process so that it would yield him the opportunity to pursue his dialectical strategy of development. During a high tide, Mao reckoned the greatest danger would be extreme "leftist" or radical excesses. During consolidation, he feared the excesses of "rightism," "liberalism," or "revisionism." To guard against these excesses and to maintain policy alternatives, Mao simultaneously advocated contradictory policy lines (one dominant, the other in eclipse) and relied on two more competing subordinates. When he promoted an upsurge, he still purposefully retained some advisers who were opposed to the unleashing of social forces at that moment and encouraged certain organizations and institutions to pursue a more moderate policy line. . . .

Retaining Key Decisions

During the peak of his rule, Mao also jealously guarded certain key policy decisions. He clearly sought the ultimate choice over whether the nature of the current situation demanded an emphasis on struggle or on unity, on economic development or on cultural change. He also sought to identify the principal contradiction or tension which was to be exploited at any particular moment. He clearly believed he had special insight into such questions as: Was the moment propitious to launch the drive for total power against the KMT? Had the time come to collectivize agriculture? Was violence necessary to rid China of its remnant capitalist class? Should the tension between state and society be tapped? He did not hesitate to stipulate policy on these questions even in the face of considerable opposition. Because of his demonstrated acumen and political resolve, he usually got his way on these issues as well.

He also sought to keep three issues in his grasp: foreign policy, rural social policy and cultural policy. These three issues concerned areas about which Mao felt passionately but which also vitally involved his power. Mao had attained power in the 1940s first within the CCP and then within China as a whole because he had articulated the aspirations of the bulk of the populace. He came to represent the force of Chinese nationalism during an era of extreme national duress, in a way somewhat analogous to Charles de

Gaulle or Winston Churchill in their countries at the same time. He came to equate his personal fate with the national destiny. And as the ultimate arbiter of Chinese nationalism, he could destroy any opponent by saying that he or she represented an alien force. This is precisely what he did against P'eng Teh-huai in 1959. Certainly, this helps explain why Mao personally was so immersed in managing the Sino-Soviet relationship and why he would tolerate no opposition on the matter. Not only did he sincerely believe in his policy, but he also probably realized that if he allowed someone successfully to challenge his policy, he would have lost his stature as the person who defined China's national interest.

Similarly, Mao deemed rural social policy to be *his* issue. Not only did he believe he had special competence in this area, but he believed he spoke for the rural poor in the councils of the Politburo. The self-identified champion of the vast majority of the peasantry, Mao claimed a popular support which could overwhelm adversaries with the Party. Given the rural origins of the Chinese revolution and the commitment of the communist movement to improving the lives of the rural populace, Mao's assertion was powerful. Not surprisingly, he did not tolerate anyone else trying to encroach on his monopoly preserve. One particularly clear instance of this came in the spring of 1959, when Mao defended his recommendation to curb the "leftist" excesses of the Commune movement of late 1958. The chairman said, "I speak for 10 million cadres at the level of production team head and for 500 million peasants. If you do not join me in firmly and thoroughly carrying out right opportunism [as contrasted to leftist adventurism against which he was arguing] I will carry it out thoroughly alone, even to the point of giving up my Party membership." . . .

Mao also sought to be the ultimate arbiter of cultural questions. In the Chinese context, "cultural matters" subsume a wider range of issues than the phrase implies in English. It includes not only policies towards the media, literature and the arts, but also embraces educational affairs, programmes in science and technology, policies towards the intellectuals, and even extends to public health and sports. Mao's focus on these issues flowed naturally from his assessment of their importance in determining China's future. But unlike the foreign policy and rural realms, Mao never established his absolute authority in this realm. For one thing, the issues could not be easily reduced to proportions manageable by one man. In addition, Mao's colleagues did not appear to believe he had special wisdom in this area. In fact, many leaders of the CCP had their own, rather definite views on the changes that needed to be made in China's culture. The notion that China demanded a cultural revolution antedated the founding of the CCP and Mao's rise within it. Whereas the CCP's attention to national resistance against Japan and to mobilizing the peasantry was partly the result of Mao's efforts, the desire for cultural change antedated Mao's rise in the Party and was one of the factors that had led to the CCP's formation. In spite of Mao's recognition of the issue's importance, therefore, he never succeeded in making it his own.

In another sense, however, he did ensure that the interpretation of the ideology remained his prerogative. That is, the basis of the Party's claim to legitimacy, the reasons it asserted for claiming the obedience and loyalty of the populace, was based on Mao's thought: his creative adaptation of Marxism—Leninism to the Chinese context. As a result of his successfully claiming to be the sole Chinese source of the ideas upon which the political system was based (the reality was much more complicated), Mao could destroy any rival by saying the opponent had departed from his thought. As Lin Piao's son noted, "The Chairman commands such high prestige that he need only utter one sentence to remove anybody he chooses." Obviously best exercised as a threat and even then sparingly, none the less Mao employed it with devastating effectiveness, especially against potential successors with whom he had grown disenchanted; Mao proclaimed the former heir apparent deficient in ideological understanding of his beliefs. It was the charge which turned Liu Shao-ch'i into a symbol of evil, a pattern repeated with Lin Piao.

Cultivating Authority

There can be little doubt that Mao carefully manipulated his image in order to elicit maximum support from his policy-making associates, the bureaucracy and the population at large. But, as noted earlier, to establish his authority, he had to project a somewhat different image to each constituency. His colleagues saw the total Mao and were exposed to the full range of his power: his willingness to coerce, his ideas, his capacity to reward, and his ability to manipulate psychologically. The bureaucrats were somewhat removed from his direct lash, and primarily were the objects of his ideas and his material rewards and denials. But to the populace as a whole, Mao remained a remote figure whose presence was felt primarily in its symbolic-ideological dimension. He sought to be held in awe, and drew upon the imperial tradition to foster a sense of reverence. In sociological jargon, those far from the chairman felt only his normative power; remunerative power was added for his bureaucrats; and a coercive dimension was added for his colleagues. To be sure, as with any classification scheme, the types of power are imperfectly drawn, the boundaries between the types of constituencies are not easily delineated, and exceptions to the generalization exist. But still, the images of Mao held by colleagues were vastly different from those seen by the remote populace. Colleagues knew him infinitely better because they were exposed to facets of Mao that the public did not see.

When the Red Guards shouted in emotional frenzy as Mao appeared before them during mass rallies in 1966, or when peasants pasted the chairman's picture on the family altar, they were responding to him as the spiritual symbol of their nation. According to one prisoner who spent considerable time in labour camps, they did not associate Mao with their harsh treatment. Even prisoners revered the chairman and blamed their condition either on their own shortcomings or on Mao's evil, deceitful subordinates. It must be added, however, that in Mao's last years he was less successful in projecting solely a benevolent image. He became inextricably linked with the violence of the Cultural Revolution in the minds of many urban dwellers and, in the "Criticism of Lin, Criticism of Confucius" campaign of 1973–74, he even encouraged mass media comparisons of him with the cruel founder of Ch'in. How much of the awe and reverence of the 1950s and early 1960s had been destroyed by the mid-1970s, particularly in urban areas, remains open to question. . . .

Mao recognized the risks of allowing the "cult of the personality." . . . As he told Edgar Snow in 1965, "Probably Khrushchev fell because he had had no cult of personality at all." In his subsequent 1970 interview with Snow, the chairman recalled that at the time of their 1965 colloquy, a great deal of power had escaped his control. That was why, he explained to the American journalist, a more extensive personality cult was needed, so as to stimulate the masses to dismantle the anti-Mao Party bureaucracy. It was hard, Mao explained, for people to overcome the habits of 3,000 years of emperor-worshipping tradition. But Mao asserted that the cult had become excessive during the Cultural Revolution and ought to be cooled down. Still, he asked, could any leader, even in the U.S., get along without some people to worship him? Mao concluded that there was always the desire to be worshipped and the desire to worship. . . .

THE EXTENT OF MAO'S RULE

China specialists have debated widely among themselves precisely how Mao's rule should be characterized. Some have suggested that the political system from 1949 to Mao's death was essentially "pluralistic," with various autonomous, bureaucratic, factional and social groupings competing for influence. Policies were the result of negotiation and compromise; budget allocations-involved bargaining among contesting sectors. In this schema, in addition to being the unifying symbol of the regime, Mao's primary role was to reconcile and balance interests. His capacity to strike compromises that coincided with his value preferences fluctuated with his own changing power position. Occasionally, his power and circumstances permitted him to sponsor major new programmes. . . .

Clearly, a portrayal of Chinese politics that places Mao in a weak position or makes bargaining central to a "pluralistic" policy process has a lot to explain away. The available evidence convincingly demonstrates that the collectivization of agriculture in July 1955, the "Hundred Flowers" episode of May 1957, the unleashing of the Red Guards in August 1966, and the invitation to President Nixon in 1970, to name some of the major initiatives, would not have occurred without Mao's power and resolve. More broadly, the commitment to reducing urban-rural inequities, the ceaseless efforts to create a responsive bureaucracy, and the boldly experimental policies in the educational and public health realms can be clearly traced to Mao's persistence and will. And we have already noted the considerable success which Mao encountered in creating a dialectical approach to development and in fostering analytical categories and modes of political discourse that permeated the entire system during his lifetime. A grave danger exists that analysts may give undue weight to his last few years in office, when he was but a shadow of his former self, and neglect the decisive impact he had on his nation's earlier political course.

Other analysts have sketched a policy process which Mao clearly dominated. All power flowed from him; all subordinates sought to obey his fickle and vague desires, competing among themselves to prove their loyalty to him. To these observers, Mao was a dictator. But this view also has its troubles, and not just with Mao's apparent inability to control rampant factional strife in his last years and with his being the alleged target of an assassination attempt by Lin Piao. For, as this essay has shown, Mao had to manoeuvre constantly to enforce his will. His resources were limited. He did have domestic adversaries who had their own power to thwart Mao's designs.

So where does the truth rest? Was Mao one politician in a pack, a monarch among barons, a figure-head, a dictator, or a captive of others? While each caricature contains an element of truth, the best answer seems to be that no static assessment of Mao's power can be accurate, for his roles changed significantly over time, as did the entire system. At a minimum and to oversimplify, one can say the system and Mao's position in it passed through five stages. To trace this evolution, it pays to conceive of the Chinese political order during Mao's era as consisting of several types of policy-making arenas: (1) Mao's arena, which was not highly institutionalized, but consisted of the mechanisms available to him to communicate and obtains his will—meetings he convened, reports he read and approved, directives he gave through the Military Affairs Commission, directives he gave while on trips, comments he issued to the press, and so on; (2) policy-specifying bodies led by Mao's associates, including the State Council under Chou En-lai, the Military Affairs Commission under Lin Piao, and the Cultural Revolution Group under Ch'en Po-ta; (3) the vast Party, government and army bureaucratic hierarchies, with their functional subdivisions and their various administrative levels; (4) the *ad hoc* campaign organizations, composed of officials from the bureaucracies who were seconded to the temporary campaign staffs to mobilize the populace for specific objectives (the campaign staffs could be variously commanded directly by Mao, by one of the policy-specifying bodies, or by a bureaucratic agency itself); and (5) local communities—factories, schools, urban neighbourhoods, commercial enterprises, Communes, hospitals and so on. The evolution of the system can be described in terms of the waxing and waning authority of each arena, of the changing agenda of decisions confronting the leaders in each arena, and the changing relationships between arenas.

21

From Revolution Toward Reform

Michel Oksenberg
and Richard C. Bush

The authors of these excerpts examine recent changes in China's political climate in terms of three interrelated factors: the change in leadership upon the death of Mao; reaction to previous political campaigns; and a reassertion of cultural traditions. They argue that cleavages between the military and civilian authorities, between generations, and between rural and urban dwellers could worsen under these reforms. Specific problems such as lagging agricultural production, inefficient industry, and population control must be overcome as well.

[T]he changes in China's political system over the past decade have been extensive. Understanding the reasons for the[se] changes is important, for they offer clues to the durability of this monumental development. At work are three interrelated factors: the change in the top leaders, the ubiquitous course of revolution; and the reassertion of Chinese cultural traditions. In none of these areas has change gone far enough to be irreversible.

The human factor—the passing of Mao and the rise of Deng and Chen—is the most obvious. Many of the changes only took place after Mao's death—the arrest of his principal allies in revolution, and the subsequent eclipse of his lingering beneficiaries. ... The Chinese system remains one which reflects the aspirations and techniques of rule of the top officials. To that extent, the system will continue to evolve and take on the coloration of Deng and Chen's successors. Should they not share Deng's and Chen's priorities, a reversal is possible.

Second, China is going through a stage in the course of any major revolution, be it France, Russia, Cuba, or Vietnam. It appears that such societies reach their limit for turmoil and become exhausted by it. Problems of legitimacy and compliance come to the fore as leaders are forced to grapple with a cynical, disenchanted population which has been coerced for too long. Authoritarian rule through bureaucracy is the usual result. ...

[In such nations,] the post-revolutionary era ... will be a specific reaction to the particular target of the mobilization effort. To an extraordinary extent, the pressing problems now [facing China] are precisely the ones

Mao neglected as he directed the nation's energies elsewhere. The contours of the 1982 system, to a considerable extent, were shaped by the successive high tides of the Maoist system. The political institutions and process Deng and his associates have called into being have been designed to cope with the particular set of problems Mao bequeathed to his successors:

- lagging agricultural production;
- an inefficient industrial system;
- high unemployment among youth;
- a low standard of living;
- widespread apathy and cynicism;
- an inadequate scientific and technological manpower base;
- specific bottlenecks in transportation, communication, and energy;
- an unacceptably high rate of population increase. . . .

In addition, the current system and set of policies generate their own set of problems, and it is not clear that the Deng-Chen system is capable of handling them. In particular, the system relies heavily on rule through bureaucracy, but it has yet to develop effective mechanisms for ensuring that the bureaucracy will be responsive either to popular will or indeed to orders from above. Over a protracted period, the Deng-Chen system could prove to be one in which social tensions accumulate but for which there are no adequate safety valves. To be sure, the new opportunity for individuals to withdraw from politics and the personnel readjustment in the bureaucracies lessen the causes of tension. Furthermore, unlike the Maoist system, the Deng-Chen system does not envision using social tensions as an engine of history.

Nevertheless, several already apparent cleavages could prove politically troublesome if allowed to persist: 1) civil-military relations, 2) generational layering, where the experiences and education of successive age cohorts have differed sharply, 3) differences between city and countryside, between which living standards and opportunities for social mobility are highly unequal, 4) tensions between coastal and interior provinces, with the benefits of China's opening to the West flowing much more rapidly to the coastal provinces, and 5) income differentials within and among localities, with perhaps rising resentment as differentials grow under the post-1978 remuneration systems. The long-term consequences of increased contact with the outside world are also difficult to foresee.

Another potential source of instability stems from the promise the leadership has made to raise the standard of living. From 1978 and 1982, real income rose dramatically for many, particularly people in the countryside, and moderately for others, especially city dwellers. Not only have wages gone up but construction of housing has increased significantly, as has the production output of many consumer durables (watches, bicycles, sewing machines, television sets, etc.). The slightly more affluent urban Chinese populace is beginning to press upon scarce leisure-time facilities, such as theatres, parks, and sports grounds.

Therefore, questions remain. Are expectations rising more rapidly than the expansion of consumer goods industries? Is it in fact wise to stimulate support for the regime through such heavy reliance on material incentives? What can happen if the economic strategy does not succeed, the growth rate falters, and standards of living stagnate? If the regime failed to make good on its promises, its fundamental stability would not necessarily be at stake. But many of the changes since 1972 would be threatened, particularly the relative importance of various bureaucracies and the mechanisms for integrating the society.

A third way of interpreting the late-Mao and post-Mao eras is from the vantage of China's cultural heritage. In many respects, what transpired from 1972 to 1982 was a reassertion of certain dominant strands in the Chinese tradition. In particular, as Columbia University Sinologist Theodore deBary has argued, the two dominant models of rule in China have been harsh dictatorship or benevolent but still authoritarian bureaucracy, with the latter the preferred alternative through the years.

Ironically, the Cultural Revolution helped revive the traditional culture it was designed to destroy. One important way the populace endured the harsh dictatorship was to confide in those whom they trusted, i.e., those with whom they shared ties. Thus, the nuclear family in many ways became more important; school, native place, or early career connections became tickets to survival. The disillusionment with the formal Maoist ideology led to increased interest in traditional religion, especially Buddhism and Taoism. Thus what makes China in 1982 at least superficially resemble the imperial system is the twin reassertion of formal bureaucracy and the informal means for coping with the state (especially use of *guanxi* and the prevalence of factions).

The present leadership swiftly jettisoned those aspects of the Maoist system which ran especially counter to the dominant strands in the Chinese tradition. These included its totalitarian quality, its emphasis on class struggle, and the campaign technique for policy implementation. To be sure, such concepts as "privacy" and "individualism," so central to Western political thought, have not been well developed in the Chinese tradition, but notions of "withdrawal," "quietude," and particularly "self-cultivation" were quite well developed. In traditional China, the ruler who prevented cultivation of private talent—poetry, painting, carving of seals—was considered threatening to culture and the attainment of virtue. Mao's fostering of struggle also ran counter to a deeply ingrained preference for harmony. Campaigns and the brawling that accompanied them brought on disorder, instead of the preferred regularity and order.

To the extent the Deng-Chen system represents a reassertion of "Chineseness," several exceptions must also be briefly noted:

- collective leadership: When unified, China has always had a single, discernible ruler. It remains to be seen if a system of shared power will work.

- the downplaying of ideology: In the absence of extensive, formal religion, the state always played a major role in the inculcation of morality; this had a major role in helping to unify the country. The current system would seem to leave a vacuum in the propagation of a unifying, coherent set of beliefs.
- the empirical basis of policy choice: The current leadership is trying to build scientific methods of research and analysis into the decision making of the bureaucracy. Many students of China would argue that these methods are antithetical to dominant Confucian precepts (the view that most facts are infused with values and hence that truly "neutral" social and policy sciences can not be developed; the preference to learn through the emulation of models rather than through the understanding of scientific principles). Whether the current effort to develop an empirically based policy process will really succeed is open to question.
- the idea of linear progress: The traditional Chinese interpretation of history as cyclical has more in common with Mao's dialectic view of history than with the current view that progress can be persistent and gradual.

In short, Deng and his associates have rekindled the century-old debate over how best to root the quest for modernity in China's intellectual heritage. China's imperial rulers had a rich diversity of traditions—Confucianism, legalism, Buddhism, for example—on which to draw, and a wide array of Western ideas—liberalism, Marxism, etc.—became available from the late nineteenth century on. Now, as then, the question is which Chinese strands should be combined with which Western ideas to create an ideological amalgam suited to Chinese needs.

22

Dynamics of Conservative Leadership in Postwar Japan

Kent E. Calder

In these excerpts from *Political Leadership in Contemporary Japan,* Calder discusses the importance of brokerage in the policy process. Brokerage involves "pork barrel" politics over the distribution of government subsidies and public works projects. Calder notes that such expenses compose a relatively high percentage of the Japanese national budget. For this reason, ideology and policy orientation tend not to be significant in selecting leaders. Instead, bureaucratic experience in what Calder calls "subgovernments," actually groups of politicians, bureaucrats, and lobbyists concerned with specific policy areas, is a more important basis for successful brokering. However, brokers do differ in their approach to the policy process. Calder argues that a basic dichotomy exists between former bureaucrats who are established in the political structure and who advocate slow growth, and political entrepreneurs who advance by currying favor and who desire economic expansion. This competition between *kanryō* and *shomin* is one that Calder believes will continue in the future.

Leaders (both formal and informal) can be seen as having at least three major functional roles in relation to policy formation—legitimizing particular patterns of policy, originating policy positions, and brokering preexisting demands for some form of policy output. The frequency with which leaders perform one or another of these functions varies significantly from nation to nation, with legitimation and brokerage particularly pronounced in Japan.

A cultural predisposition to settle major issues of policy in private through intermediaries, and in public only to ratify, rather than to decide, policy questions may account for the frequency with which formal leaders appear as legitimators rather than as originators of policy in Japan. (Some formal leaders, such as the emperor and many elderly corporate presidents, act exclusively as legitimators, participating in decision making only ceremonially to ratify decisions which have already been made.) However, structural characteristics of the Japanese political economy appear most important in explaining why Japanese conservative leaders function so frequently as brokers and why ability at brokerage has been such an important precondition for success in modern Japanese politics.

In this paper, "brokerage" is understood to mean the act of mediating between private-sector groups or individuals desiring direct material benefits or regulatory actions conferring such benefits, on the one hand, and governmental bodies perceived capable of providing such services, on the other. The mediation of more abstract demands for "national security," "clean government," "crime control," and other public goods is not construed as brokerage, nor are nonmediatory policy initiatives by public figures themselves. The heart of brokerage as considered here is the mediating role of politicians in "pork-barrel politics." . . .

Every nation, of course, has its "smoke-filled rooms" where political intermediaries hammer out patterns of compensation for private-sector clients. What is distinctive about Japanese politics is that brokerage is a major part of total political activity, and central ability at brokerage determines who leads the nation. In sharp contrast to Europe, and to a lesser degree the United States, basic ideologically oriented debates on the proper nature of the domestic political system and of class relationships do not rend the Japanese political order, nor are foreign-policy controversies high on the political agenda. Public-works expenditures, allocation of government land, and the distribution of subsidies for farmers, small business, and so on are the questions which agitate Japanese politicians, especially those in conservative ranks. The salience of brokerage-related, "pork-barrel" politics is clear from the composition of the national budget. Subsides comprised a percentage of the whole much higher than the average for the OECD over the two decades 1955–1975, and public works expenditures were also unusually high.

The correlation between brokerage skills and tenure in national leadership positions also appears unusually strong in Japan, suggesting the importance of brokerage abilities in determining who leads the nation. Of the eight United States presidents since Franklin D. Roosevelt, only three (Lyndon Johnson, Richard Nixon, and Gerald Ford) had extensive brokerage experience in national politics before being elected chief executive. Of the remaining five nonprofessional politicians, one was a former general, another a former actor, and the third a former peanut farmer. France has routinely elected aristocratic presidents like Charles de Gaulle and Valery Giscard d'Estaing, who disdain the political process and who are relative newcomers to its intricacies. Even parliamentary democracies like Britain frequently place higher priority on policy orientation than on brokerage skills in selecting leadership, as the selection of figures such as Margaret Thatcher, Edward Heath, and Winston Churchill to head the Conservative Party suggest. In Japan, however, factors other than brokerage skill (ideological orientation, charisma, rhetorical skill, and so on) have been relatively unimportant to leadership success.

Brokerage ability in Japan derives preeminently from stable, institutionalized ties with the bureaucracy which allow a politician to consistently deliver resources formally controlled by government ministries (such as budget allocations and construction permits) into the hands of private-sector groups. Former bureaucrats, with a wealth of personal contacts developed from years of government service, tend to be best able to mediate for private-sector groups. Not surprisingly, such former officials (including Yoshida Shigeru, Kishi Nobusuke, Ikeda Hayato Satō Eisaku, Fukuda Takeo, and Ōhira Masayoshi) served as prime minister for over 80 percent of the period 1952–1980. Such nonbureaucrats as have served were mostly either compromise candidates like Suzuki Zenkō, who possessed their own intraparty mediating skills, or leaders like Tanaka Kakuei, who developed institutionalized ties with the bureaucracy like those the former officials already possessed. Practically the only common distinguishing trait of all postwar Japanese prime ministers is that they have been first and foremost skilled brokers of some variety.

The central factor forcing conservative Japanese politicians into brokerage roles has been the tradition of a strong central bureaucracy capable of profoundly affecting the livelihood of citizens. This reality, combined with the uneven responsiveness of the bureaucracy to demands from various sectors of the population, has caused some interest groups to rely on party politicians, often with bureaucratic origins, to satisfy their demands. . . .

The strategic problem of all Japanese political brokers [is] establishing a consistent capability to deliver resources formally controlled by the bureaucracy (budget allocations, construction-permits, approvals of bank merger applications, and so on) into the hands of private-sector interest groups. The solution to this problem has . . . been developing close, institutionalized relations between themselves and the bureaucracy. One key element in such relations has been their bureaucratic support networks strategically placed in ministries important for brokerage operations.

John Campbell and other analysts have pointed to the importance in Japanese policy making of vertically organized "sub-governments" composed of bureaucrats, politicians, and interest-group representatives with common policy goals. (One such group is the agricultural lobby, intent on assuring high income levels for farmers.) Equally important, at a different level of analysis, are the personal "support networks" of politicians like Fukuda and Tanaka. These are also composed, like "sub-governments," of bureaucrats, politicians, and interest-group representatives—but their purpose is to sustain the brokerage deals a particular politician makes and to be compensated in return, rather than to press for any specific policy measures. . . .

Behind-the-scenes brokers (*kuromaku*) and brokers with a public role share two key traits (1) an independent power base, usually financial (giving them initial resources to facilitate brokerage), and (2) institutionalized connections with key parts of the existing power structure (allowing them to influence that structure when necessary). The greater their financial backing and the stronger their bureaucratic connections, the more influential brokers have been in national decision making. Ex-bureaucrats have an advantage as brokers. Not surprisingly, the prime ministers who have exerted the greatest impact on post-Occupation policy formation (Yoshida, Kishi, Ikeda, Satō, and Fukuda) have been former bureaucrats. The only striking exception is Tanaka Kakuei.

Resource brokerage, like most of Japanese "compensation politics," has thus far been the province largely of Liberal Democratic Party politicians, mainly from rural constituencies, and behind-the-scenes conservative kingmakers. . . .

There are important variations among Japanese conservative political brokers in their paths to political power and their leadership styles once in positions of responsibility. Broadly, Japanese conservative leadership divides between bureaucrats (*kanryō*), epitomized by Fukuda Takeo, and political entrepreneurs without elite backgrounds (*shomin*), epitomized by Tanaka Kakuei. *Kanryō* tend to rise predictably from outstanding academic backgrounds at Tokyo University to top-level posts in strategic ministries like MOF, and hence into politics. They tend to be technically proficient, often issues-oriented, and relatively passive in leadership style. *Shomin,* by contrast, are of necessity pragmatic, aggressive promoters, reliant for success on their ability to curry favor with an establishment to whom they are essentially outsiders. *Shomin* are of necessity more concerned with the dynamics of political power than with the substance of public issues and are, as a result, often more reliant on the bureaucracy in the formulation of concrete policy proposals than the former bureaucrats themselves.

The distinction between *kanryō* and *shomin* is also often important in analyzing the impact of conservative leadership on the Japanese political economy. Broadly, *shomin* tend to be more consistently expansionist because of their need to create resources to reinforce their essentially vulnerable political positions. *Kanryō,* because of their established status, can generally afford to be more dispassionate in their judgment of macroeconomic questions and occasionally oppose growth-oriented policies which they feel are leading the nation toward economic or political instability. . . .

The dynamics of Japanese conservative leadership in the 1980s could well differ significantly from those of the previous generation, if only because of the new strategic problems relating to low growth which that leadership now confronts. But cultural predispositions toward indirect, nonconfrontationist decision making, together with structural peculiarities of the Japanese economy, will assure the continued prominence of political brokers. And as long as Japan has a clear conservative establishment with "insiders" and "outsiders" vying for political status, many essentials of the *kanryō* vs. *shomin* struggle for primacy will continue to reappear long after Fukuda Takeo and Tanaka Kakuei have passed from the political scene.

23

Political Leadership
in Contemporary Japan

Robert E. Ward

In this selection from *Japan's Political System,* Ward describes some of the salient characteristics of postwar Japanese leadership. He identifies businessmen, politicians, and bureaucrats as the three groups comprising the leadership today. These men attain their positions not by appeals to the electorate but through intra-party competition. They are selected for their seniority, fund-raising skills, political connections, and their reputation for honesty. The emphasis on these criteria makes for leaders who are conservative, cautious, and experienced. It also tends to restrict women and other groups from the top levels of power.

The characteristics and quality of political leadership in postwar Japan are particularly difficult to access. Both Japanese tradition and practice place far less emphasis on individual "leaders" and "leadership" than does American culture. This tendency is reinforced by the multifactional nature of political party organization and the prevalence of committee and consensual techniques of decision making. Under such circumstances, it becomes peculiarly difficult to assign meaningful responsibility for particular political policies or actions and thus to determine what any given "leader" may have contributed to a particular decision. Despite such problems, certain persons who occupy positions of leadership in the Japanese political system can be identified. The members of the Liberal Democratic and opposition contingents in the National Diet have already been mentioned. The Cabinet, a more selective and important leadership group, represents the top level of governmental leadership.

An examination of appointments to the postwar Cabinets demonstrates the impact of war, defeat, and the Allied Occupation on Japan's political leadership. The military figures and the representatives of court circles and the aristocracy so prominent before the war are no longer encountered. Among the prewar elites, only the party politicians, the bureaucrats, and the representatives of business have survived. The onus of defeat, the American-enforced purge of military and ultranationalist elements from public office, and the provisions of the new Constitution combined to drive the traditional leaders from office; in the resulting vacuum of leadership, new faces—or at least new looks—appeared in the higher ranks of the conservative parties and for the most part remain there today.

The standing of these leaders is not based on their appeal to the masses. Just as Japan's political parties are largely associations of professional politicians rather than mass membership organizations, so too are the ranks of its leaders filled by private and closeted means rather than by any sort of popularity contest. In conservative circles, it makes very little different whether a given person is an accomplished public speaker or possessed of a personality with wide popular appeal. The meaningful criteria are more apt to be length of political service, abilities as a fund raiser, skill as a tactician, administrative ability, possession of useful connections, and a personal reputation for loyalty and sincerity. Such a system tends to bring to the fore men of experience, caution, and a generally conservative approach to political problems rather than more brilliant or venturesome types. Almost all the conservative leaders have had long experience in government. Article 68 of the Constitution requires that a majority of the ministers of state, that is, the Cabinet, must be chosen from among the members of the Diet, and custom decrees that a large majority hold seats in the lower house during their Cabinet service. In practice about 80 percent are normally chosen from the House of Representatives and practically all of the rest from the House of Councilors, with only an occasional Cabinet post given to individuals who are not elected members of the National Diet.

Since the prime ministership is the highest and most powerful political office in postwar Japan, it may be helpful to look briefly at some of the more salient sociopolitical characteristics of the thirteen men who have held that office between 1945 and 1977. . . . All but the last three were born in the nineteenth century. Their average age on assuming the prime ministerial office was sixty-three. Individual cases ranged from Tanaka Kakuei who was only fifty-four when he took office in 1972 to Ishibashi Tanzan who was briefly prime minister in 1956–57 at the age of seventy-two. The average tenure of office has been about one year, but this really distorts the picture. Of the twelve whose terms had ended in 1977, four served for a year or less; the terms of Higashikuni Naruhiko, slightly less than two months, and Ishibashi, just over two months, were the shortest. Four of the others held office for more than three years apiece, with the record for longevity (for prewar as well as postwar times) going to Sato Eisaku who served for seven years and nine months, followed by Yoshida Shigeru, six years and nine months.

The background of the prime ministers is mixed. The first two postwar prime ministers—Higashikuni, an imperial prince, and Shidehara Kijuro, an aristocrat and prewar foreign minister—are exceptional and represent a transition to the new Constitution. Yoshida and Ashida Hitoshi were professional diplomats, though Ashida resigned and served for many years in the House of Representatives before becoming prime minister. Katayama Tetsu was a lawyer and Ishibashi a journalist, but both had also long been Diet members. Hatoyama Ichiro and Miki Takeo were really professional politicians; at the time they became prime ministers, Hatoyama had served twenty-five years in the lower house and Miki had served thirty-seven. Kishi Nobusuke (Ministry of International Trade and Industry), Ikeda Hayato and Fukuda Takeo (Ministry of Finance) and Sato (Ministry of Transportation) were all career bureaucrats who in the latter stages of their service were elected to the postwar Diet and had extensive legislative and Cabinet-level experience before becoming prime ministers. Only Tanaka came from a business background. With the exception of Tanaka, all were university graduates; eight of the thirteen were from Tokyo University's Law Department. All seem to have come from prosperous families. Two were brothers—Kishi and Sato (Sato was adopted, left his own family, and changed his name).

The following generalizations [can be made] about Cabinet members. Practically all postwar Japanese Cabinet members have been male. In the 1946–73 period, 275 men and 2 women attained Cabinet rank. On the average, they first attained this high office between the ages of fifty-one and fifty-five, but the modal figures are probably more representative. When first appointed, 58 percent were fifty-six or older, and only 11 percent were under forty. They held Cabinet office for an average of two years in the course of their entire political career—not necessarily, or even normally, on continuous sequence. About 57 percent served for less than one year and 77 percent less than two years—a testimonial to the postwar practice of rapid rotation of the Cabinet to reward as many deserving party members as possible. These brief terms are, however, somewhat offset by the relatively few (about 10 percent) major figures who have held Cabinet for periods of four to more than seven years.

This generally high rate of turnover in the Cabinet is, of course, calculated. The factionalized nature of the ruling parties in postwar Japan requires a prime minister to maintain a majority coalition of factions within his party—the mainstream group—if he hopes to stay in office. Therefore, factional leaders belonging to the mainstream group—and, to a limited extent, others as well—must be continuously rewarded and kept in line. In order to retain the allegiance of their followers in the Diet and to attract new members, these factional leaders must also dispense rewards for loyal service. In addition to campaign and operational funds, the major prize for factional leaders and their followers is access to Cabinet positions, especially the most important and prestigious ones such as finance, international trade and industry, or agriculture and forestry. These are prizes that only the prime minister can bestow. Obviously, the higher the turnover rate in Cabinet office, the more often he can reward the virtuous and punish or mollify his intraparty opponents. Major reorganizations of postwar Cabinets have occurred frequently.... Starting with the fourth reorganization of Yoshida's Cabinet in October 1952 when the postwar pattern really established itself and ending with the last Tanaka Cabinet of 1974, the average ministerial term was only about nine months. Thus, although the normal

Japanese Cabinet member may be a person of high intelligence and ability, the probability is that he or she will hold office too briefly to acquire a real feel for the job or to formulate and enact any sort of program. These are circumstances calculated to enhance the importance of bureaucratic at the cost of political leadership. This is not equally true of prime ministers, however. In recent years they have served for much longer terms. In some degree, this brevity of tenure for the Cabinet ministers may be compensated for by experience gained in the course of multiple terms in the Cabinet. About one-third of the Cabinet members have over the years held more than one Cabinet post; one has actually served at the ministerial level in seven different posts.

Postwar Japanese Cabinet ministers have generally been well educated. Most (88 percent) have been university graduates, usually from law departments. Almost 47 percent of these have graduated from the same university, Tokyo, followed by Kyoto (8 percent) and Waseda (7.6 percent). A few have attended universities in Western Europe (3.6 percent) or the United States (2.2 percent). Another 17 percent have had significant experience abroad. There is no notable pattern of geographic areas from which postwar Cabinet ministers originally derive.

Finally, it is of some interest to note the professional backgrounds of Cabinet ministers. Over the 1946–73 period, about 46 percent have been career politicians, usually with prior service in prefectural assemblies as well as the National Diet. About 18 percent have been former bureaucrats in the national service who, after retirement or resignation, have run successfully for the Diet. Another 19 percent come from careers in business, while about 15 percent were professionals from fields such as education, law, or journalism. Unlike the United States, relatively few lawyers achieve Cabinet status or, for that matter, figure prominently in politics at any level. The military are totally unrepresented because Article 66 of the postwar Constitution requires all ministers to be civilians.

The number of ex-bureaucrats in the Cabinet has been a subject of prolonged and bitter controversy in Japan. Almost without exception, former bureaucrats who run for the Diet do so on the Liberal Democratic ticket. This is even more applicable to the forty-odd who have achieved Cabinet office. This combined with a fairly widespread tendency to regard ex-bureaucrats as an elite and anti-democratic force in Japanese politics has made bureaucrats as a group a frequent target for abuse, suspicion, and condemnation by opposition elements and the press. There is little evidence to document a blanket accusation of this sort, but it has figured prominently in the political discourse of postwar Japan.

We come finally, therefore, to a deeper truth about the nature of political leadership in postwar Japan. Obviously, Cabinet ministers are in no position to exercise effective or continuing control over national policies. The prime minister, by experience, tenure, and authority, is better equipped to do so, and in fact, he is without doubt the single greatest source of ultimate direction and control. To assert this, however, is not to claim or to clarify a great deal. The prime minister is limited by and dependent upon the support of the factional leaders in the mainstream group. He is continuously and vitally dependent upon the higher reaches of the professional bureaucracy for technical and policy advice and for action of any sort. His own and his party's essential financial support derives largely from big business sources that are only partly subject to his influence. He is even somewhat dependent upon the leadership of the opposition parties to maintain that degree of civility in the Diet without which a parliamentary system cannot function or long survive. Beyond all this lies the great, unmobilized but potent force of Japanese public opinion. For all these reasons and more it would be a serious error to regard a prime minister as an independent force of great and autonomous authority in Japanese politics. Neither his autonomy nor authority rival that of an American president, although the president is also subject to similar external influences.

Who then rules Japan? Some years ago Japanese commentators occasionally employed an analogy based on an old children's game called *Jon-kem-po.* ("scissors-paper-rock"—scissors cut paper, paper covers rock, and rock breaks scissors). These commentators so portray the complex interactions of the party in power, which can allegedly control the bureaucracy, which can in turn through its regulatory powers make or break big business, which has the capacity to nourish or starve the party in power by granting or withholding financial support. This imagery dramatizes in simple terms the interactions and interdependencies of three major elements in the Japanese pantheon of political power: the party in power (particularly the prime minister), the higher civil servants, and big business. It is, however, far too simple to be either accurate or very useful. It imputes a wholly spurious unity to the major elements involved and tempts the incautious or the credulous to assume that any or all of these three elements share common interests and goals, concert common policies for their realization, or act as a unit in striving to effectuate such policies. None of these theses are even remotely true. There are actually very few issues of practical importance on which there is anything approximating general agreement within the ranks of the party in power, the bureaucracy, or big business. Much more common—indeed, normal—are varying degrees of internal suspicion, rivalry, competition, and outright strife. Furthermore, any significant issue in which this normal dissension prevails automatically creates an occasion and incentive to improvise ad hoc alliances, first, among like-minded elements within each of these three camps and, second, with potential allies in the other two camps. The possible combinations and permutations are numerous and are regulated only by the nature and importance of the policy issue or action at stake and by the ranges of loyalty or obligation that can be invoked by the several parties in their search for allies. Some very improbable bedfellows are apt to emerge from so complicated a process.

The complexity of the distribution of political power and influence is important in any modern political system, but it is especially true of Japan. There is no single or satisfactory answer to the question, Who rules Japan?

It varies with time, with issues, with specific circumstances, and with personalities. It is always more complex and more obscure than it seems to be. Throughout Japanese history political power has seldom, if ever, really been wielded by those whose official position apparently entitled them to do so. In this sense the degree of real, albeit qualified, authority inherent in the postwar prime ministership probably represents something of a departure from tradition. In systems in which authority and decision-making power are diffuse, it is extraordinarily difficult to assign responsibility for particular governmental policies and actions. This is certainly true in Japan, as in all modern political systems. To some extent, however, the legal fiction that holds the party in power and its leadership formally and legally accountable for all governmental acts provides a viable substitute for another more accurate means of assigning responsibility.

24

The "New Japanese" Leaders

Gerald L. Curtis

In these excerpts from an article originally published in *Foreign Policy* magazine, Curtis discusses recent changes in the leadership of the Liberal Democratic Party (LDP), Japan's largest and most powerful political party. The essential difference Curtis sees is the trend toward selecting leaders from the ranks of professional politicians rather than from the bureaucracy, as has been the norm. The "professionalism" of Japanese leadership and the tendency of younger officeholders to seek party rather than Cabinet posts actually strengthens the role of the bureaucracy. Because new party leaders are removed from bureaucratic decision making, the responsibility for day-to-day decisions devolves to the bureaucrats themselves. While party leaders may still set long-range goals and policy, bureaucratic competition could prevent consensus on these objectives. Without consensus on clearly defined national goals, Japan might find itself unable to respond to dynamic changes in the international arena.

This decade is seeing a major change in LDP leadership, as a large number of politicians who were able to enter the Diet in the late 1940s are now approaching the end of their political careers. The men who are now coming into power are neither more nor less nationalistic than the ones they are replacing, nor do their policy orientations differ in fundamental ways; what is more important in this regard is the shift that has occurred in attitudes and in policy orientations that cut across generations.

But the new leaders in the LDP do share certain characteristics which differentiate them from their predecessors—and, interestingly, from the new generation of leaders that is emerging in the business community or in the bureaucracy, many of whom have had extensive international experience and are cosmopolitan, fluent in English and comfortable in non-Japanese settings. Many, though by no means all, of the new political leaders come out of long involvement in professional political life rather than from careers in the central government bureaucracy such as characterized many of their predecessors. Like those who have served before them, however, almost all of these new leaders are from rural or semi-rural parts of the country, a consequence not so much of the rural orientation but of the party or of district imbalances that favor rural areas, but because seniority, measured in terms of the number of times elected, remains a critical factor in leadership recruitment. Since the party was a predominantly rural party in the 1950s and early 1960s, those Dietmen who now have the most seniority come from rural districts, and it will not be until sometime in the 1990s that the LDP shift to a more urban base will be reflected in its leadership.

Most of these new political leaders have over the past decade sought important party rather than cabinet posts; where they have served in the cabinet, it has been in ministries that have a primarily domestic focus. Very few of them have extensive international experience or close personal relationships with foreigners, in the United States or elsewhere. Thus, while they may not be any more nationalistic than their elders, many of them are less internationalist—unaccustomed to extensive contact outside Japan and not deeply familiar with many of the critical issues of importance to Japan. Consequently, in a country for which foreign relations are critical and in a society in which personal relationships are carefully cultivated and play an extremely important role in decision-making processes, there is emerging a new leadership group that has neither close personal links nor deep experience with the outside world.

It is not entirely clear how such leadership characteristics will affect policy but, given the complexity of many of the issues that confront Japanese policy-makers and the relative lack of policy expertise among these new leaders, there may be an increasing tendency to rely on the bureaucracy to provide the lead in determining policy. Strong bureaucratic intervention in the policy process has been true in the past as well, but it can have rather different consequences in the 1980s than it had in past years.

Through most of postwar Japanese history the bureaucracy has gone about its business within a framework of clearly defined national goals and foreign policy priorities, its efficiency in making day-to-day decisions and in implementing government policies made possible by the existence of such a framework. But in Japan as elsewhere it is only the political leadership that can structure the consensus that must exist if bureaucratic institutions are to avoid adopting inconsistent and contradictory policy orientations. In the absence of such leadership Japan will drift with the trends of the time, with its cautions, time-consuming and reactive patterns of decision-making unable to adjust to a situation in which expectations are high that Japan will play a more dynamic leadership role in a variety of international forums and on a wide range of international issues.

Thus, if the 1970s are any guide to the kinds of issues that will confront Japan in the 1980s, there are likely to be an increasing number of foreign policy issues that will be left initially to the bureaucracy to handle, only to escalate into major political controversy; the political leadership will have little choice but to enter into the fray. And, as the older generation of politicians who have dominated the highest positions in the government and the party leaves the scene, the absence of close personal relationships abroad and the lack of extensive international experience, combined with the forceful personalities and the self-confidence that characterize many of the most outstanding new leaders, could lead to a pattern of decision-making for which the outside world, and the United States in particular, will be ill prepared. The reliance, for example, on the exercise of often heavy-handed outside pressure to force Japan to adopt certain policies is apt to come up against much stronger resistance than was true in the past.

Unit VI

Government-Business
Relationships

In both China and Japan, the government plays an important and active role in coordinating economic activity and promoting economic growth. However, there are important distinctions between the "central planning" approach taken in China and the "administrative guidance" approach used in Japan. China's command economy is patterned after the Soviet model in which all productive activities are owned and organized by the government. Allocation of resources, distribution of finished goods, wages, employment, and financial activities are all under the direct control of the state. Japan, on the other hand, is a developmental state in which the government attempts to lead the economy by working closely with privately owned businesses in setting economic goals and in deciding how these goals will be achieved. Tax, investment, tariff, and research and development policies are all used as incentives to encourage businesses to cooperate with government.

As China enters an era of intensive economic growth (that is modernization and increases in productivity and efficiency, as opposed to extensive growth-high rates of capital investment and expansion of capacity) and Japan moves away from manufacturing and into information and other high-technology industries, both countries face problems that are not unlike those facing U.S. policymakers. Specifically, both countries are being required to make increasingly difficult decisions about how best to abandon low-growth industries and increase the scope and activities of high-growth sectors.

China has been involved in national economic planning since the 1930s. At that time, the Chinese Nationalist government targeted select critical industries in which rational allocation and distribution were considered absolutely essential to national security. Soon after the Chinese Communists came to power in 1949, all private enterprises were absorbed into the state sector. Central planning was considered necessary both for economic growth and to meet ideological goals inherent in Marxism.

Similarly, in Japan there has also been a tradition of government intervention in the economy, particularly since the end of World War II. In the immediate postwar years, government officials saw planning and cooperation as the primary keys to achieving economic growth. Japan's lack of natural resources and its dependence on imports made rational allocation and distribution essential to the continued expansion of the economy. While such planning has not been without conflict and discord, the heart of the nation's economic success has been the ability of business, government, and political parties to form a consensus on long-range goals and strategies to meet them. This situation is changing, however, as Japan moves into high-technology fields.

The recession of 1978–79 was a particularly bitter experience for many Japanese corporations. Japan already had a high rate of small business bankruptcies. Many large corporations were forced to reduce their staffs and to move production overseas to avoid a similar fate. The need to move out of high-wage, low-profit manufacturing industries has been a source of much tension between business and government leaders. The government has traditionally attempted to spread the burdens of declining industries through subsidiaries or voluntary production decreases, much to the dismay of profit-minded corporate executives. Furthermore, other factors, such as bureaucratic competition, international criticism of the country's "anti-competitive practices," the independence and influence of large conglomerates, high energy costs, competition from newly industrialized nations like South Korea, and changes in public attitudes toward growth have all exacerbated or contributed to the increase in tensions between government and industry. As it becomes more difficult to reach a consensus on goals and methods, the government has found itself regulating industry more and planning less.

Chinese leaders would welcome a decreased role for government in economic administration. Although China has enjoyed high growth rates, much of that growth has been achieved at the expense of efficiency and economic rationality. Consumer goods industries have been continually underfunded and agricultural production has been allowed to stagnate. Bureaucratization and overcentralization, problems that plague all centrally planned economies, have been no less apparent in China. Indeed, these problems have led to high levels of waste, inefficiency, and low productivity among workers and managers alike. Political conflicts have weakened an already inadequate planning apparatus. And localism,* insufficient statistical information, and supply and transportation bottlenecks have been sources of additional problems.

The Deng Xiaoping leadership has moved to decrease the state's role in direct productive activities and to improve the level of planning. Enterprises have been given greater autonomy to make decisions concerning production levels, wages, employment practices, and marketing. And the use of limited market mechanisms, such as profits and free markets, has gradually increased. These mechanisms, in combination with improved methods of economic planning, have emerged as the most viable solution to the problems of modernizing China's economy.

However, as in Japan and the United States, conflicts have occurred over inefficient industries. Because prices are still centrally set, many efficient factories producing low-priced goods cannot make a profit. Conversely, some inefficient enterprises making high-priced items achieve high rates of profit. More importantly, the increased emphasis on market mechanisms has threatened the "iron rice bowl"† of Chinese workers, who face the possibility of reduced wages, decreased benefits, and unemployment. Managers must scramble to find ways of making an enterprise profitable despite the constraints of a centralized sys-

---

*The tendency for lower level officials to put the interests of their organizations ahead of the national interest.

†Guaranteed permanent employment.

tem of allocation and distribution. If they cannot ear a profit, such enterprises may have little chance of obtaining financial aid from budget-conscious planners in Peking.

There is a subtle change taking place in both China and Japan which is transforming the traditional relationship between government and industry. Although faced with radically different situations, China and Japan nonetheless share many similar problems. China is responding to those problems by intervening less in the economy and by improving planning. Japanese planners, in contrast, constrained by the tensions between themselves and business leaders, are finding that their ability to plan has been severely impaired. As regulation of the Japanese economy increases, there will be a corresponding change in the government's role in the economic sector.

In "The Japanese 'Miracle,'" Chalmers Johnson describes the major characteristics of the Japanese "developmental state" and explains how it differs from other economic systems, noting that the Japanese system is ideologically closer to the centrally planned economies of the Soviet Union and China than to the market economies of the United States and Western Europe. In "Inside MITI: How Japan Forges Industrial Consensus," Sam Jameson and Tom Redburn shed light on the role of the Ministry of Trade and Industry (MITI) in promoting economic growth in Japan since the end of World War II. Analyzing the factors that contributed to Japan's extraordinary postwar economic success, the authors show how changing conditions both at home and abroad, along with overall economic growth, have triggered conflicts between MITI and Japanese industry that may eventually lead to a decline in MITI's prestige and power.

In "How Japan Helps Its Industry," Steve Lohr points to the unique collaborative arrangement between Japanese government and business as the key factor in the success of Japan's much-heralded "industrial policy." Lohr also notes that in contrast to the United States, where roughly half of all government funds for research and development are channeled into military projects, Japanese research and development efforts are largely concentrated in civilian areas, which socializes the risks of failure and thus encourages businesses to cooperate and innovate in high-risk areas.

In "Formulation and Implementation of Central Plans," Chu-yuan Cheng describes the role that the state bureaucracy has played in promoting growth in China's centrally planned economy. Cheng first explains how China's economic planning apparatus is organized, then discusses some of the problems currently facing Chinese planners and their strategies for solving them.

25

The Japanese "Miracle"

Chalmers Johnson

In these excerpts from *MITI and the Japanese Miracle,* Chalmers Johnson focuses on several aspects of the Japanese "developmental state," arguing that the real issue in a developmental state is how the state intervenes in the economy and for what purposes. Japan plans its economy according to rational economic principles. The USSR, in contrast, plans according to ideology while the United States does not plan but regulates. Although Japan has shown some signs of increasing regulation in recent years, planning remains the dominant approach. The bureaucracy is extremely powerful in Japan and bureaucratic infighting is much more important in the policy process than political rhetoric. Effectiveness in achieving goals, not efficiency, is the measure of success of a policy whose long-range goals are identified by consensus. Johnson points out that these characteristics actually place Japan much closer to the centrally planned economies of China and the Soviet Union than to the market economies of Europe and the United States.

What do I mean by the developmental state? This is not really a hard question, but it always seems to raise difficulties in the Anglo-American countries, where the existence of the developmental state in any form other than the communist state has largely been forgotten or ignored as a result of the years of disputation with Marxist-Leninists. . . .

The issue is not one of state intervention in the economy. All states intervene in their economies for various reasons, among which are protecting national security (the "military-industrial complex"), insuring industrial safety, providing consumer protection, aiding the weak, promoting fairness in market transactions, preventing monopolization and private control in free enterprise systems, securing the public's interest in natural monopolies, achieving economies of scale, preventing excessive competition, protecting and rearing industries, distributing vital resources, protecting the environment, guaranteeing employment, and so forth. The question is how the government intervenes and for what purposes. . . . Economies of the Soviet type are not *plan rational* but *plan ideological.* In the Soviet Union and its dependencies and emulators, state ownership of the means of production, state planning, and bureaucratic goal-setting are not rational means to a developmental goal (even if they may once have been); they are fundamental values in themselves, not to be challenged by evidence of either inefficiency or ineffectiveness. In the sense I am using the term here, Japan is plan rational, and the command economies are not; in fact, the history of Japan since 1925 offers numerous illustrations of why the command economy is not plan rational, a lesson the Japanese learned well.

At the most basic level the distinction between market and plan refers to differing conceptions of the functions of the state in economic affairs. The state as an institution is as old as organized human society. Until approximately the nineteenth century, states everywhere performed more or less the same functions that make large-scale social organization possible but that individuals or families or villages cannot perform for themselves. These functions included defense, road building, water conservancy, the mining of coins, and the administration of justice. Following the industrial revolution, the state began to take on new functions. In those states that were the first to industrialize, the state itself had little to do with the new forms of economic activity but towards the end of the nineteenth century the state took on *regulatory* functions in the interest of maintaining competition, consumer protection, and so forth. . . .

In states that were late to industrialize, the state itself led the industrialization drive, that is, it took on *developmental* functions. These two differing orientations toward private economic activities, the regulatory orientation and the developmental orientation, produced two different kinds of government-business relationships. The United States is a good example of a state in which the regulatory orientation predominates, whereas Japan is a good example of a state in which the developmental orientation predominates. A regulatory, or market-rational, state concerns itself with the forms and procedures—the rules, if you will—of economic competition, but it does not concern itself with substantive matters. For example, the United States government has many regulations concerning the antitrust implications of the size of firms, but it does not concern itself with what industries ought to exist and what industries are no longer needed. The developmental, or plan-rational, state, by contrast, has as its dominant feature precisely the setting of such substantive social and economic goals.

Another way to make this distinction is to consider a state's priorities in economic policy. In the plan-rational state, the government will give greatest precedence to industrial policy, that is, to a concern with the structure of domestic industry and with promoting the structure that enhances the nation's international competitiveness. The very existence of an industrial policy implies a strategic, or goal-oriented, approach to the economy. On the other hand, the market-rational state usually will not even have an industrial policy (or, at any rate, will not recognize it as such). Instead, both its domestic and foreign economic policy, including its trade policy, will stress rules and reciprocal concessions (although perhaps influenced by some goals that are not industrially specific, goals such as price stability or full employment). Its trade policy will normally be subordinate to general foreign policy, being used more often to cement political relationships than to obtain strictly economic advantages.

These various distinctions are useful because they draw our attention to Japan's emergence, following the Meiji Restoration of 1868, as a developmental, plan-rational state whose economic orientation was keyed to industrial policy. By contrast, the United States from about the same period took the regulatory, market-rational path keyed to foreign policy. In modern times Japan has always put emphasis on an overarching, nationally supported goal for its economy rather than on the particular procedures that are to govern economic activity. The Meiji-era goal was the famous *fukoku-kyōhei* (rich country, strong military) of the late nineteenth and early twentieth centuries. This was followed during the 1930's and 1940's by the goals of depression recovery, war preparation, war production, and postwar recovery. From about 1955, and explicitly since the Income-doubling Plan of 1960, the goal has been high-speed growth, sometimes expressed as "overtake Europe and America" (*Ōbei ni oikose*). Amaya lists the goals of the past century in detail:*shokusan kōgyō* (increase industrial production), *fukoku-kyōhei* (rich country, strong military), *seisanryoku kakujū* (expand productive capacity), *yushutsu shinkō* (promote exports), *kanzen koyō* (full employment), and *kōdo seichō* (high-speed growth). Only during the 1970's did Japan begin to shift to a somewhat regulatory, foreign-policy orientation, just as America began to show early signs of a new developmental, industrial-policy orientation. But the Japanese system remains plan rational, and the American system is still basically market rational.

This can be seen most clearly by looking at the differences between the two systems in terms of economic and political decision-making. In Japan the developmental, strategic quality of economic policy is reflected within the government in the high position of the so-called economic bureaucrats, that is, the officials of the ministries of Finance, International Trade and Industry, Agriculture and Forestry, Construction, and Transportation, plus the Economic Planning Agency. These official agencies attract the most talented graduates of the best universities in the country, and the positions of higher-level officials in these ministries have been and still are the most prestigious in the society. Although it is influenced by pressure groups and political claimants, the elite bureaucracy of Japan makes most major decisions, drafts virtually all legislation, controls the national budget, and is the source of all major policy innovations in the system. Equally important, upon their retirement, which is usually between the ages of 50 and 55 in Japan, these bureaucrats move from government to powerful positions in private enterprise, banking, the political world, and the numerous public corporations—a direction of elite mobility that is directly opposite to that which prevails in the United States. The existence of a powerful, talented, and prestige-laden economic bureaucracy is a natural corollary of plan rationality.

In market-rational systems such as the United States, public service does not normally attract the most capable talent, and national decision-making is dominated by elected members of the professional class, who are usually lawyers, rather than by the bureaucracy. The movement of elites is not from government to the private sector but vice versa, usually through political appointment, which is much more extensive than in Japan. . . . American economic decisions are made most often in Congress, which also controls the budget, and these decisions reflect the market-rational emphasis on procedures rather than outcomes. . . .

Another way to highlight the differences between plan rationality and market rationality is to look at some of the trade-offs involved in each approach. First, the most important evaluative standard in market rationality is "efficiency." But in plan rationality this takes lower precedence than "effectiveness." Both Americans and Japanese tend to get the meanings of efficiency and effectiveness mixed up. Americans often and understandably criticize their official bureaucracy for its inefficiency, failing to note that efficiency is not a good evaluative standard for bureaucracy. Effectiveness is the proper standard of evaluation of goal-oriented strategic activities. On the other hand, Japanese continue to tolerate their wildly inefficient and even inappropriate agricultural structure at least in part because it is mildly effective: it provides food that does not have to be imported.

Second, both types of systems are concerned with "externalities," or what Milton Friedman has called "neighborhood effects"—an example would be the unpriced social costs of production such as pollution. In this instance, however, the plan-rational system has much greater difficulty than the market-rational system in identifying and shifting its sights to respond to effects external to the national goal. The position of the plan-rational system is like that of a military organization: a general is judged by whether he wins or loses. It would be good if he would also employ an economy of violence (be efficient), but that is not as important as results. Accordingly, Japan persisted with high-speed industrial growth long after the evidence of very serious environmental damage had become common knowledge. On the other hand, when the plan rational system finally shifts its goals to give priority to a problem such as industrial pollution, it will commonly be more effective than the market-rational system, as can be seen in the comparison between the Japanese and American handling of pollution in the 1970's.

Third, the plan-rational system depends upon the existence of a widely agreed upon set of overarching goals for the society, such as high-speed growth. When such a consensus exists, the plan-rational system will outperform the market-rational system on the same benchmark, such as growth of GNP, as long as growth of GNP is the goal of the plan-rational system. But when a consensus does not exist, when there is confusion or conflict over the overarching goal in a plan-rational economy, it will appear to be quite adrift, incapable of coming to grips with basic problems and unable to place responsibility for failures. Japan has experienced this kind of drift when unexpected developments suddenly upset its consensus, such as during the "Nixon shocks" of 1971, or after the oil shock of 1973. Generally speaking, the great strength of the plan-rational system lies in its effectiveness in dealing with routine problems, whereas the great strength of the market-rational system lies in its effectiveness in dealing with critical problems. In the latter case, the emphasis on rules, procedures, and executive responsibility helps to promote action when problems of an unfamiliar or unknown magnitude arise.

Fourth, since decision-making is centered in different bodies in the two system—in an elite bureaucracy in one and in a parliamentary assembly in the other—the process of policy change will be manifested in quite different ways. In the plan-rational system, change will be marked by internal bureaucratic disputes, factional infighting, and conflict among ministries. In the market-rational system, change will be marked by strenuous parliamentary contests over new legislation and by election battles. For example, the shift in Japan during the late 1960's and throughout the 1970's from protectionism to liberalization was most clearly signaled by factional infighting within MITI between the "domestic faction" and the "international faction." The surest sign that the Japanese government was moving in a more open, free-trade direction was precisely the fact that the key ministry in this sector came to be dominated by internationalistic bureaucrats. Americans are sometimes confused by Japanese economic policy because they pay too much attention to what politicians say and because they do not know much about the bureaucracy, whereas Japanese have on occasion given too much weight to the statements of American bureaucrats and have not paid enough attention to Congressmen and their extensive staffs.

Looked at historically, modern Japan began in 1868 to be plan rational and developmental. After about a decade and a half of experimentation with direct state operation of economic enterprises, it discovered the most obvious pitfalls of plan rationality: corruption, bureaucratism, and ineffective monopolies. Japan was and remained plan rational, but it had no ideological commitment to state ownership of the economy. Its main criterion was the rational one of effectiveness in meeting the goals of development. Thus, Meiji Japan began to shift away from state entrepreneurship to collaboration with privately owned enterprises, favoring those enterprises that were capable of rapidly adopting new technologies and that were committed to the national goals of economic development and military strength. From this shift developed the collaborative relationship between the government and big business in Japan. In the prewar era this collaboration took the form of close governmental ties to the zaibatsu (privately owned industrial empires). The government induced the zaibatsu to go into areas where it felt development was needed. For their part the zaibatsu pioneered the commercialization of modern technologies in Japan, and they achieved economies of scale in manufacturing and banking that were on a par with those of the rest of the industrial world. There were many important results of this collaboration, including the development of a marked dualism between large advanced enterprises and small backward enterprises. But perhaps the most important result was the introduction of a needed measure of competition into the plan-rational system.

In the postwar world, the reforms of the occupation era helped modernize the zaibatsu enterprises, freeing them of their earlier family domination. The reforms also increased the number of enterprises, promoted the development of the labor movement, and rectified the grievances of the farmers under the old order, but the system remained plan rational: given the need for economic recovery from the war and independence from foreign aid, it could not very well have been otherwise. Most of the ideas for economic growth came from the bureaucracy, and the business community reacted with an attitude of what one scholar has called "responsive dependence." The government did not normally give direct orders to businesses, but those businesses that listened to the signals coming from the government and then responded were favored with easy access to capital, tax breaks, and approval of their plans to import foreign technology or establish joint ventures. But a firm did not have to respond to the government. The business literature of Japan is filled with descriptions of the very interesting cases of big firms that succeeded without strong governmental ties (for example, Sony and Honda), but there are not many to describe. . . .

Within the developmental state there is contention for power among many bureaucratic centers, including finance, economic planning, foreign affairs, and so forth. However, the center that exerts the greatest *positive* influence is the one that creates and executes industrial policy. MITI's [Ministry of International Trade and Industry] dominance in this area has led one Japanese commentator to characterize it as the "pilot agency," and a journalist of the *Asahi* who has often been highly critical of MITI nonetheless concedes that MITI is "without doubt the greatest concentration of brain power in Japan." MITI's jurisdiction ranges from the control of bicycle racing to the setting of electric power rates, but its true defining power is its control of industrial policy (*sangyō seisaku*). Although the making and executing of industrial policy is what the developmental state does, industrial policy itself—what it is and how it is done—remains highly controversial.

Industrial policy, according to Robert Ozaki, "is an indigenous Japanese term not to be found in the lexicon of Western economic terminology. A reading through the literature suggests a definition, however: it refers to a complex of those policies concerning protection of domestic industries, development of strategic industries, and adjustment of the economic structure in response to or in anticipation of internal and external changes which are formulated and pursued by MITI in the cause of the national interest as the term 'national interest' is understood by MITI officials." Although this definition is somewhat circular—industrial policy is what MITI says it is—Ozaki makes one important point clear: industrial policy is a reflection of economic nationalism, with nationalism understood to mean giving priority to the interests of one's own nation but not necessarily involving protectionism, trade controls, or economic warfare. Nationalism *may* mean those things, but it is equally possible that free trade will be in the national economic interest during particular periods, as was true of Japan during the 1970's. Industrial policy is, however, a recognition that the global economic system is *never* to be understood in terms of the free competitive model: labor never moves freely between countries, and technology is only slightly more free. . . .

26

How Japan Forges Industrial Consensus

Sam Jameson and Tom Redburn

The role of the Ministry of International Trade and Industry (MITI) in Japan's postwar economic development should not be underestimated. In the years immediately following the war, only the government was capable of providing the assistance that was needed to rebuild the country's damaged industries. Industry was willing to cooperate with government not only because it had traditionally played a leading role in the economy but also because the government's goals corresponded closely to their own. In recent years, however, this close relationship between government and industry has begun to change. The successful growth of such economic giants as Toyota, the end of the "growth at all costs" philosophy, and international pressures have combined to create conflicts between MITI and Japanese industry whose outcomes remain to be seen.

After the devastation of World War II, the Japanese government was the only institution capable of assuming jurisdiction, under Gen. Douglas MacArthur's occupation, for reviving the economy of the war-torn nation. [As former MITI official Shiro Miyamoto put it,] "No socialist country in the world now exercises the kind of complete control the government exercised in those days—under the authority of the general headquarters (of the U.S. Occupation authorities)."

"It was a completely controlled planned economy," he said.

With industrial facilities in ruin, production of consumer goods had fallen to 30% of prewar levels. To ensure even a minimum standard of living and to rebuild the economy, MITI had to adopt a "priority production system," allocating raw materials, capital and foreign exchange to key industries, such as electric power, coal mining, steel and chemical fertilizer, Miyamoto said.

The allocation policies, together with the strong boost given the Japanese economy by the demands of the Korean War, worked to revive industry, and, by the mid-1950s, the economy had regained prewar production levels and was launched on a high growth trajectory. Because so many analysts had been pessimistic about Japan's economic future, MITI's boldness in pushing for an industrial transformation of Japan dramatically enhanced its prestige. It was a pivotal success that cemented the relationships that, in modified form, continue to exist today between MITI and business, Miyamoto said.

SOUGHT GOVERNMENT'S GUIDANCE

Two key reasons help explain why the Japanese government continued to play such a leading role in the economy.

One reason why Japanese businessmen, unlike their American counterparts, have often responded favorably to government guidance lies in a tradition dating to Japan's feudal era.

"Exalt the rulers and disparage the ruled" is an age-old saying, explains Shigenori Hamada, known as the "godfather" of Japanese electronics for his continued promotion of a vigorous national industry. "It is the national characteristic of the Japanese people for the government to play the role of taking initiatives," said Hamada, who now heads the Japanese Electronics Council, a think tank.

Another more prosaic reason is that, for years, MITI served to protect and promote the goals of Japan's leading industries. "No one with any insight into the Japanese way of conducting affairs could imagine that the government or the bureaucracy dictates policy to private industry," wrote G. C. Allen, a British scholar who is a leading authority on the Japanese economy. "The Japanese normally arrive at decisions by consultations that everyone expects will lead to a consensus.

"It may well be that the government's most important role in the economy has been to assist private firms to develop on the lines that they have persuaded officials to approve (after also being) convinced that the national interest was being served."

'INVITATION FROM OLD FRIEND'

MITI's persuasion, which comes after long internal battles have already been fought among all the affected groups, Hamada said, usually works because, when the government proposal finally emerges, "It is like an invitation from an old friend."

Every year, 25 engineering graduates and 25 law and economic specialists enter the ranks of MITI's top-echelon bureaucrats—an elite from which MITI will choose its section chiefs, bureau chiefs and, ultimately, one vice minister, to run the 12,000-person ministry. With careers normally lasting 30 years, MITI is staffed at the top by about 1,500 of those cream-of-the-crop leaders. This year, 1,370 of Japan's top college graduates competed for the 50 posts, which gave the ministry the ability to skim even more selectively from Japan's brightest students.

Eventually, about six of the 50 entrants will have a chance to direct, usually for a 2-year period, one of MITI's 12 bureaus—the level at which Miyamoto ended his career.

At the pinnacle of the agency is the vice minister, a post reserved for a career officer, who also usually serves for two years. The person chosen to this post thus represents the survival of the fittest from about 2,700 initial applicants.

With many technological jobs in the Ministry of International Trade and Industry, officials with backgrounds in law and economics and those with engineering degrees keep close contact with businessmen and make it a point to follow technological developments around the world, Miyamoto said.

"We are a kind of consultant to private business," Miyamoto said.

CLOUT IS HIDDEN

But Hiroshi Yamada, director of Fujitsu Laboratories Ltd., acknowledged that MITI is something more than a consultant, that its invitations to participate in joint research projects contain a strong dose of hidden clout.

"There would be no specific punishment for turning down a specific invitation. But in relations in this country, ties do not end with just one job. Over a long period of time, some adverse effects (on business) might be expected (if an invitation is rejected)," he said.

While many companies are growing increasingly reluctant to wholeheartedly participate in such joint projects, Yamada pointed out that it is important not to miss out on the benefits that flow from a successful research endeavor. "MITI bureaucrats are very competent. They have studied advanced technology well, and to go along with their judgment is generally not a mistake," he said. . . .

In recent years, conditions at home and abroad have changed, forcing the ministry to change and posing problems that increasingly have grown to dimensions beyond MITI's power to deal with them, Miyamoto said.

Some firms, such as Toyota Motor Corp., became "giants," no longer as pliable as they had once been, he said.

Although Toyota has now decided to set up a joint venture with General Motors Corp. to manufacture small cars in California, several years ago the company reacted with anger when MITI's vice minister tried to persuade Toyota officials to invest in the United States, Miyamoto said.

A change in the public mood in the 1970s—away from the growth-at-all-costs atmosphere of the 1950s and '60s—created cracks in MITI's ties with business as the ministry started insisting that industries adopt anti-pollution measures, he said.

Overall economic growth also made MITI's job harder.

With Japan producing 10% of the world's economic products, "no longer was there room for maneuvering," Miyamoto said. At the same time, Japan came to face demands to assume international economic responsibilities; it was deprived of the use of tariffs and import quotas, which MITI officials acknowledge were used into the early 1970s as protection for developing industries.

BALANCE OF POWER FRAYING

Using a folk tale to illustrate his point, Miyamoto also suggested that the triangular balance of power among Japan's politicians, bureaucrats and business leaders is coming apart.

In a well-known Japanese children's story, Miyamoto said, a balance of power is maintained among a village chief, hunters of the village and foxes in the fields nearby. As members of his village, the hunters are controlled by the village chief, the foxes held in check by the hunters and the village chief himself restrained by fear of attack by the foxes.

Miyamoto said the comparison does not apply with precision, but he equaled the village chief to Japan's politicians, the hunters to Japan's businessmen and the foxes to MITI.

"There is a gradual change toward the village chief and the hunters ganging up on the foxes—the politicians joining with businessmen to oppose government officials," he said.

27

How Japan Helps Its Industry

Steve Lohr

In this selection, Steve Lohr points to the unique cooperative relationship between Japanese business and government in explaining Japan's phenomenal success in targeting new growth industries, in directing the orderly decline of ailing industries, and in keeping unemployment rates at levels far below those of any other advanced industrialized country. But, as Lohr points out here, increased energy costs and competition from industrializing nations are forcing Japan to make major cutbacks in production in several industries. Meantime, the focus of most criticism from abroad, especially from America, has to do with the targeting of such high-growth industries as microchips. While the United States spends much more on research and development than Japan, most of America's effort is restricted to military projects. Japan, on the other hand, concentrates on research and development in civilian areas and thus socializes the risks of failure. This policy naturally encourages Japanese businesses to cooperate and innovate in costly and/or high-risk areas.

The rapid strides made by Japan in computers and semiconductors are generally viewed as the best recent examples of the payoff from the Japanese brand of industrial policy.

The Japanese approach emphasizes cooperation between business and Government. While the teamwork that characterizes Japanese industrial policy has accomplished much in the rising high-technology field, perhaps its biggest achievement has been in maintaining an unemployment rate of less than 3 percent, the lowest of any major developed country.

"The most impressive thing about Japan's industrial policy is the way they manage the rational adjustment of their declining industries with a minimum of social pain and political obstruction," said Frank A. Weil, a former Deputy Secretary of the United States Commerce Department.

The key Government player in this process is the Ministry of International Trade and Industry. The agency directs the orderly decline of ailing industries and nurtures up-and-coming industries. In doing so, Japan and its trade ministry have been criticized in the United States and elsewhere for what are considered anticompetitive practices. The Japanese reject the charges, saying they stem from the success of the policies. . . .

Today, Japan again faces the problem of paring declining industries—mainly businesses that have lost their competitiveness because of high energy costs in Japan or lower labor costs in newly industrializing nations.

The petrochemical industry is an example, and the 12 main producers recently reached an agreement to cut capacity by 36 percent by early 1985. . . .

HIGH-TECHNOLOGY SUCCESS

The ministry-orchestrated project begun in the mid-1970's to conduct research on sophisticated semiconductors, called very large-scale integrated circuits, is viewed as the most successful example of Japanese industrial policy in high technology.

The integrated circuits project also illustrates what the American Government finds "objectionable" in Japan's industrial policy, according to Lionel H. Olmer, Under Secretary for International Trade in the United States Commerce Department.

In the project, five major semiconductor companies—NEC, Hitachi, Toshiba, Mitsubishi Electric and Fujitsu—conducted cooperative research under the ministry's aegis from 1976 to 1980. The agency contributed $123 million at current exchange rates, while the companies put up $186 million. There were 150 researchers donated from the five companies, and their main laboratory was in Kawasaki City, south of Tokyo, in space provided by NEC.

The Government paid to equip the laboratory. "At the start, the biggest beneficiaries were American companies," one Japanese executive said. "They supplied most of the equipment that MITI bought."

Still, the payoff for the Japanese industry seems to have been considerable. The work yielded more than 1,000 patents spanning a wide range of semiconductor technologies. Many industry analysts have said that the project enabled Japan to attain leadership, with two-thirds of the world market, in one key product, the 64K RAM, or random access memory, a chip that stores data.

SOME RESISTANCE

Before the project began, a couple of the big semiconductor companies resisted joining but were persuaded. One of the companies that bridled at first was NEC, Japan's largest semiconductor maker.

Apparently, the company made the right decision in going along. "We would have been delayed six months to a year without the cooperative project," said Tomihiro Matsumura, the NEC director responsible for semi-conductor operations.

But Mr. Matsumura said the trade ministry project was by no means the major reason for his company's success in the 64K RAM's. While NEC had 30 researchers lent to the cooperative lab, it had 200 assigned to an in-house team doing related research.

"We would not trust MITI entirely," Mr. Matsumura said. "And frankly, the in-house work was more important to us than the MITI project."

Japanese executives note, however, that the integrated circuit project did help with the development of fundamental technologies in design and manufacturing. But for mass production many adjustments were required, which were made on a company-by-company basis. And, they note, more efficient mass production is their advantage over American producers of 64K RAM's.

INDUSTRIAL 'TARGETING'

Nonetheless, it is the integrated-circuit-type coordinated research focusing on a particular product area that Japan's critics call industrial "targeting." Because its effect can be to nurture a new industry that can take over markets abroad, targeting is an unfair trade practice, they say. . . .

However, the so-called targeting is difficult to measure, and by measures that do exist Japan hardly appears to be an offender. For instance, the United States Government finances a much larger portion of domestic research and development than does the Japanese Government.

The Government contributes 47 percent of all funds for research and development in the United States. In Japan, the Government's share is about 27 percent. One significant difference, however, is that roughly half of the Government-financed research in America is for military purposes, while in Japan the military portion is about 2 percent. Thus, thanks partly to the defense umbrella the United States provides, Japan is free to use more of its research financing to develop commercial products.

REDUCING RISKS

Far more important than the money the ministry spends, according to foreign critics, is its role in reducing the risk in industries whose development it marks as a national priority. Once the ministry is involved, they say, bank loans and other essential services are more readily provided by the Japanese corporate community to companies in the chosen industry.

"MITI's endorsement results in a leveling of the competitive plane for the selected companies," said Clyde Prestowitz, United States Deputy Assistant Secretary of Commerce for International Economic Policy.

Japanese officials reply that the Government provides no guarantees against losses for companies in chosen high-technology fields. Some will succeed and some will fail, as in any business, they say.

Yet to some degree, they agree that Japanese industrial policy has resulted in a "socialization of risk," but without Government subsidies. "Because the Japanese Government has played that role is one of the main reasons our industrial policy has been successful," said Eisuke Sakakibara, a senior Finance Ministry official. "And as far as I'm concerned, there is nothing to be criticized in that."

The effects of industrial policies elude measurement since no one can say what would have occurred in their absence. For that reason, some analysts believe, foreign governments will have difficulty rationalizing actions against Japan.

"If you can't measure it," asked Thomas Pepper, one of the Hudson Institute consultants who prepared a study of Japanese industrial policy for the United States State Department last October, "how do you justify going after it?"

28

Formulation and Implementation of Central Plans

Chu-yuan Cheng

In China's centrally planned economy, which is based on the Soviet model, the central planning apparatus is hierarchically organized. In China, the State Planning Commission and the State Economic Commission, the two highest planning authorities, are responsible for formulating and implementing economic plans that involve productive units throughout the country. In addition, provincial and local governments are responsible for planning regional production. Pointing out that the primary goal of central planning is balanced, proportionate growth, Cheng notes that although China has managed to achieve high rates of capital formation and a more balanced distribution of goods and resources, it still faces a number of problems. Today, a major goal of the Chinese leadership is to reestablish the primacy of planning while at the same time allowing for the flexibility of market forces.

THE CENTRAL PLANNING APPARATUS

Essentially, central planning in a Soviet-type economy is a hierarchical system of organization, a pyramid-type structure with a planning elite at the top issuing orders concerning output and production technique and a multitude of production units at the bottom carrying out those orders. In a central planning economy, virtually all government organs are in some degree concerned with plan construction and implementation.

The Chinese administrative system consists of three levels. At the top of the hierarchy is the central government, with the National People's Congress (NPC) serving as the highest organ of the state authority and the State Council serving as its executive organ. Under the State Council are thirty to eighty ministries, commissions, general bureaus, and special agencies—the number depends on the emphasis on centralization or decentralization.

The second level of administration includes twenty-one provinces, five autonomous regions and three centrally administered cities (Beijing, Shanghai, and Tianjin). Under the provinces and autonomous regions are several hundred prefectures (special districts) or autonomous prefectures, each of which controls several *xian* (counties) or autonomous counties (banners) and cities. . . . The third level of administration encompasses 2,138 *xian*, which are further broken down into people's communes and towns.

Of the central and local government organs, three sets of agencies are directly involved in economic planning. They are, respectively, responsible for information collection and evaluation, plan formulation and coordination, and plan implementation and supervision. . . .

The State Planning Commission [is] China's highest planning authority. It establishes broad budget parameters for each component of the economy and engages in both long-range and annual planning. The SPC sets the guidelines, and other planning bodies draw up plans in conformity with them. [T]he SPC has bureaus for production, foreign trade, communications, agriculture, and construction, as well as other bureaus corresponding to each industrial ministry. The State Economic Commission . . . is charged with implementing the production plans of the SPC. Specifically, the SEC coordinates the details of annual and quarterly production plans for the industrial and communications sectors and coordinates the supply and demand of industrial raw materials, energy, and other inputs. As a result, supply shortages in any given sector normally come to the SEC's attention first. If domestic sources are unavailable, the commission may order the necessary items from abroad through the Ministry of Foreign Trade. . . . Generally, the implementation of plans rests on the ministries, and the SEC becomes involved only when a ministry does not pay enough attention to a particular problem or when there is a conflict of interest between two ministries. Each month, the SEC holds meetings with ministry heads to discuss such problems. . . .

Often the appearance or disappearance of the planning apparatus appears to have been the result of changing attitudes in the Party's leadership toward planning and control. During periods when Maoist ideology was the paramount concern, as in the Great Leap Forward and the Cultural Revolution, careful planning and control were generally eschewed, the power of the planning commissions was circumscribed, and their organizations were abolished or cut to the bone. During periods when the pragmatists were in the saddle, planning and control became prime concerns, and the power and organization of the planning machinery were usually greatly expanded. In the First Five-Year Plan period and in the adjustment years after the Great Leap, the influence of the planning commissions was notable. In November 1962, for instance, when more moderate policies were in favor, the State Planning Commission had twenty-two vice-chairmen, which indicates the immensity of its organization. . . .

Most of the government agencies in economic affairs are directly responsible for industrial and agricultural production. The number of ministries in charge of a single industry has fluctuated almost constantly through mergers, regroupings, and divisions over the years. . . .

The purge of the radicals in October 1976 presaged the resurrection of many central ministries. Under the subsequent drive for modernization, many ministries, commissions, and other offices under the State Council regained their separate identities. . . .

Most of the central ministries . . . are at the apex of a vertical system and have corresponding departments or bureaus in the provincial and city governments. These vertical functional systems have a great influence on plan formulation and implementation. In a sense, the ministries resemble holding companies or large, multidivisional, multiplant corporations in the West. Although the corporation is the principal financial, juridical, and accounting unit in the West, in China, the individual enterprises, rather than a ministry, perform those functions. Frequent changes have resulted in a fairly high degree of administrative instability on the national level, but because bureaus and other subministry bodies have often remained essentially intact—still performing many of their basic tasks despite mergers or splits on the ministry level—there has been more continuity in functions and institutions than one might expect.

FORMULATION OF THE ECONOMIC PLAN

The primary goal of central planning is balanced and proportionate growth. The methodology employed in central planning is called comprehensive balance—between state revenue and expenditures, between the supply of and demand for commodities, and between the inflow and outflow of cash. The process involves a two-way vertical movement from the central planning organs down to the enterprises and vice versa.

The national plan is formulated in three stages. In the initial stage, the State Planning Commission issues control figures, based on the long-term plan, to the State Economic Commission. The SEC then formulates yearly control figures and directives and passes them on to the central economic ministries and the provincial economic organs, which in turn issue control figures and directives to their subordinate units. The control figures include (1) the rate of growth for national income, industry, agriculture, transportation, and so on; (2) major industrial and agricultural production quotas; (3) investment in capital construction; (4) distribution of important materials; (5) purchase and allocation of major commodities; (6) state budget and currency issuance; (7) number of new workers; and (8) wages for and prices of major industrial and agricultural products.

To translate these targets into concrete action, the central economic plan includes various subordinate plans: (1) a financial plan dealing with the national budget, accumulation and allocation of capital funds, banking, and credit-monetary flow; (2) a material plan dealing with the allocation and supply of materials, the flow of commodities among various geographic areas and trade organizations, and imports and exports; and (3) a production plan dealing with the temporal allocation of users and the maximization of the rate of growth, including a labor plan and a technological plan.

A major portion of the control figures used initially in plan construction and subsequently as instructions to the operating agencies consists of commodity output targets. How are the particular goods and output targets selected? There is no uniform criterion. In the case of some intermediate goods, such as pig iron, the physical output targets can be deduced from the corresponding targets for end products (e.g., finished steel) under the assumption of fairly stable technical input coefficients. In the case of some final products, such as most essential consumer goods, minimum requirements can be estimated on the basis of the physical needs of the population, modified by export requirements. In the case of a number of final and intermediate goods in chronic short supply, the production targets are set at the level of full capacity production by existing plants. The domestic production targets of some products that use import components as input are set by the availability of those components.

Based on these tentative plans, each business bureau will send compulsory targets to the enterprises under its jurisdiction. Prior to November 1957, the Chinese planning system, following the Soviet model, was highly centralized. There were twelve mandatory targets; total quantitative output of major products, total value of output, total number of employees, new varieties to be trial manufactured, total wage bill, important technical and economic norms, amount of cost reduction, rate of cost reduction, number of manual workers at the end of the year, average wage, labor productivity, and profit. . . .

The number of mandatory targets, like the entire planning system, has varied over time. During the Cultural Revolution, considerable flexibility characterized the planning system, and it is unclear whether the central planners still provided compulsory targets. In 1972, a visitor to the Anshan Iron and Steel Company found that there were six major targets: the output of major products (in physical terms), the value of sales, specified product quality, supply of raw materials and fuels, cost reduction, and profit.

In April 1978. as the central planners resumed tight control over the economy, the CCP Central Committee issued the (Draft) Resolution on Some Problems of Accelerating Industrial Development. The number of control targets was raised to eight: output of major products, variety of product, quality, cost, profit to the state, rate of raw material consumption, labor productivity, and liquid capital. These control targets remained in effect as of the end of 1980.

In the formal planning process, workers and the technical and managerial staffs of the enterprises receive the targets; evaluate the output quotas against production capacity, input requirements, and technological conditions; and map out a concrete plan. Plans submitted by the various enterprises are then aggregated by the business bureaus and transmitted upward to the ministries and the State Economic Commission. The central planners reconcile the enterprises' input requests, using certain goods with output assignments of firms producing those goods to ensure a balance between supply and demand. The method used is the Soviet "material balance" approach. A balance sheet must be drawn up for each of the approximately 200 key materials under unified distribution by the state. The two sides of a material balance are supposed to be estimated separately. The supply side represents the planner's best estimate of what each plant may be capable of producing, and the demand side is based on the material input norms (technical coefficients) the central planners regard as feasible for the enterprises. If the demand and supply sides balance, the consistency problem has been solved for that particular commodity or industry; if the two sides are unbalanced, adjustments must be made. The balancing task is often tedious and time-consuming. The whole process of drafting the annual plan therefore entails some tough bargaining concerning input norms between planning organs and enterprises. Because this bargaining takes time, annual plans have often been promulgated in final form only after the start of the planning year.

After the balance between the input and output of various industries has been worked out, a final plan will be approved by the State Council, the Central Committee of the Communist Party, and, in a purely formal sense, by the National People's Congress or its Standing Committee before the plan becomes the law of the land. Each enterprise and department has the obligation to implement the plan and to fulfill the quotas assigned.

In the planning process, there is an inherent conflict between planning organs and enterprises. Planners have a strong interest in economizing on raw materials and in guaranteeing that output will be maximized per unit of raw materials used. Often planners tend to set "tight" norms in the preliminary plans that are sent down to the enterprises. Enterprises, on the other hand, want to protect themselves against the risk of not fulfilling the output plan and thus have a strong tendency to demand low output quotas and high input requests. Moreover, plan formulation involves a process of aggregation and disaggregation. The commands of the central planners must be disaggregated so as to become meaningful to the individual producers. Yet the production plans of each individual producer are beyond the limited comprehension of the central planners until they are aggregated and presented to the central planners by the ministry. This process inevitably results in distortions. Final plans may be out of balance in that the aggregate may balance, but its components may not. This problem is particularly keen in China, where the territory is vast and economic conditions vary widely. . . .

IMPLEMENTATION OF THE PLAN

At the heart of central control is the direct distribution of key intermediate inputs and important capital goods to individual enterprises in accordance with the plant targets. The number of items subject to unified distribution rose quite rapidly during the First Five-Year Plan. . . . Materials under unified distribution could not be purchased on the market. Through the allocation of inputs, the central authorities hoped to guide production activities. This method, however, created contradictions between output targets and input requirements, and in many cases, the input allocated by the center was inadequate. Under the impact of decentralization in industrial management, the number of items subject to centralized allocation was reduced to 132 in 1959. Although there is no information on the precise number after 1959, visitors to China in 1972 estimated that there were probably 100 to 200 items under central control. In March 1980, an official source mentioned 100 major industrial products in the state plan. Adding agricultural products to that number, the total number of items subject to centralized allocation must have been around 120 in mid-1980.

Although central planners regard the central allocation of key materials as an effective way to force individual plants to comply with state plans, the central government has often been unable to maintain a firm grip on the distribution of even the most important raw materials. The barter system has prevailed between cities and between enterprises. The situation was particularly severe during the Great Leap Forward and the Cultural Revolution, when central control was loose. In recent years, exchanges of major materials among individual plants have become a common practice, which, according to official reports, has severely "affected the fulfillment of the state production plan, undermined the Party's economic policy, and impeded socialist marketing."

To back up administrative and physical controls, an elaborate system of financial controls was also initiated during the 1950s. Starting in 1950, all state enterprises had to conduct their business with other similar units through the People's Bank of China. All transactions were to be cleared through the bank, and only minor operations could be financed by currency. Copies of all contracts involving any unit within the system had to be deposited with the bank, so that it could act as the government's watchdog in making payments and could play a role corresponding to that of the controller of a giant Western corporation. . . .

The financial control system, like the other control mechanisms, was not as effective as expected, and after the 1958 decentralization, there was a considerable volume of investment financed out of extrabudgetary funds. In 1958, local authorities were encouraged to use their initiative to provide funds for above-plan investment by diversion of funds from other uses. Investment from extrabudgetary funds had amounted to only 4 percent of the investment from budget in 1957, but it rose sharply to 23 percent in 1958 and 19 percent in 1959. Many enterprises also diverted working capital from bank loans for various unauthorized purposes, such as covering the losses of the enterprise, paying wages for extra workers, and so on. During the Cultural Revolution, the control function of the People's Bank was further curtailed. In more recent years, the People's Bank has been concerned only with wage funds and a part of the capital construction investment, and it has played only an insignificant role in enterprise operations. . . .

PROBLEMS AND PROSPECTS

Despite the fact that China has had a central planning system since 1953, a highly centralized command system has never been fully put into effect, and the performance of the planning system during the past twenty-eight years has proved to be mixed. The central planning system has achieved two significant goals: a high rate of capital formation and a more balanced spatial allocation of investment resources. In the pre-World War II years, China's rate of investment (i.e., gross domestic capital formation as a percentage of gross domestic product) averaged only 5 percent in terms of 1933 prices and 7.5 percent in terms of 1952 prices. As a result of the central allocation of financial and physical resources, the rate of investment in the 1952–1957 period rose to 18.2 percent in 1933 prices and 24 percent in 1952 prices. The central planning system enabled the government to allocate larger portions of current output for accumulation, and from 1959 to 1960, the accumulation rate reached 40 percent of national income. The average accumulation rate from 1970 to 1978 was more than 31 percent, and in 1978, it reached 36.6 percent. In view of the extremely low per capita income, these accumulation rates are exceedingly high.

The guiding principle concerning consumption and investment as expounded by Bo Yipo, former chairman of the State Economic Committee, was that the rate of increase in people's consumption should be less than that of social output and should also be lower than the rate of increase in accumulation. . . . Without a central planning system, such a high rate of capital formation would have been impossible.

Moreover, the centralized economic planning and budgetary processes enabled the central authorities to constantly transfer income and wealth from the well-developed provinces to the backward areas, thus reducing the degree of interprovincial inequality. Under the centrally controlled financial system, the maximum level of expenditures permitted in each province is determined by the central government. After estimating the total revenues available to each province, the central government then calculates a revenue remission rate for each province. This rate is set so that each province will have just enough revenue to finance the initially determined level of expenditure. Because of the central government's commitment to reducing regional inequality, backward provinces typically have low remission rates, or may even retain all of their revenues and receive additional subsidies, while the more prosperous provinces are allowed to spend only a small portion of their revenues, the rest being remitted to the central government. In 1955, the five developed provinces (Sichuan, Jiangsu, Zhejiang, Shandong, and Guangdong) were required to remit some

60 percent of their revenues, and the five less developed provinces (Qinghai, Xizang, Gansu, Xinjiang, and Nei Monggol) retained all of their revenues and received additional subsidies from the central government. This system has generated a far-reaching redistributive effect in interregional economic development.

The system also became the source of increasing economic inefficiency, however. This was due both to the difficulties inherent in all central planning and management systems and to the size, diversity, and backwardness of the Chinese economy. When China began its central planning in 1953, each of its twenty-one provinces had more people than all but a handful of the other developing nations. In the 1950s, China had more than 100,000 individual industrial firms. In 1979, the number of state-owned and collective-owned enterprises had increased to 350,000, but the enterprises differed widely in technology, scale of operation, and efficiency. Consequently, the central ministries could not manage their geographically far-flung empires with any single set of technical coefficients as the foundation of the material balance. The rudimentary level on which accounts were kept and the lack of vital statistics prevented the formulation of realistic and comprehensive plans.

The leadership of the Chinese Communist Party was in no better shape. Most of those in charge of planning and economic administration had become leaders during the period of guerrilla warfare in the 1930s and lacked any training in planning and management. In 1955, for example, less than 6 percent of the leadership personnel (plant managers and the like) had a university or an equivalent level of technical education. A more recent official investigation revealed that in some provinces in 1980, none of the leaders on the prefectural and county levels were university or college graduates, and few of the leaders were capable of handling scientific, technical, or managerial matters. In many enterprises, only one or two leaders had a good command of production and planning techniques.

As of 1980, implementation of the central plan was still impeded by several factors: the inability of the central planners to formulate economic plans ahead of the planned period, the absence of horizontal coordination of the plans, and the promotion of self-reliance and self-sufficiency. To serve as an effective guide for the national economy, an economic plan must be formulated ahead of the planned period and must demonstrate a high degree of consistency. The Chinese experience in the past three decades has breached those requirements. . . .

During the tumultuous years of 1967–1969, most of the bureaucrats in charge of planning and economic administration were purged, and it was not possible to implement any long-term planning. . . . This background indicates that long- and medium-term plans have played a rather limited role in shaping the Chinese economy. In most years, the Chinese planning system has concentrated on annual plans, but even the annual plans have not been ready at the beginning of the year. This delay suggests that for most of a period, individual enterprises have operated without a nationally integrated economic plan.

The absence of horizontal coordination of economic plans on a regional basis has been a frequent source of inefficiency and waste. It was quite common for both a central government ministry and a local government to construct factories in the same area to use local raw materials. Since there was no effective means of coordinating these projects, they competed for the same materials. As a result, both factories operated below capacity. A similar lack of horizontal coordination has also existed in national supply planning. . . .

The promotion of regional self-sufficiency during the Great Leap Forward and the Cultural Revolution also conflicted with overall planning. Under the principle of self-sufficiency, local authorities tended to ignore the central plan and to pursue local interests. One typical example was the reduction of acreage for cotton and cash plants in order to concentrate on food grain production for local consumption, regardless of the local natural endowment. This kind of problem made it very difficult to achieve material balance on a national scale. At the same time, self-reliance implies the ability to improvise out of one's own resources rather than rely on planned coordination and state investment grants. In recent decades, enterprise expansion has no longer relied on budget appropriations of capital but has mostly resulted from the plowing back of profits or from the diversion of working capital. The economy was leading toward what Audrey Donnithorne has called a "cellular economy"—one consisting of numerous small, self-sufficient units without a unified national plan.

The entire command structure was severely weakened when most members of the experienced economic elite in the fields of planning and administration were purged during the Cultural Revolution. . . . The loss of the services of those experienced experts had a devastating effect on the central planning system. . . .

PROPOSALS FOR REFORM

The post-Mao leaders have deemed it necessary to transform the semiplanned, semianarchist state into a fully planned state, and strenuous efforts have been made to restore the planning structure and control mechanisms since Deng Xiaoping regained power in July 1977. . . .

The second major reform was the enlargement of the decision-making power of individual enterprises. For three decades, the central departments had imposed rigid norms and regulations on regions and individual enterprises for output, funds, machinery and equipment, marketing, and salaries and wages. The state had not only drawn up production plans, supplied materials, and marketed the products, but it had also taken most of the enterprises' profits and had made up their losses. Consequently, an enterprise's success or failure had had no direct bearing on the economic welfare of the enterprise or its staff and workers. In 1978, more than a quarter of the state enterprises had suffered a loss. To promote management efficiency, experimental reforms were first introduced in 100 industrial enterprises in Sichuan Province and soon extended to 6,600 different types of enterprises in all parts of the country, which contributed 45 percent of the nation's total industrial output value in 1979.

In mid-1979, the State Council issued five directives that formally granted selected state-owned enterprises the right to (1) draw up their own production plans and sell above-quota output directly to other units; (2) retain 5 percent of their assigned profits and 20 percent of their extra profits after state quotas had been fulfilled; (3) promote workers according to the principle of "more pay for more work" and control their own welfare and bonus funds; (4) receive bank loans for investment; and (5) negotiate directly with foreign companies and retain a share of their foreign exchange earnings.

Another new thrust in the same direction was the issuance of bank loans to replace state budget appropriations for capital investment. In the past, all capital construction projects, once approved by the state, had been automatically financed by state budget. That system had caused a great waste of capital and an undue prolongation of the construction period. Between July 1979 and early 1980, 150 capital construction projects were undertaken solely with bank loans. In 1980, textile, power, tourism, metallurgical, building materials, machine-building, and light industries in Shanghai and in eleven provinces were experimenting with the new system. Funds derived from bank loans accounted for 30 percent of the investment in capital construction in Hubei Province and 28 percent of such investment in Fujian Province. Eventually, all capital investment will shift to bank loans.

All these experimental plans seem to have one goal in common: to abolish the highly centralized planning and management system, which seriously shackles the initiative of managers and workers, and to build a system that combines central planning with a market mechanism similar to the market socialism of Yugoslavia and some Eastern European Communist states.

Unit VII

_____ Bureaucracy _____

If the bureaucracies of China and Japan have long histories, so too does the struggle against bureaucratism. In China, this struggle dates back to the time of Confucius, whose instructions on good government included an admonishment to government officials to be responsive to the needs and demands of the people or risk losing their right to rule. In Japan, the idea of the divine nature of the emperor precluded such "practical" philosophies. However, since the end of the war several Japanese political parties, most notably the Komeito, or Clean Government Party, have pressed hard for bureaucratic reform and an end to bureaucratic corruption. The limited influence of such parties testifies to the fact that Japanese bureaucrats enjoy much higher prestige than do their counterparts in China. In fact, Japanese bureaucrats are considered by many to be the most efficient and responsive in the world. And, indeed, the Japanese bureaucracy has for the most part managed to avoid the problems of inefficiency, waste, and ineffectiveness that have plagued China's bureaucracy.

Throughout his political career, Mao Zedong was obsessed with the idea of building a responsive and politically loyal bureaucracy. Mao conducted frequent campaigns and purges of the bureaucracy in an effort to combat sloth, waste, corruption, inefficiency, and political conservatism. He used similar campaigns to combat his political opposition. More often than not, however, these methods only served to make a bad situation worse. As the risks in bureaucratic life increased, so too did the caution and conservatism of the Chinese bureaucracy. Bureaucrats became increasingly protective of their territories. To shield themselves from the vicissitudes of political life, many sought political alliances through patron-client ties. These clientelist networks, which can reach from the highest level of government down to the lowest, form the basis for factional cleavages within the Chinese leadership and play an important, if not fully understood, role in the political and policy-making processes. Furthermore, innovation and criticism of problems in administration were stifled by fears of being targeted in future campaigns.

Mao's efforts to remold Chinese bureaucrats culminated in 1966 with the Great Proletarian Cultural Revolution. Many bureaucrats were purged from their posts and sent to "May 7th Cadre Schools" for ideological reeducation. Today, many of those same cadres are returning to their former posts in the state and party administrations. Unfortunately, these posts did not go vacant during the turmoil of the Cultural Revolution decade. Mao and his supporters appointed and promoted members of their faction to all levels of the bureaucracy so that in many ministries and departments today, former enemies must share desks. An upcoming purge planned by the present leadership is expected to replace any politically unreliable or disloyal appointees with rehabilitated or new cadres.

The cleavages that divide present-day bureaucrats are factional as well as ideological. There are factional divisions even within the Deng leadership. However, ideological divisions do play a much greater role in creating political cleavages in China than they do in Japan or the United States. Generational conflict is also a problem. Many Chinese bureaucrats remain in their posts until a very old age, which tends to frustrate the ambitions of some of the younger cadres. Clearly, it will not be easy to reform the existing system. The sheer size of the civil service alone, 20 million people at five levels of government, makes efforts to formulate new reform policies even more difficult. Yet, Deng and his supporters are determined to reform the state administration and to raise the prestige, morale, and technical expertise of its bureaucrats.

Bureaucrats in Japan do not suffer from low morale or low prestige. Although recruited from all the top schools in the nation, Japanese bureaucrats are drawn predominantly from the Law Faculty at Tokyo University. Recruitment to a ministry occurs through a rigorous selection process in which inductees are required to pass difficult civil service examinations in competition with others in their own "class," usually individuals of similar age and experience. It is the extraordinary selectivity of the Japanese bureaucracy that accounts for much of its uniqueness. The training process for civil servants is equally rigorous and excellence is demanded at each stage. Consequently, Japanese bureaucrats tend to be well read and extremely well versed in all areas of government policy. Moreover, shared experiences and values tend to forge a cohesive bond among civil servants and frequently co-workers are given promotions at the same time.

Part of the explanation for the excellence of the Japanese bureaucracy lies in its high status, which is a result of both its successful management of Japan's economic "miracle" and its selectivity. Moreover, the limited policymaking role of politicians and the relative weakness of competing institutions such as the judiciary and local governments further enhances this status. Still, most important in explaining Japan's avoidance of bureaucratism is the practice of *amakaduri*. This policy requires that all bureaucrats must retire at age 55, a frightening prospect for Chinese leaders. Many bureaucrats must retire even earlier if a member of their recruitment group is promoted to a level beyond that of the other group members. Usually, retired bureaucrats move to positions in private business, where their bureaucratic connections and experience are highly valued. For this reason, most bureaucrats want to maintain close and cooperative relations with their peers in order to benefit their new employers. This also helps promote cooperation and excellence within the bureaucracy.

In "China's Economic Bureaucracy," Michel Oksenberg discusses the impact of recent reforms on bureaucratic management methods. He focuses particularly on the structure of the Chinese bureaucracy, the characteristics of the bureaucracy that influence economic planning, and some of the problems that represent major obstacles to current bureaucratic reform efforts.

Two selections by Chalmers Johnson, "The Japanese Bureaucracy" and "Japan's Economic Bureaucracy," focus on various aspects of the Japanese bureaucracy. Johnson argues that despite its enormous power, Japan's bureaucracy is not "bureaucratic" but rather efficient, prestigious, and dynamic. Johnson points to several factors in explaining how the Japanese have managed to avoid bureaucratism—informal norms, such as school, family, and regional ties, which inspire loyalty, ease communications, and generate new ideas; tradition; and, most important, *amakaduri,* the mandatory retirement of all civil servants at age 55.

29

China's Economic Bureaucracy

Michel Oksenberg

In these excerpts from an article that originally appeared in *The China Business Review,* Oksenberg discusses some of the recent reforms in the Chinese bureaucracy. The present leadership is seeking to create a more efficient, durable, and technologically proficient government bureaucracy. Although the number of ministries and personnel has been reduced and there is evidence of greater consensus on goals than during the Cultural Revolution, a number of serious problems remain to be solved.

The most significant obstacle to bureaucratic reform is the problem of personnel. China has approximately 20 million civil servants at 5 levels of the state administration. The Cultural Revolution left few bureaucrats untouched. Personnel are factionalized. Much of the power within the state administration is still in the hands of individual faction leaders rather than in the bureaucratic institutions. Unreliable statistics and discipline problems are two results of factionalism. Interagency competition is another. Oksenberg argues that with problems such as these, bureaucratic reform must remain an ongoing policy.

In February 1982, the Chinese leadership began to restructure the State Council and its ministries, reduce the number of government personnel at all levels of the central and provincial bureaucracy, crack down on corruption, and complete the drafting process for a new state constitution. The leadership intends to shape a more efficient, durable, technologically proficient government. Among the principal changes now under way:

- The number of ministries and ministry-level agencies under the State Council is being reduced from 98 to 52.
- The number of personnel staffing State Council bureaucracies is being reduced from 49,000 to 32,000.
- Officials above the age of 60 (65 if a minister or vice-minister) are to retire. Equally significant, officials who gained their positions through their rebellious behavior during the Cultural Revolution or through affiliation with Lin Biao or Jiang Qing are to be dismissed. . . .

To be sure, considerable time must pass before the full consequences of the changes can be assessed. In China, as elsewhere, bureaucratic reform is more easily proclaimed than implemented. Indeed, some of the changes appear more sweeping than in fact is the case. For example, the merger of the Ministry of Commerce and the All China Supply and Marketing Cooperative brings together two agencies that were merged once before and still share the same building. The actual reduction in personnel may end being less than implied, if older officials become "advisors," for example.

Nonetheless, a major effort is under way to make the Chinese system more effective. In some ways, the reforms entailing major personnel shifts—that Deng Xiaoping, Premier Zhao Ziyang, and Party Chairman Hu Yaobang have initiated since 1978—will probably be the most difficult to implement. The leadership—no doubt itself divided—recognizes that they are presiding over a faction-ridden, slothful, duplicative, cumbersome bureaucratic apparatus. The effort to invigorate the bureaucracy is neither the first such effort since 1949, nor is it likely to be the last. No nation with 20 million civil servants, working at 5 tiers of government (center, province, special district, county, and commune) can escape bureaucratism. Repeated efforts are necessary to keep Chinese organizations lean and responsive. . . .

LEGACY OF THE CULTURAL REVOLUTION

At the time of Mao's death in 1976, China's top planning agencies lay in total disarray. Few government departments either in Beijing or the provinces had been exempt from the initial terror imposed by marauding Red Guards in 1966–69, and by the subsequent campaigns as "Struggle, Criticism, and Transformation," "One Hit, Three Anti's" and "Criticize Bourgeois Rights."

Scores of top officials had been sent to May 7th Cadre Schools for thought reform. Others, while still officially listed on their organizational rosters, were in humiliating circumstances, forced to reside in "cow sheds" and assigned menial tasks. Gradually, from the early 1970s on, leaders who had been identified as "capitalist roaders" reappeared as rehabilitated officials.

As administrative units regrouped, officials quietly stored memories of previous injustices and lost battles, to be acted upon when the opportunity presented itself. In the typical Party or government agency, tensions ran high. The decade of chaos and turmoil left personal animosity and distrust, hindering cooperation between work units. Exploring ideas and sharing information without fear of retribution were limited to one's most intimate and reliable friends. Rather than breeding ideological cohesion, in short, the external pressures of the Cultural Revolution had splintered each government agency into warring factions staffed by extraordinarily cautious, circumspect, and isolated individuals. As of 1981, the wounds of the tumultuous years had not yet healed.

Power is still vested as much in individuals as in institutions. All attuned bureaucrats that I met were consummate "Pekingologists," closely charting how their chief was doing in the government pecking order. The situation reminds one of Washington in the Nixon, Carter, and Reagan administrations, bureaucrats begin their day turning to read *The Washington Post* and the *New York Times* to see how their bosses fared yesterday against rivals and in the eyes of the president, and how the president fared in the eyes of the press.

A high-level policymaker in Beijing is similar to a patron or sponsor, with many loyal followers and subordinate staffers, who in turn are patrons of lower level groupings. The ravages inflicted on China's administrative structure during the Cultural Revolution deepened the sense of loyalty, mutual obligation, and, given the atmosphere of the times, shared vulnerability that seems to have created the notoriously tight-knit administrative units that puzzle foreign executives who try to get quick answer, or, more commonly, explanations for the lack of answers. . . .

In the summer of 2981 the premier and vice-premiers in charge of the economy were members of the Standing Committee of the State Council, a group that met once a week, usually on Friday afternoon, both to discuss broad policy issues and to resolve particular problems. In the spring of 1982 the government formalized this system by announcing that the committee had been replaced by a new State Council Standing Committee consisting of the premier, two vice-premiers, a secretary general, and ten members with specific responsibilities.

The agenda of these committee meetings, as of mid-1981, was set by the State Council Staff Office. The secretary general of the State Council played a key role in preparing the circulating the documents for the meetings. These documents provided the background for the discussion. If the issue was a large policy issue, then the relevant information may have included statistics generated by the State Statistical Bureau, reports from the field as to how particular units had coped with the problems at hand, and policy analysis prepared either by one of the research offices within the State Council or a research institute within the Chinese Academy of Social Sciences (CASS). The search was for consensus, and, in the absence of agreement, a decision on a difficult issue frequently was postponed. . . .

INSIDE THE STATE COUNCIL

Inside the State Council's Zhongnanhai premises in the august grounds of the Forbidden City, the premier and vice-premiers each have only two or three personal secretaries or administrative assistants. As of mid-1981, they did not provide policy advice. The premier and vice-premiers turned to three places to secure the policy support they needed. First, they drew on a common staff in the Zhongnanhai complex, which included economic specialists. Secondly, commission heads often turned day-to-day management of their commissions over to the ranking vice-commissioner in order to devote time to policy questions. Thirdly, research could be carried out at one of the institutes under the Academy of Social Sciences. In this case, the research team's terms of reference might be set through consultation between the premier and vice-premier, the institute director, and the designated head of the research team.

Large numbers of interagency and interprovincial disputes cascade upon the State Council. In fact, a major structural weakness of the Chinese bureaucracy is the inadequate means for resolving interagency disputes. The SPC [State Planning Commission] and State Economic Commission do act as filters. They are forced to become embroiled in disputes, according to my interview sources, because most interagency differences involve either efforts to alter the plan in midcourse or instances of nonfulfillment of, or noncompliance with, the plan.

In the summer of 1981, if the dispute involved ministries within the jurisdiction of a single commission, then the pertinent commission made an effort to reconcile the differences. But since commissions did not possess line authority over the ministries, they were able to reject commission recommendations and plead their cases before the State Council Standing Committee and its economic staff.

The minister appeared personally to plead his case. To be sure, such appeals carried inherent risk, since the vice-premier whose commission had recommended a remedy sat on the State Council Standing Committee and outranked the petitioning minister. Nonetheless, I sensed that the vice-premiers were overburdened by various interagency disputes, and much negotiation was necessary to resolve them.

With the vice-premiers immersed in energizing the bureaucracy and settling disputes, it was no wonder that they turned to brain trusters and troubleshooters to assist them. . . .

While the economic vice-premiers had distinctive responsibilities, they also shared in many decisions. In a very real sense, many of the most important policies were collective decisions, requiring a high degree of consensus. On some specific decisions, in fact, many agencies had to concur. For example, the importation of machinery from abroad, depending on its value, level of technology, source of funding, and implications for capital construction and the plan, could easily have required the approval of half a dozen agencies. No one figure, not even Deng Xiaoping, was so dominant that he could unilaterally circumvent the process and impose his will.

While our description concentrates on the daily and weekly routine, the policy guidelines which established the parameters for daily activities were decided at Central Party Work Conferences and enunciated in programmatic speeches of the leaders and central directives issued by the Party Central Committee. . . .

The SPC clearly is the first among equals, the commission with the broadest mandate: to formulate and supervise the annual and five-year plans; and to control all financial aggregates, including the money supply, the budget, and the nation's balance of payments. The SPC, in some respects, serves the functions of the US Office of Management and Budget.

Without making all the necessary qualifications, the SPC currently draws up annual production targets for around 300 commodities such as coal, steel, nonferrous metal, lumber, cement, sulfuric acid, and even motor vehicle tires. On January 1 of each year, the responsibility for achieving these target passes to the State Economic Commission. Since its Beijing staff consists of just a few hundred individuals, the SEC must turn for help to the ministries and provinces, which elaborate more detailed plans covering nearly 600 "category two" commodity categories. Local planning bureaus, in turn, plan for over 10,000 "category three" commodities. Because there categories are still rather broad, municipal planning bureaus regularly convene material allocation conferences so that enterprises can get together and write into their purchase and delivery contracts the specific type of, say, cement, bicycle, or industrial boiler that is desired. At least in theory, the system makes it possible for Beijing's "desk-top" planners to communicate their priorities right down to the shop supervisor....

Clusters of bureaus in different commissions and ministries have very similar functions. For example, the SPC, Ministry of Finance, and the State Bureau of Supplies all have energy bureaus, while the various energy ministries such as Coal and Petroleum have planning and capital construction bureaus. Greater informal communications exist among these overlapping bureaus than conventional wisdom acknowledges, at least during the planning process. Indeed, the SPC deliberately staffs its bureaus with personnel from bureaus in other agencies with similar responsibilities, so that any given SPC bureau has personal connections with other agencies. The US Office of Management and Budget employs a similar personnel practice, where officers are drawn from throughout the US government to facilitate interagency understanding....

An even stronger impression I gained was that each agency has its own sense of mission and purpose, or "organizational ideology." On only a very few occasions did I leave an interview doubting that were it not for that agency, the Chinese economy would collapse, that this agency played an indispensable role in maintenance of the economy, be it setting prices, allocating labor, designing and approving capital construction projects, setting the budget, or making the plans. My interviewees were impressive in delineating the turf of their "system" nationwide. The boundaries tended to be expansive, intruding into other chains of command at lower levels. For example, the State Statistical Bureau included in its "system" statistical personnel in other ministries or in factories. It was not unusual, therefore, for me to be assured by the national agency that it was at the apex of a system of several hundred thousand personnel.

While agencies tended to be expansive in identifying their personnel, the tendency was quite the reverse when describing the scope of their responsibilities. An example suffices to make the point. The State General Bureau of Labor is responsible for, among other things, securing employment for urban middle school graduates. When asked whether unemployed youth existed in Shanghai, however, the bureau's spokesman assured me that the situation was under control, and that few youths were unemployed. When pressed, the spokesman said the bureau's task was to find employment for youths at their place of official registration, or *hu-kou*. To be sure, the official admitted, many youths whose *hu-kou* was in Xinjiang in Northwest China had returned illegally to their family homes in Shanghai. Since employment awaited them if they returned to their locale of official registration in Xinjiang, as far as the Labor Bureau was concerned, they were employed and the bureau had no responsibility for them. The spokesman did admit that from the perspective of Shanghai's municipal leaders who had to deal with the problems of idle youth, an unemployment problem existed. But as far as his agency was concerned, no problem existed. . . .

The single most important factor, which the middle-level bureaucrats implied determined their fate, was the political strength and interest of the premier or vice-premier responsible for their agency. For example, one frustrated bureau chief intimated that his agency was suffering from having a lower ranking vice-premier holding the portfolio of his agency. He saw hope in the signs that a higher ranking vice-premier was taking an interest in the work of his agency, though he despaired that an agency closely affiliated with his own was under yet another vice-premier. Under these circumstances, he doubted sufficient coordination would be achieved in his area. . . .

Personal connections are not the only source of an agency's strength. Its financial resources also are important. Agencies that preside over revenue-producing enterprises speak with greater power than agencies that run chronic deficits. The latter are known as "red" agencies. The ministries of Public Health and Grain, for example, are considered to be "red" agencies. This does not mean "red" agencies inevitably lose when their views conflict with those of revenue-producing agencies; they just labor under a handicap. One example, I discovered, had to do with cigarette smoking. Public Health was convinced of the dangers smoking poses to health, and wished to undertake a range of measures to reduce smoking. But the Ministry of Finance reaps sizable tax revenues from smoking, and the relatively poor provinces of Yunnan and Guizhou make money on tobacco. Against this weight, Public Health lost. This aspect of bureaucratic politics in China, of course, helps explain both the reluctance of agencies to surrender revenue sources and their eagerness to seek additional sources.

LOW CAPACITY TO PLAN

The low capacity of agencies to make accurate plans was particularly revealing. Obviously climatic uncertainties make long-range forecasting difficult in China's predominantly agriculture-based economy. But a more decisive factor limiting the capacity of the leaders to develop accurate plans is inadequate, unreliable statistics on many aspects of the economy. The statistical network is still recovering from the damage of the Cultural Revolution. On the eve of the Cultural Revolution, the professional manpower ceiling of the State Statistical Bureau central office was roughly 400. At its nadir, when made into a section in the Planning Commission, the office had a staff of only 13 or 14 people. After 1971, it expanded to 40—its number at Mao's death. Its ceiling in the summer of 1981 approached 350, and there were plans to keep growing to its pre-Cultural Revolution level. However, since no statisticians had been trained in Chinese universities in the past 15 years, the bureau was unable to fill its available slots, and its actual manpower was about 280. Thus, a group of 280 professionals was expected to direct and monitor the activities of the statisticians in the ministries, provinces, and basic level units. They were struggling valiantly with the challenge, but did not indicate to me that they were fully on top of the problem. In such professional areas as sampling techniques, questionnaire construction, and sophisticated techniques of data control and analysis, recent computer advances in the West were just beginning to be acquired.

Without an extensive capacity to generate its own data, the Statistical Bureau was dependent on the figures supplied it by ministries and the provinces, both of which aggregated statistics from lower levels. But within line agencies, there was an awareness of the softness of some of the data. Indeed, it was not unusual for an entire agency or set of agencies to propagate figures which all knew to be inaccurate. . . .

This situation provides the context for understanding the slogan, "Seek truth from facts." In many ways, the Cultural Revolution greatly intensified the propensity, to put it bluntly, to lie. When survival was at stake, lying was justifiable. It then became a way of life in the bureaucracy, the easy way to escape responsibility.

While quick to admit its problems, the Statistical Bureau believed its figures provided an adequate guide to key economic trends. But policy makers had a different perspective. Those I spoke with believed that they presided over a society reluctant to "seek truth from facts," and that the statistics supplied them were frequently not reliable. Since important decisions could not be based exclusively on quantitative data, they often felt it necessary to dispatch factfinding teams around the country. Draft directives for solving problems could then be tested in a few locales and discussed nationwide, with the feedback altering the directive. (This method, of course, was the preferred process for generating information in the Maoist era.) The investigation and policy formulation process, however, was somewhat protracted, and as much as a year passed between recognition of an incipient problem and articulation of a policy to cope with it. In the interim, the problem could intensify, as happened with excessive capital construction in 1980.

Another factor in Beijing's inability to plan accurately was the imperfect mechanisms of control available to the central government. Plans and orders could be issued, but they were not necessarily obeyed. The excess of capital construction in 1979 and 1980 demonstrated how easily lower level units could divert resources to unauthorized projects. The decentralization measures of 1979 intensified this problem.

For all these reasons, many officials believed China really does not have the capacity to develop reliable five-year plans. Indeed, what pass for five-year plans today are just a few overall targets which are changed, if need be, every year during the five-year period. Annual plans tend to be linear projections of the previous year's trend.

The depredations of the Cultural Revolution certainly made the restoration of China's cumbersome bureaucracy a welcome return to normalcy. Though progress has been made, the government has yet to eliminate the factionalism and reliance on personal ties which the Cultural Revolution intensified. Personal relations remain at the heart of the system. Interagency conflict is rife. Separate organizational ideologies flourish.

Clearly, much has changed since 1976. Most important of all is Deng's pledge for the era: no more campaigns, and no more radical swings between periods of stability and mass campaigns. But further change can be expected if the leadership persists in its effort to build a lean, effective, technologically proficient bureaucracy.

30

The Japanese Bureaucracy

Chalmers Johnson

In these brief excerpts from *Japan's Public Policy Companies,* Chalmers Johnson sheds light on a number of factors which he believes to have contributed most to the success of the Japanese bureaucracy. He argues that the most significant of these is Japan's long experience with bureaucracy, which has taught the Japanese how to anticipate and avoid the evils of bureaucratism.

JAPAN'S BUREAUCRATIC HERITAGE

The modern Japanese state began under an oligarchy, which created and nurtured a powerful bureaucracy to serve its own interests; the common Western device for supervising the state, a parliamentary assembly of representatives of the people, has not yet developed to the point of real effectiveness in Japan. Weber commented that "the level of parliament depends on whether it does not merely discuss great issues but decisively influences them; in other words, its quality depends on whether what happens there matters, or whether parliament is nothing but the unwillingly tolerated rubber stamp of a ruling bureaucracy." Weighted by this standard, the postwar Japanese Diet must be found wanting....

Despite its heritage of strong governmental control and the postwar resurgence of the state bureaucracy, Japan nevertheless does not suffer from the worst excesses of bureaucratism. Instead, it has had a talented and generally respected state administration. How is this anomaly to be explained? Part of the answer lies in Japan's long experience with bureaucracy, its informal norms for dealing with it, the traditions and the high prestige of the bureaucrats themselves, and the existence of potent, if not omnipotent, competitors to the bureaucracy in the political and industrial worlds....

ADVANTAGES IN WEAKNESS

Given the impressive performance of the Japanese economy in the post-war world, the problem for analysts is to explain the unusual capabilities of Japanese governmental institutions, not their limitations. Even their deficiencies, however, may have features that work against bureaucratism.

For example, *amakudari* is caused by early retirement; and forcing all bureaucrats out of their sinecures by age fifty-five inhibits the tendency of lifelong bureaucrats to become rigid and complacent. It also puts them on notice that they must eventually enter and perform in a world that is much less tolerant of the arrogance and the legalistic mentality that often characterize bureaucrats. Further, the need to descend from heaven stimulates bureaucrats to learn new things throughout their active-duty service, which can be salutary, though it can also produce conflicts of interest. . . .

In Japan, the intense competition among established ministries (between the Ministry of Finance and MITI, for example) is legendary, and it undoubtedly contributes to the performance and high esprit de corps of the elite bureaucrats. . . . Advantageous competition among bureaucracies and their extensions may be impossible to institutionalize; but the mere presence of large numbers and overlapping jurisdictions is not in itself a sign of bureaucratism.

Official bureaucracy is the major growth enterprise of the contemporary world. An unintended consequence of virtually every proposed solution to the various problems of the advanced industrial democracies—depletion of resources, technological innovation, environmental protection, and so forth—is more official bureaucracy. This growth is inevitable, given the risks and the size of the investments needed to implement any solutions to such pervasive problems. Japan and societies like it, with their greater experience of and alertness to the evils of bureaucratism, may well outperform societies like the United States, in which there is no natural resistance to bureaucratism.

31

Japan's Economic Bureaucracy

Chalmers Johnson

In this selection, Johnson examines how the Japanese bureaucracy has been shaped and sustained by informal norms, such as school, family, and regional ties, and other practices and traditions that have allowed it to flourish while at the same time avoiding the pitfalls of bureaucratism. Johnson pays particular attention to the practice of *amakaduri,* or early retirement, which he considers to be particularly important in the avoidance of bureaucratism. He contends that because all civil servants know that they must retire to private industry at 55, and because they know that their success will be dependent on the strength of their connections in the bureaucracy, they evidence great loyalty to and cooperation with their fellow-workers. The sense of shared mission that results helps to defuse potential conflicts and promotes a high level of efficiency that spills over into all sectors of society.

Although relations between bureaucrats and politicians are understandably delicate in the Japanese political system, the focus of bureaucratic life is within the ministry itself—and there informal norms and their occasional violation generate real passion. . . . These informal ties sustain an organization's "culture," helping it to function effectively by inspiring loyalty, easing communications problems, socializing newcomers, generating new ideas in the clash of values and so forth. . . . [Moreover,] it is the[se] informal practices and traditions that give life to an organization and that make its formal organization interesting.

[It has been argued] that all human relations in Japanese society are based on four kinds of "factions" (*batsu*): *keibatsu* (family and matrimonial cliques), *kyōdobatsu* (clansmen, or persons from the same locality), *gakubatsu* (school and university classmates), and *zaibatsu* ("factions based on money," an indefinite use of the term that should not be confused with its specific reference to the family-dominated industrial empires, or zaibatsu, of prewar Japan). All of these occur in the bureaucracy, but the first two are of minor significance and can be dealt with speedily.

Evidence of keibatsu can be found in MITI. To cite a few examples, Hatoyama Michio, formerly a physicist in MITI's Industrial Technology Institute and after retirement head of Sony's technical department, is married to the second daughter of former Prime Minister Hatoyama Ichirō. The wife of Takashima Setsuo, who retired from MITI in 1969 after serving as vice-minister of the Economic Planning Agency, is the daughter of Kuroda Nagamichi, a former Imperial chamberlain. And Masuda Minoru, director-general of MITI's Natural Resources and Energy Agency in 1975, became a nephew through marriage of Nagano Shigeo, former president of Fuji Steel and one of the great industrial leaders of postwar Japan. Many other examples could be cited. . . .

These connections and possible influences are important in Japan, and they are not necessarily accidental. A great many young bureaucrats ask their section chiefs to arrange their marriages, and a section chief will often have keibatsu considerations in mind when he promotes a match. Nonetheless, most informed observers conclude that keibatsu is not as important in the postwar bureaucracy as it was before the war. Still, some MITI officials report that it is better for one's career to have a good keibatsu than a poor one, and Kubota notes that "on the average the 1949–1959 higher civil servants [the group that he studied in depth] more often had prominent fathers-in-law than prominent fathers." It appears that bureaucrats in Japan are good catches as husbands.

Kyōdobatsu are similarly present among bureaucrats but of comparatively slight influence. A former MITI vice-minister, Tokunaga Hisatsugu (executive director of New Japan Steel after retirement), notes that when he was vice-minister, the minister was Ishii Mitsujirō, one of the major figures of postwar conservative politics. Ishii was not only his "senior" (sempai), but they both came from the same area of Fukuoka prefecture—that is, they both belong to what is called the same kyōtō (literally, "village party"). . . . The career of Kogane Yoshiteru, a major figure in the prewar Ministry of Commerce and Industry and an ex-MITI bureaucrat turned politician in the Diet during the 1950's and 1960's, illustrates both keibatsu and kyōdobatsu. He was born in 1898 into a commoner family in Odawara, Kanagawa prefecture, but as a young official he married the daughter of the sister of Mori Kaku's wife and thereby acquired the prewar secretary-general of the Seiyūkai party as his uncle. Through this connection and his background as a native of Kanagawa, he later succeeded to Mori's secure constituency in the Kanagawa third electoral district, which he represented in the Diet for about twenty years.

Keibatsu and kyōdobatsu are part of any large Japanese organization, but gakubatsu is without question the single most important influence within the Japanese state bureaucracy. The cliques of university classmates are inseparable from bureaucratic life, because it is their university degrees and their success in passing the Higher-level Public Officials Examination that set bureaucrats apart from other elites in the society. Gakubatsu also forms the most pervasive "old boy" network throughout the society as a whole. . . .

State bureaucrats in Japan retire early from government service and then obtain new employment in big business, public corporations, or politics. This practice is obviously open to abuse, and many Japanese commentators have charged that it has been abused. MITI reporters, for example, argue that a wise bureaucrat will use his years as a section chief to generate new ideas and put pressure on the business community to adopt them, but that as a bureau chief he should become submissive toward the ministry's clients with a view to enhancing his own amakudari. . . .

Actual corruption among higher officials in Japan has occurred but is uncommon. In general, the Japanese public places greater trust in the honesty of state officials than in the honesty of politicians or business leaders. Such petty corruption as does occur—gifts from business, golf club fees, dinner parties, junkets—is more common among noncareer officials than among the higher bureaucrats, and was more common in the period of shortages in the 1950's than in later years. When such incidents do involve higher officials, the press and public are quick to condemn them. . . .

The serious issue in Japan is not the occasional abuse of office by a higher official but a pattern of cooperation between the government and big business that may have unintended consequences. Throughout its modern history Japan has experienced a series of major governmental corruption scandals, the most famous of which are the Siemens case of 1914, the Yawata state steel works case of 1918, the Teijin case of 1934, the Shōwa Denkō case of 1948, the shipbuilding bribery case of 1954, the Tanaka "money politics" case of 1974, and the Lockheed case of 1976. These are only the most sensational; numerous others have occurred, and four resulted in the fall of governments. . . .

The reemployment of retired government bureaucrats on the boards of industries currently designated as economically strategic also creates many opportunities for hand-in-glove relationships. . . .

Thus one reason for the private sector's participation in amakudari is the extensive licensing and approval authority (kyoninkaken) of the government. Companies believe that having former bureaucrats among their executives can facilitate obtaining licenses from the ministries. . . .

Preferential access to the government for the strategic industries in Japan is not an unintended consequence of the developmental state; it is in fact an objective of the developmental state. This is the true significance of amakudari. A cost of the system is occasional misuse of access to gain some private advantage. Nonetheless, from the Japanese point of view, the advantages of amakudari for smooth policy formulation and execution outweigh this cost. The Japanese refer to consultations between ex-bureaucrat seniors and their incumbent juniors as "digging around the roots" (*nemawashi*), that is, preparing the groundwork for a government-business decision. To outsiders it often looks like "consensus." . . .

The Japanese government-business relationship does not always work as smoothly as it appears to on the surface. A major check to its effectiveness, one that often alters the various relationships within the establishment in unforeseen ways, is competition among ministries—what the Japanese call "sectionalism." Some observers believe that it is the most important characteristic of the Japanese government, either limiting its potential effectiveness or mitigating its enormous powers. To judge by the Japanese term commonly used to describe it—*gunyamu kakkyo* (the rivalry of local barons)—one would think that the Japanese believe sectionalism is an inheritance from the samurai era. Certainly one demonstrable cause of sectionalism was the Meiji Constitution of 1889, with its provisions for "independent responsibility to the throne," meaning that ministers and their ministries were not accountable to the prime minister, the cabinet, or the Diet, but only to the Emperor—and hence to no one but themselves. The drafter's intent was to prevent rivals to the oligarchs from coming to power and using the government against them, but the actual result was numerous instances in which the military ministries used their radical independence to defy all authority. And many scholars believe that the lack of coordination between the army, the navy, and the rest of the government during the Pacific War was a major cause of Japan's overwhelming defeat. . . .

Japanese analysts usually characterize the basic outlook of MITI officials as "nationalistic." Kakuma observes that they like to use expressions such as *jōi* (expulsion of the foreigners) and *iteki* (barbarians) that date from the last decades of the Tokungawa shogunate. They see their function in life as the protection of Japanese industries from "foreign pressure." . . . Nagai Yōnosuke sees still another historical parallel: "With its self-assertiveness, its strong native nationalism, its loyalist posture, . . . and its terrific 'workism,' MITI reminds us of the General Staff Office of the defunct army." Whatever its roots, MITI's "spirit" has become legendary.

Unit VIII

———— Industrial Policy ————

Industrial policy in China and Japan provides a startling contrast in terms of levels of development, history, and future capabilities. Economically, the two countries could not be further apart. Japan now has the second highest per capita income in the world and is expected to surpass U.S. levels sometime in the 1990s. China, on the other hand, is struggling to reform its economic system in order to bring standards of living that have been stagnant for several decades up to a respectable level. To a certain extent, the gap between China and Japan can be explained in terms of the alternative methods the two countries have used to manage their industries.

In Japan, the process of industrialization began in the late nineteenth century. As a resource-poor, technologically backward nation, Japan found competition with already developed Western nations extremely difficult. Leaders of the Meiji Restoration recognized the need for comprehensive planning if Japan was to catch up with Western states. This "developmental" perspective capitalized on feudal patterns of paternalism, cultural homogeneity, and social harmony. Out of this perspective arose a conception of the corporation that differs strikingly from European and American thinking.

Japanese companies reflect the emphasis on consensus, the group, and social harmony that characterizes Japanese society and culture. Profits are considered together with long-term objectives as a basis for economic planning. Loyalty to the company is encouraged through the policies of age seniority and permanent employment. Low differentiation among different ranks of employees, cooperation between management and labor, and an increased role for employees in the decision-making and quality control processes are distinctive features of the Japanese company.

China's system of industrial management is significantly different from that of Japan, although recent reforms have drawn somewhat on the Japanese model. The most important feature of China's economy is, of course, that it is centrally planned. The experience of planned economies has shown that problems of efficiency, stagnating growth, declining productivity, quality, and innovation are common. China is certainly no exception. Additionally, political conflicts like the Cultural Revolution have exacerbated economic problems and made reform of the economic administrative system an urgent issue. Reforms since 1978 have attempted to address these problems.

The basic objective of these reforms is to expand production by reducing the role of the state in economic activity and by giving greater play to market forces. Therefore, planning decisions have been decentralized, profit retention has been increased, commercial contracts among enterprises have been expanded, and managers' authority over administrative and personnel decisions has been improved. In financial planning, state subsidies have become less important while loans from banks have increased in importance. Wages and bonuses have replaced ideological exhortations as an incentive for improved worker performance.

Naturally, there are groups in China which are opposed to such reforms. Heavy industry, long a favorite of central planners, has suffered greatly under austerity measures and investment reorientation. Bureaucrats now find themselves in less control of enterprise managers. Political purists object to the use of capitalist methods in their socialist motherland. Although some recentralization has been indicated, due largely to an explosion of construction financed by retained profits, the most recent pronouncements from Premier Zhao Ziyang suggest a much wider reform effort and a further evolution of reform policies. Still, problems in energy, transport, population, and employment seem destined to remain important in the short term.

This unit focuses on industrial policy in China and Japan, and considers the nature and impact of these policies on economic performance in each country. In "Industrial Modernization in China," Chu-yuan Cheng details recent efforts on the part of the Chinese leadership to modernize China's industrial system and to expand its productive capacity.

Four selections from *The Chinese Business Review* examine various aspects of Chinese industrial policy. The first, titled "The Problem of Partial Reform," by Susan L. Shirk and James B. Stepanek, describes the major economic reforms initiated by the Chinese leadership since 1978, and considers how these reforms are changing the character of the Chinese economy and in some cases creating additional problems. In "The Profit System," Barry Naughton examines the various profit schemes that lie at the heart of China's recent industrial reforms, arguing that the major accomplishment of the Chinese reform movement is that it has continued to move forward despite the emergence of many new problems. Andrew G. Walder discusses China's mounting labor problems in "Rice Bowl Reforms," and describes some of the shortcomings of wage policies aimed at linking pay to worker performance. Finally, in "Bureaucratic Competition," Susan Shirk describes how China's current economic policies have increased competition throughout the economy and led to bureaucratic warfare among rival industries.

In "The Twenty-First Century Capitalists," Frank Gibney identifies several social and economic factors which he considers important in explaining how Japan has been able to achieve such spectacular economic growth while at the same time preserving its social stability. Ezra Vogel examines the origin of the modern Japanese corporation in "The Large Company: Identification and Performance," pointing out that although Japan still faces problems in a number of areas, the cooperative environment that exists between labor and management in large Japanese firms suggests that the sacrifices necessary to resolve these problems can and will be made.

32

Industrial Modernization in China

Chu-yuan Cheng

A fundamental objective of recent reforms in Chinese industrial policy is the expansion of productive capacity. However, to achieve this objective requires a basic restructuring of industrial management. In this selection, Cheng argues that overcentralization in management decision making and planning ignores too many microeconomic processes, prevents horizontal linkages among enterprises, and inhibits initiative. Because of irrationalities (for example, supply shortages) arising from the plan, enterprises attempt to produce all necessary inputs. Current reforms aim at decentralizing the decision-making process, merging enterprises in order to avoid the "comprehensive" tendency mentioned above, and freeing more supplies form state administration. Specific reforms include more autonomy in planning at the enterprise level, profit retention for enterprises, greater control over personnel decisions for managers, and financing of expansion through bank loans. Not surprisingly, these reforms are encountering resistance from bureaucrats, planners, and subsidized industries. Price irrationalities render profits meaningless as a standard of efficiency, and bottlenecks in energy and transportation as well as unemployment continue to pose serious problems.

REVAMPING INDUSTRIAL MANAGEMENT

Apart from the expansion of productive capacity, the modernization plan hinges on the restructuring of the management and control system. Thus far, China's industry has been operating considerably below its potential, because of deep-seated organizational shortcomings. As Fang Weizhong, vice chairman of the State Planning Commission, commented:

> The system involves three basic defects: first, the mandatory plans from the top mummify extremely complicated economic activities; second, the management of economic affairs through an administrative system and by administrative fiat severs intrinsic economic links and excludes the use of appropriate

economic means, creating great waste in time and materials; third, without the power to make decisions, enterprises are bound hand and foot and employee initiative and enthusiasm are stifled.

To remedy these defects, corrective measures have been adopted in the past two years. The first major attempt to streamline the industrial structure centered around revamping industrial organization. Recently, most industrial establishments have been small but comprehensive or self-reliant enterprises, leading to tremendous duplication. These comprehensive enterprises have prevented specialization, standardization, serialization, and other hallmarks of modern industry. According to the latest reform, small enterprises of various types are to be amalgamated into specialized companies, with a major enterprise as the core....

The second major reform is the granting of decision-making power to individual enterprises. Over the past three decades, the central departments imposed rigid norms and regulations on regions and individual enterprises for output, funds, machinery and equipment, marketing, salaries and wages. The state not only set production plans, supplied materials, marketed the products; it also took away most of the enterprise's profits and made up its losses. Consequently, the success or failure of an enterprise had no direct bearing on the economic welfare of the enterprise itself, or its staff and workers. In 1978, more than one-fourth of the state enterprises operated at a loss. To promote management efficiency, an experiment in expanding enterprise autonomy was first introduced to 100 industrial and transportation enterprises in Sichuan Province. The experimentation was soon extended to 3,300 different types of enterprises in all parts of the country.

In mid-1979, the State Council issued five directives that formally granted selected state-owned enterprises the right to: (1) draw up their own production plans and sell above-quota output directly to other units; (2) retain 5 percent of their assigned profits and 20 percent of their extra profits after state quotas are fulfilled; (3) promote workers according to the principle of "more pay for more work" and control their own welfare and bonus funds; (4) receive bank loans for investment; and (5) negotiate directly with foreign companies and retain a share of their foreign exchange earnings.

In addition to organizational reforms, the restructuring process also involves changes in material management. Under the old system, all capital goods and intermediate goods were classified into three categories according to the levels of administration: those distributed by the state, those controlled by the ministries and those controlled by local government. The system created unnecessary red tape and proved to be inflexible and inefficient. The new system reclassified all capital goods and intermediate goods into those distributed under state plans, those to be sold by supplies enterprises and those to be used by productive enterprises. Vital materials and equipment, like fuel and major machinery, are still subject to state-planned distribution, but the producing enterprises can now sell part of their products to customers. For secondary capital goods and materials, like bearings, tools, chemical products, metallic materials and construction materials, the producing enterprises (after fulfilling contracts) may sell any surplus in the market. All materials not in the first two groups are available for production and sale. The new reform represents a major step in the building of a capital goods market.

Another thrust in the same direction is the issue of bank loans to replace state budget appropriations for capital investment. In the past, all state-approved construction projects were automatically financed by state budget. The system caused great waste in capital and undue prolongation of the construction period. Since the second half of 1979, 150 capital construction projects have been undertaken solely with bank loans. In 1980, textile, power, tourism, metallurgical, building materials, machine-building and light industries in Shanghai and 11 other provinces are experimenting with the new system. Funds derived from bank loans now account for 30 percnet of the investment in capital construction in Hubei Province and 28 percent in Fujian Province. Eventually, all capital investment will shift to bank loans.

All these experimental plans have one common goal: to abolish the highly centralized management system, which seriously shackles the initiative of managers and workers, and to build a system that combines central planning with a market mechanism similar to the market socialism in Yugoslavia.

PROBLEMS AND PROSPECTS

The program of readjustment and restructuring has achieved mixed results in the 18 months. While the industrial structure and management system are moving toward rationalization, the industrial modernization program has apparently encountered many barriers.

The curtailment of capital formation and construction has not been progressing smoothly. As noted in the party newspaper *Renmin Ribao,* (People's Daily)

> Many departments and areas have started projects that should not have been started; refused to suspend those projects that should have been discontinued ("dismount from the horse but do not loosen the saddle"). Some feared that cutting down accumulation and curtailing capital construction would make it possible to expand production. Others feared that readjustment might affect the speed of economic development.

Consequently, although investment covered by the state budget in 1979 remained unchanged from that for 1978, investment made by various departments, localities and enterprises showed a 25 percent increase over

1978; and the rate of accumulation still stood at 32 percent of the national income. The scope of capital construction remained overextended.

The experimentation in self-management in industrial enterprises also created new problems. First, there has been growing conflict between production enterprises and commercial establishments. In the past, all items of vital materials in the first category were exclusively distributed by the Ministry of Material Allocation. Under the new system, enterprises are allowed to sell some of these materials to customers, thus creating tension between factories and commercial departments. Both are contending for the right to sell popular products.

Second, under the new system, the level of reinvestments, bonuses and workers' fringe benefits are all linked directly or indirectly to profit, although the irrational price-fixing system means that profit generated by individual enterprises does not necessarily reflect the efficiency of the management. For instance, the processing industries make a much higher profit than the extractive industries, which barely cover their costs. In 1978, the average rate of profit calculated on the basis of sale was 40 percent for the petroleum industry, 31 percent for power, 13 percent for the metallurgical industry and only 1 percent for coal enterprises. Consequently, the 33,000 workers at Beijing's Yanshan Petroleum Corporation turned over one billion yuan in profits to the state in 1978, more than the total contribution by China's two million coal miners.

Even in the same industry, differences in natural endowments and equipment result in divergent profit rates. For example, while the profit rate in the Daqing oilfield is 67 percent, in the Yumen oilfield, the rate is only 20 percent. The new reform, thus, is bestowing the fattest profits on enterprises that enjoy arbitrarily high fixed prices or abundant natural resources.

Apart from conflicting interests, widespread resistance to reform also arises from the political and social groups who benefit least from these new initiatives. Many bureaucrats and managers, threatened by the increased emphasis on economic performance and technical expertise, tend to resist or even sabotage the plan.

The growth rate of industrial output, as anticipated, has slowed down considerably because of the cut in capital investment. In 1978, the growth of gross industrial output was 13 percent. It was 8 percent in 1979, and the 1980 target was set as 6 percent. According to Chairman Hua Guofeng, this 6 percent annual growth rate may hold throughout the 1981–1985 period. Compared with the more than 10 percent growth rate stipulated in the original eight year plan, the pace of development has been substantially scaled down. As the rate of accumulation is slated to be reduced to 25 percent of national income, down from 32 percent last year, industrial expansion faces a series of bottlenecks.

The most critical bottleneck for China's current industrail drive is the shortage of energy. Although China is rich in energy resources, its ability to exploit those resources is severely hampered by poverty, a backward technology, poor management, and the lack of an industrial infrastructute. In

1979, the production of oil increased by only 1.9 percent and coal, by 2.8 percent. The growth rate for electricity was 9.9 percent but could not keep up with surging demand. The shortage of electricity has been blamed for the idling of some 30 percent of China's industrial capacity. It is expected that in 1980, instead of increasing, the supply of energy will be reduced by 3.7 percent, although industrial output is planned to grow 6 percent.

Because of the lack of capital investment and technology, the short-term outlook for oil appears to be gloomy, but the outlook is even gloomier for coal. On the basis of recent developments, the growth rate for oil in the 1980–1985 period will probably average only 5 percent and for coal it will average 3 to 4 percent. By 1985, the output of crude oil will probably reach only 135 million tons and coal 745 million tons—both substantially lower than the original plan.

Another serious bottleneck is transportation. Between 1950 and 1978, when the country's railway mileage increased 1.4 times, the volume of freight transports rose 9.7 times. Because 85 percent of the volume still relies on the old railways in coastal areas, the capabilities of many trunk lines have reached their saturation point. The transport capabilities of many weak sections in the coastal areas can meet only 50 percent of the actual needs. The shortage of coal supplies in many parts of the country is partially caused by the deficiency in the delivery capacity of the rail system.

While the energy and transporstion bottlenecks may be eased some-what when new oilfields and coal mines are put into operation and more old railways are double-tracked, the formidable problem confronting the current industrial modernization is the built-in contradiction between mod-ernization and employment. China's total labor force now exceeds 400 mil-lion people, of whom 300 million are farmers and 100 million are workers and employees. Forty million industrial workers are employed by the 400,000 state enterprises. Most factories and plants are small-scale, over-staffed and technologically backward. Their equipment is obsolete; the man-ufacturing process is outdated, the consumption of energy and raw mate-rials are high; and quality of the product is poor. In 1979, some 25 percent of these factories still suffered a loss and required state subsidies. Unless China can modernize these plants, progress will be extremely slow. Mod-ernization not only requires enormous amounts of capital investment, but it must also substitute machines for manual labor. The process will create a huge labor surplus, which will have no apparent outlet.

In light of these barriers, bottlenecks and contradictions, the ten year plan now in preparation promises to be moderate, emphasizing the modi-fication of exisiting plants rather than building grandiose, super-modern plants. The scope of capital construction will be narrowed, and the rate of accumulation will be scaled down. More investment will be allocated to agriculture and light industry. This will meet the rising domestic demand for consumer goods and will supply more consumer goods for export to earn the foreign exchange to import more sophisticated capital goods for further industrial modernization. The target date—when China's output of major industrial products "will approach, equal or outstrip that of the most developed capitalist countries"—may not be the end of this century, as Hua Guofeng projected, but 30 to 50 years into the twenty-first century.

33

The Problem of Partial Reform

_____ **Susan L. Shirk and James B. Stepanek** _____

This selection describes some of the economic reforms initiated by the Deng Xiaoping leadership since 1978, noting that reforms in industry, agriculture, trade, and economic administration have led to a marked improvement in China's overall economic performance. Initially proposed in response to the problems of productivity and output that arose out of the Cultural Revolution, the most important of these reforms involve decreased investment in heavy industry, an expansion of light industry, increased foreign trade, and greater play for market forces, especially in the rural areas. Although there has been some resistance to these reforms from bureaucrats and ministers of heavy industry, the momentum of reform has been sustained.

In late 1978 Deng Xiaoping initiated a set of policies that have thoroughly shaken, and in many ways improved, the performance of the Chinese economy. These reforms were far-reaching, extending to industry, agriculture, foreign trade, and every facet of government administration. The reform proposals were also radical, involving fundamental changes in economic policies and institutions. Such drastic measures reflected the sense of economic and political crisis that pervaded the Chinese leadership after Mao's death on September 9, 1976 and the arrest of the "gang of four" one month later, which ended the turbulent decade of the Cultural Revolution.

The new leadership confronted an economy in serious trouble. Industrial activity was stagnant and efficiency had declined. Agricultural output had just barely kept up with population growth, so that per capita food consumption had not improved since the 1950s. The Cultural Revolution had slowed industrial production and left the society embittered. Respect for the Communist Party and the socialist system was extremely low and people were in no mood to respond to calls to continue to sacrifice for the revolution. Like the 1956 Hungarian revolution, the Cultural Revolution and its aftermath forced even the more conservative leaders to agree that political survival required economic reform. These were implemented in the months following the now-historic third plenum of the eleventh

Chinese Communist Party Central Committee, convened in Beijing during December 18–22. The main reforms:

RESTORING A BALANCE

The government's first action was to reduce China's high rate of investment in heavy industry, particularly in steel. This lowered China's accumulation–consumption ratio, so that less money was spent on capital construction and more on raising people's living standards. In hindsight the change in emphasis may have signalled a historic shift in strategy from investment-led economic growth to one of demand-led growth.

On March 10, 1979, former Vice-Premier Li Xiannian revealed to a visiting American delegation that a complete reordering of economic priorities was in progress. The weak links to be strengthened, he said, were agriculture, coal, oil, hydroelectric power, communications, transportation, foreign trade, and the construction industry. At the second session of the Fifth National People's Congress on June 18, 1979, former premier Hua Guofeng publicly terminated the grandiose Ten-Year Plan for 1976–85 and its planned expenditures on 120 giant projects announced the previous March, and said that for the first time a lower target would be set for heavy industry than for light industry. These changes, the Chinese press noted, were to be accompanied by increased decentralization.

In the five years since 1978, heavy industry's share of industrial output value has, in fact, fallen from 57 percent to 50 percent. Agricultural output has experienced a five-year period of unbroken, spectacular recovery. Consumer goods production has also expanded rapidly, and foreign trade increased from just 10 percent of GNP in 1978 to 16 percent in 1982.

The new priorities also aggravated the rivalry among industrial ministries, causing such confusion in some sectors that the reform drive, while not halted entirely, has been punctuated by efforts to recentralize the economy. Moreover, the attempt to affect a healthier economic balance between sectors exposed China's administrative and statistical shortcomings. Economic data had not been systematically collected during the Cultural Revolution, and the planners allowed to remain at their posts during those chaotic years had little time to pinpoint where the economy was, let alone steer it. But at the second session of the Fifth National People's Congress in June 1979, the government released its first comprehensive economic statistics in 20 years and shortly thereafter stepped up efforts to reform the Party and government bureaucracy.

DE-COLLECTIVIZING AGRICULTURE

About 90 percent of China's rural households today work under one of several "household responsibility" systems introduced since 1979. These have transferred decision-making power from collective production units, such as teams, brigades, or communes, to households and individuals. Peasants typically sign contracts with the collective to provide certain services or amounts of crops, and are permitted to retain or sell the excess. These contracts may even be inherited, and are more like long-term leases than rental agreements. The most widely used form of the system is similar to sharecropping, and involves assigning a plot of land to each household for cultivation in exchange for a share of its output or rent paid to the collective. Peasants are also allowed to invest their earnings in farm machinery and even vehicles to engage in private marketing. In short, farmers have acquired the right to use the land as though it were their own, indicating a clear trend toward *de facto* private ownership.

MANAGEMENT REFORMS

Beginning in 1979, enterprises were permitted to retain a certain percentage of their profits to use for their own capital investment, collective welfare, and worker bonuses. As a spur to economize on capital, enterprises were allowed to retain more of their depreciation funds, and for the first time some investment funds were provided in the form of bank loans instead of outright grants. Enterprises were also given limited authority to make their own arrangements with suppliers and customers.

Prompting these reforms was the knowledge that the Chinese economy was rife with waste, a realization that did not seem to hit home until the statistical system recovered. What the numbers showed was that China could vastly increase output simply by using what it had more efficiently.

The reforms have passed through three phases beginning in July 1979, when Beijing promulgated a profit-sharing scheme to reduce costs and increase production. Then a system of "profit contracts" was introduced in early 1981. It eventually gave way to a "tax-for-profit" system that is expected to be adopted by all profit-making state enterprises in 1983.

These and other internal management reforms were accompanied by external changes to support better management. The December 1978 plenum made the decision to broaden the role of free markets, at least for home handicrafts and the products of collectives. Later, state enterprises were encouraged to trade directly with other enterprises through state-controlled markets for industrial goods.

LABOR REFORM

To stimulate greater labor productivity, piecework-type bonuses and other types of bonuses have been introduced since 1978 and wages have been increased several times. Although basic wages are still based on seniority and national wage scales, bonuses have come to constitute at least 20 percent of total pay. The goal of these and other similar reforms has been to reduce job security while rewarding individual performance—to break the "iron rice bowl," as the Chinese say.

But Beijing has learned that it may be easier to motivate managers than workers. Though there have been two major and one minor wage hikes in recent years that affected most industrial laborers, per-worker output has yet to show strong gains. One possible explanation is that workers still look upon higher wages not as incentives, but merely as compensation for past privations. They still prefer to distribute bonuses equally in order to avoid conflict. Moreover, actual dismissals are still so rare that workers are under little pressure to achieve.

FINANCIAL DECENTRALIZATION

In order to combat the over-centralization of planning and budgeting, governments at the provincial, municipal, and country levels have been allowed to retain a certain proportion of the industrial profits and tax revenues generated by the foreign business dealings of enterprises under their control. They are free to spend these retained tax revenues and foreign exchange earnings on local projects. In short, the fiscal reform measures enacted since 1978 have generally increased the financial resources of localities relative to the central government. This has aggravated Beijing's budget crisis, and made it more difficult to prevent unauthorized investment spending by local governments. Meanwhile, state subsidies have skyrocketed since the reform movement began. Nearly one-fifth of China's national income is now used to subsidize the living standard of urban workers and their dependents, who constitute only about 15 percent of the country's total population.

34

The Profit System

Barry Naughton

Here, Barry Naughton traces recent changes in China's industrial system, describing the various profit schemes that form the basis of these reforms. He argues that while the system is still overwhelmingly bureaucratic, the new reforms have nonetheless produced some fundamental changes: a new emphasis has been placed on market forces; China has decentralized its financial system; and strides have been made toward a more appropriate price system. Unless the pace of reform accelerates, however, Naughton fears that dramatic restrictions will be placed on investment, which would effectively paralyze the reform process in the years to come.

China's industrial system has experienced a nearly uninterrupted series of reorganizations, abrupt changes, and noteworthy setbacks since the reform movement began in 1978. But in spite of the uneven progress, factories today are managed differently than they were just five years ago. Decisions are now made by people closer to the factories, and more attention is paid to market conditions than before. Enterprises consequently are marketing more goods on their own and selling less to the state. Meanwhile, Beijing has decided to do something about the one problem few though it would ever tackle: the country's irrational price structure.

From the beginning, China's industrial reformers have concentrated on drawing up an appropriate set of rules to govern the division of profits between the state budget and the individual enterprise. In the five years since 1978, Beijing has put forward three successive "reforms" of the industrial financial system. In each period of reform a different principle for dividing profits has been advocated, but the proportion of profits actually retained by enterprises has increased steadily throughout the three periods. This progressive decentralization has contributed to the increased flexibility of Chinese industry during a period of rapid change, but has also created serious new problems of coordination and control.

INITIAL EXPERIMENTS

The first wave of reforms began with the decision to let some factories keep a fixed percentage of their profits. The resumption of worker bonuses and enterprise bonus funds in 1978 had already restored a modest link between enterprise performance and employee rewards when, in July 1979, the regime drafted an experimental profit-sharing program to be implemented in a limited number of enterprises in each province. . . .

The profit-sharing experiment spread much more rapidly than planners had intended. At the end of 1979, Beijing was trying to limit the number of participating enterprises to 1,400, but within a few months was forced to recognize a total of 6,600 participating enterprises. These were the largest and most profitable, accounting for 60 percent of the output and 70 percent of the profits under the state plan. . . .

This period of experimentation ended when problems emerged. Profit deliveries to the state budget declined 17 percent in August 1980, and estimates of the government's deficit were revised drastically upward. The rise in consumer prices and runaway investment spending were also blamed on the reforms. In December 1980 Beijing halted the enterprise reform experiments, enacted strengthened price controls on consumer goods, and drastically reduced spending. Planned budgetary investment was cut by 40 percent, enterprise bank deposits were frozen, and the new program of bank loans for fixed investment was suspended. The strong medicine slowed industrial output, and profitability fell even more. It quickly became obvious that the deflationary policies were enlarging the government deficit they were intended to reduce, and by March 1981 the most drastic measures had been rescinded. In September 1981 plans were readjusted upward and expansion of heavy industry resumed.

A LOSS OF DIRECTION

As the regime labored through 1981 to undo the harmful effects of its deflationary policies, it again endorsed programs that would allow enterprises to retain profits. In the spring of 1981, a second period of change in enterprise financial regulations began, centering around the system of "profit contracts" (*yingkui baogan*). Under this system an enterprise and its supervisory body would negotiate a profit "base figure," which the enterprise had to deliver to the state. Enterprises typically were allowed to retain a high proportion, ranging from 50 to 100 percent of profits above the base figure. This program, too, was implemented rapidly. By August 1981, 65 percent of all state enterprises had adopted the profit contract system or some other profit retention program, and by early 1982 this figure had risen to more than 80 percent. . . .

The profit contract system clearly intensified a number of bad managerial practices. Since it was in the interest of local governments to maximize the amount of profits retained by their enterprises, the profit contract system increased local government meddling in the affairs of factories under their jurisdiction. Moreover, even the low levels at which the profit base figures were set did not ensure their fulfillment. Since the setting of the base figures was to some extent arbitrary in the first place, enterprises could argue that circumstances beyond their control prevented them from fulfilling their profit quotas. As enterprises began to dodge their responsibilities, it soon became clear that the vast majority were immune to the threat of serious penalties. In Chinese terms, the enterprises had become "responsible for profits, but not responsible for losses."

THE "TAX-FOR-PROFIT" REFORMS

In spite of its defects, this system was retained through 1982, and as production expanded so did the amount of retained profits. But in 1983 the "tax-for-profit" system was introduced, and so began the third phase of the reform. Tried in some 200 Chinese enterprises since the period of experimentation in 1980, this system is scheduled for adoption by all profitable state enterprises in 1983. The tax-for-profit system involves a series of taxes, paid directly to the state, that were substituted for the delivery of profit to an enterprise's supervisory body. . . .

NO MORE FREE CAPITAL

A parallel reform movement has begun to shake up another once-ossified practice: ignoring the true cost of capital by giving factories free use of money and equipment. Only in 1979 did the government require enterprises to begin paying fees for fixed capital. But the results are mixed, as implementation was left to local governments. . . .

Though modest, the imposition of these fees has tightened up enterprise finances. . . .

This is precisely the objective of the new program. By introducing a range of taxes and fees that reflect to some degree the scarcity value of capital, the system is designed to introduce a much greater degree of automaticity—and fairness—to enterprise finances. This should reduce the scope for bargaining, force enterprises to rely more on their own efforts, and make them truly responsible for profits *and* losses. In its ideal form, the new system should reduce local government interference in enterprise management and simultaneously give the central government greater control over the division of revenues between center and locality. Of course, this ideal remains a long way off.

A RUNAWAY EXPANSION DRIVE

Another problem undermining Beijing's control over enterprises is runaway investment spending, the unavoidable result of letting factories retain more of their profits. As foreign visitors can attest, China is engaged in an immense house-raising drive, as factories throw up worker apartments and attempt to make up for years of austerity in other areas. This is drawing cement, steel, glass—and money—away from projects Beijing deems more important. No longer disposing of the investment resources it once controlled directly, the central government has not yet devised any indirect instruments to control the scale of investment. As a result, investment spending during the past five years has tended to expand beyond the scale intended by central planners.

This investment binge has had a number of harmful consequences. In the first place, the competition for construction materials has led to escalating construction costs. . . .

An even more serious consequence of the continued expansion is the fact that the state is forced to make even more drastic investment cuts whenever the situation reaches crisis proportions. We have already seen how this occurred at the end of 1980. In 1983 the state is again making extraordinary efforts to control the scope of investment by confiscating a portion of "extrabudgetary" funds (local government funds beyond Beijing's reach), and by enforcing a stringent system of priorities to guarantee construction supplies for central government projects. The need for continued dramatic interventions in the economy creates a vicious cycle of administrative interference in which a climate of instability makes it increasingly difficult to hold Chinese (and foreign) enterprises responsible for their own decisions. . . .

SEEKING "BASIC" PRICE STABILITY

Further progress in industrial reforms depends crucially upon China's ability to overhaul its distorted price system. Some limited progress has been made in this direction in the past five years, both through the adjustment of planned prices and by allowing market forces a greater role in setting prices. But it must be said that the distance traveled so far is a small fraction of the distance that remains. Chinese industry suffers from the long-term undervaluation of most basic raw materials, including foodgrains. This gives processing industries artificially high levels of profit. Eventually, the government will have to raise the price of raw materials enough to provide some return on capital in those sectors (at least sufficient to provide for replacement investment), and raise wages and the sales prices of basic foodgrains to reduce the massive subsidies attached to grain consumption. But too-rapid steps in this direction could ignite serious inflation, and the regime is loathe to upset the "basic stability" of consumer prices.

During the past five years, planned prices of some of the most seriously undervalued commodities have been adjusted upward, including coal, iron, timber, and cotton cloth. At the same time, prices of machinery and some consumer durables either have been set lower, or allowed to float downward in response to excess supply. While these price adjustments have reduced the profit margins for downstream producers, they remain woefully inadequate to resolve the underlying undervaluation of raw materials. The Chinese fully recognize this problem, and are in the midst of computing a full set of new prices on the basis of an 80-sector input–output table compiled during 1982. Current plans call for the implementation of a comprehensive wage and price reform in several stages, possibly beginning in 1985. . . .

LETTING MARKETS DO THEIR JOB

Another promising development is China's greater willingness to let factories sell products on their own. This is beginning to force producers to take a serious look at what the market wants, as opposed to what planners want. The practice of "selective purchasing" is the mechanism bringing factories in closer touch with markets. Begun in 1979, and expanded nationwide in May 1980, selective purchasing releases the Ministry of Commerce from the obligation to buy the entire output of a given factory. Instead, commercial units only purchase the quantity of output that they judge to be saleable. The enterprise is then free to market on its own the output that commercial units have declined to purchase. . . .

The marketing of producer goods is more complicated. . . . Following the introduction of the profit-retention systems, enterprises increasingly have been allowed to market their above-plan output, if they can arrange inputs themselves, and sometimes a fraction of in-plan output, as well. This has released a large quantity of producer goods from the control of central planners. Materials from both these sources flow into "quasi-markets" in which materials are sold, or more commonly bartered, at relative prices that come substantially closer to what a free market might dictate than the state-set prices.

One of the most prominent of the quasi-markets is the barter trade between provinces. The province of Shanzi, China's largest coal producer, contributes 60 million tons of coal annually to the state's allocation system, but also disposes of an additional 10 million tons above and beyond its own needs. This coal is swapped with coastal and southern agricultural provinces for grain, consumer goods, and sophisticated machinery and technical advice.

The central authorities regard this trade with ambivalence. It is legal, and in some respects encouraged, but the authorities try to ensure that transactions take place at state-set prices. Because these thousands of arrangements are largely voluntary, however, and central authorities have no way to monitor them, this intention is almost certainly frustrated. Since mid-1983, Beijing has redoubled its efforts to stop large centrally run enterprises from diverting materials to quasi-markets at prices higher than the officially set prices. This is one part of the campaign to keep high-priority construction materials from being diverted to low-priority projects.

The quasi-markets, Beijing believes, are also aggravating the state's budget crisis. This is because large-scale enterprises, which turn over the most profits to the central government, are forced to buy higher-priced goods on quasi-markets each time the state supply system breaks down. This is precisely what worries central planners: If supplies are not guaranteed, the country's largest enterprises will experience rising costs that will reduce the profits the state so desperately needs. Indeed, the total amount of losses in industrial enterprises has remained roughly constant since 1978, at around 4 billion per year. . . .

Returning to the original question: How much has really changed since 1978? The country's industry certainly remains weakly planned, and overwhelmingly bureaucratic. Individual factories are still most likely to attain "economic results" by currying favor with their superiors, who reportedly are as likely to thwart initiative as to reward it. And a factory that does not wish to participate in a potentially threatening competitive environment still has ample bureaucratic nooks and crannies in which to hide.

Yet it would be unrealistic to expect such fundamental behavioral characteristics to disappear during only five years. What is most significant is that the reform movement has been sustained for five years, and the response of the regime to succeeding waves of new problem has not been to abandon the reform process. Instead, important new roles for market forces have been found, a major financial decentralization has occurred, and steps toward a more appropriate price system have been taken. If the Chinese are able to build upon these achievements and accelerate the pace of reform, we may begin to see fundamental changes in the behavior of China's managers and workers. But if the pace slows, it will probably be followed by dramatic restrictions on investment, which will paralyze the reform process for a long time to come.

35

Rice Bowl Reforms

Andrew G. Walder

China is currently facing mounting labor problems, many of them stemming from the Cultural Revolution. However, as Walder describes here, wage policies aimed at linking pay to worker performance have created even greater problems for Chinese management. China's leaders are gradually recognizing that wage reform can only move forward in conjunction with other economic reforms. Thus, many Chinese economists are calling for stricter fiscal controls over enterprises and reform of the country's irrational price structure so that profits will be more directly tied to enterprise efficiency.

By the mid-1970s China could no longer afford to ignore its mounting labor problems. A decade-long policy of extreme austerity had abolished all incentive pay and led to a substantial decline in wage levels, and consumer goods remained rationed and in very short supply. Quotas and other tools of labor discipline had fallen into disuse, or else had been abolished outright. Rules regarding labor discipline often went unenforced by managers fearful of the political consequences of punishing members of the working class. Slothful work, poor quality, and high rates of absenteeism became the normal state of affairs. The general malaise spilled over into a mini-wave of strikes in 1975. The strikes in Hangzhou were so large that the army was called out to restore order.

Several national leaders, notably Zhou Enlai and Deng Xiaoping, had urged basic changes in prevailing labor and wage policies from the early 1970s, but it was not until after the death of Mao that they could put their ideas into practice. Since that time, industrial wages have risen considerably, incentive pay had been restored, and labor discipline enforced more vigorously. These wage and incentive policies represent not so much an innovative reform of the Chinese system as a restoration of the practices of the early 1960s, widely deemed to have been relatively successful. Based on practical experience rather than ideological prescriptions, these new (or rather, old) policies are designed to meet the labor problems head-on. And as in the 1960s, these policies have created their own set of problems.

NO WAGE INCREASES FOR 11 YEARS

China's current labor problems stem from a long and sustained fall in real wages after 1964, and the total abolition of incentive pay in the decade after 1966. As originally envisaged in the mid-1950s, China's industrial workers were to be paid according to an eight-grade scale, with raises for substantial numbers of deserving workers every two–three years during national "wage readjustments." By 1958, many Chinese leaders, and especially Mao, decided that urban workers should not receive increased pay as long as there was surplus labor in the economy. This policy was enforced during the decade of remarkable austerity that began with the Cultural Revolution in 1966. There were no performance-related wage readjustments from 1963 to 1977.

The effects of this austerity are just becoming clear. Recently released Chinese statistics show a decline in the average annual state industrial wage, from the peak of ¥741 in 1964 to ¥632 in 1977. This represents a nominal decline of 15 percent, and a decline in real wages of 20 percent after adjusting for inflation. By 1977 the average state-sector industrial wage, in constant prices, had dropped so far that it was lower than it had been a quarter century earlier, in 1952. Workers coped by putting more family members to work, but such prolonged austerity took a terrible toll on motivation.

The abolition of monthly production bonuses from 1966 to 1977 compounded the problem. Instead of bonuses, workers were paid a monthly "supplementary wage" equal to the average monthly bonus of prior years. It was completely unrelated to work performance or attendance. Workers hired after 1966 did not get this supplement, and this effectively lowered the average wage of the younger generation by an amount equal to one pay grade.

Slack management practices worsened the situation. Virtually all labor management and supervision systems were abolished as "capitalist" during the Cultural Revolution, and their restoration was resisted through the mid-1970s. Setting quotas, inspecting work, and keeping production statistics—if such things were done at all—were token efforts. Rules specifying punishment and fines for absenteeism, leaving the work post, and failing to meet quotas went unenforced—not only because there were no inspection systems to detect this kind of behavior, but also because managers were afraid to be censured for "suppressing the working class."

REMOVING THE POLITICAL STIGMA

China's post-Mao leadership approached the problem with a clear sense of its causes, and with a straighforward prescription: Restore the practices that had once proved effective. Since 1977 two major wage adjustments, and one minor one, have given wage increases to 83 percent of China's industrial labor force. The average annual wage in state enterprises had risen from ¥632 in 1977 to ¥852 in 1981—a nominal increase of 35 percent and a real increase of 20 percent in only four years.

The link between pay and performance is being restored, as well. The most recent readjustment made an effort to tie raisers to evaluations of worker performance. Monthly and yearly production bonuses also have been widely revived. By 1981, 17 percent of the national wage bill was paid out as production bonuses, up from zero only five years before. These changes reflect the growing political pressure on managers to reward good performance. Managers have begun restoring quotas, shop-floor inspections, and statistics. And the political stigma attached earlier to productivity is gone.

A more innovative reform—discussed in the early 1960s but never widely implemented—was first adopted in 1978, when large-scale enterprises began to be allowed to retain a percentage of their above-target profit for the bonus fund. This reform created larger bonuses and tied them to increased productivity. Managers were also allowed to retain percentages of above-target profit for renovating their machinery or expanding capacity. Both of these funds rise and fall with a factory's profit, and are designed to give both managers and workers enhanced incentives for productivity. Since 1981 most of China's large and medium-sized enterprises have used a form of this scheme. This system goes far beyond what was permitted in the 1960s when enterprises drew their bonus funds as a fixed percentage of the wage bill (generally 6–9 percent, depending on the industry). If the factory met its targets, bonuses were paid in fixed amounts, regardless of the degree of plan overfulfillment, or the actual profit attained. Whatever profit the factory did make was remitted to the state.

THE PRODUCTIVITY ENIGMA

Despite the new measures, however, labor productivity has yet to show a marked improvement. Per-worker productivity in state industrial enterprises increased only 6.5 percent during 1978–81 in terms of constant dollars, and virtually all of this increase came in 1979. Labor productivity actually declined in 1981 and did so in 10 of 15 industries—most notably in machine building and petroleum, where the decline approached 10 percent. When one considers that workers' real wages increased 20 percent over the same period, it is clear that industry is getting less output per labor dollar than before the reforms. The decline in heavy industrial output, for example, pushed labor productivity figures down and may have masked some improved worker performance, but it is equally clear that any upward trend in productivity is not yet measurable.

Nonstatistical evidence reveals a similarly mixed picture. Emigre workers interviewed by this author in Hong Kong during 1980 generally confirm that absenteeism, theft, and indiscipline declined quickly after 1978, while interest in new skills and after-hours training increased, but output per worker reportedly responded much more slowly. Press reports and academic "investigation reports" published in China carry the usual share of model success stories, but many other articles have decried continuing sloth and worker indiscipline. Beijing's constant criticism of the "iron rice bowl" (China's system of unbreakable job security) and the 1982 enactment of harsher punishments for recalcitrant workers underscore official frustration with the limited success of the incentive reforms.

More disturbing to the government has been the emergence of undesirable labor and management practices that are the unforeseen outgrowth of the new policies. One is the reported upsurge in disputes over wages. The second is related to the first—managers and workers enjoy greater incentive pay, but seem to prefer the old practice of distributing bonuses equally to all with only a loose connection to individual performance. As a result, bonus funds have been skyrocketing as managers successfully evade accounting regulations.

COMPLICATING SIDE EFFECTS

It seems paradoxical that the sharp wage increases in recent years should lead to rising tensions over wage matters. However, many workers apparently fear, with justification, that the recent pay raises are just an expedient to make up for the losses of the past 20 years, and do not represent a new era of constantly rising wages. This fear reportedly led to widespread and disruptive haggling over the evaluations that accompanied the pay raises in 1979–80. Other issues, such as the decision to abolish as redundant the "supplementary wages" that older workers have come to regard as part of their fixed salaries, have added to the atmosphere of contention.

Efforts to tie bonus pay more closely to worker output have been vigorously resisted, as well. China's workers have become accustomed over the years to a relaxed pace of work, and the long absence of clear work rules and norms for earning quotas have made it hard for people to agree on what constitutes a fair day's work. China now faces the enormous task of reestablishing work standards almost from scratch. Such a colossal effort has led to all the predictable problems: Workers reportedly slow down when new quotas offend them, haggle over the assignment of "hard" and "soft" jobs, neglect quality standards to overfulfill their quotas and intimidate quality inspectors, engage in "chiseling," and refuse jobs that have impossible quotas. Now that labor relations revolve around money once again, China's managers confront problems that they have little experience in handling.

PLAYING IT SAFE

Managers appear to have responded conservatively and rationally to the new tensions in labor relations. The surest way to anger workers, managers quickly learned, was to put them on a tight quota system and then neglect to measure their output accurately, or make them wait for tools and parts. Some managers have understandably taken the easy way out by distributing bonuses more or less equally regardless of individual output—which they are ill-equipped by training and experience to measure or supervise anyway.

One symptom of this management response is the huge increase in the payment of bonus funds from 1978 to 1981—an increase that has outstripped state limits and exceeded any improvement in enterprise performance. In late 1978 the State Council limited bonuses to 8–12 percent of a factory's wage bill. Yet according to the Shanghai journal *Social Science,* a 1980 survey of 90 factories in Chongqing showed that bonuses comprised 40 percent of the wage bill for that year, and bore no relation to improved enterprise profit performance. In Shanghai, where labor productivity dropped by 1 percent and profits increased by only 4 percent in 1980, bonuses increased by 22 percent. In Liaoning Province in the same year, labor productivity dropped by 1 percent, and industrial output value rose by 8 percent, yet bonuses rose 53 percent. Even factories that were losing money were reporting large increases in bonuses paid.

Nor were the increased bonuses being handed out according to individual performance. Factories in the Shanghai Textile Bureau, described as typical by one *Social Science* writer, paid out one-third to one-half of their bonus funds equally to workers at the end of 1980. Even the portion of bonuses handed out monthly after the evaluation of worker performance were often being distributed with scant regard to performance. Evaluations were often superficial or pro-forma, differences in the sizes of bonuses were set too small to matter to workers, and in many cases workers took turns receiving the higher bonuses anyway. These practices have been widely decried as "egalitarianism" and "eating from the same pot," but there is little evidence that the practices have been curtailed.

Managers have often turned to a number of bureaucratic, sometimes illegal, strategies to inflate these bonus increases. The old bureaucratic game of hiding slack capacity and past output still pays dividends in a system where profit targets—the chief measure of enterprise performance—are based on past year's performance. Managers who have been most successful at this game in the past are rewarded preferentially, since they can now overfulfill profit targets in a way that allows them to retain the maximum amount of funds. Added to these old and accepted strategies are some new and illegal ones—the covert raising of prices and cutting of costs by skimping on quality; the filing of false requests for overtime pay; the use of plant welfare funds as wage supplements; and the arranging of cash kickbacks between industrial suppliers and their customers—to cite the most common practices exposed in the Chinese press.

REFORMING THE REFORMS

China's leaders appear to have drawn the only possible conclusion from their experience of the past seven years—that wage reform can move forward only in conjunction with other economic reforms. First of all, real wages cannot be raised too rapidly as long as unemployment exists. China's industry currently faces the prospect of absorbing a large and growing pool of unemployed youths, and this makes a large claim on wage funds that would otherwise go toward pay increases for currently employed workers. Secondly, workers are only one of many competing claimants on the state budget, and the fiscal austerity of the period since 1980 has curtailed further rounds of wage increases. And thirdly, sustained increases in wages require a shift in the composition of industrial production toward consumer goods in order to meet additional demand. If the shift is not fast enough, the incentive effect is dulled. Workers' wages did increase faster than did consumer goods production in 1977–80, and this is another reason why China's leaders may plan a more gradual rate of wage increase in the future.

Meanwhile, China has turned its attention to punishing workers and managers who break regulations. In early 1982 a new set of national punitive regulations for industry was released by the State Council and given wide publicity. Discipline ranging from fines to imprisonment were specified for violations by workers and managers. There is also a movement away from positive wage incentives and a return to the "spiritual incentives" of the Maoist era. Factory party secretaries are now declaring that "bonuses are not omnipotent," and that they must go hand-in-hand with intensified political education that instills a sense of duty to the nation. Other enterprises are also experimenting with "floating wages" and contract hiring systems for regular workers that threaten heretofore sacred wage and job security.

In the long run, wages can only be tied to individual performance when well-functioning—and enforceable—systems of quota-setting, record-keeping, and inspection exist. This will not happen as long as the irrationality of the current system encourages managers to evade fiscal controls and inflate their bonus funds. China's economists are now calling for more strict fiscal controls over enterprises, including taxes on fixed capital, and reform of the country's irrational price structure so that profits more accurately reflect enterprise efficiency. China's managers are already rational—what is needed are incentives to make it rational for them to be efficient.

36

Bureaucratic Competition

Susan L. Shirk

In the wake of recent economic reforms, which have stimulated competition in almost every sector of China's economy, bureaucratic warfare among rival industries has become increasingly commonplace. This selection focuses on China's heavy industrial sector, which has long played a dominant role in Chinese economic life, and examines the various political and economic advantages that have allowed it to retain its powerful status despite the new competitive situation. Although heavy industry has suffered no real loss of control under the current reforms, its leaders, along with those of other "favored" Chinese industries, clearly prefer the security of centralized industrial investment to the uncertainties of "market" competition.

Although some communist officials abhor competition and try to avoid it, the recent economic reforms have increased competition throughout China's economy. Enterprises want to break into new domestic or international markets—and protect their old markets—in order to earn more profits and foreign exchange.

Because prices are set by the state and the other monopolistic conditions of the command economy are still in effect, this rivalry is more akin to bureaucratic warfare than true "market" competition.

The contest between the heavy and light industrial ministries is particularly revealing. The Ministry of Machine Building (MMB), for example, recently decided to enter the lucrative consumer goods market for washing machines and refrigerators. When the Ministry of Light Industry resisted this challenge to its monopoly, the State Economic Commission had to call a meeting among several ministries to divide up the burgeoning market for 10 high-volume consumer products. MMB emerged victorious, with a sizeable share of the washing machine and refrigerator business. (In washing machines, it was awarded the multi-cycle and washer-dryer machines, while the Ministry of Light Industry kept the simple machines.)

Such turf warfare is commonplace. The Petroleum and Geology ministries have fought for control over offshore oil exploration, and the Finance Ministry has clashed with the industrial ministries and local governments over tax issues. Perhaps the only unique feature of the on-going heavy–light industrial dispute is its one-sided results.

Of course, the Ministry of Machine Building enjoyed advantages from the start. Since the early 1950s, for example, the ministry has benefited from investment policies that have emphasized heavy industry, and its plants have been allowed to supply equipment to domestic enterprises under virtual monopolistic conditions. Not surprisingly, the value of the ministry's output expanded at a rate of about 20 percent a year for almost three decades. By 1978 nearly one-third of all industrial enterprises in China were machinery factories. (With the increase in the number of processing plants, the number is now closer to one-fourth.)

When other industrial ministries began to modernize their factories with sophisticated equipment imported from abroad, the MMB demanded a policy of "buy Chinese." It was successful in reestablishing under its control a 1950s institution, the special Equipment Approval Division, which has the power to approve all factory equipment imports, even those for joint ventures. Requests are first submitted to the State Planning Commission, then passed on to the division. If the ministry determines that one of its factories can produce the same piece of equipment (regardless of cost), it vetoes the import. In a few instances, the MMB has even prevented the Metallurgical and Petroleum ministries from sending representatives abroad on shopping missions. Several interministerial disputes over equipment imports have had to be resolved by the State Economic Commission or State Planning Commission. Machinery industry protectionism has not always prevailed, however, especially when a foreign firm is willing to commit considerable capital and technology to its China project. But at the very least, the MMB has caused delays.

The political strength of heavy industry goes back to the First Five-Year Plan period (1953–57) when the Chinese adopted the Soviet heavy industry-first growth strategy. According to Chinese economic officials interviewed, heavy industry's priority status meant that the most talented cadres from the provinces were recruited into the heavy industrial ministries. From that time onward, it has been widely recognized that the leadership of the heavy industrial bureaucracies is of superior caliber.

The dominance of heavy industry is reflected in many features of Chinese economic life: Workers in heavy industry are paid on a higher wage scale than workers in light industry; the managers of major heavy industrial plants such as the Anshan and Wuhan Iron and Steel companies have a cadre rank higher than some provincial governors; the heavy industrial ministries have maintained central control of more of their own factories than have the light industrial ministries, which have lost control of most of their factories to local authorities; the heavy industrial ministries have successfully challenged the monopoly of the Ministry of Foreign Economic Relations and Trade (MOFERT) to establish their own trading companies, while the ministries of Light Industry and Textiles have (with a few exceptions) been unable to do so; and taxes and profits from heavy industry constitute the lion's share of the central government's fiscal base. Statistics bear out the heavy industry sector's undiminished power: During 1982 and the first nine months of 1983, heavy industrial output far surpassed the comparable growth rate of light industry; their respective performances were 10 percent and 6 percent in 1982, and 13 percent and 8 percent thus far in 1983.

The preeminence of heavy industry means that when the ministers of Machine Building, Metallurgy, Petroleum, and Coal assert themselves, they usually prevail. This is equally true of the ministries in charge of nuclear power, aviation, electronics, armaments, and aerospace, which are the agencies partially or wholly under the military.

Heavy industry supporters certainly appear to have had a hand in the effort to recentralize industrial investment since 1982. They seem to share the conviction held by some leaders that the economic reforms went too far, causing the central government to lose control over investment spending. Beijing's increased control over major national energy and transportation projects could mean more investment in heavy industry from the center, and increased demand for coal, steel, and large machinery.

In short, the officials leading China's heavy industrial sector appear to have adapted to the new competitive situation with considerable success. But like the executives of some US firms who are dependent on government contracts, these officials prefer the predictability of selling to one large bureaucracy to the risks and uncertainties of competition.

The Twenty-First Century Capitalists

——————————— Frank Gibney ———————————

How has Japan been able to achieve its spectacular economic growth without compromising its social stability? In this selection, Frank Gibney identifies several social and economic factors which he considers to be of particular importance. First, Japanese corporations are a "community" as well as a functional organization. Workers have great loyalty to their employers. Second, because most capital investment is financed through banks rather than stockholders, Japanese executives can plan for the long term. Short-term profits are relatively unimportant. Third, labor unrest is uncommon largely because of the interpenetration of corporate management and enterprise union leadership. Fourth, compromise rather than litigation is important in inter-business relations. Fifth, the government is "developmental" rather than "regulatory." And sixth, executives seek the prestige that accompanies success as well as the monetary rewards to be gained from their positions. Together, these factors allow Japan to combine a high degree of central planning with democratic institutions and values.

———

Why Japan? How did it come to be that this historically self-seclusive country, characterized as adapter rather than inventor, has made itself the wonder of the economic world? The advances of Japanese business, avowedly capitalist and free enterprise in nature, would make Adam Smith proud, if surprised—and send Ricardo, Marx, and Schumpeter alike back to their studies. The concurrent success of Japan's postwar economic policies—and the social stability accompanying them—are the envy of politicians almost everywhere else.

The growth history of Japan's postwar "miracle" is still unfolding. The economy it has built has weathered OPEC oil shocks, foreign export restrictions, and domestic recessions; and its statistics are business history. In 1960, Japan's $39.1-billion gross national product was not quite 8 percent of America's. Japan's $1-trillion GNP in 1980 was almost 40 percent of America's—in per capita GNP, Japan will probably pass us within the decade. Twelve billion dollars' worth of Japanese exports in 1968 had become $140 billion by 1980. Nowhere has the rate of productivity risen so fast or so steadily. If the 1960 level of Japanese productivity in manufacturing is set at 100, the 1980 level had passed the 450 mark. Japanese steel, Japanese cars, Japanese TV sets, ships, cameras, and chemicals—and now Japan's semiconductor chips, computers, and overseas factories—have made consumers all over the world satisfied and dependent. No other nation's private entrepreneurs have carried off such brilliant marketing strategies.

Nowhere have people worked harder either, to implement those strategies. In the process the Japanese have raised their standard of living greatly, with all the attendant creature comforts of a dynamic mass consumption society. Remarkably dedicated and efficient, their work force is better motivated and more secure than any other. Yet these modern Japanese are not automatons. They enjoy the rights and benefits of a working democracy. Their freedoms and civil rights are guaranteed as securely as ours. And they do not hesitate to lobby vigorously and successfully for consumerism, pollution-free environments, and enlargement of labor's rights and benefits. However did they do it?

How did they do it, indeed, at a time when the firmament of the American economic dream seems to be cracking and the failing productivity of the United States has become a matter of worldwide concern? One major American industry after another drifts into deep trouble—some finished off by competition (mainly Japan's), but others collapsing of their own weight. "Alienation" of the labor force has become a commonplace complaint, while American management is also criticized for concentrating on the quick paper profit instead of the lasting quality product. In business, as in other areas of our national life, we seem to experience a chronic lack of motivation, a failure of will. What is wrong with us? And what are we doing to remedy it?

The answers to these two sets of questions are related far more closely than is generally thought. They go beyond matters of work ethic or management techniques or government-business cooperation, although these are part of the whole. Still less can they be found by repeating the caricature criticism of a "Japan, Inc." peopled by grim "workaholics"—although there *are* some unlovely factors in Japan's economic success behind these caricatures which we would be foolish to ignore. We can neither understand the nature of Japan's economic success nor learn from it unless we see it in its social as well as economic context. . . .

• Where the typical American corporation is a functional economic organ, seeing itself primarily as a means of doing a job, the Japanese company is a functional organization, which also very consciously thinks of itself as a community of *people.* Many things follow from this difference. Unlike the American corporation, which hires and fires freely as it needs the particular kinds of skills that abound in the outside labor force, the Japanese community-company prefers to grow its own labor force, recruiting "the whole man" out of school or college and training him within the company, with a maximum of job security. Lifetime employment practices and the age seniority system are followed wherever the size and strength of the company permits. As Yamamoto says, "Achievement in the functional organization is naturally transformed into seniority in the community-company."

• Where American management typically raises its money by issuing and selling shares, the Japanese company still relies heavily on bank financing. Thus the American manager has to worry about his quarterly P&L and the effect current results will have on the company's stock. That is his report card. The Japanese manager, once he has satisfied his board and his banks about his long-range business plans, is relatively free to work them out, without the need either to push for short-term results or to constantly explain his situation to his board, not to mention the friendly securities analyst next door. In addition, his board of directors generally has a majority of management officers. Ask an American manager where his duty lies and he will answer, "To the shareholders." The business community—not to mention the Securities and Exchange Commission—would be disturbed if he said anything different. The Japanese manager, by contrast, generally feels at least an equal obligation to the workers in the company. If he keeps their work community flourishing and intact, he does his job. The profits can come either way, but the way they are planned and realized is very different.

• Although there is a greater percentage of union members in Japan than in the United States (31 percent as against 23 percent), most are not tightly organized on a national level. Even among those who belong to a national federation, the single-enterprise union is more likely than not a law unto itself. Although the Japanese "company" union can be a tough negotiator, belying the pejorative implied in that American term, its interest centers in the progress of the one company, not that of the union at a national level. Union executives quite normally go on to management roles.

• Although legalistic in their exasperating fondness for proper forms and procedures, the Japanese are resolutely not litigious. The public adversary procedures now riveted into American business are frowned on in Japan, both inside the company and out. Discussion and consultation are paramount. Open confrontation is strenuously avoided, as befits a country with only 12,000 lawyers. The courts are appealed to only as a last and often desperate resort. This is characteristic of a society that prizes harmony among people rather than a winner-loser type of justice.

• The Japanese government, as Chalmers Johnson put it in his recent book *MITI and the Japanese Miracle,* plays a "developmental" role in its relations with business, as opposed to the "regulatory" function of government in the United States. The Japanese economy, he noted, is "plan-rational," whereas the American is "market-rational." Which is to say that the government is a supportive force helping business attain various long-term goals and actively planning for them. This is in sharp distinction to the traditional "cops-and-robbers"—relationship between business and government in the United States. Yet the pushing and tugging between government ministries and business in Japan—and among both sides—reflect competitive differences of view belying the simplistic caricature of "Japan, Inc."

• The Japanese executive tends to think of himself as a community-builder as much as a profit-maker. Prestige considerations can weigh as heavily with him as monetary reward. His idea of community service is a narrow one, however, concentrating on a single industry or a single company—often to the exclusion of everything else. The American executive's idea of community service may be far wider; his particular company is only *one* of its components. Functionally, he might think of himself as a kind of Lone Ranger, his six (figure)-gun ready for hire in the service of efficiency and profitability. (*Whose* profitability may be a secondary consideration.) Once in charge of a corporation, he will want to make the big decisions himself and lead his people after him. The Japanese businessman's ideal is to encourage those under him to formulate decisions. Although there are "dynamic leader" types in Japan and "consensus" types in America, the ideals of the two capitalisms differ. A Japanese economist contrasted them this way: Our system is rather like an electric train, with each car having its own motor, whereas your system is more like a long train drawn by two or three strong locomotives, with no motors in the other cars. You tell your workers to follow. We like people to have their own motivation—and move together. . . .

This kind of people-centered business thinking and the society that developed it is constructing not only a new kind of capitalism, but the kind best suited to take the capitalist system into the strains and conflicts of the twenty-first century. Certainly the Japanese variety, lacking anything like our own massive natural resources and stored technological capital, has proved itself far more flexible in avoiding our peculiar problems of the past decade or two: stagflation, the decline of productivity, chronic unemployment, the factionalism of constantly warring special interest groups, the tug of adversary processes tearing at the heart of our polity, rising apathy and mistrust among the work force, while the gap between the elite manager or capitalist and the worker or middle manager grows rather than lessens. Japanese capitalism, to be sure, has the advantage of working with a tight, homogeneous society. Nonetheless, its achievement is impressive. Japan has proved that a democracy can coordinate central economic planning without sacrificing basic freedoms. It has shown that free workers, if properly organized and informed, can perform voluntarily all the feats of communal derring-do that Marxists and others contend can be done only by government order. It is the Japanese capitalist worker, more than the Chinese or Soviet Marxist, who is at once the real-life embodiment of many socialist ideals of spontaneous fraternal cooperation, and a living rebuke to modern socialism. . . .

To understand how this new capitalism works, we must be aware of the unique bureaucracy that presides over the government of this business country. We must be aware of the Japanese idea of what law is—and their rejection of the adversary method as a way of settling disputes. This is a logical development in people who cherish harmony rather than justice as the highest social good. We must realize also what are the underpinnings of the Japanese work ethic. This tradition goes back much further than one might think. Yet it is extraordinary how well it seems to fit into the postindustrial world.

There is no doubt something of the miraculous in the spectacle of a nation widely regarded in the days after the World War II defeat as an economic basket case transforming itself into the powerhouse of world industry in little more than three decades. But it was, paradoxically, a miracle by design. Japan's economic miracle was the product of many people and many institutions working together. They worked together not only because they are group-minded, but also because recent adversity had taught them there was no hope in disunity. A concurrent cooperation and competition among all these forces brought Japan's twenty-first century capitalism into being.

38

The Large Company:
Identification and Performance

Ezra F. Vogel

In this selection from *Japan as Number One,* Vogel traces the origin of the modern Japanese corporation. The roots of many contemporary corporate practices date back to the paternalism of feudal enterprises. But most policies are rooted in an understanding of the need for planning, training, and wide investment in the development of an industrialized economy. Since the 1960s, an increased emphasis on such Western techniques as econometric models, product life cycles, and advertising have been merged with more traditionally based policies such as lifetime employment, "bottoms-up" management, small group responsibility, and long-term planning. Japan still faces problems in the area of research and development investment, but the cooperative relationship that exists between labor and management in the large Japanese firms suggests that the sacrifices necessary to increase R&D can be made with little difficulty.

After touring automobile assembly lines in both countries, a visitor observed, "The American factory seems almost like an armed camp. Foremen stand guard to make sure workers do not slack off. Workers grumble at foremen, and foremen are cross with workers. In the Japanese factory, employees seem to work even without the foreman watching. Workers do not appear angry at superiors and actually seem to hope their company succeeds."

Japanese workers' pride in their work and loyalty to their company are reflected in their capacity to produce goods that are not only competitive in price but reliable in quality. Some workers, especially younger workers in small plants, may be alienated from their company, but compared to Americans, they are absent less, strike less, and are willing to work overtime and refrain from using all their allotted vacation time without any immediate monetary benefit. The average Japanese laborer may accomplish no more than a loyal hard-working American counterpart in a comparable factory, but loyalty to the company is typically higher and hard work more common. Many an American businessman, after touring a Japanese company and inspecting figures on time lost from absenteeism and strikes, has expressed the wish that he had such a labor force.

It is tempting to account for the differences by historical tradition, but American workers have become less disciplined in recent decades, albeit with the same American tradition, and modern Japanese employees of large companies are far more loyal than, for example, Japanese textile workers at the turn of the century. It is common to assign American labor problems to our affluence, but discipline has remained strong in affluent Japan. Furthermore, Japanese companies establishing plants in America have achieved with a few years of modified Japanese-style management a level of employee devotion on the average higher than in comparable American plants. Before resorting to an explanation that centers on a semimystical "Oriental spirit," one might consider whether Japanese success bears any relationship to company management and treatment of workers.

THE EMERGENCE OF THE JAPANESE COMPANY SYSTEM

The Japanese company system as we know it today began to emerge only late in the nineteenth century. Craft shops, with paternalistic masters and their apprentices and journeymen, date back centuries, but these "feudalistic" shops are not totally different from the kind of paternalistic shops of Paul Revere's America or preindustrial Europe.

Modern Japanese corporate paternalism drew on the recent feudal past, but it emerged in industries that borrowed modern industrial technology and organization and required a high level of skill. In new industries with lower skill requirements like textiles, no long training was necessary. Here, young, dexterous employees were, if anything, more useful than older experienced ones with less dexterity, and young women were at least as agile as men. Late nineteenth- and early twentieth-century Japanese textile manufacturers, therefore, offered wages based on a piece rate system without significant salary increases for seniority. Wages were so low and factory conditions so unsatisfactory that most workers left before completing two or three years, and in some factories turnover was even more rapid.

Modern industries requiring a high level of skill faced different problems. As Ronald Dore has shown, the resulting late development pattern, unlike other industrialized countries' earlier indigenous development, relied on more concerted planning, training, and investment. In sizeable companies that manufactured steel, machine tools, electric equipment, and the like, companies needed to train both a group of highly skilled laborers and a group of white-collar managerial personnel. Because these skills were not based on the experience with indigenous developments, it took considerable time and capital investment to train them. And since these new companies were in basic industries that were well-financed and ultimately backed by the government, the companies were in a position to guarantee long-term employment. They therefore developed a seniority system of wage increases such that the newly trained employees in whom the company invested so heavily would be motivated to remain. The system of seniority and permanent employment was by no means universal in Japanese industry, but it became the predominant pattern in the large-scale modern industrial sector and has since spread to the large commercial organizations as well. As the modern industrial sector expanded, a higher proportion of company employees has gradually been brought into this seniority and permanent employment pattern.

The modern form of the Japanese company has evolved considerably since the early 1900s. In the 1930s and during World War II Japanese companies were brought under increasingly tight government control. During the Allied Occupation, the large *zaibatsu* firms were split up into smaller independent firms, but they gradually recombined into the present-day loosely organized groups after the end of the Occupation. During the 1950s and 1960s under government guidance many smaller firms were consolidated in order to modernize, and new American technology and management were introduced. For a time companies even considered copying the American pattern whereby workers could be dismissed and laid off more easily and hired in midcareer: it might get rid of employees with low performance, reward bold, innovative employees held down by the system, increase flexibility, give employees stifled in one company more options elsewhere, and reduce costs in a declining sector. By the late 1960s, when Japanese businesses started outperforming companies in the West, Japanese management intellectuals were satisfied that their seniority system was preferable to the dominant Western pattern, and they began to articulate a new philosophy of management.

The new philosophy incorporates many concepts from modern Western management and has much in common with large companies of American origin such as IBM, Polaroid, and Kodak. There is attention to basic business strategy, to product life cycles, to market surveys and marketing strategy, to accounting, to econometric models, to modern advertising, to up-to-date information processing. But some basics of the pre-World War II Japanese system remain: long-term perspective, permanent employment, seniority, and company loyalty. In addition, certain features gradually developed have recently been articulated to a higher degree: separation of rank and task, low differentials in pay and status for workers of a given age, "bottoms-up" management, and small-group responsibility.

The Japanese firm is less interested in short-term profits and more concerned with the long run. Executives may disparage their success in planning and forecasting, but they continue their best efforts and, when appropriate, boldly sacrifice profits for several years to build the groundwork for later success. They take care in cultivating good relations with institutions that might potentially be useful. They provide extensive training for personnel in skills that might be needed in the future. They invest in technology at seemingly high prices if it might later pay off. They invest heavily in plant modernization even when present plants meet immediate demands. As products become competitive, they conduct extensive preparatory work to lay a solid grounding for markets.

The company's capacity to think in long-range terms is made possible in part by their relatively greater reliance on bank loans than on the sale of securities to meet their capital requirements. Since stock now accounts for less than one-sixth of a company's capital needs compared to one-half in the United States, stockholders lack power to pressure for showing a profit each year, and banks are as interested in a company's long-range growth as the company itself. When companies are able to pay interest, the banks want to continue to lend them money, for banks are as dependent on quality companies to lend to as companies are dependent on the banks for borrowing. Indeed, when quality companies with their own capital want to cut costs by repaying loans, the banks try to make it attractive to continue borrowing.

Despite their interest in the future, most Japanese companies have not considered it profitable to invest heavily in basic research and development. It has made more sense to purchase foreign technology, for even if costs seemed high at the time of purchase, in retrospect the technology was obtained at bargain prices. The company concentrates research on adapting the technology for large-scale production, sometimes in such a way that it no longer needs to pay royalties on a particular patent. Japanese laws are such that processes, not functions, are patented. Thus, the company can buy technology, make new inventions that meet the same function as the original patent, and end their dependence on foreign technology. Until the 1970s many Western companies sold technology cheaply. Some did so because it was a perishable item likely to become obsolete or to be pirated, but often they were short-sighted in licensing patents—eager for a quick profit, ignorant of the long-term Japanese competitive threat, and unwilling to take the trouble to invest in developing the Japanese market. In recent years, as foreign companies are more clearly aware of the potential value of patents to Japanese mass producers, the prices and terms of technological transfer have become much higher, and the Japanese companies have therefore begun to move selectively into more research and development. Having caught up with much of Western technology, Japanese research is more concentrated in innovative rather than adaptive areas, and in areas with high potential economic payoff. Japan now has about as many people engaged in nonmilitary research as does the United States.

Just as MITI has tried to reorient industrial structure toward industrial sectors that can compete more effectively on world markets in the future, so each individual company tries to concentrate on product lines or segments that are likely to be more profitable in the future and to reduce its activity in declining sectors well before it is no longer profitable to continue.

It is not that Japanese are not interested in profitability, but that they are prepared to defer maximizing immediate profits in order to increase market share. Beginning in the late 1970s when the Japanese growth rate started leveling off, most Japanese companies have been trying even harder to find ways to cut costs to maintain profitability. But they tend to judge their company's success less by annual profit than by the annual changes in the market share their company has compared to other companies in the industrial sector. As the Boston Consulting Group has demonstrated, profitability is closely related to market share, for as firms expand they have more low-priced young labor and more modern plants. Therefore the companies' emphasis on market share has been well-placed.

The company's interest in the long term is also related to the system of permanent employment whereby an ordinary employee remains in the firm from the time he first enters after leaving school until he retires, which in most firms averages about fifty-seven or fifty-eight. The firm is committed to the employee and provides a sense of belonging, personal support, welfare and retirement benefits, and increased salary and rank with age. Barring serious long-term depression, the employee expects that he will never be laid off, and even if the company were to disband or be absorbed by another company, he expects that a new job elsewhere will be arranged. Companies are able to offer this kind of security despite economic fluctuations for several reasons. In times of temporary growth, additional temporary employees may be hired. For example, housewives may be added to the work force with the clear understanding that they will remain only while business needs them. Employees retiring from the company may be offered special short-term assignments in the company, usually at a lower salary than before retirement. Work may be subcontracted to small companies with the understanding that these contracts imply no permanent relationship.

If a large, reliable company should encounter economic difficulty, it will not go out of business because it is backed by banks, and behind the banks are various government institutions. Japanese companies have large debts to banks, but virtually all major companies are considered important for the economy as a whole, and therefore the Bank of Japan, backed by the Finance Ministry, stands behind the city banks that lend to the companies. Every company borrows from a main bank and then from other banks. If the company should be badly in debt and need to be bailed out, the main bank arranges a new management team for the company, often from its own staff, thereby strengthening lines of control over the company, which had previously been essentially autonomous. To the company officials replaced, this is not only a loss of power for them and their followers but a disgrace, something to avoid at all costs. Similarly, even in a declining industry, management and unions consider consolidation and consequent loss of power a last resort, something to fight against as long as possible. Every large company that has collapsed in Japan had resorted to questionable practices and behaved improperly toward its main bank. There is virtually no danger of a reliable major firm collapsing, but this security does not lead companies to relax their determination to perform at a high level.

The Japanese company with a given amount of resources has much greater security than an American firm in making bold efforts to modernize and undertake new activities. In addition to financial backing through banks, the company can be sure that key government ministries are concerned with their success and will help out in unpredictable emergencies in finding land, getting resources, gaining crucial technology. They know the government will be unlikely to undertake antitrust or other legal action that will greatly upset the company's overall capacities. The Japanese company signs fewer contracts and works more with other firms with whom there is a high degree of mutual trust, especially within the same group. They can therefore make more flexible adjustments in case of unpredictable outside forces, greatly reducing legal risks which American companies would have to bear regardless of new circumstances.

A company that encounters economic difficulties has many ways of adjusting without sacrificing the permanent employment system. Usually in addition to monthly salary, the company pays sizeable semiannual bonuses amounting to several months' salary. The size of the bonus depends on company profits, and therefore in times of depression it may be reduced without affecting basic monthly salary. In the spring, when basic monthly salary is determined, salary increases can be reduced or eliminated. The company can request employees to take an immediate vacation with partial rather than full pay or to reduce working hours, or to take minor salary cuts while requesting high officials to take larger salary cuts. If the difficulty is more severe, a company will reduce its entering class or even take in no new employees, adjusting assignments within the company so that jobs that would have been done by new employees will be done by others. Since companies follow long-term trends very closely, in industries that are expected to level off or decline, as for example in family electronics products which are increasingly made in Taiwan and Korea where labor costs are lower, companies will have anticipated the decline and admitted fewer employees in the years preceding the decline. Temporary employees will be released and permanent employees reassigned to their tasks. If the situation is very severe, the products formerly made by subcontractors will be made by regular permanent workers when contracts with subcontractors are terminated. Some individual subcontracting firms may be in trouble, but until now there have been enough new opportunities that few workers still in their prime are unable to find new work. If the recession is so severe that this kind of remedy is not adequate, then the company may move into some product line where it can keep people busy, for it makes sense to the Japanese to employ steadily a devoted work force and to take a small loss in order to provide work opportunities for one's permanent staff. As a further remedy, a company may encourage its workers to retire somewhat earlier by providing special benefits. If all these strategies are insufficient, some employees may be transferred from a company in a declining sector to affiliated companies in growing sectors. In fact, however, the number of cases of permanent employees being transferred to other companies in hard times is small. The system has so many cushions that permanent employees in large companies have ample reason to feel secure. Japanese companies may trim around the edges but they are not about to abandon the system.

Because an employee has job security and knows his salary will rise with seniority, he is willing to accept moderately low wages during his first few years in the company. Also, since retirement age is normally in the late fifties, salary increments can go up fairly rapidly without a company's worrying about having very high-paid elderly employees for many years. Although the system is designed to provide incentives for the young person trained by the company to remain loyal throughout his career and to have a sense of advancement, one of the important side effects is that it creates great pressure on a company to hire young people. Companies are reluctant to hire a midcareer person not only because his sense of loyalty would be questionable but because it is to the company's advantage to employ him during his low-priced younger years. In boom years, school and university graduates usually have had several positions to choose from, and even in relatively depressed years unemployment among young people leaving school is virtually nonexistent, much lower than the general figure for unemployment, which escalated to over two percent in the late 1970s.

The seniority system in the company works much as in the bureaucracy. Although there are pay differentials later in the career based on performance and responsibility, these are small compared to those accounted for by seniority pay. Responsible executives consciously try to keep pay distinctions among those with the same seniority no larger than, and if anything smaller than, what most employees consider appropriate. New employees ordinarily receive precisely the same pay for the first several years in the company; when differentials begin to appear later, they are minor, having more psychological than monetary significance. Equal pay tends to dampen competition and strengthen camaraderie among peers during their early years. If anything, the peer group recognizes that the ablest of their group are not being fully compensated in salary for their contribution, and this tends to dull any envy of peers toward the fastest rising in their group. Even those who rise more rapidly after differentials come into play can be promoted only if they enjoy the respect and approval of their associates; this prevents the growing distinctions from being overly disruptive. In a basic social sense, all those with the same seniority are considered as equals.

Those with higher positions continue to dress like others, often in company uniforms, and peers retain informal terms of address and joking relationships. Top officials receive less salary and fewer stock options than American top executives, and they live more modestly. It is easier to maintain lower pay for Japanese top executives because with loyalty so highly valued, they will not be lured to another company. This self-denial by top executives was designed to keep the devotion of the worker, and it undoubtedly succeeds.

It is understood that no one in a management track will be skipped over in advancement and no one will serve over another who entered the company at an earlier time. The same is true for technical track personnel and for laborers. Japanese executives at times considered increasing incentives for young people by allowing them to rise more rapidly and serve over their elders, but this caused undo strain in personal relations. The embarrassment for a person serving under a younger person is greater than in the United States. A person's official position can only rise until his retirement, and this eliminates any anxiety over the possibility that a worker will be relieved of his job or dropped to a lower position. After the first several years the able person begins to take on positions associated with the elite course inside the company and gradually rises to more important posts. But the differentials among age peers in title as well as pay are slight. A very able person might become section chief a year or two before his peers, or he might become section chief at the same time as his peers but be chief of a more important section.

As with elite bureaucrats, those who come up an elite course within the company have a broad range of experience in all parts of the company. . . . Managers of a large American corporation commonly have at least as broad a range of experience, and American companies can acquire some know-how by hiring workers with certain skills. However, with more turnover American employees lack the close personal connections within the company and with peers in other key organizations that contribute so much to Japanese company effectiveness.

As in the bureaucracy, only the top handful of officers work beyond normal retirement age, and when one man in an age cohort is chosen president, all his peers resign, usually to assume a high position with a subsidiary or subcontractor. . . .

When asked to describe a Japanese company, most Japanese managers list as one characteristic the practice of "bottom up" rather than "top down." The lowly section, within its sphere, does not await executive orders but takes the initiatives. It identifies problems, gathers information, consults with relevant parts of the company, calls issues to the attention of higher officials, and draws up documents. . . . Some senior executives in companies play a central role in making decisions, but ordinarily they do so only after appropriate section leaders lay the groundwork through close consultation with other sections and only when lower levels cannot themselves resolve their differences. Section people take great pride in their work because of their initiatives and because they have a chance to develop their leadership and carry great weight within the company on matters relating to their sphere. Consequently, the morale of young workers in their thirties tends to be very high. . . .

GROUP SPIRIT AND PERSONAL INCENTIVES

In addition to providing the employee with the economic incentives for long-term loyalty, company officials do their best to reinforce employee identification with the company. They provide elaborate annual ceremonies for inducing the new employees who enter as a group shortly after the end of the school year. The official training program may be anywhere from a few weeks to years, and includes not only useful background information but emotional accounts of company history and purposes. For spiritual and disciplinary training the employee may go on retreats, visit temples, or endure special hardships. To strengthen the bonds of solidarity, the new employee may be housed in company dorms while undergoing training, even if it means being separated from his spouse or parents. But even after the formal training program is over, the young employee continues to be treated as an apprentice for some time. He continues to receive training and supervision, and he is expected to behave with appropriate deference to his seniors. In American terms it is perhaps like a combination of the behavior of the fraternity pledge, without the hazing, and the young doctor in residency training.

Companies commonly have their own uniforms, badges, songs, and mottos. Each company has a special lore about the spirit of a "Matsushita person" or "Sumitomo person" or "Sanwa person," but to the outside observer the spirit sounds strikingly similar: enthusiastic, loyal, devoted. Company reception halls are available to employees' families for receptions and celebrations. Resort houses in the mountains and on the seacoast can be used by company employees who have put in the appropriate years of loyal service. Dormitories or apartment projects are available to employees of many companies. Unlike America, where mortgages are commonly obtained directly from banks, in Japan a high proportion of mortgages are obtained from the workers' company at subsidized interest rates. The company supplies gifts for many occasions in addition to the large semiannual bonuses. Special discounts of company products are available to employees and their families. Many companies have daily ceremonies—for opening the store, commencing work, or starting physical exercise. Parties large and small bid farewell to the old year, send off employees transferred to another city, welcome them home, congratulate people on promotions or honors, greet visitors, and commemorate retirement. Weekend group trips celebrate the coming of cherry blossoms, fall foliage, or holidays. For family members there are parties, special-interest clubs, courses, lectures, and exhibitions.

In addition to providing gymnasiums and swimming pools, a large company usually has sports teams well-equipped with uniforms and often with showcase facilities. So they can do well in their leagues, many companies recruit talented athletes as company employees, much as American colleges do, and they are given only minor work responsibilities. Outstanding professional sports teams that in the United States would be privately owned and associated with a particular city are in Japan sponsored instead by companies. The very highest officials in the company commonly take off from work to attend important sports contests with their rival companies. . . .

Loyalty in a large company is a many-layered overlapping labyrinth. Employees have layers of loyalty to the group with which the company is affiliated, to the particular factory or store, to the section, and to the immediate work group. Younger employees who are in a given specialty or career line may also enjoy a special link with senior sponsors in the same career line. Even with the immediate work group, one kind of group spirit thrives when the superior is absent, another when he is present. Part or all of the peer group assembles to commemorate earlier times and gossip about current events. Informal socializing, celebrations, and farewell or welcome-home parties occur at all of these levels.

At times a senior's concern about younger colleagues borders on what Westerners would consider "mothering," for Japanese of both sexes accept personal solicitousness that in the United States would ordinarily be considered unmasculine for men to give or receive. To avoid embarrassing an individual in public, criticism is commonly expressed in private in the spirit of a superior siding with a junior to help with a problem certain to cause him trouble.

With so much security and warmth, how does the system ensure high performance? In initially hiring employees, the company aims to be as merciless as entrance examinations in selecting people of quality. In preparation for selecting among employees of a peer group for more responsible positions, key line officers spend an enormous amount of time informally evaluating the performance of juniors, for decisions about personnel are considered too important to be left to personnel specialists. Employees are generally reassigned every two or three years, and each person knows that the quality of his overall performance is being evaluated to determine his next assignment. Those who rise to the top are chosen because in addition to high innate ability they have the capacity to see the big picture, to analyze problems clearly, to convey poise and confidence, to inspire support from fellow employees in all parts of the company, and to form successful relationships with top-level people in other companies and in the government.

The Japanese company makes it clear that its substantial benefits to employees are not guaranteed. Benefits are not distributed automatically by contractual agreement to anyone simply because he is a company member or because he falls into a certain category of age, status, and length of service, for leaders believe flexibility of rewards is needed as a critical leverage to maintain discipline. Bonuses, sick leave, and use of company facilities are offered to the hard worker, but signs of disapproval to the dilatory cause doubts about how superiors will respond when they come with their next request.

For motivating the worker, superiors rarely need to talk directly about benefits. Since employees have such long-term personal relationships with each other, small systematic differentiations of treatment by superiors have great psychological significance. Those who receive subtle hints that they are likely to rise eventually to the top positions are tremendously motivated because there is sufficient continuity and predictability to ensure that the hints can be translated into reality. When peers become overly solicitous to see if they can be of help, the worker knows that others consider his performance below par, and he may be devastated. He will rise by seniority alone, but to be at the bottom of his age group is extremely embarrassing and to be at the bottom and disliked for not trying as well is something to be avoided at all costs. But unlike students at the Harvard Business School and members of the United States State Department, for example, those at the bottom of the Japanese peer group do not need to worry that they may become castoffs as long as they exert themselves; the threat of banishment is often implicit but rarely used.

The most important single criterion for assessing quality for regular term promotions is the capacity to work well with others. The person who rises more rapidly is not the one with the original ideas but the one who can cooperate with others in finding a conclusion satisfactory to everyone. Personal achievement cannot be separated from the capacity to work effectively in groups. Eventually the reward for performance and effort include salary and position, but the proximate reward which foretells the eventual success in salary and position is the esteem of colleagues. In an American company without a strong group spirit and without expectations of permanent employment, an employee might come to feel that the only significant reward is salary and position, which in his view ought to be finely tuned to match performance. In the Japanese view, this custom, like tipping which they still avoid, cheapens the sense of service and contributes to contentiousness. In a Japanese company with strong group spirit and a long time frame, the really significant reward, the thing an employee strives for, is the esteem of his colleagues. . . .

The success of Japanese companies in avoiding disruptive labor unrest must be understood in the context of long-run individual identification with the company, but it has been reinforced by company handling of labor unions. After World War II, when the Allied Occupation ordered a rapid expansion of labor unions, Japanese company executives moved quickly to make employees members of labor unions. Labor unions were thus born not from virulent struggles led by bitter union leaders but from the initiative of company leaders. Nonetheless, the labor movement, at first protected by the Allied Occupation, became a powerful and sometimes violent political force. Management moved to encourage faithful employees to take part in union activities with the hope of moderating the potentially devastating strikes. They encouraged white-collar employees to join the same company union as the blue-collar employees and provided rooms and other facilities for union activities. These same white-collar employees, after serving their stint in labor unions, then returned to their managerial career line without loss of seniority. When unions became too militant, companies sometimes used questionable tactics to break the union and sponsored a second union that was more sympathetic with company goals. Management realized that simply co-opting unions could not be successful and they eagerly sought feedback from unions to find opportunities for meeting worker complaints in order to create better working relations and a more satisfied labor force.

Japanese unions are organized by the enterprise, and national craft unions tend to be weak. Nonetheless, unions do energetically represent the interests of the workers in pushing for benefits. Otherwise, union leaders would lose the support of workers. Unions also play a role in aggregating worker opinion on issues directly affecting them as part of the root-binding process in the firm. Though very worried about the danger of unions in the late 1940s, management has come to regard their unions as friends in helping stabilize the company. To avoid an excessive adversary relationship and create a proper climate, management finds time to socialize with union leaders without waiting for disputes that engender an atmosphere of controversy.

Because Japan is a rapidly modernizing country, with a dual economy of a modern and less modern sector, workers in larger companies are elite, with better training, more security, and better working conditions than workers in small companies that are less modern. Employees in large companies therefore have felt privileged to be there. Furthermore, since companies were mostly formed by managers rather than independent owners, workers have no rich capitalist class above them but only a managerial class whose style of life is not so different from their own. Japanese executives feel that not only American company owners but managerial staff have given themselves too many emoluments compared to what they gave the workers. This modest differential between managers and workers of a given age tends to reinforce the worker's sense of identification with the firm. . . .

With growing affluence and full employment in the late 1960s, many young Japanese became confident of their ability to earn a living even if they should leave their present company, and this attitude threatened company discipline. Many worried managers therefore fought harder than ever to maintain company solidarity. At the height of rapid growth, when unemployment was less than one percent and many company employees could have found work elsewhere, they still remained in their company. Since the oil shock of 1973, with renewed fears of a depression and increased unemployment, workers have felt especially dependent on their company and discipline has improved further. Although the Japanese standard of living is now on a par with that of the most advanced countries in the world, affluence has not ended hard work.

Even in the public sector there have been few debilitating strikes in recent years. Strikes in the public sector are officially illegal, and when some unions tested this legality in 1976, the strike was stopped before the announced termination date by public opinion and not the law. Employees from private companies who worked hard and accepted what they considered reasonable salary raises would not tolerate the government providing more favorable conditions for striking workers in the public sector. Newspapers that initially had taken a somewhat favorable attitude toward strikers changed quickly with the vehemence of public reaction. They began reporting, for example, that children of striking workers were ridiculed by classmates for what their parents were doing to the general public. It would not be politically feasible for workers in the public sector to use their capacity to stop the operation of public facilities to raise salaries higher than their counterparts in the private sector. It is not simply that the majority of Japanese workers are basically satisfied because their interests are being served, but that the workers in the private sector who do not strike because of devotion to their company exert public pressure strong enough to contain strikers in the public sector.

Perhaps more important than the success of companies in mobilizing workers for production and avoiding disabling strikes is the impact the system has on the self-esteem of the individual. The American who is fired or laid off as soon as the company's financial statement is in the red and who must go on unemployment insurance finds it hard to maintain great self-respect for his capacity to work. The worker who knows he will then be out of work understandably might demand more salary now, but in so doing he begins to measure his contribution and even his own worth solely in monetary terms. Even a high American official who is dropped or demoted because his division is unprofitable or who is hastily removed when dissatisfaction rises about company performance cannot help but have doubts about himself as well as his company. Unless caught in a horrendous well-publicized scandal, no Japanese official would be comparably disgraced by his company, and even if an official were caught in such an extreme case, other company officials find a way to cushion the blow if he has indeed performed well for the company. Officials who must be demoted to take responsibility for a public problem are often given substitute rewards and honor within the company so that they may not feel especially distraught. Success and failure come from group effort and are never laid on the shoulders of a single person. At worst, if an official performed badly, his term would be brought to a close slightly more rapidly or he might not be promoted to the next post quite as readily. Former officials do not need to be discredited by new officials and generally remain on good terms with their successors. Japanese workers who feel they do more than is required and feel they are appreciated by fellow workers enjoy a greater sense of individual worth than do those who merely get by with the minimal effort, a more common American pattern.

In short, the large Japanese company, an institutional structure that originated not in traditional Japan but in the mid-twentieth century, has developed a very effective modern corporatism well adapted to the needs of the latter part of the twentieth century. It has not eliminated problems. There are bad managers as well as good ones, and workers feel unhappiness with boring assignments, anxiety over personal difficulties, disappointment at not being more appreciated. But by international standards the large modern Japanese corporation is a highly successful institution. It is successful not because of any mystical group loyalty embedded in the character of the Japanese race but because it provides a sense of belonging and a sense of pride to workers, who believe their future is best served by the success of their company. The pride and stability that so many Japanese have because a family member works in a large company helps stabilize the political process and set a tone for the society at large.

Unit IX

———— Foreign Trade Policy ————

Both China and Japan face immediate challenges in the area of foreign trade policy. Japan is being challenged by a number of international interests, including the United States, Western Europe, and many of the less developed countries, to open its domestic economy to foreign imports. The Japanese political leadership and some of the country's most influential interest groups have resisted these demands and are determined to limit foreign access to Japanese domestic markets. Chinese leaders, on the other hand, are extremely eager to expand China's role in the global economy in the hopes that increased trade will provide opportunities for the country to benefit from foreign technology, capital, and management expertise. However, pressures from domestic political groups who fear that such liberalized policies could potentially threaten their economic and political power have constrained China's leaders.

Historically, the Japanese have played a much more active role in the global economy than the Chinese. In fact, since World War II, Japan has enjoyed spectacular success in international markets. Today, Japanese exports constitute 7 percent of world totals and fully 10 percent of the Japanese GNP is generated by exports. At the same time, while Japan has gained a reputation for producing higher quality goods at lower prices, Japanese policies toward imports have been widely criticized for fostering unfair competition and high levels of domestic protectionism.

Japan is highly dependent on imported resources. In addition to being the world's largest importer of food, the country also relies heavily on foreign supplies of energy. In order to compensate for such dependence, the Japanese have followed a policy of export promotion which has enabled them to capture a significant share of the world market in automobiles, electronics, consumer goods, and ships. Japanese goods are marketed and distributed all over the world. Japan has acquired through these exports a degree of economic influence that far exceeds its global political role.

China has no such international economic influence. In fact, as in many Communist economies, Chinese manufactured products have not been of sufficiently high quality to compete in international markets. More important, under Mao Zedong, the Chinese followed a policy of "self-reliance" that emphasized the domestic production of as many goods as possible and a concomitant de-emphasis on imports. This policy has created serious irrationalities in the Chinese economy, but it has protected many domestic producers, especially in heavy industry where foreign supplied goods are more competitive in terms of quality and price. It is these producers who feel most threatened by trade liberalization.

The current leadership of China is determined to open the domestic economy despite political opposition. Thus Special Economic Zones have been established in which foreign companies can set up production facilities both for the domestic and international markets. Imports of foreign technology and investment have risen dramatically and the Chinese people are being increasingly exposed to the kinds of lifestyles that are typically associated with the "decadent" West. Opponents of trade reform have seized on the theme of "spiritual pollution" as a means of impeding the reform process. They point to the corruption of Communist youth and Communist ideas and values as the greatest danger posed by the materialism of Western and Japanese countries, arguing that such influences must be combatted if China is to remain socialist.

The political debate surrounding trade policy in Japan is much less ideologically oriented. Because one of the major targets of foreign countries, especially the U.S., is the Japanese agricultural market, Japanese farmers have emerged as the central group opposed to liberalized trade policies. And because rural populations are overrepresented in the Diet (in terms of their proportion of the population), they command a great deal of influence. Farmers have a history of supporting LDP candidates, and the leadership of the LDP, already confronting decreasing electoral support, is wary of alienating such an influential interest. They seem willing to persevere in the face of foreign complaints in order to soften the impact of trade liberalization. The LDP has moved slowly and deliberately on trade policy issues much to the aggravation and frustration of Japanese allies.

One possible solution to many of the problems facing the two countries is greater cooperation between them. Their respective economies are extremely complementary. The Chinese are able to supply Japan with many of the important raw materials Japan requires. In turn, Japan is a convenient source of investment capital, technology, and expertise from which the Chinese could benefit in modernizing their own economy. However, both nations must overcome strong domestic political opposition to liberalized trade if they are to take advantage of the opportunities presented by closer cooperation and increased trade.

The readings in this unit focus on some of the major issues currently influencing foreign trade policy choices in China and Japan. In "The International Economic Policy of Japan," Masataka Kosaka notes that while the tendency toward economic nationalism is still strong in Japan, Japanese leaders are beginning to recognize global interdependence as a factor in policymaking. Examining the historical roots of Japanese nationalism, Kosaka shows how Japan's past experiences have continued to influence its economic policy choices despite Japan's growing integration into the global economy. "Liberalization of Agricultural Produce," originally published in *The Oriental Economist,* examines recent conflicts between the United States and Japan over agricultural trade policy. The selection describes how the Japanese government is attempting to resolve such problems as agricultural inefficiency and declining output while at the same time responding to the conflict demands of various sectors of society.

Finally, in "The Domestic Political Dimensions of China's Foreign Economic Relations," Susan L. Shirk identifies the various domestic interest groups that form the basic opposition to liberalized trade policies in China. Shirk argues that inland provinces, heavy industry (especially machine building), and central state bureaucracies are opposed to these reforms because of the negative effects such reforms have had on them. Coastal regions, light industries, and local elites, on the other hand, have reaped the greatest benefits from the trade reforms and thus are the prime supporters of current policies. Shirk points out that the conflicting demands of these "political coalitions," combined with structural constraints on expanded trade, pose serious political problems for the present leadership and make trade policy one of the most potentially divisive issues confronting the present Chinese leadership.

39

The International Economic Policy
of Japan

Masataka Kosaka

In these excerpts from *The Foreign Policy of Modern Japan,*
Masataka Kosaka examines various aspects of Japan's foreign trade
policy. Increasingly, he notes, Japanese leaders are recognizing
global interdependence as a factor to be considered in policy-
making, although economic nationalism still tends to prevail. Kosaka argues that there are three important historical roots to this
nationalism: the weak position of Japan as it emerged from isolation in the nineteenth century; the need to export in order to pay
for resources; and the racist policies of Western countries during
the 1920s and 1930s. These experiences have continued to influence Japanese trade policy despite Japan's growing integration
into the global economy. Foreign pressure on Japan has led to
some liberalization, but the "administrative guidance" of MITI as
well as high tariffs on finished, luxury, consumer, and labor intensive goods are still sticking points in trade negotiations.

Many observers of Japan have been impressed by the contrast between Japan's worldwide economic activity and the nationalistic orientation of its economic policy. Certainly the global character of Japan's trade
in the mid-1970s is indisputable. Only twenty years ago Japan's trade, which
was then mainly with the United States and other Asian countries, represented only 1.5 percent of total world trade. But Japanese economic activities expanded throughout the 1960s to every corner of the world and, in
the 1970s, accounts for more than 6 percent of total word trade. The decline of Southeast Asia's share in Japan's trade is revealing. In 1955 Japan
sold more than 20 percent of its exports to Southeast Asian countries; in
the 1970s it amounts to little more than 10 percent, less than Japan's current trade with Western European countries. . . .

A global approach to economic matters, which tries to avoid dependence on any one place, is emerging in Japan. The country has achieved some
good results with its policy of diversification, especially in expanding its
sources for raw materials. With the exception of oil, Japan does not rely on
any specific country or area for particular materials. . . .

283

Japan's attempts to spread its economic interests more widely reflects it geographic position. As an island country, it has easy access to every nation with ports. Moreover, modern transportation technology has nullified the distance factor, and big tankers and bulk carriers have brought a sharp reduction in freight charges.... Modern technology has also increased average transportation mileage which, in effect, has reduced the distance between Japan and other countries and helped the global expansion of Japan's economic activities.

The second characteristic of Japan's economy, the nationalistic orientation of its economic policy, is also indisputable, although it has sometimes been exaggerated and the recent modifications have been underestimated. The basic principle of Japan's trade policy has been, at least until recently, to enhance exports and limit imports, and to achieve this end it has adopted an intricate system of trade regulation. After Japan joined GATT in 1955, it built up a tariff system characterized by (1) low rates for primary products and high rates for finished goods—tariff escalation; (2) low rates for capital goods and high rates for consumer goods; (3) low rates for products not currently produced in Japan or likely to be produced in the future and high rates for those that were or could be produced in Japan; (4) protection for infant industries; (5) protection for industries that employed many workers even if they were declining or stagnating; (6) low rates for daily necessities and high rates for luxury goods; (7) low rates for special goods such as materials used for education, cultural purposes, or medical care.

With the growing liberalization of the trade system of the world in the 1960s, Japan experienced increased pressure to liberalize its own trade, but it did not respond quickly....

After 1968, when Japan's balance of trade began to record a substantial surplus, the demands for liberalization of its trade policies became stronger, and in the beginning of the 1970s Japan finally took substantial measures to correct the situation. Unfortunately Japan's attitude during this period was not a positive one; rather it represented a passive adaptation to the outside pressure. Such an attitude created distrust among other countries and retarded desirable changes in Japan's economic structure....

What are the roots of Japan's nationalistic economic policy? One must begin the query by examining Japanese history, for the economic policy of Japan today is a product of its history. First, Japan had to start life in the international community as a weak and undeveloped country. Japan had closed its doors to the world for more than two hundred years before the Western powers forced them open again. It was a natural psychological reaction for the Japanese to regard these Western powers as a threat. There were practical reasons as well. Japan experienced serious disturbances in its economy—for example, in its monetary system—when it was forced to discard isolationist policies and enter the international order. Moreover, the Western powers were industrialized whereas Japan was still agrarian. Many manufactured goods streamed into Japan, which could export only raw materials and foods in exchange....

Moreover, as most studies on Japanese trade have indicated, Japan did not have the capability to manage the trade business due to its inexperience and the lack of appropriate organizations. Dependence on foreign trading companies put Japanese manufacturers in a disadvantageous position, and with the loss of its tariff autonomy Japan could not mitigate the impact of Western industrial power. Therefore, the aim of Japan's early international economic policy was to secure the country's continued existence by recovering tariff autonomy, creating trading companies and a merchant marine, and stimulating the growth of industry and the export of finished industrial goods. As the task was urgent and Japan was underdeveloped, the state took primary responsibility. . . .

Japan had a tremendous need to export because it had to import raw materials for its industry. Thus, the balance of payments problem appeared during the initial stages of industrialization and became chronic. The difficulties increased after the First World War when the system of free trade collapsed and the trends toward protectionism appeared. Even in the 1920s, world trade did not grow rapidly, but the situation deteriorated as many countries adopted outright protectionism after the Great Depression of 1929. Such developments put Japan in an agonizing situation, for it could not retaliate against those countries that provided its raw materials. . . .

The virtual ban on Japanese emigration influenced the Japanese attitude toward international society, even though it was not directly related to trade policy. In the early 1920s many Japanese sought a solution for Japan's overpopulation in emigration. . . .

Thus, Japan discarded its brief experiment with internationalism to follow the course of ultranationalism. Ultranationalism was discredited by the Second World War, but the views and experiences of the 1920s and 1930s have remained in Japanese consciousness: as Japan has no natural resources, its first priority must be their acquisition; extraordinary efforts to increase exports are necessary in order to pay for raw materials; Japan is in a weak position because it is less industrialized than the Western countries; and Japan is in a disadvantageous position politically because it is the only nonwhite industrial country. These feelings make up the underpinnings for Japan's defensive and nationalistic international economic policy.

As the contemporary situation is very different from that of the past, one might expect that the old memories and attitudes have been weakened and largely replaced with a new perspective. The remarkable success of Japan in the past twenty years, however, has not only made Japan powerful, but also vulnerable, and some of its weaknesses are now more visible. It is true that Japan currently finds it less difficult to export its industrial goods; in some sectors (steel and shipbuilding, for example) the Japanese dominate the scene. Thus, the traditional objective of Japanese economic policy—promotion of exports—is no longer a difficult task. But even before the recent oil crisis, there was growing apprehension among Japanese policy-makers concerning the future of the nation. As Japanese economic activities have rapidly expanded in scope and increased in volume, they have encountered higher barriers abroad. The Japanese consider many of the barriers counter to the principles of free trade, and sometimes they attribute them to the fact that Japan is the only non-Western industrial nation in the world. To this must be added the increasingly difficult task of obtaining the raw materials necessary for their industry at reasonable prices—not merely oil, but other products as well. Thus, the Japanese have discovered that the old problems—the unique nature of Japan and the lack of raw materials—still persist, although in different form.

Recent events clearly indicate that these concerns are not without reason. The uniqueness of Japan and the lack of raw materials create real problems, ones difficult to solve. Moreover, the resistance that the Japanese have increasingly encountered abroad is a natural consequence of the increased strength of their economy and their slowness in making adjustments to the new situation. Some criticism of Japan's protectionist policy and its delay in import liberalization is justified, but the adjustments needed have never been simple. . . .

It is not always easy to determine what constitutes protectionism. Many Japanese feel that they are unjustly accused of protectionism, especially with regard to their so-called non-tariff barriers. Much of the criticism of Japanese economic policy touches on these non-tariff barriers, the most notorious of which is the "administrative guidance" that MITI provides to Japanese industries. Some criticism is certainly well-founded, but often the picture is overdrawn. Although it is true that many foreigners have difficulty operating in the Japanese market, some too easily attribute their troubles to non-tariff barriers because these represent a vague concept that can be used in many ways. Non-tariff barriers, however, are not something that the government can create or demolish at will. They consist mainly of the differences in business conventions and customs as well as the differences in the social structures within which businessmen operate in different societies. Therefore, those who do not have sufficient knowledge of the business and social conventions of a given country are adversely affected. Non-tariff barriers exist in every nation in one form or another, but the Japanese language and conventions are so different from those of other industrial nations that it is difficult to assimilate them quickly. Theoretically, Japanese should suffer from similar difficulties when operating abroad. But the Japanese have had to operate in Western countries for a long time, so they have managed to learn Western conventions. The rest of the world, however, has long neglected the Japanese market. Still, the much-criticized hard-sell methods of Japanese merchants can be attributed to their insufficient understanding of the conventions of others. On the whole, the uniqueness of Japan's society and culture seems to be the root of the trouble. . . .

As noted, the lack of raw materials is a primary cause for concern among Japanese today. After World War II, two conditions operated to reduce the problem of raw material supply for Japan. First, the postwar world economic system guaranteed free trade and free access to raw materials fairly well. Therefore the Japanese could survive by processing imported raw materials and exporting the product to gain money with which to import more raw materials. Second, the volume of raw materials that Japan needed was small and could be obtained by one means or another. Toward the end of the 1960s, however, these conditions changed and the Japanese began to experience difficulties.

Due to its rapid growth since the 1950s, the volume of raw materials that Japan must now import to maintain its industrial activities has become colossal. [Ninety] percent of Japan's raw materials now comes from abroad, including all its aluminum and nickel and 99.7 percent of its oil. Japan is least dependent on others for lead and zinc, but half of these needs are still supplied from abroad. Japan's dependence on outside sources for raw materials has existed for a long time, and the difficulties have not proved insurmountable. But toward the end of the 1960s, Japan's share in the total world consumption of raw materials rose to nearly 10 percent. In the non-Communist world, Japan is second only to the United States in the amount of raw materials it consumes. As the United States has considerable natural resources of its own, Japan has become the largest importer of raw materials. Its share in the world trade of raw materials is now roughly 12 percent, and under present conditions it is destined to grow.

In the meantime, the international situation with regard to raw materials has changed. By the end of the 1960s, total world consumption had become enormous, and the supply of several mineral resources began to fall short of demand. Moreover, some supplying countries have become dissatisfied with the terms of trade or the fact that they have remained the suppliers of raw materials but have not succeeded in their own industrialization. Thus they have become more demanding in their terms of trade and have begun to ask for new types of economic relations with the industrial nations so that they themselves can become industrialized. These factors have made it more difficult for Japan to obtain the raw materials required....

The lack of raw materials presents two special problems for Japan. First, reliance only on commercial transactions will not be sufficient to guarantee the necessary supply of raw materials in the future, given Japan's economic projections. Therefore, a 1971 MITI White Paper proposed diversification in the acquisition of raw materials by adding two new methods for obtaining them: (1) to advance funds to countries that produce raw materials in exchange for guarantees of supply; and (2) to invest in the exploration for raw materials at Japan's own risk. The White Paper particularly emphasized the second approach because (1) it would contribute directly to an increase in world production of raw materials; (2) it would guarantee supply through the development of special ties with the countries that own the raw materials; and (3) it would improve the terms of trade. Such efforts will certainly improve the situation if they succeed, but this type of policy demands substantial political capabilities, because the close and special ties

produced through investment tend to create complicated political problems. Unless direct investment is accompanied by wise political action, the
situation can easily deteriorate.

Second, importation of large amounts of raw materials can create a
formidable balance of payments problem. Japan must export an enormous
flow of manufactured goods to pay for the vast supply of raw materials from
abroad. As most supplier countries do not have large home markets, Japan
has contrived to have a surplus in trade elsewhere—with the United States,
Southeast Asian countries, and Europe. But Japan may find it difficult to
maintain such a trade surplus now that the amount necessary to pay the bill
has become so great. Japan's trade surplus with countries other than those
that supply raw materials can become greater than they can tolerate, as past
events has so graphically illustrated. The difficulties have recently increased,
with the sharp rise in the prices of raw materials—a trend that promises to
continue. The development of the supplier countries, which are in most
cases the less-developed ones, will help alleviate the problem but will not
eliminate it. Importing a large amount of raw materials and financing it by
trade surpluses elsewhere is not an uncommon policy, but to seek to practice it on such a large scale as is necessary for Japan creates a difficult problem both for it and for the world.

In exerting a greater effort than others to promote exports, therefore,
Japan must pay special attention to the composition of its trade, and in this
respect it will continue to be different from most other industrialized nations. In sum, Japan is unique, not only socially and culturally, but also economically. Although it is not easy for Japan to maintain and enhance its
livelihood under such circumstances, it is also not easy for other nations to
accommodate to such a nation in the world system. Naturally, therefore,
Japan has become an object of criticism and various countermeasures as it
has risen from a negligible position in the world economy to one of the
largest traders. Naturally also, such reactions have caused deep anxiety in
Japan and revived the traditional fear that the country may be isolated from
the world. Many Japanese are obsessed with the vulnerability and weakness
of their country; the result is their continued defensive and nationalistic
approach to the international affairs. . . .

Even minor domestic interests cannot easily be sacrificed for the sake
of necessary adjustments to the outside world, because the first priority is
to obtain consensus within the country. The Japanese attitude on the protection of its agricultural sector represents a typical case. Japan's protectionist policy toward agriculture has not been criticized only by foreign
countries, but has also caused notoriously high food prices in Japan and hurt
such groups as blue- and white-collar workers and artisans. Only the farmers
benefit directly. If food imports were liberalized, the majority of Japanese
could obtain food more cheaply. Yet the movement in Japan for the liberalization of food imports has been much delayed. The majority interest is
clearly with the critical foreigners and the Japanese nonagricultural sectors;

but although these groups are not powerless, they are also not decisive. Unless and until the farmers themselves are persuaded to accept a different policy and a consensus is created, change with respect to agricultural trade policies will be slow.

40

Liberalization of Agricultural Produce

The Oriental Economist

This article from *The Oriental Economist* focuses on the problems of agricultural trade between the United States and Japan. Agricultural quotas are the single most important point of friction in U.S.–Japanese trade relations. Of the 27 commodities currently under import restrictions, 22 are agricultural commodities. Given the United States' comparative advantage in this sector, it is natural to expect some conflict over Japanese trade policy.

Japan's politically influential farmers strongly oppose any further import liberalization on farm produce, arguing that Japan is already the world's largest net importer of produce; that other countries take measures to protect their agricultural producers; that the balance of trade with the U.S. cannot be solved by liberalization of agricultural quotas alone; and that the real trade problems arise from declining American productivity, quality, and competitiveness. Japanese business groups, on the other hand, generally support the liberalization policies. Many, like *Keidanren,* believe that the lifting of import restrictions will not only lead to improved relations with the U.S. but will also enhance the modernization and rationalization of Japan's agricultural sector. Still, the issue of security continues to be of primary concern to Japanese policymakers. Since President Nixon sharply reduced soybean exports to Japan in 1972, the Japanese have been less amenable to increased dependence on the United States. But the problems of continued inefficiency and declining output are real and require intelligent solutions.

The crux of Japan's trade frictions with the United States is now rapidly boiling down to the question of to what extent Tokyo is prepared to go in liberalizing imports of agricultural produce.... The trouble ... is that there is no easy solution to the import problem of agricultural produce as

Japanese farmers are strongly opposed to further import liberalization for agricultural produce.

The American rationale for demanding Japan to step up its purchases of agricultural produce is quite clear. The United States ran up a huge deficit totaling $18 billion in its trade with Japan last year and is now strongly required to correct the situation.

[In 1982], Japan [had] 27 commodities under its residual import restrictions and a great majority of them (22, to be more exact) [were] agricultural produce, the field in which the United States has strong international competitiveness. It is only natural under the circumstances that the U.S. Government should now be strongly calling on Japan to eliminate import restrictions on agricultural produce.

Japanese farm organizations, on the other hand, are strongly opposed to any further import liberalization on farm produce and have been heavily pressuring Diet members to take up their cause. There are four major reasons for farmers' diehard opposition to any stepped-up imports of farm produce.

One is that Japan is the world's largest net importer of farm produce and that it is unreasonable for the United States, on which Japan already is heavily dependent for supply of grains and soybeans, etc., to zero in on farm produce as symbols of Tokyo's closed-door policy and press Japan to further lift its residual import restrictions.

Another is that agriculture is one of the most basic of all industries and that every country in the world is resorting to some kind of import restriction or the other. Japan is by no means laggard, in comparison with the United States and European countries, in opening its doors to foreign farm produce, according to Japanese farm organizations. The United States, as a matter of fact, is controlling, by force of law, imports of dairy products, wheat and related products, while EC member countries are jointly protecting intra-community agriculture by placing import surcharges on most of agricultural produce and providing promotional grants to export efforts.

The third reason, on the other hand, is that, even if Japan completely lifts import restrictions on agricultural produce, the total import amount will be limited to only several hundreds of millions of yen and will not make any appreciable dents on Japan's export surpluses with other countries. Such imports, though very much limited in view of Japan's entire imports, will have devastating effects on Japanese farmers as the produce still on the nation's residual import restrictions list are the very mainstays of Japanese agriculture. Complete lifting of import restrictions on agricultural produce are certain to lead to serious political and social problems.

The fourth reason cited by Japanese farm organizations it that agriculture is by no means the true crux of the trade problems now existing between Japan and the United States. A series of unhappy developments, including the relative decline of the international competitiveness of American products, sustained high interest rates in the United States and the resultant stagnation of the U.S. economy, are largely responsible for the trade frictions between the two countries, according to Japanese farmers, and so are the heavy dependence of Japanese manufacturers, especially those of motor vehicles, on the U.S. market. Japanese farmers maintain that the trade frictions caused by manufactured goods should be handled by industrial companies, not at the cost of farmers.

Even among the Japanese, however, there are many who are in disagreement with this line of thinking. Such people believe that lifting of protection will lead to modernization and rationalization of Japanese agriculture. One of the most outspoken endorsers of such a point of view is *Keidanren* (the Federation of Economic Organizations), the virtual command center of the Japanese *zaikai* (the business and industrial community). The prestigious economic organization has recently published "an opinion on improving the trade frictions between Japan and other countries" and again called strongly for lifting import restrictions on agricultural produce at the earliest possible date.

"Japan should play its due role as an economic giant," the Keidanren report says, "Continued protection of inefficient agriculture only aggravates foreign countries' criticism of Japan." The report then advocates for: 1) early enforcement of complete import liberalization of agricultural produce, and 2) announcement of a clear-cut item-by-item liberalization timetable if immediate decontrol is deemed advisable for some of the produce involved. As a means of compensating for the farmers who are certain to suffer from the liberalization and the resultant inflows of low-priced agricultural produce from foreign countries, Keidanren calls for creation of a subsidizing system for the farmers.

Zenchu (the National Federation of Agricultural Cooperative Associations), the virtual spokesman for Japanese farmers, summarily dismisses Keidanren's proposal simply as irrelevant. It claims that full liberalization is sure to destroy Japanese agriculture and put the nation's food security in serious jeopardy.

The Japanese Government thus is faced with a very difficult choice: whether it will allow inefficient parts of its industry simply to perish or whether it will continue to place top priority on security in food supplies even at a considerable cost to its treasury.

The farmland liberalization policy of the Occupation Forces immediately after World War II has destined Japanese agriculture to small, and often cottage-level, operations. Under the Agriculture Basic Laws formulated in 1961, Japan tried: 1) to elevate income levels in the agricultural sectors in parallel with the sharp revenue growths in manufacturing sectors, and 2) to drastically improve productivity in agricultural sectors by merging small and cottage-level operations into far larger units. Although farmers' income levels have improved drastically in the following years thanks considerably to price supports, farmland productivity has largely failed to improve. The biggest reason for the continued low productivity in agriculture is the skyrocketing of land prices in Japan. Many small and cottage-level farmers have come to find high asset values in their farmlands and become reluctant to part with them even though their farming is only of a half-hearted nature. Male members of such small farms go to cities and factories to find employment, while their wives and old folks are dabbling in farming.

This is one of the reasons why many people, especially those in the manufacturing sectors, are demanding elimination of protective means for such part-time farmers, thereby helping farmlands to fall into a smaller number of farmers who are determined to specialize in farming on a large and truly efficient scale.

At one time, Japan seemed to take a definite step in this direction. Everything, however, virtually went up in smoke in 1972 when the United States announced that it would stop soybean shipments to Japan. This action on the part of the Americans proved to be a [serious] shock even to Japanese consumer organizations which had, up to that time, been strongly calling for greater imports of low-priced foreign agricultural produce. Many Japanese have come to believe that they should maintain a reasonable level of self-sufficiency in food supply, even at a considerable cost.

If the Americans truly want their agricultural produce to have free entry into the Japanese market, they should first of all announce their willingness to make long-term and stabilized supply of agricultural produce to Japan, thereby helping the Japanese consumers' fear about food shortages to rest.

41

The Domestic Political Dimensions
of China's Foreign Economic Relations

Susan L. Shirk

In this selection, Susan L. Shirk identifies a number of domestic interest groups that make up the basic opposition to liberalized trade policies. The Chinese government has pursued an
open-door policy since 1978 in the hope of attracting the foreign
capital and technological expertise needed to modernize the
Chinese economy. Shirk argues that the major opposition to recent policies comes from a "communist coalition" of inland provinces, heavy industries, and central planning agencies and industrial ministries which was favored and protected by earlier
policies that encouraged self-sufficiency. The bulk of the support
for the new policies comes from a coalition of coastal regions,
light industries, and local elites, which has reaped the greatest
benefits from the reforms. Combined with structural constraints
on expanded trade, these groups pose serious political problems
for the present Chinese leadership and make trade policy one of
the most potentially divisive issues confronting domestic political
leaders today.

Since the death of Mao Zedong, China has entered a new era in its
economic relations with foreign countries. Foreign trade had been revived
in 1972–73 under Mao's reign, but only after his death and the overthrow
of the Gang of Four did trade become a major component of China's economic development strategy. Two-way trade was expanded almost 200 percent, from about $15 million U.S. in 1977 to over $43 billion in 1981. The
post-Mao leaders took the even more momentous step of opening-up China
for foreign investment. Foreign companies were invited to enter into joint
ventures and other forms of cooperative production in China. At the same
time the monopoly of the central foreign trade officials over foreign trade
and investment activities was shattered by the policy permitting local officials and factory managers to make foreign business deals on their own. . . .

In an effort to revive and modernize the Chinese economy, beginning
in 1979, Deng [Xiaoping] and his fellow-leaders invited foreign businesses

to enter into joint ventures and other forms of cooperative production in Chinese factories. They encouraged Chinese industries to produce for export, and allowed them to import foreign equipment. They granted local governments and factories a considerable degree of autonomy in negotiating trade and investment contracts with foreigners, even permitting them to retain and spend a percentage of the foreign exchange they earned in the process. Deng declared that there was no longer any danger of exploitation at the hands of the foreign imperialists because China was now able to control its own "door" and adopt an open-door policy on the basis of safeguarding national interest.

The expansion of China's role in the world economy will undoubtedly have major international ramifications. Although China's total trade is still comparatively small ($43.1 billion in 1981), she could eventually become a major exporter of agricultural products, petroleum, coal, nonferrous metals, textiles, pharmaceuticals, and even electronic equipment and machinery. A China market of potentially over one billion people has attracted foreign producers seeking to revive lagging international sales. Even though eighty percent of China's population consists of rural peasants too poor to afford many domestically produced consumer goods—much less imported ones—the nation has an urban consumer market of over 200 million people and an industrial economy badly in need of modern equipment. Many foreign firms have been willing to undertake co-production in China largely in the hopes of eventually gaining a share of this huge import market. Foreign banks are eager to lend to China because in contrast to Third World countries already burdened with heavy international debts, China has a healthy balance of payments, substantial gold reserves, a budget which is almost balanced, and modest foreign indebtedness. (The Bank of China is itself becoming active in lending abroad.) China's place in the international economy is potentially very significant, but much depends on what policies the Chinese leaders decide to pursue in the future. . . .

CHINA'S POLITICAL ECONOMY, 1949–78

Before the shift in economic policies which began in 1978, a set of regions, industrial sectors, and bureaucratic institutions were favored, protected, and subsidized by Chinese economic policies and structures. This set of groups, which could be called the "communist coalition," consisted of the inland provinces, heavy producer goods industries (especially iron and steel and machine building), and the planning agencies and industrial ministries in the central government.

The favoritism of these regions, industrial sectors, and bureaucratic institutions stemmed from the fundamental features of the Chinese economic and political system since 1949. Despite periodic policy shifts, the Chinese system exhibited continuity in certain basic structural characteristics. . . .

How has the expansion of foreign trade and investment affected the set of group interests—inland provinces, heavy industry, the central bureaucracies—that were favored prior to the open-door policy? How does the structure of the Chinese political and economic system shape the way these groups attempt to stem the current tide? And what kinds of policies are these group pressures likely to produce?

REGIONAL CONFLICTS

The new foreign trade and investment opportunities, combined with the policies allowing local governments and enterprises to negotiate independently and retain a proportion of their foreign exchange earnings, have stimulated economic competition among Chinese cities and provinces. Local political authorities seek to develop their local economies with the profits of trade and foreign investments in a manner reminiscent of the local authorities of the mid-nineteenth century who sought to build local armies with the *likin* taxes collected along domestic trade routes.

In this new competitive environment, the coastal provinces appear to be winning most of the prizes. Foreign investments are concentrated in a few coastal provinces and municipalities, especially Shanghai and the Special Economic Zones (areas granted special powers to offer concessionary terms to foreign investors) in Guangdong and Fujian provinces. The four Special Economic Zones in Guangdong and Fujian were able to attract sixty percent of direct foreign investment in China in 1981. As centers of light industry, the coastal areas are the source of a large percentage of China's manufactured exports. For example, 1700 of Shanghai's 8000 factories are now engaged in producing for export. The coastal ports also ship exports for many inland enterprises; despite increasing competition from inland ports up the Yangtze, the port of Shanghai still handles one-fifth of total national exports. . . .

The inland provinces, on the other hand, have obtained few benefits from the new open door and see the gap between themselves and the coastal provinces widening because of it. The inland economies are based on the extraction of minerals and the manufacture of industrial equipment. These industries were thrown into a slump because of national economic readjustment policies diverting investment funds from heavy industry to light industry and agriculture (see below). Officials in the inland provinces are trying to break into the light consumer goods industries but have a hard time competing with the brand name products (bicycles, watches, television, etc.) from Shanghai and Tianjin which are widely preferred by consumers. The inland provinces would like to find export markets for their raw materials—especially coal and nonferrous metals—but they are short of capital for exploration, production, and marketing. When inland provinces have succeeded in attracting foreign funds for large construction projects to extract and transport coal, the joint ventures have been plagued by the uncertainties in international energy markets.

Today, the inland provinces in China rely on administrative regulations and conservative cultural appeals to defend themselves against the threats of foreign and domestic competition. They have established local blockades and other forms of what central leaders sometimes condemn as "administrative interference" to protect their infant consumer goods industries by keeping out high-quality brand-name merchandise from Shanghai and other light-industrial centers. In 1982 Anhui objected to an exhibit of Shanghai products held in their province. Anhui officials argued that since many of the products were now being produced in local factories (because of the readjustment and profit-retention policies favoring the development of light industry), the exhibition ought to be closed-down. The dispute had to be resolved by the State Economic Commission, which ruled that Shanghai was entitled to hold the exhibition but not to display products identical to those made in Anhui. . . .

The inland areas have also publicized the danger of corrosion of Chinese culture by decadent ideas and lifestyles from abroad. Many of the scare stories about the infiltration of bourgeois foreign culture come from the inland provinces. Complaints about pornographic pictures and tapes (called "yellow materials") imported from abroad have been heard from areas as deep in the interior and remote from foreign contact as Shanxi. . . .

Officials from the coastal areas have also launched a counterattack against accusations that their cities have abandoned socialism for capitalism and have become dens of iniquity due to the open door. They began to fight back at the National People's Congress in late 1982. One Guangdong official protested that some inland provinces were discriminating against travelers from Guangdong by searching their luggage and separating them from other travelers in order to prevent smuggling. Ren Zhongyi, First Communist Party Secretary of Guangdong, made a speech in which he replied to "some people at home and abroad [who] still have various concerns about our open-door policy" and "some comrades [who] are afraid to mix with foreigners." He reminded them that Japan's economic progress was achieved through trade, and he held up Guangdong as a positive model of what can be accomplished when China "smashes the blockade of imperialism" and opens the door to foreign countries: "The experience of Guangdong Province shows that where the door is kept wide open to the world, economic and cultural development is quicker." Other officials cited statistics showing that the open door had resulted in average economic growth rates over the past three years which were higher (7.4 percent) in Guangdong than in the rest of the nation (6.7 percent). They also claimed that some of the reports about Guangzhou youth wearing U.S. army jackets, rampant gambling, and other examples of bad lifestyles imported from the West, were false. . . .

An even greater potential threat to the political power of Beijing is the economic power of Shanghai. This pre-1949 center of industry, trade, and commerce was until very recently kept on a tight leash by the central government. When Guangdong and Fujian were given the freedom to deal directly with foreign businesses and offer them concessionary terms, Shanghai was not. When the local governments were given the right to retain a share of their domestic and foreign exchange revenues, Shanghai, along with Beijing and Tianjin, were not given similar financial autonomy. These restrictions reflect not only the dependence of the national treasury on the economies of Shanghai and the other two municipalities, but also the central leaders' distrust of Shanghai. . . .

SECTORAL CONFLICTS

The expansion of foreign trade and investment has had a differential effect on heavy and light industries in China. Light industries have been better able to take advantage of the new opportunities for exporting, while heavy industries feel the threat of competition from imports more strongly. At the same time heavy industrial enterprises and bureaus have felt threatened by domestic economic policies and reforms. Industrial readjustment policies cut their capital investments from the center and lowered their output quotas. New policies designed to motivate managers to cut costs and raise efficiency by permitting enterprises to retain a portion of their profits worked to the advantage of light industrial enterprises but not heavy industrial ones. As a rule, light industrial products, especially consumer goods like televisions, have been assigned higher prices than raw materials and heavy industrial products. Therefore regardless of how well the enterprise is managed or how hard the workers work, a tape recorder factory will always earn—and be able to retain—more profits than a steel mill. . . .

All Chinese industries, both light and heavy, would like to promote their export prospects by upgrading their production processes with imported equipment, but they are continually frustrated by their comrades in the Chinese machine building industry. The machine building industry was a major beneficiary of the extensive growth and self-sufficiency policies of the past. It supplied equipment for almost all Chinese factories under monopolistic conditions and expanded at rapid rates, about 20 percent a year during the 1950's–70's. By 1978, there were over 100,000 machinery manufacturing enterprises in China, nearly one-third of the total number of industrial enterprises. The Ministry of Machine Building (MMB) administers 11,000 of these enterprises, which employ 5½ million employees.

The Ministry of Machine Building is an important source of protectionist pressures in the Chinese system. The Ministry reacted with alarm when Chinese factories began to modernize with purchases of imported equipment. The machine building industry's monopoly was being challenged by foreign competition. The Ministry flexed its bureaucratic muscles and demanded a policy of "buy Chinese" for factories upgrading their equipment. As a result, the Ministry revived a 1950's institution, a special Equipment Approval Division empowered to approve all factory imports of equipment, even those in joint foreign-Chinese enterprises. The request for imported equipment is submitted to the State Planning Commission, which in turn sends it to this Division in the MMB. If the Ministry determines that one of its factories can produce the same piece of equipment (regardless of cost), it vetoes the import....

Chinese heavy industries, especially machine building, urged further measures to protect local manufacturers. They complained that the "blind importation" of cars and other vehicles cost the country three to four times the total investment for the domestic car industry. They cited examples of products like the industrial steam turbine engine of the Hangzhou Steam Turbine Plant, which although of sufficiently high quality to be exported to ten countries, was having difficulty selling to the domestic market because of enterprises' "blind faith in foreign merchandise." Some newspaper articles described the purchase of domestic equipment as "an important test of patriotism." Protectionist pressures caused the Chinese government to decree in January 1981 that in principle, equipment that could be produced locally should not be purchased abroad. In 1982 import duties on such equipment as cranes, engines and other machinery were raised (duties on some raw materials and parts that were in short supply were lowered), and import licenses were required for vehicles, computers, and various types of equipment. Subsequently there has been a trend toward the Chinese purchase of licenses for foreign technologies rather than the outright import of equipment; those equipment imports which are permitted are justified by the goal of import substitution. Machine industry protectionism has clearly resulted in a decrease in purchases of foreign equipment: imports in the first half of 1982 declined 43 percent from the same period in 1981....

Government efforts to protect the domestic market, however, have impeded the efforts of light industrial plants to attract foreign investment. Periodic increases in customs duties on imported materials and product prices which are controlled by the State Planning Commission, combined with restrictions on domestic sales make it difficult for the foreign partner in a joint venture to make a decent profit....

[W]e may expect continued tension between the machinery industry and light industry over the import of foreign equipment and incentives for foreign investment and exports. Because the Machine-Building Ministry appears to have more political strength at the level of central governmental policy-making, will light industrial enterprises begin to call upon their foreign partners to bolster their influence in foreign economic policy-making? Will they press for restructuring of the state bureaucracy in order to right the political imbalance between light and heavy industry?

BUREAUCRATIC CONFLICTS

A major obstacle to economic reform in China is resistance from the Communist Party and People's Liberation Army. Party officials, worried that economic reforms will make their political skills obsolete and diminish their power, often fail to implement the reforms or even attack them for deviating from political orthodoxy. Army officers also are concerned about loss of power and status and about cuts in military spending. Military critics argue that the reforms will destroy the Maoist legacy of "politics in command."

The politics of economic reforms such as the open-door policy are, however, much more complex than just a struggle between the reformist leaders and the conservative Communist Party and People's Liberation Army. There are also conflicts within the government bureaucracy—for example, between the Machine Building Ministry and other industrial ministries over the import of foreign equipment and between the Trade Ministry and other ministries over control of imports and exports—which are highly significant in shaping foreign economic policies in China. . . .

In a socialist command economy all economic sectors (for example, the machinery industry, the electronics industry, the coal industry, the petroleum industry, the iron and steel industry, and the light consumer goods industry) are organized into vertical national bureaucracies headed by ministries in Beijing. Each minister is like a division head in a huge conglomerate called "China Incorporated." The minister, sitting in Beijing, is able to articulate the interests of the industry he represents. In this way the structure of the socialist economic and political system gives industrial sectors a powerful voice in policy-making. . . .

The [central government frequently] contends with the provinces over who should pay for the infrastructural investments which are needed to attract foreign investment and facilitate trade. For example, Fujian and Beijing clashed over the financing of the new Fuzhou airport which is vital for tourism as well as foreign business. The center won, and Fujian must pay for the airport itself out of the retained profits of their trade and industry. Guangdong Province is also being required to pay for its new rail line. Both of these projects would have been financed by the central authorities in the past. Large energy projects have also sparked conflict between the provinces, which seek to guarantee their own energy needs, and the central government which is concerned about maintaining a balance among regions, energy sources, and foreign and domestic equipment.

STRUCTURAL CONSTRAINTS

In addition to the conflicts between regions, industrial sectors, and bureaucratic organizations which influence China's foreign economic relations, the character of China's economic system itself also constrains her dealing with foreign firms. The centralized structure of the command economy limits the ability of enterprises, localities, or bureaucratic agencies to engage in international business. The national plan regulates almost all activities related to production. Factory managers cannot freely hire labor, raise wages, choose products, set prices, or invest profits in other enterprises. An enterprise that wants to import, export, or engage in joint production with a foreign firm inevitably comes into competition with the plan, which is enforced by the central planners and industrial ministers. . . .

The most striking innovation [in the Chinese economy] is the four Special Economic Zones (SEZ) in Fujian and Guangdong and their bureaucratic representative, the SEZ Office under the State Council. The Zones were placed outside the plan in order to give them the flexibility to attract foreign investors. The Zones have attracted skilled manpower with higher-than-usual wages, and their foreign connections have given them a strong claim on electric power supplies. According to SEZ officials, being outside the plan, however, makes it difficult for them to obtain building materials and other supplies for joint venture operations. The supplies problem is so acute that the SEZ Office recently demanded a change in policy which in effect incorporates supplies for SEZ enterprises back into the national plan. Enterprises outside the SEZ which want to export or engage in co-production with foreign firms have similar, albeit smaller difficulties because the plan never specifies their complete sources of supply. Managers must procure 10 to 25 percent of their annual supplies on their own initiative. . . .

The advent of foreign trade and investment also puts pressure on administered prices in China. Most Chinese economists acknowledge the irrationality of using prices which have remained unchanged since the early 1950's and which bear no relationship to supply or demand. Nevertheless policy-makers fear a thorough price reform because its redistributive consequences would be so politically divisive. Partial rationalization of prices often does not work. . . .

The discrepancy between domestic administered prices and the international price distorts the incentives of enterprises and trade companies to import and export. As one journal article put it, "The prices of some commodities, for instance, are high at home and low abroad, resulting in a loss when exported, while the prices of others are low at home and high abroad, producing a profit when exported." In order to encourage the exports of certain manufactured goods, the central government through the MOFERT [Ministry of Foreign Economic Relations and Trade] trading companies, must subsidize the manufacturers. And in certain product lines, the trading companies make more of a profit from importing than from exporting. In this way, China's involvement in international business creates pressures for price reform.

Unit X

—————— Agricultural Policy ——————

The two nations of China and Japan are facing very different problems in the area of agricultural policy. Whereas China is seeking ways to free the productive energies of a rural workforce that makes up 80 percent of its total population, Japan is attempting to rationalize its highly subsidized yet small,* inefficient, and unproductive agricultural sector. The major question for present-day Chinese leaders is how to elevate the living standards of China's 800 million peasants, who have been effectively ignored since 1949. The question for Japanese leaders, on the other hand, is how to protect a declining but highly influential farm sector while at the same time satisfying the demands of an increasingly urbanized consumer society.

In some respects, the Chinese Communist Part (CCP) and the Liberal Democratic Party (LDP) could both be described as peasant-based parties. Were it not for the support of China's rural populations, the Chinese Communists might never have gained power. Although the LDP achieved its power through an entirely different process, its main support also came from the rural areas. Indeed, it has been primarily from these conservative rural groups that the party has continued to receive consistently high levels of support. Meantime, because the Japanese farm lobby has been able to maintain a high degree of influence in the Diet, policies governing agricultural subsidies and price supports have gone unchallenged. In contrast, Chinese peasants, farm from *being* subsidized, have, in fact, effectively *subsidized* industrialization efforts. The forced extraction of profits from collectivized

———————————

*Ed. note: In 1977, Japan had an active farm population of 6.2 million (or 11.5 percent of the total active population). Since that year, the number of Japanese actively engaged in agriculture has been steadily declining.

agriculture has provided the financial underpinning of Chinese industrial expansion since the early 1950s. Japan's urbanized, consumer society demands that agriculture either be made more efficient or be abandoned. In China, where no such choice exists, agricultural reform is an absolute necessity.

Reform is the primary goal of China's agricultural responsibility system, which was instituted by Vice Premier Wan Li in Anhui Province in 1979 and later expanded to the national level. The responsibility system shifts control over production from large collectives to individual households. Under this system, peasant families are given plots of land for a term of 15 or more years in exchange for their promise to sell a certain amount of their production to the state at recently increased prices, pay agricultural taxes, and deliver grain to collective reserves. They may then retain the rest of the production (usually 92 to 93 percent of the total) to sell or consume as they wish. Rural markets are expanding to handle the increased private trade.

Although the results of this program have been promising and peasant living conditions have improved substantially, problems have arisen concerning the political values inherent in such "capitalist" modes of agricultural production. Still, the single greatest problem in China is controlling population growth, which, if left unchecked, could pose a serious threat to the country's standard of living and lead to even higher levels of unemployment in the rural areas. Michael Parks elaborates on these problems in "China—The Rural Road to Prosperity," a first-hand account of the impact of recent reforms on the lives and living standards of Chinese peasants.

Unfortunately, the responsibility system has had an unexpected negative effect on family planning. Stewart Fraser, in "One's Good, Two's Enough," explains why the Chinese government is attempting to limit population growth, and describes some of the major obstacles that are impeding these efforts. The fact that the government provides only limited aid to the rural elderly, making older peasants dependent on their children for support, combined with the fact that under the new system peasants are encouraged to take greater initiative in farming and production, has created a situation in which children—especially males to work the family plots—have become an economic necessity. Harsh economic sanctions and other measures have been adopted to counteract these problems, but many of these have been met with growing resentment among China's rural dwellers. These measures are described in greater detail by P.-C. Chen and Adrian Kols in "Population and Birth Planning in the People's Republic of China."

There has been a gradual decline in Japan's farm population in recent years, but the real problem for Japanese agriculture can be found in the skyrocketing value of farm land. As Bernard Bernier point out in "The Japanese Peasantry and Postwar Economic Growth," the high price of land has made many farmers reluctant to sell or consolidate their farms; without consolidation, efficiency and productivity cannot be increased. Business and consumer groups are pressuring the LDP to come to terms with this contradiction and to remove tariff barriers that protect inefficient agricultural producers, but the strong political influence of farmers makes it unlikely that this will occur in the immediate future.

42

China—The Rural Road to Prosperity

Michael Parks

Here, Michael Parks provides a first-hand account of the impact of recent agricultural policy reforms on the living standards and lives of the Chinese peasantry. This selection is particularly interesting because it focuses on a town in Anhui Province, the home province of Vice Premier Wan Li, who originated many of the reforms. It is also interesting for its acknowledgment of some of the problems inherent in these reforms, the most important of which is the high rate of unemployment among China's rural population. But the political squabble over the long-term implications of these reforms for Chinese socialism should not be ignored. These problems may be overcome if increased levels of productivity are sustained, but, as Parks points out, this is not very likely. Recollectivization may be necessary to maintain growth rates and productivity and, if so, a new set of political problems will have to be reckoned with.

FENGYANG, China—When beggars appeared in Fengyang county early this spring, the peasants here knew it was not a dream—they were becoming rich.

For centuries, Fengyang, in Anhui province, had sent its own people by the thousands to other provinces to beg for food, and the county was so poor that ballads were sung about the droughts, floods and famines that struck it nine years out of 10.

For the last four years, however, Fengyang has had bumper harvests of wheat and rice, and its peasants are emerging from the poverty and backwardness that have long been associated with the county.

Peasants whose family income totaled about $190 in 1977, then the best year the people of Fengyang could remember, now earn $992, according to county officials, and some enterprising families netted $6,000 and more last year.

NEW HOMES, CONVENIENCES

New brick houses with tile roofs are replacing the old ones of packed earth and straw. Wristwatches, bicycles, sewing machines and radios, once undreamed-of-luxuries beyond the reach of three-quarters of Fengyang's people, are being bought by the thousands now. And construction has begun on the schools, cinemas, roads and power stations that the county could not afford in the past.

Fengyang's new prosperity makes it a showcase for the rural reforms begun four years ago under Deng Xiaoping, China's top leader, and the county is taking those new policies further than most, becoming an experimental model for the vast changes under way in the Chinese countryside.

What will work in Fengyang, once one of the 20 poorest counties in China, should work elsewhere, Chinese leaders have reasoned, and measures that were introduced here to cope with the threat of famine have gradually evolved into a new agricultural policy, first in the rest of Anhui province in east-central China and then throughout the country.

ENDED COLLECTIVE FARMING

Fengyang was the first county to drop collective cultivation, introduced by the Communists in the 1950s, and to return to family farming in a system that has now been adopted by nearly 80 percent of China's 180 million rural households.

"The new policy was merely an expedient at first something to get us through a bad drought in 1978." Xin Sheng, the head of Anhui's Rural Policy Research Center, recalled in an interview, "But the response of the peasants was so enthusiastic at being able to farm their own plots of land that we extended and developed these measures into a long-term policy.

"The impact has been profound. Anhui's grain production is up 29 percent over 1977, and nationally we had a record harvest last year. The explanation is deceptively simple: The peasant's income depends on how well he farms and how hard he works, and so there is considerable incentive for him."

Fengyang is now pioneering in the establishment of privately or co-operatively owned rural businesses, ranging from stores and repair shops to flour mills and trucking companies, which under another major policy change are permitted to hire workers, pay dividends on invested capital and compete with state enterprises.

"We have only begun the changes," Chen Tingyuan, the Communist Party secretary for Fengyang, said in an interview. "So far, we have solved only the problem of growing enough grain to feed our people. Rice in the belly is a bigger need than money in the pocket, but we cannot say that our peasants are really better off.

"Although their living conditions are improving, this is a matter of catching up. That there has been such a dramatic development of the economy here shows how backward things were. More changes, bigger changes are needed."

These changes, judging by the direction of Fengyang's current experiments, have the potential to redefine Chinese socialism and to reshape the lives of the country's 800 million peasants.

INDIVIDUAL ENTREPRENEURS

Chen, other Fengyang officials and peasants themselves see more and more farmers working as individual entrepreneurs, the cultivation of grain becoming less and less important as agriculture is diversified and rural industries established and the government gradually lets people manage their own affairs.

"We are looking for a system that will work for us," said Yang Jingxian, 34, a farmer and bookkeeper in Houyang village outside Fengyang town, the county seat. "What we had before—the people's commune, collective cultivation, cadres telling us what to do, egalitarianism—did not work, and we were so poor here, in fact, that half the men in Houyang were bachelors because no girl would marry them, and people still went out begging each year so their families could survive. This has changed, but we need to go further."

Chen is hesitant about predicting where these changes will take Fengyang and the rest of China.

"We have made no decisions about the future," he said, "because it must be decided largely according to the wishes of the peasants. We are waiting to see where their initiatives and desires lead us. . . . Whenever we have tried something that was beyond the wishes of the people, however well-intentioned we were, it failed, and sometimes it brought great catastrophe."

The Great Leap Forward, during which the late Chairman Mao Tsetung launched the people's commune system in 1958, and its aftermath are remembered with particular bitterness in Fengyang. Peasants who had been given land to farm only a few years earlier, after the Communist victory, lost it to the communes and found themselves lumped in agricultural work gangs. To underwrite the country's crash industrialization, they then had to deliver virtually all their produce to the state.

"Those were the worst years, the Mao years," a 59-year-old widow said, recalling how her husband "just got weaker and weaker and finally could not get out of bed and died" in 1960 because he was unable to live on the diet of rice husks, roots and sawdust.

Another peasant, 64, said that just the walk to the fields each morning tired everyone.

"At night, some were too weak to go home, and we were too weak to take them, and most would be dead in the morning," he said.

If life is better in Fengyang now, it is because "we have our land back," said Chai Daowu, 63, who farms 3⅓ acres at Nanchai village with his two sons and their wives.

"If we have land, we can farm," he said, "and if we can farm, we can eat."

This was the logic applied during the severe drought of 1978—there was no rain for 138 days straight in the spring and summer growing seasons—when Vice Premier Wan Li, then the Anhui party secretary, authorized the province's 410,000 production teams to lease their land to small groups of peasants to farm.

One of Fengyang's teams, in Xiaogang village, about 15 miles from the county seat, went further and divided its 57 acres among its 20 families.

"They hid what they were doing because it was forbidden by party policy," Chen, the party secretary, said. "Others wanted to force them to do it the prescribed way, but I felt, why not let them try, as it was only one small team."

Xiaogang village got through the drought, as did Anhui province, without the usual famine, and in 1979 its harvest was 3½ times that of 1977.

Chen then took Wan Li to visit Xiaogang, and Wan was so impressed that when he moved to Peking a few months later, as vice premier in charge of agriculture, he pushed through major policy changes based on his experience in Anhui.

FAMILY GETS LAND

Under the new household farming system, a family is allocated a portion of the village's land, from one-third of an acre to a full acre per person in Anhui, and required by contract to sell minimum amounts of produce to the state at set prices, pay an agricultural tax and deliver some grain to the collective reserves.

Altogether, this rarely comes to more than 7 percent or 8 percent of the harvest, based on quotas pegged to the harvest back in 1977, and the family is free to consume or dispose of the rest as it wants. Families get a mix of good and bad land and have been promised they will be able to keep their plots for eight to 10 years before any adjustments in order to encourage improvements.

At the same time, the state raised its prices for most produce and began paying premium prices for above-quota production, increasing the peasants' incentive to grow more and, equally important, giving them sufficient money to finance the purchase of fertilizers, quality seeds and agricultural equipment they needed.

"Peasants call 1979 the 'second liberation,'" Wang Changtai, a Fengyang party official, said. "In 1949, we had political liberation (with the Communist victory), and in 1979 we won economic liberation."

But the rural policy changes have also brought problems that cloud the future of the reforms and could turn them into political controversies.

The major question is whether China is turning back from socialism to capitalism in the countryside, a highly sensitive issue of profound importance for the national leadership as well as the peasants.

"We have definitely not abandoned socialism," Chen said. "We are experimenting with the different possible forms of socialism, trying to find what is right for us, but we have not reversed our commitment to socialism."

Chen, Xin and other Anhui officials argued that because farmland is still collectively owned, there is public ownership of the principal means of production, and that because each person derives most of his income from his own work, rather than from invested capital, the other main criterion for socialism has been satisfied. They also note that the state retains overall control through its purchasing quotas, tax collections, sales of fertilizer and other agricultural items, and general economic planning.

Yet Chinese newspapers are full of success stories about peasant entrepreneurs earning 40 and even 50 times the average rural income of $143 per person by investing in either cooperative or privately owned businesses. Although they themselves are working, they also are clearly making some money from the labor of others.

"There is a very small bit of exploitation since there is a return on (an entrepreneur's) investment," Xin, the head of the research center, said, discussing the earnings of an Anhui farmer now known as "20,000 Liu" because of the profits from his sesame oil business (20,000 yuan is the equivalent of $10,600).

"But the state limits and regulates such earnings," Xin went on. "An employer is allowed to have a larger income because his work is more complicated and thus should have a higher reward. Often, he also is bearing the risk of failure of his enterprise and the consequent financial loss, and this also justifies a higher return."

The issue is certain to grow. Rural officials already see that future economic development will require the creation of more jobs through investment in agricultural processing industries, service companies, transport firms, shops and similar enterprises, and that most of the investment required will have to come from the farmers themselves.

"We see these not as a rebirth of capitalism, but new forms of economic integration," said Li Jinlan, party secretary of Fengyang's Kaocheng township, 66 of whose 83 enterprises were begun with private or cooperative investment. "Some people contribute labor, a few technical skills and managerial ability and others money.

"These types of cooperatives and individual businesses existed a long time ago, in the 1950s, but were abolished due to the leftist line we took in 1958 with the Great Leap. People were too tightly bound together after that. Unified management is good, but when it becomes too rigid it hurts.

We nearly strangled ourselves by the way we tried to bind everyone together in the name of socialism."

Kaocheng's problems with the new system are typical, Its 5,300 acres can easily be farmed by half of its 7,300 workers (out of a population of 16,000), leaving the rest looking for jobs in various rural enterprises.

As crop yields, which have doubled in the past four years, level off after three or four more good harvests, the small plots distributed among various families will have to be unified again if productivity is to be increased through mechanization and other modern farming techniques, and the displaced field workers will be looking for new jobs.

Finally, the slower growth in agricultural production will mean that in five years the area's continued economic development will depend on the industrial and service enterprises, not farming.

MORE NON-FARM JOBS

"There is a complex of problems that we will confront in several years whose basic solution lies in creating more jobs outside of traditional cultivation," Deng Zheyuan, another Fengyang official, said. "The trend off the land is irreversible, but only the peasants themselves have sufficient funds to finance new development. We therefore have to rely on their ingenuity in developing new forms of economic cooperation. This is the reality of Chinese socialism."

In Fengyang county, new jobs are tied to investment. If a peasant family wants to place a son or daughter in a new flour mill in Kaocheng, for example, it invests about $530. The new worker gets his regular monthly wage, the family gets an annual dividend equivalent to bank interest on its investment and the surplus profits are put aside for the enterprise's expansion.

"The peasants are now doing many things in what the state had previously reserved as its domain," said Li, who recalls with some irony how he had fought "capitalist roaders" in the town and forced them to give up their private plots and small sideline businesses in the mid-1970s.

RELATIONS WITH NEIGHBORS

For those families remaining below the poverty line, Anhui province has a welfare "safety net" of loans, state subsidies, preferential treatment and advice from a senior cadre. A similar program provides for major medical care and help for the disabled. And those peasants whose farming skills have turned them into wealthy men overnight are urged to maintain good relations with their neighbors by helping them to prosper too.

Chen said frankly that the Chinese leadership is counting on solutions developing more or less spontaneously as the problems come to a head—

that the number of non-agricultural jobs will grow and siphon off surplus labor, that new farming arrangements will be worked out as families specialize in rice-growing or pig-raising or construction, and that money for all this will come from the peasants themselves.

"If we can solve the problem of the surplus labor, then the solutions to the other problems will appear," Chen said.

43

One's Good, Two's Enough

Stewart Fraser

In recent years, the Chinese leadership has intensified its effort to limit population growth. As Fraser points out here, the best arguments for stricter birth control policies are the high levels of unemployment that continue to plague the country and the economic impact of China's already enormous and still-growing population. Yet, despite the government's firm commitment to family planning and other birth control programs, a number of factors exist that are in direct conflict with these policies. One problem stems from recent agricultural reforms that provide economic incentives for peasant families to have more children, especially males to work the land. Cultural dispositions favoring male children present still another problem. Finally, and perhaps most important, the lack of any real social security for the elderly has made male children an economic necessity. Under the circumstances, it is not surprising that opposition to current birth control policies runs high in China, especially among rural families.

The generation born in the late 1960s and early 1970s is going to be asked to make, by Chinese social standards, a painful sacrifice and limit their families preferably to one child and certainly to no more than two. The vigorous, unrelenting, but still uncertain one-child family campaign is, in simple demographic terms, a rigorous strategy to prevent any recurrence of China's disastrous baby booms of the late 1950s and 1960s, when birth-control programmes proved ineffective.

The two-stage campaign first aims to reduce the natural growth rate to five per 1,000 by 1985. This is to be achieved by eliminating all third and subsequent births, and by persuading at least 60% of families to have only one child and allowing for rural families to have no more than two children. The second stage of the campaign is to reduce the national growth rate to zero through the gradual extension of the one-child norm throughout China.

In 1978 the campaign was cautiously launched in key cities with its attendant package of incentives and disincentives. In 1979 the national targets were established to persuade 80% of urban couples and 50% of rural couples to keep to a single child. In 1980 even higher goals were discussed and Chen Muhua, then a vice-premier responsible for family planning, suggested that "95% of married couples in cities and 90% in the countryside will have only one child in due course so that the total population of China will be contained at about 1.2 billion by the end of the century." The figure of 1.2 billion is still ever-present in all China's future planning needs.

There has been considerable opposition at various levels throughout China to the concept of a nation having generation after generation of single-child families. Poor families, especially rural dwellers who still account for more than 80% of the population, remain largely unconvinced. Urban dwellers, on the other hand, apparently are more amenable to the directives which are enforceable now by administrative regulations, economic sanctions and social censure.

But many party officials, as well as academics, are still not fully sure of the social ramifications and political implications of the policy. Mostly they appear to be more or less convinced on demographic and economic grounds, but are uncertain as to the efficacy of the draconian methods of carrying out the policy. For example, during the National People's Congress held in the summer of 1980, the delegates were somewhat divided in their views. The military made a case that a "large country needs a large army" and suggested that a fall-off in male recruits, due to the policy, would eventually damage the ability to stave off Soviet military threats. Moreover, the army asserted that peasants would be unwilling to see their only sons serve with the People's Liberation Army.

The rural delegates emphasised that girls were still not the best guarantee for parents' security in old age, especially if parents had to rely for support in their later years on a single child. It had been expected at the start of the congress that there would be whole-hearted endorsement of the policy and that the groundwork would be laid for the establishment of a national law with a clearly spelled out national, regional and local system of incentives and disincentives.

Thus the divided congress and the zealous government came to a compromise. The party central committee published an open letter to all party and Youth League members exhorting them to lead in vigorously promoting the one-child family concept among the masses. While provinces and major municipalities have promulgated systems of rewards and punishments based on localised conditions, it still has not been possible to formulate a national law on family size or on incentives and disincentives.

In China, where children are considered important culturally—and have economic value in rural households—it would be impossible to suggest childless marriages. The relentless pursuit of the concept of a single-child family is harsh enough for city dwellers, many of whom still try to circumvent the restrictions. Many rural couples are barely content with being allowed officially to have two children. In response to the official campaigns, as of last year, a gradual reduction in the size of urban families was noticeable. The reaction from rural areas was mixed, indicating resistance from peasants.

After the reintroduction of a stricter family-planning programme in 1971 the natural growth rate dropped from 2.34% to 1.17% in 1979. This decade-long decline, however, has shown signs of being reversed and the rate rose to 1.2% in 1980 and to 1.35% in 1981 with a strong likelihood that it will be 1.5% by the end of 1982. There are probably three major reasons for this upsurge: a baby boom 20 years ago, the application of a new marriage law in 1980 and the introduction of the so-called production responsibility system (PRS).

The baby boom of the 1960s resulted in larger numbers of people eligible for marriage in the 1980s. The marriage law of 1980 reduced the minimum marriageable age, putting further pressure on population growth. The injunction of the so-called three great delays—delay marriage, delay childbearing and delay forever having a second child—has evidently not been heeded sufficiently in many parts of rural China.

But the third and perhaps more subtle reason is the PRS in rural areas, which, linked with the dismantling of the commune system, has encouraged greater peasant initiative in farming and sideline production, allowing peasants to sell their produce on the free markets. While the PRS is said to have boosted certain areas of agricultural production significantly during the past two years, it also has produced an unexpected negative impact on family planning:

It is playing havoc with the application of birth planning quotas in some parts of rural China. The peasants believe that increased production, especially on private plots, requires extra hands and these can be easily produced by ignoring the calls for a one-child family and proceeding well beyond the limit of two children now permitted for rural inhabitants. A current saying goes: "While the party has a five-year plan for anything and everything the peasant has only a seven-year plan for producing a child worker." At the village level, cadres are now becoming anxious because they believe the peasants are deliberately sabotaging the population plans and ignoring birth quotas set by higher echelons.

Sichuan, with its 100 million people the most populous of China's provinces, has long been a barometer for effective family planning programmes and in May it reported several recent problems. By late 1981 there were unexplained reductions throughout the province in the rate of couples marrying late, having only one child and signing up for single-child incentive bonus certificates—so much so that the natural population growth rate which had declined significantly during the period 1975–80 started to move upward. A similar situation, reported in February, has occurred in Hunan which also has the PRS. Hunan officials reported that "the phenomenon of unplanned births had started to emerge in some places." The birth rate, which had fallen, had started to rise again.

44

Population and Birth Planning
in the People's Republic of China

P.-C. Chen and Adrian Kols

In these excerpts from *Population Reports,* some of the problems of population control in China are discussed. The lack of a rural "safety net" for the elderly, the absence of collective organizations for birth control in the rural areas, and cultural factors are all important. To combat these problems, the Chinese leadership has imposed strict economic sanctions on families who fail to comply with the "one's good, two's enough" policies.

DIFFICULTIES OF THE ONE-CHILD GOAL

Despite achievements to date, there are serious problems inherent in the goal of a one-child family. Until China builds an adequate social security system in the countryside, it will be difficult to sustain a one-child rate of more than 50 percent over a long period of time. Peasants' preference for a son is not a curse of Confucian heritage but a rational calculation. In China today, as in the past, the average person looks to a son for support in old age. There is an adequate old-age pension system only for those employed in the state-owned, urban-industrial sector, and these workers constitute at most 10 percent of the total population. In rural areas the agricultural collective's "five guarantees"—food, shelter, clothing, medical care, and burial—provide only limited aid and are no substitute for the physical and psychological support provided by one's own child. Couples living with the bride's parents if her parents have no male child is not a solution. If an only son marries an only daughter, the couple can live with and take care of only one of the two sets of parents. At the same time, they must financially support both sets of parents, straining their resources relative to those who have only one set of parents to support. Therefore, it makes sense for parents to have a minimum of two children, regardless of sex. Presumably, even if the average peasant couple did stop at one child if the first was a boy, they would have a second child if the first was a girl. Given an almost even number of each sex at birth, in the long run no more than 50 percent of all couples are likely to have only one child. . . .

Some recent birth planning reports have called the full responsibility system a serious threat to birth planning—as serious as the increasing size of the population groups reaching marriageable age. The new system gives the households a greater incentive to produce more children to work in the fields, earn money for the household, and support aging parents. Moreover, households are reluctant to contribute to collective services, so that primary education systems and cooperative medical services are on the verge of financial insolvency in some areas. This, of course, cripples the community distribution system for contraceptive devices and operations. The national government has become concerned over the problem and is now mandating collective support for personnel such as barefoot doctors. Because the full responsibility system has taken root in the areas where birth planning has traditionally been least successful, its adverse impact is all the greater.

Local units have quickly responded with new measures to reconcile birth planning with the full responsibility system. In many areas the birth planning norms are now built into the households' annual production contracts. These contracts now stipulate that couples with one or more children will use an effective birth control method (sometimes even specifying a birth planning operation) and will have an abortion if contraception fails. Newlyweds without children pledge not to have a child before receiving a birth quota. When a pregnant woman refuses to have an abortion or has a child in violation of the contract, her family's farm plot can be taken away and other types of economic sanctions applied. Also, local cadres are being put under a new "cadre job responsibility" system as a part of these changes. The cadres' annual bonuses, which form up to 25 percent of their annual income, are dependent on their units' birth planning performance as well as on grain production and general economic prosperity. The cadres must fulfill both grain and population targets to be eligible for the bonus. Because of these adaptations, the full responsibility system has had no effect on birth planning efforts in certain provinces. The most successful of the local innovations probably will be designated models for other rural areas, and successful adaptations to the new conditions will diffuse throughout the country.

45

The Japanese Peasantry
and Postwar Economic Growth

Bernard Bernier

In this excerpt from the *Bulletin for Concerned Asian Scholars,* Bernier examines the sources of Japanese agricultural policy. He traces many of the government's policies to the Land Reform Act of 1946–47, which was imposed by the American Occupation Command (Supreme Command of Allied Powers, or SCAP) to undermine support for rural radicals. The Act broke the authority of landlords and parceled out agricultural lands to the tillers. A combination of factors have conspired to render the policies connected with land reform inefficient and outdated. Of greatest importance is the increase in the value of Japanese land. Farmers, even of inefficient farms, are reluctant to sell or consolidate their farms because the value of land is increasing so rapidly. Meanwhile, the proportion of agricultural production in GNP is declining, farm lands are shrinking under the impact of urbanization, and agricultural workers are fleeing to the cities to find jobs in manufacturing and services. This leaves much of the farming to elderly and female workers who are supplementing other family incomes. Inefficiency is widespread. And, because the LDP gains so much of its support from rural voters, agricultural subsidies, import restrictions, and price supports are difficult to defeat. Public outcry from consumers as well as the concern of businessmen who must deal with nations that complain about import quotas could lead to changes in agricultural policies in the near future.

The Land Reform of 1946–1947 marks a definite break in the history of Japanese rural society. It thoroughly eradicated the landlord-tenant class relation which had been a dominant feature of the Japanese countryside since the late Edo period (1600–1868). The Reform was imposed on the Japanese government by the Supreme Command of Allied Powers (SCAP). One of its basic tenets was that landlordism had been a major cause of the jingoistic and militaristic tendencies which characterized Japanese society in the 1930s and 1940s. It thus had to be eliminated. But a more important goal of the Reform was to stamp out rural radicalism which had been an important aspect of agrarian Japan in the 1920s and 1930s. Rural intransigence, prompted by the misery of the peasants under the landlord system, was a major potential source of social unrest, and it was feared that the peasantry might support left-wing parties. In order to eliminate all dangerous socialist tendencies in the countryside, it was necessary to return the land to the tillers, that is to transform the majority of agriculturalists into small property owners. This rural "middle class" would hopefully become a conservative political force, thus insuring that Japan remained in the anti-communist camp.

The Land Reform has in fact been successful, at least until recently, in transforming the peasantry into a conservative bloc. Since 1948 the countryside has voted overwhelmingly for right-of-center parties, despite mounting difficulties for peasants and growing protests against various aspects of the State's agricultural policy. But the Reform never achieved its goal of creating a "middle class" of farmers. In the first place, the Reform did not equalize land holdings. For example, in 1950, 73 percent of all farm households owned less than one hectare of arable land. Secondly, since about 1955, Japanese agriculture has had to bear up under the pressures of rapid economic growth whose prime moving force has been the heavy and chemical industries dominated by monopoly capitalism. Thus it will be necessary both to assess the various forces at work within the agricultural sector itself and to examine the national context in which these tendencies occur, taking into account the effects of Japan's "economic miracle" and the State's agrarian policy. Perforce it will be useful to examine, albeit briefly, Japan's place in the international farm market.

THE AGRICULTURAL SECTOR
SINCE THE LAND REFORM

Demographic Aspects

Throughout the twentieth century, the rural population has been decreasing in proportion to the total Japanese population. From a level of about 60 percent around 1900, it fell to 48 percent in 1950, 31 percent in 1965, and 19.9 percent in 1977. In absolute terms, the rural population had grown between 1900 and 1950 (from 26 to 37 millions, with various ups and downs), but thereafter, a sharp decline has occurred, dropping to 22.5 million in 1977. Of course, the 1950 figure is inflated because of the influx of population to the rural areas after the war, due to the destruction of homes and industrial installations in the cities and the repatriation of Japanese soldiers and former colonists. But this decline was still noticeable even after industrial production had attained its prewar level in 1953. In fact, the average annual decrease in the 22 year period between 1955 and 1977 was about 2 percent, and nearly 8 percent since 1968.

... From 1950 to 1960, the number of farm units remained relatively stable at the unprecedented high level of about 6 million. Only between 1965 and 1970 was the prewar level reached—a level that had been maintained from the late Edo period until 1945 at between 5.3 and 5.5 million families. Thereafter a sharp decrease occurred, and in 1977 the number of farm households was 4.8 million. The decline between 1960 and 1970 can be viewed as a process of elimination of the excess farm households created by the unusual conditions of the immediate postwar period, but the downward trend that has prevailed since 1970 cannot be explained in this way. In fact, in 1975, for the first time in two centuries, the number of farm families fell below 5 million. This trend has continued. According to most observers, the quasi-mystical attachment to the land is now breaking down among many Japanese peasants. An important feature of the feudal period when land was for many the only means of survival, this attachment has persisted because, until now, farming has been the only way for most rural inhabitants to earn a living. Now survival can be secured by non-agricultural work, and the sale of land, which until recently was thought of as disrespectful toward the family ancestors who bequeathed the land, is now based on cold economic calculations. This is the case in peri-urban areas but is also true of outlying regions.

Agricultural Production

Agricultural production has accounted for an increasingly low percentage of the Gross National Product. From a level of 16.5 percent in 1934–1936, it reached 31 percent in 1946, but settled back to its prewar level in 1954. Thereafter, it has decreased constantly, falling from 13 percent in 1960, to a mere 2.5 percent in 1977. The major reason for this decline is the fantastic development of the industrial and service sectors. Overall agricultural production has increased however, at least until 1968. In fact, from 1960 to 1968, the average annual rate of increase of agricultural production in current prices has been near 4 percent. But since 1969, there has been a slow decline every year, except 1972 and 1975 (good harvests, higher prices.)

A main reason for the decrease in farm production is, first, a reduction in the total area of land under cultivation. For example, between 1969 and 1976, an annual average of 50,000 hectares were transferred out of cultivation. While much of this is the result of urban and industrial development, it is also due to the abandonment of agriculture by many peasants, partly because of the government's policy of encouraging the curtailment of rice production. Secondly, rice yields per hectare have decreased. For example, between 1967 and 1971, the yield per hectare on large farms fell from 45.4 qt. to 41 qt. Finally, many farmers have abandoned winter crops, and consequently, the rate of land use has declined from 134 percent in 1960 to 100 percent in 1973. Since then, it has risen somewhat to 103 percent in 1976. . . .

Agricultural Products

Japanese agriculture is still strongly centered on cereals, particularly rice. However, since 1950 specialization in other crops has been gaining ground. In 1950 cereals accounted for more than 70 percent of total farm production. This is only slightly lower than comparable figures for the early 20th century. But since 1950 the importance of cereals has decreased. In 1960 they accounted for 55 percent of total agricultural production but this percentage had fallen to 36 percent by 1973 and to about 33 percent in 1977. The decline has been much more dramatic for cereals other than rice (wheat, barley, buckwheat, corn). In 1950 these other cereals accounted for more than 10 percent of the total farm output, but less than 1 percent in 1976. The major reason for this rapid drop in production lies in the fact that cereals cultivated in Japan are expensive. In 1969, Japanese wheat sold at more than double the international price. However, this in itself is not a sufficient condition, for in the same year the price of Japanese rice was about three times that of American rice. A second important factor is U.S. pressure on the Japanese government to import large quantities of American farm goods. This pressure has been applied more or less consistently since 1945. Just after the war, the Japanese government had little power to resist. The U.S. was producing large surpluses, especially of wheat and soy beans, and Japan proved to be an ideal market both because of the immediate food shortage and because of low farm productivity. Agreements were even signed in 1954 to insure the flow of certain American agricultural products into Japan. The net result was a slackening off in production of many Japanese crops, including wheat, barley and soy beans.

Conversely, the production of livestock, dairy goods, fruits, and vegetables has increased tremendously. From 35 percent of total production in 1960, these products have grown to 57 percent in 1972 and almost 60 percent in 1975. The increase in the production of fruits, vegetables, meat, milk and eggs, together with the decline of cereal production, is a sign of a more diversified diet, a consequence of the higher standard of living brought about by the economic growth of the 1960s. However, the sustained growth of non-cereal production has been possible only through heavy tariff protection. Since 1971 international pressure has been applied, especially by the United States, to force the easing of Japanese trade barriers on many agricultural goods. These pressures, which are analyzed in more detail below, have strained the growth of many types of products, including beef, dairy products, and citrus fruits. To offset the effects of liberalization on the peasants, the Japanese government has had to ease up on its policy of rice production control, thus putting an end to its 10-year-old farm diversification program. This policy change has led to new rice surpluses. However, by 1973, the policy of restricting rice production was again revived, resulting in a drop in Japan's overall agricultural output. . . .

The reasons for these trends are complex. One is that farm owners are hesitant to sell their land even when they engage in farming only as a secondary activity. As I mentioned previously, the ideological restraints on selling farm land have been weakened and peasants actually sell more than they did previously. . . . But despite this increase in land sales, the general tendency remains for farmers to hold on to the soil. The reasons for this "attachment" to the land are usually very concrete. Many cultivators own land whose price is rising faster than the interest they could obtain on the amount of money they would receive for their land, so, if the price is not high enough or if they do not really need to sell, they prefer to keep their land. Moreover, many farm owners prefer converting their land partly to other uses, such as apartment building, near the cities. Still others, and they are in the majority, want to keep the land as an insurance against hard times. Many farmers still remember the famine of the middle '40s and they want to be protected should the same difficulties arise again. Besides, given the inadequacy of social security programs in Japan, old people generally have a hard time of it particularly when they own nothing, and this encourages peasants to cling to their land as a form of old-age insurance. Finally, prices for land or houses are so high that even should a farm owner sell at a good price, he/she is likely to spend most of it on the purchase of a new house. . . .

The consequences of these trends are complex and far-reaching. In the first place, the refusal of small holders to sell their land, coupled with high land prices resulting from urban development, have retarded farm consolidation. Thus the constitution of a substantial group of prosperous family farms has been thwarted. Secondly, the possibility of keeping the land while working outside of agriculture has led to an increase in the number of farms short of even one full-time worker (man or woman). In 1973, as well as in 1977, 50 percent of farm households were of this type. Another 15 percent had only one woman as a full-time worker. In this case, it is considered "normal" for women to keep on doing household chores, a fact that cannot but diminish their effectiveness as farm workers. Moreover, if we take into account the fact that a sizeable proportion of farms with full-time employees are geared to subsistence farming and worked by old people, the percentage of farm operations run on a less than adequate basis is very high, probably near 75 percent. This leads to the type of farm management that has become the trade mark of Japanese agriculture. Farming is done part-time either in the evenings or on weekends by women and old people.

A third consequence is that part-time cultivators tend to withdraw from cooperative ventures and deal with their problems individually. The net result is the breakdown of village cooperation and the purchase of agricultural machinery at a pace much faster than is really needed. Each household requires its own machinery in order to complete the farmwork in the short periods when manpower is available.

Fourthly, as has been mentioned earlier, there has been a reduction in the yield per hectare for many types of crops despite an increase in farm productivity. The replacement of labor by industrial goods does not result in as productive a use of the land. Besides, it increases the danger of toxic poisoning.

A fifth consequence is the growing strain on village and family life. Although conditions for seasonal workers have improved, it remains that, with the departure of so many villagers for the cities, the families left behind encounter serious problems and many villages have become deserted, with schools closed, etc. . . .

THE NATIONAL CONTEXT

The State's Agricultural Policy

An analysis of agricultural programs in Japan since the Land Reform is not easy because the policy-making process has many contradictory aspects which have forced the government to change course at different times or even to devise and implement contradictory measures. One important aspect is the fact that, since the end of World War II, the Japanese government has been structured to accommodate even more closely than before the war the interest of giant business concerns. Since the economic strength of dominant *zaikai* interests is based on the export of manufactured goods, and since it is necessary to compensate for these exports by importing foreign products, the *zaikai* and its related organizations (*Keidanren,* etc.) have, since 1955, applied pressure on the government to liberalize agricultural imports, terminate government control of the rice market and consolidate farms and encourage their mechanization.

A second aspect is the dependence of the ruling Liberal Democratic Party, whose relations to the *zaikai* are well known, on the rural vote. In order to get the agricultural producers to vote conservative, the government has had to make concessions to them, mainly by maintaining rice prices at a high level. This points to another important aspect of agricultural policy: it must take into account the fact that agriculture is at one and the same time an economic sector and the means of livelihood for several million people.

A final aspect is the pressure exerted by foreign countries, especially the United States, to liberalize the Japanese farm market. The policy on rice prices has had the greatest importance for the peasantry since 1945. At first, the rice-price policy was geared to the regulation of foodstuffs needed for the war effort. The first government controls on the rice market were imposed in 1939, but only in 1942 were these controls explicitly applied to prices. . . .

Under rural pressure, the government, with the implementation of the Fundamental Law on Agriculture in 1961, adopted a new way to determine rice prices by adding to the production costs of the least productive farms an amount of money intended to raise the standard of living of farm families. This method of calculating rice prices has in fact led to an increase in rural incomes, but it also resulted in a doubling of the price of rice paid to producers between 1960 and 1968. It is during this period that the price of Japanese rice rose far above international prices. Moreover, so as not to accelerate inflation, and to keep wages at a fairly low level while avoiding a public outcry, the government has not allowed the sales price of rice to rise at the same pace as the purchase price at the farm. . . .

What prompted this curiously contradictory policy is, first of all, the necessity for the LDP to please its rural constituency. The party is elected by the rural vote. With the defection of the urban working class, the LDP has had to make some concessions to the peasants to acquire their votes. Furthermore, with a higher standard of living, rice had lost its importance as the main food item in workers' diets, and its price has been able to rise. Before 1955, it was necessary to guard against increases in the price of rice in order to keep wages low; rice was the major food item and low wages were a must for small enterprises. However, it is important to note that, even though it became possible to let rice prices climb after 1960, the rate of increase was not high enough to prevent the spread of part-time farming. In fact, with the rapid progress of mechanization, the new rice policy encouraged this development by allowing small holders who normally would have been evicted from agriculture to maintain a certain level of rice production while working only part-time in agriculture, thus obtaining good secondary incomes. However, given price levels, social needs, the size of farm plots, and agricultural productivity, it was impossible for the majority of rice producers to depend mainly on agriculture for their income. Most of them have had to rely increasingly on wage labor, usually in low-paying industrial jobs. Actually, the rice policy has had to accommodate the need of many industrial sectors for a steady supply of low-paid rural labor, and the price of rice has had to satisfy rural voters while insuring a constant outflow of cheap labor to factories, shops and construction sites. . . .

All through the '60s, the government attempted in various ways to speed up farm consolidation, mechanization and diversification—in short, the establishment of viable family farms. However, these efforts went contrary to the necessity, for electoral reasons, to maintain the majority of peasant families on the land. Furthermore, since diversification had to be backed up by high tariff barriers, this policy drew fire from the *zaikai* whose interests required a more open internal market for agricultural imports. Criticism also came from the U.S. government which was pushing for trade liberation. Nevertheless, the Japanese government succeeded temporarily in its efforts to protect local producers in key sectors of livestock, dairy, fruit and vegetable production. But this was done at the expense of cereal production (except rice), raw materials for fodder, and soybeans. . . .

The "Nixon shock" of 1971 was the main blow to the government's diversification program. As a result of U.S. pressures, the Japanese government had to lower or abolish trade barriers on agricultural products. This led to difficulties for many agricultural producers. To compensate, the government decided to raise the price of rice, which encouraged many producers to revert to rice production. However, international pressures were not limited to the Nixon shock alone. The year 1972 saw the disappearance of the world's agricultural surpluses which had been maintained for the previous 25 years, and world food production became insufficient. Japan, whose degree of self-sufficiency in food had plummeted from about 80 percent in 1960 to less than 50 percent in 1973, thus faced severe problems in obtaining badly needed farm goods on the international market. The most acute problem centered on soybeans. In 1971, Japan imported 96 percent of its soybeans, 97 percent of which came from the U.S. In 1972, the U.S., for various reasons, put an embargo on soybean exports to Japan. Because of such difficulties in the international market, many groups in Japan have proposed a return to food self-sufficiency partly for security reasons. But still, in 1975, Japan depended for 97 percent on imports of soybeans, 92 percent of which came from the United States.

Confronted with these many-sided problems, the government has remained indecisive since 1971. There have been tentative plans to reduce the number of farm families and industrialize the countryside, etc. But most of these have been as severely criticized by the representatives of Japanese capital as by peasants and workers. However, the vacillation of the government has not prevented the uncontrolled implantation of industries in the countryside. The city continues to encroach on rural areas, and pollution is increasingly hazardous to farm villages. Rural unrest has been increasing and the rural constituency to the interest of the *zaikai*. But what would become then of this stabilizing force that is the peasantry?

Unit XI

Energy Policy

China and Japan, along with the rest of the world, were profoundly affected by the energy crises of 1973 and 1978. In 1973, world oil prices rose astronomically. The 1978 crisis served to remind the world that such price increases were not events of the past and that, in fact, energy prices would continue to rise in the years to come. For an oil-dependent country like Japan, which was importing over 90 percent of all its energy supplies at the time of the first crisis, continued price hikes threatened economic destruction. For China, rich in coal and hydroelectric capabilities and possessing huge, untapped reserves of oil, the crises signaled an opportunity to expand energy production, increase exports, and finance through those exports the modernization of industry, agriculture, and technology. However, both nations found that the effects of increased energy costs would not be so direct. Oil prices eventually declined and then leveled out. Japan did not experience the economic instability it expected and China most certainly did not find the economic bonanza which its leaders predicted. Still, neither nation remained unaffected.

The energy crises of the 1970s were a coming of age for Japan. The interdependence of the global economy and Japan's own vulnerability to that interdependence were brought home sharply by the Arab oil embargo. The United States, Japan's traditional protector, could do little to shield the Japanese from the harsh realities of the post-OPEC* world. Instead, the Japanese were forced to expand their diplomatic and economic efforts at securing independent sources of energy supplies. While this did not preclude cooperation with the United States and Western Eu-

---

*Organization of Petroleum Exporting Countries, which initiated the dramatic increases in the price of oil during the 1970s.

rope, that cooperation has been difficult to achieve and maintain. As Margaret A. McKean explains in "Japan's Energy Policies," Japan has sought, through a variety of independent policies, to secure stable supplies of oil while simultaneously reducing its dependence on imports. One such policy involves investing in production of facilities in oil-producing nations like Iran and Indonesia. Another involves the establishment of Japanese oil exploration capabilities.

Prior to 1973, Japan had only half an oil industry. Refining industries and petrochemicals had been the focus of Japanese investment and there was little or no exploration and recovery capability. Although the Japanese have made some attempts to develop such capabilities, the emphasis still lies on investment in production overseas. Such investment has not proven to be without risk, however. Attempts to invest in China, for example, have been stymied by reversals in modernization plans, political conflict within the Chinese leadership concerning foreign investment, and Japanese concern over the stability of the present Chinese leadership and the long-term security of supplies from its neighbor.

The Japanese have, therefore, concentrated primarily on conserving energy, making industries more energy efficient, and on developing alternative energy supplies. The government has instructed business to reduce its consumption of oil by switching to coal or by modernizing existing plant. This "administrative guidance" has been augmented by market forces, which have raised the price of oil and led to reduced consumption. Nuclear and solar energy technologies are also being explored and developed.

While the Japanese have been successful in reducing oil consumption and dependence, the Chinese have failed to reap significant economic benefits from energy shortages. The Chinese have taken great pride in their indigenous capabilities in energy production. The Daqing oil fields were frequently referred to by Mao as fruits of China's policy of self-reliance. During the Cultural Revolution extensive debates took place concerning the necessity and wisdom of employing foreign technology to increase productivity at the fields. In the early 1970s, elements of the present

Chinese leadership began to articulate their reform policies, stressing the need to modernize energy production for reasons of defense and economic expansion. When oil prices began to rise, there was a hope that expanded production could lead to increased exports which would finance other modernization programs. In "China's Energy Plan for the 80s," Christopher M. Clarke discusses the current energy crisis in China and identifies five obstacles to resolving these problems.

Unfortunately, as Clarke points out, the Chinese leadership did not expect domestic energy consumption to increase as quickly as it has. Part of this increase has been an unintended consequence of economic reform, as Thomas Fingar describes in "Energy in China." Retained profits have been used to expand plant thereby increasing energy use. This has been somewhat balanced by a shift from energy intensive heavy industry to more efficient light industries, but a problem still exists. Additionally, development of reserves, both coal and oil, is difficult. Many fields are inaccessible; existing technologies and supporting infrastructures (for example, railways, ports, and pipelines) are antiquated or insufficient; and the foreign technology necessary to develop the reserves is expensive and resisted by members of the leadership who fear excessive dependence on the West. The Chinese have not forgotten their experiences with Soviet technicians who abandoned oil and coal fields in 1960 at the time of the Sino-Soviet split.

The Chinese have therefore embarked on a cautious course of allowing foreign investment in oil and coal production, but only after very hard bargaining. (Negotiations have been complicated by fluctuations in the world market prices for energy supplies, though the Chinese seem determined to overcome such complications and to secure investment for long-term production.) They have also imposed strict regulations on the use of energy. Plants are being upgraded and made more energy efficient; investment decisions are frequently based on existing energy supplies and projections of supply and demand; and bank loans, increasingly a source of financing plant expansion, are partially determined by an enterprise's success in reducing energy consumption. The state economic and planning commissions are taking an active part in seeing that such regulations are enforced.

As China and Japan enter the 1980s, energy remains a serious concern, as the readings in this unit reveal. Despite their success at conservation, the Japanese must still face the fact that over 75 percent of their oil supply is imported from the Middle East. Moreover, coal is a source of environmental pollution, and nuclear power, while "clean," arouses political opposition from environmentalists and opponents of nuclear weapons. Declining industries are still energy inefficient, and the move to more efficient, high-tech industries is a long-term policy goal. Some type of complementary energy policy with China, in which Japan invests in production in exchange for oil, is attractive. But any such cooperative ventures are threatened by China's own increased consumption of energy, a global market fluctuations, and political conflict within the Chinese leadership.

46

Japan's Energy Policies

Margaret A. McKean

In these excerpts from an article that originally appeared in *Current History,* McKean discusses some of the features of Japanese energy policy since the oil embargo of 1973. Perhaps the most distinctive feature of that policy has been the extent to which individuals and industries have voluntarily complied with government conservation measures. Dependence on oil, and especially Middle Eastern oil, has declined markedly. This is the result of diversification of supplies as well as a switch to alternative energies such as coal and nuclear power. Although attempts to secure Chinese supplies of oil have been disappointing, the Japanese are still pursuing investment in production facilities in other countries, including Iran and Indonesia. Still, the major reason that conservation has succeeded has been voluntary cooperation, a cooperation that McKean argues is based on the Japanese practice of "administrative guidance" and allowing prices to rise in accordance with the market. Thus, by a combination of planning and market forces, the Japanese have succeeded in reducing their dependence on unreliable foreign sources of oil as well as diversifying energy inputs.

Since the 1973 oil crisis, Japan's energy policy, both foreign and domestic, has tried to reduce Japan's unfortunate dependence on oil in general and on Middle East and OPEC (Organization of Petroleum Exporting Countries) oil in particular. Japanese reactions to anticipated shortfalls in oil supply have ranged from panic to businesslike calm. Official policies have ranged from relatively silly public information campaigns (encouraging businessmen and bureaucrats to abandon neckties and wear safari suits during the summer) to a very serious and thorough overhaul of the industrial structure.

The Japanese speak almost obsessively of their frightening dependence on imported energy, which would lead one to expect stringent controls on energy use. Instead one finds mild-mannered conservation policies consisting almost entirely of exhortations to accept government suggestions voluntarily, with almost no legal compulsion to modify energy use. Nonetheless, in Japan we find perhaps the most impressive performance among the industrial democracies in terms of conservation, the achievement of IEA (International Energy Agency) and Tokyo Summit targets for reducing oil consumption, and the restoration of relative health to the Japanese economy after a bad year in 1974.

If the Japanese are so anxious about their dependence why are they doing so little about it? If they are doing so little about it, how do they manage to accomplish so much? If they are doing so well why do they persist in being nervous? And why are they doing so well if the dependence that makes them nervous is indeed more serious than in other countries?

To answer these questions, we must understand certain features in the profile of Japanese energy consumption. First, the rapid growth in Japan's energy-intensive industrial sector, for years made possible in part by the supply of cheap oil, resulted in a relatively high share of energy consumption for industry and relatively low shares for the transportation and residential-commercial sectors, respectively. Second, Japan has made more use of oil and oil derivatives and has been more dependent on them for functions ordinarily performed by other fuels in other countries—most notably, using oil and natural gas rather than coal or water power to generate electricity.

Japanese politicians came easily to the conclusion that Japan should diversify its geographical sources of oil away from all OPEC nations. This task was made easier by the convenient development of new non-OPEC oil fields in China, Mexico and the North Sea. Japan is also trying to persuade the United States Congress to alter legislation that prevents the United States from exporting Alaskan oil. In 1976, 79.5 percent of Japan's oil imports came from the Middle East, but by 1981 only 69.3 percent of all oil imports came from the Middle East.

It was also easy for Japan to diversity the contractual arrangements under which oil was imported—that is, to depend as little as possible on purchases through the international majors and to begin making more direct deals between domestically financed oil firms and supplier countries, to buy more oil on the spot market and, wherever diplomatic opportunity presented itself, to make government-to-government deals for oil as well. The attempt to reduce dependence on the majors has long been an element of Japan's energy policy, and threats in 1973—1974 by the majors to reduce supplies sold through their Japanese subsidiaries if the Japanese government tried to put ceilings on oil product prices confirmed the wisdom of this policy. . . .

One element of diversifying supplies and contractual arrangements is to concede to the demands of supplier nations that the importing nation invest in the supplier nations' economic development, particularly in refineries and petrochemical plants at the wellhead, instead of removing the crude oil for processing and profits elsewhere. In return, suppliers would offer a guaranteed volume or share of the resources to the Japanese market.

In view of the political instability or difficult negotiating styles of many OPEC and non-OPEC supplier nations, these investments are very risky, and private firms have been reluctant to engage in these adventures without government backing. For years, the Japanese government and its business leaders have negotiated with the Soviet Union and China about the development of energy resources and the export of Japanese industrial plants, with an eye to Japanese purchases of energy from these countries. Results have been disappointing. Frustrating negotiations with the Soviet Union have prevented most of these projects from materializing, and enthusiasm about many Sino-Japanese projects faded quickly after the abrupt cancelling by China of the steel plant at Baoshan (even though China did pay compensation to the Japanese firms that had already incurred losses). The Japanese government regarded its arrangement to purchase large quantities of Chinese oil as a political coup, but Japanese oil companies protested because the high paraffin content of Chinese oil would require very expensive modifications of petroleum refineries in Japan. . . .

Another way to diversify supplies and contractual arrangements is to cooperate with other consumer nations—eventually through the International Energy Agency—in order to share "responsibility" in the industrial world for reducing oil consumption, conserving energy, building up emergency stockpiles, sharing oil in a supply crisis, and negotiating jointly with OPEC. Although Japan has done well at containing its oil consumption, conserving energy, and building a more than 120-day stockpile for its own use, cooperation with the IEA nations has proven more difficult. All the members are understandably reluctant to increase their dependence on anybody else, whether OPEC or IEA, in a crisis that will naturally give national interests top priority. Ironically, the commitment to conservation and the anxiety about depending on others appear to go hand in hand.

Therefore the United States, with its enormous domestic supply of oil, is most enthusiastic about consumer collaboration and most sluggish about conservation; Japan, dependent on imports for virtually all its oil, is most skeptical about collaboration and thus far more talented at conservation.

Japan has made modest headway in reducing its demand for oil and diversifying its sources of oil wherever unilateral action (a Japanese decision to purchase from one source rather than another) works, but it has encountered far more trouble wherever bilateral action (Japanese investment in supplier nations) or multilateral action (cooperation with consumer nations) is involved. Not only are bilateral and multilateral negotiations more complex and therefore less likely to yield agreement, but the high risks and subsidiary issues involved also increase internal conflict among Japanese participants over how to proceed.

Japan's search for alternatives to oil can be divided into interim and long-term goals. The only immediately available alternatives to oil are conservation (the substitution of investment in technology and behavioral change for fuel itself) and coal (Japan's own dwindling domestic supply can still be mined if the price is right, and world supplies of coal are plentiful and varied). As longer-term alternatives the Japanese establishment has some interest in renewable forms of energy but places its greatest faith in nuclear power.

Japan's official policies to encourage energy conservation are extensive and impressive (if ludicrously detailed) until one realizes that most of them have been voluntary. Measures urged on business and the general public after the 1973 oil crisis were forgotten when the government declared an end to the state of emergency on September 1, 1974, but the same measures were revived when the second oil crisis convinced the government that as long as Japan depended so heavily on a material that came from politically unstable countries, shortages could be endemic. The government formally adopted a comprehensive list of voluntary measures as official policy in 1979 and 1980, based on predictions from the Economic Planning Agency that these measures could save 20 million kiloliters of oil and could thereby achieve a seven percent reduction in projected oil consumption.

In addition to voluntary measures, the government also launched a public information campaign to keep energy conservation a high priority—setting aside one energy conservation day each month, declaring every February to be an energy conservation month of intense public awareness, doing spot surveys of compliance with the government's suggestions, considering the adoption of daylight savings time and the five-day (as opposed to the six-day) workweek, and funding an Energy Conservation Center to run these campaigns.

A few policies involved legislative changes and offered either rewards for conserving (above and beyond the savings to the conserver) or punishments for not conserving. The government provided special depreciation allowances and tax credits to businesses on investments in energy-conserving equipment and guaranteed the availability of loans (at ordinary terms) to businesses and households for such investments. These loans turned out to be very popular, and the government had to expand the budget for them in 1980. The IEA would like Japan to increase the availability of such inducements still further and especially to make the terms more favorable relative to other kinds of tax breaks and loans. In 1978, the government launched the Moonlight Project, essentially a research fund to develop large-scale energy conservation technology with applications in industry.

The Diet passed an Energy Conservation Law in June, 1979, requiring 4,500 firms that together consumed 75–80 percent of the nation's industrial-sector energy to employ "energy managers," specialists in waste heat and electricity who would go through a rigorous government training program, and then return to their companies with the right to inspect company records, give binding instructions to employees, and thus enforce the government's standards for energy conservation in productive processes and the insulating, heating, and cooling of buildings. There are small penalties of 200,000 yen and 100,000 yen respectively for any firm that refuses to hire energy managers or keeps inadequate records for the energy manager.

The law also regulates the energy efficiency of cars, refrigerators and air conditioners.

The IEA's reaction to Japan's measures, especially to the purely voluntary ones, was that they were entirely insufficient. It comes as a surprise, then, to see how impressive Japan's actual performance is in conservation. In every area, during the 1970's Japan's performance was better than that of other IEA countries. Japan's performance also improved steadily over time, breaking old myths about the relationship between energy consumption and gross national product (GNP), with one exception: energy consumption per capita in the residential sector is increasing in Japan, though thus far energy conservation in industry more than makes up for this to produce steady improvement in the overall national record of conservation.

How did Japan achieve such an impressive performance—most of it occurring after 1978 in a very brief period? First, although the conservation measures were largely voluntary, the government has enormous leverage over the behavior of major industries through its system of administrative guidance, an informal, extralegal form of persuasion developed and used principally by the Ministry of International Trade and Industry (MITI). Technically unenforceable, it is in fact backed up by MITI's assorted legal powers over the licensing of technology, permission for construction or expansion of facilities, allocation of materials, and permits to commence operations. MITI has particularly extensive legal powers at its disposal where energy is concerned—as opposed to some other sectors where MITI's legal powers are fewer and its extralegal guidance has traditionally been much less effective.

By exercising administrative guidance over the behavior of firms at a stage in the processing or distribution of a commodity where there are only a few firms to monitor, MITI can powerfully influence not only the behavior of those few firms but also the far greater number of enterprises further along in the distribution of that commodity. Thus MITI's control over fewer than 40 oil companies gives it influence over more than 59,000 gasoline stations. . . . Conversely, the fact that many small firms organize themselves into trade associations in order to exert political pressure gives MITI the opportunity to influence countless small firms indirectly through a quid pro quo: MITI will consider the association's interests in return for its cooperation in transmitting administrative guidance to its member firms. . . .

A second and equally powerful reason for the success of these voluntary measures is that, after a very bad experience in 1974 (attempting to keep a lid on the prices of oil and related commodities to soften the impact on both industrial users and individual consumers and witnessing the frivolous use of kerosene and liquid propane gas, whose prices were kept low), the Japanese government decided to let prices rise as high as the market would take them. This was politically possible because all Japanese recognized that the factors responsible for rising oil prices were outside Japan and beyond the control of the Japanese government, which therefore did not have to live up to the expectation that it could make oil materialize at low prices. Thus high prices constituted the motive to conserve, and the government's public information campaign merely served as the method, teaching eager firms and citizens how to do what they already wanted to do.

Since 1973, the Japanese government has used administrative guidance to encourage energy-intensive industrial uses of oil, from cement to electric utilities, to switch when possible from oil to coal. . . .

The search for alternatives to oil does not stop with coal and other fossil fuels. With the establishment of the Sunshine Project in 1974, the Japanese government also indicated an interest—some would say a rather feeble low-budget interest—in the eventual adoption of renewable energies: solar heating and cooling, solar electrification, geothermal, wind, thermal gradient, tide, hydrogen, biomass conversion, and similar forms of energy, most of which require considerable technological study before they can be commercially practicable. Japan's most noteworthy advances to date in these long-term technologies are in geothermal power (available in considerable abundance by virtue of Japan's volcanic origins), solar electrification, and the applications of solar heating and cooling to large office buildings and multifamily housing. In addition, millions of private households have already installed simple solar hot water systems. . . .

NUCLEAR POWER

Japan must import all its uranium, currently under rather stringent contracts with its suppliers that restrict experiments with uranium enrichment, reprocessing spent fuel, development of advanced thermal and fast breeder reactors, and waste disposal. Nonetheless, the government is making headway in a round of negotiations begun in August, 1982, with Canada, Australia and the United States (its major suppliers) to procure blanket permission in advance for this research. Japan hopes soon to acquire control over the full fuel cycle and to find a permanent disposal site for nuclear wastes—perhaps on an island already contaminated with radioactivity from nuclear tests in the 1950's that the Marshall Islands are offering to Japan. The government expects to have advanced thermal reactors using plutonium fuel in operation by 1990 and commercially practicable fast breeder reactors by 2010. . . .

Even though opponents of nuclear power have not yet brought about a moratorium in plant construction, they manage to cause delays, raise costs (both for construction and in the price per head of compensation that the government and utilities must eventually pay), and embarrass the government and the utilities every step of the way for virtually every plant proposed. . . .

[O]pponents are deeply disturbed about how little consideration is given to the opinion of local residents during the planning stages. MITI and the Nuclear Safety Commission [NSC] hold two public hearings per plant, but they select the speakers, control the agenda, limit speeches (to about 5 minutes each), limit question time (to a total of perhaps 30 minutes for each hearing) and, in the final analysis, may ignore the proceedings entirely. Until May, 1983, opponents boycotted such hearings and held demonstrations outside instead. In early 1983, MITI and the NSC decided to abandon public hearings and instead conduct even more stringently controlled closed hearings and solicit written opinions from local residents.

As their opposition to nuclear power increases, opponents are becoming progressively more skilled in causing delays if not in stopping construction. In addition to demonstrating at the hearings in order to get press coverage, they file lawsuits (a technique borrowed from the environmental movement) and recall pro-nuclear mayors; most recently, they have begun drafting municipal ordinances to require mayors to abide by the results of local referenda.

Even though nuclear power capacity has increased tenfold since 1973, its contribution to Japan's primary energy supply is still small. All in all, it seems likely that Japan's nuclear power program is headed for further difficulties and may not provide the panacea that government, business, and even much of the population still hope for.

Although the Japanese are anxious about their dependence, they have adopted policies that appear faint-hearted and indecisive to some observers because they prefer to let the market provide the motive for conservation. Unfortunate experiences in 1973–1974 with relatively modest forms of intervention confirmed their preference for market solutions.

If the Japanese are doing so little, how do they accomplish so much? First, market solutions work as long as the political waters remain calm. Second, because industry can usually pass on some of its increased costs (economizing to make up for those costs that consumers refuse to absorb), industry has been willing to pay these additional costs. Third, because the industrial sector is the largest consumer of energy in Japan, the strong stimulus to conservation in that sector made an enormous difference in overall conservation.

If Japan is doing so well why are the Japanese nervous? First, most conservation thus far has been in the industrial sector, but the Japanese have expectations about increasing domestic comfort and increasing their use of automobiles as a convenience, and energy experts doubt that Japan can easily achieve much conservation in the transportation or residential-commercial sectors. Second, the Japanese fear that Japan has already achieved the "easy" increment of conservation and that further progress will require technological breakthroughs that may not come at convenient times. Third, success at conservation undermines the conditions that stimulate conservation. The industrial world's reduced appetite for oil is nibbling away at OPEC's ability to function as a cartel, causing a worldwide oil glut, and pushing the price of crude downward. Japanese energy experts fear that this situation may produce overconfidence and a drop in energy efficiency.

If Japan is doing so well, is its vulnerability to another energy crisis really so serious? That Japan depends for more of its energy on imported fuels than other nations is a hard fact. Japanese energy experts recognize that their next best choice in their own eyes (nuclear power) is also at bottom an imported energy, and that it is very difficult to achieve rapid or radical change in patterns of energy use. They believe that they have done well thus far only because oil still flows; but they are still competing with other energy-importing nations to increase their flexibility and independence in energy matters before the next crisis.

47

China's Energy Plan for the 80s

Christopher M. Clarke

In this selection, Clarke argues that China is facing five major obstacles in attempting to resolve its current energy crisis: inadequate transportation facilities leading to transport bottlenecks; inadequate ports and pipeline facilities; imbalances in the regional distribution of energy supplies and demand; low recovery rates for existing fields (oil and gas); and poor or inexperienced management of energy supplies, production, and distribution. Two strategies that the Chinese leadership has employed in attempting to overcome these obstacles are conservation and energy resource development. Conservation involves government sanctions against inefficient industrial users of energy as well as incentives for managers to modernize existing plant and equipment to make them more energy efficient. However, the Chinese are interested in developing and modernizing the extraction of their huge coal reserves. And, they are interested in alternative sources of hydroelectric, nuclear, and solar energy. Each of these alternatives poses its own peculiar problems, such as cost effectiveness and availability of appropriate technology for development. These problems must be solved, Clarke argues, if China is to escape its crisis.

Only three years ago the Chinese were confidently, even jubilantly, expecting an oil bonanza that would pay for their ambitious program of the "four modernizations." Ten new Daqing-sized oilfields, eight major new coal bases, and 30 new electric power stations were to be supported by new trunk-line railroads and a major program of port development. Expected revenues from foreign sales of oil were to help build a modern heavy industry by the year 2000. But almost as quickly as US pumps dried up in 1973, Chinese petroleum production dreams were dashed. The country now faces an energy crisis as severe as the West's, and perhaps even more difficult to solve.

At least five major factors contributed to China's energy shortages. Historically, the country has underinvested in the transportation lines supporting the energy sector. Railroads offer a key example: 43 percent of all rail traffic in China, and some 60 percent of north-south traffic, carries coal—about two-thirds of China's output. Rail traffic increased about tenfold between 1948 and 1975, yet route length since liberation has only doubled; overall track (because of double tracking) has expanded about three times. Similarly, the production of rolling stock has shown negative growth in the past two years.

As with the rail system, underinvestment in pipelines and ports has hampered China's ability to deliver energy. Some 47 percent of the water transport under the Ministry of Communications is coal-related, yet only recently has a concerted effort been made, with Japanese assistance and financing, to improve the port system.

China's widespread regional imbalance of supply and demand has compounded the energy problem. Most of China's coal supply lies in underpopulated and underdeveloped northern provinces, far from the heavy energy demands of the South and East. . . .

Energy recovery in China is nearly as inefficient as energy use. Coal mines recover only about 60 percent of their known deposits, while only about 30 percent of the oil in China's developed oilfields is ultimately recovered.

The country's aggregate conversion rate for primary energy resources is only a little more than half that of the US. Energy consumption per unit of output ranges from twice that in Japan for chemical fertilizer and steel, to about ten times per motor vehicle.

A final cause of China's energy crisis is poor coordination, planning, and management. Until recently, China had no comprehensive energy plan. Even since the establishment of a State Energy Commission last August, responsibility for various parts of the plan remain shared by the State Planning Commission, State Economic Commission, State Science and Technology Commission, State Machine Building Industry Commission, State Capital Construction Commission, Ministry of Petroleum, Ministry of Chemicals, Ministry of Coal, Ministry of Electric Power, Ministry of Water Conservancy, Ministry of Geology, and other agencies. Consequently much equipment, up to and including oil rigs, has been sitting crated and idle. [In late 1980] Premier Zhao Ziyang admitted that nearly $2 billion in equipment purchased abroad was sitting in storage (although it was not all energy-related equipment). . . .

ENERGY PLANNING

Since 1978 China's leaders have come to see the need for a comprehensive energy program, now being formulated. For the first time planners are seeing energy as one element of an interrelated socioeconomic system; forecasts of China's energy needs are being related to population growth, for example.

Similarly, energy consumption patterns are being viewed in the context of a shift from heavy to light industry. The Chinese point to the fact that light industry uses about 80 percent less energy than heavy industry, and that for each percentage change in the ratio, China can save about 6 million tons standard coal equivalent. Moreover, for each ¥1 million of investment, Chinese light industry provides more than 250 jobs; fewer than 100 would be created in heavy industry.

Finally, planners recognize the energy implications of budget deficits, inflation, and uncontrolled capital construction. China's leaders realize that their inability to fuel existing industries adequately makes it foolish to construct new high energy-consumption facilities. Uncoordinated local development disrupts national coordination of energy production and distribution. New construction will now be coordinated by the SPC, taking into account China's financial, technical, and energy capabilities.

CONSERVATION

Chinese leaders recognize their principal short-term task as initiating strong conservation measures and improving the efficiency of existing machinery and plants. Conservation plans in 1980 called for saving 23 million tons of coal, 3 million tons of gasoline and diesel fuel, 1.5 million tons of fuel oil and coke, and 7 million megawatts of electricity. This year's plans are reported to be similar. As of November 1980 no new petroleum-fueled equipment will be designed, manufactured, or imported without the approval of the SPC. Moreover, all oil-burning industrial boilers and furnaces must be converted to coal by May 1985. Inefficient and wasteful facilities have been ordered to conserve energy or change product line, or face shutdowns. Work teams have been sent out from Beijing to assess the efficiency of energy use in industrial facilities—some 350 people went in March 1980 alone. . . .

COAL

Although conservation is intended to relieve the immediate strain of China's energy shortage, new resources obviously must be developed. Coal is the first priority. With known reserves totaling some 600 billion tons, China trails only the Soviet Union and the United States in coal output. Most important, China can develop its coal with relatively unsophisticated technology and low investment.

There are significant technical problems attached to coal development: coal fields are far from eastern population centers; transportation is inadequate and costly; and coal, relatively inefficient as a heat supplier, creates high levels of pollution. In addition, some half-dozen key questions on the development of this resource must be resolved.

To begin with, officials must compromise on the disparate goals of mechanizing China's coal mines on the one hand, or utilizing its massive labor force on the other. The 1978 policy stressed rapid, high-level mechanization and high production targets. Since 1980, Gao Yangwen and his Coal Ministry have seemed resigned to a slower pace of mechanization, and have advocated lower production targets over the next year or two while stepping up investment in tunneling and mining infrastructure to compensate for past neglect. But the idea of cutting back output, even temporarily, does not sit well with other high-ranking officials, many of whom favor using China's abundant manpower to maintain output over the next few years until mechanized production can be more widely introduced. . . .

ELECTRICITY

Following conservation and coal, China's third energy priority—electricity—currently has a green light for development.

This year, although the amount of available investment funds has been reduced, electric power's slice of the capital construction budget has risen from 6.9 percent in 1980 to 9.1 percent. Reflecting this increased emphasis, Vice-Minister of Electric Power Li Rui said in February, "The absolute value of capital construction investment in the power industry ranks first compared with what other industrial departments receive. All the capital construction projects under construction in the power industry are being allowed to continue."

Hydroelectric power in 1979 provided about 17 percent of China's electric output. Plans are to increase this amount to 25 percent or more in the next 20 years. As a result, 1981 investment in hydropower will increase by 2 percent over 1980 to 50 percent of investment in power generation.

The development of hydro projects, however, involves some serious problems, the first of which is money. The Gezhouba dam reportedly costs ¥3.5 billion ($2.2 billion at current exchange rates). The Three Gorges project will cost about ¥9.56 billion ($6.0 billion). In addition, the construction of such large projects takes as long as ten years and displaces people and farmland. The Three Gorges ultimately will cause the relocation of about 1.4 million people, and will cost China 44,000 hectares of cultivable land. The regional political implications of such issues will create another serious constraint on the development of massive hydro projects. Similarly, because of the location of most of China's hydro potential, the costs of transmission infrastructure will be huge.

Nonetheless, China's hydropower potential is abundant. It is a clean and renewable resource in known quantities and locations, providing such ancillary benefits as fisheries, irrigation, and water transport. Moreover, small, locally developed hydroprojects are within the technical and financial capabilities of many of China's communes. Such installations can provide electric power for agriculture, small industry, and domestic consumption which otherwise would be unavailable. . . .

China's prime source of electricity—thermal power—accounts for about 75 percent of its electric generating stations and provides about 83 percent of China's electricity. Of this, approximately 80 percent comes from coal, and the balance from oil. In general, thermal plants are less expensive and more quickly built than hydropower or nuclear electric generating plants.

Whatever combination of hydro and thermal installations China opts for, three issues remain. The first is infrastructure development. For example, China currently has no 500,000-volt lines, although plans call for completing two in 1981, one in the Northeast, and one in Central China. Recognizing this deficiency, the leadership this year increased the percentage of electric power investment for transmission lines from 22.2 percent in 1980 to 28.1 percent in 1981.

A second issue is the size of the installations. China currently has about 90,000 small plants generating some 7.1 million kilowatts. Most of these have been developed locally. National investment is being channeled into large plants. This is reflected by the fact that while the 1981 production of 180,000 megawatts of generating units is down slightly from 1980, the average annual capacity of each unit is 155 megawatts, or about twice that of last year. In its search for larger-capacity generating units, China's First Ministry of Machine Building has signed licensing technology agreements with Westinghouse and Combustion Engineering for the production of 300- and 600-mw generators and boilers for coal-fired power plants.

The third electric power issue involves the intended user of the power plant; that is, will a power plant be built with a specific heavy industrial enduser in mind, or will planners ensure that such plants are integrated into the economy of the region? The Metallurgy Ministry, for example, has been a strong advocate of building power plants designed to fuel particular heavy industrial complexes like Baoshan. However, with the recent postponement of Baoshan's phase two, planning authorities have decided to go ahead with construction of its attendant power plant, with its output to be diverted to Shanghai. Similarly, the Longtan hydro project in Guangxi, originally envisioned as the power supply for an aluminum plant, is now being integrated into the Hongshui regional development scheme.

PETROLEUM

That China's oil development now has dropped to fourth priority points out the high costs, lengthy development time, and serious risks associated with this sector. Neither quantity nor location of oil reserves is certain, and from that standpoint at least coal and hydro seem safer bets. But of course petroleum has advantages as a clean, easily transported fuel that, in today's world market, is well worth developing.

The crucial issue in China's oil development is whether to concentrate resources on offshore or onshore drilling, or on both at once. For now the shortage of personnel and finances has precluded the dual strategy. More-over, the decision clearly has been made to concentrate on offshore devel-opment. French and Japanese companies have signed exploration agree-ments with China, and in February 1981 Total Chine, a French company, struck oil in the Gulf of Tonkin, while another French company, Elf Aqui-taine, discovered encouraging signs in the Bohai Bay. . . .

Petroleum development has, of course, been a center of political con-troversy in the past three years. The failure to make good on the grand designs of 1978, associated with top leaders like Hua Guofeng, Li Xiannian, Yu Qiuli, and Gu Mu, has caused substantial political fallout. Disagreement with the advocates of readjustment came to a head in August and September 1980 when Yu Qiuli was shifted from the SPC to the newly created State Energy Commission, and Minister of Petroleum Song Zhenming was fired. The most recent development in this conflict was Kang Shien's appointment as minister of petroleum and his removal from the State Economic Commission.

The primary responsibility of the SEC is to coordinate supply and de-mand in China's annual planning process. Kang became SEC chairman when a continued oil supply seemed assured. Kang's career and expertise cen-tered on the production of more oil, not managing the consumption of less. Thus, it made both economic and political sense for him to be "demoted" to the position of minister of petroleum. If he is successful in increasing output, his transfer will be interpreted as a wise one. If he is unsuccessful, it will be substantially easier to eliminate one of the "energy clique's" main supports in the leadership.

NUCLEAR POWER AND ALTERNATIVES

As discussed in the January–February, 1981, *CBR,* nuclear power is receiving new attention in China. Provincial officials have combined with scientists from State Science and Technology Commission and the Chinese Academy of Sciences and officials from the Second Ministry of Machine Building in advocating nuclear-generated electric power as a major energy source for the future. Despite the price tag of $1 billion or more, and the ten-year construction period, nuclear power is seen as a clean, safe, and relatively inexpensive source of energy. . . .

Another important element in redressing regional imbalances and pro-viding energy to China's rural areas is the development of alternative sources. Biogas or methane is the most popular of these alternatives. China now has about 7 million rural biogas pits, seven times as many as in 1975, supplying about 30–40 million peasants. Less (but still substantial) attention is also being paid to developing local shale-oil deposits, solar power, wind power, geothermal tidal power, and forests for wood fuel. While there is little political support for massive national-level investment in most of these areas, localities have been strongly encouraged to make maximum use of alternate energy sources through the employment of low-level technology and local funds and manpower.

Since 1978, China has come a long way in the direction of establishing realistic energy policies and plans. Its current short-term priority is to conserve energy while nudging the economy away from heavy industry toward a light industrial, consumer-oriented system. Even as the rate of increase for energy demand is being reduced, development of coal, hydroelectricity, thermal electricity, petroleum, nuclear power, and alternate energy sources will increase supply. Whether China's plans are realistic, or can succeed, is uncertain. But it is encouraging to see Chinese planning become more sophisticated in the 1980s.

48

Energy in China

Thomas Fingar

In these excerpts, Fingar discusses some of the connections between economic reforms and energy policy. The post-Mao leadership once believed that China's sizable oil reserves, if developed for export, could finance China's four modernizations. They not only failed to take into account international market fluctuations in supply, demand, and price of oil, but they also failed to comprehend the domestic constraints on increased production and export. Many new oil fields are inaccessible. Transport and distribution infrastructures do not exist. Foreign technology is key to developing many reserves. And many of the economic reforms since 1978 have exacerbated the problem.

The retention of profits, for example, has allowed enterprises to expand their plant and productive facilities but has increased energy consumption. This increased consumption is usually very inefficient and is not outweighed by shifting investment from inefficient heavy industries to more efficient light industries. Since most centrally distributed energy supplies are directed to urban areas, increased consumption by industry can only further hinder attempts at agricultural mechanization, which depends on increased supplies to rural areas. The state planning and economic commissions are playing a greater role in coordinating supplies and overseeing conservation and efficiency measures. Rural areas are being urged to cooperatively plan energy usage. Finally, bank loans to expanding enterprises are now partially dependent on the plant's efficient use of existing supplies.

Twenty-one American oil firms have submitted bids to the China National Offshore Oil Corporation (CNOOC) for the right to explore for petroleum on China's southern continental shelf. The Atlantic Richfield Corporation, which signed a contract with CNOOC on September 19, 1982, has already begun exploratory drilling south of Hainan Island. Occidental Petroleum has signed a contract to do a feasibility study for a major coal mine in North China. As part of the US-PRC Hydropower Protocol signed in 1979, the Army Corps of Engineers is advising the Chinese Ministry of Water Conservancy and Electric Power on a major project in Southwest China. China's search for new supplies of energy promises to tie the country to the United States—and to the world economy in general—in complex and unprecedented ways.

As natural as this may seem to Americans, China's leaders have been very reluctant to allow foreign corporations to play a major role in the development of China's energy resources. Their reluctance stems from a mixture of pride, fear, and inexperience. They were—and still are—proud of China's indigenous capabilities, fearful of becoming dependent on and victimized by foreign firms, and unfamiliar with the technical, financial, and legal requisites of large-scale joint ventures with capitalist firms. If they could, they would prefer to rely on outsiders only to a limited extent; for example, for advanced equipment that China cannot produce. Indeed, the policies first adopted by Mao's successors embodied precisely this approach. It made superficial good sense, but soon foundered on historical, logistical, technical, and political obstacles. By the late 1970s, shortages of fuel and power had become chronic, in spite of the fact that China produces more commercial energy than all but a handful of nations.

The current approach recognizes the difficulties involved in opening new mines and oil fields and in sustaining production in older fields. China probably could develop its energy resources without foreign assistance, but neither the country nor the political leadership can afford further delay. Energy demand and the Chinese populace's expectations for a higher standard of living are rising inexorably. Forced to choose between economic stagnation *and* popular dissatisfaction, on the one hand, and partial reliance on foreign firms, on the other, the leadership has opted for a less restrictive definition of self-reliance. But the door to the capitalist world could be pushed shut by the forces that made self-reliance so attractive in the first place.

THE INITIAL POST-MAO ENERGY POLICY

The strategy of development adopted shortly after the 1976 death of Mao Zedong (Mao Tse-tung) and purge of the "gang of four" assumed that energy production could and would increase steadily. This was a critical assumption because large and rapidly growing amounts of fuel and power were needed to realize the "four modernizations" (agriculture, industry, national defense, and science and technology). This would enhance the legitimacy of the Communist Party and the "socialist system" by restoring political and economic stability, improving economic performance, and generating tangible and substantial social benefits.

Without expanded energy supplies, it would be impossible to achieve promised improvements in the performance of farms and factories. Mechanization was supposed to raise agricultural output while easing the lot of the peasantry. Freed from the "irrational" (i.e., political) constraints imposed by the discredited "gang of four," industry was to provide consumer goods for town and countryside alike. Chinese planners believed all this was possible because they assumed that energy would be cheap and abundant.

This ambitious modernization effort was to be financed as well as fueled by the country's energy resources. Exports, primarily of crude oil, were expected to earn vast amounts of foreign exchange. Revenue from oil sales would, in turn, be used to purchase advanced technologies, completed industrial plants, and other ingredients needed for China to leapfrog across intermediate stages of development to become a "powerful, modern, socialist state" by the end of the century. Again, obtaining adequate supplies of energy was treated as a nonproblem. . . .

[Chinese leaders] knew that their country had vast deposits of fossil fuel. Although the precise magnitude of China's reserves is uncertain, because much of the country remains unexplored and the quality of available data is uneven, they clearly are substantial. Recoverable coal reserves are now estimated at more than 600 billion metric tons (bmt), roughly the same magnitude as those of the United States and the Soviet Union. Estimates of both total and recoverable oil reserves vary widely but, on the basis of current information, probably fall within the range of 3–10 bmt. In the mid-1970s, when the initial plan was being drafted, Chinese officials frequently used substantially higher figures when describing their country's potential. Little is known about the size of natural gas deposits, but they too are impressive—perhaps on a par with those of the United States. China also has the largest theoretical hydropower potential in the world (500 million kilowatts); less than 5 percent of this potential has been tapped.

But resources in the ground do not fuel economic development; they must be exploited. Here too, Chinese leaders had cause for optimism because by any standard their country had achieved steady, even dramatic production increases. . . .

Finally, assumptions about future earnings from oil exports were buttressed by favorable market conditions. OPEC-led price increases and the scramble to find alternatives to Mideast oil seemed to bode well. Growing foreign interest in Chinese fields, where production increases had reached roughly 20 percent per year in the mid-1970s, also contributed to the general sense of optimism about the future.

In retrospect it is clear—to the Chinese as well as to outside observers—that the post-Mao leadership had too rosy a view of the country's energy balance. But it is important to point out that they had lots of company. It has been less than a decade since the Arab oil embargo and predictions of impending energy crises forced political leaders around the globe to focus on and learn more about the production, transport, and use of energy. Others also made easy but erroneous projections on the basis of past experience. However, the Chinese had—and still face—four special problems in perceiving and responding to the new verities, problems of logistics, history, technology, and politics.

Logistics

China's leaders appear to have assumed that the exploration and exploitation of fuel and power resources would follow the same general pattern as that found in China's recent past or the experience of other nations. But such reasoning by analogy was misleading. Major producing areas (for example, the giant Daqing [Ta-ch'ing] oilfield and the Kailan coal complex) were exploited first both because they were located near industrial centers, and, more importantly, because they were easiest to develop. In contrast, most of the larger untapped reserves, especially of hydropower but also of oil, coal, and natural gas, are in remote, inaccessible areas. Each new investment will be more difficult, more costly, and more technically demanding. The Chinese will have to face such obstacles as transport over long distances and difficult terrain, removal of heavy overburdens atop coal seams, working in deep water and violent weather in promising offshore areas, and unusually heavy silt loads in major rivers. These problems are not insoluble, but they are certainly more formidable than was appreciated in the 1970s and may be more difficult than China can handle, at least in the short run.

History

The Chinese approach to energy development under Mao shaped the perceptions of his successors in three important ways. The first was a strong faith in self-reliant mobilization. Chinese leaders are justifiably proud of the Daqing oilfield, which is located in a remote and harsh region of the country and now supplies roughly half of China's annual production. Daqing was built without foreign assistance. Successes in the expansion of coal mines, development of small-scale and a few large hydropower projects, and in tapping Sichuan's (Szechwan) rich reserves of natural gas also contributed to the general sense of optimism.

All this suggested that even the most formidable obstacles to further exploitation of known reserves could be overcome. China had scored great accomplishments in the past and could surely do so again, especially since the country was no longer shackled by the infamous "gang of four," or so many leaders thought in 1976–77. For example, officials and media commentaries proclaimed that it was possible to open "ten new Daqings" by 1985.

Second, history constrained as well as misled political officials. The "Soviet model" of economic development, adopted in the 1950s, stressed heavy, energy-intensive industry, and relied on extensive rather than intensive growth. This approach ignored energy efficiencies: efficiency did not matter because fuel and power were underpriced and no competitive or other mechanisms existed to induce efforts to limit costs. As a result, China has hundreds of thousands of aging and energy inefficient enterprises and a deeply ingrained approach to capital investment that makes it difficult to switch to more efficient, less energy-intensive construction and retrofitting. Moreover, since efficiency mattered little for thirty years, tens of thousands of enterprises continue to operate, even though they waste resources and serve more of a welfare than a production function. (According to official figures more than 25 percent of state-run enterprises operate at a loss.) The technically or economically rational course is clear, but it is extremely difficult to change attitudes, expectations, and behavior, or to close factories that waste energy.

The third historical legacy is the government's near continuous failure to devote adequate attention or resources to the energy and transportation sectors. Despite considerable rhetoric and a few major achievements, construction of mines, oilfields, railways, transmission lines, pipelines and highways failed to keep pace with the growing demand for fuel and power in the cities and rural areas. This failure is particularly striking in a state which advocates central planning and claims an almost religious faith in the advantages of planned development. Decades of neglect cannot be overcome in just a few years.

Technology

The geographical, geological and other logistical factors noted above combine in ways that preclude rapid development of energy resources without substantial infusion of advanced technology; both equipment and know-how. China has done quite well with the technologies acquired from the Soviet Union in the 1950s, but, generally speaking, has pushed those technologies about as far as they could be pushed. Tapping deeper oil deposits, opening new mines, and exploring for offshore gas requires knowledge and equipment not available in China. The needs cover a very broad spectrum, from heavy-duty trucks for use in open-pit mines to the computer hardware and software for processing seismic data. Moreover, to make effective use of many items requires simultaneous acquisition and absorption of many others. Almost without exception, the technologies and equipment needed are expensive. . . .

Politics

Tapping China's energy resources is complicated by both domestic and international politics. On the domestic side, one finds the same types of regional, bureaucratic, and personal rivalries that bedevil other political systems. Various agencies, interests, and coalitions jostle one another at the budgetary trough and compete for other limited resources. Despite rhetorical homage to "scientific socialism," most decisions are made using political as well as purely technical or economic criteria. Thus, investment must be spread to satisfy many claimants rather than concentrated in an economically optimal way. Short-term demands often overwhelm arguments in favor of technical solutions that might be better in the long run. In short, energy decisions in China are at least as political as they are in the United States. But the impact of confused and contradictory energy policies is worse in China than in the U.S. because China lacks the moderating effect of myriad private sector decisions.

International politics, or, more specifically, domestic debates over China's foreign policy and the way those debates are shaped by external developments, also affect China's ability to develop its energy resources. The logistical, historical and technical factors outlined above make it imperative for China to rely, at least in part, on foreign assistance if it is to meet its energy requirements. But such reliance is an anathema to some officials and unpalatable to many others. They recall the history of "exploitation" at the hands of imperialist states and foreign companies. As nationalistic leaders dedicated to restoring China's prestige and independence, they view the role of transnational energy companies through ideologically tinted glasses. They are understandably reluctant to allow foreigners to play a direct and central role in the development of so critical a sector as energy. Part of the attractiveness of the 1977–78 strategy of development was that it promised to keep the foreigners at arm's length; they would merely supply equipment and advice.

As officials came to realize that exploiting China's energy resources— and attaining broader developmental goals—would be impossible without substantial foreign involvement, they faced two unpalatable alternatives: (1) the undermining of political legitimacy through failure to produce immediate and tangible economic benefit, or (2) dependence on foreign firms and governments. One reason it has taken China so long to conclude the first sizeable contracts for development of coal and offshore oil is that officials are unwilling to make politically risky decisions. They fear, with good reason, that support for foreign involvement (that is, "underestimating China's potential" and "selling out to the capitalists") might come back to haunt them.

Involving foreigners effectively and absorbing advanced technologies raise other political issues as well. Current efforts to "readjust and reform" the economy are linked to the effort to achieve greater energy (as well as economic) efficiency and they tread on deeply entrenched interests. Aggrieved or endangered interests (e.g., inefficient factories, and local Party leaders in relatively disadvantaged areas) mobilize support and use every available political tool to alter decisions they do not like. This has had, and will continue to have, a major impact on the implementation of energy policy.

CURRENT POLICIES AND PRIORITIES

Confronted with this complex mixture of opportunities and difficulties, China's leaders have moved, albeit by fits and starts and with a degree of trail and error, to formulate integrated, comprehensive and effective energy policies for the entire nation. After decades of neglect, the energy sector has been accorded high, if not highest, priority. Although the military still commands the lion's share of the budget and agriculture retains rhetorical preeminence, investment in energy production and distribution is at an all-time high, and energy considerations are central to the evaluation of all capital construction projects. Implementation has lagged behind the articulation of energy policies and, naturally, individuals and organizations have interpreted guidelines to accord with their own wishes. However, generally speaking, China appears to be moving in a sensible direction. Cataloging the dozens of specific measures adopted is less useful than describing the four fundamental elements of Chinese energy policy: conservation, concentration, cooperation, and coordination.

Conservation of Existing Resources

Chinese fondness for the slogan of "walking on two legs" has continued into the post-Mao era. Under that rubric officials now proclaim the need to pursue both exploitation (i.e., greater production) and conservation of energy. They immediately add, however, that production cannot be increased significantly in the short term and that primary emphasis must be placed on conservation through more efficient use of the energy that is produced.

Official pessimism about the ability of China to produce more energy has been justified by recent statistics showing little or no growth. Even allowing for the inaccuracies that almost certainly exist in Chinese statistics, the trend is clear and stands in sharp contrast to that of the early 1970s.

To implement the call for energy conservation, departments and localities were instructed to prepare concrete plans to reduce wasteful consumption. Enterprises must monitor the amount of fuel and power used and strive to reduce consumption per unit of output. Inefficient factories will be penalized, presumably by having their allocations of energy reduced, and those able to use energy most efficiently will be given additional supplies if the addition will enable them to operate at higher capacity. This is in keeping with a general shift to what are termed "economic methods." Other conservation measures include retrofitting plants as part of the emphasis on tapping the full potential of existing enterprises, the introduction of "modern" principles of management and techniques associated with systems engineering and operations research, and closer monitoring of energy consumption.

To conserve oil, oil-burning industrial boilers are to be converted to burn coal. Current policy specifies that "all" oil-fired boilers must be converted and no new ones may be constructed except in extraordinary cases. Reasons for making such a change include freeing more oil for export and other forms of domestic consumption, and for taking full advantage of China's large coal reserves. But there are also costs and problems associated with this policy. For example, increased use of coal will require additional transport capacity, opening and/or expanding mines, and greater attention to pollution problems—not to mention the direct costs of conversion. Thus far, officials seem to be paying little attention to these implications.

Concentration of Investment

Another Maoist aphorism adopted by his successors is to "concentrate resources to fight a war of annihilation." This injunction has been construed to mean that available resources (human, fiscal, technical, etc.) must be dedicated to the construction of a relatively small number of projects that can be completed quickly and will produce tangible and immediate benefits. Applied to energy decisions, this approach has produced three notable developments.

The first and most significant development is increased investment in the energy sector. Despite substantial reduction in expenditures for capital construction, the amount and percentage of funds earmarked for energy production (and conservation) have climbed to an all-time high. Having identified energy shortfalls as the principal obstacle to realization of economic, social, and political goals, officials have made the politically difficult decision to shift resources from other sectors with aspirations, requirements, and supporters of their own.

Resources have been concentrated more heavily than heretofore in the energy sector; within that sector, they have been concentrated in relatively few facilities. In order to bring new facilities on line as quickly as possible, the number of concurrent projects has been reduced sharply in the past three years. More care than previously is being devoted to the evaluation of alternative projects to ascertain the optimal sequence of development. Existing facilities will be expanded and modernized before new ones are built *if* doing so will produce better results in the short run.

Principles and priorities guiding the retrofitting of existing facilities to conserve energy are similar to those guiding new construction. Since industry consumes more than 70 percent of all commercial energy in China, and since the chemical, petrochemical, and metallurgical industries account for most of that figure, initial efforts are directed at the biggest sources of waste in these major consuming industries. This approach has certain clear advantages but it is also quite new in China where it has been far more common to dissipate resources in order to "do a little for everyone at the same time."

Second, the general economic policy of "readjustment" serves to concentrate investment in ways that affect the energy sector. A key component of this approach has been to shift resources and emphasis from heavy to light industry. One frequently proclaimed reason for doing so is that light and textile industries consume far less energy per unit of production than do heavy industries. Reducing the targets and operating time of one heavy industrial facility "frees up" enough fuel and power to supply several light industrial plants. The latter generate higher profits, produce goods needed to satisfy rising consumer demand at home, and earn foreign exchange from exports.

Concentrating resources in this way has raised the productivity of energy inputs, but it has also infringed upon the interests of powerful groups. These include representatives of the defense industries and their allies in the military, centers of heavy industry such as Shenyang and Anshan, and officials linked by factional ties and logrolling arrangements. These political forces—Nikita Khrushchev used to refer to their Soviet counterparts as "steel eaters"—will no doubt make new claims on the country's fuel and power in the near future.

Finally, the energy supplies produced under central direction will be consumed primarily in the cities. Since total energy production will grow slowly and demand in the urban and industrial sector will steadily increase, the supply of commercial energy to the rural areas will not increase significantly during the remainder of the decade. Consequently, the ambitious plan to mechanize agriculture by 1985 has been abandoned. Even if there were no other obstacles (which of course there are), the energy requirements (diesel fuel, electricity, gasoline) would be prohibitive.

In one sense the 800 million people living in the countryside are being told that they must once again defer to the needs of their urban cousins, but there are significant differences between present policies and past neglect of the rural areas. For the first time in PRC history, the central government appears to be making a substantial effort to help the villages to help themselves in the energy field.

As part of this effort, investigation teams have surveyed the potential energy resources, capabilities, and needs of all (approximately 2,000) rural counties to determine, among other things, the potential for development of small hydrogenerators, local coal pits, biogas, solar energy, and fuelwood. Recognizing the impossibility of formulating detailed plans for 2,000 counties, the energy research institute (subordinate to both the state economic commission and the Chinese Academy of Sciences) has assigned each country to one of twenty-six categories or "zones." Counties in the same zone have the same general mix of resources and requirements. When the process of analysis and clarification has been completed, central officials will formulate twenty-six rather than 2,000 specific rural energy policies. Small hydro projects will be encouraged in some counties, for example, while tapping natural gas deposits will be promoted in others. The allocation of funds, assignment of skilled personnel, and development of local industries will be made accordingly.

Cooperation: Foreign and Domestic

After years of delay and agonizing efforts to find an acceptable alternative, China's leaders have finally begun to sign major contracts with foreign firms for the development of energy resources. At the same time, the government is encouraging cooperation across formerly hermetic administrative boundaries within China. Both forms of collaboration have encountered political resistance.

Domestic opposition to foreign involvement is fueled by economic concerns as well as chauvinism. Investment in the development of energy resources is, to some extent, a zero-sum game. Some regions, industries, and enterprises will benefit from joint projects with foreign partners while others will be disadvantaged, at least in the short run. Those with something to lose have joined those opposed to foreign involvement on ideological or xenophobic grounds. Politics is omnipresent. By mid-1982, however, Deng Xiaoping and his allies had converted, neutralized, or removed enough of those opposed to foreign involvement to clear away the remaining obstacles.

Willingness to permit major energy companies and foreign governments to participate in the search for and exploitation of China's energy resources is neither a sudden development nor an invitation to foreigners to write their own ticket. While combating and conquering domestic opposition, key officials (e.g., Deng, Zhao Ziyang [Chao Tzu-yang], Hu Yaobang [Hu Yao-pang], and Yao Yilin) and legal, technical, financial, and other specialists have been preparing the way for restricted but effective foreign investment in the energy sector. Preparation of the joint venture, corporate income tax, petroleum, and other laws; decisions as to how and where foreigners will be allowed to invest; and analysis of how to reap maximum benefits from training, technical information, and sale of equipment and support services has proceeded slowly but steadily during the past three years. Hence, when it became politically possible to invite the foreigners in, it was also technically possible to do so. These developments are not unrelated; it is likely that political opposition diminished as safeguards were devised.

Cooperation within the country is at least as significant and as fraught with political controversy as allowing foreigners to invest in and operate mines and oilfields. The government is promoting a variety of new (for China) ways to induce joint projects between, and capture scarce investment funds from, different administrative and functional units. For example, provinces with limited or low-quality deposits of coal have been urged and enabled to invest in the development of mines located in other provinces.

They do so with the promise of reaping economic benefits (e.g., equipment sales and a return on investment) and guaranteed energy supplies. At lower levels of the system, new ways are being tested to facilitate cooperation among villages (teams, brigades, and even communes) in the same river basin or astride the same deposit of coal.

As reasonable as it seems, the policy of encouraging domestic cooperation faces several obstacles. For years, farms, factories, and administrative units were urged to be self-reliant: their willingness to be so was reinforced by traditional rivalries and the perils of depending on others. As a result, cooperation was problematic and infrequent. Better guidance, better leadership, and material incentives are now seen as critical to overcoming the attitudes and behavior of the past. It is too soon to declare current policies a success, but, again, they are a step in the right direction. . . .

Overall responsibility for formulating the energy sector plans and coordinating projects to ensure adequate supplies of fuel and power now rests with the state planning commission and the state economic commission. The evidence to date suggests that considerable progress has been made toward overcoming energy bottlenecks caused by unplanned or poorly coordinated construction and operation of industrial enterprises. Better coordination has also been achieved through the remerging of the former ministries of water conservancy and electric power (both of which had constructed hydro facilities). The major restructuring of state agencies undertaken in the spring of 1982 also should enhance coordination of energy policy. With fewer organizations, fewer layers of bureaucracy, and fewer redundant functionaries, project review and approval procedures will be simplified and, it is hoped, lead to greater efficiency.

The tenor of economic policy in general facilitates coordination in energy development. Provincial, municipal and enterprise officials are on a shorter leash when it comes to beginning new projects. As a result, there has been a sharp reduction in the amount of new construction, which, in turn, has slowed growth of energy demand.

Several additional steps have been adopted to enhance coordination. Provincial governments and Party committees have been instructed to establish special groups to oversee energy-related matters and to assign clear responsibility for the implementation of energy policies. Regulatory mechanisms are hence forth to be supplemented by a type of outside review effected through the various branches and arms of the People's Bank. More investment capital is to be allocated through loans approved and monitored by agencies of the Bank than through direct grants from central ministries. Before approving any loan, Bank cadres are supposed to review projects to ensure that requisite supplies of fuel and power will be available. There are reasons to question the ability of Bank personnel to conduct thorough reviews of all projects, but this is another step in the right direction.

Coordination does not just mean centralization, however. Indeed, separate corporations more independent of central ministerial control have been established to perform specific functions. Some of these corporations have entered into joint ventures with foreign firms; the China National Off-shore Oil Corporation is an obvious example. Moreover, even as the government has tightened planning and control over critical sectors of the economy, it has allowed market mechanisms to operate more freely in secondary areas. This should lead to better energy planning and policies by enabling the small band of overworked statisticians, analysts, and planners to focus on fewer projects and relationships.

PROSPECTS

China's leaders have undertaken nothing less than the total restructuring of their economic system. Energy plays a key role in their approach and success or failure in the energy sector will strongly influence, perhaps even determine, the outcome of the broader effort. What are the prospects of success on the energy front? What are the implications for the United States?

If left in place long enough, the general approach and specific policies concerning energy now dominant in China could, perhaps will, produce the desired results. On balance, the policies are both appropriate and sound; the unaddressed and unanswerable question is whether or not they will produce enough tangible benefits fast enough to satisfy skeptics, opponents, the public as a whole, or even key supporters.

If one were to predict the future on the basis of China's recent past, the inescapable conclusion is that prospects for policy continuity are not very good. Leaders and constituents eager for dramatic advances have repeatedly demonstrated impatience with policies that "worked" but were too slow. Given the visibility and inherently political character of current economic policies, including those dealing specifically with energy, it seems certain that those who fare relatively badly under policies now in place will do what they can to force change. Rising expectations among the leadership as well as the rural and urban populace will inevitably lead to increased demands and reduced willingness to delay gratification in the name of abstract goals or the larger good. These pressures will be intensified by demography and disenchantment with Marxism, the Communist Party, and contemporary Chinese society. Cynicism and the implicit question, "What has the Party done for me lately?" undermine the authority of the regime and individual leaders. To restore lost legitimacy, current policies must succeed. If success comes too slowly, current leaders may be tempted to experiment with other alternatives in an effort to substitute motion for movement and to buy more time for themselves.

Though possible, the above scenario is probably less likely than one of basic policy stability with continuous adjustments at the margins, and with intermittent removal of scapegoats who can be blamed if policies fail to deliver as much or as quickly as people have been led to expect. Perhaps the strongest reasons for assuming such continuity are that the approach is unlikely to fail miserably and that there are no ready alternatives. Weary of unsuccessful experimentation and eager for sustained, predictable, and "sensible" policies, a significant portion of the public is likely to support continuity and to "give the leaders and their approach more time." As long as things do not get worse, they need not improve dramatically to satisfy "the masses." Ironically, greater participation in the world economy and a larger role for transnational and foreign government-owned energy companies will increase pressures favoring preservation of the status quo.

Without substantial policy stability, China will not be able to exploit its rich energy resources fast enough to satisfy growing domestic demand or to provide revenue-generating exports to finance the imports of grain, equipment, and technologies needed to prevent slipping even further behind the advanced and rapidly modernizing states with which China wants to be compared.

China's energy balance will not improve significantly during the 1980s. Projects initiated in 1982–83 will not come on line until the latter part of the decade; when they do, output will barely meet increased domestic demand. Even if offshore deposits prove as rich as many hope, China probably will not earn much additional foreign exchange until well into the 1990s because it will need to retain its share of the output for domestic use. It is possible, especially if efforts to locate oil offshore prove unsuccessful, that China might have to import small quantities of oil during the 1980s.

For many reasons, the United States and American corporations will play a central role in the development of China's energy resources. Many technologies and much of the capital needed to locate and exploit deposits of oil, coal, and natural gas must come from the United States. For better or worse, China is going to become more dependent on U.S. firms and its political relations with the United States will become hostage, up to a point, to these economic and energy relationships. Similarly, the U.S. government can be uniquely helpful in the development of China's hydroelectric potential. The government-to-government agreement for cooperation in hydroelectric power and related water resources and the annexes agreed to and currently under negotiation could be extremely helpful to the Chinese and very profitable for American firms.

Should relations between Washington and Peking deteriorate significantly at some future point, it is unlikely that American firms would undertake new energy development projects. Depending on the outcome of President Reagan's attempt to block the sale of equipment embodying U.S. technologies to the Soviet Union for use in constructing the natural gas pipeline to Western Europe, American firms may find it undesirable to operate in China and China might treat American firms as suppliers of last resort.

While it is true that deterioration of official relations between China and the United States could, probably would, interfere with the development of China's energy resources and realization of its broader economic, social, and political goals, both sides recognize how undesirable that would be. At some point that is likely to be reached relatively quickly, increased energy ties will strengthen and add to the stability of the political relationship.

Unit XII

———— Education Policy ————

Both China and Japan are firmly committed to the development of human resources as a means of providing the skilled manpower needed to insure continued economic growth. But the two countries face different types of problems and their particular values and traditions have shaped different strategies for achieving this "education for human capital." In recent years, both countries have implemented policies aimed at improving the quality of education and increasing educational efficiency, but some of these measures have led to inequalities in educational opportunities.

In Japan, for example, the various reforms undertaken in the public school sector have produced a situation that in effect encourages *less* equality, at least in terms of actual outcome, since they have merely served to strengthen the private schools and to perpetuate an elitist, nonegalitarian system that favors the well-to-do. While the Japanese government has equalized opportunity for students during the first nine years of compulsory schooling, there is a distinct inequality of opportunity at the secondary and postsecondary levels. A rigorous selection process based on stiff entrance examinations bars all but the most highly qualified students from admittance to the country's first-rate universities and has forced parents to turn to private schools and examination cram schools to insure that their children will have an equal chance to receive a higher education. Widespread popular acceptance of Japan's examination system, and a general belief in its fairness, has not only provided support for a policy many consider unfair, but has also stymied educators' attempts at reform.

In spite of its problems, however, Japan has been more successful than China in raising educational levels. In an effort to make up for educational losses sustained during the Cultural Revolution, the present Chinese leadership is reverting to earlier policies that favor educational efficiency over egalitarian objectives. Under the new system, elite schools and classes, ability tracking, and competitive placement have been reinstated. Moreover, with educational investment concentrated in urban special schools and opportunities distributed on the basis of academic achievement, the peasantry (which accounts for over 80 percent of the Chinese population) stands to lose the most.

The readings in this unit focus on a number of issues related to education policy in contemporary China and Japan, including the effects of recent policy choices on educational quality and equality and the role of cultural values in shaping these policies. In the first selection, "Basic Education: Quality and Equality," Ezra Vogel analyzes the role of Japan's central government in raising educational levels and in equalizing opportunities in the primary schools. In "Is Japanese Education Becoming Less Egalitarian?," Thomas P. Rohlen details the inequality of opportunity that emerges at the high school level, showing how the more affluent Japanese are favored by the examination system. T. J. Pempel, in "The Politics of Enrollment Expansion in Japan's Universities," explains how the central government's "laissez-faire" policy has not only resulted in poorer facilities but has perpetuated social stratification based on educational attainment. In all these selections, there is evidence of the important role Japanese cultural values have played in the shaping of educational policy.

In the final reading in this unit, "The Politics of Education in Post-Mao China," Susan L. Shirk outlines the policy shifts that now favor educational efficiency over equality of opportunity and shows how these policies, along with the practice of sending students abroad for higher education, are creating new privileged classes based on educational opportunity. Shirk identifies the groups most disadvantaged by the new policies and raises important questions regarding the ultimate political impact of the government's current policy choices in education.

49

Basic Education: Quality and Equality

Ezra F. Vogel

Japan's advances in expanding educational opportunities and raising competency levels have brought it to the front rank among modern nations. In this selection from *Japan as Number One,* Vogel compares Japanese approaches to American practices and examines the problems as well as the successes of the Japanese education system. He also analyzes the relationship between high school and college entrance examinations and educational standards, discipline, responsibility, and achievement.

. . . [I]t is difficult to find a meaningful quantitative measure to compare the educational level of the adult population of different countries. Probably the most meaningful cross-national comparisons can be made in fields like mathematics and natural science, where cultural and historical factors play a relatively smaller role than social science and humanities. Where data is available for such cross-national comparisons, no country outperformed Japan overall. Nathan Glazer points out that on the 1964 twelve-nation achievement tests in mathematics for thirteen-year-olds, Japan scored second to Israel. However, these were selected samples, and when adjusted to estimate the average in the age group, Japan ranked third, although the first and second place countries edged Japan by only an insignificant amount. When adjusted to estimate the top three or four percent of the entire age group, Japan was first both for mathematics majors in the preuniversity group and, by an even larger margin, for nonuniversity majors.

In the 1970 international science test given to ten- and fourteen-year-olds in nineteen countries, Japanese youth performed comparably well. Among ten-year-olds, the Japanese were first in the subtests for earth sciences, chemistry, and biology. Although they ranked fourth in information, they ended overall in first place because they were first in understanding, in application, and in higher mental processes. Fourteen-year-old Japanese scored second to their Hungarian counterparts in biology but first in physics, chemistry, and practical science. Although they ranked only second in information, they were also first overall because of their test results in understanding, application, and higher processes. These findings are not unrelated to the fact that Japanese middle schools have science labs, and ninety-three percent of the science teachers were trained in science at universities, a record unrivaled in other countries. In grand total score America ranked fifteenth of nineteen countries. . . .

The Japanese drive to extend formal education has been as vigorous as their efforts to increase their GNP. In 1955 only about one-half of Japanese youth entered high school and less than ten percent postsecondary institutions. By the late 1970s over ninety percent of both Japanese girls and boys were completing high school, compared to approximately eighty percent of all American youth. Virtually all Japanese who enter a school complete it. In 1975, for example, ninety-seven percent of those entering high school completed it, compared with seventy-nine percent in America. At the postsecondary level in Japan, approximately the same number of males and females enter colleges, but females more commonly complete two-year courses and males more commonly four-year courses. Although approximately thirty-five to forty percent of college-aged youth were attending a university both in the United States and Japan, because of sizeable numbers of American drop-outs Japanese more often complete their training. Almost forty percent of Japanese males in their mid-twenties have completed four-year colleges compared to about twenty percent of Americans (although the American figure rises to about thirty percent by the late twenties). Very few Japanese attend graduate school. However, the desire for higher education in Japan is greater than enrollment figures suggest, for university openings are still not adequate to meet the demand. In America virtually any high school graduate can find a college or university to attend, but in Japan there are roughly three openings for four applicants. Even after students have completed their schooling, an extraordinarily high number continue taking a variety of correspondence courses and special study programs in their place of work, whether or not they are required to do so by their company. A very high percentage of the Japanese continue to read serious books and to master new bodies of knowledge.

Japanese education is not without major problems. Universities have an important function in certifying students, but faculty devotion to teaching and to students is limited, student preparations are far less than prior to the entrance examination, analytic rigor in the classroom is lacking, and attendance is poor. University expenditures per student are unreasonably low, and the level and variety of advanced research are highly limited. The Japanese student in his essays is more likely to follow guidelines than to develop his originality. Entrance examinations to high schools or universities can be so competitive as to cause students to restrict their intellectual breadth, eliminate extracurricular activities, neglect their social development, and, in case of failure, become psychologically depressed.

Americans are not about to import these problems, which show deep failures in Japanese education. Yet the maintenance of high motivation for learning, the uniformly high quality of the nine years of compulsory education, and the wide scope of educational television in Japan are remarkable achievements worthy of emulation.

Japanese are not satisfied just to attend school more hours per day and more days per year than Americans. Over half of Japanese youth at some time attend supplementary schools (*juku*) during their elementary or secondary school years. Supplementary schools come in all shapes and sizes, but the vast majority are to improve the students' chances of passing an entrance examination to a slightly more desirable high school and college. Most students have a good idea of what institution they might qualify to enter by entrance examinations if they prepare thoroughly for one or two years. Yet after entrance examinations are over, about eighteen percent of the men and a somewhat smaller percent of the women who fail to pass an examination to their desired institution remain for one year or more as *ronin* (masterless samurai), without institutional affiliation, preparing for another try at entrance examinations.

The pressure surrounding entrance examinations derives from the fact that they are the exclusive means for determining admission to institutions of higher learning and for obtaining that all-important first position. In fact, the American student who attends a good university and receives a good first job is likely to be significantly more successful than one who does not, but there is somehow an American hope that one will have many opportunities to move throughout one's career. In Japan the widely acknowledged importance of the university attended for determining later success concentrates life-long career ambitions on the entrance examinations.

The entrance examinations measure acquired knowledge on the assumption, widely accepted, that success depends not on innate ability, IQ, or general aptitude but on the capacity to use innate ability for disciplined study. It is acknowledged that native ability may affect the capacity of an individual to absorb information, but in the Japanese view there is only one way to alter the result: study. Those who spend a year or more going through special cram courses in order to enter what they consider an acceptable institution are not criticized for plodding but are praised for perseverance.

Entrance examinations are much maligned for causing excessive tension, rote memorization, and one-sided intellectual development, and for eliminating extracurricular activities and destroying the joy of youth or preexamination students. Horror stories of examination preparation receive ample publicity, although extreme cases are in fact small in number. There are suicides over exam failures but these have declined since the late 1960s, and the overall Japanese suicide rate is not high by European standards. Educators have urged and undertaken a variety of reforms to reduce examination fever, albeit without appreciable success, for the desire to achieve through entrance examinations remains unabashed.

No one defends extreme cases of "examination hell," and if the system were imported to America, it would probably not be carried to such extravagant lengths. It should be noted, however, that entrance examinations have a great deal of logic in their favor. They are highly predictable so that schools, students, and their parents know what to prepare for. The teacher's authority in judging a student's record is negligible, since grades or written recommendations are unimportant for college admission. It is unmistakably clear to students that their future depends on meritocratic performance as measured by entrance examinations. Motivation comes from the inside, and the student, mindful of his responsibilities to parents and school and concerned about his future, wants to learn so that he may be prepared for the entrance examination. As shown by the questionnaire returns accompanying the science achievement tests in nineteen countries, Japanese children enjoy school more than students in other countries. The teacher becomes an ally who is trying to assist the student in facing the examination. The Japanese teacher has a broader sense of responsibility for helping the student outside classroom hours and is typically available in school many days during summer recess.

The motivation for achievement through examinations is increased by the tight-knit membership of a variety of groups. Families are, in a sense, competing with other families, and the child's success in examinations is seen as directly reflecting on a family's success. As Thomas Rohlen has shown, the small, intact family does much better in preparing the child for entrance examinations than the large family, the broken family, or the family with one parent deceased, for the intact family exerts itself, sending the child to supplementary classes, assisting him at home, and arranging family life to ensure the sanctity of study. Parents, and especially mothers, take a great interest in how well the school prepares their student for the examination. Through the junior high school level it is unrealistic for most parents to send their children to schools other than their local public school; therefore parents take an active role in local school activities, supporting teachers of excellence and school administrators who try to maintain quality education.

Furthermore, there is intense competition between schools to place their students well. Just as villages compete to erect the best most modern buildings, so schools strive to get a higher share of their graduates admitted to the best schools at the next higher level. Since teachers are responsible for their students' personal and motivational life as well as for classroom behavior, they feel responsible for the success rate of their students.

The system thus reinforces the key actors—students, teachers, and parents—in their identification with the student preparing for the examinations. Given the tendency to relax that comes with affluence, schools in Japan, as in other modern countries, face the danger of lax standards. From his interviews in various Japanese schools, Rohlen concludes that having the entrance examination system in the background is necessary to maintain discipline and high standards.

Compared to examinations that would certify high school graduation—an idea now being considered in America—entrance examinations have clear advantages. With certification examinations, it is unlikely that many students, teachers, and parents would be positively motivated since only those close to the margin of failure would be at all concerned. On the other hand, entrance examinations make sense to the Japanese because they are not simply arbitrary evaluations by authorities but a legitimate demand by educational institutions that those who enter meet a certain standard. Most of the ninety percent of the age group who wish to enter high school and the fifty percent who wish to go on for higher education are highly motivated to prepare for entrance examinations to be able to enter an institution of their choice. Once a student enters an institution, examinations do not end, but he does not need to worry about being terminated for academic failure, and this allows the student to develop a feeling of belonging in a mutually supportive group environment. . . .

It is impressive how well schools throughout Japan ensure that virtually every pupil achieves minimal standards. No student is failed, and all students of the same age proceed together up through grade nine. The threat of failure or of being held back is considered neither desirable nor necessary to encourage students to maintain minimal performance standards. Approximately ninety-five percent of lower secondary students attend public institutions. There is no tracking, and all students are expected to acquire the basic materials of that grade. Some teachers have complained that this system slows down the more talented students and that some of the poorer students still do not catch on to many things in the class. However, the assumption that everyone can and will get through puts pressure on the teachers and the poorer students. Americans are much more prepared to accept that some students are unteachable and to give up on difficult students. Japanese teachers exert themselves to see that every student in the class has achieved a certain level before the end of the school year. They mobilize other students and parents to work with students with difficulties, for they are responsible not just for presenting the material and giving the students an opportunity to learn but for making sure that they do learn.

To assure that every school has the financial resources to provide a minimal level of compulsory education, the Japanese government provides subsidies to poorer prefectures and isolated school districts. A good part of the educational budget is met by the prefectures and some by the local community, but the national budget constitutes about one-fourth of the budget for the nine years of compulsory education. In a relatively wealthy prefecture like Tokyo, about eighteen percent of the public funds for the elementary school budget comes from the national budget, but in a poor prefecture like Aomori about thirty-three percent of the elementary school budget comes from the national government. Within a prefecture an effort is made to supply equal facilities for all pupils, and therefore in isolated rural areas with a smaller number of students the expenses per pupil are actually greater than in the metropolitan areas. As a result, there is much more uniformity in school facilities and expenses between school districts than in the United States. In most American states, where major costs of education are still met by local taxes, rich suburban schools can sometimes spend twice as much per pupil as poorer suburbs or urban areas. Furthermore, American dollars spent per pupil in the poorest states are substantially lower than that in the richest states despite special programs of federal aid.

50

Is Japanese Education
Becoming Less Egalitarian?

Thomas P. Rohlen

Japanese are well aware of the crucial connection between education and socioeconomic status, but opportunities for education are not so equal and open as most Japanese believe. Here, a scholar who has closely studied Japanese education focuses on the secondary level and the pervasive impact of high school entrance examinations, and points out how parents' attitudes have helped to frustrate educators' efforts toward high school reforms.

That public education during the last century, especially since 1945, has been an important source of upward mobility in Japanese society is a virtually uncontested element in our picture of modern Japan, and compared to the rigidity of Edo Period arrangements and their attitudinal legacies this interpretation is undoubtedly correct. The image of the poor, but bright lad who graduates from Tokyo University and eventually wields great power remains widely popular. Most certainly this quite romantic portrait serves to color the impression the average man has of Japan's leaders. This notion, in turn, colors his view of such matters as governmental authority, the character of the Japanese elite and, in fact, the very legitimacy of Japan's modern structure.

Educational achievement is not only an avenue to elite status in Japan, it is a widely applied measure of character, ability, and modern virtue. The formula "ability + hard work = educational achievement = elite status" is a powerful one in Japan and its power hinges on the assumption that public education provides a very high degree of equal opportunity. In this paper I will discuss several aspects of the question of educational equality as it existed in post-war Japanese cities to date and as it appears to be changing under the influence of certain reforms in the high school system....

GETTING INTO HIGH SCHOOL
IN KOBE

Although the attention of Western scholars has been focused primarily on the problem of college entrance in Japan and particularly on the formation of future elites at this juncture, the time of high school entrance represents an even more crucial juncture in the *total* process of educational stratification in Japan. The entire population of students are involved, not just the college-bound minority, and the educational tracks into which students are shunted at this stage are both more diverse and more fundamental to their ultimate social identities. We must realize that ranking of high schools in a given locale is as clear if not clearer than for universities on a national scale. At the local level, what high school a person attends carries lifetime significance and the finely etched stereotypes of student character associated with each high school becomes an indelible part of individual identity. At the high school level in Kobe, where I did field work for one year during 1974–75, the various spectra of differences in such things as academic ability, career prospects, family background, and school reputation are all tightly interwoven into a single hierarchically ordered fabric. Furthermore, these differences have marked significance for the actual conduct and ethos of each school. Urban high school sub-cultures, that is, illustrate a definite tendency to stratify in a manner parallel to social class stereotypes.

In the spring of 1975, 15,103 students graduated from junior high schools in Kobe and of these 95 percent indicated a preference to go on to high school. A poll of these students the previous autumn revealed that fully 80 percent wanted to matriculate to public, "academic" high schools. We must note at this point that the three top boys' private schools in Kobe, which draw the top 1–2 percent of students from the entire Kobe-Osaka region, admit primarily at the junior high school level, thus, it is the remaining 99 percent of the students that we are considering at this point. Because their costs are low, *public* schools are definitely preferred by most ninth graders. And because prestige is high and the chances of going on to college much greater, public *"academic"* high schools are the most preferable (after the top elite private schools). Public vocational high schools have the advantage of low tuition, but the disadvantage of not being geared to university preparation. Due to a continuing lack of space in public, academic schools (only 6,165 places were available), however, no more than 40 percent of each year's junior high school graduates can enter public high schools designed for university preparation. . . .

Once the approximately eight percent that did not go on to high school (in 1972) are added, we have an outline of the rudimentary categories into which the entire spectrum of fifteen year olds in the city is divided. These categories are inevitably ranked in popular thought. Academic schools are always superior to vocational schools and vocational schools, in turn, are always ranked above night schools. There are both elite private schools (very few in number) and low stature private schools (numerous). Of course, at the very bottom of this elaborate totem pole are those whose education terminates with junior high school graduation.

High school entrance procedures vary today from city to city in Japan—one example of post-war local government autonomy. In Osaka, entrance is governed solely by examination, much as in the case of universities. Each student is limited to applying to only one public high school per year and, as at the university level, this creates a small population of fifteen and sixteen year old *"ronin."* In Tokyo, on the other hand, as the result of a recent reform (to be discussed later), many students are assigned to a public, academic high school by a computer once they qualify in a general examination. . . .

The heart of Kobe's high school system is its "large district" form of organization. Within the city's three large high school districts are many public high schools and application to any one of them is open to a resident of the district. Consequently there is competition (focused on good grades leading to a high teacher evaluation at entrance time) and a thorough system of ranking among the schools of each district. Each level of academic ability is shipped off to a separate high school. Students in their last year of junior high school are sorted on a one to ten scale and it is into even more narrow strata that they are separated in the process of being advised to apply to particular high schools. This practice annually confirms the ranking of all high schools, a ranking that embraces the private school world, too, although the story there is somewhat more complicated.

The very top private high schools in Kobe today are head and shoulders academically superior to the best in the public system. They admit their students strictly through competitive examinations and typically students are accepted for six years of schooling, beginning with seventh grade. Only the top one percent of sixth graders are encouraged to apply. Elite schools of this sort, however, are but a small percentage of the private schools in the city. It is important to note also, that they have gradually emerged as academic power houses in the post-war period with acceleration of this trend during the last ten years.

Another small group of private schools are ranked more or less parallel to the better public, academic high schools. These schools take their students from 1) those few who fail the examination to the better public high schools and 2) families willing to pay for a higher level of schooling than their child's teacher has "recommended." As upper and middle class parental displeasure with public schooling increases, these second rank private schools get more and better students and as a consequence their place in the overall city-wide ranking based on university entrance performance is raised. Recently, such schools have been moving up steadily. Paralleling this middle-level set of schools are some girls' schools with the aura of finishing schools. They are not critically involved with the overall academic competition, yet neither are they repositories of the academically least qualified.

The largest set of private high schools, however, have been traditionally at or near the bottom of the secondary school hierarchy, usually standing just above night schools. Essentially they exist to serve the students who fail to enter even public vocational high schools—typically the bottom quarter of junior high school graduating classes. Obviously, competition and the anxiety over entrance to high school is not simply an elite or middle class phenomenon in Japan, but as our attention passes from areas of high academic performance to those involving the bottom one-third of the junior high school graduating population, we find parental concern shifting from the goal of university attendance to that of saving the family money in the process of gaining a high school diploma and perhaps saving the child from a bad reputation as a graduate of a low status school. Private high schools charge approximately $600–700 per year plus a sizable entrance fee and in Kobe the majority of parents shouldering this not inconsequential burden do so not out of ambition for their child's university chances, but simply because he or she has performed below average academically and cannot enter public high school. Since there is a solid correlation between family impoverishment and poor school performance (as we shall see), it is clear that typically the costs of private schooling fall most heavily on families least able to afford them. These families are not only reluctant to carry this extra economic burden, but they are often anxious that their children avoid the problems of delinquency and peer group troubles associated with the worst private schools. The fact that they send their children to high school at all is vivid testimony to the powerful drive at all levels of society for attaining "at least" a high school education, even if the content is so poor as to have primarily negative influence on the students, a fact I believe to be true in at least thirty percent of Kobe's high schools today. The crucial point here, however, is that the shortage of public high schools clearly works to the disadvantage of the less well off. . . .

PRIVATE EFFORTS
TO SUPPLEMENT EDUCATION

Students attending elite private high schools typically enter this inside track at the seventh grade level, meaning that in the minds of most parents, particularly urban parents, the first six grades, and even kindergarten, are as crucial to the race to enter top universities as are any succeeding levels. It is almost unheard of to leave the crucial matter of academic priming exclusively in the hands of elementary school teachers, especially since today most of them candidly admit a personal revulsion with the university entrance syndrome. Tutors (*katei kyōshi*) and cram schools (*juku*), heavy parental attention and every sort of special study aid and gimmick are the solutions to which parents turn, and quite naturally competition to master more and more material earlier develops among the children submitted to this regimen.

. . . Tutoring is now even becoming common for families in lower income brackets, and for high level academic achievement it has become virtually mandatory. The typical after-school tutoring "academy" is a neighborhood affair which costs an average of ¥4,400 a month in 1974. A private tutor costs three times this amount. The costs of study aids, such as practice test forms and encyclopedias of exam-relevant facts, can mount up. In Kobe, a recent survey indicated that more than half of all sixth graders receive extra academic attention of this sort. None of these by now almost normal supplementary activities compares with the costs in time and money involved in a high-powered cram effort—the kind more and more bright, urban, middle and upper middle class children are undergoing in the large cities in order to meet the competition to enter the best private secondary schools. Such cram schools, typically offering courses that involve three-hour classes almost every night (and sometimes all day Sundays), study camps in the summer, frequent tests, and a frankly competitive atmosphere for elementary and junior high students, have been rapidly growing in number and public attention. . . .

To take this point one step further, in each large city, the top post-high school cram schools (*yobiko*) are considered harder to enter than the top public high schools. . . .

Public school officials are particularly appalled at the growth of super-cram schools at the lower levels, for they have begun to supersede the regular public school instruction (especially in philosophy, pace, and balance of subjects). In a nation long known for its exam-oriented education and stiff educational competition, the new cram schools thus represent a further escalation of this old tendency, one that underlines the tremendous drive for educational achievement present in most levels of society. This drive, however, is finding expression primarily in the private spheres of education as steps to undercut or at least dampen the exam-oriented competition syndrome are effected in the public school system. . . .

In summary, cram materials, private tutors, special schools, private elite high schools, and the many other aids to educational success that are purchased on the market by parents acting in a private capacity all have the effect of creating less equality of educational outcome. Families are not equal in their capacities to compete in the "private sphere," that extensive part of education over which public schools and public policy have little or no influence. Nor is the question of inequality just a matter of income differentials, although this appears to be a central and increasingly important factor. Children of teachers do very well in Japan despite parental income, for example, while rich and poor families in rural areas suffer a disadvantage because tutors, cram schools, and so forth, are not available. Economic resources, in other words, are but part of the total family resources relevant to a student's success in school.

The question remains as to the relative importance of the "private sector" in the overall outcome. Obviously, the enormous drive of most Japanese parents to assure their children a satisfactory future social status through educational achievement generates much of the dynamic behind the "private sector," but this is only part of the story, for what occurs in the area of public education is also very relevant.

The establishment of greater equality of educational *opportunity* in the public school system rather than cooling off parental (and student) drive is only likely to encourage more "private sector" activity given the high level of competitiveness focused on educational achievement. Secondly, since private goals of educational success are dominant in the minds of most parents, their appreciation of public schooling will focus on the advantages their children's public schools provide in the overall competition. As Japanese post-war public education has periodically attempted to extricate itself from the exam competition syndrome, it has diminished its value in the eyes of parents. Thus, increased parental reliance on private sector education can be seen as to some degree stimulated by public school policies that deemphasize exam-oriented preparation. . . .

THE MOVEMENT FOR HIGH SCHOOL REFORM

. . . Long before the new Minister of Education, Nagai Michio, announced to the press that reform at the high school level would pave the way for university reform, city and prefectural school boards throughout Japan had been laying cautious plans to end the rigid academic hierarchy among public high schools through a combination of redistricting and redefinition of the function of entrance exams. . . .

The occupation, of course, set out to achieve a rather similar reform in 1946 and a close look at the history of education in any locality will reveal that the occupation's reforms were instituted for at least a few years. In Kobe, and I assume in most other cities, the American-inspired high school system faced enormous difficulties due to 1) the lack of schools, 2) traditional understandings of high schools as places for university preparatory training, 3) the weight of each school's tradition within the old differentiated and ranked system, and 4) the general social and economic chaos of the times. With few schools (none of which had been initially located with districting criteria in mind) and most of them adamantly vocational or academic in tradition and preference, city school officials in 1946 were presented with almost insurmountable problems in sorting out students, on the one hand, and attempting to merge, integrate, divide, and in other ways transform high school facilities and faculties on the other. With no money to build new high schools (a matter of local finance under the occupation's reform) and heavy pressure from large numbers of applicants, the City Board of Education between 1951 and 1953 progressively retreated from the position of one district—one high school to a plan, still in effect today, in which the city was divided into three approximately equal "large districts" (each today with about eight public high schools). Vocational and academic high schools were successfully merged in only one case. The old elite public schools became the new elite public schools (one in each of the three districts) resting at the top of "large district" based hierarchies. As new public schools were built they joined the status ladder at the bottom. . . .

Today, . . . [n]early all urban children are going to high school and while many are forced to attend low status private schools, the number of public high schools has increased greatly since the early fifties. Officials feel the time is right to end the present "large district" system and, in doing so, end the problems of gross differences among high school sub-cultures and the educational advantages and disadvantages they represent. The reform movement, then, is in one sense restorational, since the precedent for all this lies buried in the occupation's legacy and, of course, behind that in an inclusive, egalitarian philosophy of secondary education. Ironically, American educational reform today seems headed in the opposite direction, being aimed at superseding the effects of its traditional one district–one high school policy. . . .

It is rare indeed for teachers, school boards, and the union to see eye to eye in Japan and most certainly there are many teachers rather skeptical about reform, just as there are many disagreements over details among the various supporting parties. The fact is, however, that a sense of deep dismay about secondary education exists—focused both on the "examination hell" syndrome that affects the more able students from elementary school on and the inequities and demoralization that await the less able. High school reform has had great appeal within educational circles because it appears to provide answers ultimately to both kinds of problems, and because it could be undertaken by each prefecture or large city without entanglement in the politics of national educational policy, something not true of university level reform.

The progressive parties, incidentally, are encouraging the movement while the Liberal Democratic party remains rather reluctant, but publicly noncommittal. Both sides naturally hope to make political hay on this issue as it develops.

The conservatives may well have chosen the more popular cause in political terms, however, for there has been much public opposition to the reform idea. The reasons many parents oppose reform are somewhat hard to nail down in precise terms. Awareness of status distinctions does not undermine the readiness of many to remain convinced that the present form of public high school education offers equality of opportunity. What parents worry most about is any development that threatens the opportunity for their children to retain at least the social status level the family has already achieved. The school board's and union's problem in urging reform, therefore, has not been one of having to prove that differences of family background are involved (which may explain the lack of detailed studies), but rather of establishing that the high school level pattern of differentiation is unjust and impractical for society, while simultaneously trying to convince a majority of parents that no fundamental threat to their children's future status is involved.

Privately, middle class Japanese seem generally convinced that school performance is a reflection of the character of the student and the household. Divorce or many children or a lack of parental discipline, they intuitively feel, are not the fault of the school system, but of the parents. Quite naturally these factors affect a student's ability to do well in school. Schools to them are not properly instruments of social leveling, but arenas of fair competition. Good students, people will say, come from stable, hard working, educated and, most of all, concerned families. If families are well off, their success is also an illustration of the same point, good family character.... People opposing reform are firm in their belief that there is formal equal opportunity in the public schools (all the while straining every effort to get their children into a "better" school), and they will always have before them the exceptional cases of "rags to Todai" that illustrate this notion.

But more crucial than rationalizations and abstract perspectives is the dismay middle and upper class parents experience when they realize that reform may disadvantage their own children. The present system rewards the great Japanese values of hard work, family concern, and stability. Why should such virtue be punished? Whether the people who feel this way are a majority cannot be proven, but clearly they are the most vociferous. The families most certain to benefit from high school reform, the poor, have spokesmen in educational circles, but as a group they are not politically active and often they share the same viewpoint as the middle class regarding the rewards of hard work.

So while the teachers' union, leftist groups, and school boards push for reform, the general population of parents remains unconvinced and often adamantly opposed to any changes that will work against the chances of their own children in the educational race. Finally, while it would be erroneous to say that parents like the enormous pressure exams put on their children, most remain convinced that objective exams and high school stratification represent the only way to give the best students a chance to the best education. In the competition with the best students of other cities to enter the top universities, their children need the education that only first class public high schools can provide. The parental view of education as a crucial status race, thus, has made high school reform a very tricky business....

The shift to private schooling by perhaps most of the top quarter of the students has also revealed the lesson that public school policy, at least at the high school level, could not unilaterally control the shape of education and educational change in the big cities, a point American experience might have taught. The option of private schooling in Tokyo, Osaka, Nagoya, and Kobe is sufficiently broad that significant declines in the quality of public high school student populations (as Japanese view them) can occur very rapidly, and for all the bravado of the reformers' claims that the well-off and especially able should not be the public system's main concern, the fact remains that a new kind of inequality—one in which wealth and elite educational opportunities are closely tied together and institutionalized—has emerged as a result of their efforts. The higher costs of private universities await those middle class and lower class average students who may have avoided the costs of private secondary schools, but lost out in the opportunity to enter public universities by doing so....

. . . Public high school reform will not eliminate social stratification or educational elitism given the private school option. Furthermore, cities like Osaka that have not acted to reform are sending an increased number of their public high school graduates to Todai while they watch Tokyo squirm, and in Japan this remains a significant feather in a city's cap.

Ironically, nothing has caused the private side to grow in strength more than the various reforms undertaken in the public school realm. These reforms undertaken in the name of equal opportunity end up producing a situation that actually encourages less equality of actual outcome, for, as in the Tokyo example, it is the private high schools that are strengthened when public high schools are reformed. . . .

51

The Politics of Enrollment Expansion in Japanese Universities

T. J. Pempel

The *Journal of Asian Studies* published an article in 1973 which remains a key analysis of higher education in Japan. In these excerpts from it, the author describes how the Japanese government's "non-interventionist" policy has led to a decline in the quality of university facilities and fostered a class bias in higher education that favors children of the affluent.

From an administrative standpoint, there are three types of universities in Japan: those under the direct control of the national government; those under the control of local governments, such as prefectures or cities; and finally those under private administration. The great bulk of the expansion that has taken place since the end of the Occupation has come in privately administered universities.

In 1952 there were a total of 221 four-year universities in Japan. Of these, seventy-two (thirty-three percent) were national, thirty-three (fifteen percent) were local public, and 116 (fifty-two percent) were private. In 1972 the total was up to 399 universities, representing an increase of 178 institutions. This gain came almost exclusively as a result of new private universities. From 1953 to 1972, 175 new private universities were chartered so that in 1972 there were seventy-six national universities (nineteen percent), thirty-two local public universities (eight percent), and 291 private universities (seventy-three percent). In terms of student enrollment, a similar shift can be seen. Even though there has been a significant increase in the absolute number of students enrolled in public universities, increases there have been far less significant than those in the private institutions. In 1952 thirty-nine percent of the total university student body was enrolled in national universities; four percent in local public universities; and fifty-seven percent in private institutions. By 1972 the composition had shifted dramatically so that nearly eighty percent of the student body was enrolling in private universities....

... [A] decreasing portion of the money that is being spent within Japan for higher education is coming from public sources. During the period from 1950 to 1968, government's share of the total bill for higher education shrank from 67.2 percent to 51.4 percent, and government expenditure per pupil is at present only about two-thirds what it was in the prewar period. Finally, both as a percent of national income and as a percent of total government spending for education, the Japanese government's outlay for higher education falls far below the levels in other major countries of the world, as is clear from [Table 51–1]. In fact, a recent survey of government spending for higher education as a percent of total governmental spending for higher education for thirty-one countries showed that only six allocated lower percents to higher education than Japan. . . .

[T]he government, while encouraging the expansion of enrollments in institutions of higher education by easy charters and nonenforcement of standards, has done so at minimal cost, with funding for the university system in general and for private universities in particular being at a level of niggardliness unmatched in the industrial world.

What then are the consequences of the government's policy and the manner in which it has been effected? Because of their socio-political implications, two stand out above any others: the deterioration of educational conditions and the class bias of the system as a whole. . . .

. . . Since nearly twenty-five percent of the age cohort are able to attend institutions of higher education, the Japanese system could hardly be called "elitist" in the sense that the word is normally used. However, the expansion of opportunities has not been felt at all evenly throughout Japanese society. Rather it has been the sons and daughters of the more financially endowed who have been most able to take advantage of the broadening of opportunities. . . .

No governmental policy is formulated in a valuational vacuum, and the enrollment expansion in Japanese higher education is no exception. Three interrelated facets of extent values have been strongly congruent with, and supportive of, the present policy and its social consequences,

TABLE 51–1 Government Spending for Higher Education in Various Countries (1968)

Country	As % of National Income	As % of Total Government Educational Expense 1965
Japan	0.7	15.7
U.S.S.R.	0.9*	17.4
U.K.	1.0*	22.9*
West Germany	1.1**	24.6**
U.S.A.	1.9	27.6

Source: Ministry of Education, *Educational Standards in Japan, 1970* (Tokyo: Ministry of Education, 1971), pp. 145–6.
    *1967
    **1966

namely, the popular importance of the university diploma, a laissez faire attitude toward the acquisition of such a degree by both government and private sectors, and the general governmental policy of high, rapid economic growth.

In Japan, as in most countries, there is a high correlation between a person's level of education and his economic success. Thus, in 1967, the starting salary for male university graduates in Japan averaged nearly seventy percent above that for middle school graduates, forty-five percent above that for high school graduates, and twenty-four percent higher than that for junior college graduates. Moreover, this gap widens with age and length of employment, so that even allowing for the seven years when a middle school graduate is working and a university graduate is in school, the latter's lifetime earnings remain far superior. A university education is statistically a wise investment. Above and beyond the purely economic "payoff," one must recognize that the status of one's occupation as well as the type of work one does is also largely dependent on education with the most desirable positions almost invariably demanding a university diploma as a prerequisite to employment.

Such differences are not lost on Japanese parents. There is a very high concern among parents for the education of their offspring. . . .

Parental desires are mirrored in part by the attitudes of the business community. Firms generally will hire their employees only from a limited number of specific schools. Close ties are frequently maintained between university officials and various business firms with mutually acceptable quotas worked out as to the number of graduates a particular firm will hire and what a university will agree to provide for the firm, so that career success depends much less on actual skills than on school standing and a school's alumni connections, the entire syndrome pointing to the greater importance of the university one graduates from as compared to what one learns there. . . .

. . . [P]rivate universities in Japan do operate as profit-making institutions. Those with the best connections and placement records can command not only high tuitions but also high "voluntary" contributions, which are often inversely proportional to the attractiveness of a student's academic record, a factor which contributes to the class bias in the system as a whole.

More politically salient, the government, for its part, also treats the relationship between students and private universities in precisely this same sense by its hands-off attitude regarding funding, tuition raises, deviations from official quotas, etc. Perhaps the most pertinent facet of this attitude, however, concerns scholarship aid to students—whether in public or private universities. In this area there is nothing to suggest any sense of government responsibility for insuring that the individual be allowed to receive a university education regardless of his, or his family's, economic well-being. . . . [A]mounts which by no means begin to cover normal expenses of tuition and fees are loaned to some fifteen percent of the total university student body, giving Japan the lowest percentage of students receiving aid, and the lowest amounts received among the major countries of the world. In fact, Japan seems to be the only such country which in fact has no genuine government program of scholarship grants at all, clearly indicative of the pervasive attitude in Japan that higher education is by and large a private sector relationship beyond the purview of the government.

Such a non-interventionist policy is fully complementary with, and perhaps partly the consequence of, a final factor in present attitudes, namely, the dominant consideration given to high growth economics in the formulation of Japanese governmental priorities. To the extent that conservative political dominance in the postwar period has been at all related to governmental policies, it is fair to say that they have been heavily bolstered by the ability to deliver "peace and prosperity." Beginning with the Hatoyama Cabinet's "Six Year Plan for an Independent Economy," through the Ikeda Cabinet's "Plan to Double the National Income in Ten Years," and the industrial development plans in present Prime Minister Tanaka's "Plan to Remodel the Archipelago," the conservatives have consistently relied on economic growth and its fall-out as a mainstay of their political power. These economic policies have been based most fundamentally on the concept of growth through cyclical investment and reinvestment in high and rapid return items. For a highly industrialized country such as Japan, higher education does not constitute such an item.

Economists by no means agree fully on the reasons for Japan's phenomenal growth, but one thing is clear: despite the fact that Japan's high level of education may have been a *prerequisite* to such growth, further investment in education would have produced no appreciable returns in terms of *added* growth. A comparison of the relative importance of several factors to Japan's growth during the period 1955–68, shows the minimal role played by investment in education. In terms of international comparisons, one study interestingly showed the role of education to be less significant in Japan than in any of the thirteen industrial countries or regions studied with the exception of one. Ministry of Education officials have thus been in a weak bargaining position in any demand for more funds which has had an unmistakably negative effect on standards and funding.

It thus becomes clear that regardless of the immediate causes of the problems of quality and class bias, there are much more significant and much more deeply rooted values and attitudes that have exacerbated the situation. The importance of the diploma, the notion that higher education is essentially a private business transaction beyond the realm of government intervention, and finally, the dominance of economic growth as a criterion in the assessment of governmental priorities must all be seen as the attitudinal props behind both the manner in which higher educational enrollment has been expanded as well as the decline that has taken place in the quality of university facilities over the past decade and a half, and the class bias which remains a part of the higher educational system.

The policy of the Japanese government then, in this area of higher educational enrollment, emerges as the non-fiduciary encouragement of rapid and uncontrolled expansion. But it has been an expansion lacking the democratic characteristics of parallel improvement, or at least parallel maintenance, of educational facilities and lacking also a concern for improving the mobility opportunities among the lower economic classes. Instead it has developed in such a way that overall physical quality has deteriorated markedly and new university admissions resulting from it have, because of funding policies, been accessible primarily to the offspring of the more affluent sectors of the Japanese population.

52

The Politics of Education
in Post-Mao China

Susan L. Shirk

In order to speed up modernization after the overturn of the
Cultural Revolution, the government of the People's Republic of
China has instituted a number of changes in educational policy
which are shifting the patterns of advantage within the system. In
this essay, excerpted from a longer paper prepared for the Asia
Society's China Council, Susan L. Shirk analyzes the varying effects
of the new policies and the resulting political implications for
China's leadership.

. . . China's education system was devastated during the Cultural Revolution decade of 1966–76. The late Mao Tse-tung used that mass political
campaign to attack what he saw to be growing elitism and bureaucracy, for
which schools and universities were in part responsible. One positive result
was increased primary and high school opportunities for peasants. On the
other hand, there was a decline in the quality of education and a disruption
of scientific research.

Some have asserted that changes in the curriculum were the cause of
the problem. In practice, however, the content of education has changed
very little since 1950. Rather, university selection procedures adopted after
1968 were primarily responsible for the deterioration in quality. With entrance examinations abolished, universities were unable to screen applicants recommended by factories, communes, and military units. Many university freshmen had only one or two years of post-primary education.

College enrollment policies also had an effect in high schools. Students lost motivation because they knew they would have to work for several years after graduation, usually in the countryside, before they could be
considered for college. Teachers were robbed of the "carrots and sticks" to
enforce classroom order.

To make matters worse, the Cultural Revolution procedures resulted
in new inequalities. The recommendation system, designed to benefit peasants and workers, actually favored officials and their children. In rural villages, where traditional patterns of power and deference persist, local leaders' children were often chosen for college admission. Higher officials were

able to exploit their connections and get their children in through the "back door."

Even before Mao's death, Vice Premier Teng Hsiao-p'ing and other leaders concluded that the Cultural Revolution education system, for all its good intentions, was creating a serious obstacle to economic modernization. With the purge of the "gang of four" (Mao's widow, Chiang Ch'ing, and her radical associates) in October 1976 and Teng's rehabilitation in July 1977, the dismantling of the Cultural Revolution system began. Chinese education officials are now trying to build a structure similar to the one that existed before 1966.

Academic excellence is again the top priority, and making up for lost time is the chief concern. "We have to find the most competent people and train them faster," says one high education official. Resources are concentrated on the best students and the best schools. Higher education and research are getting more of the budget pie. Entrance exams have been reinstituted to screen junior high, senior high and university applicants. Ability tracking—assigning students to fast, average or slow classes according to their ability—has begun.

Sending students and scholars to universities abroad further accelerates the process of rebuilding, quickly producing qualified university professors, scientific researchers, and factory engineers. China's leaders recognize that foreign study is expensive, but they believe the country cannot afford to wait for its own universities to recover. . . .

. . . The modernization program has had its detractors, especially concerning education policy. Education Minister Liu Hsi-yao was fired in early 1979 for not implementing the new program with sufficient speed or enthusiasm. In Anhwei province, "a tortuous and fierce struggle" unfolded at an education conference in 1978, with defenders of the Cultural Revolution system holding out for days. The stress on quality over quantity works to the disadvantage of several groups. These groups might be molded into a potent political force under certain conditions, with serious consequences for students returning from abroad.

The peasantry is the group that stands to lose the most under the new system. With educational investment concentrated in urban special schools and universities, with opportunities distributed largely on the basis of academic achievement, the 80-plus percent that lives in China's villages is once again a disadvantaged majority.

Young people undoubtedly have mixed reactions to the new approach. Only the most talented can take advantage of the educational route to status and power, while others will be shut out. Competition is more intense than ever before: the number of high school graduates is growing at a much faster rate than university enrollments, and only two to three percent of college age youth will be able to matriculate (compared with about 40% in the U.S.). Moreover, current politics will create new status distinctions and potential conflicts (for example, between elite-school graduates and those of ordinary schools, and between foreign-trained and China-trained scientists).

Opposition and dissent will most likely come from the "lost generation" of former Red Guards and graduates of the Cltural Revolution system. Few of them will have the opportunity now to enter university, study abroad, or get the best jobs. Many are still working in the countryside or are unemployed in the cities. But as they proved in recent wall posters and demonstrations, members of this "lost generation" are ideologically articulate, daring, and experienced in political protest.

Many *local officials* find the new policies contrary to their interests. Large numbers of educational bureaucrats find their jobs threatened by the rehabilitation of older officials purged during the Cultural Revolution. More generally, local officials have been able to use their positions to get their children into universities—a practice that the examination system will now deter. Generalist politicians worry about being eclipsed by technocrats important to the modernization effort.

With the proper kind of leadership from the highest levels, these groups could be molded into a political movement attacking the modernization program, its education policies, and its foreign-trained specialist. Such specialists might be branded as experts without political commitment, as agents for the foreign countries and cultures in which they lived.

For the moment, the leadership in Peking seems stable and united enough to keep one of their number from leading such a populist challenge. Even Party Chairman Hua Kuo-feng, who at times has cast himself as a Mao-like defender of the have-nots, is backing Teng's program for now.

But things could change, and history is not on the side of the foreign students. In the 1950s, many Chinese went to the Soviet Union to study from the Communist "elder brother." Within a decade, the Soviets' "advanced experience" was deemed inappropriate for Chinese reality. During the Cultural Revolution, those tainted by Soviet contact were under a cloud of political suspicion.

China has long been ambivalent about the outside world. To gain "wealth and power," it has alternated for more than a century between trying to learn from technologically advanced countries and relying on an isolationist cultural superiority. A large group of students sent by the Chinese government to the United States in 1872 was soon called home because conservatives felt that contact with the West was doing more harm than good.

By sending students abroad, the 74-year-old Teng Hsiao-p'ing is doing more than trying to raise their level of knowledge. He is recruiting supporters of irreversible modernization. But he is also creating a new group of technocrats, vulnerable to a change in the political climate.

Unit XIII

_____ Social Welfare Policy _____

It is not surprising that the systems of social welfare in China and Japan differ. A fundamental tenet of Communism is "from each according to his ability, to each according to his need," a principle that Mao aspired to throughout his leadership of the Chinese political system. Japan, as a capitalist and developmental state, has downplayed the role of government in providing services to the needy and has concentrated instead on expanding the economy in order to guarantee a steady rise in living standards for its people. The Japanese have traditionally depended on the private provision of social welfare among members of a company, a profession, or a family.

Nor is it surprising that both countries have encountered problems as their respective economies have grown and matured. What is surprising is that in their responses to these problems the two countries are coming to resemble each other more and more. Increasingly, Chinese workers are discovering that the "iron rice bowl" of guaranteed employment is somewhat cracked. Social services in rural areas are declining and peasants are being urged to cooperatively finance schools, clinics, and other public works projects. The Japanese, on the other hand, are making increasingly strident demands on their government for the construction of more parks and schools, improved retirement security for the elderly, better health care facilities, and unemployment benefits for those workers not employed in the large companies that provide extensive benefits to employees. In short, China is moving toward a policy of lower burdens on public resources for social welfare while Japan is evolving in the direction of greater burdens on government for the provision of public services.

Both China and Japan have great success in advancing social welfare since World War II. Japan emerged from the war with a shattered economy, cities that lay in ruins, and few guarantees against mass starvation. Likewise, China, after more than twenty years of internecine warfare, invasion, and civil war, faced a similarly bleak future. Its urban economy was fragile, millions of refugees crowded the cities, and the population of the countryside was surviving at subsistence levels. Malnutrition and starvation were not uncommon, and disease was endemic. In the less than four decades since the war's end, both nations have ended starvation, malnutrition, and mass poverty; effectively controlled disease; and increased life expectancy. But they have achieved these successes in radically different ways.

In China, the central objective has been to widen the scope of social services to include rural peasants and the urban poor. The emphasis has been on increasing the number of services available to the population. The central government has financed such programs as the "barefoot doctors" (teams of trained medical personnel who deliver health care services to the countryside), as well as programs guaranteeing housing, health care, food, and wages to workers through their firms. The *danwei,* or work unit (such as a factory), assigns workers to housing, obtains health care for employees, and grants registration permits (*hukou*) for obtaining food and other rationed commodities. As June Kronholz describes in "Urban Policy in Contemporary China," these registration permits are the most effective means of controlling the growth of China's urban areas and thereby limiting the demands placed on the country's already overburdened social welfare agencies. Rural services, which are funded through the earnings of commune members instead of with government funds, have always been less extensive than those in the urban areas.

As Richard M. Goldstein, Kathrin Sears, and Richard C. Bush point out in -"Material Welfare, Education, and Public Health," recent reforms in China have further increased this gap. Under the current leadership, urban social services are funded by enterprise profits. More profitable enterprises can afford more extensive services for their employees, the most frequently established benefit being new housing for company workers and their families. Less profitable enterprises are less able to guarantee services, thereby creating inequalities among urban workers. Reforms have also broken up the traditional communes through which peasants cooperatively funded health care clinics, schools, and other services. Since the advent of private farming, no new forms of cooperation have been established so that gaps among peasants in terms of income have now been augmented by gaps in the obtainment of basic social welfare. Additionally, the new leadership has attempted to break the "iron rice bowl" within which Chinese workers were guaranteed a wage regardless of work performance, absenteeism, or productivity. If such policies are implemented, an already critical unemployment problem could be exacerbated. It is doubtful that the central government, strapped for cash under the impact of profit retention among enterprises, could afford to finance unemployment compensation.

Finally, education policy has changed under the reforms. The emphasis is no longer on increasing the number of students educated; rather, the focus is now on increasing the caliber of students in order to produce the technically skilled workers required by a modern economy. It is perhaps this change, so antithetical to Mao's ideas about education, that best indicates the extent of the transformation of social welfare policy in China since 1976.

Japan has never aimed at egalitarianism in the provision of social services. As Ezra Vogel points out in "Welfare: Security Without Entitlement," the Japanese government has traditionally relied on private firms to fund social welfare. In many large corporations, this took the form of "permanent employment," the practice of keeping workers until retirement and then finding positions for them in subsidiaries so that they would be guaranteed an income in their old age. Housing, health care, and other services were also provided by the firm. Workers joined a particular firm in expectation that they would receive such "fringe" benefits, thereby building loyalty and trust between the firm and its employees. The government took responsibility for "guiding" economic development in the hope that an expanding economy would benefit both the firms and, indirectly, their workers. Steadily rising standards of living would indicate success. However, in recent years the system has begun to change in response to demographic and economic factors.

The 1978–79 recession forced many firms to lay off workers for the first time in their histories. Permanent employment only covered one-third of Japanese workers to begin with, so their unemployment suggested even greater effects on employees of small firms. Additionally, the Japanese populace is beginning to age, straining the ability of many firms to finance retirement benefits. Changes in family structure have forced many elderly, who would have formerly lived with their children to fend for themselves. The elderly have demanded improved security from the government and their demands have been joined by those of working women demanding government day-care facilities for "latch-key" children, minorities demanding special services, and citizens who desire greater spending for parks, recreational facilities, and public works. In short, Japan's low-burden welfare system is being increasingly challenged by demands for expansion from almost every segment of the society. In contrast to Chinese workers, who must increasingly rely on their enterprises' profits for housing and health care, Japanese workers are finding their employers unable to finance their demands and needs. The era of privately supplied welfare may be coming to a close in Japan while in China, the experiment is just beginning.

53

Urban Policy in Contemporary China

June Kronholz

One of the greatest accomplishments of the Chinese government since 1949 has been its successful avoidance of urban sprawl that so plagues many other developing countries. As Kronholz points out here, modernization often means urbanization, as peasants crowd into new cities in search of jobs and the often extensive welfare services that accompany city dwelling. Quite frequently, however, the influx of peasants is too great for the city to support. Social services and physical plants are quickly exhausted and massive slums develop. China, despite its rapidly growing population and the ever-widening welfare gap between its rural and urban areas, has managed to avoid these problems, in part because of the CCP's penetrating control of all aspects of Chinese social life. Through a system of neighborhoods and work units (*danwei*) and household registrations (*hukou*), Party cadres can insure that people live only where they are assigned to live, work only at jobs to which they are assigned, and consume only the ration of certain commodities that has been assigned to them. Mobility is difficult, job transfers are not easily obtained, and squatting, or living in unassigned housing space, even if with relatives, is nearly impossible.

These conditions are changing somewhat under the effect of recent reforms. Because private businesses are now allowed in China, jobs are more easily found. Private markets are increasingly a source of unrationed food and goods. And the problem of rusticated youth, sent down to live with peasants during the Cultural Revolution and who are now returning in great numbers to the cities, has weakened enforcement of household registrations. Shanghai alone has nearly 900,000 such immigrants. The problem for the Chinese leadership is to find new ways to slow urbanization. And as Kronholz argues, this becomes increasingly difficult as the Chinese economy modernizes.

WUHAN, China—Tang Yueh Xian runs Yong Ching Street in Wuhan, a steelmaking city that sprawls along the banks of the Yangtze. Among other duties, Mrs. Tang oversees a shoe factory, restaurants and grocery stores, a kindergarten and a clinic. She sees to it that everyone has a job, plants flowers, takes in the laundry when it rains; she looks in on her neighbors to make sure their floors are clean.

And any time a stranger is on the street, even just a country cousin come by for a visit, Madam Tang sends a report up the administrative line. Should the cousin want to move in, well, "it just isn't allowed," Mrs. Tang says.

Two decades ago, after a famine forced millions of peasants into its cities in search of food, China adopted the most rigid urban policy in the world. Wuhan, with 4,179,600 people already, will find room for university graduates assigned to jobs here by the government, for technicians if it needs their skills, and perhaps for their wives or husbands "if it fits the plan," say the mayor, Wu Guanzheng. No one else is allowed to move to Wuhan. "There is no flexibility in our policy," he insists.

URBAN MARCH

The Third World's cities are exploding, doubling in size every 10 to 15 years and putting profound strains on poor countries that haven't the industry to support big cities, the agriculture to feed them or the know-how to make them run. The United Nations predicts that by the end of the century, all but a dozen of the 100 biggest cities in the world will be in the developing countries; China alone, despite its controls, will have 50 cities with more than a million people.

The move to town is only normal. With new technology on the farms—tractors, fertilizers, better seeds—fewer people are needed to grow food. Men move to new factory jobs in the cities. This is the process that created the big cities and industrial base of Europe and North America.

"It's the definition of development," says Anthony Churchill, the director of the World Bank's urban-development department. But the boom in the Third World's cities has stretched thin their capacity to cope.

Two-thirds of Calcutta's 10 million people live in shanties and squatter camps. Khartoum generates enough electricity to keep the lights on only three hours a day. There are nine times as many people looking for work in Nairobi as there are formal jobs.

NO ADMITTANCE

China copes by building an administrative fortress around its cities and cementing shut the drawbridge. It's a policy that has mothballed surplus labor in the countryside, hobbled farm productivity and kept the peasants poor.

"It made the rural areas bear the costs of China's inefficiencies," say John Aird of the U.S. Census Bureau, who is studying the results of last year's Chinese census. It is also a policy that is likely to become harder to enforce as China modernizes its creaky economy.

A vast pyramid of committees runs China's cities—its industries, social services and private lives. And it they sound meddlesome, they also explain how China copes with some problems that baffle big cities elsewhere.

Wang Shu Fang lives in four rooms at 78 Danien Road in Wuhan with her husband, daughter, son, son-in-law, daughter-in-law and grandchild. By Chinese standards they are wealthy, with the equivalent of a $196 monthly income, two bicycles, a color-television set and, come summer, a refrigerator.

STAYING PUT

Both Mrs. Wang and her husband work for the telephone company, which transferred them to Wuhan in 1961. A transfer isn't common in China. "We don't understand you foreigners, moving all the time," Mrs. Wang says. But it is about the only way to change jobs or move to a different city. A Chinese can't just quit his job; he needs permission from his *danwei,* the committee of 10 or 20 people he works with, which clears it first with management.

Finding another job is tricky. The government in Peking bloats factory work forces with demobilized soldiers and with other politically deserving sorts. There aren't any firings or layoffs in China. The constitution gives everyone the right to a job, but anything better than hauling construction materials across town in a handcart is difficult to find.

At Wuhan Iron & Steel Co., the second largest steel mill in China, boys inherit jobs from their fathers; fathers retire in favor of their sons. The steel factory, with 120,000 workers and with a target this year of three million tons of steel, has about 18,000 employees too many, the deputy director concedes.

Moving to a different city is trickier still. You need a city registration to rent an apartment in China, to collect your rice ration and old-age pension, to send your children to school, to go to the hospital for treatment and to claim your cotton allocation of six yards a year.

The steel mill won't give a job to a worker who isn't registered in Wuhan; on the other hand, no one can register in Wuhan unless he has a job. If it sounds like a Catch-22, well, "that's why it's very difficult to move here," says Tsai Chen, an official of a Wuhan district registration office.

Registration doesn't cover a man's family, either. Pun Qing Yuan was aboard a Yangtze River steamer recently, making the three-day trip back to Wuhan from Fuling. Mr. Pun is a carpenter, and because of the housing shortage in Wuhan he got a job and registration 13 years ago. But it didn't include his wife. In recompense, the government gives Mr. Pun one month a year to visit her.

The mayor says Wuhan has built housing for 100,000 families in the past three years, but that isn't nearly enough. Staggered by the size and cost of housing its huge population, China in 1978 ordered its factories and industries to help. The telephone company built Mrs. Wang's apartment building; she pays about $3.50 of the family's $195 monthly income in rent. That's about twice the rent of the average apartment in Wuhan, but then with four rooms it also is about twice the size.

NO SPITTING

There are 500 households in Mrs. Wang's neighborhood, 15 neighborhoods in Yong Ching Street—and a committee to run each of them. "We do the propaganda work," says Madam Tang, who heads the street committee. There is the Spirit of Civilization march, Civic Virtue month and the Patriotic Sanitation Campaign, during which her neighborhood committees discourage spitting, inspect everyone's housekeeping and see to it that everyone plants flowers and shrubs.

They run social services—nursery schools, corner clinics, lunch counters where meals begin at 27 cents, and take-out restaurants where Yong Ching's working women buy the family supper.

But they have weightier obligations, too. China doesn't admit to unemployment, but it concedes it has people "waiting for jobs," Sometimes the wait can be years. So Yong Ching Street has its own factories, where the jobless sew cloth shoes, string rope beds or make candy.

In Shanghai, the problem is compounded by the recent return of 900,000 people who as youths had been bundled off to do field work during the Cultural Revolution. When their agitation for jobs threatened to become ugly two years ago, Shanghai found work for them. But that meant that thousands of new high-school graduates hadn't any jobs to go to.

SMART SHOPS

In Shanghai's Tien Shan Street, with 12,7000 households, Mrs. Wan Ye of the street committee says she has found temporary work—it has lasted two years already—for 1,264 "young men waiting for jobs." To acknowledge their educational achievements, however, they work in outfits called the Young Intellectuals Grocery, the Young Intellectuals Restaurant and the Young Intellectuals Hotel.

China's courts were demolished in the Cultural Revolution, so in Wuhan, Madam Tang's street committee also mediates disputes and investigates divorce petitions. If there are grounds, she refers the case to court. She refers few cases. "We will educate the couple first," she says. "Sometimes it will take 20 visits or more."

The street office also registers newly married couples and all girls when they reach puberty, and it checks that they are all using birth-control measures. When a couple want to have a baby, Mrs. Tang's committee helps them fill out the application they send to their factories for approval. The factory, in turn, decides who may get pregnant this year.

There are 10 streets like Yong Ching in each of Wuhan's districts and six districts in the city, with a committee to run each of those, too. The state owns the production and distribution in a socialist country like China, and in China "the state" usually means the cities and their administrative districts.

RETAINED EARNINGS

Wuhan, for example, owns 3,300 industries. (An exception is the steel mill, which belongs to the government in Peking.) The city also owns 5,158 shops and restaurants and 45,000 acres of farm land. Wuhan used to own even the shoe-repair stands and sidewalk tailor shops, but China's new economic policies allow individuals to start small businesses, and 12,000 have done so in Wuhan in the past few years.

The district collects taxes from all those businesses, whoever owns them, and forwards the money to Wuhan and on to Peking. That is a change, too. Until recently, businesses didn't pay any tax but simply turned over all their profits to the government.

The government figured on a 40-year life for industrial equipment, so it returned little of the money for reinvestment. In 1982, the first year it went on the tax system, the Wuhan steel mill says it paid $200 million in taxes and kept $62 million—the biggest cash infusion in its history—for investment, production incentives and still more housing.

LOOSENING THE BONDS

With those new economic policies, China is aiming to quadruple production by the end of the century, and it already is showing stunning results. The gross national product, the sum of all goods and services, grew 9% in the past year, the Chinese reported recently. Consumer spending is booming: The country doubled its output of washing machines and refrigerators last year, and Wuhan estimates its retail sales were up $330 million.

But as the economy grows, China's cities can't help but grow with it. The U.N. predicts that two Chinese in five will be living in cities by the end of the century, up from one in five now. "China is entering the Latin American stage of development," says the World Bank's Mr. Churchill. "Rapid growth of the economy is going to result in rapid growth in the cities."

The freer economy also is likely to weaken China's controls over how its people live. Since the government began allowing farmers to sell their surpluses freely, Chinese haven't been restricted to the state food stores— where city registration is checked. The new policy toward private businesses means it now is possible to find work without registration. And in experimenting with production incentives, China may find that the freedom to change jobs and move is the biggest incentive of all to workers stuck in dead-end jobs.

"It takes either administrative controls or economic resources to enforce an urban policy," says the U.S. Census Bureau's Mr. Aird. It is possible that China soon may have the resources but begin to lose the controls.

54

Material Welfare, Education, and Public Health

Steven M. Goldstein, Kathrin Sears, and Richard C. Bush

In this selection authors Goldstein, Sears, and Bush provide a wealth of statistical information on material welfare, education, and health care. Since 1949, the Chinese have made great strides in all these areas. Technological change and economic progress have eliminated starvation, malnutrition, and mass poverty. A "floor of subsistence" has been laid that provides most Chinese with at least minimum requirements for health, education, and economic well-being. There are problems, however, Despite a stated policy of egalitarianism, income inequalities exist, and these gaps are becoming wider under the impact of economic reforms. Cadres, technicians, and professionals have traditionally fared better economically (if not politically) than other social strata. But new reforms are increasing these income gaps as well as creating new sources of inequality through bonuses and wages tied to production, and agricultural policies that encourage production through profit retention. A related problem is educational policy. During the Cultural Revolution, students were admitted to schools based on class and family background. This "affirmative action" program has since been scrapped in favor of more meritocratic criteria, so as to increase the number of technically qualified workers and scientists needed for the modernization effort. Similarly, health care policies are changing to give greater emphasis to urban areas, and rural areas are being told to fend for themselves. This could succeed if rural reforms provide the regionally generated funds needed to fund public services and if peasants can form the cooperative organizations to fund and maintain them. For now, the Chinese must balance their previous successes in expanding the scope of social services with the need to improve the quality of these services.

All the characteristic problems of very poor societies plagued China in 1949. Distribution of wealth and income was quite unequal and most people were at or below subsistence level. Malnutrition, starvation, and infectious diseases were widespread. As a result, only 80 out of every 100 infants survived to their first birthday; the average life expectancy was between 35 and 40 years of age. Social services were minimal and concentrated in urban areas. The ratio of patients to doctors trained in modern science was around 35,000:1. There were only 17 million primary school students, 20% of the total age group. Only a million of those could expect to get any secondary education. And probably a substantial majority of adults were illiterate.

How has post-1949 economic development . . . affected the welfare of the Chinese people? The Communist Party has undeniably ended the mass poverty that it found when it took power in 1949. Through institutional and technological change, through expanding production and improving distribution, the regime has for the most part laid a floor of subsistence so that very few people must relive the horrors of the past. Public health services have reduced serious infectious diseases. Basic education is now available to many instead of the very few.

But progress beyond subsistence has come slowly to China's growing population. Consequently, Party leaders have continually argued over whether poverty or inequality is the greater political liability, and over how to rectify the situation. One group, led by Mao Zedong before his death, has held the inequality breeds political alienation, which in turn breeds economic stagnation. It has advocated reducing the gap—in material goods, in education, in health care, etc.—between the relative "haves" and the relative "have-nots." It favors fostering political consciousness to spur productivity. The other group, epitomized by Deng Xiaoping, believes that this egalitarianism has only perpetuated backwardness. It believes that all will benefit to some degree from rapid economic growth, but that those who are more productive should receive a greater material reward.

MATERIAL WELFARE

Estimating the quality of life in China is not an easy task since statistical information is limited and of uncertain validity and reliability. Per capita GNP has risen slowly over the past 30 years, declining after the Great Leap Forward and rising more rapidly in the years following Mao's death. Per capita supplies of basic necessities—grain, cotton cloth, processed sugar, for example—grew rapidly in the early 1950s and then stagnated until after Mao's death. Data on average food consumption indicate a diet limited in both quantity and quality.

The post-Mao leadership has admitted that there is a good bit of variation around these national averages. It was revealed in March 1979, for example, that about 100 million people (10% of the population) suffered from malnutrition. Only rough estimates of the extent of social inequality are available at this point. . . . [These] suggest that China has been fairly successful in limiting income inequality within urban and rural communities, though less successful in reducing disparity between city and countryside. It is clear, however, that the material incentives now being used to spur productivity will widen the gaps that still exist, with unpredictable political and social consequences.

A recent province-by-province comparison of industrial and agricultural output value indicates wide disparities in levels of development. The major cities and provinces of the east and northeast (Shanghai, Tianjin, Beijing municipalities; Liaoning, Jiangsu and Heilongjiang provinces), where economic development began before the communist victory in 1949, remain the leading areas in value of output. Most striking is Shanghai municipality, where per capita output value is twice as high as in Tianjin and Beijing and 18 times that of Guizhou province. Shanghai thus continues to play a primary role in the national economy, just as it did pre-1949.

More detailed information on urban wages and family budgets suggests some of the sources of inequality in cities. For the individual, occupation and seniority level are the key factors. Senior cadres, professionals, and technicians receive substantially higher monthly incomes than juniors in their own field or ordinary workers. For families, the proportion of workers to non-workers in the household is crucial. The size of the family work force is even more important in the countryside, and ranks with natural conditions as the chief determinants of rural income. . . . Introduction of the "responsibility system" in rural areas has allowed private income to increase. Private income as a percentage of collective income still varies between areas, however. The post-1978 economic reforms are contributing to greater diversity in sources of income and, while raising income levels in general, also are increasing inequality in earnings.

It would be incomplete, however, to concentrate only on income as a measure of inequality. Foreign observers and the Chinese themselves have pointed out that those in positions of power have special access to material goods and social services, and can, if they choose, use their posts for personal or family gain. This form of corruption—its prevalence is unknown—lends a definite political cast to inequality caused by economic factors.

EDUCATION

How best to use scarce educational resources has been an issue of continuing controversy in China. Quality and quantity have been competing goals. On the one hand, economic development requires increasing numbers of technicians and managers. On the other, spreading basic knowledge is essential to rural development and fostering upward mobility. The rival priorities are evident in the evolution of the educational system and enrollment statistics.

The pre-Cultural Revolution approach emphasized training technical specialists. Middle school and college enrollments grew at a faster rate than primary school enrollments. The Cultural Revolution attacked this focus on expertise: schools were closed for varying lengths of time from 1966 on, with universities not reopening until 1970. The approach that then emerged stressed the expansion of primary and secondary enrollments, especially in the rural areas, and the selection of university students on the basis of political commitment rather than tested academic ability. The post-Mao leadership has reemphasized expertise. Expanding higher education is the highest priority, universalizing middle school education is now a goal for the long term, and entrance exams have been restored as a screening device. Short-term colleges and "TV universities" have been opened and the government has encouraged the creation of rotational training programs for cadres. Graduate degree programs have been reintroduced and the number of students sent abroad greatly increased. By the end of 1982, approximately 6,000 Chinese government-sponsored students and research scholars and 3,500 privately sponsored students were studying in the United States alone.

An educational balance sheet reveals pluses and minuses in both quality and quantity. Primary education is now nearly universal, and secondary education has expanded considerably. The adult literacy rate is said to be about 85%. However, rural schools still lag behind their urban and suburban counterparts, and closing the gap does not seem to be a high priority of current policy. The Cultural Revolution turmoil and the enrollment policies adopted after 1970 are said to have caused a decline in school discipline. In contrast to the interest in expanding opportunities for high education, tighter standards, demographic trends, and introduction of the "responsibility system" in rural areas have caused primary and secondary enrollments to decline.

Concerning quality, the higher education system has over the past 30 years trained a corps of specialists in fields appropriate to modernization—science, engineering, teaching, and medicine. But here the Cultural Revolution took a tremendous toll, damaging or destroying the careers of older specialists and preventing the training of younger ones. The revival of the higher education system will remedy this shortage of skilled manpower only over the long term. To further deal with the problem of lack of specialized skills, senior high schools in many provinces are focusing upon vocational training.

If one uses aggregate enrollment statistics to measure equality of educational opportunity, the following becomes clear:

- As noted above, primary education has become increasingly accessible, with about 93% of the age group in school.
- Secondary education has become increasingly accessible (middle school enrollments were about 10% of primary school enrollment in 1957, 13% in 1965, 25% in 1974, 39% in 1977, and 38% in 1980),

but total enrollments declined in 1980 and 1981.

- As secondary education expanded to 1980, university education became relatively less accessible (enrollments for the latter were 7% of the former in 1957, 4% in 1965, and around 1% in 1974 and 1977). That trend, which actually continued during the Cultural Revolution, has now been reversed to a limited extent (the ratio was 2.1% in 1980).
- Primary school enrollments have more than doubled since 1957. The probability of the average primary school student getting into university is somewhat better at present (around 1 in 128 in 1980), after decreasing opportunities from 1957 to late 1970s.

But these general trends mask an underlying question: whether specific groups—for example, urban youth, particularly children of officials and the well educated—are getting better access to scarce secondary and higher education resources. The renewed emphasis on academic admissions criteria, especially for university, would seem to favor these groups. Mao's mid-1960's belief that elite groups held a disproportionate share of college enrollments, at a time when the number of high school graduates was growing, was a partial basis for the Cultural Revolution attack on the educational system. The current leadership's emphasis on improving quality may create similar political discontent among those who have gained and would stand to gain from the Maoist stress on education for all.

HEALTH CARE

As with education, medical services have expanded gradually, but not without political conflict over how they are distributed. The number of hospital beds and doctors has increased over time, with public health campaigns to combat specific problems supplementing the more formal medical institutions. This combination has brought about the "modernization" of China's health problems. Infectious and endemic diseases are now fairly rare. According to Chinese estimates, life expectancy is now 67 years for men and 69 for women; infant mortality is around one-tenth of its 1949 rate. As in the industrial world, cancer and cardiovascular problems are now the main cause of death. Although epidemiological statistics for one district of Beijing are not representative of the country as a whole, they do demonstrate the dimensions of the transformation.

Despite this progress, there has been substantial political controversy over which groups should receive what level of medical services. Public health work before 1966 tended to focus on the urban areas, although some progress was made in rural health care. With the launching of the Cultural Revolution, the countryside was given special emphasis. Subsequently, health services spread much more broadly, so that by 1979 each of the country's 2,000 counties had at least one general hospital, and each of the 55,000 communes had at least one clinic. By 1981 urban and rural areas were served by over 2 million medical and health personnel, more than three time the number in 1950. The total number of hospital beds increased from less the 100,000 to more than 2 million during the same period.

But this quantitative improvement came at the expense of quality of care, especially in the cities. Upgrading urban hospitals and improving the skills of medical personnel—especially paramedics and full doctors trained after 1966—are now of high priority. It remains to be seen whether there will be sufficient resources (scarce to begin with) to maintain and improve services in the countryside, where peasants have become used to basic health care.

Evaluating the quality of life in China depends in large measure on the yardstick employed. If the standard is the dark days of the 1940s, then there has been substantial progress. Basic subsistence and services are available to the great majority of the population, an accomplishment which many developing counties have yet to achieve. How to meet the needs of the poorest 10–20% of the population, whose nutrition, education, and health levels are significantly lower than the rest of the population, will be an immense challenge. Even if the standard is the still spartan existence of China's cities and wealthier communes, then a large proportion of the population has a long way to go. If one judges by the expectations of Chinese themselves, there can only be a tentative verdict. Those who experienced China at its pre-1949 worst seem fairly content. Less satisfied are those for whom the past is only their parents' reminiscences, who have lived the contradiction between socialism's promise and its mixed performance. Unless the "four modernizations" soon bring them palpable rewards, they may be unwilling to sacrifice for an uncertain future.

55

Welfare in Japan: Security Without Entitlement

Ezra F. Vogel

Japan has the highest life expectancy of any nation in the world. Yet, its health care system does not enjoy a significant level of government support, nor does the government have much of a role in providing health care insurance or benefits to cover medical expenses. In fact, as Ezra F. Vogel argues in this selection, beyond provisions of unemployment compensation and retirement benefits for the elderly, the Japanese government plays only a minimal role in the country's social welfare system. Instead of relying on the government for their economic security, most workers are covered by employer-funded health care plans, housing services, pensions plans, and other services. Rather than negotiate for sick leave and vacations, workers look for home loans or homes provided by their firms. Employers, rather than funding expensive pension plans, provide work for older workers in subsidiaries and augment their salaries with retirement benefits. Moreover, the fact that no one in Japan likes to admit to the embarrassment of collecting benefits is another factor in the continual underfunding of the country's social welfare system. The private funding of welfare has several advantages, as Vogel points out here, but the system is rife with inequalities according to occupation, seniority, and locality. Despite these shortcomings, the present system does seem to lead to satisfactory levels of welfare (even if privately funded) without necessitating massive government spending.

In 1955 the average Japanese life expectancy was sixty-five years for males, sixty-seven years for females. One might have expected that in the 1960s and early 1970s, with frantic economic development and environmental pollution, health would suffer. Since 1962 companies with fifty employees or more given annual physical examinations to all employees. With the exception of small rises in 1966, 1973, and 1974, the rate of illnesses observed through these examinations has gone down annually. By 1977, when Japanese longevity surpassed Sweden's to become first in the world, life expectancy was 72.7 for males, 77.9 for females.

In the 1950s as urban areas grew rapidly and expenditures on social benefits lagged behind economic development, one might have expected alienated city dwellers. Sewage facilities and park areas still rank behind those of other advanced countries. Although from 1970 to 1975 Japan had more than eighty percent as many new housing starts as the United States (about 8.6 million, compared to 10.5 million) with only fifty percent as much population, the average Japanese still has only about two-thirds as much housing space as his American counterpart. Yet large urban districts with defaced personal and public property and accompanying degradation and alienation, found so frequently in large American cities, are virtually absent in Japan.

Since pension and old-age security payments are just catching up with modern Western countries, one might have thought that Japanese old people would have been discouraged and forlorn. There are discouraged old people in Japan, and suicide rates rise with old age as in other countries, but as Erdman Palmore finds in his comparative study of aging in the United States and Japan, Japanese old people are more active than their American counterparts, and, based on large sample surveys of different age groups, their sense of satisfaction does not decline with age as in America.

In the 1960s as Japanese production was catching up with world levels, politicians began to talk of the need for more expenditures on social benefits to balance economic growth. Fashionable speakers replaced the term "gross national product" with "net national welfare" in order to show they were not narrow economic animals but were concerned with the quality of life. More funds began to flow into the welfare sector.

However, by the mid-1970s government and business leaders, at first quietly and then increasingly in indirect public comments, began expressing a new consensus. The essence of the consensus is that the welfare state, with "high welfare and high state burden" as found in England, Sweden, and the United States, is undesirable. By emphasizing the tax burden, Japanese leaders have achieved a measure of public support, but because opposing welfare lacks popular appeal, the new consensus has not been sloganized and enshrined with a fully developed rationale. Nor has it necessarily carried the day with the Diet, which has voted and established more welfare than bureaucrats and business leaders consider desirable. Yet the basic rationale for the new consensus is understood by all in leadership positions and in muted form ("in a period of low growth, with a heavily strained budget, funds are not available") occasionally appears in the public media. These leaders prefer to keep funds flowing into the productive sectors of the economy, to encourage the working place and the family to share welfare burdens, and to supplement private welfare with state funds only when it is essential to do so.

MINIMAL STATE WELFARE

The Japanese lag in welfare expenditures is not necessarily permanent, but the new consensus has already slowed down the rate of increase and it is tailoring the welfare program in a certain direction. In part the long-range strategy of Japanese leaders after World War II was to concentrate first on industrial growth, next on wages and consumption, then on welfare expenses. By 1973 only twenty percent of public expenditure in Japan went to social benefits, compared to twenty-six percent in Great Britain, twenty-eight percent in the United States, and substantially more in all other Western European nations. As welfare expenditures increased, they were concentrated in health (in the early 1960s) and pensions (in the early 1970s) while other areas were virtually neglected.

In the health field the percentage of the GNP spent for medical expenditure grew rapidly for several years after national health care was established and then remained fairly steady except for 1973 to 1975, when it grew to keep pace with inflation, while the GNP remained steady.... Japanese expenses on health care, including the ratio of doctors, nurses, hospitals, and hospital beds to the population now compares favorably with the Western European average.... Yet the system of private physicians, low standard fees for doctors' visits and hospital service, and patient responsibility for as much as thirty percent of health care provides more frequent doctor visits for all elements of the population than the American delivery system.

Following heightened attention to the problems of the elderly in the late 1960s, annuity and pension payments began to increase very rapidly. There are two major pension plans covering about ninety percent of Japanese pensions: those for former company employees (*kōsei nenkin*) and those for unattached independent citizens (*dokumin nenkin*), further divided between contributory payments (for those young enough to be part of recent payment plans) and noncontributory (those for the very old and infirm unable to pay their own way)....

Aside from health and old age, welfare payments are still minute by American standards. Unemployment insurance is low because of the low unemployment rate; companies find it cheaper to set aside their own funds and pay for disguised unemployment when necessary than to support a very large bureaucratic system of unemployment insurance that is then paid out to workers laid off or fired....

Aside from health care and old-age pensions, people do not have a sense of entitlement about welfare, there is a sense of stigma about accepting it, and it is given out sparingly. The family (including relatives beyond the nuclear family) and the workplace are expected to bear a much bigger responsibility and to put aside funds to provide for their own security.

GROUP WELFARE

Historically, the Japanese government did not establish a single comprehensive welfare system for everyone, but progressively developed special schemes for various occupational categories. It basically followed the Bismarckian model of the government's encouraging private organizations to set up welfare programs and keeping to a minimum the direct involvement of the state.... Just as the government holds to the principle that polluters should bear the costs of polluting, so it has generally accepted the principle that companies should be responsible for all the welfare costs of their employees. These programs did not necessarily stem from the most benevolent motives; many of the original programs concentrated on productive workers with the purpose of keeping a healthy working population, but the programs have since been extended to the nonworking population.

Since the employer in all lines of work is responsible for welfare, the employee know he will be better looked after if he remains loyal to his company or his government branch. When the economy is very vigorous the individual can find other opportunities, but nonetheless the system tends to reinforce the tie between the individual and his place of work....

The scheme of providing welfare through separate occupation groupings rather than through a single system is quietly but enthusiastically supported by big-businessmen. According to a recent survey, large companies provided twice as many benefits as they were required to provide by law. Businessmen oppose the government's assuming heavy welfare burdens, for they want to pay less in taxes and to avoid the large governmental administrative overhead required for a large public welfare system. Perhaps even more important, they want to maintain the advantage that large companies enjoy over small companies, for if a potential employee is offered an equivalent salary at a large and a small company, other things being equal, he will take the large company because it can provide more security over the long run. This broader sense of security strengthens the identification of the worker with his company. Big-businessmen prefer to offer the benefits because the system reinforces the loyalty of the worker.

Although it is difficult to compare the welfare benefits in a Japanese and an American company because the categories are so different, Japanese companies concentrate their benefits in areas that will keep the employee attached to the company over a long period of time. Benefits in the United States include substantial paid sick leave, vacation time, and coffee breaks— benefits rarely provided by Japanese companies in comparable amounts. In contrast, some seven percent of the Japanese population live in housing supplied by employers. An additional fifty percent—almost as much of the population as in the United States—own dwelling where they live, and over half of the money that company employees borrow to buy housing is lent by employers. In 1975 the average interest rate for money borrowed from employers was three to four percent, compared to nine to ten percent for private loans in general. Even small companies unable to buy housing often lease housing and rent it to their employees below cost.

Large companies often have their own medical facilities, including hospitals and recuperation homes; these provide a much higher level of service than facilities supported by the national health plan. Since company retirement age is usually between fifty-five and sixty, most employees need a second job after retirement, and a company ordinarily assists a faithful employee in finding this post-retirement work. Many benefits provided by the company for longtime employees, such as the use of company mountain and seaside cottages and entertainment halls, are not easily calculated in value. Entertainment allowances are generous, but it is not easy to distinguish what portion should be considered company needs and what portion employee welfare. However difficult to calculate, as Robert Immerman, longtime American labor ataché in Tokyo, has noted, it is clear that the total Japanese company welfare package is larger than the American.

The Japanese company avoids tight contractual arrangements with employees and unions, leaving considerable discretion to company executives. The company tries to keep abreast of worker desires and offer more services than seem minimally necessary to meet union demands. By avoiding contractual agreements, company officials retain the leverage to give more rewards to those who have been faithful and hardworking. Especially in allocating company loans, assisting with post-retirement employment, and allowing the use of special company recreation sites, company officials enjoy considerable leeway, conveying the message that perquisites are not automatic and that loyalty will be rewarded. . . .

Although it is difficult to match the security of the large companies, independent professionals and small businesses respectively form groups not only to make payments for mandatory welfare benefits but to provide additional collective security to their members. Their associations commonly offer collective insurance through private companies, and large organizations often create their own independent welfare funds. . . .

The Agricultural Cooperative, a very powerful organization to which every farm household belongs, has in effect an extensive program of security benefits for its members. Farmers make mandatory government welfare payments through the Cooperative, and the Cooperative buys and invests on a broad scale, providing greater security for investment than the farmers could hope to attain individually. . . .

The family farm also provides a form of social security. The typical farm is small (two or three acres) as a result of the land reform policy of the Allied Occupation and the accompanying legislation discouraging reconcentration. By the mid-1960s, with increased mechanization, much less labor power was required on the farm. Young farmers therefore go out to work in towns and cities, in a variety of industries. With good transport facilities and automobiles, most of them are now able to commute to work from their homes. Even if they are retired from urban employment at age fifty or fifty-five, they can return to farm work, earning enough to cover food and other expenses for the household until well into old age. This is the dominant pattern for the five million rural household in Japan, one that provides old-age security and a sense of pride and activity for the elders in almost twenty percent of the nation's family households. . . .

Families, rural and urban, have expected to provide funds for themselves in their old age, although it is likely that the very rapid increase in pension payments in the early 1970s will have an impact, lessening family financial responsibility. In 1973 Japanese saved twenty percent of disposable personal income, compare to Americans, who saved eight percent. Survey research data collected during the last several years show increased savings since the mid-1970s. In households where heads are approaching retirement, savings rates have increased beyond the national household average. . . . In Japan the family has been clearly responsible for the education of its children, and families put aside money for that purpose. In the United States, where there is less clarity about whether the family, the government, or private institutions are responsible for the education of the student, there is virtually no family saving for educational purposes.

Japanese family members also assume a much larger share of the responsibility for caring for the sick than American family members. Hospitals not only encourage family members to help out but often supply mats or cots and cooking facilities at the hospital, providing quality personal care without great financial burden.

The Japanese family still accepts a large responsibility in caring for the aged. In 1952 eighty-one percent of the Japanese over sixty-five were living with their children, and in 1974 this had declined only to seventy-five percent. As John C. and Ruth Campbell have noted, less than two percent of Japanese over sixty-five were in nursing homes and other institutions, compared to almost six percent in the United States. Palmore notes that in 1973, seventy-nine percent of Japanese couples over sixty-five live with one of their children, compared to between fourteen and eighteen percent in Denmark, the United States, and Great Britain. Among Japanese widowers, eighty-two percent over sixty-five live with children, and of widows, eighty-four percent. Only about ten percent of Japanese over sixty-five are not living with a spouse or child. The pattern of elders living with their children does impose a burden on the young couple, especially upon the young housewife, and this is a cost that needs to be considered in this system. The advantage for the elderly is quite clear. Even in old age the Japanese continue to be active, to maintain strong social ties to their families, and to engage in work and hobbies. . . .

There are many in Japan, including the leaders of the Japanese Medical Association, who would argue that the system of having different welfare schemes for different companies and other groups of the population is a feudalistic holdover that should be rationalized by having a more unified standardized national welfare program for everyone. Clearly, the greatest disadvantage of the system is that the unattached individual does not receive as complete a coverage of various benefits as those attached to the largest companies. . . .

MINIMAL BUREAUCRACY, MAXIMUM IMPACT

In the health and welfare fields, as in other fields, the Japanese bureaucracy is highly centralized. It has broad scope but tries to play a minimal role in direct administration. Compared to the United States, which has confusing and overlapping national and state jurisdictions with many inconsistencies, Japan has simpler, more consistent national plans. Although the varying program for different groups is not without administrative problems, services are nonetheless standardized throughout the country. With less duplication, Japan is able to streamline its welfare bureaucracy.

Just as the economic bureaucracy accepts a broad responsibility for promoting the economic health of the nation, so the national health bureaucracy accepts a broad responsibility for looking after the health of the populace. As in other fields, bureaucrats take more initiative than their counterparts in the United States. For example, they make for more frequent inspections of restaurants, hospitals, and other institutions to see that they observe standards of nutrition and cleanliness. They take a more active role in health examinations for youth, providing dental and medical checkups for all school children. They make more use of schools and neighborhoods for giving vaccinations and injections of all types, and therefore the Japanese population is better protected against such diseases than people in the United States. . . .

In the United States politicians are at the mercy of welfare pressure groups, and the result has been that fees and payments for certain welfare programs have risen astronomically, sometimes at the expense of a coherent, equitable plan. In Japan the bureaucracy, which has a greater measure of power relative to politicians, is somewhat better able to resist special pressures and to provide a sound fiscal base, although it is by no means immune from pressure groups, as John C. Campbell has shown in his analysis of Diet decisions to raise welfare payments prior to crucial elections. . . .

REDISTRIBUTION AND WELL-BEING WITHOUT DEPENDENCE

One of the tenets of the Japanese approach to welfare in the broad sense is that there should be economic employment opportunities for everyone and that those who work and exert themselves for their organizations should be appropriately looked after. The government's policy of distributing wealth throughout the society is not based on public welfare but on fine calibrations of wages, taxes, budget redistribution to poorer prefectures, and subsidized rice price paid to farmers. People are not entitled to anything but the barest essentials unless they contribute to their groups. As a result, there is no sizeable group that feels indignant out of a sense of entitlement or self-deprecatory out of a sense of inadequate achievement. Nor is there the deep social cleavage between taxpayers who object to supporting those who work less and the recipients who object to the inadequacy of their payments, their uncertainty, and the spirit in which they are given. . . .

The Japanese are reluctant to sing the praises of their modest public welfare system, but Japanese who travel to American cities are invariably struck by the run-down nature of American slums, the lack of respect for public property, and the general degradation of American cities. As paradoxical as it may be to Americans, the Japanese, with a poorly financed welfare system aside from health and pensions, have managed much better than we to avoid the despair that underlies this degradation.

Ample employment opportunities help maintain high morale, a sense of purpose, self-respect, and group effort; the opportunity to work more than compensates for the inadequate welfare payments. How well the system would work if the Japanese economy were to decline precipitously is speculative, but with the vigor of the national efforts, this may not be tested in the foreseeable future. In short, the Japanese have been able to provide for the well-being of their population without requiring many except the very old and infirm to become economically dependent on the state, and they have done it in such a way as to reinforce their communitarian ideals.

Unit XIV

__ Policy Toward the Military __

China and Japan face difficult decisions regarding defense policy in the 1980s. In both countries, the need for defense modernization has come up against economic and political obstacles. Defense spending enjoys very low priority in the budgets of the two nations, and in both countries the military suffers from low prestige. Moreover, defense policy is an issue of great political significance to domestic political leaders, as well as the leaders of other nations. In both China and Japan, the issue of defense is the basis for fundamental cleavages in the political structure and is certain to influence domestic politics in the future.

The military is regarded quite differently in the cultural traditions of China and Japan. Whereas in China the military is the lowest of the four social strata (scholar, peasant, merchant, soldier), in Japan the figure of the *samurai* (or warrior) is an heroic one, celebrated in literature, visual arts, and film. It was military men who guided the Meiji Restoration and who reinvigorated the idea of Japanese nationalism in the latter part of the nineteenth century. The growth and strength of the Japanese military, marked by the defeats of Russia in 1905 and successes in Manchuria between 1931 and 1937, symbolized the growth and power of the Japanese people and nation. Then, Japan's humiliating defeat in World War II and the agony of Hiroshima and Nagasaki dealt a devastating blow to the military's prestige. The postwar Constitution severely limited the size and power of the newly created Self-Defense Forces. Article Nine, the peace clause, provided for no standing Japanese army and swore off war as an instrument of Japanese foreign policy. Nuclear weapons were never to be allowed on Japanese soil.

China's People's Liberation Army (PLA), the combined forces of the army, navy and air force, emerged from World War

II with a distinctly different public image. It was the PLA that had enable China to resist Japanese aggression throughout the thirties and forties. An army of the peasants, the PLA never oppressed the populations of the areas it occupied. It defended the Chinese Revolution and the philosophy of Mao Zedong and protected the motherland, whether in Korea or along the border with the Soviet Union.

Then, in 1967 and 1968, the PLA was called in to quell the civil disturbances of the Cultural Revolution. Under the leadership of Lin Biao,* the PLA actively struggled against the opponents of Mao Zedong. Mao in turn upheld the PLA as a revolutionary model to be emulated by the Chinese masses. "Learn from the PLA" became a popular slogan of the period. But, in reality, the PLA was not a perfect model. PLA commanders moved troops into factories, schools, and housing blocks and remained there until the mid-1970s. In 1978, there were several public demonstrations against the PLA occupying forces. Four generals were put on trial with the "Gang of Four" and tried for their actions during the decade of the Cultural Revolution (1966–76). Chinese writers, poets, and filmmakers all denounced the military for its attitude of superiority toward civilians, its corruption, and its behavior in the conflicts of the 1970s. Today the PLA enjoys little prestige and suffers from extremely low morale.

Interestingly, both China and Japan are confronted by the need for enhanced defense capabilities while being simultaneously constrained by their recent military history. Japan must respond to changes in the global arena engendered by the decline of American military and economic power by forging a more autonomous and independent military force. At the same time, it must be sensitive to the concerns of former World War II victims in Asia, who fear a resurgence of military adventurism. The Japanese leadership must also take into consideration the strong domestic political opposition to rearmament. While most Japanese have accepted the Self-Defense Forces as meeting the requirements of the Constitution, few are convinced that any further

---

*Mao's chosen successor, also known as Lin Piao, who was killed fleeing China after his attempt at a coup was foiled in 1971.

increases in defense spending are necessary. Leftist parties have capitalized on the pacifism that runs deeply in the electorate and have made defense modernization a controversial political football. Moreover, defense has even become an issue of factional conflict within the LDP, some of whose members advocate a great deal more autonomy, some of whom advocate enhanced defense within the context of the American alliance, and some of whom maintain that enough is already being done in the area of defense. American pressures for a greater regional and international role for Japan increase the complexity of the debate and make it harder to resolve the conflicts over defense policy.

Donald C. Hellmann, in "Japanese Security and Postwar Japanese Foreign Policy," examines the important role of domestic political conflict in shaping defense policy in present-day Japan. In "Japanese Security Policies and the United States," Gerald L. Curtis focuses on recent reforms in Japanese defense policy, many of them initiated in response to U.S. demands that Japan assume greater responsibility for its own defense, and then goes on to describe some of the domestic political concerns that present the greatest obstacles to continued reform.

American policies concerning weapons sales also play a key role in Chinese defense policy making, though not to the same degree that they do in Japan. Unlike Japan, China has no security treaty with the United States, though there has been some indication that American leaders would appreciate a stronger relationship with the PRC to counter Soviet strength in Asia. However, as June Dreyer points out in "China's Military Power in the 1980s," the key factors in Chinese defense policy can be found in the domestic political arena.

There is a fundamental cleavage in China between reformers in the present leadership and leftist holdovers from the Cultural Revolution who are still members of the PLA. In the late 1960s, after the weaknesses of the military were revealed in border clashes with the Soviet Union, these elements were able to agree on the need for military modernization. However, the current leadership has consistently deemphasized the place of military modernization in the program of modernizations now underway. Despite wage hikes and some new weapons procurement, many members of the armed forces are upset over the severe budget cuts the PLA has been forced to accept. Moreover, recent agricultural reforms have encouraged many peasants, once the backbone of the PLA, to stay home and farm rather than join the army. Morale is not going to be improved by upcoming personnel reductions involving more than a million people. Analysts expect that the primary targets of such reductions will be older, less politically reliable officers. There are also conflicts within the military itself concerning strategic doctrine, the issue of ranks (abolished during the Cultural Revolution), and the adaptation of Maoist guerrilla tactics to today's nuclear world.

In sum, China and Japan face similar but essentially different problems. On the one hand, both countries must modernize their defense systems. However, the constraints on modernization differ. Japan is facing external demands from its allies that conflict with popular and opposition parties' demands. China, constrained economically by its lower level of development, is also confronted by serious political cleavages that could threaten its present leadership. As the readings in this unit suggest, in both countries defense policy promises to be a major issue in domestic politics for some time to come.

56

Japanese Security and Postwar Japanese Foreign Policy

Donald C. Hellmann

Aside from the Mutual Security Treaty with the United States, Japan has not real defense policy. Security has been defined as defense of Japan's territorial integrity. Hellmann argues that there are two reasons for this. First, Japan has no clear conception of long-term defense objectives that might involve any independent action. Second, domestic considerations, as opposed to external factors, play too great a role in defense policy making.

Defense spending in Japan is primarily a budgetary question, not a strategic issue. The requirements of economic expansion and political opposition from strict interpreters of Article Nine of the Japanese Constitution combine to make defense a low-priority issue. Furthermore, given the destruction of Hiroshima and Nagasaki, and Japan's unique position as the only nation to constitutionally forbid war as an instrument of foreign policy, increased defense spending is a controversial issue. Hellmann argues that the controversy surrounding defense policy makes it likely that any change in policy will be caught up in factional politics within the LDP. Moreover, leftist politicians who have traditionally defended Article Nine and who advocate pacifism have increased the political risks of raising defense policy to a more important status. Therefore, he concludes, the present lack of attention to defense issues will likely continue and an independent defense posture will not emerge without considerable domestic political conflict.

Security has been a pivotal issue in postwar Japanese foreign policy. During the Occupation, deep concern for the past and future role of Japan in world affairs underlay the sweeping American-sponsored constitutional and political reforms and established the conditions on which independence ultimately was granted. During the ensuing Cold War years, alliance with the United States served both as the foundation for the integration of

Japan into the international economic and political order and as the focal point of Japan's internal conflict between the conservative and opposition parties. With the emergence internationally of a more pluralistic, multipolar era, the linkages between political security affairs and economic relations have posed fresh dilemmas for Japan's most serious strain since 1952. Security policy has been the point at which Japanese domestic and external politics have converged most fully and dramatically, so in considering that policy, one must look beyond the modest military forces and defense plans of the government. An evaluation of the past crises and current strategic problems from a broad political and historical perspective is required.

Japan's strategic policy can be seen simply as one dimension of Japanese-American relations. Since 1945, Japan has been either a country occupied by American troops or a defense satellite under a hegemonical alliance arrangement that has ultimately treated Japan security interests as identical with those of the United States. The explicit ties on defense matters have been reinforced both by the cultivation of extensive bilateral economic and political relations, and by the shrill anti-American campaigns of the Japanese Left which have served to narrow the focus of the foreign-policy debate to an obsessive concern over relations with the United States. With the unfolding of the so-called Nixon Doctrine, and in the face of the monetary, trade, and resource crises that have devastated the international economic system in the last few years, this one-sided defense relationship has undergone significant changes. Still, the United States continues to hold the key to Japan's security policy; when and how Japan will move to an expanded defense posture will be shaped as much by what is done in Washington as in Tokyo. . . .

ECONOMICS AND POLITICAL-SECURITY ISSUES

Japan's approach to the issue of security has been that of an expanding international trading company, not that of a nation-state. The Japanese have become a major global economic force and the preeminent power in the East Asian region. They are more dependent on imports of critical raw materials than any major industrial nation and have highly vulnerable shipping lines to these resources, but they have steadfastly refused to acknowledge the need for an overseas security role. Not only has Japan refused to dispatch forces abroad, but up to now there has been no linkage between its overseas economic interests and national military capabilities. In this still-prevailing vision of global affairs, economics and politics are seen as separable, and armament and power politics are rejected as critical ingredients for a successful Japanese foreign policy. The assumptions on which this dimension of Japanese foreign policy rest are also derived from the American diplomatic tradition. They have been perpetuated by the singularly salutary international economic relations that prevailed under United States leadership from 1950 to 1970 among both Western industrial powers and underdeveloped nations.

The separability of economics and politics in foreign policy has been an implicit (and often explicit) premise in the policies of all postwar Japanese governments and a perspective widely shared by many left-wing critics as well. In short, there has been a consensus that defined Japan's international role in narrowly economic terms within the framework of the nation-state system. . . .

Until the enunciation of the Nixon Doctrine, American security policy made it possible and appropriate for the Japanese to conduct a one-sided economic foreign policy in keeping with the principles of their new liberal diplomatic tradition. Power politics, however, were not peripheral to the postwar international system; the international economic order in which Japan operated so well rested on the political-security arrangements that served to underwrite the Western bloc. Pax Americana was the foundation on which an "American world economy" rested. Even in bilateral Japanese-American relations, the security tie was at least as important as mutual economic interests in establishing the special economic relationship marked most notably by easy access to the United States market.

The world in which Japanese liberalism flourished was shattered in the early 1970s by a series of events that has brought together the high politics of a changing politicomilitary era and international economic relations. Economically, the erosion and collapse of the postwar monetary system and the perpetration of a global resource crisis by the producing nations' political use of economic resources have seriously jeopardized the fragile arrangements fostering global interdependence during the period of the "American world economy." The specter of economic nationalism is made more real by a climate conducive to political nationalism, which features the proliferation of nuclear weapons and an explicit recognition by the superpowers (as well as other nations) that the commitments and capabilities of the United States and the Soviet Union are no longer global in the Cold War sense.

In these new circumstances, Japan has been forced to reconsider its international economic policy side-by-side with its political role in the world, especially with regard to the oil-producing states. This shift implicitly repudiates a basic premise of the foreign policy consensus of the past two decades, but its meaning for security policy has not been fully recognized, far less developed. . . .

Japan's approach to defense has been remarkably unvarying and subdued, being built around full and unqualified United States security guarantees. Beyond the American alliance, there has been virtually no strategic policy regarding external threats or regional conflict. Security has been defined in the narrow sense of preserving national territorial integrity. Government defense measures have been aimed first at maintaining internal order and, second, at supplementing American forces to cope with a conventional invasion—a contingency that has been singularly implausible since the early 1950s. Every Japanese government has supported this narrow definition of security as defense of the home islands, within which there is unlikely to be a clear or present military danger from any country that could not be met by its own modest conventional forces.

The development of the Japanese Self-Defense Forces, despite the fact that they are structured around five-year plans, displays two general characteristics of Japanese foreign policy—a lack of clear, long-term goals involving more independent actions by the nation and an emphasis on domestic over external considerations. The very extensive dependence on the United States has allowed defense plans to develop in a kind of international vacuum, in which the direction and tempo of expansion have been treated more as a budgetary issue than a strategic one—in essence, as kind of weapons procurement review. The extraordinarily modest level of military expenditures—a record completely out of line with comparable expenditures of other industrial powers—has many causes, including political opposition to rearmament and the demands of rapid economic growth. However, the basic causes lie in the dynamics of decision-making and in the low priority (indeed, almost inadvertent attention) that has been accorded the question of external defense. With no independent strategic goals beyond providing a holding operation for the United States, and with no immediate political incentives for establishing such goals, even the limited appropriations requests of the Defense Agency have been grist in the mill of the Finance Ministry and other powerful elements of the bureaucracy, which have reduced them to proportions in line with other ministries' demands.

Within the ruling conservative party, there has been a consensus on the need for the Mutual Security Treaty, the principle of collective defense, the gradual strengthening of the Self-Defense Forces, the education of the public on national defense requirements, and (with some dissent) the preservation of the constitution. Two aspects of the conservative politicians' posture on defense are notable: a reluctance to speak out on the security issue because of potential domestic political repercussions; and a willingness to keep a wide range of policy options open. Because the security issue is such a highly politicized and controversial question within the LDP (as with all the parties), it will inevitably be caught up in factional politics if and when a shift to a new strategic posture is undertaken.

The nature of the foreign-policy-making process in Japan has prevented bold leadership not only on security policy, but on all major questions involving political rather than economic matters. The fragmented structure of the LDP—a style of authority that requires at least tacit consensus among all the responsible participants involved in policy-making (in this case the party faction leaders)—and the extreme degree to which intraparty politics has been involved in all major foreign policy moves have produced a kind of immobilism in conservative decision-making.

Furthermore, the vehement and unqualified opposition of the Japanese Left to a more activist position has discouraged government initiatives by increasing the domestic political risks that would be involved. More recently, the proliferation of opposition parties and the shrinking margin of the conservatives' control of the Diet has further limited the capacity of the government to act. Barring an unexpected reversal of past trends, which would alter the relative strength and modes of operation of the parties, or the sudden emergence of a nationalist consensus, this style of policy formulation will continue to restrain leadership no matter what the personalities or issues of the moment. Further, it will prevent a Gaullist-type move in the direction of a more autonomous political and military role in the world. Rather, basic shifts in security policy, if they occur, will be closely tied to changes in the international milieu, not one independently initiated by policy-makers in Tokyo.

Security has been the central concern to all of the opposition parties, and this has given broad definition to Japanese public opinion as well as structure to the debate in the mass media and intellectual journals regarding the defense question. Despite many differences regarding details, the two most significant effects of the opposition parties' actions have been to fuel anti-American feelings and to give political identity to pacifism. The Left has made Article 9 into the most dramatic symbol of the new constitution, so that aside from the weak and abortive challenges offered by several conservative leaders in the 1950s, the issue of the peace clause has not been directly and effectively raised. In consequence, the government has operated in a pacifist milieu and has been placed continuously on the defensive with respect to all efforts to develop a security policy. As the very legality of the military forces has been vehemently questioned by a portion of the Left, it is not surprising that it has proved difficult for the government to articulate clear and positive national strategic objectives. Above all, the idealism embodied in Article 9 has given all matters of defense a peculiarly moral cast; it has drawn the question of security deeply into the issue of constitutional revision and a consideration of the basic attitudes regarding the very foundations of the postwar political order—reaching even to the relationship between citizen and state. Thus, the emotional and political legacies of Article 9 stand as major imponderables affecting the future direction of Japanese defense policy.

Each of the opposition parties has different reasons for opposing the current military alliance with the United States, but the substantive differences among their respective positions are less important than the overall political effect: to feed protonationalist and anti-American sentiments. Much of the public partisan clamor against the security treaty has been provoked by periodic campaigns to exploit the issue. In a world featuring détente with Communist powers and intensified economic competition among all states, the conservatives will be increasingly vulnerable to attacks leveled against Cold War style dependence on the United States, with such attacks having an implicit nationalistic appeal.

Even a cursory examination of the nature of foreign-policy-making in Japan and the substance of the security debate raise profound doubts about the capacity of Japan to devise a security policy for a world of fluidity, uncertainty, and conflict. The decision-making process is most appropriately described as immobilist, and even under optimal conditions it ensures that Japan proceeds incrementally from one issue to another without a strategic calculus. Beyond the American alliance, there has been no real consideration of strategic options, and the debate over defense policy takes on highly moral and emotional forms. Therefore, any attempt to devise a fresh policy will raise issues challenging the assumptions of the new diplomatic tradition and threatening the stability of the domestic political system. The main result of this situation is to assure a passive role for Japan in foreign affairs, at a time when change and uncertainty have come to characterize both the political and economic dimensions of the international order.

Japanese Security Policies
and the United States

Gerald L. Curtis

In this selection, Gerald Curtis describes recent changes in Japan's defense policy and the major obstacles to continued reform. He argues that a central feature of the Japanese-American relations is maintaining a balance between alliance and autonomy. Recently, the United States has demanded that Japan assume greater responsibility for its own defense. Japanese leaders and their constituents have noted with alarm the decline of American hegemony during the past decade. They have seen that the United States can guarantee neither a stable international currency nor secure energy supplies. They are, therefore, willing to assume more responsibility for defense, but the question is how to do so.

Curtis notes that a substantial effort is already underway to modernize the military in Japan. Recent increases in defense spending are higher than those in Europe. The Japanese defense budget is already large and is growing at a faster rate than the national budget. Per capita outlays for defense are still low and defense as a percentage of the national budget has declined markedly since the 1950s. Nonetheless, there is a growing recognition of the Soviet threat to Japan among political leaders and the public alike.

Despite this recognition and the willingness to face the threat with improved defense capabilities, there are major obstacles (both within Japan and in Asia) to increasing the defense budget. Japanese foreign policy, in general, is characterized by risk minimization and cost analyses. Public opposition to nuclear weapons and adherence to Article Nine make defense a sticky domestic political issue. Additionally, the Southeast Asian nations that remember Japanese militarism during the 1930s and World War II fear a resurgence of Japanese nationalism and a concomitant rise in military adventurism. Finally, the Japanese public will accept no substitution for American power. Consequently, any defense improvements must take place entirely within the context of the U.S.-Japan alliance. Curtis suggests that Japan might further absorb the costs of American troops in Asia, buy more American weapons, and increase its aid to developing nations to secure stable growth and diminish conflict.

Americans who follow trends in Japanese security policies tend to divide into those who see little significant change, particularly in terms of the central importance of the U.S. alliance, and those who believe that Japan is poised to embark on a more assertive and independent course involving independent military capabilities and an important role in regional security. Which view is more nearly correct, and how the balance is struck between autonomy and alliance, are crucially important questions, both in themselves and in terms of U.S.-Japan relations.

There can be little doubt that Japanese thinking has entered a new phase, over the last decade but especially in the past few years, and that the central factor underlying Japanese concern with what has come to called "comprehensive security" is a marked shift in Japanese perceptions and attitudes concerning the United States. In an important and illuminating report for then Prime Minister Ohira, a group of specialists headed by Masamichi Inoki noted this shift in July 1980 in no uncertain terms: "the most fundamental change in the international situation which emerged in the 1970s was the end of American superiority both militarily and economically." No longer could the United States be depended upon to underwrite a stable international currency system, to guarantee Japanese access to energy and raw materials, or to secure Japanese political interests in a stable political order.

Such a view, with sometimes takes the form of an exaggerated perception of American weakness and decline, has been reflected to some extent in Japanese policy—in its relations with the Association of Southeast Asian Nations (ASEAN), in its Arab tilt after the 1973 oil boycott, in the new interest in military defense, and in the willingness of some of its leaders to express their views more forthrightly than in the past on a variety of international issues.

But the perception of the end of the age of *pax Americana* has not yet had a more fundamental impact on Japanese security policies. This is not particularly surprising. Declining confidence in the credibility of American support does not necessarily lead to a desire to abandon it. As Fritz Stern recently wrote of West Germany's leadership, mainstream Japanese leaders—however apprehensive about American policy they may be—are not ready "to commit suicide out of a fear of death." Few but the most extreme elements on the Right and the Left favor a Japanese security policy independent of the U.S. security treaty structure.

Moreover, the shift in attitudes toward the United States has not yet worked its way through the political system. Public opinion is not ready for new bold policy directions, nor is there a clear sense of the options available to Japan. Thus there is an ambivalence in attitudes about the United States, a fluidity in current Japanese thinking about security, and a tentative and limited quality to the consensus that presently prevails.

Furthermore, caution, a risk-minimizing orientation to international political affairs, and a conviction that more costs than benefits would result from a major military role that would move beyond a limited conception of conventional self-defense remain keynotes of Japanese foreign policy. But there is also a new assertiveness that arises not simply from an awareness of the country's economic power but from a new sense of confidence in the strength of the nation's economic, social, and political institutions and in the Japanese way of doing things. The feeling that Japan should "do something" in international affairs more than doggedly pursue its own economic self-interest has become widespread. But agreement about what than "something" should be has yet to be forged....

[T]he specific issues of Japan's own defense posture have now engaged the wider Japanese public. Both Japanese leaders and the public at large are giving military issues more serious though than has been true for many years, with matters long treated as taboo more openly discussed, and with movement toward a strengthening of Japan's military capabilities.

Overall, support for the security treaty and for the existence and gradual strengthening of the self-defense forces has markedly increased. The political opposition has now for the most part accepted the treaty and recognized the legitimacy of the self-defense forces. Even the Socialist Party has moved to a position of defending the status quo, though it retains a formal commitment to unarmed neutrality in its official doctrine. But growing support for a Japanese defense role still leaves the crucial issue of how much, and how fast, Japan should expand its defense capabilities, and this question has generated enormous public controversy. Public opinion surveys show increasing public support for a strengthening of the self-defense forces but they also show an increase in support for Article Nine of the constitution— and they give no indication of change about desirable priorities in government expenditures, which still overwhelmingly favor increased social welfare-related programs and a limited defense budget.

Within mainstream Japanese leadership opinion, one can identify three major viewpoints concerning Japan's defense policy. One group sees a growing Soviet threat, diminishing U.S. power and credibility, and the opportunity and desirability for Japan to develop its own *autonomous defense* and to move away from what is perceived as a subordinate relationship to the United States. Another, well reflected in the Inoki commission report cited above, argues that the Soviet threat is real and that Japan can and should do more to contain it *by gradually increasing defensive capabilities within the context of the U.S.-Japan alliance,* an alliance essential to securing Japan's national interests. A third group adopts a *minimal response* position, arguing that the major threats to Japanese interests come not from the Soviet Union but from the vulnerabilities inherent in an economy totally dependent on outside sources for its food, energy and raw material supplies, that Japan's most important relationship is the one with the United States, and the Japan's defense buildup therefore should be the minimum necessary to avoid a crisis in Japanese-American relations.

Among these three groups, it is largely the views of the minimal response group, well represented in the bureaucracy and among the political leadership, that have been most influential in formulating Japanese defense policy to date. But the balance has been shifting. The Afghanistan invasion in particular appears to have reinforced and made more widespread Japanese awareness of the essentiality of the U.S. alliance for Japan's well-being, hence weakening at least at the current time the appeal of the supporters of autonomous defense and strengthening the position of those who advocate greater Japanese efforts within the U.S. alliance context.

However, one should not exaggerate the degree of movement toward a more forthcoming defense posture or underestimate the domestic opposition to major departures in Japan's defense policy. Voices within the conservative establishment that have for a long spoken of the desirability of Japan developing greater military power are now heard more loudly but, contrary to the impression conveyed in much of the Western press reporting on the Japanese defense debate, they remain a minority within leadership circles and obtain little support among the population at large. There is not much evidence that Japan can be pressured to do considerably more in expanding its defense capabilities than it currently plans to do, or that the deterioration in the international security environment that was both symbolized and furthered by the invasion of Afghanistan will shock Japan into doing more.

For one thing, many Japanese leaders feel that they are already making a substantial effort. The real rate of increase in defense expenditures over the past decade has been higher than that of America's European allies, not to mention the United States itself, and in 1980 and 1981 the increase in spending on defense was higher than the increase in the budget as a whole. Japan now contributes more than $1 billion annually to the costs of U.S. forces in Japan, and its forces are involved to an unprecedented degree in joint military exercises with the United States, including maritime self-defense force participation in 1980 for the first time in a Rim of the Pacific (RIMPAC) exercise that involved Canada, Australia and New Zealand as well as the United States.

Furthermore, the absolute size of the Japanese defense budget is large and the proportion going for procurement of new weapons and other equipment has been rising considerably faster than the increase in the total defense budget. Personnel expenses have declined from 56 percent of the budget in 1976 to 49.3 percent in 1980 while the budget share for procurement rose in the same period from 16.4 percent to 20.7 percent. The proportion of the defense budget allotted to personnel expenses can be expected to fall a little further assuming a continuation of a pattern of moderate wage increases for government employees (as well as in the private sector) and no major increases in the size of the land self-defense forces.

But it is equally evident that Japanese defense efforts, even in the aftermath of Afghanistan, have been extremely limited. While it is true that in fiscal year 1980 Japan spent approximately ten billion dollars on defense, making it number eight in the world in terms of absolute outlays, this amounted to only 0.90 percent of gross national product (GNP) and translates into a per capita expense of $87 compared to $520 for the United States and $396 for West Germany. The Japanese defense budget has quadrupled in the past ten years (from 569.5 billion yen in 1970 to 2230.2 billion yen in 1980), a growth rate averaging seven percent annually in real terms, but defense expenditures as a percentage of the national budget have steadily declined (from 13.61 percent in 1955 to 7.16 percent in 1970 and 5.24 percent in 1980).

The Suzuki government, prior to the Ministry of Finance compilation of a draft budget for the fiscal year 1981, announced that the Defense Agency would seek a 9.7 percent increase in its budget compared to the 6.5 percent increase it received in 1980 and an MOF ceiling of 7.2 percent for other ministry requests for increases in the 1981 budget. But when the budget finally was compiled it contain an increase of only 7.6 percent for the Defense Agency. On the one hand, this is the first time in the postwar period that the percentage increase in the defense budget was as large as that for social welfare-related programs, cut from a 9.8 percent increase in 1980 to 7.6 percent in the proposed 1981 budget. But is also is only the second time in recent years (1980 was the first) that the annual increase in defense expenditures will have fallen below ten percent. This makes it doubtful that Japan will achieve the buildup goals specified in the Defense Agency's 1979 midterm program estimates even with the five years originally projected, much less in four years as the Carter Administration had been urging. . . .

How to approach the issue of Japan's defense is one of the central questions facing the new U.S. Administration. It is not that the defense issue has not suddenly emerged as a potential source of friction in the Japanese-American relationship; it has been a troublesome one throughout the postwar period. But in the 1950s and roughly through the middle of the 1960s Americans generally assumed that they could afford to pay for Japan's "free ride"; and in the 1970s, with the United States preoccupied with economic issues in its bilateral dealing with Japan, differences over the issue of Japan's defense efforts were seen largely as a "spillover" effect of frustrations created by the intense quality of many of the economic disputes that characterized the relationship. But in the 1980s, given Japan's economic strength and the United States' economic problems, the increase in the Soviet Union's military power relative to that of the United States, and almost certain American demands on NATO countries to make greater military efforts, the issue of Japan's defense policy is likely to come into its own. If not carefully managed, it could result in a reverse "spillover"—with Japanese resistance to demands for a greater military effort adversely affecting American, and most particularly congressional, attitudes toward Japan not only on defense but on other issues in the relationship as well.

How far, and in what terms, is it reasonable for the United States to press Japan on this issue? Let us look first at two fundamental judgments that have long guided the thinking of successive American administrations—and which I believe remain basically correct today.

The first of these is that a major and rapid Japanese expansion of military capabilities and a broadened definition of the mission of the self-defense forces to give them a regional security role would represent a fundamental reordering of the power balance in East Asia in ways that would not only raise the level of tensions with the Soviet Union but also arouse fears among other Asian countries about Japanese intentions. Although the non-communist countries in the region are no longer as fearful as they once were of a Japanese military role per se, I believe they would view with intense apprehension any Japanese effort to play a regional role.

Secondly, welcomed or not, the Japanese simply are not going to play this kind of regional role, at least not for several year to come. People who argue that the Japanese are poised for a military takeoff and who see the possibility for constitutional revision in the near-term are either engaging in wishful thinking or are giving more credit for influence than is deserved to a highly vocal minority element in the Japanese conservative camp.

I would maintain that the only conceivable development that would galvanize Japanese public opinion to support a greatly expanded military role would be a radical decline in American strength and commitments and an almost total collapse of American credibility. One hardly need note that there would be nothing more destabilizing to the security of the East Asian region than the spread of such perceptions. In Japan they would strengthen the advocates of autonomous defense rather than the supporters of a close U.S. alliance, they would result in policies that would raise the level of threats to Japan, and given the fact that they would be premised on and made possible by the decline in American power, they would be part of a general deterioration in the security environment in East Asia.

It follows that the United States should avoid policies and postures that deliberately or inadvertently encourage declining confidence in American commitments and contribute to an exaggerated perception of U.S. weakness. It is for this reason in particular that proposals such as having the Japanese build two aircraft carriers and lend-lease them to the United States are less than attractive. Neither Japan nor other Asian countries would be reassured by the presence in the region of two carriers under the command of a country that did not have the ability to mobilize the economic resources or the political consensus necessary to build them. There is, after all, no substitute for American power in the region. Japan can supplement but not substitute for it, and though this is not always an easy distinction to make, it is an important one to maintain to the extent possible in considering East Asian security and Japan's role in it.

Overall, a slow and steady increase in Japan's military expenditures, directed to the strengthening of its air and naval defense capabilities in particular, would in my view serve U.S. interests well. Of course, Japan could do more to speed up the implementation of its defense expansion plans— especially to improve its mining, patrol, surveillance and anti-submarine warfare capabilities and its air defenses—and bilateral consultations to seek ways to increase areas of cooperation between American and Japanese forces in the sea and air spaces surrounding Japan should be pursued. But it seems to me doubtful that much would be gained by visible American pressure for a more rapid development of Japanese military capabilities.

There are of course other contribution Japan could make. While the Status of Forces Agreement between Japan and the United States does not oblige Japan to do more than it currently is doing to pay costs for maintaining American forces in Japan, it does not preclude them from doing more. Further Japanese financial support for maintaining these forces would be an important contribution to the alliance. Japan also could do more in the way of buying "off the shelf" American weapons systems and other necessary material rather than emphasizing, as current policy does, licensing arrangements and expanded domestic production.

Japan also could make more generous contributions than it has so far in non-military aspects of comprehensive security, in the area of economic assistance, for example, or in massive investments in large-scale projects to develop new energy resources. In 1980 Japan allotted 0.31 percent of GNP to official development assistance. Though this was a sizeable increase over the previous year's 0.26 percent, it still left Japan below the 0.36 percent average for the countries in the Development Assistance Committee of the OECD; even present Japanese government plans to double official assistance in the five-year period from 1981 to 1985, given current projections of Japanese economic growth rates during this period, are not likely to result in a significant increase in the percentage of GNP Japan allocates to assisting the less-developed world.

But by all odds the most constructive step the Reagan Administration could take, in my judgment, would be to encourage the Japanese to define their security role for themselves. And this gets back to the importance of engaging Japanese leaders more fully in careful consultations about regional and global security matters. The objective, in other words, should be to change a deeply entrenched postwar pattern of Japanese-American security relations, in which Japanese leaders ask the United States what it wants them to do and then, after feeding this American "demand" through the domestic political system, emerge with a "concession" that leaves everyone dissatisfied and resentful.

This is a pattern that cannot be changed suddenly—both side have been too comfortable with it for too long. But it is a patter that, if continued, can only lead to increasingly serious difficulties and misunderstandings. And, above all, it is a pattern that simply does not accord with the realities of Japan's present power. Rather, with both countries still deeply committed to the alliance relationship, it is time for Japan to formulate its security policies, not on the basis of responses to the United States asking, or pressing, Japan to do more to "help" a weakening America, but in terms of how the world's two wealthiest democracies can cooperate to secure their mutual and common interests.

I do not mean to underestimate the difficulties involved in moving in this direction. The postwar relationship, after all, has been an exceedingly successful one and the temptation for the leaders of both countries to stick to time-tested approaches in dealing with each other remains strong. But surely there can be little doubt that new approaches are called for if the security policies of both countries are to evolve within the context of a healthy alliance relationship.

58

China's Military Power
in the 1980s

June Teufel Dreyer

China has the world's largest standing army, but it is an army possessed of antiquated weapons, outmoded battle tactics, and low morale. Defense modernization, one of the four modernizations pursued by the post-Mao leadership, is a low priority. And, as Dreyer argues in this selection, the failure to pay attention to defense modernization has exacerbated conflicts between military and civilian leaders, between military and civilian populations, and within the military itself.

Recent economic reforms in agriculture have lowered the attractiveness of a military career for rural youth, once the backbone of the People's Liberation Army (PLA). The inclusion of four generals in the trials of Cultural Revolution leaders has further diminished the status of the military in Chinese society. Military interventions in factories and schools during the Cultural Revolution, and the usurpation by military commanders of civilian housing and other commodities angered many civilians. Mass demonstrations have been staged to force the military to return housing space and other goods commandeered during the chaos of the Cultural Revolution. And such demonstrations of popular discontent have only intensified conflicts within the military over strategic doctrine, technological modernization, and the adaptation of Mao's military principles to contemporary geopolitical realities.

The immediate future looks no better. Although some progress has been made in cost-cutting measures such as weapons maintenance and although morale has improved with recent wage hikes, the military still suffers from lack of funds. The present leadership plans to trim the PLA by as many as one million men. This will reduce costs as well as weaken leftist opposition that is centered in the PLA. Moreover, under the draft constitution of 1982, the military has been placed firmly under government control. This is partially a precondition for the upcoming purge of leftists and partially a result of military demonstrations that Dreyer identifies as a threat to the civilian political leadership. Finally, popular discontent with the military is still being voiced through plays, poems, and other forms of demonstration. As Dreyer points out, such animosity is especially striking in a country that once revered its military as a revolutionary model.

The PRC's armed forces are in a state of flux. There is general agreement in China on the need for military modernization, but less accord on pace, direction, and funding. In recent years, the Chinese elite has argued over questions of strategic doctrine, procurement, organizational structure, size, training methods, recruitment practices, and the relationship of the military to the Communist Party and the civilian population. How these debates are resolved will have a profound effect on the character of the armed forces, their capabilities against various adversaries, and, therefore, on the potential effectiveness of military cooperation with the United States.

SIZE AND STATUS OF FORCES

Not surprisingly, the world's most populous country maintains the world's largest armed forces, approximately 4.5 million persons. The overwhelming majority, 3.6 million, are enlisted in the army. Though small by comparison, China's navy (360,000) and air force (490,000) rank third in manpower size after those of the Soviet Union and the United States. The three services are known collectively as the People's Liberation Army (PLA), which itself is backed by an armed militia estimated to be between twelve and fifteen million people strong.

The PLA's numerical superiority must, however, be balanced against its technological weaknesses. Weapons are mainly copies of much older Soviet models. While some Chinese equipment has been updated, much is still twenty to thirty years behind the state-of-the-art. The country's infrastructure remains weak, and its economy is fragile. China's ground forces are hampered by a lack of mobility, and much of the country's artillery is not self-propelled and must be hauled by draft animals. There is also a shortage of armor.

The PRC's navy is mainly a coastal defense force. Its guided missile patrol boats, though numerous, are vulnerable to electronic countermeasures, and its submarines, to antisubmarine warfare. Chinese warships and submarines rarely venture beyond the PRC's territorial waters.

The air force possesses large numbers of combat aircraft, although the obsolescent avionics with which most are equipped would make fighting at night or in poor weather conditions very difficult. Most navigation is visual.

Design problems have thus far plagued the development of aircraft capable of achieving supersonic speeds. The PRC's ground-based air defense system, despite considerable upgrading during the United States-Vietnam war, has serious weaknesses. The PLA air force was probably weaker in the 1970s than it was in the 1950s.

The PRC possesses a modest nuclear capability. It successfully tested an ICBM, designated the CSS-X-4, in May 1980, though its deployment is believed to be several years in the future. IRBMs were deployed in the mid-1970s, giving China the capability of striking targets throughout the Soviet Union and much of Asia. Although China is not capable of launching a successful first strike against the Soviet Union or the United States, its own missile sites are well-concealed, and an adversary is unlikely to succeed in a preemptive strike against China. . . .

OBSTACLES TO THE MODERNIZATION
OF CHINA'S NATIONAL DEFENSE

Because of China's precarious military situation, national defense was one of the "four modernizations," the program of economic development first enunciated in 1975 and pursued since Mao's death in 1976. How fast the PRC will attempt to close the technological gap between it and its neighbors is another question. Clearly, a shift in leadership and policy that took a Maoist direction would, for the military spell a greater emphasis on "people" (politics) than on "weapons." Whatever the policy line, the overall state of China's economy sets limits on investment in new military hardware.

Even assuming leadership continuity and moderate economic growth, military modernization will probably be slowed by conflict between military leaders and civilian leaders, between the military and the civilian population, and with the military itself.

Military vs. Civilian Leaders

The most significant bone of contention in this arena, and perhaps the most enduring, is financial. National defense was given lowest priority in the "four modernizations" program, although apparently only after a good deal of internal debate during which some, but not all, PLA leaders came to accept that defense must depend upon the overall modernization of the economy.

Problems in the civilian economy further lowered the priority given to military modernization. The ambitious effort of the immediate post-Mao period to expand heavy industry rapidly caused economic imbalances, inflationary pressures, and large deficits in the government budget. In 1979, the leadership embarked on a three-year program of "readjustment," which was recently extended to five years. This retrenchment involves a good deal of budget-cutting, with adverse effects on the modernization of defense. . . .

Although the brunt of the cuts will fall on personnel, these cuts are also expected to affect the amount spent on weapons. An August 1981 news release noted that budgetary restrictions will "temporarily affect" Chinese efforts to build warships. The PRC's ability to purchase arms from the West will, of course, be further restricted.

Austerity in personnel expenditures has already adversely affected PLA morale. There have been complaints from the ranks about the problems of primitive barracks and poor diet. Soldiers are also grumbling about having to make do with substandard equipment that is apt to malfunction—there are almost no funds for manufacturing new weapons or for inspecting old ones. The government has curtailed certain privileges traditionally extended to soldiers' dependents (who for the most part live in the countryside), causing serious hardships in some cases. In another cost-cutting measure, the PLA recently demobilized a large number of troops, many of whom were unable to find jobs. One thousand such disgruntled and angry veterans reportedly demonstrated on Hainan Island during the winter of 1980, demanding jobs. And in a neighboring county of Guangdon (Kwangtung) province, an estimated 3,000 jobless demobilized servicemen, who called themselves the "Disillusioned Army," staged a revolt. Several months later, troop cutbacks totalling one million persons were announced.

The PLA is also at odds with the civilian leadership over several political issues that the politicians regard as evidence of "leftism within the army." First is the treatment of Mao's legacy, which the PLA has generally regarded as close to sacrosanct. The Deng leadership has sponsored a massive educational campaign in the military to counter that view. Military cadres of the Nanjing (Nanking) Military Region, for example, were told that the "main trouble of a considerable number of cadres" stemmed from "their erroneous concept that to emancipate their minds [a Dengist slogan] means to chop off Chairman Mao's banner." Other cadres were told: "We would be defeated in battle if we cherished and retained outmoded concepts. . . . We should apply Chairman Mao's thinking in a flexible way, emancipate out thinking, dare to break away from old conventions, study the new situation, and solve new problems."

A second point of conflict is the regime's current economic policies of instituting material incentives and bonuses in factories, and encouraging share-cropping as an alternative to collective farming. Many in the military regard these approaches as insufficiently socialistic. Also, the new rural policies damage troop morale and complicate recruiting, because they benefit those peasant families with the greatest number of able-bodied workers. There is now more money to be made in the countryside than in the PLA. Another traditional fringe benefit of military service—the right to switch one's registration permit from countryside to city at the time of demobilization—has also been suspended, further reducing the appeal of military service for a number of potential recruits. The Deng leadership, determined to stem the flow of rural people into urban areas whose economies cannot efficiently absorb them, cancelled this privilege. Urban young people have been unenthusiastic about filling the gap left by rural youth, and it is not clear that they would be acceptable substitutes in any case. Although better educated than their rural peers, city-bred young people are regarded as less suited to the rigors of military life as well as less amenable to discipline. There are also fewer of them. Not surprisingly, the 1981 draft failed to attract high-quality recruits for the first time in history.

Third, some in the PLA objected to Deng Xiaoping's revival of the "Lin Biao (Lin Piao) clique" as an object of political criticism, along with the "gang of four." Lin, the former defense minister who died in 1971 while allegedly plotting a coup against Mao Zedong, had already been subject to intense criticism in the early 1970s. Publicly trying five elderly generals, who were purged in the wake of Lin's death, along with the notorious "gang" was particularly insulting. The trial also sparked rumors of a massive purge involving the estimated two-fifths of the PLA who are alleged to have fallen under Lin Biao's influence. This group is thought to include several high-ranking military leaders who were promoted during the years of the Cultural Revolution. Anger at Deng Xiaoping's efforts to remove Hua Guofeng (Hua Kuo-feng) as Party chairman reportedly caused a PLA unity located in the Peking Military Region to plan a rebellion; other, officially confirmed rebellions have occurred in Guangdong, to the south, and in Xinjiang, in the far northwest. Fears that these may prove the precursors of other PLA moves against the government persist.

The Military vs. Civilian Population

Many Chinese—how many it is impossible to say—have come to believe that the military has garnered excessive privileges over the past three decades. Among the ones that are most resented are those that were acquired during the Cultural Revolution. The army was the only force capable of restoring order during this chaotic period and it was able, as a result, to greatly improve its position vis-a-vis civilian society.

Control over housing is one example of conflict. In 1969, PLA units were ordered into factories and schools to quell factional fighting. In the process, troop units took over dormitories attached to those institutions. In many cases the troops never vacated the premises, even after military personnel gave up day-to-day leadership in those units in the early 1970s. Civilians certainly did not appreciate this aggravation of urban China's chronic housing shortage.

The army intervened again in civilian politics in the wake of the brief period of democratization introduced by Deng Xiaoping in late 1978. When local public security forces and militia were unable to cope with the breakdown in social order that occurred when individuals pushed the new freedoms beyond the limits the government was willing to tolerate, army troops were ordered to patrol the major cities of China. Members of the democracy movement resented this restraint of their activities; other resented the almost inevitable instances of excesses of PLA authority.

Resentment took many forms, from the literary to the violent. Poetry criticized corruption and extravagance within the PLA elite, and controversial Shanghai play portrayed the evils of excessive military privilege. In Peking, over 2,000 students shouting "down with militarism" protested the army's refusal to end its decade-long occupation of several campus buildings. In Guangshou (Canton), the army was persuaded to vacate premises, claimed by the provincial people's congress, that it had occupied over fifteen years before.

By itself, the erosion of popular support for the fighting forces will not hinder the modernization of the PLA. But it is not insignificant in a country that proclaims officially that "the army is the fish and the people are the water," and that without the water the people could not survive.

The PLA seems to have nursed some resentment of its own. It cannot have been happy about having to abandon its accustomed quarters, particularly since equivalent alternative facilities are unlikely to be available. And military units performing tasks that benefit civilians (defense industries are turning out consumer goods, for example) are dragging their feet. Indeed, a PLA construction and engineering corps that had been ordered to construct buildings for civilian use had to be prodded to complete the task. Clearly the move to reduce the number of privileges accorded the PLA, coupled with the assignment of non-military tasks to military units, has negatively affected the PLA's self-image and inevitably detracted from improving the PLA's military capabilities.

Conflict Within the Military

Although the majority of the PLA appears to accept the need for modernization of both strategic doctrine and weapons technology, substantial disagreements remain on how best to accomplish these goals.

An important area of disagreement is over whether to reinstitute military ranks, which were abolished on Mao's orders in 1965. Yang Dezhi, chief of the PLA's general staff, declared in an August 1981 speech that: "In order to strengthen the modernization program in the army, we are planning the reinstate a system of military ranks." This part of Yang's statement was broadcast in the Chinese-language transmission of the official New China News Agency. But it was deleted from an otherwise identical English-language translation broadcast a few hours later, and from a "corrected" Chinese version issued the next day. Apart from the stimulus that the reintroduction of ranks is expected to have on military morale, proponents of the reintroduction of rank consider that the increased specialization that a rank system would allow is an important part of the military modernization process.

Another subject of debate has been the geographic allocation of China's defense forces, specifically whether the defense of Xinjiang should be given equal or lower priority than the defense of the northeast. In typical Chinese fashion, the controversy has been waged through allegorical articles purporting to deal with a superficially similar debate between the nineteenth-century officials Li Hongzhang (Li Hung-chang) and Zuo Zongtan (Tso Tsung-t'ang).

Third, while most PLA commanders can agree on the need to adapt Mao Zedong's military theories to modern conditions, there exist many differences on which particular concepts should be modified and in what ways they should be changed. For example, some military leaders doubt the wisdom of replacing the strategy of luring enemies deep with one of forward defense, fearing that PLA troops will be surrounded and destroyed.

Finally, differences of opinion are inevitable on a wide spectrum of other, technical military options. These include command, control and communication equipment, target acquisition and fire control systems, strategic and tactical reconnaissance systems, systems to counter atomic, biological, and chemical warfare, logistical support and mobility, and the entire range of modern battlefield support systems. Such differences can, of course, be resolved. But in the present context of limited resources, compromise will not be quick, easy or without complex factional conflict. In the process, military modernization will be retarded.

REMOVING OBSTACLES TO MILITARY MODERNIZATION

China's leaders are well aware of the problems facing the PLA and the military modernization process, and have sought to deal with them in a variety of ways. In an apparent attempt to strengthen central leadership and reduce tendencies toward regional military independence, in late 1979 and early 1980, Deng Xiaoping transferred the commanders of nine of China's eleven military regions and engineered a series of other changes in the upper echelons of the PLA as well. Deng also succeeded in having his personal choice, Geng Biao, appointed minister of defense, although opposition from within the PLA apparently delayed the appointment by a full six months. The new state constitution, which was introduced in draft form during the spring of 1982, put the military more firmly under government control by subordinating it to a central military council whose chairperson is responsible to the National People's Congress and who may not serve for more than two consecutive five-year terms. Meanwhile, newspaper articles and discussion sessions enjoined the military to "avoid endless quibbling over matters of the past, ... observe discipline, and consciously defend the Party's unity."

During the summer of 1981, the PLA's General Political Department issued a fourteen-point document designed to improve relationships between the military, the government, and civilians. It contained directives forbidding the military to construct unauthorized buildings, and admonishing PLA personnel on guard duty to be polite to civilians. The need for better relations between the army and the people formed a major focus of speeches on Army Day (August 1) 1981, although traditionally the theme of army-civilian ties has been emphasized only at the time of the spring festival (traditional Chinese New Year).

Other measures were aimed at softening the army leadership's reputation for arrogance. In a ritual show of humility, army leaders were publicized doing hard physical labor "in an effort to perform good services for the people." Commanders have also been ordered to take public trains or car pools to their meetings rather than forming majestic convoys with one officer per military vehicle, as in the past.

At the other end of the military hierarchy, efforts are being made to alleviate some of the difficulties facing the rank-and-file. In several instances, measures have been taken to improve the worst of long-standing problems among certain units, including such basic issues as improperly constructed barracks, the lack of fresh drinking water, and inadequate food supplies. Plans have also been announced to transport demobilized soldiers and, where possible, new recruits, via passenger train rather than in boxcars as had been the case heretofore. And at least one area has instituted courses to prepare demobilized army cadres for jobs in civilian life.

In a further move to improve military morale, large parades—the first of their kind since 1959—were held in honor of Army Day. During the following month, military exercises, said to be the largest held since the founding of the PRC, were conducted near Peking. Heavily publicized and lavishly praised by the media, they were reviewed by virtually all of the PRC's top party, government, and military leaders. An accompanying article in the official army newspaper stressed that "the army must be regularized in order to be modernized," and for the first time, army, navy, and air force units were identified separately rather than collectively referred to as the PLA.

CONCLUSION

China's leaders have devised these and other well-conceived schemes to reduce dissension, create harmony, and alleviate problems to the maximum degree possible given the minimal funds available. However, there are no easy solutions to many of the problems connected with military modernization, and the solution to one problem may in fact exacerbate another. One case in point is the demobilization of large numbers of veteran soldiers. While desirable in that it reduces personnel costs and produces a younger, more energetic fighting force, the demobilization has also produced a large number of disgruntled, unemployed persons. They have a deleterious effect on military morale and a proven capacity to disrupt the social order. Moreover, they must compete with civilians for the few available jobs, thus aggravating civilmilitary tensions. . . .

[A]lthough the Chinese leadership has introduced timely and appropriate measures to effect military modernization during a time of financial stringency, their effect on battlefield performance is apt to be marginal, and it is unlikely that there will be a significant improvement in the PRC's military capabilities before the end of the decade. One analyst, writing in the winter of 1979–80, before the magnitude of the military budget cuts became obvious, stated that, even with substantial Western help, the chances were not good that weapons systems and defense technologies could be incorporated soon enough to meet the PRC's pressing security needs. He predicted that it could be the late 1980s or even beyond before the technology of the early to mid-1970s could be adequately introduced into the Chinese armed forces. Since the potential for xenophobic backlash is always present he maintained that "the qualitative gaps between indigenous output and the state-of-the-art will remain at least ten years."

The array of problems facing military modernization has become greater since this best-case scenario was written. Although some improvement in the PLA's training methods and technical proficiencies should result from the palliative measures discussed above, it is entirely likely that the gap between Chinese military capabilities and those of the Soviet Union will widen rather than narrow by the end of the decade. Much will depend on the leadership's ability to achieve levels of economic growth high enough to enable a gradual rise in civilian living standards while expanding China's industrial base and easing the pressure on the PRC's military budget. Given such factors as the population-land ratio, the less than enthusiastic mood of the population, and the existence of considerable disagreement within the leadership on how to proceed, it seems unlikely that China can succeed in achieving high enough economic growth rates to permit an escape from this impasse in military modernization.

Unit XV

—————— Foreign Policy ——————

The foreign policies of both China and Japan are in a state of continual flux. Many of the most recent changes can be traced to the 1971 visit by President Nixon to the People's Republic. That event marked the return of China to the global political arena and led the Japanese to reconsider their role in the American-led Western alliance. While relations between the two Asian powers are warm, the problems that each faces require difficult political choices which could alter their relationship.

Japan has been a member of the Western alliance since 1945. Its devastated postwar economy was in fact rebuilt with American aid. Its constitution was written by Occupation forces under the direction of General Douglas MacArthur. Many of its cultural styles have been imported from the United States. And its security, until quite recently, was perceived by Japanese leaders to be entirely a matter of American protection.

In 1971, however, Japanese leaders began to reconsider their ties with the United States. President Nixon's surprise visit to China shocked the Japanese. This first "Nixon shock" was soon followed by a second jolt when the President announced import restrictions and currency regulations that would have a significant impact on Japanese economic performance. The lack of consultation from its ally revealed a vulnerability to American actions that concerned Japanese political leaders. Their response was to begin considering a more independent and autonomous foreign policy, yet one that would operate within the structure of the American alliance.

Japan's allegiance to the American alliance was weakened, however, by the impact of the oil crises of the 1970s. Clearly, America could no longer guarantee Japan's oil supplies. In fact, American leaders used Japan's vulnerability to cutoffs in energy supplies to argue for an enhanced military role for Japan in protecting the East Asian sealanes. The Soviet invasion of Afghanistan intensified American pressure for increased Japanese defense spending. The Japanese leadership is now confronted with the problem of having to increase military spending despite opposition from both domestic groups and other Asian nations.

Although the Japanese have been slow to increase their military power, this does not mean that they are not anxious to assume a more active role in world affairs. Japan's economic success has been and will continue to be greatly dependent on a stable international environment—that is, one that is conducive to trade. Yet, the Japanese still have some distance to go before their global political role will match their global economic role. Since the Nixon visit of 1971 and the oil crises of 1973 and 1978, the Japanese have made efforts to expand their relations with Europe, Southeast Asia, the Arab countries, and the Third World. And in this respect, as much as in any other, they resemble the Chinese.

The Chinese have long maintained that the Second and Third World nations—that is, industrialized states like Great Britain and Japan and underdeveloped states like China—are equally vulnerable to and exploited by the two superpowers, the United States and the Soviet Union. Since the mid-1950s, China has advocated that Second and Third World nations seek improved communications and relations to jointly struggle against superpower domination. In fact, China proposed to lead the Third World in the pursuit of that objective.

In the early 1960s, however, China grew further and further distant from the USSR. This development was a result of political disagreements between the two states, problems in their economies and economic relations, and Mao's belief that the Soviet Union's leaders were restoring capitalism or "revisionism" in the USSR. The Sino-Soviet split left China with few allies other than the developing states. Diplomatic interaction declined even more precipitously with the advent of the Cultural Revolution and its emphasis on "self-reliance" and xenophobia. For many years, China was almost totally inactive in international forums and in the global economy.

After the Nixon visit in 1971, China emerged as a politically divided, militarily weak, and economically underdeveloped country, unsure of its international role. Border disputes in 1969 with the Soviet Union had clearly exposed China's vulnerability to invasion and defeat. Economic stagnation seemed unavoidable without massive inputs of foreign technology. Chinese leaders tried to strengthen relations with the U.S., other Western nations, and Japan, and such initiatives caused a great deal of conflict between Maoists and their opponents. And openness to the West continues to be a problem for the Chinese leadership today. Some Chinese leaders perceive the West to be a source of "spiritual pollution," and fear the corruption of Chinese society by Western capitalist values. For this and other reasons, there is an uncertain future for the foreign policy of tilting toward the West that has been carried out since 1971.

The Chinese had counted on American might to offset the expanding influence and "hegemonism" of the Soviet Union. However, problems over technology transfers, arms sales, and the future of Taiwan have somewhat soured the Sino-American relationship. While a return to the Sino-Soviet alliance is unlikely, the Chinese have sought to improve relations with the Soviet Union and pursue a more balanced posture toward the two superpowers as a means of solving their conflicts with Vietnam and of coping with the demands of regimes in North Korea and Cambodia. They have also hoped to once again appeal to the Third World and Second World states, such as Japan, for greater cooperation in achieving their goals.

These developments portend an alteration in Sino-Japanese relations as well. As the Chinese move closer to the Soviets and the Japanese respond to American demands for increased military spending, there is the possibility that the two neighbors will find themselves divided by international alliances. Yet, the economies of the two countries are so complementary as to balance that possibility with the alternative of increasingly close cooperation in the fields of technology, research, and production. The Japanese have always depended more on economic than political criteria to formulate foreign policy. And the Chinese have now rejected the Maoist idea of placing "politics in command." Thus it is unlikely that their complementary needs will be easily frustrated by superpower conflicts.

This unit's readings focus on various aspects of Chinese and Japanese foreign policy as well as on the major issues involved in foreign policymaking in each country in the 1980s. In "China's International Posture: Signs of Change," A. Doak Barnett describes how China's relations with the United States and the Soviet Union have changed in recent years, arguing that the present stalemate between the U.S. and the USSR has forced the Chinese to assume a more flexible international posture. In "China and the Great Power Triangle," Gerald Segal traces the evolution of China's postwar foreign policy from a bipolar approach based on its alliance with the USSR to a more balanced, tripolar strategy, with itself as the third leg in the power triangle.

J. A. A. Stockwin discusses the major features of Japan's postwar foreign policy in "Issues of Foreign Policy and Defense." Arguing that the so-called "Nixon shocks" of the early 1970s marked a turning point in Japanese foreign policy, Stockwin describes the series of events that forced Japan to reevaluate its foreign policies, particularly its alliance with the U.S., and to begin seeking a more autonomous means of operating in the global arena. In "Japan's Foreign Policies," Gerald L. Curtis examines Japan's current relations with China and the Soviet Union, noting that Sino-Japanese relations have steadily improved and expanded since the early 1970s. Japan's relations with the Soviet Union are not so warm. In fact, says Curtis, they are marked by caution, suspicion, and distrust, and are conditioned at least in part by political concerns arising from the U.S.–Japanese alliance.

59

China's International Posture:
Signs of Change

A. Doak Barnett

China's relations with the United States and the Soviet Union have changed in recent years. In this selection, Barnett argues that the present stalemate between the U.S. and the USSR has forced the Chinese to assume a more flexible international posture. Underlying this change is the recognition that the U.S. is a power in decline while the USSR is a power in ascendance. The Chinese have thus moved away from uncritical support of U.S. foreign policy toward a more critical appraisal of its policies. Similarly, China has softened its criticism of the Soviet Union and maintained silence on such issues as the Polish Workers Movement, Solidarity. The biggest shift however, according to Barnett, has been the renewed Chinese emphasis on the theory of Three Worlds. China is attempting once again to position itself as a leader of the undeveloped countries. It has been outspoken in defense of Third World demands for a new international economic order and the redistribution of wealth between "northern" and "southern" hemispheric states. To Barnett, this signifies a shift back to China's "united front" policies, including an alliance between Second World developed states and Third World undeveloped nations. Still, relations with the U.S. are important. Despite political conflicts over arms sales to Taiwan, the Chinese leadership hopes for the continued expansion and improvement of U.S.–Chinese economic relations.

INTRODUCTION

During 1981–82, there have been serious strains in US–China relations over the issue of arms sales to Taiwan. During this same period, at least some Chinese leaders seem to have been reassessing their overall foreign policy posture. Starting in 1981, there was evidence that some began to have doubts about the wisdom of aligning too closely with the Americans on broad international issues, and as US–China tensions over the Taiwan arms sales issues grew, there were increasing signs of adjustments in Peking's posture on many other international questions.

The Chinese began to be more overtly critical of a broad range of US domestic and foreign policies. From 1978 until 1981, most publicly expressed Chinese opinions about the United States and its policies were remarkably favorable. Peking's leaders seems determined to paint as bright a picture as possible of the United States as a society and deliberately played down differences between Chinese and American foreign policy, linking Chinese and American interests to an unprecedented degree.

By the second half of 1981, however, the tone of Chinese discussions of the United States and its policies clearly had begun to change. Once again, Peking's leaders and the Chinese press were inclined to highlight rather than to gloss over Sino-American differences. The new criticism dealt with both American domestic policies and US foreign policy.

WANING CONFIDENCE IN THE UNITED STATES

In early January 1982 the *People's Daily,* in an article titled "A Difficult Year," argued that the Reagan administration's policies in general had been unimpressive during the previous year. "In an economic sense," it declared, "things have proved contrary to expectation"; moreover, the article stated, "Reagan's revitalization plan was not well-founded and was mostly guesswork."

The article made a sweeping criticism of the narrow view and short-sightedness of the Reagan administration's overall foreign policy. It asserted that his administration's "decision-making machinery is not operating smoothly," and US "foreign policy has been marked by a lack of consideration of the overall situation and a lack of consistent guidelines." "In the United States of today," it said, "and the world of today, many things and tough problems can never be solved by just relying on the US president's will or just relying on the strength of the United States itself. If it is thought that the United States can do whatever it likes and if the United States lacks a farsighted strategic view of the whole world and overlooks the existence and role of various other factors in the world, then it will surely come to grief."

Many Chinese press articles now highlighted US domestic problems—unemployment, inflation and others. For immigrants from China to the United States, one article declared, "actual life in the United States turns out to be quite a blow to them." The analysis presented by China's papers of the economic situation in the entire Western world was extremely gloomy. One article, for example, discussing the "long-term stagnation of the Western economies [which] started in 1974," asserted that "a mood of despondency pervades the whole Western world."

CRITICISM OF WASHINGTON'S
STRESS ON ARMS

One broad criticism of US foreign policy that was particularly striking, in light of the fact that for a decade Peking had urged Washington to build up its military strength and be tougher in dealing with Moscow, was contained in an article titled "Weakpoints of the United States," which stated: "As a superpower, the United States had another weakness, namely, blindly worshipping weapons and not knowing how to generate mass support."

Although "Reagan claims that the United States respects the sovereignty of other nations, he has consistently displayed an unjust and irresponsible attitude towards them," the article asserted. "He has also interfered in their internal affairs. Washington's influence is waning in the third world because of US support for Israel, South Africa, and other reactionary regimes." An accompanying article on "Moscow's Policy" stated: "In contrast to Reagan's hard-line policy, Moscow has pursued a policy of moderate gestures and big sticks."

Chinese criticism of the Reagan administration's policies toward third world nations because increasingly sharp over time. "The United States has not established fair and responsible relations with the third world," declared one article. "On the contrary, the United States has frequently pitted itself against the vast third world countries. . . . Apparently among the advanced Western countries, the United States is the toughest on the question of North-South relations." It went on to say: "In Central America, the Reagan administration has opposed the Soviet and Cuban intervention in the Central American countries' internal affairs, while posing as the enemy of the local national and democratic movement, trying its utmost to obstruct changes in these countries which the United States dislikes." Several articles specifically criticized US policy toward El Salvador.

DOUBTS ABOUT US RELATIONS
WITH EUROPE AND JAPAN

The Chinese press also began to give increased attention to evidence of growing differences between the United States and its allies in Western Europe and Japan. In general the tone of articles on Europe was sympathetic to Western European rather than America views. For example, a deputy director of a research institute attached to the Chinese Foreign Ministry published an analysis in which he asserted: "Western Europe wishes to become independent in every aspects of its foreign policy . . . [and] an increasing number of people in Western Europe believe that in the 1980s, the Europe–US alliance must be fundamentally reformed."

The author discussed European desires for detente with Moscow, with surprisingly little criticism:

The West European countries have tended to emphasize the need to maintain "detente" with the Soviet Union.... [They] have considerable economic and military strength, and they have their own calculations for support "detente," not entirely resulting from their weakness or the lure and pressure of the Soviet Union.... It is possible, if "detente" is implemented, for Western Europe to impose certain restraint on the Soviet Union and strengthen its position vis-à-vis the United States. Some Europeans believe that in the stalemate between the two superpowers, this policy will provide Western Europe with the key to a greater opportunity for diplomatic maneuvering.

Discussions of US–Japanese relations in early 1982 also highlighted growing problems. A major article in the *People's Daily* was titled "Japanese–US Contradictions Seem To Be Intensifying." Analyzing recent "contradictions" in the fields of trade and defense, the author argued that present conflicts between Washington and Tokyo appear more serious than those in the past. He asserted:

The future is by no means promising.... [T]here has been an atmosphere of suspicion between Japan and the United States. People in Japan and the United States are worried that such an atmosphere will consequently lead to a political movement and the friendly relationship between the two countries will be shattered.

"SUPERPOWERS" AND "HEGEMONISM"

Articles in the Chinese press increasingly referred once again to the United States as well as the Soviet Union not only as a "superpower" (a derogatory term in China's political lexicon) but also as a country following a "hegemonist policy." One such article asserted: "In Washington there are not only politically blind men, but also a considerable number of Yankee fools who are not blind but are foolish all the same." Some of the articles emphasized US weaknesses and inconsistencies in dealing with worldwide problems posed by the Soviet Union....

As 1981 drew to a close, one Chinese journal carried a year-end analysis (based largely on reports from the foreign correspondents of the New China News Agency), which was titled "The Present World Is Very Disquieting." To a striking degree the analysis stressed the failings and weaknesses of both Soviet and US policy. Much of the article was devoted to analysis of the struggles in Kampuchea, Afghanistan, and Poland; the continuing conflicts in the Middle East; and "the pacifist tide" in Western Europe. However, throughout the article, both the United States and USSR were portrayed as being unable to cope effectively with existing problems. "The polar bear" [the USSR] has been bogged down in a quagmire in Afghanistan and Kampuchea. Failing to pull itself out from the quagmire, it has no alternatives than to drag on and wear itself out."

The news agency's Washington correspondent contributed this analysis:

> US and Soviet military capabilities [are] generally comparable. . . . The Reagan administration takes a stronger stance toward the Soviet Union . . . [but] when a real problem has arisen (for example, the invasion of Afghanistan and Kampuchea), no strong determination is likely to be made, nor any significant measures worked out. . . . The situation is rather passive. . . . [These] tactics are not likely to bring about quick results. The reason is that the United States has shortcomings [and] the minds of its people and the thinking of its allies are unstable and not at ease. . . . [A] weakness often ignored by a superpower is that it has blind faith in arms but does not see the need to rely on the masses and the majority. . . . If the United States does not adjust its policies in good time, its weakness will be more obvious.

The United States correspondent added, "While the United States assumes a hard line toward the Soviet Union, the actual policy carried out toward that country has been rather confusing."

Increasingly, the Chinese press tended to blur the distinctions between the two superpowers. Previously, for years Peking had focused its harshest criticisms almost entirely on the Soviet Union, labeling it as the superpower posing the principal immediate threat to the world, against whom all others should unite. Now some Chinese articles (especially those that dealt with the Taiwan problem) again stressed the similarities of the two superpowers. One, for example, asserted:

> There are people in the United States who live in the 1980s, but believe that China's sovereignty is limited and that of the United States is boundless. Their conception of American authority reminds people of Brezhnev's theory of limited sovereignty. . . . Is it simply because the United States is a superpower and has a big nuclear arsenal that some Americans claim the right to unlimited power in affairs on Chinese soil?

Discussing the arms race, another article asserted: "The debate over who is threatening whom has no longer been considered as news. Both the superpowers . . . are arguing that . . . each feels militarily threatened by the other. . . . This reminds us of the age-old argument of whether the chicken or the egg came first. It is in the course of this continual wrangling that the arms race of the two superpowers grows fiercer and fiercer, constituting in [an] increasingly serious threat to world peace. . . . It seems that this debate will go on forever and the world will never be able to enjoy true peace."

CHANGING TACTICS IN DEALING WITH MOSCOW

There was also a noticeable change in tone in many Chinese articles and statements on the Soviet Union. The Chinese press continued strong criticism of Soviet foreign policies and still warned that the Soviet threat remained very serious worldwide. But criticism of Soviet domestic policies clearly declined. The Chinese no longer carried bitter denunciations of Soviet "revisionism" (one explanation being of course that China's own domestic policies had swung in directions that the Maoists had previously denounced as "revisionist"). While still warning against Soviet expansionism, the Chinese now increasingly stressed the domestic and foreign factors constraining Moscow. An article titled "Whither Soviet Global Strategy?" began, for example, with the statement: "The Kremlin staggered into the new year [1982] burdened with problems at home and abroad that defy easy solution." Although the article discussed in some detail the dangers posed by the Soviet Union's continuing military buildup, repeating Peking's long-standing warnings about the resulting threats especially to Europe and the Middle East but also in "the East," it asserted that

> [the Soviet Union's] ailing economy ... coupled with the protracted war in Afghanistan and the Polish crisis, has more or less shackled the feet of the Soviet giant in pressing ahead with its expansion abroad.... Looking at the crystal ball, one may say that there probably won't be another Afghanistan for some time to come. But unfortunately, temperature in the world's hot spots remains dangerously high and there is always the possibility of new trouble spots coming into being.

A number of developments during 1981–82 raised questions about whether or not Peking might be modifying its long-standing posture of rigid hostility toward the Soviet Union. There were signs of improvement in bilateral state-to-state relations. At least two leading China specialists in the Soviet government made private visits to China. In late 1981, a Chinese gymnastics team participated in an international meet in Moscow and reportedly had "friendly conversations" with their Soviet counterparts. At the end of the year the director of Radio Peking broadcast greetings to the Soviet people, in which he said, "Dear friends: Allow me ... to warmly congratulate you on the new year and wish you in the new year lots of happiness, good health and success in your work.... We hope that in the new year our relations and friendship will be consolidated even more." In early 1982, a leading member of the Soviet–Chinese Friendship Association made an unofficial visit to Peking. At about the same time, a Chinese journal stated succinctly: "China is not afraid of the Soviet military threat."

The Chinese also were remarkably silent about the crisis in Poland. Privately, Chinese diplomats admitted that Peking was far from enthusiastic about the emergence of an independent trade union in any socialist country, but they also stressed that, although the Soviet Union had clearly exerted threatening kinds of pressures on Poland, it had not directly intervened, as it had in Czechoslovakia. They asserted that they opposed outside intervention by either superpower. Publicly, Li Xiannian, a member of the Chinese Communist Party's Standing Committee, stated in an interview that China opposed "all foreign interference" in Poland ... [and] when we speak of interference, we understand by that all interference."

More important, there were hints that Peking was at least considering a resumption of the Sino-Soviet border talks that had been suspended following the Soviet invasion of Afghanistan in 1979. On September 25, 1981, Moscow's leaders proposed resuming negotiations. They were fully aware of the new strains in US–China relations and doubtless hoped that these would influence Peking's attitudes toward talks with the Soviet Union. The immediate Chinese response came in a Foreign Ministry statement which simply stated: "We have always maintained that the boundary question should be settled through negotiations, but owing to reasons from the Soviet side, no agreement has been reached so far. We are studying the Soviet proposal." Near year-end, a Chinese government spokesman then revealed somewhat cryptically that China had "recently responded," adding: "The two parties must prepare themselves well before resuming negotiations. Any date should be discussed through diplomatic channels."

The most noteworthy public statement made by any high Chinese official during this period regarding the possibility of Sino-Soviet talks was one made by party Vice Chairman Li Xiannian, in an interview with the correspondent of the Italian Communist party newspaper *L'Unita* in January 1982. A report from Rome on the interview stated, "In the Chinese view [perhaps it should simply have said Li's view] as it emerged from the interview, the dangerous rivalry between the two superpowers threw ominous shadows over Europe, Japan, and the developing world." Li was quoted as saying: "We all know that the United States remains an imperialist country" even though it is now in a defensive position while the Soviet Union is on the offensive. Paraphrasing Li, the report stated that he reiterated the Chinese position that:

> China and the Soviet Union must still find a solution to their border problems. ... China has no impediments to opening a dialogue with Moscow, although such talks would surely touch on the need for a withdrawal of Soviet troops from Cambodia. It would not be easy for the Soviets to give an answer to these things.

Li was directly quoted as saying: "We are not against the US–USSR negotiations underway in Geneva, so why should be be against Sino-USSR negotiations."

An Agence France Press report from Peking on the same interview quoted Li as saying, "We are not setting any preconditions," even though it was inevitable that, in the talks, Afghanistan and Cambodia as well as the "withdrawal of Soviet forces deployed along our borders and in Outer Mongolia" would be raised.

Nothing in these reports suggested that Peking had significantly eased its stand on the intractable substantive issues that China and the Soviet Union have tried to deal with in intermittent negotiations ever since the border talks started in the 1960s. However, the reports suggested that China might be more flexible tactically in dealing with Moscow than it has been in recent years.

Statements such as Li's seemed to encourage Moscow to step up its efforts to reopen border negotiations. On March 24, Leonid I. Brezhnev himself made a new proposal for negotiations that sounded more conciliatory than any in years. Brezhnev underlined the fact that Moscow rejected the two-Chinas concept and recognized Peking's claim to Taiwan. He stated that Moscow was prepared to discuss possible "measures to strengthen mutual trust along their border" and "to come to terms, without any preliminary conditions, on measures acceptable to both sides." In March there were additional direct contacts of significance. Most important of these was a visit by three Chinese economic experts to Moscow to study Soviet management methods.

The official Chinese response to Brezhnev's March 24 statement was noncommittal. On March 26, a Foreign Ministry spokesman in Peking said that China's leaders "have noted the remarks" and "firmly reject the attacks on China" contained in them, but he did not say that China had rejected the idea of renewed talks; instead he simply declared that "what we attach importance to are actual deeds."

RENEWED EMPHASIS ON THE "THREE WORLDS"

Of all the changes in emphasis in China's posture on broad international problems that became apparent during 1981, perhaps the clearest were Peking's strong reassertion of the Chinese concept of "three worlds" (classifying all nations into three groups—the superpowers, the other industrial nations, and the developing countries), its renewed emphasis on China's support for the developing nations (as a self-proclaimed member of the third world), and its increased criticism of US policies toward the third world.

From 1977 through 1979, China had said relatively little about the "three-worlds concept," its press commentaries on North–South issues had decreased, and its rhetoric on such issues was noticeably more restrained than previously. In 1980, however, this changed. The Chinese again gave very extensive coverage to North–South problems, reasserted China's role as a third world leader, and strongly criticized American as well as Soviet policies toward the developing nations.

In the fall of 1981 one major Chinese article strongly reemphasized

China's third world ties. "Chairman Mao's strategic conception of the three worlds is correct," it said. "China will always be a member of the third world and never seek hegemonism. . . . Developing relations with the United States does not mean that China supports its erroneous policy toward some third world countries."

Throughout this period, a stream of articles in the Chinese press criticized the Reagan administration's policies on a wide range of third world concerns and North–South issues. In early October 1981, one article, after declaring that the US position on aid to developing nations "caused anxiety and resentment among the developing countries," added: "North–South economic relations is [sic] by no means a simple economic issue. It should be considered from the viewpoint of the immediate international politics." Later in the same month, the author of another article declared that "one of the main weak points of the Reagan administration's foreign policy [in 1981] was that it neglected the important role played by the third world in the present international situation. It overemphasized East–West relations or even subordinated North–South relations to those between East and West."

Shortly thereafter, in early November, in an article about the United Nations, the Chinese charged that in the 1950s the United States ("with US dollars in one hand") had "manipulated the veto machine," and declared that this era was forever gone. "At present," the article stated, "the third world countries . . . can neither be bribed nor coerced. They will not take orders from Washington and will not submit to Moscow."

At year-end, a New China News Agency review of US foreign policy during 1981, titled "Talking About US Foreign Policy," declared:

> Perhaps the most crucial aspect of US foreign policy is that toward the third world countries. There is no denying the fact that the thrust of Soviet expansionism is the most threatening in the third world and the Middle East and South Asia in particular. . . . Still, the question remains whether the United States has the resolve to make bolder adjustments of its policy toward the third world. . . . Often the United States as a great power fails to treat the third world countries as equals and to act impartially toward them all. Those political groupings, whether they are in power or overthrown, are taken as its old friends so long as they are pro-American and anti-communist. . . . [Washington] often does not scruple to interfere in the affairs of other countries, even at the expense of its own long-term strategic interest. . . . The United States government has proclaimed opposition to hegemonism of any country as its basic policy. Well, it is much easier to oppose the hegemonism of others than to oppose one's own. This perhaps is the crux of the problem of US foreign policy.

Throughout this period, not only did Chinese publications increase their verbal criticism of US policy toward the third world, the Chinese government became much more diplomatically in support of third world causes, and it became notably more assertive in the United Nations. The most striking example of this was Peking's decision in late 1981 to fight hard—despite strong US support for a new term for Kurt Waldheim as UN secretary-general—to insist that someone from a third world country be chosen for that post. For the first time, the Chinese used their veto power in the UN repeatedly until their view prevailed, and, ultimately, they were able to ensure that a third world representative (though not the one Peking originally had supported) was approved as Waldheim's successor.

SIGNIFICANCE OF THESE TRENDS

The coincidence of increasing strains in bilateral US–China relations over the Taiwan arms sales issue and signs of possible broader changes in China's general international posture was clearly not accidental. As of early 1982 it was impossible to foresee how far the broader changes might go.

Some of the new Chinese criticisms of US policies toward other countries—not only toward the third world but toward the United States' closest allies as well—were unquestionably intended to be oblique criticism of the Reagan administration's policy toward China, especially as it related to Taiwan. Charges that the United States, as a superpower, is prone to interfere in the internal affairs of other countries, frequently violates other nations' sovereignty, supports "old friends" even if they have been "overthrown," ignores the desires of some of its closest supporters to be truly independent, tends to act unilaterally and to impose its own views on others, and (the most bitter charge) on occasion seems to operate on premises close to Brezhnev's doctrine of "limited sovereignty," unquestionably were not simply criticism of US policy toward other countries; they were not very subtle indirect criticism of American attitudes and policies on the Taiwan issue as well.

Yet, despite the mounting criticism of general US policy, the tone of most Chinese statements did not suggest that Peking had abandoned its desire for friendly US–China ties or had reverted to a policy of hostility toward Washington. On issues other than Taiwan, the tone of the Chinese statements usually seemed to reflect feelings of sorrow or regret more than of anger. Many of the Chinese criticisms, in fact, were no more harsh (and sometimes less so) than those directed at Reagan administration foreign policies by certain critics in the United States or in other Western and third world nations. Moreover, even as the strains in US–China political relations regarding the Taiwan issue escalated to a point of real "danger," US–China economic relations and educational and scientific interchanges continued throughout 1981 and early 1982 to develop in a very positive way. In 1981,

US–China trade rose to a new peak (over $5.5 billion), and in early 1982 Peking opened bidding for oil exploration rights in key South China Sea shelf areas to foreign oil companies, including major American companies.

The Chinese continued to assert that they wished to maintain and further develop strong, friendly US–China ties, and in their foreign economic policy in particular they appeared to be operating on the assumption that, despite their new demands for changes in US policy on arms sales to Taiwan, somehow it would be possible to prevent any major setback in overall US–China relations. Privately, however, Chinese diplomats stressed that the outcome of talks on the Taiwan arms sales issue would be crucial, and that, if relations reached an impasse over this issue, the consequence probably would be a downgrading of official relations. Generally, during 1981 and 1982 they argued that a political setback would have an adverse impact on trade and other ties in the future. However, as the impasse over Taiwan arms sales continued without progress toward compromise and as the possibility of a political setback continued, top Chinese leaders began expressing the hope that key economic ties could be protected from the effects of any political setback.

It was very difficult to judge what the long-term significance might be of the shifts in Peking's broad international posture that accompanied mounting US–China tension over Taiwan. However, it was impossible to exclude the possibility that the shift foreshadowed a gradual move away from—or at least a modification of—the dominant central theme of Peking's overall international strategy from the late 1960s until 1981, namely the coalescence of a worldwide united front in which the United States and all the other major industrial nations would play key roles in close cooperation with China and as much of the third world as possible.

China's official statements and press commentaries during 1981 and early 1982 certainly did not indicate in any clear fashion that Peking's leaders had yet decided to alter this decade-old strategy in any radical way; Peking still labeled Moscow as the main threat to world peace. Nevertheless, many statements did suggest that the Chinese were positioning themselves for possible further shifts in their global posture.

What such a shift might involve, if it were to occur, could be inferred from the kinds of statements quoted earlier. These statements suggested that Peking's leaders could decide to reemphasize further their theory of three worlds and their primary identification with the third world, and also stress the two superpowers' similarities rather than their difference, place increased priority on strengthening China's ties with the "second world" (Japan and Western Europe), and take steps deliberately to distance China politically from the United States, underlining Peking's determination to avoid political dependence on Washington.

In early 1982, while there were many hints that the Chinese could decide to move further in these directions, it remained unclear to what extent these were mainly tactical, designed to remind Washington that Peking does have options other than increasing its reliance on US strategic and economic support. In part, the hints undoubtedly were intended to exert leverage on Washington to make further compromises on the Taiwan issue, but they clearly were more than that. The change in Peking's overall foreign policy had not gone so far, however, that the trend could not be checked or reversed by Peking, especially if compromise on the Taiwan issue could be reached. If the discussions initiated after [Assistant Secretary of State] Holdridge's trip to Peking [in January 1982] could produce a new compromise on this issue, it would not be difficult for the Chinese to renew primary emphasis on the importance of US–China cooperation and to try to strengthen relations, playing down rather than highlighting the differences between the two countries' policies.

Nevertheless, the clear signs of changes in China's international posture did raise the possibility that Peking was not only reexamining policy because of the Taiwan problem, but was also—as a result of a reassessment of broad international trends—considering major adjustments in its overall foreign policy. Leaders in China now seemed to view general world trends differently from the way they had during 1978–80. They seemed to have less confidence in the United States' intentions and capabilities, and they appeared to take a less alarmist view of Soviet capabilities.

One important clue to a direction in which overall Chinese policy might move was contained in the statement cited earlier, in which the author (a Chinese scholar close to Peking's Foreign Ministry) asserted that "some Europeans believe that in the stalemate between the two superpowers," Europe might, through detente, be able to "impose certain restraint on the Soviet Union and strengthen its position vis-à-vis the United States," which could provide "the key to a greater opportunity for diplomatic maneuvering." It is plausible that by 1982 some Chinese felt that in the stalemate between the two superpowers Peking too might be able, if it adopted more flexible policies, to discover a "key to a greater opportunity for diplomatic maneuvering."

If Peking does decide that global trends argue in favor of greater flexibility and maneuverability in Chinese policy—whether or not there is a major setback in Sino-American relations—what changes in overall Chinese policy would be likely? Under existing circumstances it is improbable that Peking would suddenly decide on a dramatic shift of policy comparable to that which took place when the Sino-Soviet split and the initial steps toward US–China detente occurred. What seems more likely is that the Chinese might decide to move cautiously toward a more independent position between Washington and Moscow to try to increase Peking's flexibility in dealing with both.

Even under such circumstances, there is little possibility that any far-reaching Sino-Soviet rapprochement would occur; however, gradual steps toward a limited detente between Peking and Moscow would certainly be possible. Nor do the Chinese seem likely, under foreseeable circumstances, to revert to a hostile general policy toward the United States. Even if there were to be a political setback in US–China relations over the Taiwan issue,

Peking probably would still try, to the extent possible, to continue having Chinese trained in the United States and to maintain certain important cooperative economic ties with the Americans, especially in the fields of agriculture and energy and in some high-technology fields as well—though they might turn increasingly to Japan and Europe for the latter.

In March, Deng Xiaoping (Teng Hsiao-p'ing) himself made clear that he hoped US–China economic relations would continue to expand even if there was a setback in political relations. He was reported to have said to Armand Hammer, chairman of a major US oil company, that while there was "no room for a deal" over Taiwan, this issue "will not affect business with China." (Some Americans were less sanguine about the prospects of protecting economic relations from politics, however.)

Assuming no reversion to outright Sino-American hostility and conflict, the Chinese probably also would continue to see some convergence of US and Chinese interests on particular international issues, above all the problem of balancing Soviet power, which they doubtless would continue to see as the greatest potential threat to China's security. Even if their confidence in US policy is weakened, they are likely to continue to view the United States as the strongest global counterweight to Moscow and recognize some continuing parallelism in the efforts of both China and the United States—even if not closely coordinated—to check Soviet expansionism. If so, there would continue to be at least an indirect linkage of Chinese and American security interests.

However, even if all of these judgments prove to be correct, any serious setback in US–China political relations over the Taiwan issue—or any decision by Peking to deliberately distance itself politically from Washington—would undoubtedly alter the tone of US–China relations and limit the possibilities for expanding US–China cooperation or increasing parallelism in the two countries' policies. A major shift in China's overall international posture, especially if it is perceived to be the result of a political crisis between Washington and Peking over the Taiwan issue, could have more farreaching—and more unpredictable—effects on other nations in East Asia. Most of these nations would view the future with greater uncertainty, and virtually all would feel compelled to reassess the regional balance and consider adjustments in their own policies toward the major powers. It is difficult to predict what the long-run consequences would be.

60

China
and the Great Power Triangle

Gerald Segal

In these excerpts from *The China Quarterly,* Gerald Segal
analyzes the postwar evolution of Chinese foreign policy. From a
bipolar approach based on an alliance with the USSR, China has
moved toward a more balanced, tripolar strategy, with itself as
the third leg in the power triangle. After the 1960 split with the
Soviet Union, China attempted to forge an independent foreign
policy based on the theory of Three Worlds, and proposed to lead
the underdeveloped nations in demanding greater economic eq-
uity among nations. 1969 border clashes with the Soviet Union
convinced the Chinese leadership of the vulnerabilities of such
nonalignment and led the Chinese to seek improved relations
with the U.S. In a sense, the Chinese played the American "card"
against the Soviets. However, Sino-Soviet relations are not static.
The 1979 border war with Vietnam provided a basis for reconsi-
dering Sino-Soviet relations. The Chinese now recognize that improved relations will reduce the need for border troops along
both the Vietnamese and Sino-Soviet frontiers. Additionally, improved relations with the Soviets will prevent regimes such as the
North Koreans and Cambodians from playing China off against the
USSR. This rapprochement has been made possible, Segal argues,
by the post-Mao leadership's willingness to heal old wounds, such
as the withdrawal of Soviet aid in the 1960s, and by recent economic reforms that resemble similar Soviet reforms criticized by
Mao. However, factional politics within the Chinese leadership
are influential in shaping Sino-Soviet relations and must be considered when making predictions about the future of these
relations.

The notion of a great power triangle composed of the U.S., U.S.S.R. and
PRC, and the "card games" played within this geometric configuration, are
now particularly prevalent in the field of international politics. It is the pur-

pose of this analysis to study the relevance of the great power triangle concept for Chinese foreign policy. A primary assumption will be that an understanding of Beijing's previous policies in a tripolar system will be a useful guide to the policies and problems of the present. Therefore we will begin with a review of the development of tripolarity and China's past attitudes. We will then concentrate on some crucial aspects of the triangle, the difficulties facing the Chinese leaders, and some possible policy options derived from our focus on the great power triad.

It is frequently claimed that the terminology of the great power triangle, "card playing," and the "balance of power" concept that it presupposes, is not applicable to China and the formulation of its foreign policy. The following analysis takes the view that tripolarity and its great power manoeuvres are not foreign to China and that indeed the "game" is particularly well understood in Beijing. Chinese history and culture provide an adequate basis for this kind of approach to politics. *The Romance of the Three Kingdoms* with the tripolar interaction of the kingdoms of Shu, Wu and Wei in the third century, as well as the ancient parable of the monkey sitting on a hilltop "watching two tigers fight," are cases in point. More recently, Henry Kissinger has suggested that in his negotiations with Beijing, it was clear that Chinese leaders understood triangular politics better than most powers. This view is also supported by J. D. Armstrong's study of Chinese policy showing the predominance of the "alliance" model of Chinese foreign policy over the "united front" model in the post-1949 period.

THE EVOLUTION OF THE
GREAT POWER TRIANGLE

It can be argued that one of the first steps in the PRC's emergence as a third great power upsetting the bipolar equation can be found prior to the declaration of the People's Republic. Even as the Chinese Communist forces overran their U.S.-supported rivals, Zhou Enlai reportedly issued a secret appeal to Washington for assistance so that China could ". . . serve in (the) international sphere as (a) mediator between (the) Western Power and (the) U.S.S.R. . . . and make (the) U.S.S.R. discard policies leading to war." Shortly afterwards Mao Zedong reportedly said that in the event of a U.S.-U.S.S.R. war, China was not committed to joining the Soviet Union. However, it seems that as a result of certain trends in U.S. policy-making on China and the extreme sensitivity of the Chinese leadership due to delicate factional politics, Zhou's offer was never acted upon, and the great power configuration developed into its essentially bipolar form. This possible opportunity to encourage the emergence of China as an important third independent actor on the international scene was lost.

Towards the end of the 1950s, the bipolar configuration began to be overtaken and a major aspect of this was the Sino-Soviet split. When the

U.S.S.R. began moderating its foreign policy in a fashion that China found increasingly unacceptable, the Moscow-Beijing rift widened. It is now clear that one of the major aspects of the split was the divergence of views regarding the formulation of the "correct" attitude towards the U.S. As the Communist conflict worsened in the late 1950s, Moscow found itself under increasingly conflicting pressure from the U.S. and China to pursue radically different policies. Thus the interaction of these three powers was emerging as a major facet of the international system. While there already were polycentric tendencies and indicators of multipolarity in the international system at the time, China stood out as the single most important factor which regularly figured in both the U.S.'s and U.S.S.R.'s calculations. By virtue of its being the great power with the most co-operative and least conflictive relations with the other two powers, the U.S.S.R. can be seen as the pivot power in the great power triad. Because conflict and co-operation are relative terms, the concept of a pivot is also relative. Nevertheless, in the analysis that follows it will be useful to study the role of the pivot and its position in tripolar interaction. For the U.S.S.R. in particular, the 1960s was not an easy decade: the passage was rough when sailing the choppy waters between the U.S. Scylla and the Chinese Charybdis.

One of the first major signs of the emergence of China as a third independent great power actor upsetting bipolar equations, was evident in the Laos crisis of 1961. Even during the early stages of the conflict, China was intricately involved in the great power negotiations. At the 1961 Geneva conference convened to discuss the Laos question, China was beginning clearly to assert its crucial role. The U.S. and U.S.S.R. sought to minimize the importance of China, and in a blatant attempt to re-impose the bipolar "rules of the game," formulated an agreement whereby both superpowers would "guarantee" the behaviour of their respective "allies." Known as the Pushkin Pact, this secret accord between Averell Harriman and deputy foreign minister Pushkin surprised the U.S. because of Moscow's readiness to assume responsibility for China's actions. In retrospect it seems clear that the Kremlin's actions can be explained by the desire to retain the bipolar configuration and prevent the evolution of China as an important third pole. The Chinese, for their part, apparently feared just such a "secret deal" between the super-powers and began to evolve a policy of opposing both the U.S. and U.S.S.R. despite rhetoric of undying Sino-Soviet friendship.

After a lengthy period of ignoring the Communist rift, the U.S. was beginning to undertake significant studies of the new international environment. However, one of the elements most limiting U.S. policy was the pressure from Taiwan. For example, in 1962 there were loud noises from Taipei that the time was ripe for the "liberation of the mainland." The resulting entirely spurious crisis in the Taiwan straits in June 1962 worsened Sino-American relations and made it less likely than ever that the U.S. would take advantage of the Sino-Soviet rift and improve relations with China. Hitherto classified U.S. documents from this period indicate that such obstructionist policies were not new for Taiwan. In April 1955, Eisenhower asked Chiang

Kai-shek to withdraw from Quemoy and Matsu while offering in return a U.S. blockade of the PRC coast, but Chiang angrily refused. By 1958 even Dulles was ready to throw the offshore islands issue to the United Nations as he recognized that the costs of standing firm were greater than the losses from leaving. Thus, despite the great opportunities provided by the break-up of the Sino-Soviet alliance, the U.S. failed to act and the great power triangle evolved very slowly.

A significant reason for the slow evolution of the nascent tripolar system was the predicament faced by the pivot power, the U.S.S.R. The dual pressures on Moscow from Washington and Beijing were clearly seen in the pattern of Soviet reactions to the Sino-Indian war of 1962. In the first period, in late October, the U.S.S.R. required Chinese support during the heat of the Cuban missile crisis and so Moscow "tilted" towards Beijing in its policy on the Asian conflict. After the tension in the Caribbean passed its peak, the U.S.S.R. "tilted" to India (and by implication to its supporters in the U.S.) in order to stop the Chinese advance. The pivot's shifts were, however, not enough to cope with the demands from the two other great powers. Especially in the negotiations on the Test Ban Treaty, it was seen that the U.S.S.R. would eventually have to lean more decisively to one power or the other. By mid-1963 Moscow's signature on the Test Ban led to an open Sino-Soviet break and the distinct emergence of China as the third independent great power.

The evolution of China's attitude towards the global configuration had undergone a major change in the 1963–64 period. From the autumn of 1963 the international system was seen as having entered a new era wherein the two super-powers formed a new "Holy Alliance." The PRC's self-image was as leader of the revolutionary world that remained ever vigilant against the super-powers' conspiracy to limit world revolution. Mao, the main architect of China's foreign policy, had initially held that China along with the Soviet bloc opposed the imperialists, with the non-aligned forming a vague intermediate zone. This trilateralism, as first expounded by Mao to Anna Louise Strong in 1946, was hinted at again in the post-Korean War period and then stated explicitly on 6 November 1957 by Mao to the Supreme Soviet. Even in the late 1950s such an emphasis on a "third world," or the Chinese equivalent comprising essentially the same actors, was highly unusual. It presupposed that these states in the intermediate zone were somehow a more solid and permanent unit than the U.S.S.R.'s perception of states in a transition phase of neutralism on the "inevitable road to socialism." Nevertheless, China still viewed the collection of these states as very fluid, something along the lines of an international united front framework.

At the 10th plenum of the eighth CCP Central Committee, Mao again mentioned the intermediate zone and then in January 1964 a *People's Daily* editorial outlined in detail the theory of the two parts of the intermediate zones. In this view of a triangular international system composed of the U.S., the U.S.S.R. and the intermediate zones, Mao made it clear that China was not to be counted among the Soviet bloc and that it probably lay some-where in the intermediate zone, perhaps between the first and second zones. Thus Beijing had taken the lead in viewing the international system in triangular terms (albeit its own type of triangle) and it also began evolving basic foreign policy objectives accordingly. Three of the more fundamental Chinese principles can be stated as follows. (1) Try to stay independent of entangling alignments with either of the two super-powers. (2) If necessary, try to unite with the weaker power (as seen by China and not based necessarily on conventional measures of power), but keep any alignments to the absolute minimum. (3) Try, if possible, to sit back and watch the other two tigers fight. China, as the power whose pursuit of an independent role was the single most important cause of the break-up of bipolarity, was thus the first to come to terms with the tripolar system.

The U.S.S.R. responded in September 1964 to the theory of the intermediate zones and denounced what it saw as "nationalist sentiments." *Pravda* understood Mao's theory to mean that essentially there were only two worlds: the U.S. and the U.S.S.R. versus China and its intermediate zones. If one accepts that Moscow would clearly reject the notion of the U.S.S.R. and the U.S. in the same zone, then we are left with basically a great power triangle. As the power whose bloc was split by China's departure, it was not surprising that the U.S.S.R. had soon come to terms with the tripolar system. The Soviet Union also indicated one of the possible implications of the triangle when it spoke of its fear of Sino-American collusion against the U.S.S.R. *Pravda* asked what would happen if U.S. leaders ". . . find it advantageous for themselves to reconsider their policy of non-recognition of the Chinese People's Republic and offer it economic co-operation. Will they too be issued credentials as 'fighters against imperialism'?" This perceptive prediction of tripolar dynamics was to be confirmed in 1971.

After the political demise of Khrushchev in late 1964 and the growing U.S. war threat in Vietnam, China had to decide whether or not to engage in "united action" with the U.S.S.R. against the U.S. Thomas Gottlieb has recently produced an excellent analysis of the Chinese strategic debate on the proper policy for the great power triangle. It seems clear that China's options in the tripolar world were well understood in Beijing. By mid-1966, Mao led the Chinese leadership into rejecting what in effect were Soviet overtures for an anti-U.S. coalition, and with the severance of inter-party ties, the Sino-Soviet rift deepened and Moscow's pivotal role in the triangle became increasingly difficult to maintain. However, Beijing's position also deteriorated, especially as a result of the self-imposed isolation and radicalism of the Cultural Revolution. For example, in Hanoi the Soviet position gradually improved at China's expense and by the Tet offensive in 1968 the Vietnamese decided that Beijing's extreme hostility towards negotiating with Washington had to be abandoned. At the same time, the U.S. and U.S.S.R. were regularly engaged in secret discussions about China and the two super powers seemed to have accepted the need for trilateral communication in the new system. However, China was not ready to hold such extensive discussions with the U.S. and U.S.S.R., and because of its radical mood during the Cultural Revolution, had become too isolated. It lacked the room for manoeuvre when new challenges developed, basically because the radical leaders had a tendency to view great power relations, and especially Sino-American ties, in overwhelmingly conflictive terms and could not envisage partially co-operative elements co-existing with the conflictive ones.

Following the double shock of the Warsaw Pact invasion of Czechoslovakia and the March 1969 Sino-Soviet border clash, the "moderate" faction in Beijing led by Zhou Enlai was able to predominate and the simmering debate on altering China's options in the triangle began to be resolved in favour of those who wanted to open contacts with the U.S. Zhou's group sought an important "card to play" against the perceived threat from the U.S.S.R., and this roughly coincided with the new U.S. administration's desire to open contacts with Beijing in order to play the "China card" against Moscow. This coincidence of desires brought about the most significant alteration in the great power system since the Sino-Soviet split, when, by virtue of having the most co-operative and least conflictive relations with the other two powers, the U.S. emerged as the great power pivot. The tripolar communication process was also becoming more balanced as now Beijing and Washington were discussing their relations with Moscow, much as Washington and Moscow had discussed Beijing several years previously.

In 1973, China's strategy in the triangle became somewhat more clear. In Beijing's view the U.S.S.R. was clearly the aggressive great power directing its main threat towards the U.S. as it "contended and colluded" with Washington for global hegemony. This was an alteration of the Chinese line immediately after the 1969 border incidents when Moscow's aggression was seen as being directed towards China. The diminution of the Soviet threat, coupled with a stalemate in Sino-American relations in 1974–75, meant that the conceptual basis of China's global posture was being undermined. For Beijing, the "U.S. card" was meant to counterbalance the threat from the U.S.S.R., but with the minimization of the Soviet factor, the broad Chinese tripolar policy once again became the focus of debate. Overtures were apparently made to the Kremlin as some forces in Beijing tried to "play the U.S.S.R. card" against the U.S. It seems clear that the understanding of the great power triangle was present in China but at least for the time being there was no major alteration in the configuration of the great power system.

The debilitating Watergate scandal, and the hiatus as Chinese factions struggled in anticipation of Mao's imminent death, ensured that the development of the tripolar system was largely halted for a time. Washington managed to hold the pivot position by tilting in China's favour in order to offset what were perceived as Soviet aggressive tendencies. This was apparent in the careful process of tripolar communication in the 1971 India-Pakistan conflict and in 1974 when Kissinger followed the Vladivostok summit with a visit to Beijing.

Towards the end of 1976 a new, crucial phase in great power relations began as Mao died and the U.S. changed Presidents. Just as in late 1964 when President Johnson assumed full control of the office and Khrushchev was removed, so in 1976 new political options were opened for Moscow, Beijing and Washington. China essentially had three courses of action: to maintain the *status quo,* to continue the process of normalization of relations with the U.S., or to improve Sino-Soviet relations. As a result of domestic problems and an internal debate regarding policy towards the U.S. and U.S.S.R. in the triangle, it chose to maintain the *status quo,* while the U.S. attended to other external relations. By 1978, under the guidance of Deng Xiaoping, China broke the stalemate in its great power foreign policy and improved Sino-American ties. In pursuit of the desire to modernize, China turned to the great power pivot for aid and arms.

The normalization of Sino-American relations in December 1978 and Deng's call for "unity" with the U.S. and Japan against the "polar bear," was a less rigid policy as compared with foreign policy during the Cultural Revolution, but Chinese options remained restricted. It seems probable that in China's calculations, it had to establish a position of strength *vis-à-vis* the U.S.S.R. prior to the opening of negotiations with the latter. What is more, the Chinese advances to Rumania, Yugoslavia, Iran, Western Europe, Japan, and especially the U.S., preceding the anticipated Vietnamese drive against the China-supported Kampuchean regime, can probably be understood as an attempt to strengthen an anti-Soviet coalition. If China's overtures to these states had followed Hanoi's success, then China would clearly have been seen as weak and scurrying to the West for aid. Furthermore, given Chinese planning to "punish" Vietnam for the invasion of Kampuchea, China would require at least tacit U.S. support in order to deflect expected pressure from the Kremlin on Hanoi's behalf. It must have been obvious to Beijing that normalization of relations and support were unlikely to be forthcoming if China invaded Vietnam before reaching an agreement with the U.S. In any case, it is apparent that the anti-Soviet character of Chinese foreign policy may now be doing China more damage than good. There are signs that the U.S. and Japan in particular will no longer tolerate having their Soviet policy made in China. If it intends to continue its strident anti-Soviet policy, Beijing is likely to find that it has reached the end of the road as far as Washington is concerned. The time may well be ripe for a modicum of Sino-Soviet détente.

Following the Sino-Vietnamese war in early 1979 the U.S.S.R. and China indeed seemed to be searching for a new type of relationship. The process began in March with China's termination of the Sino-Soviet Treaty of Friendship. The Chinese continued to take the initiative and suggested the timing and agenda for future discussions. In the April/May Sino-Soviet exchange of notes China dropped its previous demand that Moscow withdraw its troops from the frontier prior to the opening of talks, and the problems resulting from the Sino-Vietnamese war were said to be an important factor in China's new moderation. By June, the prospect for a degree of progress in Moscow-Beijing relations seemed to increase and in July the Chinese agreed to meet in Moscow at deputy foreign minister rank. The precise outcome of this is not clear, but whatever the case, it was becoming increasingly apparent that with the continuing coolness in Sino-Soviet relations, the powers, and China in particular, had more options in the great power triangle than they were exercising. . . .

From China's point of view, clearly the concept of triangular politics, a pivot power, and card playing are not considered in the same way in which we have been using the terms. Nevertheless, some of the more important aspects of tripolarity do still have some relevance for an analysis of Chinese policy; pre-eminently the question of an improvement in Sino-Soviet relations. In fact, the state of Moscow-Beijing ties has been a major focus of previous Chinese debates on the triad, and is likely to continue to be a crucial issue.

For several years in the early and mid-1960s, China avoided any alignments with either the U.S. or U.S.S.R., but in 1968–69, due to the resolution of a foreign policy debate on tripolarity, Beijing realized that a policy of isolation from both super-powers rendered China extremely vulnerable. By and large, the course of Beijing's actions in the triad has been an attempt to remain safely in the middle ground between these two extreme tactics. However, most recently China appears to have been drifting to the extreme of forming a close alignment with the U.S., and now there is reason to believe that a degree of détente with the U.S.S.R. will bring benefits along both of Beijing's great power axes.

The U.S.-China axis would be improved because, as pointed out above, the U.S. is feeling constrained by the tension between the Communist powers. The recent debate in the U.S. as to whether to grant most favoured nation status to both the U.S.S.R. and China and the fear of upsetting Moscow if only the latter obtains the status, has upset Washington. A reduction in Sino-Soviet tension would lessen the contention between the "pro-détente" and "pro-China" groups in the U.S. What is more, some degree of U.S.S.R.-China rapprochement might make the U.S. feel that it can assist the Chinese modernization drive without fear of a negative reaction from Moscow as occurs now when even the smallest step is taken to improve U.S.-China ties. Furthermore, a reduction in Sino-Soviet tension might make less likely such actions as the Chinese invasion of Vietnam, and that would improve the domestic U.S. feeling about China. Particularly in Washington's conservative circles, the attack on Vietnam raised disturbing questions as to China's true intentions regarding Taiwan. As long as any U.S.S.R.-China détente is not based on anti-U.S. sentiments, Beijing is likely to find Washington pleased with the reduction of tension. If there is also less Sino-Soviet competition in extremism regarding struggles for national liberation, for example, in Southern Africa, U.S. satisfaction will increase. China might also find that by improving its Soviet ties it will be able to play off the U.S.S.R. against the U.S. At present, China has no such leverage as most talk of China's rapprochement with the U.S.S.R. is viewed with favour in Washington.

Clearly, there is a certain point beyond which the U.S. would not like to see Sino-Soviet détente develop, but only by moving part of the way down the road towards Moscow will Beijing be able realistically to threaten to cross the line that the U.S. fears and thereby gain some leverage in the triangle.

Although the Sino-American axis is important, it is apparent that for China the main appeal of a degree of Sino-Soviet détente lies along the U.S.S.R.-China axis. First, there are advantages for China's modernization that will result from troop reductions along the Sino-Soviet frontier. The recent revelations regarding the growth in the Chinese Defence Ministry's allocation to 18 per cent of the total budget and the deputy defence minister's pledge not to exceed that total, indicate tension in Beijing on the subject of the allocation of scarce resources in the modernization drive. What is more, Beijing is also likely to find its position in various conflicts involving the U.S.S.R. improved. For example, the degree to which Kim Il-sung and Pol Pot hold China "hostage" to their radical positions as a result of their knowledge that Beijing does not want to do anything to improve the Soviet position, would be reduced if Sino-Soviet relations become less tense. A reduction in the Vietnam-Kampuchean conflict and, more to the point, a reduction in China-Vietnamese tension, would lessen Hanoi's dependence on the U.S.S.R.: an objective that must be crucial for Beijing. In sum, Beijing's unbending opposition to Sino-Soviet rapprochement has prevented China from benefiting from the triangle. Although the U.S. and U.S.S.R. also stand to gain from an easing of Moscow-Beijing relations, China clearly has much to gain itself.

The discussion of such an important issue as Sino-Soviet détente naturally involves important considerations from the realm of internal Chinese politics. In the previous debates in Chinese factional politics the question of what type of ties should be maintained with Moscow has been controversial, and it seems that more recent Chinese politics are no exception. In the course of this paper, we have already pointed to several persuasive analyses of continuing Chinese factional debates on the proper policy for the tripolar world. Although there is some dispute regarding which leaders are in which faction, it is apparent that China's policy-makers do take into consideration the strategic import of their behaviour for the great power triangle and the significance of improving relations along the Sino-Soviet axis.

A Chinese faction supporting a degree of détente with the U.S.S.R. would be likely to support the factors noted above, but might also include a few other arguments. For example, the reduction of U.S.S.R.-China tension would remove yet another reason for the apparently wasteful Chinese military moves against Vietnam. Particularly at present, with already intense demands for other areas of military modernization, the Sino-Vietnamese hostilities cannot please the PLA professionals. Furthermore, and despite claims to the contrary, the new Chinese economic policies have reduced the differences between the internal policies of the so-called "revisionist" U.S.S.R. and those of China. The death of some personalities with more rigid anti-Soviet credentials (pre-eminently Mao himself) removes yet another factor which had kept Sino-Soviet relations so frozen. While China has been cautious about casting off the burden of Mao's legacy in foreign policy, the process of de-Maoization on internal issues may well make it easier for China to break away from the limitations imposed by Mao's refusal to consider an improvement in relations with the U.S.S.R.

61

Issues of Foreign Policy and Defense

J. A. A. Stockwin

The evolution of Japan's postwar foreign policy is the subject of this selection, in which Stockwin identifies three continuities: a movement toward decreased dependence on the United States; a consolidation of Japan's global economic role; and the modernization of Japan's defense capabilities. Stockwin contends that the turning point in Japan's foreign policy occurred in the early 1970s, following the so-called "Nixon shocks," that is, the rapprochement with China and the floating of the U.S. dollar. These twin surprises forced Japan to reevaluate its foreign policies (especially its alliance with the United States) and to seek more autonomous means of operating in the global arena. Japan has since expanded its diplomatic presence in many states, has strengthened ties with Middle Eastern oil-producing nations, increased aid to Asian and Third World countries, and begun a long process of re-examining its defense policy and its commitment to the "peace clause" in its constitution. Still, the basis for Japanese foreign policy measures is, and will be for some time, Japanese economic relations. To secure such relations, the Japanese are likely to pursue a foreign policy characterized by caution and risk-avoidance.

The rapidity of Japanese economic growth in the past quarter of a century has given rise to a mixture of expectations and anxieties about her future role in world politics. However, even from the perspective of the early 1980s it is difficult to argue that Japan has already emerged on the world scene with a clearly definable and positive role. In part, however, this may be because the most commonly proposed ideas for a positive Japanese role in world affairs tend to have American authorship and envisage greatly enhanced military capacity and responsibilities. From a Japanese perspective a fairly limited capacity—in terms of international comparisons—to wage war has not necessarily been seen as a barrier to positive involvement in world affairs in other, particularly economic, ways. Even though since the late 1970s there has been a perceptible shift in the climate of official opinion in favour of a more positive defence policy, it is still too early to say that there has been a 'breakthrough' or a conclusive departure from past attitudes and practices.

At the same time Japan is now clearly an important factor in international affairs, with a fairly complex foreign policy. She is not a 'superpower' in the generally recognized sense of that term, but being both a major (and highly successful) trading nation and the second largest economy in the non-Communist world, her ability to affect events is considerable. Whether, as is sometimes argued, she would acquire greater capacity to influence events in her own interest were she to become a major military power is highly debatable.

By far the most salient factor in Japan's foreign policy since the Occupation has been her relationship with the United States. As events in the early part of 1981 clearly demonstrated, the American connection remained both the most central and the most problematical part of Japan's relations with the outside world. The possibility of any decisive break with the United States was extremely slight, but Japan in the early 1980s could be seen as searching for a way of reconciling American demands for enhanced Japanese participation in the maintenance of global security with a domestic preference for maximum freedom of action and minimum military commitment.

As Japan's economy has grown, her relationship with the United States has naturally evolved into something different from what it was in the early postwar period. Having been under American rule between 1945 and 1952, she remained in a kind of tutelary relationship for a number of years. The ramifications of this were extensive. Through the Security Pact of 1951, revised in 1960 as the Mutual Security Treaty, Japan received guarantees of protection in case of attack at fairly low cost in terms of her own defence expenditure. . . .

. . . Diplomatic relations were not established with the Soviet Union until 1956, but even then the two countries could not agree on a peace treaty or on the northern territories issue. (Both of these issues remain unresolved.) Formal relations with South Korea were not entered into until 1965; with North Korea they are still to be established; and with the People's Republic of China, despite enormous pressure from within Japan itself, they were not established until 1972. Japanese businessmen, helped by a series of reparations and aid agreements, soon penetrated the markets of Southeast Asia in strength, but relations with most Southeast Asian countries remained on a strictly economic level, with few specifically political initiatives being recorded.

It followed from the closeness and one-sidedness of Japanese–American relationships stemming from the Occupation period that any development of Japanese foreign policy could only be in the direction of greater independence from the United States. It was scarcely surprising if the two countries should have given the appearance of drawing somewhat further apart simply by virtue of the fact that Japan was developing a wider range of international contacts. Nevertheless, mutual co-operation held remarkably firm until the early 1970s, although it was shaken very briefly by the 1960 crisis revision of the Security Treaty.

When change came it came suddenly and, from the Japanese point of view, in a curiously disconcerting manner. In July 1971 President Nixon took a dramatic new initiative, without prior reference to the Japanese Government, by announcing his coming visit to Peking. This was followed the next month by his announcement of a series of economic measures, including the floating of the dollar in terms of gold and a 10 per cent surcharge on imports entering the United States. A principal target of these measures was the exchange parity of the yen, since it was calculated by the American Government that the lifting of the surcharge could be traded for an upward revaluation of the Japanese currency, and thus make Japanese exports less competitive in the American market. The 'second Nixon shock' (as it came to be called in Japan) eventually succeeded in this objective and in the new era of floating exchange rates the yen became a much more expensive currency.

The two Nixon shocks precipitated an intensive debate among articulate Japanese about the future direction of foreign policy, and there was a great deal of questioning about the long-term viability of a policy of continuing as a military satellite of the United States. Although the Japanese reactions to the Nixon shocks were curiously similar to later reactions to American initiatives, relations between the two Governments at that time had also been poisoned by a lengthy wrangle over textiles, in which personal ill-will between President Nixon and Japanese Prime Minister, Satō Eisaku, was an exacerbating factor.

More broadly, at about this time protectionist pressures had been building up in the United States, with Japan as the chief target—a problem that was to recur later—while in Japan, foreign policy makers were beginning to explore a wider range of options than they had needed to contemplate before.

Only just over a year after the Nixon shocks, Japan under a new prime minister recognized the People's Republic of China. This was widely heralded as a turning point in Japan's foreign policy, marking the end of passive adherence to American policies. Clearly, President Nixon's visit to Peking was a major reason why the new Tanaka Government was so eager to shift diplomatic relations from Taipei to Peking, and thereby reverse the strong stand in favour of Taipei that the Satō Administration had taken for so long. . . .

While the Nixon shocks and the return of Okinawa seemed major events at the time they occurred, they were dwarfed by the impact of the first 'oil shock' of 1973–4. The quadrupling of the oil price had a massive and immediate impact on an economy in which inflationary pressures were already building up, and temporarily halted economic growth. Psychologically the impact was also very great. Resource vulnerability came to be seen as Japan's most pressing international problem, and politics designed to reduce dependence on oil imports in particular were devised and put into effect with urgency and skill. The policies included the search for alternative energy sources (including nuclear), and the reduction of wasteful usage. On raw material generally, Government and industry sought as far as possible to avoid excessive dependence on one source of supply and rather to develop resource flexibility. The Government, as we have seen, following the economic disruption of the first oil crisis, was able rather quickly to put the economy back on the rails, and when the oil price was once again increased substantially in 1979–80 the disruptive effect was much less. The Government was now much better able to handle the second oil crisis because of its experience in handling the first, and because of the long-range policies to cope with resource vulnerability that had been coming into operation since the mid-1970s. Nevertheless, the potential for economic disaster posed by severe interruptions in supply, especially of oil, continued to be a source of great anxiety for policy-makers.

In the specifically diplomatic area, the most important event of the late 1970s was the much-delayed signature of a peace and friendship treaty with the People's Republic of China in 1978. The significance of this may be regarded as both less and greater than was commonly supposed at the time. First of all, the confident expectations that a trade bonanza for Japan would stem from the friendship treaty (and an associated trade agreement) soon had to be scaled down in the face of manifold difficulties of economic modernization in China. On the other hand fears about an adverse Soviet reaction to the treaty proved rather exaggerated, though relations between Japan and the Soviet Union have been anything but happy. The other side of the picture, however, is that a key issue which had long divided the Government and Opposition in Japan was largely removed from the arena of contentious political debate. Undoubtedly this has contributed to a certain coming together of political forces in Japan in their views on foreign policy in general.

The Soviet invasion of Afghanistan in December 1979 wrought substantial changes in US Government policy towards the Soviet Union, and as a consequence of this, led to increased pressure upon Japan to contribute more to an American-led security system whose main purpose was to counter what was seen as an unacceptably rapid Soviet arms build-up. . . .

Clearly, Japan is in the early 1980s a power of great importance in world affairs, and almost unrecognizable from what she was in 1952 when the Occupation ended. Nevertheless, if one examines Japanese foreign policies since the 1950s, a sense of continuity of development is very evident. This should not be too surprising given that the same political party has been in power since the 1950s, that it is ideologically conservative and business-oriented, and that under its leadership Japan has enjoyed a sustained high rate of economic growth. Although significant changes in the leadership of the LDP have taken place, there has been no large shift in the domestic balance of political power such as might have entailed any really fundamental reorientation of foreign policy. Changes in foreign policy have tended to come from shifts in the external environment, and from the need to adjust to becoming a major economic power.

The basic continuities in Japanese foreign policy can be reduced to three long-term trends, all of which have developed with some consistency over a number of years. It would perhaps be an exaggeration to say that they represent aims of policy which have been specifically and consistently pursued, since many policy decisions have been prompted more by short-term considerations of expediency than by any long-term plan. Nevertheless, as trends they are clear enough.

The first such trend has been the development of a multi-lateral diplomacy within, and to some extent constrained by, the framework of the security relationship with the United States. Though it is arguable that there was more rhetoric than substance to the phrase 'multilateral diplomacy' used by governments in the late 1970s, it did have substance in the sense that there was a pragmatic broadening of international contacts and a strong reluctance to maintain a foreign policy which could be seen as having been dictated by the United States. At the same time, however, this exercise was carried out strictly within the strategic assumption that the Japan—US Security Treaty would continue and that Japan's military security would be looked after by the United States in co-operation with the Japanese Self-Defence Forces. Pressures upon Japan, especially after the Soviet invasion of Afghanistan, to contribute more to the 'alliance' created difficulties for the policy and strains within the Government. Nevertheless, there seemed little alternative other than to continue a balancing act of this kind. The theoretical alternative of breaking with the United States was seen as far too expensive and dangerous, while the other alternative of simply following the American line and becoming part of a full-fledged military alliance against Soviet expansionism, though favoured by some, was also strongly opposed by many within the Government. In these circumstances it looked as though Japan would continue to pursue a kind of multilateral diplomacy while attempting to retain a special relationship with the United States. It was unlikely that the future course of the policy would be smooth.

The second trend has been the consolidation of Japan's position as a major trading power, with an increasingly important role to play in world trading arrangements. The status of Japan as an accepted member of the 'club' of first-class economic powers is now generally accepted, but a considerable amount of positive diplomacy was required over the years to establish it. In this respect 1964, the final year of the Ikeda administration, was a key year, for it was then that Japan gained entry to the Organization for Economic Co-operation and Development (OECD) and had her status under the International Monetary Fund (IMF) changed from that of an article 14 nation (with substantial exchange controls) to an article 8 nation (moving to a convertible currency). She also entered the General Agreement on Tariffs and Trade (GATT) at this period, and negotiated the ending of discrimination against her exports authorized by article 35 of GATT.

More recently, Japanese interest in the economic development of third world countries, particularly those in Southeast Asia, led to her heavy involvement in the Asian Development Bank, and to an interest in proposals for the establishment of some kind of Asia–Pacific, or 'Pacific Basin', community. During the 1970s Japan in a sense acquired global economic interests, and having previously established her credentials as a leading advanced economy, became involved in North–South problems. Much of this was, not surprisingly, motivated by national interest, and in particular by the advance of her capital into Southeast Asian countries. The rather blatantly self-interested nature of Japanese economic policy towards the third world, especially as reflected in her foreign aid policies, adversely affected her popularity, if not her influence, in some third world countries.

Liberalization of trade and capital imports was a feature of Japanese trading policy in the 1960s and early 1970s, but Japan continued to be the object of complaints from foreign companies and governments that it remained far too difficult for foreign interests to operate effectively inside the Japanese market. Since Japanese imports also remained out of balance with exports, the problem of 'friction' in trading relations between Japan on the one hand and the United States and the European Community countries on the other remained a continuing obstacle to the full acceptance of Japan as an equal partner in the world economy. To some extent, as has been suggested earlier, this kind of criticism reflected factors other than deliberate obstacles imposed by Japan to the penetration of her market.

Thirdly, there has been a slow but steady trend towards the development of more sophisticated and better equipped defence forces. The whole issue of defence is one of great political delicacy in Japan, with Opposition parties and substantial sections of public opinion having opposed any increased expenditures on defence, and even at times arguing that the existing Self-Defence Forces should be abolished. The controversy over article 9 of the Constitution has been discussed in chapter 10 and elsewhere. Public opinion now shows majority support for the existence of the Self-Defence Forces, but broad uncertainty about their role, and support for the present Constitution which includes the peace clause remains strong. Of the Opposition parties, the Democratic Socialists now favour a clearer statement of defence policy, while there has been some shift of view in that direction on the part of the Kōmeitō. The Socialists and Communists, however, are still strongly opposed to increased spending on defence, and within the LDP itself, as was evident from the controversy following the Suzuki–Reagan talks of May 1981, there are divisions of opinion on the desirable rate of military build-up.

Despite the lack of consensus on defence, however, Japan already has substantial, well-trained, and comparatively well-equipped armed forces. They do not compare remotely with the forces of the United States or the Soviet Union, and they conspicuously lack nuclear weapons. Their role in the defence of Japanese territory has nevertheless been increasing. . . .

As already indicated the achievement of greater equality and independence within the relationship with the United States has been a persistent theme of Japanese foreign policy debates since the early 1950s. Thus [Japan's] policy of resisting American demands for a massive Japanese military commitment had considerable success, although under the 1951 Security Treaty and the Mutual Security Assistance Agreement of 1954 Japan found her freedom of action in the sphere of defence and foreign policy quite severely restricted by the American presence. Negotiations for revision of the Security Treaty between 1958 and 1960 were motivated on the Japanese side largely by the search for greater equality within the framework of continuing security guarantees. Although it was obscured at the time by the domestic political discord which the whole issue aroused, it was Kishi's* achievement to have obtained, through tough bargaining with the Americans, a number of quite significant concessions which in effect placed Japan in a more equal and favourable position than she enjoyed under the old Treaty. . . .

[An] indication of the greater equality which Japan achieved—at least on paper—in the new Treaty was the fact that she assumed greater obligations to contribute to a mutual defence effort. Article III of the 1960 Treaty in effect committed Japan to a continuing programme of rearmament, though the phrase 'subject to their constitutional provisions' was a ritual obeisance by the Americans to the peace clause of the Japanese Constitution. There was a similar proviso in article V, which provided that the two countries would act together in the event of 'an armed attack against either Party in the territories under the administration of Japan'.

The 1960 Treaty contained three separate references to the 'peace and security of the Far East'. This was the subject of a lengthy debate in the Diet during the early months of 1960 about the precise geographical definition of the term 'Far East'. Government spokesmen at the time came out with differing answers to the question, but it seemed to be accepted that it included not only the Japanese islands themselves, but also South Korea and Taiwan, at the minimum. As the Government subsequently interpreted the Treaty, however, there was no question of Japanese forces being sent overseas in joint defence with the United States of the 'peace and security of the Far East'. Government ministers repeated frequently that the despatch of troops overseas would be in violation of article 9 of the Constitution, and this ban was extended even to cover participation in UN peacekeeping operations.

It need not be supposed that the Japanese Government was acting here out of a scrupulous regard for the Constitution as such. But a combination of domestic political pressures, suspicion of Japanese intentions on the part of other countries in the area and a preference not to be too closely identified with American policies in the Asian region all contributed to an

---

*Ed. note: Kishi Nobusuke was Prime Minister of Japan from 1957 to 1960.

official interpretation of the Security Treaty which virtually confined the Japanese contribution to a role in the defence of Japanese territory, while providing facilities for American operations elsewhere. . . .

Relations between Japan and the Soviet Union have not had the same cultural overtones as relations with China. Since 1956, when diplomatic relations were entered into but no peace treaty was signed because of the northern islands dispute, the two countries have regarded each other coolly. Memories of the way Stalin unilaterally broke the Neutrality Pact in August 1945 and of the treatment of Japanese prisoners after the war have not entirely disappeared, and the two countries have had little in common either culturally or politically. Nevertheless, relations at the economic level have gradually developed in recent years, largely as a result of Japanese interest in the natural resources of Siberia. Although the grandiose Tyumen project to supply oil from Western Siberia through a pipeline to the Pacific coast was still-born, other more modest projects in eastern Siberia have been pursued.

The northern islands dispute appears no closer to solution than it was in 1956, and no Japanese government has been prepared to act on the suggestion of Miki Takeo's adviser Hirasawa Kazushige during the former's prime ministership, that the question of Etorofu and Kunashiri (the southernmost two islands of the Kurile chain) be shelved until the twenty-first century. Proposals from the Soviet side for a treaty between the two countries always run up against a Japanese refusal to consider such a treaty until the northern islands are returned. . . .

If relations between Japan and her near neighbours on the mainland of Asia were greatly complicated by political factors, her contacts with the countries of Southeast Asia were largely dominated by economics. In part on the basis of reparations agreements with a number of Southeast Asian countries, Japanese firms were quickly able to establish trading links with the area, and as the Japanese economy grew, trade with Japan became a dominant factor in the external trade of practically every Southeast Asian country. The series of riots against Tanaka, when as Prime Minister he toured Southeast Asian capitals in January 1974, prompted a certain degree of reconsideration of the role of Japanese businesses in the region, but the central point that the Japanese economy is enormously dominant in Southeast Asia remains. Apart from the important Japanese role in the Asian Development Bank, the impact of Japanese capital investment and Japanese-based multinationals has been increasingly important. Politically, Japan has maintained close relations with the ASEAN nations. So far as possible she has avoided becoming entangled in the international politics of Indochina.

Large-scale contracts for the sale to Japan of iron ore, bauxite and other minerals were the basis for a major trade expansion from the 1950s between Japan and Australia (wool has been the other major factor). On the whole the relationship developed without serious frictions, aided no doubt by the fact that Australia has had a consistent trade surplus with Japan. The Basic Treaty of Friendship and Co-operation between Australia and

Japan, signed in 1976, gave Japan what was essentially most favoured nation treatment in matters of entry and stay, as well as investment. The changing structure of the Japanese economy in the 1970s and 1980s was requiring substantial adjustments to the mutual economic relationship. Moreover, there was a certain impetus between the idea of sorting out economic problems in the Asian and Pacific area—an area of rapidly increasing regional economic exchange—in a multilateral rather than a purely bilateral context.

Japan's economic relations with Western Europe have also greatly increased, but the 'friction' entailed by an excess of Japanese exports to Europe over imports from Europe was far from resolution as of early 1981.

From the above picture it can be seen that, whereas Japan's economic impact on much of the rest of the world has been spectacular, her foreign policy remains fairly unassertive and 'low key', even though changes have taken place since the 1960s. A number of explanations have been advanced to explain this caution. One is that Japan, having known the bitter taste of defeat and the horrors of atomic attack, and possessing a 'peace Constitution' which commands widespread respect among the electorate, cannot aspire to more positive, nationalistic or adventurous foreign and defence policies because this would not be acceptable to public opinion. Another explanation is that politics in Japan is seriously fragmented, with the politics of factional advantage and the constant search for a watered-down consensus of what can be agreed between rival groups inhibiting clear and sustained policy initiatives. A third explanation is that, by concentrating on building up the economy and developing a strong position in international trade, Japan has maximized national advantage at minimal cost, and that the policy is continued because it is successful and recognized as such.

All these three explanations contain a considerable element of truth, but they need to be looked at critically, and also tested against Japan's changing domestic and external situation of the early 1980s.

The anti-war sentiment based on the Constitution is still a factor to be reckoned with in the Japanese electorate, although the fervent pacifism of the postwar years has declined, and the existence of the Self-Defence Forces is more readily accepted than it was. The Opposition parties remain generally hostile to rearmament and continue to champion the Constitution, though the Democratic Socialists in particular had changed by the early 1980s to a more forward attitude on defence. The Liberal Democrats, having been returned in 1980 once more with a comfortable majority, may not be too much inhibited by Opposition attitudes, but the prospect of disruption of Diet proceedings and popular demonstrations in the streets, has in the past tended to encourage caution.

Factionalism and consensus politics have also in the past tended to make it hazardous for the Government to pursue obviously innovative policies in ideologically charged areas of foreign policy and defence. The crisis which Kishi faced in 1960 over revision of the Security Treaty is the classic case of this, but there have been a number of examples since, including the passage of the non-confidence motion which led to the downfall of the Ōhira Government. Nevertheless, one ought not to exaggerate the degree to which foreign policy-making has been hamstrung by internal division during the long period of Liberal Democratic rule. Taken in broad perspective, Japan's foreign policy-making processes have been cautious and conservative not solely because they are the product of compromise, but because the Liberal Democrats, together with influential businessmen and civil servants, have seen advantage to lie in the policies actually pursued.

This leads on to the third explanation, that the successes hitherto of a foreign policy emphasizing economic development rather than military strength or political assertiveness have been such as to convince a generation of decision-makers that it is worth while. The Government, by concentrating on economics, or more specially by allowing businessmen the freedom to pursue their natural interests for growth, while itself working vigorously for maximum resource security and a stable economic environment, has succeeded in establishing Japan as a global economic power without resort to military power politics.

On the whole, this third explanation appears to be the most convincing, although the other two should certainly not be discounted. The three are of course connected, in the sense that the line of least resistance, of avoiding controversial political decisions because of the domestic complications they involve and the resistance of public opinion, has through a combination of luck and astute judgement been made to work in such a way that it has paid off.

Whether it will continue to pay off, however, is more problematical. Japanese foreign policy is already having to contend with some difficult and important political problems. Perhaps the most worrying long-term issue is the nature and credibility of Japan's security arrangements with the United States. All things considered, Japan is likely to depend for a long time upon security guarantees given by the United States simply because she has no real alternative. Short of a massive shift of the ideological balance within Japan itself, she has no other obvious ally. How long, however, the United States will be prepared to underwrite the security of a nation as economically advanced and independent-minded as Japan is problematical. Under the late Carter and early Reagan presidencies Japan has come under greater pressure than ever before to stop 'taking a free ride on the Security Treaty' and to contribute more to the 'alliance'. Moreover this corresponds with the increasing prominence of such sentiments in some sections at least of the Japanese Establishment.

One course of action that is open is to embark upon a substantial build-up of Japanese armed strength, and to an extent this is already happening. In military terms however Japan has a long way to go before she can remotely match the superpowers, and the cost of attempting to do so could well be grave in terms of alienating her neighbours, promoting political instability at home and imposing strains upon her own economy and environment. The nuclear option would be the most striking instance of this kind of dilemma, and to take it would be for Japan a step with the very gravest of implications. Indeed, one may well question whether anything recognizable as a democratic system of government would be likely to survive a decision for massive rearmament including the development of nuclear weapons.

Japan has succeeded in weathering the international economic crisis of the late 1970s and early 1980s with her economy in remarkably good shape in comparison with the economies of many other countries. Despite the perennial problems of resource vulnerability, it is at least arguable that Japan is headed for a situation where her economic leverage is internationally so great that she can afford to 'write off' particular markets and sources of supply because she has adequate supplies and markets elsewhere. Oil is an obvious exception to this scenario, but as we have seen, Japan's dependence on external sources of oil for her vital energy supplies has been diminishing under government guidance. The continued competitiveness of her most advanced industries, and the flexibility of her industrial structures as a whole, mean that nothing short of massive international protectionism could stop her in her tracks. And it needs to be remembered that Japan herself is an integral part of the world economy, so that serious harm to the Japanese economy tends to affect adversely the international economy as well.

There is a sense, however, in which the Japanese economic success story has been achieved at the expense of the outside world. Americans and Europeans, not to speak of Southeast Asians, are not entirely without reason when they argue that Japan has done well economically because of a light defence burden, the 'free ride on the Security Treaty', low spending on genuine foreign aid (as distinct from aid designed to further the commercial success of Japanese industries overseas), and official policies encouraging exports and discouraging imports. Even though such views are frequently expressed in exaggerated form, they contain the proverbial grain of truth. It is therefore in the interests of the outside world generally, to encourage Japan to develop more internationalist attitudes, and within Japan itself there is a distinct trend in this direction.

One thing, however, that is often overlooked about Japan's foreign policy record in discussions such as these is that while in one sense she has been 'reluctant to bear a defence burden commensurate with her economic capacity', this very fact has been an integral part of her economic success. While other nations groan under an excessive defence burden and their economies fail to recover from 'stagflation', Japan with her concentration on economic efficiency and motivation rather than international politics has continued to expand and prosper. Moreover, whether her military security has actually suffered as a result of these policies is a more difficult question than it sounds. Perhaps the only way of resolving it is to ask what Japan would look like today if since the war she had been spending a similar proportion of her GNP on defence (including presumably nuclear weapons) as the United States, the major European countries or the two Koreas. Quite apart from the domestic political impact of such a policy, one needs to ask whether, had it been pursued, China and the Soviet Union might not have developed strategies of Asian defence directed primarily against Japan rather than primarily against each other. Of course, had that been the case, Japan would have been forced into still greater military efforts, and one wonders how her economy would have fared in that case.

While the foreign policy and defence policy problems of Japan in the 1980s may well be complex and difficult to resolve, the caution and restraint which have been characteristic of Japanese policy for several years have put down deep roots, and are unlikely to be abandoned lightly.

62

Japan's Foreign Policies

Gerald L. Curtis

Japanese relations with the People's Republic of China and the Soviet Union could not be more different. Since the Sino-Japanese rapprochement of 1972, economic relations between China and Japan have steadily improved and expanded. Japan now supplies 25 percent of China's imports and China is Japan's fastest growing market. The trade relationship between the two countries is highly complementary, with China supplying Japan with foodstuffs, energy, and low-priced consumer goods and Japan investing capital and transferring technology to the backward Chinese mainland. Relations with the Soviet Union are not so warm. The USSR and Japan have yet to sign a peace treaty for World War II; the Russians still occupy four northern Japanese islands; and Soviet activities in Cambodia, Afghanistan, and the Eastern Pacific are of great concern to the Japanese public and Japanese leaders alike. Despite some economic activities in Siberia, Japanese relations with the Soviet Union are marked by caution, suspicion, and distrust.

In this selection, Curtis argues that the different character of Japan's relations with China and the Soviet Union can best be understood in the context of U.S.-Japanese relations. Japan's relations with China are basically bilateral and do not concern the United States. Its relations with the Soviets, however, are conditioned by larger geopolitical concerns which arise from the U.S.-Japanese alliance. While U.S. relations with the People's Republic affect Sino-Japanese relations, the effect is not as direct as in the case of Japan-USSR relations.

Japan is not pursuing an equidistant policy toward Moscow and Peking, nor is it likely to seek a balance in its relations with its two large communist neighbors for the foreseeable future. There are strong indications that economic relations with China will continue to grow more than those with the Soviet Union, that cultural relations with China will expand

while those with the Soviet Union will stagnate, and that political rela-
tions—assuming the absence of major policy shifts on the part of either the
Soviet Union or the People's Republic—will be generally positive with the
PRC and relatively acrimonious in the case of the U.S.S.R.

The last time two-way trade between Japan and the Soviet Union exceeded that between Japan and China was in 1976. Since then trade with
China has grown at a much faster rate than that with the Soviet Union, the
gap growing wider in the aftermath of Afghanistan. Two-way trade with
China in the first half of 1980 amounted to $3,992 million while that with
the Soviet Union was $2,158 million. Japanese exports to the Soviet Union,
in fact, declined absolutely in dollar terms in the first half of 1980 compared
to the first half of 1979.

Anti-Soviet sentiment in Japan is strong, and it is growing. The reasons
are not hard to discern: increased Soviet naval power in the waters surrounding Japan, a military buildup on the disputed northern islands and
total intransigence on the issue of their reversion, Soviet support for Vietnam's efforts to impose a client regime in Kampuchea, the Afghanistan invasion, and more generally a Soviet diplomatic style toward Japan which is
marked by an almost total inflexibility and a seemingly purposeful indiffer-
ence to Japanese reactions. Though few serious people worry about a Soviet
attack on Japan in the absence of a wider conflagration, the perception of
the Soviet Union as posing a threat to Japan has grown both among elite
groups and the public at large. It has been a major factor in spurring Japanese to consider military issues more seriously than before.

Both for these reasons and because of then Prime Minister Ohira's
determination to demonstrate the importance Japan attaches to the U.S.
alliance, the Japanese government, after an initial hesitation, moved in step
with the Carter Administration in imposing sanctions on the Soviet Union
to protest its invasion of Afghanistan. In addition to forcing the Japanese
Olympic Committee to boycott the Moscow games, the government
brought a halt to most trade talks then ongoing. Negotiations relating to 14
projects valued at $4–5 billion were suspended; new Japanese plant exports
to the U.S.S.R. virtually ceased; and a freeze was put on new loans through
the Japanese Export-Import Bank for exports to Moscow on a deferred-
payment basis.

Japan's position was considerably more cooperative with U.S. policy
than that of key West European countries, and as 1980 progressed Japanese
businessmen began complaining, with considerable justification, that they
were losing contracts to European competitors. In the first half of 1980
Japan ceded to France its erstwhile position as the Soviet Union's second
largest non-communist trading partner (the first being West Germany). So
it is hardly surprising that Japanese support for sanctions is now waning.
They see the American determination to retain sanctions wavering, and are
convinced that the Russians are in Afghanistan for a long time to come and
that further Japanese fidelity to U.S. policies will only lead Moscow into
deals with European, and possibly American, firms. At the end of 1980 Japan

agreed to extend new credits by its Export-Import Bank totalling 208.8 billion yen for coking coal development in South Yakutsk and for the exploitation of Siberian forestry resources.

Even with sanctions removed, however, it is unlikely that trade between the Soviet Union and Japan will expand very greatly. At the best of times Soviet trade has not exceeded more than about two and a half percent of Japanese total trade, and some of the Siberian projects on which Japanese participation was most sought by the Soviet Union failed to elicit an enthusiastic Japanese response long before Afghanistan or the recent expansion of Soviet military capabilities in the Far East. Considerations of cost, security of supply, the absence of American participation, and the potential military uses of the projects proposed, as well as a concern for Chinese sensitivities, have made Japanese government and business leaders cautious about Soviet economic relations.

The Japanese government does not appear to be prepared to take any initiatives to try to improve Soviet relations. While there are disagreements among Japanese leaders as to how to deal with the Soviet Union, the dominant sentiment at the moment is that any improvement in the relationship will have to come on Soviet initiative. The Soviet Union, according to this view, has as much if not more to lose from a further deterioration in relations, and hence Japan can refuse to offer concessions or move to improve the relationship without incurring serious costs. Thus there is a curious mixture in current Japanese thinking: on the one hand, anxiety about Soviet intentions and capabilities; on the other, a new degree of self-confidence that Japan can live perfectly well with the present unsatisfactory state of the relationship.

At the same time, precisely because the Soviet Union is potentially Japan's most dangerous neighbor, there is a widespread view that efforts should be made to avoid policies or actions that would worsen the relationship. Japan continues to try to reassure the Soviets that it is not lining up with the Chinese in an anti-Soviet bloc; it will attempt to keep the door open for expanded Soviet ties should Soviet diplomatic strategy toward Japan change. But given the record of Soviet diplomacy toward Japan, the possibility of a more intelligent strategy must be regarded as extremely small.

What about the Japanese view of American policy toward the Soviet Union? Despite their own anti-Soviet views, Japanese leadership groups share a general lack of confidence in American leadership and a feeling that Japan has been pulled to and fro by excessively wide swings in American policy, especially during the Carter Administration. Indeed, some influential Japanese have interpreted these swings as being, at least in part, an effort to deflect public attention away from, and an unwillingness to come to grips with, a variety of difficult domestic problems. The Inoki report cited earlier more than hints at this perception: "Unfortunately, it is easier to take a hardline anti-Soviet stance given the opportunity presented by the Afghanistan problem than to come to grips with energy conservation, easier to criticize the 'invasion' of Japanese-made goods than to work to increase productivity or change industrial structure."

It is still too early to say how Japanese leaders perceive the Reagan Administration's Soviet policy. Clearly there is support for the new Administration's efforts to strengthen America's military position. Just as clearly, there is apprehension lest U.S. policy become totally confrontationist and increase the risks of conflict. One hardly need underscore the ambivalence evident here. Japan will go along with a tough U.S. policy toward the Soviet Union up to a point, because it perceives the need for toughness and because it views positive relations with the United States as essential to its security. But it would be unlikely to associate itself with a posture that effectively closed off avenues to possible accommodation with the U.S.S.R., particularly if Western Europe persists in efforts to preserve détente at the cost even of considerable discord in European-American relations. And should American policy include what were perceived to be attempts to build an anti-Soviet entente with China and Japan, the Japanese reaction would be even more negative, on all present indications. Japan is in a sharp tilt toward China, but it is not about to fall into an anti-Soviet tripartite alliance or a de facto security relationship.

Although the normalization of Sino-Japanese diplomatic relations in 1972 came in response to the new political situation created by the Nixon Administration's opening of relations with the PRC, the thrust of Japanese policy toward China since then has been overwhelmingly economic. As China's internal policies turned more pragmatic and development-oriented, the Japanese became for a time enthusiastic boosters of trade ties with China, signing a long-term trade agreement in 1978 and entering into contracts to export large-scale plants and equipment needed for China's crash modernization drive.

However, shortly after the signing of that trade agreement, it became evident that China's planners had set totally unrealistic targets, and the Japanese settled down to more modest appraisals of the short- to medium-term potential of China both as a source of needed supplies and as a market for Japanese goods. Like the Chinese themselves, the Japanese have come to realize the difficulties of modernizing the economy and the long period of time that will be required. The Chinese cancellation of contracts for some 17 Japanese steelmaking and petrochemical plants this February removed any doubts on that score. Nonetheless, Japan, unlike the United States, has a long-term economic strategy, and in that strategy China continues to occupy a significant though limited position.

Of Japan's total exports in 1979, 3.6 percent went to China. On the other hand Japan accounts for nearly a quarter of total Chinese imports. Although Japan's market share has declined slightly in the past couple of years and may decline a little further, given a PRC policy that seeks to diversify China's sources of imports, the size of Sino-Japanese trade and its continuing expansion remain impressive by any measure. The annual volume of trade between the two countries increased almost six times in the seven years following the normalization agreement in 1972, at an average annual growth rate of 29 percent. Excluding transactions with OPEC nations, this is a faster rate of growth than Japan had with any other country in the world.

In terms of exports, China in 1979 was Japan's seventh largest market, with chemical fertilizers, steel, and machinery and equipment, especially machinery for textile production, cargo handling, mining, construction, and agriculture being the major export items. The increases in machinery and equipment exports within the past few years have been dramatic, increasing from 11.2 percent of Japanese exports to China in 1977 to 30.7 percent in 1979 and 40.2 percent in the first half of 1980.

But the important feature of Japan's economic intercourse with China is not only the size of the exchange but the direct link between Japan's trade and loan policies and China's modernization program, particularly the development of agriculture, textile industries, and energy-related exploration, development and transportation. The successful modernization of those particular sectors would enable Japan to increase imports precisely in those areas where it has no significant domestic capability, i.e., energy and foodstuffs, and those where it is phasing out its own industry, as in fairly simple textiles.

The energy picture, however, has so far been a disappointing one. The 1978 long-term trade agreement between the two countries called for shipment of 9.5 million tons of crude oil in 1981 and 15 million tons in 1982, targets that clearly will not be met. In drawing up these targets the Chinese simply failed to anticipate the difficulties they would face in bringing new wells into operation or even keeping production increasing from existing wells. Total Chinese crude oil production in 1980 appears to have declined somewhat compared to the previous year, and the target for 1981 is to try to keep production at 1980 levels. Chinese crude oil exports to Japan in 1980 totalled about 8 million tons, and this total appears likely to rise only slightly, if at all, in 1981 and 1982. In terms of Japan's total oil imports of 242 million tons (1979), this is but a drop in the bucket.

From the Chinese standpoint, however, crude oil is the vital element in its trade balance with Japan: even though the volume has not gone up significantly in the past three years, price rises have dramatically increased its value, so that crude oil accounted for 42.4 percent of Japanese imports from China in the first half of 1980 and was the major factor in nearly wiping out the previous pattern of Chinese deficits in the bilateral trade balance. Both countries have obvious major stakes in the development of China's energy resources—coal and gas as well as oil—and Japan is deeply involved financially in efforts to expand production. But current prospects are not encouraging, either in terms of Japan's desire to diversify its energy sources or China's need for foreign exchange.

In the late 1970s some Americans (and a few Japanese) were concerned about Japan's getting too big a share of the Chinese market, to the point of creating political frictions with the United States. In the three years from 1977 to 1979, however, U.S. exports to China rose tenfold (from $171 million to $1,723 million), and while most of this was agricultural commodities, the proportion of manufactured goods has grown steadily and is now a substantial 35 percent of total exports. While U.S. investment and capital equipment exports to China are still well below those of Japan, the United States has established a competitive position; this is healthy from every standpoint, as a foundation for the overall Sino-American relationship and also because a situation in which Japan gained major economic benefits while the United States concentrated on issues of higher strategy would indeed contain the seeds for major discord in bilateral U.S.-Japan relations. While there surely is room for Japanese-American joint efforts to contribute to Chinese economic development, one should not equate the desirability of cooperation with an absence of competition. The critical challenge to U.S. policy in terms of economic relations with China is not to lessen competition with Japan but to foster it.

A similar point can be made about American economic intercourse with Asian countries as a whole. An inability on the part of the United States to maintain an economically competitive position would eventually undercut domestic support for a major political and military role in the region. It could lead to political problems in the bilateral U.S.-Japan relationship, particularly if a pattern emerges in which Japan retains a dominant position in the export of machinery and equipment for industries in the middle-income Asian countries that find their major export markets in the United States.

What, then, of the Japanese view of their own political relations with China, and of the Sino-American political relationship? From 1972 onward, Japanese leaders were intensely concerned about the possible impact on their Soviet relations of the appearance of a close Sino-Japanese political relationship. They refused to accept the anti-hegemony clause proposed by China for inclusion in a Sino-Japanese peace treaty and thus delayed conclusion of the treaty until 1978, when a compromise was struck to replace the language proposed by the Chinese—which was clearly anti-Soviet in intent—with a more general statement opposing hegemonism.

The Japanese were not only determined to decouple their China and Soviet policies but also reluctant to face up to the implications for Japan of the strategic thrust of the American rapprochement with China. After the establishment of full diplomatic relations between the United States and China in 1978, many Japanese leaders became concerned with what they saw as growing American enthusiasm for playing a "China card" to contain Soviet expansionism. But their response was largely confined to reassuring the Soviet Union that they were not playing the same game.

This basic orientation has not changed. At the present time, however, though there continues to be no substantial support in Tokyo for a China policy that would align Japan with China and the United States in an anti-Soviet united front, there appears to be a much less anxious attitude than was evident a couple of years ago both about Sino-American cooperation and about the impact on the Soviet Union of Japan's own policies toward China.

Japanese reactions to the meeting of Premier Hua Guofeng with President Jimmy Carter in Tokyo in June 1980 are indicative of the current Japanese mood. Contrary to the worries of some, Japan did not appear at all nervous about the impression of an emerging triple alliance that might be created in Moscow by having Hua and Carter meet in Tokyo. On the contrary, the whole country seemed to delight in being host to that meeting—because it put the Ohira memorial service at least on a par with Tito's in terms of "funeral summitry," because it made Japan the stage for what was seen as a historic event, and because it was a neat way to take a slap at the Russians who sent no one higher than the Ambassador to Japan to represent the country at the service.

It may well be that the relaxed, even nonchalant, attitude with which many Japanese political and business leaders view U.S. China policy results from a belief that the United States will not move very far in developing a security relationship with China or that the course of Sino-American relations will not, in any case, have an adverse impact on a Japanese policy committed to keeping the country divorced from efforts to manipulate China ties for purposes of restraining the Soviet Union in its political behavior. But there are other factors that contribute to this Japanese attitude and which reflect significantly on a number of more general features of Japanese foreign policy orientations.

Japanese increasingly talk of a division of responsibility between the United States and Japan in helping China modernize its economy, with the United States, as is appropriate to its great power status, assuming primary responsibility for geopolitical concerns while the Japanese extend loans, technical assistance and in other ways contribute to China's economic development. In this new version of the separation of economics and politics, it is difficult for Japan to be openly critical of U.S. policy on matters relating to geopolitical strategy and at the same time avoid being drawn more directly into this strategy. There remains a tendency in Japan to view Sino-Japanese relations in an almost completely bilateral context, while Sino-American relations are seen as part and parcel of a larger geopolitical game.

Thus, for Japan, American China policy is important primarily to the extent it affects Japan's bilateral ties with Peking and with Moscow. From such a vantage point the best way to limit any potentially adverse impact on these relationships is for Japan to tend to its own business and stay out of the geopolitical game. The issue of U.S. military assistance to the PRC is a case in point. No matter how seriously it might privately express its concerns, Japan would rather not have to take a public position. It does not lose much in its Soviet relations by failing to make public its concerns about the direction of U.S. China policy, and the improvement in Soviet relations that might result from openly criticizing trends in Sino-American relations it considers worrisome would probably not be as great as the strains that would arise in its relations with both the United States and China. And since the U.S. government, despite its rhetoric of viewing Japan as the cornerstone of its East Asian policy, has not sought to consult with Japan in formulating its China policies, the Japanese are under no pressure to take a position—even though the course of Sino-American relations will in the long run affect their interests as much as anyone else and could also lead to serious difficulties between Japan and the United States.

But it is not only the legacy of a small power mentality which accounts for the spectator posture Japanese often adopt vis-à-vis Sino-American relations. Japanese also are realistic about the implications of Chinese modernization, cognizant that an economically developed China would not remain a militarily backward one and aware that their own exports and economic assistance contribute, both indirectly and directly, to greater Chinese military strength. Japan, for example, is helping China develop a capacity to produce special metals such as aluminum, magnesium, titanium, cobalt and nickel which are necessary for the building of modern aircraft and for ballistic missile development. Thus Japanese leaders do not see any reason to get excited over minor U.S. military-related exports that do not in any case threaten Japan, even though the seriousness with which some Americans see such military assistance, or the threat of it, as a powerful constraining factor on Soviet behavior is widely viewed as naïve.

At the present time there is a strong complementarity in U.S. and Japanese policies toward the PRC. As has often been pointed out, this is one of the few periods in modern history when the United States has had positive and friendly relations with both China and Japan. But whether this complementarity prevails in the future largely hinges on the evolution of Sino-American relations. Japanese leaders do not accept assumptions popular with some American leaders about the feasibility of managing China relations for purposes of constraining the Soviet Union, nor do they accept the view that a major effort to build up Japan's military capabilities would contribute to maintaining the balance of power in East Asia. Japan will go along, up to a point, with American policy toward China for all the reasons mentioned above and, most of all, because of the simple fact that Japanese continue to view close ties with the United States as absolutely essential to their country's security. But, to repeat, there is a clear limit to Japanese willingness to be drawn into any effort to align the United States, China and Japan in an anti-Soviet entente. Such an effort could well lead Japan to try to repair its relations with the Soviet Union, especially if Western Europe, and West Germany in particular, move away from Washington on Soviet policy and toward accommodation with Moscow.

Appendix A

Chronology of Events—China

14th century   European missions to China by Franciscans, Alani Christians, and Marco Polo confirm what earlier Mongol invasions into Eastern Europe had suggested—the existence of the great civilization known as Cathay.

1557   Portuguese colony is established at Macao.

1583   Matteo Ricci, a Jesuit missionary, arrives in Ming dynasty China and by the time of his death in 1610, Jesuit missions will have been set up throughout South and Central China.

1624   Dutch traders, based on Formosa, begin commerce with merchants in Fukien and Chekiang Provinces.

1637   Five English ships shoot their way into Kuangchow Harbor and dispose of their cargoes.

1664   The Ming dynasty is overthrown and replaced by the alien Manchus who assume the name Ch'ing. European contacts, resisted by the Ming rulers, increase in scope and frequency, despite all efforts of the Ch'ing to curtail them.

1779   The British East India Company (BEIC) is granted a monopoly over the growing tea trade between China and England. As trade imbalances grow, the BEIC begins to import opium to China from India in order to balance payments. Silver (originally imported from the New World by the British as a basis of exchange and constituting the third leg of what historians call the "triangular trade") begins to flow out of China. As silver reserves are depleted and the social problems of opium addiction become more widespread, the Chinese search for ways to halt the trade.

1793   The MacCartney mission is presented to the Chien-lung emperor and is received as a tribute-bearing mission.

1834   In response to the British public's revulsion toward the opium trade, Parliament strips the BEIC of its monopoly. Far from halting the trade, however, this action only serves to expand it as merchants rush to enter the lucrative opium business. Further complicating British-Chinese relations is a basic lack of understanding. When the Napier mission arrives in Canton to negotiate a new trade agreement, it, like the MacCartney mission before it, is treated as a tribute-bearing mission. Efforts to negotiate with the Canton authorities on an equal basis meet with failure, since such a conception goes against the Chinese ideal of their nation as the Middle Kingdom.

1839   Lin Tse-hsu, appointed commissioner in the Ch'ing anti-opium campaign, arrives in Canton and confiscates 20,000 chests of opium. British forces withdraw to offshore islands and await assistance from England.

1840   Expedition commanded by Admiral George Eliot arrives in Hong Kong.

May 1841   After failed negotiations the British attack Canton. Poor organization of the locally formed militias, divisions between the army and local populations, and the general weakness of the Chinese troops all contribute to a quick British victory. Canton is ransomed for $6 million.

August 1841–
August 1842   Henry Pottinger, Eliot's replacement, continues the campaign taking Amoy, Ningpo, Shanghai, and finally Nanking.

August 1842   The Treaty of Nanking is signed, ending the first Opium War. The treaty cedes Hong Kong, opens five new ports to trade, and results in an indemnity of $21 million.

1844   Similar treaties are signed with France and the United States, beginning the era of unequal treaties. Provisions will grow to include joint tariff control, extraterritoriality, free movement of missionaries, and the granting to all foreign powers any concession granted to one.

1847–1858   Disagreements over treaty provisions, increased xenophobia linked to anti-Manchuism, and the organization of better trained local militias lead to increasingly frequent incidents between Chinese and Westerners. The "Arrow Incident," in which Chinese crew members of a British ship are arrested for smuggling opium, leads the British, with French, American, and Russian approval, to begin a campaign to seize Canton. Lord Elgin is appointed to direct the expedition and by March of 1858 takes Canton and Tientsin.

1859   Negotiations on the Tientsin treaties conclude and as foreign signatories arrive in the city they are fired upon by Chinese troops.

1860   The Allied Expeditionary Force takes Peking, forcing the emperor to flee to Jehol. With Prince Kung acting as negotiator the new treaties reconfirm the provisions of Nanking, extend foreign commerce and tariff powers, give greater freedom to missionaries, and insultingly allow foreigners to reside in Peking.

1850s–1864   In addition to foreign incursions, China is racked by internal rebellions. The most serious is the Taiping (or Great Peace) movement. Led by a failed examination candidate, Hung Hsiu-chuan, the Taipings appeal to minority Hakka and working-class elements. With a philosophy based loosely on socialist and quasi-Christian elements, the Taipings grow quickly and establish a capital at Nanking by 1853. With much of south and central China under their control, the Taipings pose a serious threat to the Manchu government. In response, the Manchus decentralize control of taxation and militias and come to depend on Western powers for the support of their rule. With the defeat of Nanking in 1864, the Manchus face a more influential foreign presence as well as extremely capable local military leaders. It is estimated that 30 million Chinese die during the ten years of internal strife.

1869   The Alcock Convention limiting some of the more oppressive and insulting treaty provisions is negotiated and submitted to the British Parliament. Under the leadership of Prince Kung and the Empresses Dowager Tz'u hsi and Tz'u an, and with the aid of farsighted local military commanders such as Tseng Kuo-fan and Li Hung-chang and intellectuals like Feng Kuei-fen, the 1860s and 70s are relatively calm. Bureaucratic reform proceeds with the establishment of the Tsungli Yamen, a modern foreign service, in 1861. Modernization of the military and formation of capitalist enterprises are encouraged. As the Tung Chih restoration (as it came to be called) continues, it seems as if China is on the road to political modernization and equality with the West. But the Alcock Convention is rejected by the British and powerful conservative elements within the Chinese leadership hinder progress.

1870   The Tientsin Massacre of French missionaries occurs in an eruption of anti-Christian sentiments.

1880   Western competition for Chinese resources increases, especially in the case of the French, who are active in Indochina. They attack Foochow in 1884.

1894–1895   Japan and China clash over control of the Korean peninsula, a traditional Chinese tributary state. In February of 1895, a defeated China signs the Treaty of Shimonoseki, ceding Taiwan, the Pescadores, and the Liaotung Peninsula to Japan.

1895–1898   Although Japan is pressured by Western powers to return Liaotung, the "scramble for concessions" is on. The Germans take Shantung in 1897; the Russians take Port Arthur and Dairen the following year; Britain seizes Kowloon; Japan takes Fujien Province; and France invades three southwestern provinces.

1898   The fear of partition leads many Chinese intellectuals to petition the court for reforms. From June 10 to September 20, intellectuals like Kang Yu-wei and Liang Ch'i-ch'ao, who had jointly organized the Society for the Study of National Self-Strengthening in 1895, besiege the court with recommendations. Conservatives triumph, however, when Empress Tz'u hsi assumes control of the administration on September 21, bringing to a close the 100 Days Reform.

1900   In June, an anti-foreign uprising begun by a quasi-mystical group known as the Boxers besieges foreign embassies in Shantung. The Empress declares war on June 21. By August the allies have taken Peking. An Anglo-German agreement inspired by the American

"Open-Door" policy protects China from further partition. A peace agreement is signed in September of 1901.

1904–1905   The defeat of Russia in the Russo-Japanese War signifies to the Chinese the possibility of an Asian nation gaining equality with the West. Chinese advocates of reform are encouraged.

1905   The Imperial Civil Service exams are abolished and with them the raison d'etre of the Chinese educational system. Over 8,000 students are sent abroad in 1905 and 1906, the majority to Japan where the Sun Yat-sen Revive China Society (organized in 1895) and dozens of other revolutionary and reformist organizations are centered.

1906   Bureaucratic reform is again attempted and a constitution is advocated.

1910   Provincial assemblies are opened. They are seen as the first step in the formation of a national assembly. Dominated by the local gentry, they become increasingly independent of Peking's control to the point that when the central government in an attempt to recover railroad rights from imperialist interests nationalizes the Hankow-Canton and Szechwan-Hankow lines, the assemblies revolt. (Many of the assembly members had a financial interest in these lines.) The uprising succeeds in capturing Wuhan in October of 1911, and by February of 1912 the Empress abdicates in favor of a republican government formed by General Yuan Shih-kai.

1913   Dissatisfied with the selection of Yuan and angered by his negotiations to secure a $125 million loan, a revolt is begun in the summer of 1913. Yuan responds by dissolving Parliament in 1914.

1915   With an ever-increasing presence in China, Japan presents Yuan with the 21 Demands. In May, they give Yuan 48 hours to decide and he grants them concessions in Manchuria and in the former German concession of Shantung.

1916   The National Protection Army begins a rebellion in response to Yuan's attempt to enthrone himself as emperor. Yuan dies in June.

1917   Sun Yat-sen attempts to form a national government in Canton. But with Japan in the northeast and powerful "warlords" controlling sections of the nation, the task is difficult and China again faces dismemberment.

1917   The Lansing-Ishii agreement recognizing Japan's "special interests" in China is signed by the U.S. and Japan.

May 4, 1919   Conditions of the Treaty of Versailles, ending World War I, are announced in Peking. Japan is granted many of Germany's former holdings in China and students around the country respond with protests. Youth plays an especially active role in the cultural and political events of the next several decades, known collectively as the New Culture or May Fourth period. The magazine, *New Youth*, founded by Chen Tu-hsiu in September of 1915, is the bible of the movement, advocating women's rights, antitraditionalism, and the adoption of a common, nonliterary language.

July 1921   Li Ta-chao and Chen Tu-hsiu found the Chinese Communist Party. One of the original seven members is a young library assistant at Peita named Mao Tse-tung.

1923   The CCP and Sun's party, the Kuomintang (KMT), hold discussions on forming a United Front against Japanese aggression. The KMT had held its first party congress in 1920 with the aid and direction of a Comintern advisor named Borodin.

March 12, 1925   Sun Yat-sen dies of cancer of the liver.

May 30, 1925   British troops fire upon a crowd of demonstrators in Shanghai, killing twelve people.

June 23, 1925   A second demonstration in Shanghai against British and French legations leaves 52 Chinese dead. The resulting boycott against British trade seriously affects the Hong Kong economy.

January 1926   The second KMT National Party Congress is held and confirms Russian alliance but indicates a significant opposition to radical elements within the party.

July 1926   The Northern Expedition to establish KMT control of northern and eastern China begins under the direction of General Chiang Kai-shek.

March 1927   With Shanghai and Nanking taken, Chiang feels secure enough to begin a bloody suppression of radical elements both within his own party and the CCP.

August 1927   Under the direction of Mao Tse-tung, an attempt is made to organize the peasants of Hunan Province. Known as the Autumn Harvest Uprising, it quickly fails and is suppressed.

December 1927   The CCP attempts to establish a commune in Canton, but again its efforts meet with failure; by April 1928, the movement is suppressed. During this time serious splits within the CCP leadership are forming around the issues of Comintern guidance, United Front policies, and the possibility of an agrarian-based (as opposed to an urban-based) socialist revolution.

April 1928   The Northern Expedition is resumed and in June, Peking is captured. In October, Nanking is established as the capital of the Republic of China.

1935–1936   Deprived of most of its bases in south China, the CCP finds itself threatened on all sides. In an heroic attempt to salvage the movement, the Communists march 6,000 miles to Yenan, a base in northern China. Along the way internal rivalries split the leadership, but Mao Tse-tung emerges as the unchallenged leader. Most of those on the "Long March" die en route, leading many of the survivors to develop an almost mystical belief in their own indestructibility.

1930–1937	The Japanese steadily expand their control of Manchuria. In 1937, they bomb Shanghai and threaten the coastal provinces. In July of the same year, the Japanese Kwantung army (which in 1935 had initiated the "Mukden Incident" as a justification for seizing parts of Manchuria) again seizes upon a Chinese "provocation" to threaten Peking. Troops clash on July 7, 1937, and by September war has been formally declared between China and Japan.
December 1936	While in Sian to encourage local leaders to stiffen resistance to Communist insurgents, Chiang Kai-shek is kidnapped by the local military commander and turned over to the Communists. A second United Front policy is agreed upon, leading to the formal declaration of war with Japan.
1938	Japan now controls most of coastal and northern China, forcing the KMT to abandon Nanking and establish their capital at Chungking. The Communists are more active against the Japanese and simultaneously organize peasants for land reform and political education. The KMT allows the CCP to bear the brunt of Japanese military might, husbanding its resources for the coming conflict with the Communists.
1941	KMT forces attack the Communist New Fourth Army fearing Communist dominance of Shantung.
1944	The Hurley mission from the U.S. attempts to mediate CCP-KMT differences. The failure of the mission foreshadows the coming civil war for control of the Chinese nation.
1945–1949	The war against Japan ends and the Nationalists and Communists begin the civil war. On October 1, 1949, the Communist Red Army enters Peking and establishes the People's Republic of China (PRC).
1950	China enters the Korean War.
1952	The initial phase of land reform is completed with land redistributed among the peasants and perhaps as many as two million landlords executed.
1953	The Korean Armistice is signed and the First Five-Year Plan is begun. The Plan imitates the Soviet model, emphasizing heavy industry in national economic development.
1956–1957	Khrushchev's denunciation of Stalin and political protests in Hungary and Poland, both Communist bloc nations, lead Mao to relax political controls in China. He calls for letting "a hundred flowers bloom and a hundred schools of thought contend," thereby christen-

ing the Hundred Flowers Movement. However, when blooming and contending attack the legitimacy of Communist political leadership, an antirightist campaign is organized to suppress the critics.

1958–1959   Disappointed in the slow pace of economic development, Mao calls for a Great Leap Forward. The campaign is to rely on the mass mobilization of labor, utilization of native techniques and skill, and the organization of huge communes in the countryside. While successful in some respects, inefficiency, maladministration, as well as general confusion brought about by the haste with which the campaign was initiated lead to severe failures in productivity and levels of agricultural yields. Three years of near famine ensue and an estimated 27 million die. Peng Te-huai, defense minister and critic of the Great Leap policies, is replaced by Mao's handpicked successor, Lin Piao.

1960–1966   To meet the economic crises engendered by the Great Leap Forward and the withdrawal of Soviet advisors in 1960, more pragmatic economic policies and objectives are put forward by Liu Shaoqi and Deng Xiaoping. Their policies meet with success and China recovers from the Great Leap in three years.

1964   China explodes a nuclear bomb.

1965   Mao begins a Socialist Education Movement to indoctrinate the populace against what he sees as the resumption of bourgeois elements and ideology in Chinese society. Lin Piao carries on a campaign to indoctrinate the People's Liberation Army with Maoist thought.

1966–1969   Mao calls on Chinese youth to spearhead a Great Proletarian Cultural Revolution. Millions of youths and students join the Red Guards and attack Party bureaucrats, intellectuals, and some units of the People's Liberation Army. Party leaders, including Liu Shaoqi and Deng Xiaoping, are purged and sent to labor camps along with millions of lower-level cadres. Eventually, Mao must call in the army to quell student disorders. The campaign leaves the Chinese population divided, the Party structure in a shambles, and the economy in complete chaos.

1971   Lin Piao, named as Mao's successor in 1969, attempts a coup and dies in a plane crash as he tries to flee to the Soviet Union.

1972   President Richard Nixon visits the People's Republic, the first U.S. President to do so. He signs the Shanghai Communiqué, recognizing that there is only one China.

1974   Zhou Enlai, Deng Xiaoping, and other moderate leaders begin to alter or mitigate some of the harsher Cultural Revolution era policies. Radicals respond by initiating a "criticize Confucius and Lin Piao" campaign, a thinly veiled attack on Zhou Enlai and his allegedly "feudal" thought.

1976   In January, Zhou Enlai dies. When mourners commemorate his death in April, their wreaths are removed from Tienanmen Square sparking mass demonstrations. Deng is blamed for these outbreaks and is once again purged. Hua Kuo-feng is named as Chou's successor and when Mao dies on September 9, Hua succeeds to the chairmanship of the Party. In October, he arrests the four leading radicals of the Cultural Revolution: Jiang Ching, Mao's wife; Zhang Chunqiao; Wang Hongwen; and Yao Wenyuan. They are branded the "Gang of Four" and are held responsible for all the excesses of the past decade.

1977   The campaign against the "Gang of Four" shifts into high gear. Hua advocates the "four modernizations" (industry, agriculture, science and technology, and defense) as the new economic policy, stressing material incentives as a means to accomplish them. In the fall, 60 percent of Chinese industrial workers are granted pay increases and bonuses are again used to spur productivity. Deng is rehabilitated.

1978   U.S.-China relations are officially normalized. Economic policies continue to be liberalized allowing for direct foreign investments and more international borrowing. Hua visits Romania, Yugoslavia, and Iran and Deng visits Japan as China "opens up." Educational and political reforms are advocated and in the general atmosphere of liberalization the Democracy Wall movement begins in spring. Posters criticizing Mao, the Party, the Cultural Revolution, and many other aspects of Chinese society appear during Peking Spring.

1979   The Democracy Wall movement falters as leading dissidents are arrested and one, Wei Jingsheng, is sentenced to fifteen years. Deng's visit to the United States is widely covered in the Chinese media, which emphasizes the material wealth of America. Conservative critics attack Deng for his liberal policies, social unrest, and the poor showing of the military in the invasion of Vietnam. However, Deng maintains his political predominance and his policies, especially those concerning the reform of agriculture, are approved by the Party's Central Committee.

1980   Hua is replaced as CCP head by Hu Yaobang and as Premier by Zhao Ziyang. Criticism of Mao and Maoist philosophy mounts and public portraits of the "Great Helmsman" are removed. The "Gang of Four" go on trial as the campaign against their political allies continues. Connected with these developments is the renewed emphasis on Party reform. In international arenas, China continues to develop its new-found internationalist image and is admitted to the World Bank.

1981–1983   Deng Xiaoping, Hu Yaobang, and Zhao Ziyang consolidate their leadership of the Communist Party and state administration. Economic reforms continue in the areas of private farming, enterprise autonomy, and managerial authority. A long-awaited purge of the Party is scheduled for 1984. Negotiations with the Soviet Union appear hopeful, but little tangible progress is made in improving relations.

Appendix B

Chronology of Events—Japan

1543	Portuguese are shipwrecked off southern Kyushu.
1549	A Jesuit missionary, Francis Xavier, arrives in Kagoshima and stays two years. Local leaders known as *sengoko daimyo* protect missionary activity in order to reap the profits of trade with Christian Portugal. Lower-class population responds to missionary medical and social welfare aid by converting.
1600	Tokugawa Ieyasu wins the battle of Sekigahara and unifies Japan. The feudal class system crystallizes into warrior, farmer, artisan, and merchant divisions. Local *daimyo* acknowledge the political supremacy of the Tokugawa *shogunate,* which will last until 1867.
1612	Tokugawa prohibits the propagation of Christianity, fearing an alliance of Christian elements with his political rivals. He does, however, open Japan to trade with Protestant Britain and Holland.
1635	Tokugawa Ieyasu's successors, fearing too great an influence from the West, forbid overseas Japanese to return to Japan and outlaw overseas travel. In 1637, in response to these prohibitions as well as to high taxes, the Shimabara Rebellion breaks out. It is led by masterless, Christian *samurai.*
1639	Fear of the West, exacerbated by such incidents as Shimabara, results in the closure of Japan to all nations but the Dutch, whose trade is restricted to an island off Nagasaki. The Japanese begin their development of *"shima guni konjo,"* or insularity.
17th century	Under the prevailing peace of the *shogunate,* Japan prospers. Trade, industry, and culture flourish. By the early years of the eighteenth century, Edo (now Tokyo) will have become the largest city in the world.
18th century	As commercialization progresses, problems develop. Farm prices rise and the urban poor experience periodic famines. Rice riots occur in 1730 and again in the years 1783–1787.
1789–1801	Kansei Reforms attempt to alleviate the problems of the poor. Debts are cancelled, cultivation is encouraged, and an exam system for government officials is implemented. But court intrigues hinder progress and force the resignation of reformers.
1792	Adam Laxman, Russian envoy, lands at Nemuro and requests trade.
1804	N. P. Rezanov, Russian envoy, arrives in Nagasaki to establish commercial relations. When he is refused, he attacks Etoforu island. His

495

actions lead the central government to begin a program of defense building.

1808	English warship *Phaeton* enters Nagasaki harbor.
1811	Another Russian envoy, V. M. Golovnin, lands on Kunashui island and is arrested by the Japanese. Defensive measures decline as foreign aggressiveness declines.
1830s	Famine is again frequent and causes urban and rural unrest. An 1836 rebellion in what is today Yamanashi Prefecture involves more than 50,000 rebels. A rebellion in Osaka in 1837 is led by a former government official.
1841–1843	The Tempo Reforms are initiated by Mizuno Tadakuni in order to meet the twin challenges of foreign aggression and internal unrest. Though his reform measures often met with serious resistance, his initiation of them encouraged many young, local, middle-class *samurai* to press *daimyo* for reforms. Many of these young *samurai* would play a role in later attempts at political reformation.
1844	Dutch request greater trade relations and opportunities.
1844–1846	British and French make repeated visits to Ryukyu islands to request trading relations. In 1845, the *kaibo gakari* (or coastal defense office) is established.
1846	Commander James Biddle of the U.S. Navy enters Uraga harbor with two warships to negotiate trade treaties. He is turned away.
1853	Admiral Perry "opens" Japan to the West.
1850s	Inability of the *shogunate* to prevent foreign intrusions increases opposition to the Edo rulers. The *sonno-joi* (Revere the Emperor, drive out the barbarians) movement gathers strength. As the central government relaxes centralized control in order to free localities for defensive buildup those same localities become extremely antiforeign.
1863	Extremists shell foreign ships in Shimonoseki Straits.
1864	Foreigners bomb Shimonoseki. As a result, a coup brings antiforeign military men into power as counselors to the local *daimyo.*
1866	War breaks out between the forces of the *shogunate* and those reformers in present-day Yamaguchi Prefecture. A new *shogun* succeeds to the position, but his forces are defeated at Kyoto in the following year.
1867	The Meiji Emperor is enthroned and the Meiji Restoration begins. In power the reformers are not as virulently antiforeign as they were while out of power. They ally themselves with fief leaders and court nobles in pursuit of the twin goals of "rich country and strong arms."

1869   Feudal lands are returned to the throne checking the tendency towards decentralization. In 1871, feudalism is declared abolished and the 300 fiefs become 72 prefectures and 3 metropolitan districts. The *samurai* are released from military service and forbidden to wear swords or their identifying hair style. In 1873, a national conscription deprives them of their monopoly on military service.

1872   A system of universal education is established.

1873   Christianity is legalized, land reform is implemented, and capitalist enterprises are encouraged with the help of government-sponsored pilot plants.

1880s   Government plants are increasingly sold to private individuals. Monopoly interests begin to form as small numbers of financial leaders come to dominate industry. These financial cliques are termed *zaibatsu.*

1881   The Liberal Party is formed, followed by the formulation of the Progressive Party in 1882.

1884   The upper house of government or Peerage is established, and the Cabinet, in the following year. Economic problems lead the government to suspend party and press activity. Expansionist policies concerning the Ryukyus and Korea foreshadow problems with China.

1889   Japan's first constitution is promulgated and elections follow in 1890. Nationalism is encouraged by the government through the establishment of national deities, Shintoism, and a nationalist educational curriculum based on Confucianism and Shinto.

1894   Japanese missions attempt to have unequal treaties revoked and in this year the practice of extraterritoriality is changed. Relations with China degenerate, however, as sovereignty over Korea becomes a major issue. In July, hostilities break out and within months, China is defeated. The Treaty of Shimonoseki cedes to Japan the Pescadores, Formosa, and the Liaotung Peninsula. Additionally, Japan is granted all rights granted to European powers in China as well as an indemnity.

1898   The Liberal and Progressive parties merge and briefly form a government. As a result of Japan's victory in the Sino-Japanese War, the influence of the military grows.

1902   An Anglo-Japanese agreement guarantees that if either party is attacked by more than one country, the other party will come to its aid. It also guarantees neutrality of the second party if the first is involved in a war with any one country.

1904   The Japanese fear a growing Russian influence in the area of the Korean peninsula and so attack the Russian naval base at Port Arthur. Peace is signed in September of 1905 granting Japan privileges in

Korea, Manchuria, and southern Sakhalin.

1910	Korea is formally annexed by Japan.
1912	The Meiji Emperor dies and his successor finds himself increasingly influenced by business interests.
World War I	During the war, Japan seizes former German holdings. In January of 1915, it presents China with the 21 Demands. Japan's behavior leads to an intense anti-Japanese nationalism among the Chinese.
1918	Japan participates in an Allied intervention in Siberia against Bolshevik forces.
1922	The Japanese Communist Party is formed and the Washington Agreement setting shipbuilding limits for Japan, Britain, and America is signed.
1924	Legislation extending suffrage, reducing the size of the army, and promoting social welfare is enacted. The United States enacts discriminatory immigration laws and conservative elements within the Japanese leadership demand intervention in the Chinese civil war.
1925	Leftist activity increases despite recently enacted police laws. Fear of subversives unites business and bureaucratic interests.
1926	Hirohito succeeds to the throne.
1928	Agitating against private property or state policy is made a capital offense.
1929	The American stock market collapses and with it, the single largest market for Japanese silk. Financial panic ensues.
1930s	Population expansion, economic collapse, and Western racial discrimination all contribute to the growing belief that Japan's future lay in military expansionism. The military distrusts agreements like that signed in Washington in 1922 and demands stronger action against the KMT's northern expeditions and anti-Japanese boycotts in China. Ultra-rightist organizations grow in numbers and strength and terrorist activities such as political assassinations become more frequent. Junior military officers are especially active in these incidents, thereby threatening civilian government.
1931	The Mukden Incident takes place. Japanese troops accuse the Chinese of attempting to plant a bomb on a train. The Kwantung Army seizes Mukden and soon all of Manchuria.
1933	Japan withdraws from the League of Nations in protest over Western proposals on the future of Manchuria.
1934	The Japanese submit to military pressure and reconstitute Manchuria as the puppet kingdom of Manchukuo.
1936	A regiment leaving for Manchuria revolts and holds downtown To-

kyo for three days. There are several assassinations but the revolt is put down.

1937   Elections suggest that the new civilian parties are very popular with the voters. The sinking of the U.S. gunboat *Panoy* on the Yangtze river turns American sentiments against Japan. In July, Japanese troops fire on a Peking regiment and advance as far as Nanking, Hankow, Canton, and parts of Shensi and Shansi provinces. A puppet regime will be established in Nanking by 1940.

1938   National mobilization laws grant sweeping powers to the central government.

1940   Japan signs a tripartite agreement with the axis powers and occupies Indochina.

1941   Japan signs an agreement with Vichy France for joint sovereignty of French Indochina. In response, the U.S. freezes Japanese assets in America and boycotts oil shipments. General Tojo, Minister of War, replaces Prime Minister Konoe and continues negotiations with the U.S. on the embargo. As the negotiations continue, Pearl Harbor is attacked on December 7, 1941.

1942–1943   The war in the Pacific rages with the Japanese taking Manila in January 1942, Singapore in February, and Indonesia in March. But heavy losses in the Battle of Midway in June and defeats in the Solomons and at Guadalcanal foreshadow Japanese defeat in the war.

1944   Tojo is replaced by Koiso Kuniaki as prime minister.

1945   Every major city in Japan except Kyoto is firebombed. Okinawa is taken and Admiral Suzaki Kantaro replaces Koiso as Prime Minister. The Potsdam Conference declares that Japan will not be "enslaved as a race or destroyed as a people." On August 6, 1945, Hiroshima is destroyed by an atomic blast. Two days later, the Soviet Union declares war on Japan and on August 9, a second atomic blast wrecks Nagasaki. On September 2, 1945, a peace agreement is signed in Tokyo Bay aboard the USS *Missouri.*

The Occupation   Supreme Commander of the Allied Powers (SCAP) is established to oversee the demobilization of Japanese forces. As SCAP, General Douglas MacArthur is under no direct authority due to the confusion over Allied and/or American responsibility for Japan. He and his staff promote major reforms designed to ensure that Japan will become a peaceful and democratic society. State Shinto is abolished as is central control of compulsory education. Officers and businessmen active in wartime organizations are dismissed from their posts. General Tojo and seven others are sentenced to death for war crimes.

1946   A Cabinet committee prepares a revision of the Meiji Constitution. Dissatisfied, MacArthur has his own staff write a constitution. In April, the first postwar Diet elections are held and in November a constitution renouncing war as a right of the Japanese nation is promulgated. The Emperor renounces his claim to divinity.

1946–1947   SCAP implements a land reform program to distribute land more equitably among the rural poor. Rural prosperity increases dramatically. Imposition of a war-profits tax wipes out many large fortunes. However, of the more than 1,200 *zaibatsu* scheduled to be broken up, SCAP decides to break up only 28. Additionally, the large banks responsible for the financing of many of the *zaibatsu* are left untouched.

1947   The establishment of a Labor Ministry and the freeing of all political prisoners, many of whom belonged to the Japanese Communist Party, mark the beginning of a period of labor unrest. Leftist organizers help to form a strong labor movement.

1948   A general strike in 1947 (which was forbidden by SCAP) is the basis for Prime Minister Katayama Tetsu's socialist Cabinet ordering that government and communication workers be deprived of the right to strike. SCAP fears communist influence in labor unions and so issues ordinances on political activity. Sohyo (General Council of Japanese Trade Unions) is organized as a counterbalance to leftist-dominated unions.

1950   The Korean War breaks out and the Japanese economy profits immensely from Japan's position as a staging area for the war effort. A National Police Reserve (renamed the Self-Defense Forces in 1954) of 75,000 men is authorized by SCAP. SCAP orders the removal of all Communist Party members from politics. (The JCP had garnered 10 percent of the vote in the 1949 elections and had placed 35 members in the lower house of the Diet.)

1951   MacArthur is replaced as SCAP by General Matthew B. Ridgway. In September, the peace treaty signed in San Francisco renounces all Japanese claims to Taiwan, the Pescadores, Kuril islands, and southern Sakhalin. It also recognizes the independence of Korea. Soviet objections prevent their participation in the signing. A U.S.-Japan security treaty provides for the removal of U.S. troops from Japan as soon as Japan is capable of defending itself.

1952   With the peace treaty in full effect, many financial interests begin to recombine with the approval of the government.

1953   An unofficial trade pact between Japanese businessmen and the People's Republic of China is signed.

1954–1958   Peace treaties with many southeast Asian nations, formerly colonies of Imperial Japan, are signed providing generous indemnities.

1955   The Liberal Democratic Party (LDP) is formed.

1960s   The 1960s mark the emergence of Japan from the shadow of World

War II and suggest possible difficulties in future U.S.-Japan relations. The Japanese economy experiences exponential rates of growth, prompting Prime Minister Ikeda Hayato to put forward a "ten-year doubling of national income" plan. Hosting the 1964 Olympics renews Japanese national pride. Japan's role in the formation of the Asian Development Bank is evidence of its newly recognized international position. There are problems, however. Rightists assassinate Asanuma Inajiro, a socialist leader, in 1960. Urban migration creates a mass society with all its inherent problems. The latter part of the decade witnesses massive student protests against American involvement in Vietnam and Japan's aid in that effort. And the fall of Prime Minister Kishi's government in 1960 is at least partially attributable to popular opposition to the U.S.-Japan Security Treaty being renewed for ten years.

1971   President Richard Nixon travels to the PRC. This is the first of the three shocks Japan will receive in the 1970s (the other two being the twin oil crises of 1973 and 1978 and rapprochement with the PRC).

1972   Tanaka Kakuei is chosen as prime minister and begins steps to normalize relations with the PRC. The Ryukyu islands, including Okinawa, are returned to Japan.

1973   The first oil crisis sets off a financial panic in Japan and reveals the precarious nature of Japan's economy.

1974   The Lockheed scandal is uncovered, implicating government officials, including Prime Minister Tanaka, in a series of illegal deals with the Lockheed Corporation. Tanaka resigns and is replaced by Miki Takeo.

1976   Tanaka is arrested and indicted for accepting bribes. The December election ends the LDP's absolute majority in the Diet. Fukuda Takeo becomes prime minister.

1978   Ohira Masayoshi is elected prime minister amidst growing international resentment over Japan's export policies. An eight-year, $20 billion agreement for industrial contracts is signed with the PRC.

1980   Ronald Reagan is elected U.S. President and immediately begins to pressure Japan to assume a greater financial burden for its defense as well as to exercise greater restraint in exports.

1982–1984   Yosuhiro Nakasone is elected prime minister with the backing of still powerful former Prime Minister Tanaka. He tells the Japanese that they are a great nation with a greater international responsibility. He refers to the nation as an "unsinkable aircraft carrier," upsetting the pacifist elements in Japanese politics. He promotes more harmonious relations with distrustful Asian nations and in 1983 signs a U.S.-sponsored statement backing deployment of U.S. missiles in Europe, the first time Japanese security has been explicitly linked with general Western military policy. Amidst growing international distrust and anger over Japanese economic policy, Nakasone seeks a more influential role for the nation.

Bibliography

Unit I:
China and Japan Today

China

Butterfield, Fox. *China: Alive in the Bitter Sea.* New York: Bantam, 1983.
    A highly critical discussion of life in contemporary China. The author, a former Peking bureau chief for *The New York Times,* is vehement in his condemnation of Communist leadership, social control, and repression, and the low standards of living endured by the great majority of the Chinese population.

Eberhard, Wolfram. *China's Minorities: Yesterday and Today.* Belmont, Calif.: Wadsworth Publications, 1982.
    Detailed descriptions of the many minorities in the PRC. National minorities number in the tens of millions. This work explores their cultures, values, and place in Chinese society and how that position continues to change as China modernizes.

Pye, Lucian. *China: An Introduction.* 3d ed. Boston: Little, Brown, 1984.
    An extensive but thorough investigation of Chinese culture, society, and politics by a leading American scholar of Chinese politics. This work combines incisive analysis with a straightforward style enabling students to approach even the most complex issues in China studies.

Thomson, John. *China and Its People in Early Photographs.* New York: Dover, 1983.
    A handsome collection of images and scenes from China. While not a scholarly work, the photographs presented here reveal much of the Chinese character, the beauty of the Chinese people, and the poverty of their nation.

Japan

Aoki, Michiko, and Margaret B. Dardess, eds. *As the Japanese See It.* Honolulu: University of Hawaii Press, 1981.
    A beautiful collection of Japanese prose in translation. Selected readings include contemporary and historical speeches, sermons, short stories, folktales, myths, and excerpted novels. The authors bring a particular Japanese style to a wide variety of themes and issues.

Massabuau, Jacques Pezeu. *The Japanese Islands: A Physical and Social Geography.* Trans., Paul C. Blum. Rutland, Vermont: C. E. Tuttle, 1978.
    A comprehensive survey of the people, regions, environment, and resources of the Japanese archipelago. The author brings important historical perspectives to bear on contemporary features of Japanese society, focusing especially on the constraints placed on economic development by resource scarcity.

Yoshida, Kenichi. *Japan Is a Circle: A Tour Round the Mind of Modern Japan.* Tokyo: Kodansha International, 1981.

A noted Japanese author conducts a humorous investigation of Japanese society, modern customs, values, and behavior. The humor masks perceptive criticisms of the contradictions in Japanese life.

Unit II:
China and Japan Yesterday: The Cultural Background

China

Crozier, Ralph C. *China's Cultural Legacy and Communism.* New York: Praeger, 1970.
   A wide-ranging collection of readings in Chinese culture. The particular focus here is on how traditional values and beliefs have influenced recent political thought and to what extent tradition has been maintained in the modern context.

Moore, Charles A., ed. *The Chinese Mind: Essentials of Chinese Philosophy and Culture.* Honolulu: University of Hawaii Press, 1967.
   An exploration of Chinese traditions, religions, and political thought. The author, a noted specialist in Asian studies, focuses on the major schools of Chinese philosophy, including Confucianism, Taoism, and Buddhism, and discusses the influence of these tradition philosophies on contemporary values.

Morton, W. Scott. *China: Its History and Culture.* New York: McGraw-Hill, 1982.
   An extremely useful survey of Chinese history and cultural development. Contains excellent descriptions of the major events in economic and political evolution and covers broad topics concisely and simply.

Japan

Jansen, Marius. *Japan and Its World: Two Centuries of Change.* Princeton: Princeton University Press, 1980.
   A short yet incisive discussion of changes in Japanese world views over the past two hundred years. Based on a series of lectures delivered in Japan by the author, a well-known authority on Japan.

Moore, Charles A., ed. *The Japanese Mind: Essentials of Japanese Philosophy and Culture.* Honolulu: East-West Center Press, 1967.
   A companion volume to *The Chinese Mind,* this collection covers such topics as Shinto, Buddhism, the conception of the individual, and the relationship of the individual to the group.

Sansom, George. *Japan: A Short Cultural History.* New York: Appleton-Century-Crofts, 1962.
   Though more than two decades old, this work by an eminent scholar of Japan still provides an insightful analysis of Japanese cultural development. The period covered extends from early history and the influence of China to feudalism, the Tokugawa shogunate, and modern times.

Unit III:
China and Japan Yesterday: Response to the West

China

Ch'en, Jerome. *China and the West: Society and Culture, 1815–1937.* Bloomington: Indiana University Press, 1980.
    The 1937 Japanese invasion of China was both the climax and the beginning-of-the-end of foreign influence in China. A leading American historian examines the impact of that influence during the more than one hundred years of extensive Western involvement in China.

Rossabi, Morris, ed. *China Among Equals: The Middle Kingdom and Its Neighbors, 10th–14th Centuries.* Berkeley: University of California Press, 1983.
    An extremely detailed examination of Chinese foreign relations before the era of Western imperialism. The readings in this volume provide a basis for making the often startling contrasts and comparisons between traditional Chinese foreign policy and those adopted in response to Western intrusion.

Salisbury, Harrison E. *China: One Hundred Years of Revolution.* New York: Holt, Rinehart & Winston, 1983.
    An exciting, colorful, and eminently readable account of the climactic changes in Chinese society since the mid-nineteenth century. No nation has had as traumatic a recent history as China, and the author gives life to those events and people that have transformed the country.

Japan

Keene, Donald. *The Japanese Discovery of Europe, 1720–1830.* London: Routledge and Kegan Paul, 1969.
    An informative study of early Japanese and Western interaction, concentrating on the influence of "Dutch learning" in Japanese thought. The author is a renowned scholar of Japanese history.

Moulder, F. V. *Japan, China, and the Modern World Economy: Toward a Reinterpretation of East Asian Development.* New York: Cambridge University Press, 1977.
    Why, among Asian nations, was Japan the only state to modernize and industrialize in response to Western imperialism? Using a comparative international perspective, the author examines questions of development and underdevelopment in East Asia from 1600–1918. The discussion of Ching dynasty and Tokugawa economies is especially interesting.

Warshaw, Stephen, and C. David Bromwell. *Japan Emerges: A Concise History of Japan From Its Origins to the Present.* Berkeley: Diablo Press, 1983.
    This book, along with its companion volume, *China Emerges,* is an exhaustive survey of Japanese (or Chinese) political, economic, and cultural development. The authors touch on all the important events, personages, and systems of thought that have played roles in Japanese (or Chinese) history.

Units IV and V:
Political Parties and Political Leadership

China

Brugger, Bill, ed. *China Since the Gang of Four.* New York: St. Martin's, 1980.
    An anthology of articles on the sweeping transformations in Chinese society since the arrest of Mao's widow and her supporters. Combines concise accounts of the Cultural Revolution, its leaders and policies, with extensive descriptions of the reforms underway in China today.

Dunster, Jack. *China and Mao Zedong.* New York: Lerner Publications, 1983.
    The most recent of a large number of books on Mao's role in the Chinese revolution. What makes this particular account so interesting is the discussion of post-Mao China and the influence that Maoist thought and values continue to have in Chinese politics.

Elegant, Robert S. *China's Red Masters: Political Biographies of Chinese Communist Leaders.* Westport, Conn.: Greenwood, 1971.
    While dated and somewhat biased, this work is singularly important. The information, descriptions, and analyses of Chinese leaders that it contains are not easily found in other sources. The author has assembled a thorough compendium of biographies that convey a sense of great importance of individuals in the Chinese political process.

Guillermaz, Jacques. *The Chinese Communist Party in Power, 1949–1978.* Boulder, Colo.: Westview Press, 1976.
    A historical account of Communist leadership of the world's most populous nation. Free of the ideological biases that plague most other analyses of Communist rule, this book presents a straightforward and insightful analysis of three decades of Communist administration in China.

Hsu, Immanuel. *China Without Mao: The Search for a New Order.* London: Oxford University Press, 1983.
    Given Mao's extensive influence in Chinese politics, how has his death affected the policy process, ideology, and political life of his native land? The author, a well-known expert in Chinese history, explores the great changes in China since Mao's death and effectively captures the character of a nation in transition.

MacFarquhar, Roderick, ed. *China Under Mao.* Cambridge: MIT Press, 1966.
    This now classic anthology is the best of a large number of accounts of Mao's influence in Chinese politics. Readings deal with Mao's role in political thought, culture, education, and politics.

Saich, Anthony. *China: Politics and Government.* London: Macmillan, 1981.
    A penetrating analysis of the Chinese political process, the institutions of administration, and the informal rules that guide policy making in the PRC.

Japan

Beckman, George M., and Okuba Genji. *The Japanese Communist Party, 1922–1945.* Stanford: Stanford University Press, 1969.
    An overview of the history of the JCP, from its establishment in 1922 to

the end of World War II.

Curtis, Gerald L. *Election Campaigning Japanese Style.* New York: Columbia University Press, 1971.
    A dated though still illuminating and colorful look at one Japanese politician's campaign for public office. Concentrates on the important issues of party endorsement, support groups, and the role of political organizations.

Ishida, Takeshi. *Japanese Political Culture: Change and Continuity.* New Brunswick, N.J.: Transaction Books, 1983.
    A provocative comparison of Japanese and Western political values and institutions from a Japanese perspective. The author is particularly sensitive to the contradictions in Japanese society, such as that between social harmony and competition. He raises important questions about bureaucratism, tradition, and pacifism in Japanese political life.

Palmer, Arvin. *Buddhist Politics: Japan's Clean Government Party.* The Hague: Martinus Nijhoff, 1971.
    An examination of Soka Gakkai and Komeito—their organization, leadership, electoral support, ideology, and role in the Japanese political system.

Scalapino, Robert A. *The Japanese Communist Movement.* Berkeley: University of California Press, 1967.
    This book concentrates on the postwar history of the JCP, its dissolution under SCAP, the tilt away from Moscow to Peking, and current problems the Party faces.

Steiner, Kent, and Scott C. Flanagan. *Political Opposition and Local Politics in Japan.* Princeton: Princeton University Press, 1980.
    An anthology addressing the issues surrounding local government in Japan. Readings include studies of rural, urban, and suburban areas, citizen's movements, and progressive regional governments that oppose the ruling LDP.

Stockwin, J. A. A. *The Japanese Socialist Party and Neutralism.* New York: Cambridge University Press, 1968.
    A narrowly focused examination of the role of the JSP in foreign policy making. Penetrating analyses of the Japanese political process, the unique role of the JSP in that process, and the ways in which the JSP brings its influence to bear on policy.

Valeo, Francis R., and Charles E. Morrisson, eds. *The Japanese Diet and the U.S. Congress.* Boulder: Colo.: Westview Press, 1982.
    A collection of essays by Japanese and American scholars, discussing the national legislative bodies of their respective homelands. The readings provide a basis for startling contrasts and even more striking similarities between the two countries' institutions.

Units VI and VII:
Government-Business Relationships and Bureaucracy

China

Chan, Anita, Richard Madsen, and Jonathan Unger. *Chen Village.* Berkeley: University of California Press, 1984.

A fascinating case study of a Chinese village, its social and political life, and the impact of Communist rule on village life. Special attention is given to the role of rural cadres, their position in rural society, and the connections between national policies, party cadres, and the rural population of the PRC.

China from Mao to Deng: The Politics and Economics of Socialist Development. Armonk, N.Y.: M. E. Sharpe, 1983.

An incisive and illuminating study of the often conflictual evolution of Chinese development strategy and the influence of leaders, bureaucrats, and factions on economic policy.

Harding, Harry. *Organizing China: The Problem of Bureaucracy.* Stanford: Stanford University Press, 1981.

A thorough, well-documented analysis of the various approaches to eliminating bureaucratism and reforming Party and government organizations since 1949.

Masi, Edoarda. *China Winter: Workers, Mandarins and the Purge of the Gang of Four.* Trans., Adreinne Foulke. New York: Dutton, 1982.

Although primarily concerned with the political struggles surrounding the arrest and trial of the "Gang of Four," this work provides as well a fascinating portrait of ideological conflict and bureaucratic in-fighting. The author traces the interplay of various factions and social groupings in the leadership struggle that ensured after Mao's death, illustrating the complexity of Chinese politics and the influence of bureaucratic groups in the political process.

Meisner, Maurice. *Mao's China.* New York: The Free Press, 1977.

The textbook for courses in modern Chinese history. The author emphasizes the importance of antibureaucratism in Maoist ideology, the violent conflicts between Mao and Party cadres, and the continuing influence of an antibureaucratic tradition in Chinese politics.

Pye, Lucian. *The Dynamics of Chinese Politics.* Cambridge, Mass.: Oelgeschlager, Gunn & Hain, 1981.

Factions, campaigns, and policy making are among the issues addressed in this slim but incisive analysis of Chinese politics. Contains illuminating discussions of the roles of bureaucrats in Party politics, the policy process, and social life in China.

Japan

Dimock, Marshall. *The Japanese Technocracy: Management and Government in Japan.* New York: Walker/Weatherhill, 1968.

Describes the alliance of academic, government, and corporate elites who rule Japan. The study focuses on several important issues including bureaucratic growth, departmentalism, public corporations, and corruption.

Kubota, Akira. *Higher Civil Servants in Postwar Japan.* Princeton: Princeton University Press, 1969.

An in-depth examination of the postwar Japanese bureaucrat—his social origins, educational background, and career patterns.

Titus, David Anson. *Palace and Politics in Prewar Japan.* New York: Columbia University Press, 1974.

This colorful yet scholarly description of the role of the Japanese emperor and court in Japanese politics originated as a study of contemporary politics. As such, it creates a fascinating foundation for comparisons of traditional and contemporary values among Japanese politicians and civil servants.

Unit VIII:
Industrial Policy

China

Byrd, William. *China's Financial System: The Changing Role of Banks.* Boulder, Colo.: Westview Press, 1982.

One of the most important reforms of the Chinese economy involves the ways in which capital investment is allocated. Until recently, the state subsidized expansion; today, however, banks and loans are playing an increasingly important role. This study explores the strategic but little known institution of the Chinese bank and analyzes its growing influent on economic planning.

Dernberger, Robert F., ed. *China's Development in Comparative Perspective.* Cambridge: Harvard University Press, 1980.

A collection of readings on the Chinese economy edited by a leading American scholar of Chinese economics. The comparative perspective adopted by the authors makes for fascinating contrasts with both capitalist and socialist economies.

Donnithorne, Audrey. *China's Economic System.* New York: Praeger, 1967.

Although dated, this masterful text is still a fine, thorough, detailed description of all aspects of the Chinese economy.

Eckstein, Alexander. *China's Economic Development: The Interplay of Scarcity and Ideology.* Ann Arbor: University of Michigan Press, 1975.

The two most important factors in Chinese development strategy are the scarcity of many critical goods and an ideology of self-reliance that demands that such goods be produced domestically. A well-known analyst of Chinese trade policy uses this as a starting point for his investigation of Chinese development and economic policy since 1949.

Feuchtwang, Stephan, ed. *Chinese Economic Reforms.* New York: St. Martin's, 1983.

An anthology of essays, many by leftist authors, critically analyzing recent reforms in the Chinese economy. Although biased, these analyses provide a comprehensive and disturbing picture of the prospects for reform policies.

Howe, Christopher. *China's Economy: A Basic Guide.* New York: Basic, 1978.

A thorough and comprehensive discussion of the Chinese economy—planning, management, trade, agriculture, industry, and labor policies.

Tung, Rosalie L. *Chinese Industrial Society After Mao.* Lexington, Mass.: Lexington Books, 1982.

A discussion of Mao's influence on Chinese industrial policy and the changes that have occurred in that policy since his death. Industrial policy in China is intimately connected to other policy areas such as development strategy and educational policy. The author makes a complex topic easily comprehensible.

Japan

Clark, Rodney. *The Japanese Company.* New Haven: Yale University Press, 1979.
    A thoroughgoing analysis of the Japanese company—its history, organization, and role in society. Special emphasis is given to hierarchy and mobility within the firm, management techniques, labor relations, and the formation of industrial groups.

Kamata, Satoshi. *Japan in the Passing Lane: An Insider's Shocking Account of Life in a Japanese Auto Factory.* Trans., Tatsuru Akimoto. New York: Pantheon Books, 1983.
    A stirring indictment of the Japanese economic model. The author, a native Japanese, rejects the traditional attention given to such issues as lifetime employment and concentrates on the underbelly of corporate Japan—worker stress, hazardous working conditions, company unions, and cultural conformity.

Woronoff, Jon. *Japan: The Coming Economic Crisis.* Tokyo: Lotus Press, 1980.
    A disturbing revisionist study of Japan's so-called "economic miracle." The author challenges many widely held beliefs about the Japanese economic system, raising provocative questions about social hierarchy, welfare rights, working conditions, and sexual inequality.

Unit IX:
Foreign Trade Policy

China

Azif, Herbert B. *China Trade: A Guide to Doing Business with the PRC.* Coral Springs, Fla.: Intraworld Trade News, 1981.
    Although intended for a corporate audience, this guide is suitable for students of Chinese trade policy as well. It is a revealing look at the problems and prospects faced by foreign businessmen hoping to do business with the huge communist state.

Buxbaum, David C., ed. *China Trade: Prospects and Perspectives.* New York: Praeger, 1982.
    A collection of essays on trade with the PRC. Aims at an understanding of the major issues and influences in Chinese trade policy.

Fingar, Thomas, ed. *China's Quest for Independence: Policy Evolution in the 1970's.* Boulder, Colo.: Westview Press, 1980.
    A reader in Chinese policy making in the 1970s that attempts to explain the reasoning behind the opening to the West in the early 1970s. Fingar and the other contributors do an excellent job of explaining the issues confronting the Chinese leadership in the 1970s and in detailing the various responses offered by elements within the Party.

Japan

Japan in the World Economy. Tokyo: Press International and MITI, 1972.

This book, published in conjunction with the Japanese Ministry of International Trade and Industry, presents a Japanese view of international economic relations. It describes the underlying principles of Japanese trade policy and the global political context for trade. It also suggests some ways the international trade and monetary organizations might be reformed.

Okimoto, Daniel. *Japan's Economy: Coping With Change in the International Environment.* Boulder, Colo.: Westview Press, 1982.
An investigation of the prospects and problems facing the Japanese economy in the 1980s. The author discusses such issues as protectionism, interdependence, and resource scarcity, highlighting the dynamic character of the global marketplace.

The following journals are excellent sources of current information on foreign trade policy in China and Japan:

> *The China Business Review*
> *The Far Eastern Economic Review*
> *The Oriental Economist—Japanese*

Unit X:
Agricultural Policy

China

Barker, Randolph, and Radha P. Sinha, eds. *The Chinese Agricultural Economy.* Boulder, Colo.: Westview Press, 1982.
An anthology of essays on Chinese agricultural policy, peasants, and the role of agriculture in Chinese economic performance.

Barnett, A. Doak. *China and the World Food System.* Washington, D.C.: Overseas Development Council, 1979.
A leading American scholar of Chinese foreign policy discusses China's food production, its connection to global markets, and the factors involved in recent Chinese food policy.

Buck, John L. *The Chinese Farm Economy.* New York: Garland Publications, 1982.
A study of that 80 percent of the Chinese population that still resides in the countryside. The role of peasants in China's economy and the specific features of the agricultural sector are among the topics discussed.

Zeng, Liu, and Song Jian. *China's Population: Problems and Prospects.* Peking: China Books, 1981.
A defense of Chinese population policies offered from the perspective of Chinese planners. An illuminating discussion of the rationale behind present policies and some of the factors influencing those policies.

Japan

Fukutake, Tadashi. *Rural Society in Japan.* Tokyo: University of Tokyo Press, 1980.
An examination of Japanese rural society, the social structures of village and hamlet, and rural influence on national politics. Special emphasis is given to

the farm family and changes in agricultural and family systems since World War II.

Sanderson, Fred H. *Japan's Food Prospects and Policies.* Washington, D.C.: Brookings Institution, 1978.
  Japan is the largest net importer of food in the world. What effect does this dependence have on Japanese agriculture, trade and economic policy? The author describes some of the issues facing Japan in the areas of food and agriculture and suggests some possible solutions to the problems facing Japanese policy makers today.

Unit XI:
Energy Policy

China

Carlson, Sevinc. *China's Oil: Problems and Prospects.* Washington, D.C.: Center for Strategic and International Studies, 1979.
  A study of China's future role in global energy markets and the implications this has for Chinese foreign and domestic economic policies.

Harrison, Selig S. *China, Oil and Asia: Conflict Ahead?* New York: Columbia University Press, 1977.
  Many of China's energy resources lie in disputed geographical regions. This work analyzes the potential for military and political conflict over those resources and the long-term implications of such conflict for Chinese foreign policy.

Smil, Vaclav. *China's Energy: Achievements, Problems, and Prospects.* New York: Praeger, 1976.
  A survey of the issues confronting Chinese energy planners, the problems of a developing nation in establishing energy independence, and the possibilities of expanded investment in energy production for export.

Japan

Wu, Y. L. *Japan's Search for Oil: A Case Study of Economic Nationalism and International Security.* Stanford: Hoover Institute Press, 1977.
  A penetrating examination of the complex problems faced by Japan in the realm of energy policy. The author concentrates on Japan's responses to the 1973 Arab oil embargo and how those responses have altered Japanese foreign policy and international alliances.

Unit XII:
Education Policy

China

Bernstein, Thomas P. *Up to the Mountains, Down to the Villages: The Transfer of Youth from Urban to Rural China.* New Haven: Yale University Press, 1977.
  An extensive investigation of "sent-down youth," the policies that led to

their transferral to the countryside, and an examination of the rationale behind such policies.

Shirk, Susan L. *Competitive Comrades: Career Incentives and Student Strategies in China.* Berkeley: University of California Press, 1982.
    A vivid description of student life in city high schools in the China based on interviews with former students of the 1960s.

Unger, Jonathan. *Education Under Mao: Class and Competition in Canton Schools, 1960–1980.* New York: Columbia University Press, 1982.
    A well-argued, thorough discussion of changes in educational policy and their impact on students.

Japan

Krauss, Ellis S. *Japanese Radicals Revisited: Student Protest in Postwar Japan.* Berkeley: University of California Press, 1974.
    The Japanese educational establishment is a bastion of leftist political ideology. This case study of political socialization and mobilization is especially concerned with the roles of schools, the family, and political organizations in "radicalizing" youth.

Rohlen, Thomas. *Japan's High Schools.* Berkeley: University of California Press, 1983.
    A narrowly focused look at Japanese society through the high school system. The author, a noted specialist in the field of Japanese education, first describes the historical development and social context of Japanese schools, then moves on to look at the organization, politics, and instructional methods of the high school.

Thrush, John C., and Phillip R. Smith. *Japan's Economic Growth and Educational Change, 1950–1970.* Lincoln, Nebr.: EBHA Press, 1980.
    A survey of the changes wrought in Japanese education policy by the Japanese " economic miracle." The stratification and expansion of school, increased competition for admission, the growth of private schools, and the influence of the educational establishment on policy are among the topics discussed.

Thurston, Donald R. *Teachers and Politics in Japan.* Princeton: Princeton University Press, 1973.
    An absorbing history of the leftist teachers' movement in Japan. Concentrates on the formation of unions in the prewar era and the increasing radicalization of those unions after the war. Provides an excellent description of the conflicts between teachers and education policy makers, as well as of teachers' influence in national politics.

Unit XIII:
Social Welfare Policy

China

Eberstadt, Nick. *Poverty in China.* Bloomington: Indiana University International Development Institute, 1980.
    A disturbing look at standards of living in China, the efforts of Communist

leaders to raise those standards, and the relative success of the policies designed to accomplish this goal. The author brings a comparative perspective to the issues he raises.

Henderson, Gail E., and Myron S. Cohen. *The Chinese Hospital.* New Haven: Yale University Press, 1984.
    A fascinating study of one Chinese hospital by two Americans who spent five months there.

Lucas, Elissa. *Chinese Medical Modernization: Comparative Policy Continuities.* New York: Praeger, 1982.
    An overview of Chinese public health policy from a comparative perspective.

Japan

Fukutake, Tadashi. *The Japanese Social Structure: Its Evolution in the Modern Century.* Trans., R. P. Dore. Tokyo: University of Tokyo Press, 1982.
    A critical examination of the evolution of Japanese society since the middle nineteenth century. Written by one of Japan's foremost academicians, this work looks at the societies of pre- and postwar Japan in order to trace the sources of contemporary values and institutions.

Patrick, Hugh, ed. *Japanese Industrialization and Its Social Consequences.* Berkeley: University of California Press, 1976.
    An anthology of articles on Japanese industrialization and the formation of a working class. Topics include income equality, poverty, welfare, and pollution—and the relation of industrialization to each of these areas.

Woronoff, Jon. *Japan: The Coming Social Crisis.* Tokyo: Lotus Press, 1981.
    Changes in demography, economics, and politics are transforming Japan, placing an increasing burden on the government to respond to such changes. The author surveys such problems as an aging population, alienated youth, dissatisfied minorities, and inadequate welfare, and describes the options open to Japanese leaders.

Unit XIV:
Policy Toward the Military

China

Carlson, Evans F. *The Chinese Army: Its Organization and Military Efficiency.* Westport, Conn.: Hyperion Press, 1975.
    An overview of PLA history and an examination of the limitation placed upon it by inadequate weaponry, planning and military strategy.

Godwin, Paul H. *The Chinese Defense Establishment: Continuity and Change in the 1980's.* Boulder, Colo.: Westview Press, 1983.
    An impressive examination of the issues facing Chinese military planners in the coming decade. The author notes the contradictions facing planners who must attempt to modernize an institution (the PLA) having strong ties to the past, a revolutionary tradition, and a Maoist ideology.

Nelsen, Harvey W. *The Chinese Military System: An Organization Study of the Chinese PLA.* Boulder, Colo.: Westview Press, 1981.
   Describes the organization, structure, and ideology of the People's Liberation Army and the role it plays in Chinese politics.

Japan

Buck, J., ed. *The Modern Japanese Military System. Beverly Hills, Calif.: Sage Publications, 1980.*
   Readings on the history and evolution of the Japanese military—its organization, relations with civilian government, relations with business, and the role of the military in a nation that forbids war as an instrument of foreign policy.

Emerson, John K. *Arms, Yen and Power: The Japanese Dilemma.* New York: Dunellen, 1971.
   A probing study of Japan's global role in the 1970s and 1980s. Concentrates on the changing U.S.-Japan alliance, Japan's emergence as an economic superpower, and Japan's security role in Asia.

Johnson, U. Alexis, ed. *The Common Security Interests of Japan, the US and NATO.* Cambridge, Mass.: Ballinger, 1981.
   A selection of essays on issues of Japanese defense policy. The primary emphasis is on Japan's role in the Western alliance and the implications of that alliance for East Asian security, relations with the USSR and PRC, and for Japan's self-defense strategies.

Unit XV:
Foreign Policy

China

Burchett, Wilfred. *The China, Cambodia, Vietnam Triangle.* Chicago: Vanguard Books, 1982.
   A timely study of the region in which China faces its greatest military and diplomatic challenges.

Chiu, Hungdah. *China and the Taiwan Issue.* New York: Praeger, 1979.
   A slim but thorough discussion of the chief irritant in Sino-American relations and the prospects for its resolution in the future.

Dulles, Foster R. *China and America: The Story of Their Relations Since 1784.* Westport, Conn.: Greenwood, 1981.
   An exhaustive but absorbing history of Sino-American relations. The author gives life to often dry material, describing the unique attraction of China for Americans that continues to exist today.

Larkin, Bruce D. *China and Africa, 1949–1970: The Foreign Policy of the PRC.* Berkeley: University of California Press, 1971.
   A key part of Chinese foreign policy has been its leadership of the Third World. The author examines China's relations with and aid to African states and raises questions about the success of such policies and the potential for PRC leadership of nonaligned states.

Stewart, Douglas T., and William T. Tow, eds. *China, the Soviet Union and the West: Strategic and Political Dimensions for the 1980's.* Boulder, Colo.: Westview Press, 1981.

An informative examination of current relations between the two Communist states and the Western allies. Readings cover such issues as USSR-PRC rapprochement, trade and technology transfer, and European relations with the Communist states.

Japan

Braddon, Russell. *Japan Against the World, 1941–2041.* New York: Stein and Day, 1983.

An examination of Japan's place in the international order—its cultural isolation, military weaknesses, and image among allies and enemies.

Chapman, J. W. *Japan's Quest for Comprehensive Security: Defense, Diplomacy, and Dependence.* London: F. Pinter, 1983.

An excellent discussion of the major issues in Japanese foreign policy. Covers the expansion of Japanese economic power, allies' demands for a similar increase in defense spending, and the contradictions inherent in such policies for a nation that eschews war.

Jain, R. K. *China and Japan, 1949–80.* Atlantic Highlands, N.J.: Humanities Press, 1981.

An overview of the evolution of relations between the Communist giant and the economic superpower since 1949. Provides a good, concise history of both nations' development in the postwar era.

Glossary

administered prices—Prices set by government planners. In China, administered prices that not reflect actual production costs are a major obstacle to the success of many current reforms.

administrative guidance—In Japan, the cooperation of government and business in pursuit of national economic objectives. The government, primarily through the Ministry of International Trade and Industry (MITI), "guides" industries in the selection of investment, production, and research policies.

administrative interference—In China, the practice on the part of local and regional officials of blocking the sale of nonlocal goods in their administrative areas. The aim of such policies is to protect local industries.

agricultural responsibility system—See responsibility systems.

amakaduri—The practice in the Japanese bureaucracy of retirement at age 55. Most bureaucrats "descend from heaven" into private corporations. Their close relations and connections to the bureaucracy are a basis of government-business cooperation.

Article Nine—The "peace clause" of the Japanese Constitution forswearing the use of armed forces for anything but defense of the Japanese islands. Signifies a continued pacifist orientation in Japanese public opinion and serves as a basis for opposition to increased military spending.

ASEAN—Association of South East Asian Nations. A six-member organization consisting of Indonesia, the Philippines, Thailand, Singapore, Malaysia, and Brunei. ASEAN states have experienced rapid economic growth in recent years. They are a major market for Japanese goods and are strategically important to U.S.-Asian policy.

back door—In China, the practice of securing opportunities and rewards through nonofficial channels.

Bank of China—The central bank of China. Destined to play a more influential role in the Chinese economy under current reforms. Bank loans are increasingly replacing government funds as a source of enterprise investment funds.

barefoot doctors—Health care personnel serving in rural China. The barefoot doctor program was popularized by Mao during the Socialist Education Movement (1963–64) as one response to what he saw as a decline in commitment to socialist goals.

"bottoms-up" management—In Japan, the practice of involving lower level employees and supervisors in corporate decision making.

bourgeois revolution—Marxist term for the destruction of feudal traditions and their replacement with modern, democratic institutions. In Marxist theory,

517

every society passes through a bourgeois-democratic stage on the path to socialism and communism.

brokerage—"Pork barrel" politics. The process of mediating the demands of interest groups and bureaucracies.

bucho (Japanese)—Higher-level civilian bureaucrats.

Buddhism—Originally an Indian religion transmitted to China sometime before the Fifth Century A.D. and to Japan in 552 A.D.

bureaucratism (bureaucratization)—Generally, the stratification process in which government officials develop into an elite that is removed from the masses and that enjoys a disproportionate share of political and economic privileges.

"buy Chinese"—The rule that, wherever possible, domestically produced goods should replace imports of foreign products.

cadre—In China, a government official, usually, though not necessarily, a member of the Chinese Communist Party.

campaigns—Political movements in China used to mobilize the public in support of new policies or to implement these policies. Rectification campaigns usually concentrate on the bureaucracy and are meant to instill official values and habits in cadres. Other campaigns have aimed to economic objectives (e.g., the Great Leap Forward), intellectual freedom (e.g., the Hundred Flowers Movement), or have arisen out of political conflict within the leadership (e.g., the Cultural Revolution).

Canton system—The system of monopoly trade between merchants that was licensed by the Chinese emperor and Western traders. The Canton system was a compromise between the traditional tributary system and Western demands for free trade.

capitalist roaders—In China, a disparaging term applied by Mao and his followers to Party leaders who advocated more moderate policies.

CASS—Chinese Academy of Social Sciences. A "think tank' composed of Chinese intellectuals, scholars, and planners that advises the central government on policy.

CCP (or **CPC**)—Chinese Communist Party founded Beida (Peking University) in 1921. The ruling party of China since 1949.

Central Committee (of the CCP)—Composed of the top officials of the Communist Party, the Central Committee ratifies the policies adopted by its standing committee (Politburo).

centrally planned economy (also command economy)—Economic system in which the government plays the major role in setting investment, production, labor, and fiscal policy for industry and agriculture.

Ch'ing—The Manchu dynasty that governed China from 1644 to 1911.

class labels—In China every individual is categorized by the status of his or her family at the time of Liberation (1949). Good, or "red," classes include cadres, peasants, and soldiers. Bad, or "black," classes include landlords, rich peasants, and capitalists. Class labels were employed during the Cultural Revolution to determine personnel and educational opportunities. Labels such as "rightist" have also been used to identify political enemies of the regime.

clientelist networks—The basis for factions in Chinese and Japanese politics. Essentially, clientelist networks involve exchanges of rewards for political support between superiors (patrons) and subordinates (clients). Such networks extend from the highest levels of government to the lowest level of society.

collectivization—Process of organizing peasants into progressively larger and more complex forms of cooperative associations, from mutual aid teams to communes. Collectivization, essentially completed by the mid-1950s, became controversial during the Great Leap Forward period (1958–59) when Mao urged the formation of large communes. Agricultural difficulties have led current leaders to "decollectivize" or "privatize" farming once again.

command economy (also centrally planned economy)—A type of economic system in which central government planners set wage, price, investment production, and fiscal policy. Allocation of supplies (inputs) and distribution of output are centrally managed. Enterprises must meet centrally set targets or quotas that determine enterprise output, quality of goods, number of laborers, wages, bonuses, and availability of supplies. Overcentralization is considered a basic cause of many of the economic bottlenecks and irrationalities that plague command economies.

Communist coalition—term denoting the major groups opposed to current Chinese economic reforms—specifically, the inland provinces, central planners, heavy industries, and the PLA. All of these groups have been negatively affected by reforms.

company union—In Japan most labor unions are organized within companies rather than along occupational lines. Officials of these unions are usually junior managers of the company.

comprehensive enterprises—In China, enterprises that supply many of their own inputs for production. Supply bottlenecks lead many managers to invest in capital construction that can supply them with scarce inputs. Economically inefficient over the long term, such capital construction has exploded under recent reforms giving managers greater discretion and autonomy in investing retained profits.

comprehensive security—In Japan, a military and defense policy that acknowledges global interdependence, the end of American hegemonism, and the need for Japan to modernize its military and become more involved in international affairs.

Confucianism—The ethical and political philosophy upon which imperial administration in China, and to a limited degree in Japan, was based. Confucian values are still important to large numbers of Asians despite political and economic modernization.

contract system—Reform effort in China under which peasants contract with the State to produce certain types and quantities of commodities in return for the retention of the remainder of their production. Peasants farm plots leased to them for periods of up to 15 years and are free to sell their retained output. The system also covers fish, timber, and livestock production, sideline industries, and has recently been extended to manufacturing enterprise.

criticism/self-criticism—In China, thought reform. All Chinese are expected to engage in regular study of Marxist texts and to criticize their own and others' mistakes. Through this process, they are expected to become "new socialist" men and women.

Cultural Revolution—Although much of the violence associated with this political movement was quelled by 1969, most analysts speak of the Cultural Revolution "decade" (1966–76). During this 10-year period, Mao and the "Gang of Four" mounted attacks against rightist revisionism in the Party and State administration. Many cadres were purged, with planning agencies being especially hard hit. Wages were frozen under a policy of "moral incentives" that led to a stagnation of agricultural and industrial production. Current reforms represent an attempt to repair the damage of of economic and social policies implemented during the Cultural Revolution.

daimyo—Japanese feudal lords who oversaw regional administrative units in conjunction with the central government of the shogun.

danwei—In China, a neighborhood or work unit. Housing, health care, and food rations are all distributed through the danwei. Moreover, under current reforms the danwei plays a key role in enforcing birth control policies and settling civil disputes.

defense modernization—In Japan, defense modernization includes an increased global military role, a reinterpretation of Article Nine of the Japanese Constitution, and a redefinition of American-Japanese security policies. In China, defense modernization refers to the acquisition of high-tech weaponry, the reform of the PLA, and a reevaluation of Mao Zedong's guerrilla warfare strategies, which have been the basis for Chinese defense policies since 1949.

democratic centralism—The organization strategy of Leninist parties and communist states. Centralism refers to the hierarchical structure of the Party and State administration, in which lower-level organs are subordinate to higher-level organs. This discipline is balanced by "democracy"—that is, by the right of subordinates to voice opinions on policies in the early stages of formulation.

Deng Xiaoping (also Teng Hsiao-p'ing)—Foremost of the triumvirate of leaders (which also includes Zhao Ziyang and Hu Yaobang) now leading China. Deng advocates the moderate use of market mechanism to modernize the Chinese economy.

developmental state—Broadly speaking, a state in which the government leads an industrialization drive. Developmental states, because they are late industrializers, require a mixture of public and private sector efforts to modernize their economies and catch up with developed economies. Central governments, through a combination of tax, investment, and other economic policies, "guide" the development and transformation of their national economies.

Diet—The Japanese Parliament. The two houses of the Diet are the House of Councillors and the House of Representatives.

divided authority—Refers to the "parallel structure" of Party and State. At lower levels of government, party committees frequently compete with factory managers for management of an enterprise.

DSP (Democratic Socialist Party)—A splinter group of the Japanese Socialist Party (JSP).

dualism (dualistic industrial structure)—In Japan, refers to the distinction between large financial and industrial concerns (*zaikai*) and small enterprises. Social welfare provisions, such as lifetime employment, are more comprehensive in large corporations. However, 70 percent of the workforce is employed in enterprises not covered by such benefits. Efficiency and productivity are also lower in small firms.

economic liberalization—Similar to economic rationalization but emphasizes classic liberal economic theory of competition and free trade. Liberalization can refer both to the "opening up" of an economy to foreign competitors and the removal of domestic restrictions on competition.

economic rationalism (rationalization)—Generally, a term denoting the use of some form of market mechanisms to allocate supplies and distribute goods. Can refer to both free market economies (where allocation and distribution are determined by market forces and constrained by government planners "guide" economic development through tax, investment and tariff policies or through state ownership of the means of production).

exam system—In China, the series of examinations in Confucian doctrine that was the basis for appointment to the imperial bureaucracy. Abolished in 1905 by the Ch'ing Dynasty, the examination system served for thousands of years as the foundation of political and economic administration in Imperial China.

examination hell—In Japan, refers to the grueling competition among Japanese students for entrance into the best universities and high schools.

extensive growth—The expansion of national productive capacity through a fast-paced program of industrialization that emphasizes heavy industries like steel, mining, and electric generation.

factions—Groupings within political and bureaucratic institutions based on patron-client relations and extending through all levels of Japanese and Chinese government.

five guarantees—The provision of food, shelter, clothing, medical care, and burial to all members of agricultural collectives. Increasingly, under the impact of the privatization of Chinese agriculture such services are no longer guaranteed to all in the rural population.

"four modernizations"—The modernization of industry, agriculture, science and technology, and defense, first announced by Zhou Enlai in 1971. In the post-Mao era, the "four modernizations" have served as the basis for economic reform policies.

GATT—General Agreement on Tariffs and Trade. An international agreement concerning the management of international trade. GATT signatories promise to promote free trade and to negotiate tariff regulations with co-signatories.

"Gang of Four"—Jiang Ching (Mao's widow), Wang Hongwen, Yao Wenyuan, and Zhang Chunqiao. Mao's supporters responsible for many of the leftist policies of the Cultural Revolution. The present leadership has vilified these leaders and blamed them for the host of problems plaguing the Chinese economy.

gentry—A strata of rural Chinese society consisting of wealthy landowners, scholars, and government officials. Gentry leaders played important roles in reform movements of the nineteenth century.

Great Leap Forward (1958–59)—A campaign directed by Mao to increase the pace of industrialization and collectivization. During this period Mao announced the advent of communism in China, which was marked by the establishment of communes throughout the country.

group welfare—In Japan, the system of social welfare that is provided by private organizations and employers.

guanxi (Chinese)—Commonly refers to the exchange of favors between managers, bureaucrats, or workers through nonofficial channels.

habatsu (Japanese)—Factions.

han—Feudal domains in traditional Japan.

horizontal linkages—The relations between enterprises and consumers or among enterprises and commercial departments.

household responsibility system—See responsibility systems.

hsien (or xian)—In China, the administrative unit equivalent to an American county.

Hua Kuo-feng—Immediate successor to Mao. Hua's economic policies proved too ambitious and in 1978 were modified under the slogan of "readjustment and restructuring." Hua has slipped into obscurity and has been replaced by Deng Xiaoping as the preeminent policymaker in the present Chinese leadership.

Hu Yaobang—Present CCP Secretary who, with Deng Xiaoping and Zhao Ziyang, is overseeing current reform policies.

hukou (Chinese)—Household registration. Permits for residence and food rations that force Chinese citizens to reside in assigned areas or forfeit guarantees of food and shelter. With the increase of free markets, the effectiveness of the *hukou* system is declining and many rusticated youth are returning to urban areas.

human capital—Training and skills in a workforce.

Hundred Flowers (1957–58)—A political campaign promoted by Mao to free the energies of the Chinese intelligentsia for economic modernization.

ie (Japanese)—House. Refers to cultural patterns of "groupism," consensus, and family cohesiveness.

Income Doubling Plan—1960s Japanese economic policy under which Japan evolved into a global economic power through a strategy of domestic protectionism and expert promotion.

industrial policy—Generally, a combination of programs designed to protect domestic industries, develop strategic industries, and ease the adjustment of the economic structure to change.

intensive growth—Economic policy that emphasizes the efficient use of resources, increasing productivity (as opposed to capacity), and a move into high technology and consumer goods industries away from heavy mining and manufacturing sectors.

iron rice bowl—In China, a term referring to the guarantees of employment, shelter, clothing, and medical care provided by work units to their employees.

Japan, Inc.—American term for the close cooperation of Japanese government and business.

JCP (Japanese Communist Party)—Outlawed during the American postwar occupation, the JCP has recently begun to expand its influence in Japanese politics.

joint ventures—In China, cooperative efforts of foreign investors and Chinese enterprises.

juku (Japanese)—"Cram schools." Schools whose curriculum is designed to help Japanese students pass the rigorous college entrance examinations.

kana—The Japanese syllabary.

kanryō—Politicians who emerge from the Japanese bureaucracy, as opposed to *shomin,* who are professional politicians.

Keidanren—The Japanese Federation of Economic Organizations. An industrialists' group and key source of support for the LDP.

Komeito—In Japan, the Clean Government Party.

KMT (Kuomintang or Guomindang)—The Chinese Nationalist Party, founded by Sun Yat-sen and which now administers Taiwan.

Land Reform (China 1949–52, Japan 1946–47)—Generally, land-to-the-tiller programs in which peasants are granted ownership of the land they farm.

latch-key children—In Japan, the children of working mothers.

law of avoidance—In Imperial China, the practice of not appointing officials to home provinces in order to prevent favoritism in decision and policy making. The policy forced local officials to rely on local leaders for information and support concerning local conditions and administration.

LDP (Liberal Democratic Party)—The political party that has ruled Japan since the party's founding in 1955. Currently headed to Prime Minister Yasuhiro Nakasone.

Leninist Party—The political party, organized according to the principles of Marxism and democratic centralism, which is at the vanguard of socialist revolution. As a "vanguard" party, the Leninist Party believes itself to be the only group capable of formulating policy for the achievement of Communism.

lifetime employment (permanent employment)—In Japan, the practice of regularly promoting workers according to seniority, then finding positions for them in subsidiaries upon retirement. Lifetime employment is the foundation of management-labor relations in many large companies. It eases the welfare burden on the public sector by shifting responsibility for pension, housing, and health care to private sector employers. Similar to the "iron rice bowl" in Chinese enterprises.

Lin Piao (also Lin Biao)—Chinese defense minister under whose leadership the PLA became a bastion of leftist influence and the chief promoter of Mao's personality cult.

localism—In China, the practice of putting local needs and goals above national priorities. Localism is one aspect of bureaucratism and is related to "departmentalism," the practice of putting one's work unit's goals above general national objectives.

lost generation—In China, the generation raised during the tumultuous years of the Cultural Revolution (1966–67). These young men and women, denied schooling, sent to the countryside, and prevented from returning home, are now faced with the prospect of long-term unemployment from a combination of economic conditions and their lack of training. They form a potentially explosive core of alienated youth and are of particular concern to the current Chinese leadership.

Manchus—Tribe from Manchuria that defeated Ming Dynasty armies to rule China from 1644 to 1911.

Mao Zedong (also Mao T'se-tung, 1893–1976)—Leader of the Communist revolution and Chairman of the Chinese Communist Party from 1949 to 1976.

market mechanisms—The use of competition, consumer demands, floating prices, free trade, wage hikes, material incentives, private plots, free markets, and managerial autonomy in running an economy.

market rational—An economic system in which market forces determine the distribution and allocation of resources. In a market rational system, there is no industrial policy, trade policy is subordinate to foreign policies, and the government regulates rather than plans.

May 7th Cadre Schools—During the Cultural Revolution in China, work camps for purged cadres.

Meiji Restoration—the 1860s overthrow of the *shogun* that led to the restoration of imperial power in Japan.

MITI—Ministry of International Trade and Industry. The Japanese governmental agency credited with guiding Japan's postwar economic policy.

moral and material incentives—Moral incentives include the praise of colleagues, medals, prizes, certificates and other nontangible rewards. Material incentives include wage hikes, bonuses, and improved standards of living. The debate over which to emphasize in domestic economic policy has preoccupied Chinese leaders since 1949. The current leadership has placed greater emphasis on the latter.

Nakasone, Yasushiro—Japanese prime minister since 1982.

Nixon shocks—In Japan, a term referring to the twin surprises in the 1970s of Sino-American rapprochement and the floating of the U.S. dollar (along with other economic policies like soybean export reductions and import quotas). Because Japan was caught unaware by these policy shifts, confidence in the reliability of the U.S.-Japan alliance was shaken. These surprises or "shocks" are considered to be one reason for the deterioration of relations between the two states during the 1970s.

nontariff barriers—Barriers to trade not involving tariffs but stemming mainly from differences in language, customs, and systems of economic organization. In Japan, nontariff barriers such as monopolized distribution and marketing systems, contribute to imbalances in trade and are a major source of friction in trade relations with foreign countries.

Northern islands (or Southern Kuriles)—The islands occupied by the USSR at the close of World War II. Because Japan and the USSR never signed a peace treaty following WWII, the Northern islands remain a serious issue of contention in Soviet-Japanese relations.

North-South debate—Refers to the ongoing conflict between the developing countries of the Southern Hemisphere and the industrialized economies of Europe, Asia, and America. China and Japan are on opposite side of this debate, though the issues arising from the conflict are critical to both nations' foreign policies.

NPC (National People's Congress)—In China, the national parliamentary body that is indirectly elected and serves largely as a rubber stamp for Central Committee and State Council decisions.

OECD (Organization for Economic Cooperation and Development)—Organized in 1960 to promote constructive world economic policies. Its members now include the United States, Japan, Australia, New Zealand, and nineteen European countries.

oil shocks—The economic problems arising from the 1973–74 and 1978–79 Arab oil embargoes. In Japan, the oil shocks revealed the extent of the country's vulnerability to global economic changes and are one reason for Japan's increased attention to international affairs.

open door—Originally, the forced opening of Chinese and Japanese markets to Western trade. Today, the term refers to China's policy of increased trade, expanded technology transfers, and improved contact with foreign countries.

overcentralization—In a planned economy, refers to the problems of too many decisions being made at the center rather than at the enterprise level.

parallel structure—The administrative system in China in which at every level of State administration there is an equivalent Party unit that instructs the State agency on Party policy. Party committees are usually identical or overlapping with State agencies, making it difficult to delineate responsibilities.

permanent employment—see lifetime employment.

PLA (People's Liberation Army)—In China, the combined defense forces of the navy, the air force, and the army.

plan ideological—Denoting a type of economy in which state ownership, planning, and bureaucratic goal-setting are themselves values and not merely a means whereby to achieve developmental objectives (e.g., industrialization).

plan rational—A planned economy in which industrial, agricultural, and economic policies are employed as a means to achieve national economic goals. A plan rational system does not preclude the use of market forces or any other instruments of obtaining goals.

politics in command—Maoist slogan describing the importance of political and ideological considerations in all policy choices.

price reform—In China, attempts to link prices with supply, demand, and/or production costs.

profit contract system—Recent Chinese economic reform under which enterprises contract with the central government to turn over a certain portion of their profits in exchange for the right to retain the remainder for investment purposes, wages, or bonuses.

protectionism—Trade policy that aims to protect domestic industries through tariff and nontariff barriers.

readjustment/restructuring—In China, the twin policies adopted in 1978 aimed at shifting investment to light industry and agriculture and introducing market forces into the centrally planned economy.

red agencies—In China, refers to bureaucratic agencies subsidized by money-making State units.

Red Guards—In China, factions of students that battled among themselves and with the PLA during the Cultural Revolution.

regulatory state—An economy in which the government regulates, rather than guides, the economy.

responsibility systems—The package of reforms in Chinese agriculture and industry giving greater autonomy to producers in order to step up production. Provisions include private plots, profit retention, wage hikes, and the withdrawal of the party from economic administration.

revisionism—A term of opprobrium denoting the betrayal of true Marxist revolutionary theories for short-term economic benefits.

ringi—In Japan, the process of consensus-building and consensual decision making designed to foster support and cooperation among workers and managers for company policies.

ronin (Japanese)—Literally, "masterless samurai," Slang expression for students preparing for the college entrance examination.

runaway expansion—In China, the explosion in construction due to the retention of profits by private enterprises.

rusticated youth—Chinese youth, many of them former Red Guards, sent to the countryside beginning in 1969.

samurai—In Japan, a stratum of warriors, intellectuals, and administrators who, in their capacity as advisors to the Feudal *daimyo,* were chiefly responsible for many of the reforms of the Meiji era.

sankin kotai—In Japan, the practice during the Tokugawa *shogunate* of having the *daimyo* spend alternate years at Edo, the capital. Under this policy, the *daimyo* and their families were held hostage as a means of preventing local rebellions.

SEC (State Economic Commission)—In China, the agency responsible for overseeing the implementation of central plans. The SEC also arbitrates disputes among Ministries.

sectionalism—In Japan, putting the goals of the smaller unit above those of the larger collective. Specifically, in the bureaucracy, the practice of placing too much emphasis on the work unit at the expense of policy objectives.

Security Treaty (or Mutual Security Treaty)—The U.S.-Japanese Agreement covering foreign and defense policy issues, the stationing of American troops in Japan, and U.S. nuclear weaponry. Originally signed in 1960, the treaty was revised in 1970 amidst large and vocal Japanese opposition to American global military policy. The stationing of nuclear submarines in Japan and nuclear weapons in Okinawa remain a controversial issue in Japanese politics.

"seek truth from facts"—A Maoist slogan employed by Deng Xiaoping to justify pragmatism in economic policy. The opposite of "politics in command."

seiji shikin—Political funds. In Japanese factional politics, fund raising is a key criterion of factional leadership.

Self-Defense Forces—The Japanese armed forces. Though the Japanese Constitution forbids militarization other than for defense of the Japanese islands, the Self-Defense Forces are the seventh largest armed force (army, navy, and air force combined) in the world.

self-reliance—In China, an economic policy that stresses reliance on indigenous resources and technologies.

SEZ (Special Economic Zone)—In China, designated areas where foreign businesses may operate joint ventures and enjoy low tax rates, investment incentives, and cheap labor.

Shinto—An indigenous Japanese religion that combines emperor-worship with the worship of nature.

shogun—The supreme military commander in feudal Japan.

Sohyo—General Council of Japanese Trade Unions. The chief shource of electoral support for the Socialist Party Japan (SPJ).

Soviet model—A centrally planned economy in which profits are extracted from the agricultural sector in order to fund investment in heavy industry.

SPC (State Planning Commission)—In China, the government organ responsible for economic planning.

spiritual pollution—In China, refers to the growing influence of Western capitalism on Chinese society and values.

SPF—Socialist Party Japan.

study system—In China, the system of propaganda and indoctrination in Marxist theory and CCP history and policy. The standard technique involves regular study of texts and Party documents followed by "criticism/self-criticism" sessions.

Sun Yat-sen—The father of the modern Chinese Revolution.

Taiping Rebellion (1857–64)—Originally a religious-political movement in southern China that gradually developed into a civil war that threatened to topple the Ch'ing Dynasty.

targets—Each Chinese factory receives centrally formulated targets for production, wages, investment, quality, and dozens of other "indicators" of economic performance.

Ten-Year Plan—Economic plan introduced by Hua Kuo-feng in 1976 and designed to modernize the Chinese economy by 1985. Like previous long-term plans, it concentrated investment in capital construction and heavy industry.

Three Worlds—Theory discussed by Zhou Enlai in 1954 at the Bandung Conference of nonaligned states. The theory imagines three worlds with the United

States and USSR composing the first, Europe and Japan the second, and China and the underdeveloped countries the third.

trade liberalization—Generally, the lowering of tariff and nontariff barriers to trade; the opening up of domestic markets to foreign competition; increasing participation in global economic systems; and a reduction of government subsidies to noncompetitive or inefficient firms.

treaty system—The system imposed on the Chinese after the Opium Wars. Chinese ports were opened to Western trade and the Chinese hinterland was made accessible to missionaries and traders.

tributary trade—The traditional trading system to Imperial China in which foreigners paid tribute to the Chinese emperor in exchange for trade with China.

virtuocracy—Basing opportunities and rewards on political virtue rather than on meritocratic criteria.

Wan Li—Chinese vice-premier responsible for current agricultural reforms.

zaibatsu—In Japan, privately owned industrial empires.

Zenchu (National Federation of Agricultural Cooperative Associations)—In Japan, the spokesman for farmers and a major support group of the LDP.

Zhao Ziyang—Premier of the People's Republic of China. With Deng Xiaoping and Hu Yaobang, oversees current reform policies.

About the Contributors

Hans H. Baerwald is professor of political science at the University of California, Los Angeles.

A. Doak Barnett is professor of Chinese studies at the School of Advanced International Studies at Johns Hopkins University.

Bernard Bernier is a professor in the department of anthropology at the University of Montreal.

Richard C. Bush is a member of the staff of the House Committee on Foreign Affairs.

Kent E. Calder is assistant professor of politics and international affairs at the Woodrow Wilson School at Princeton University.

P.-C. Chen is professor of political science at Wayne State University in Detroit.

Chu-yuan Cheng is professor of economics at Ball State University in Muncie, Indiana.

Christopher M. Clarke is a China analyst with the Bureau of Intelligence and Research in the U.S. Department of State. He was formerly Associate Director of Research at the National Council for U.S.-China Trade.

Albert M. Craig is a professor in the department of history at Harvard University. He is also Director of both the Yenching Institute and the Japan Institute at Harvard.

Gerald L. Curtis is professor of political science at Columbia University.

June Teufel Dreyer is professor of political science and Director of East Asian Programs at the University of Miami.

John King Fairbank is Francis Lee Higginson Professor of History, Emeritus, at Harvard University.

Stewart Fraser is a writer and contributor to *Far Eastern Economic Review.*

Thomas Fingar is director of the U.S.-China Relations Program at Stanford University.

Frank Gibney is president of the Pacific Basin Institute in Santa Barbara, California, and vice chairman of the Board of Directors of Encyclopedia Britannica.

Steven M. Goldstein, a professor of government at Smith College, is currently Director of the China Council of The Asia Society.

Donald Hellmann is professor of political science in the School of International Studies at the University of Washington, Seattle.

Sam Jameson is a staff writer for the *Los Angeles Times.*

Chalmers Johnson, a political scientist, is Walter Haas professor of Asian Studies at the University of California, Berkeley.

Adrian Kols was formerly a staff writer for *Population Reports* at Johns Hopkins University.

Masataka Kosaka is professor of international politics in the Faculty of Law at Kyoto University, Japan.

June Kronholz is a staff writer for the *Wall Street Journal.*

Marion J. Levy is professor of sociology and international affairs and Chairman of the Department of Asian Studies at Columbia University.

Melinda Liu is a correspondent for *Newsweek* magazine.

Steve Lohr is Bureau Chief in Manila for the *New York Times.*

Margaret A. McKean is associate professor of political science at Duke University.

Maurice Meisner is professor of history at the University of Wisconsin, Madison.

Tom Morganthau is a correspondent for *Newsweek* magazine.

Barry Naughton is an assistant professor of economics at the University of Oregon.

Michel Oksenberg is professor of Chinese politics at the University of Michigan.

Michael Parks is a staff writer for the *Los Angeles Times.*

T. J. Pempel is professor of government at Cornell University.

Tom Redburn is a staff writer for the *Los Angeles Times.*

Edwin O. Reischauer is professor emeritus at Harvard University, History.

Thomas P. Rohlen is a consultant and research associate at Stanford University and associate editor of *The Journal of Japanese Studies.*

Larry Rohter is a correspondent for *Newsweek* magazine.

Franz Schurmann teaches sociology and history at the University of California, Berkeley.

Kathrin Sears is Program Assistant at the China Council of The Asia Society.

Gerald Segal is a lecturer in international politics and strategic studies at the University of Wales, Aberystwyth.

Barbara Slavin is a correspondent for *Newsweek* magazine.

John Bryan Starr is a lecturer in the political science department at Yale University. He is also executive director of the China Association at Yale.

James B. Stepanek is the editor of *China Business Review.*

J. A. A. Stockwin is Nissan Professor at the University of Oxford.

Ezra Vogel is professor of sociology at Harvard University.

Andrew G. Walder is associate professor of sociology at Columbia University.

Robert E. Ward is professor of political science at Stanford University.

Kozo Yamamura is professor of economics at the University of Washington, Seattle.

About the Editors

SUSAN L. SHIRK is associate professor of political science at the University of California, San Diego. She holds a master's degree in Asian Studies from the University of California, Berkeley, and a Ph.D. in political science from Massachusetts Institute of Technology. Dr. Shirk has written extensively on Chinese economic policy and education and is the author of *Competitive Comrades: Career Incentives and Student Strategies in China* (1982). She is currently doing research in China as a Rockefeller Foundation International Relations Fellow for a book on the implementation of the post-1978 economic reforms in China, with special emphasis on foreign trade and investment.

KEVIN KENNEDY received a bachelor's degree in Chinese Studies from the University of California, San Diego. He is currently enrolled in the J.D. Ph.D. program in law and political science at the University of Michigan, Ann Arbor.

LINDA WOOD, a free-lance writer, has been an editorial consultant at University Extension, University of California, San Diego, since 1979. Most recently, she has served as editorial director of print materials for two political science courses developed by the Global Understanding Project at National Public Radio. Ms. Wood holds a bachelor's degree and a master's degree from the University of California, Berkeley, and a diploma in French civilization from the Sorbonne. Her publications include the *Study Guide to Accompany Contemporary Western Europe, The Psychology Primer,* the *Reader/Study Guide* and *Viewer's Guide* for Carl Sagan's "Cosmos," *A Land Called California, Working: Changes and Choices,* and *Understanding Space and Time.* She is also the coauthor of an award-winning children's book, *Windows in Space,* published in 1982.